The Child and the English Language Arts

Third Edition
The Child and the English Language Arts

Mildred R. Donoghue
California State University, Fullerton

wcb
Wm. C. Brown Company Publishers
Dubuque, Ia.

To Charles

Contents

Preface

The English language arts discipline has been described by some as being at once the most basic, the most complex, and the most potent in the entire curriculum. That the English language arts constitute the foundation for all other subjects commonly taught in elementary schools has finally become evident empirically. And a growing body of research has begun to justify the emphasis on an integrated rather than on a segregated approach to language arts instruction.

All of the language arts and skills reinforce and complement each other so strongly that none can be taught or learned in total isolation from the others. Nor can a child gain appreciably in the mastery of one such art or skill without triggering some degree of advancement in at least two of the others.

Consequently, this third edition replaces the previous editions' tripod organization of literature, composition, and language with a new, pervasive concern for the young student. Ways of meeting the current federal mandate for educating handicapped and other exceptional children are included in various chapters throughout the volume. And one of the two new chapters is simply entitled "The Child."

The second new chapter relates to the child's vocabulary, stressing factors that affect its growth and describing curriculum guidelines and instructional activities for this area. Other changes in this edition include two new appendices: Appendix 1 presents specific questions for teacher use in evaluating language arts textbooks; and Appendix 2 concerns guidelines for avoiding sexist language in teaching materials and other literature. Besides these major textual additions, every section of the book has been revised substantially in an effort to keep current and future teachers aware of pertinent scholarship and research findings.

Pedagogical aids in this revision include summary statements which precede each chapter and pinpoint several highlights. Also, discussion questions, suggested projects, and recent related readings conclude each chapter.

Finally, as in the previous edition, discussion of the skill of reading has been omitted deliberately from this volume. This is because I believe that a chapter or two devoted to reading in a book of this size can scarcely prepare the modern teacher for the caliber of reading instruction demanded today by both the public and the profession itself.

For this edition I have relied on my colleagues and graduate students for commentary and criticism, and I wish to thank them for their efforts. I also wish to express my appreciation to three California school districts for contributing photographs of children and teachers engaged in meaningful classroom activities: Fountain Valley, Fullerton, and Ocean View (Huntington

Beach). And I am equally indebted to the hundreds of elementary school master teachers who have graciously invited me into their classrooms during the past decade.

Fullerton, California   Mildred R. Donoghue

The Language Arts Program

1

The four general language processes or skills

The foundational competencies for English language arts programs

Evaluating behaviors in the three educational domains

Types of activities that develop language readiness

Small children are not taught a language but learn it by themselves without conscious effort and application. Since they seem to possess an inborn faculty for language generally, the language they learn depends wholly on the language —or languages—to which they are exposed until about the age of puberty.

By the time children are ready for kindergarten, they already have marvelous control over the pronunciation and syntax of their native American English as they have learned it from their families and playmates. The school then begins to share the responsibility for the children's language development with the home and the community. Both inside and outside of the school environment the children are continually increasing their command of the language through informal means: conversing; playing; listening to records and to adult dialogue; watching films and television; reading signs, magazines, and books; and writing notes and creative pieces. Therefore, and to a greater extent than in any other discipline, the language arts program demands a knowledge of each child's social, emotional, cultural, and intellectual background and development.

Due to the variety of student experiences in any level or grade, an effective program in language learning must focus upon children as individuals. Boys and girls must be involved actively and positively in genuine learning situations that have meaning for them.

As children progress through the grades, they must be permitted greater responsibility in choosing learning experiences because as Figure 1.1 shows, these experiences influence their gradual acquisition of the productive and the receptive operations in the English language arts. The productive or expressive areas stress composition in both oral and written forms. The receptive areas concern reading and listening. Yet all these areas are so intricately interrelated that none of them can be learned in complete isolation from the others, and growth in one area promptly promotes growth in the others.

Figure 1.1. Central Role of the Student in the English Language Arts Curriculum.

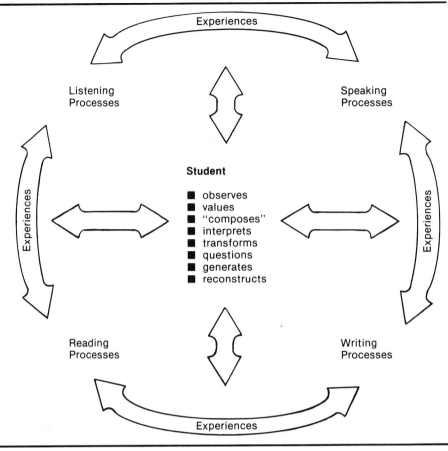

Source: *English Language Framework for California Public Schools: K–12* (Sacramento: State Department of Education, 1976), p. 15.

Universal Considerations

The teacher that introduces young learners to formal language instruction currently incorporates into the curriculum certain language basics drawn from many specialized areas in linguistics, psychology, sociology, and educational philosophy and practice. These "universal statements" or guidelines have been organized by Fillion, Smith, and Swain according to three classifications: (1) statements about the nature of language; (2) generalizations about language learning; and (3) considerations about language in school.[1]

The Nature of Language

1. *Natural language is never independent of meaning.* Language is a vehicle for communication. Since words that have no context have no meaning, teachers cannot present isolated words for study or use terms to which pupils are unable to relate what they already understand.
2. *Natural language is never independent of function.* Language without a

function is pointless. There are many functions that language does serve, including problem solving, controlling behavior, and acculturation. Language is not something divorced from human purposes.

3. *The four general language skills or processes are largely independent.* As students develop one skill, they increase their potential development of the other skills. Each skill also appears to grow through individual practice. Lack of skill in one area, however, does not necessarily reflect lack of skill in one or more of the others.

4. *Comprehension always exceeds production.* Listening comprehension is generally superior to the other language skills. Therefore, teachers must be cautious about making statements regarding a pupil's level of comprehension since both children and adults can understand language which they themselves cannot produce.

5. *Comprehension entails an understanding of both function and content.* Full linguistic competence demands learning to understand purpose as well as literal meaning. Second-language students, for instance, must learn not to reply with a lengthy speech about the state of their health when asked "How are you?" Despite the literal content of this question, its linguistic purpose is a friendly greeting and not a demand for extensive knowledge.

6. *All dialects can potentially convey the same meanings and serve the same functions.* In effect, all dialects and language are intertranslatable. Dialect does not in itself indicate linguistic or intellectual ability. Consequently, more time should be spent on developing an awareness of linguistic variation and the relation of dialect to social and geographical factors.

7. *Language is initially based on an individual's reality but it also constructs its own reality.* Much of human reality (such as historical events) exists, in a practical sense, only in language and therefore is subject to its limitations. For instance, terms used to characterize the world and its people influence the perceptions and reactions of listeners and readers.

1. *The processes of language learning are not directly observable or manipulable.* Language learning takes place at the deeper levels of an individual's prior knowledge and cognitive processes. It is not primarily a matter of the "correct" expression of a particular order of elements. **Language Learning**

2. *Language is not learned independently of meaning or function.* Children do not learn anything about language from anyone (including authors) unless there is a shared sense of purpose and a shared understanding of meaning. If teachers try to present language as a subject consisting of abstract rules and information, the language skill of children will be virtually unaffected.

3. *Meaning and function are learned as language is learned.* The learning process may be beyond a teacher's direct control, but it is influenced by the child's need and opportunity to use language for varied purposes.

4. *Skill in some functions of language does not mean that all functions of language have been mastered.* A pupil who can compose a poem, for instance, is not necessarily able to compose a business letter.

5. *Language used for a function that has not been mastered will not contribute to learning.* Language skills are generally developed and acquired because boys and girls perceive these skills as useful. On the other hand, teacher demands which interfere with a language function deemed important by the children may interfere with language expression and development in the classroom.

6. *Individuals learn the languages and language functions of persons with whom they wish to identify.* Learning adult uses of language is often resisted by children because such uses appear contrary to their goals and needs. In much the same way, children learn to value creative drama, second-language learning, or appreciative listening if school friends do too.

7. *Motivation and perseverance are both required for language learning.* Both factors can be negatively affected by repeated failure or by teacher demands which appear futile.

Language in School

1. *The language of instruction differs from much out-of-school language.* The meanings, functions, and forms of classroom language are distinctly different from the language that children use in other situations. Teachers must be aware of the distinctiveness of their own language. They also must realize that while pupils need classroom language, most of them will acquire it slowly and laboriously.

2. *Teachers and students speak different languages.* Teachers are well-educated adults who discuss subjects and employ terminology generally unfamiliar to young pupils.

3. *Children set the norms for their own language in school.* They use language in much the same way that their classmates do. Should they be asked prematurely to use language in the way that adults do, they may react with apathy or hostility.

4. *Demands for unfamiliar language use inhibit spontaneous speech or writing.* Such demands can lead to speechlessness or writing blocks. A pupil's repeated inability to respond should suggest to the teacher that there is a critical need for a revision of program goals.

5. *Education is mostly a matter of learning school language.* A major goal of education should therefore be the ability to handle classroom language.

6. *No specific statements about language instruction are universally valid.* Any particular practice can fail occasionally with some pupils or with some teachers. There must always be flexibility in language programs.

Language Competencies, Program Goals, and Educational Domains

In recent years there have been expressions of concern coupled with mounting evidence that too many children and adults have not attained the language competencies required for success in everyday life. Such competencies require sustained attention in the primary grades as well as at all other teaching levels because they must be functional for every person in American society. Although there are obvious differences in their use by particular individuals, the essence of these competencies lies not in their specific manifestations but in the processes.[2]

Essential Competencies for English Programs

I. Competencies Essential for Receiving Communication from Others

  A. Basic Understandings and Attitudes
1. To understand that reading and listening skills are needed for learning in school, for most occupations, and for daily living.
2. To understand that symbols and signs other than those which either graphically or auditorily represent words may transmit meaning.
3. To understand that the purpose and the degree of involvement of the receiver affect communication.
4. To understand that reading and listening are means for gaining pleasure directly as well as indirectly in terms of finding avocational and recreational information.
5. To understand and appreciate various types of language: dialects, levels of usage, jargon, figurative language, and so forth.

  B. Receptive Comprehension Abilities
1. To follow directions, determine main ideas, recognize important supporting information, and perceive relationships.
2. To use language structure, context clues, dictionaries, and other aids in gaining meaning.
3. To relate information received to previous experiences and present knowledge and to draw inferences.
4. To distinguish between fact and opinion and between the relevant and the irrelevant.
5. To recognize bias, prejudice, and propaganda and avoid judgments based upon inadequate evidence.
6. To gain pleasure and self-development from receptive communication acts.

  C. Abilities Needed for Aural Decoding
1. To identify and discriminate among common speech sounds.
2. To recognize words, phrases, and larger units of aural communication.
3. To use the pitch, stress, juncture, and tone of speech in gaining meaning.

  D. Abilities Needed for Visual Decoding
1. To distinguish and identify individual letters and letter groups in a wide variety of type and script styles.
2. To recognize by sight a core of words and to be able to use structural and phonemic-graphemic knowledge to determine others.
3. To use punctuation marks and other nonword symbols as aids to reading.
4. To make use of facial expressions, physical movements, and graphic and picture symbols as aids in gaining meaning from nonreading communication acts.

II. Competencies Needed for Expression to Others

  A. Understandings and Attitudes
1. To recognize that the content of what is said is more important than the mechanics of saying it.

2. To understand that the mechanics of writing and the manner of speaking are aids to communication rather than ends in themselves.
3. To understand that, to communicate effectively, one must be willing to acquire the specific skills or learnings needed for the performance of particular speaking or writing tasks.
4. To recognize that there are levels of usage appropriate to varying occasions.
5. To recognize that one's own personal language or dialect is worthy of respect and is suitable for many situations.
6. To recognize that standard English is needed for certain kinds of oral and written communication.
7. To be sensitive to the opinions and feelings of one's reader(s) or listener(s).

B. Abilities Needed for Organization and Composition
1. To speak or write for particular purposes:
   a. to seek information
   b. to give directions
   c. to make explanations
   d. to give information
   e. to express feelings and/or opinions
   f. to persuade
   g. to make requests
   h. to comply with social amenities
   i. to provide entertainment, pleasure, or comfort
2. To choose content appropriate to the intended audience—that is, the reader or listener.
3. To use varied structures in accord with the purpose, the audience, and the situation.
4. To use language—one's own personal language or dialect or standard English—that is suitable to the occasion, the content, and the audience.
5. To organize ideas and information in ways such as:
   a. using sequential development
   b. using supporting details
   c. giving examples or illustrations
   d. showing cause and effect
6. To use accurate facts and valid sources of information to support ideas.

C. Abilities Needed for Oral Communication
1. To participate in informal as well as formal speaking situations that involve exchange with others without being either overly dominant or reticent.
2. To speak distinctly and to articulate sounds clearly.
3. To use volume, pitch, rate, and tone appropriate to the audience and the occasion.
4. To use suitable gestures and facial expressions.

D. Abilities Needed for Written Communication
1. To write legibly and neatly.
2. To spell correctly the words that are needed.

3. To use accepted punctuation and capitalization.
4. To use accepted form and appropriate language in varying types of written communication.

III. Competencies Needed for Locating Information

A. Understandings and Attitudes
1. To have the desire to acquire knowledge and pleasure from sources outside one's immediate environment.
2. To understand that most sources of information—from the telephone directory to the card catalog in the library—list items alphabetically.
3. To understand that the ability to locate information aids in achieving self-determination and acquiring knowledge.
4. To be aware that it is sometimes desirable and necessary to ask for assistance in locating information.

B. Locational Abilities
1. To know the sequence of the letters of the alphabet.
2. To use alphabetical order to locate information of varying kinds.
3. To give specific information desired when requesting aid in locating someone or something.
4. To use various aids for finding information in books, such as tables of contents, indexes, and format clues.
5. To use such aids as card catalogs, computer searches, building directories, diagrams, maps, and the like to locate facts, materials, places, or people.

Program Goals

In addition to incorporating foundational competencies appropriate for all English curricula, the elementary language arts program must also identify several more specific goals in its efforts to help children communicate efficiently and properly at their individual ability levels.[3]

The program must aim first to develop students who, in terms of their maturity and potential, understand that people use language to create literature which records their experiences, expresses their emotions and perceptions, and responds to the expressions of others. Literature provides the models and the stimuli to extend children's mental horizons and to nurture their sensitivity and imaginations. At every grade level, children should hear or read a rich variety of literature—stories, dramas, and poems.

Secondly, it must hope to develop students who, in terms of their potential and maturity, realize that people communicate both verbally and nonverbally in formal and informal speech situations. Skills of oral communication are prerequisite to the development of all language skills. They are worthy of organized classroom instruction because speech is so integral to every personality and so much more commonly used than the written word.

The program must also aim to develop students who understand, according to their maturity and potential, that verbal systems of communication convey precise, unequivocal, and time-binding information which is obtained primarily through purposeful and attentive listening. Objectives related to the lexicon of the English language can be included here.

Fourthly, it must hope to develop students who, in terms of their potential and maturity, realize that the written form of a language records and preserves spoken language and is subject to certain organizational and mechanical conventions. Increasing attention is being paid to the importance of children's writing as a means for self-discovery, self-expression, and self-education in the arts of language use.

In addition, the language arts program must aim to develop students who, in terms of their maturity and potential, understand that a living or spoken language is continually changing. Oral usage may be introduced to elementary school children as early as the kindergarten year. Dialectology and the history of spoken and written language teach both primary and intermediate pupils that pictures can be used to communicate and record ideas, that certain words have interesting and known origins, and that language changes in response to various influences.

Finally, it must aim to help students understand, according to their potential and maturity, that language and thought are inseparable. The instructional objectives included under this goal are a kind of translation of the cognitive domain from the taxonomy of educational objectives and are relevant at every grade level from kindergarten through the sixth grade. This goal represents a major concept about the function or use of language.

Educational Domains and Evaluations

The cognitive hierarchy just mentioned includes those objectives which deal with the recall or recognition of knowledge and the development of intellectual abilities and skills. Much of the work in curriculum development has taken place in this domain.

Two other major educational orientations have also been isolated for the purpose of identifying outcomes of learning goals—affective and psychomotor.

Behaviors in the affective domain generally include the interests, attitudes, values, appreciations, and adjustments of the individual. The affective behaviors, emphasizing the emotional processes, begin with the simple behaviors of receiving and responding and continue through the complex process of characterization.

The third domain is the manipulative or motor-skill area—psychomotor. Levels of behavior in this domain generally have been based on the concept of coordination. These behaviors include muscular action and require neuromuscular coordination.

A problem of semantics arises when people attempt to describe or communicate learning behaviors. Most specialists and researchers of learning behaviors use and apply these levels of behavior:

Cognitive Domain

1. *Knowledge*—the learner recognizes and recalls facts (e.g., defining terms, recalling names, etc.).
2. *Comprehension*—the learner demonstrates the ability to restate knowledge in new terms (e.g., giving examples, explaining, summarizing, translating, etc.).

3. *Application*—the learner applies the knowledge (e.g., predicting, solving, using, etc.).
4. *Analysis*—the learner separates the knowledge into parts and makes comparisons and relationships between elements (e.g., inferring, relating, selecting).
5. *Synthesis*—the learner combines elements and arranges them into a structure that was not clearly evidenced before (e.g., planning, designing, creating, organizing, etc.).
6. *Evaluation*—the learner judges and selects knowledge based upon a given set of criteria (e.g., making decisions, finding fallacies, comparing standards, etc.).

Affective Domain

1. *Receiving*—the learner is aware of or attends to an event or stimulus (e.g., listening, attending, etc.).
2. *Responding*—the learner reacts to an event or stimulus (e.g., obeying, participating, speaking, etc.).
3. *Valuing*—the learner displays an acceptance or preference for a value or belief (e.g., desiring, preferring, etc.).
4. *Organization*—the learner organizes a set of values, determines interrelationships, and accepts some as dominant (e.g., identifying characteristics which the child admires, judging the responsibilities of people, relating to ethical standards, etc.).
5. *Characterization*—the learner acts in accordance with personal values and beliefs (e.g., developing a consistent philosophy of life, exhibiting respect for the worth and dignity of human beings, etc.).

Psychomotor Domain

1. *Perception*—the learner becomes aware of objects, qualities, or relations through his or her senses.
2. *Set*—the learner makes preparatory adjustments mentally, physically, and emotionally.
3. *Precision*—the learner practices and performs components of complex acts. Errors are minimal.
4. *Articulation*—the learner coordinates a series of acts by establishing sequence and harmony. Performance involves accuracy, control, time, and speed.
5. *Naturalization*—the learner performs automatically and spontaneously. Performance becomes smooth and natural.

Evaluation of Behaviors

In most instances *cognitive* behaviors can be evaluated through written or spoken work of the individual (e.g., standardized and nonstandardized tests, teacher-prepared materials, written reports, discussion). Until recently, more emphasis was placed on the measurement of cognitive behaviors than on affective behaviors even though the affective domain is applicable to a majority of language skills.

Measurement in the *affective* domain has utilized teacher observation, checklists, rating scales, and so forth. Often the affective behavior instrument measures only the receiving and responding levels of behavior. Measurement of valuing, organization, and characterization levels in the affective domain is best accomplished through open-ended activities in a threat-free situation where the individual is not expected to comply. Examples of objectives at the various levels of the affective domain could include:

Receiving
> Listens (carefully) when others speak
> Listens for specific sounds or words
> Displays interest in language study

Responding
> Complies with conventions and mechanics of writing
> Observes procedures used for language games
> Voluntarily seeks new information about the history of language
> Participates in research and language projects
> Uses good speaking and listening habits
> Finds pleasure in reading
> Enjoys working with others on projects

Valuing
> Has desire to improve abilities in the communication skills
> Displays desire and interest in learning
> Has a sense of responsibility about the quality of his or her work
> Assumes responsibility for helping others attain their goals

Organization
> Identifies characteristics in people he or she admires
> Forms judgments about the responsibilities of people
> Judges various people as individuals in terms of their behaviors

Characterization
> Revises judgments in light of new evidence
> Views problems objectively
> Depends upon scientific procedures for investigating a problem
> Exhibits respect for human worth and dignity

Instruments for measuring *psychomotor* behavior include observation systems, rating scales, and checklists. Operation in the psychomotor area takes place during handwriting, speaking, cutting out pictures, drawing, constructing bulletin board displays, using gestures, and doing pantomime.

The Environment and the Teacher

The language development of children admittedly varies widely as they enter school and proceed through the grades. However, these differences should be cherished and preserved so that originality of speaking and thinking will be apparent as children mature. Language skills are developed best in a classroom where pupils are grouped informally and where they discuss topics meaningful to them.

In fact, the key to the teaching of language, argues Weber, is the creation of a community in which children feel the need as well as the desire to communicate with a variety of individuals and groups, both adult and peer.[4] That, in turn, means providing an environment in which children can be involved in a range of different activities, an environment in which they can see different possibilities in the same material or exercise, and an environment in which they are encouraged to express their understandings of their own experiences in different ways and at different levels. The two things that are built in are people to communicate with and things to communicate about.

In an effort to establish a more student-oriented classroom, the teacher might wish first to consider the distinctions between formal and informal program structures in the English language arts as presented in Table 1.1. The teacher might next examine the features of six different organizational models appropriate for the elementary school, as published by the California State Department of Education (Table 1.2).

It is the teacher who sets the tone for the environment. Depending upon the teacher's philosophical stance, even an open classroom may reflect prescriptive teaching while a self-contained classroom may stress most of the traits of informal structure. The teacher must communicate genuine interest and concern for the total development of each child. The teacher must respect

Table 1.1.
Formal and Informal Language Arts Program Structures.

Formal Structure	Informal Structure
Basic Material Scope/sequenced textbooks and workbooks for each language arts skill area	*Basic Material* A variety of textbooks, trade books, magazines, newspapers, and other media resources
Setting Traditional self-contained classroom	*Setting* Self-contained or open-space classroom
Instructional Process Ability groups and whole class instruction	*Instructional Process* Small groups/individual instruction according to diagnosed instructional needs and learning styles
Instructional Style Teacher-directed instructional skills—emphasis on assigned/memory learning	*Instructional Style* Group process and classroom management skills—emphasis on experience/discovery learning; accommodates the team-teaching approach
Teacher as educational disseminator	Teacher as educational facilitator

Source: *English Language Framework for California Public Schools: K–12* (Sacramento: State Department of Education, 1976), p. 65.

Table 1.2.
Organizational Models for the Elementary School.

Model 1.   Traditional Classroom in the Elementary School.

Salient Features	Other Aspects
Guarantees that all children have similar experiences and exposure to similar predetermined concepts	Emphasizes subject matter rather than children's needs and interests
Has easily perceived structure	Limits chance for student input
Tends to emphasize content over process	Minimizes opportunities for teachers and students to exchange ideas to provide variety and depth
Provides, through structure, security for children who need it	Minimizes integration of subjects with each other
Provides an instructional program familiar to most parents	Maintains status quo

Model 2.   Open Classroom in the Elementary School.

Salient Features	Other Aspects
Provides informal educational setting conducive to growth of language	Language program lacking structure, thereby not providing that all children have similar experiences and exposure to similar concepts
Emphasizes student-centered curriculum rather than content alone	Some children lacking maturity to be responsible for decisions necessary in an open classroom
Emphasizes process (how to learn) as well as content (what to learn)	Lacks structure; not carefully planned and well organized
Integrates oral and written language with classroom activities	Limits opportunities for all students to participate in same activity
Capitalizes on students' existing language facility through first-hand experiences	Lacks supportive structure for children who need more supervised activities

Model 3.   Open Space Schools at the Elementary Level.

(NOTE: Open space schools are designed without interior walls or partitions to provide for flexibility in instruction, resources, and function of students and teachers.)

Salient Features	Other Aspects
Fosters a comprehensive language arts program through close staff planning	Requires teachers to compromise with other teachers; difficult for some
Provides an atmosphere of freedom which encourages interaction with others	Requires children who have maturity to cope with much freedom
Enhances flexibility of activities due to the possible variety of space arrangements	Demands more time for cooperative staff planning

Model 4. Nongraded Program in the Elementary School.

(NOTE: The nongraded program model is based on the use of cross-aged grouping.)

Salient Features	Other Aspects
Delays the problem of whether to promote until junior high school	Demands additional time for cooperative staff planning
Groups students according to levels of performance to facilitate learning	Emphasizes subject matter rather than children's needs and interests
Encourages teachers to collaborate and coordinate their efforts in development of a language arts program	May accentuate differences between bright and slow for a given age, which may foster racial and ethnic stereotyping (Reasons for placement may vary; problems of an accelerated child are different from those of a remedial child working at the same skill level.)
	Allows little flexibility for transferring students within the school when interpersonal conflicts arise

Model 5. Individualized Program in the Elementary School.

Salient Features	Other Aspects
Identifies specific objectives for language arts learning	Demands both range and variety of appropriate materials to meet prescribed needs
Provides specific activities to meet identified language needs of students	Requires a consistent method of recordkeeping
Enables students to progress at their own learning rates	Requires parental and community orientation to understand progress reports in terms of individualization
Progresses through steps, enhancing possibility for success	Becomes repetitive for some students if restricted to programmed model

Model 6. Media/Resource Emphasis in the Elementary School.

Salient Features	Other Aspects
Provides experiences to enrich, extend, and practice language use	Requires adequate space, equipment, repair of equipment, and check-out systems
Circumvents the problem of students' reading difficulties which impede their language skill development	Confines the learning experience
Provides for various developmental levels and learning styles	
Enhances and extends, through a variety of language arts programs, the concepts developed by the teacher	

Source: *English Language Framework for California Public Schools: K–12* (Sacramento: State Department of Education, 1976), pp. 66–67.

the children's individual personalities, provide the pupils with opportunities to work at tasks suited to their abilities, and create a climate of mutual acceptance and rapport. In a practical sense, both printed and nonprinted materials should be displayed within reach of the boys and girls, seating arrangements should accommodate physical differences or needs, and adequate lighting and ventilation should be provided.

The teacher must plan for a correlation of expression in art, music, drama, writing, and rhythmic games and replenish learning centers, bulletin boards, and other displays with fresh materials as new areas of study begin and interests shift. In addition, the teacher must continually provide activities which foster creative thinking or promote problem solving. And the teacher must demonstrate a personal interest in learning by sharing personal books and nonprinted resources with the class.

Developing Language Readiness

Language readiness activities cannot be differentiated from other language learning experiences, except that they are those experiences which are recommended before children begin the routine use of readers and textbooks.

Major Types of Beginning Language Activities

Firsthand Experiences

A language is a system of arbitrary verbal symbols. Children cannot listen, speak, read, or write very well until they have learned a large number of symbols and the concepts related to these symbols. Consequently, children must have extensive firsthand experiences with places, such as the zoo, the airport, and the supermarket, and with concrete objects, such as a flower, an aquarium, or an umbrella, in order to attain a functioning vocabulary. Children must also have experiences to help learn the meanings of a myriad of abstract concepts such as fairness, kindness, and responsibility. The development of vocabulary is a necessary prerequisite to language fluency.

Imaginative Experiences

Looking for forms in the clouds and listening for messages in the wind or rain are all experiences that stimulate the imagination. Such activities offer occasions for use of descriptive words and figurative speech that help children to enjoy poetic literature and increase their language power.

Sensory Experiences

The experiences of smelling, seeing, touching, tasting, and hearing are related to firsthand experiences but imply greater refinement. Children need to learn to identify numerous objects by shape, texture, or sound. Appropriate experiences include making and classifying collections, playing identification games when blindfolded, and participating in tasting parties. As the children learn to use their senses, they extend their vocabularies and store up percepts that will help them in their reading and writing.

Picture Interpretation

Pupils can tell a story illustrated by a single picture, "read" a story from a wordless picture book or a sequence of pictures, and sort and classify pictures according to various topics or word elements. They can illustrate concepts with pictures and play matching games with pictures. Picture dictionaries help teach early work-study habits. And it is possible for the teacher to stimulate concept development through the use of pictures collected from magazines, discarded schoolbooks, and used workbooks.

Listening to well-selected stories gives children opportunities to learn listening and comprehension skills and to become acquainted with the various qualities of literature that make it enjoyable. Probably nothing has more effect on the development of the pupils' desire to learn to read than listening to appealing stories.

Story Listening

Language readiness activities include a variety of both first-hand and imaginative experiences. (Photo courtesy of James Ballard.)

Young children readily appreciate the poet's ability to paint word pictures and to express different moods; they quickly learn to sense the rhythm and listen for rhyming sounds. Repetitive phrases aid them in hearing varied speech sounds, and nonsense verse leads them into their own efforts at creative expression. Poems can help the pupils to see their own selves, to develop a healthy sense of humor, and even to acquire increased ease in communication situations.

Poetry Experiences

In these types of activities children step into other people's shoes and portray others' personalities. In learning to identify with others pupils learn to think creatively, to use common courtesies, and (in dramatic play) to use the mechanics of oral communication to express themselves in clear and colorful ways.

Dramatic Play and Pantomime

Classrooms often display puppets, but paper dolls are not frequently utilized in teaching. Children love to work with both devices, however, and through such experiences they grow in eye-hand coordination. Puppets and paper dolls have the advantage of permitting shy children to hide behind their characters, thereby making it easier for boys and girls to speak freely.

Puppetry and Paper Dolls

Puzzles	Jigsaw puzzles that have large pieces provide purposeful practice in differentiating shapes and sizes. They develop eye-hand coordination and habits of concentration. A variety of durable puzzles can be obtained from Creative Playthings.
Musical Games	Singing games such as "London Bridge" and "Looby-Loo" teach articulation and the rhythm of the language.
Word Games	The children whose home backgrounds cause them to use words habitually in patterns that are considered nonstandard will be handicapped in speaking, reading, and writing in many situations. Most word and sentence games provide practice in standard English usage.
Use of Educational Television	Programs, such as "The Electric Company" and "Sesame Street," promote language development among many young viewers. Children may watch them on the classroom set or at home. Research has shown that viewers of "The Electric Company" make significant gains over nonviewers in the reading skills which the program is designed to teach and that the program is an effective instructional supplement for target-age pupils in the bottom half of their class who are just beginning to experience reading difficulty.[5]
Experience Charts	These charts may be employed for constructing group experience stories, recording plans, displaying information, and a number of other purposes. Through their use children learn page orientation, sequential organization, initial sight vocabulary, and various language functions.
Conversation Periods	It is essential that the daily schedule provide some periods when children work quietly on individual projects and other periods when they can learn the give-and-take of lively, polite conversation. A short session for sharing out-of-school experiences may stimulate conversation, especially if the class is broken into small congenial groups for the activity so that simple social responsibilities and courtesies may be taught. Classroom snack times also offer occasions for teaching and learning language usage.
Use of Films and Filmstrips	Motion pictures and filmstrips effectively develop concepts, foster literary appreciation, and teach language patterns. The filmed experience must be followed, however, by a related verbalization if maximum benefits are to be obtained. Some teachers find the loop projector especially worthwhile. (Titles of selected films and filmstrips are provided in Appendix 4.)
Use of Recordings	Records that are available can be classified into three language instruction categories: concept development, literary appreciation, and auditory discrimination. They may be used well as early as kindergarten and first grade. (Titles of selected recordings are included in Appendix 4.)

The ways in which a tape recorder can be employed for language development are so numerous that every classroom should have its own machine. In speech arts, for example, the initial taping of puppet plays provides an opportunity for pupils to listen critically and suggest changes in the production. The tape recorder can also be used for gathering outdoor sounds for indoor listening or for bringing an evening radio program to school for a daytime lesson.

Use of the Tape Recorder

During unit study children discover new ways in which language may be used in group planning, in recording of experiences, and in evaluating outcomes. Frequently they may learn how to make and read labels and how to use books (with the teacher's help) as sources of information.

Unit Experiences

Children's first writing experiences may be the drawing of their initials in manuscript capitals on booklets related to unit activities. When they are ready to learn to write their full names they should be taught to use both uppercase and lowercase letters so that there is no problem of relearning writing habits later. Next, the more advanced children can learn to make signs as part of their unit work.

Beginning Writing

The early retelling by children of stories they have heard aids them in learning to relate events in sequence. Experience chart planning and picture interpretation projects also add to creative skills. The first expression usually consists of recounting personal experiences, and some beginners never progress any further. Others can compose an entire original story several sentences long. Young children who can express their ideas with some degree of sensitivity and imagination are well along the road to language fluency.

Telling Original Stories

It is only a short step from telling personal experience stories and original stories to dictating them for the teacher to record. As boys and girls dictate and watch the teacher write the dictation, they learn page orientation and gradually attain a sight vocabulary. With guidance, children generalize that certain letters and letter combinations stand for specific sounds which appear in words. Each child's dictated stories contain his or her own vocabulary and are as long or short as attention span and ability permit them to be. Since the work is so completely individualized, one immature pupil can enjoy participation in the activity without learning to read a single word, while another may advance to the second- or third-grade reading level. Dictated stories lead toward experiences in writing one's own stories and in reading books and so are important milestones in a coordinated language arts curriculum.

Dictated Stories

1. Of the ten subgroups of essential competencies for English programs, which two do you feel should receive the least attention in the elementary school? Can you justify your ratings?
2. Why are teachers and parents often fearful of the evaluation of affective behaviors? How can such concern be properly managed?

Discussion Questions

3. As an aide or student teacher, how can you adapt phases of the language arts program to pupils who (a) use gestures or noises in order to communicate; or (b) have a limited range of concepts and vocabulary useful for school; or (c) lack interest in work and study?
4. Which of the major types of beginning language activities would you use with less advantaged first graders enrolled in a school district noted for its limited financial resources?

Suggested Projects

1. Prepare for the grade of your choice a list of goals that are appropriate for the language arts program of the school where you observe or work.
2. Locate the teacher's edition for one elementary language arts text series, such as *Language for Meaning* (Houghton Mifflin, 1978) or *Patterns of Language* (American Book Company, 1977). Categorize the instructional objectives in one chapter or section, first according to the three educational domains and then according to the level within each of them.
3. Draw and label on a sheet of graph paper a classroom arrangement conducive to language development. Then, on the other side of the paper, list briefly other items which would further stimulate the language arts program in such an environment.
4. Role play: A classroom teacher justifies the expenses involved in the language arts program before a group of parents determined to slash school costs.

Related Readings

Adams, A. et al. 1977. *Mainstreaming Language Arts and Social Studies*. Santa Monica, California: Goodyear Publishing Co.

Becker, W. C. 1977. "Teaching Reading and Language to the Disadvantaged." *Harvard Educational Review* 47: 518–43.

Chase, N. C. et al. 1976. "Preparation of the Elementary Language Arts Teacher." *Language Arts* 53: 363–69.

DeStefano, J. S. 1978. *Language, the Learner, and the School*. New York: John Wiley.

Flanagan, M. C., and Boone, R. S. 1977. *Using Media in the Language Arts*. Itasca, Illinois: F. E. Peacock Publishing Co.

Goodman, Y. et al. 1976. "Forum: Guidelines to Evaluate the English Component in the Elementary School Program." *Language Arts* 53: 828–38.

Graves, D. H. 1977. "Research Update: Language Arts Textbooks—A Writing Process Evaluation." *Language Arts* 54: 817–23.

Stelzer, C. A. 1976. "Language Alive!" *Teacher* 93: 74–77.

Weinstein, C. S. 1977. "Modifying Student Behavior in an Open Classroom through Changes in the Physical Design." *American Educational Research Journal* 14: 249–72.

Zahorik, J. A. 1976. "The Virtue of Vagueness in Instructional Objectives." *Elementary School Journal* 76: 411–19.

The Child 2

The two major theories of language acquisition in children

Ways in which maturing children change linguistically in their orientation to the world

The Piagetian stages of intellectual growth in children that concern the elementary school teacher

Some of the individual variations in the heterogeneous classroom for which the teacher must plan

A knowledge of child development is essential to the design and implementation of a solid language arts program. Also, coupled with this knowledge of the child's total development, there must be an awareness of the child's acquisition and growth in language.

Language Acquisition and Development

Young children in all cultures appear to master the complex task of acquiring an abstract system of linguistic knowledge. This knowledge or competence enables them to produce an infinite variety of sentences, to understand and make judgments about sentences, and to develop an unconscious awareness of both the limitations and creative capacity of language. Yet most of this knowledge is attained early in life (*primarily* between the ages of two and five) without direct instruction. Psycholinguists are still investigating the attainment of this knowledge because to date there has been no complete explanation acceptable to everyone.

Since the mid 1960s two major theories about language acquisition in children have evolved. First, there is the *behavioristic theory* which holds that boys and girls learn their language through imitation. Proponents argue that stimuli and reinforcement bring about changes in children's language. Boys and girls who produce desired language patterns receive social and material reinforcements as rewards. Opponents contend however that (1) children utter certain expressions which they have never heard anyone say (so that their language is hardly a faithful imitation); (2) children's speech is highly resistant to alteration by adult intervention; and (3) the practical task of memorizing all of the possible language structures is virtually impossible. The behavioristic theory is known also as the *environmental* or *empiricist* or *associationist* view.

The second prevalent theory is the *nativistic theory* which maintains that boys and girls learn their language from within themselves because language is innate. Proponents contend that (1) the onset and accomplishment of minimal language development seem unaffected by linguistic or cultural variations; (2) language cannot be taught to nonhuman forms of life whereas the suppression of language acquisition among humans is almost impossible; and (3) only humans have the necessary physiological and anatomical features to engage in sustained language. The nativistic theory is also known as the *genetic, generative, mentalist, rationalist,* or *biological* view.

Both theories appear to be umbrellas. Parents, teachers, and other adults who observe children's language daily notice imitative sounds as well as nonsocial speech. So until there is a better understanding of the complex process of language acquisition, concerned adults should be aware of both major theories and use the insights from each. They should be equally aware of the development of language performance or behavior because mastery of the spoken language has been found to be basic to achieving success in reading and writing.

Studies of the stages of that development vary to some extent depending upon the observer and the techniques used. Clear-cut delineations are not possible. Nevertheless, authorities generally agree upon certain age ranges which may indicate progressive stages of speech development in young children, as shown in Table 2.1.

The *undifferentiated cry* occurs during the first month of life and appears to be wholly reflexive; it is part of the total bodily response to a new environment. The *differentiated cry,* observed between the second and third months of life, varies with the type of situation or stimulus: thirst, hunger, pressure, or fear; each arouses a selective response and cry with regular recurrence. All of the characteristic sounds exercise the speech apparatus. Data from these early months of life contain all the speech sounds that the human vocal system can produce.

· *Babbling* appears between the third and sixth months and consists primarily of vocal play in which children produce a great variety of sounds. Children emit sounds which occur in a language other than that of their speech community, numerous sounds that far surpass those prevalent in any one language. In fact, infants of all nations and cultures babble the same sounds and in the same order, following a highly stereotyped pattern. The babbling, however, is not as random as it might appear: infants use a front-to-back mouth action for vowel-like sounds but use a back-to-front mouth action to produce consonant-like sounds. During this period the first evidence of the role of hearing in speech can be observed. In the case of the congenitally deaf child, speech development terminates with the babbling period because deaf children lose interest in playing with mouth movements and exercising their vocal muscles.

Critical to the process of early language acquisition is the role of adults and siblings. If they focus the infant's attention on sounds produced that are approximations of words, the infant is likely to repeat those sounds again due to the positive reinforcement. By rewarding selective responses, families are apt to motivate infants to produce *phonemes* or the significant speech sounds comprising the language.

The production of phonemes steadily increases so that a thirty-month-old child is using vowels and consonants with a frequency approximating that of an adult. Age three represents the upper-age limit for mastery of most diphthongs (or blends of vowel and semivowel sounds) and of most vowels as well as the consonants *m, p, b, w, h, t, d,* and *n.* By age four most of the remaining consonants are being produced correctly and the child's phonological system closely approximates the model system of the language, lacking only those sounds which do not fit the stage of phonemic development that the young child has attained. Complete mastery, including two- and three-consonant blends, is attained at about eight years for most boys and girls. *Phonological development is not complete when children enter kindergarten.*

While the phonemes are being acquired, the child is combining them appropriately to express words. The age for the appearance of the first word, as reported by twenty-six nonbiographical studies, ranges from nine to nineteen months for normal children with the average set at eleven to twelve months.[1] Some handicapped children do not produce words even at sixty months, depending upon the environment, physical involvement, and degree of retardation.

The child's first words are likely to be *holophrases* or single words used to express a more complex idea. In order to interpret such a word correctly, information is needed about the situation that generates the holophrase; the more cues provided by the child, the greater are his or her chances to be understood. The single-word utterance tends to express an important idea and generally takes the form of a noun, pronoun, verb, adjective, or adverb. While anecdotal studies and case histories show that first words are the monosyllabic or reduplicated monosyllabic *mama, daddy,* and *bye,* research indicates that more functional words than these may appear first. For instance, a recent study of middle-class Hebrew boys revealed that the first words elicited by their mothers in the home were *this, that, here, no,* and *food.*[2] These words, together with gestures, resolve most children's problems by age twelve months. By twenty-four months some boys and girls have a vocabulary of more than 150 words (although others have a vocabulary of less than 5 words). By forty-eight months many children have a vocabulary of 1,000 words.

In contrast to their gradual mastery of phonology, children use syntax correctly (though incompletely of course) from the very beginning. Syntax concerns the arrangement of words in a sentence as well as the way each word relates to the other words. By age two, and sometimes as early as eighteen months, children begin to string together two-word and three-word sequences that have been termed "telegraphic speech." They form these sequences through *imitation and reduction;* i.e., children imitate what their parents say but reduce it by omitting prepositions, conjunctions, determiners, auxiliaries, and inflections. Such orderly sequences are the precursors of the sentence. Generally, normal children may be expected to have acquired at least a few hundred such presentences by the time they are thirty months of age.

Table 2.1.
Checklist of Language Behavior of Preschool Child.

Average Age	Question	Average Behavior
3–6 months	What does he do when you talk to him?	He awakens or quiets to the sound of his mother's voice.
	Does he react to your voice even when he cannot see you?	He typically turns eyes and head in the direction of the source of sound.
7–10 months	When he can't *see* what is happening, what does he do when he hears familiar footsteps . . . the dog barking . . . the telephone ringing . . . candy paper rattling . . . someone's voice . . . his own name?	He turns his head and shoulders toward familiar sounds, even when he cannot see what is happening. Such sounds do not have to be loud to cause him to respond.
11–15 months	Can he point to or find familiar objects or people, when he is asked to? *Example:* "Where is Jimmy?" "Find the ball."	He shows his understanding of some words by appropriate behavior; for example, he points to or looks at familiar objects or people, on request.
	Does he respond differently to different sounds?	He jabbers in response to a human voice, is apt to cry when there is thunder, or may frown when he is scolded.
	Does he enjoy listening to some sounds and imitating them?	Imitation indicates that he can hear the sounds and match them with his own sound production.
1½ years	Can he point to parts of his body when you ask him to? *Example:* "Show me your eyes." "Show me your nose."	Some children begin to identify parts of the body. He should be able to show his nose or eyes.
	How many understandable words does he ·use—words you are sure *really* mean something?	He should be using a few single words. They are not complete or pronounced perfectly but are clearly meaningful.
2 years	Can he follow simple verbal commands when you are careful not to give him any help, such as looking at the object or pointing in the right direction? *Example:* "Johnny, get your hat and give it to Daddy." "Debby, bring me your ball."	He should be able to follow a few simple commands without visual clues.
	Does he enjoy being read to? Does he point out pictures of familiar objects in a book when asked to? *Example:* "Show me the baby." "Where's the rabbit?"	Most two-year-olds enjoy being "read to" and shown simple pictures in a book or magazine, and will point out pictures when you ask them to.
	Does he use the names of familiar people and things such as *Mommy, milk, ball,* and *hat?*	He should be using a variety of everyday words heard in his home and neighborhood.

Source: *Learning to Talk: Speech, Hearing and Language Problems in the Pre-School Child*
(Bethesda, Maryland: National Institutes of Health, 1977), pp. 22–24.

Average Age	Question	Average Behavior
2 years (cont.)	What does he call himself?	He refers to himself by name.
	Is he beginning to show interest in the sound of radio or TV commercials?	Many two-year-olds do show such interest, by word or action.
	Is he putting a few words together to make little "sentences"? *Example:* "Go bye-bye car." "Milk all gone."	These "sentences" are not usually complete or grammatically correct.
2½ years	Does he know a few rhymes or songs? Does he enjoy hearing them?	Many children can say or sing short rhymes or songs and enjoy listening to records or to mother singing.
	What does he do when the ice cream man's bell rings, out of his sight, or when a car door or house door closes at a time when someone in the family usually comes home?	If a child has good hearing, and these are events that bring him pleasure, he usually reacts to the sound by running to look or telling someone what he hears.
3 years	Can he show that he understands the meaning of some words besides the names of things? *Example:* "Make the car go." "Give me your ball." "Put the block in your pocket." "Find the big doll."	He should be able to understand and use some simple verbs, pronouns, prepositions and adjectives, such as *go, me, in,* and *big.*
	Can he find you when you call him from another room?	He should be able to locate the source of a sound.
	Does he sometimes use complete sentences?	He should be using complete sentences some of the time.
4 years	Can he tell about events that have happened recently?	He should be able to give a connected account of some recent experiences.
	Can he carry out two directions, one after the other? *Example:* "Bobby, find Susie and tell her dinner's ready."	He should be able to carry out a sequence of two simple directions.
5 years	Do neighbors and others outside the family understand most of what he says?	His speech should be intelligible, although some sounds may still be mispronounced.
	Can he carry on a conversation with other children or familiar grown-ups?	Most children of this age can carry on a conversation if the vocabulary is within their experience.
	Does he begin a sentence with "I" instead of "me"; "he" instead of "him"?	He should use some pronouns correctly.
	Is his grammar almost as good as his parents'?	Most of the time, it should match the patterns of grammar used by the adults of his family and neighborhood.

By age three, most boys and girls are constructing simple affirmative-declarative sentences, putting together a subject (or a noun phrase) and a predicate (or a verb phrase). Then the length and complexity of utterances begin to increase in several ways. One major factor responsible for the increase is *adult expansion and extension* of child speech. Another is *child induction of the latent structure of language;* that is, children apparently process the speech they hear and induce from it general rules of structure which they later use in their own speech.

The rule system which boys and girls construct makes it possible for them to generate an infinite number and variety of sentences, including many never heard from anyone else.[3] The system is a set of rules for sentence construction, rules which neither the children nor their parents know explicitly. It consists of a series of grammars that have their own phonological, syntactic, and semantic components at each successive stage in the development of language. Boys and

Table 2.2.
Development of Syntax and Fluency in Children Ages Five to Twelve.

Ages 5 and 6

The average number of words per oral communication unit (independent clause with modifiers) will be about 6.8 with a variation between 6 and 8 for those who speak with strong or weak oral proficiency. The Tennessee research found slightly higher scores, about 7 as an average, with a range of 4 to 9.5, but their subjects represent a somewhat more affluent socioeconomic background than those in the Oakland study.

Children at this stage settle their use of pronouns and of verbs in the present and past tense. Complex sentences appear more often. As early as age two, "pre-forms" of causality and conditionality occur in which the ideas expressed by *if, because,* and *why* are implied in the children's language.

Ages 6 and 7

The average number of words per oral communication unit will be about 7.5 with a variation between 6.6 and 8.1. The research group in Ypsilanti, Michigan, known as High Scope, found the average number of words per written communication unit (grade two) ranging from 6.9 to 8.3.

Progress occurs in speaking complex sentences, especially those with adjectival clauses. Children begin to use conditional dependent clauses, such as those starting with *if.*

Ages 7 and 8

The average number of words per oral communication unit will be about 7.6 with a variation between 7 and 8.3. The Far West Laboratory for Educational Development in San Francisco found the average number of words per written communication unit (grade three) ranging from 6 to 7.

---

girls construct the rule system by using some general concepts about language. While psycholinguists do not agree on what these general concepts are, McNeill believes that the concept of a sentence is the guiding principle in children's efforts to organize and interpret linguistic evidence which fluent speakers make available to them.[4] Children take all speech, interact with it, and somehow develop the systems that constitute the grammar of their language.

Syntactical development is not complete when children enter kindergarten. The language development of 211 subjects who began as kindergartners in the Oakland, California area was studied by Loban for thirteen years.[5] He compiled a chart describing syntax and fluency during elementary school years. The chart combined his findings with those of Hunt in Florida, Watts in England, and O'Donnell, Griffin, and Norris in Tennessee.[6] An abridged version of this chart appears in Table 2.2.

Source: Adapted from Walter Loban, *Language Development: Kindergarten Through Grade Twelve.* Research Report No. 18 (Urbana, Illinois: National Council of Teachers of English, 1976), pp. 81–84.

Children now use relative pronouns as objects in subordinate adjectival clauses (*I have a dog which I feed every day*). They begin to use the subordinate clauses starting with *if, when,* and *because* more frequently.

Ages 8, 9, and 10

The average number of words per oral communication unit will be 9 with a variation from 7.5 to 9.3. The average number of words per written communication unit found by Loban was 8.0 with a range from 6 to 9, but the average number of words per T-unit (communication unit) in writing was 8.1 for boys and 9.0 for girls in the Hunt study.

Children begin to relate specific concepts to general ideas, using such connectors as *meanwhile, even if,* and *unless.* Some 50 percent of the children begin to use the connector *although* properly. They begin to use the present participle active and the perfect participle.

Ages 10, 11, and 12

The average number of words per oral communication unit will be about 9.5 with a variation from 8 to 10.5. The average number of words per written unit found by Loban was 9 with a range from 6.2 to 10.2.

All students show a marked advance in using longer communication units and in the incidence of subordinate adjectival clauses, both in writing and in speech. Nouns modified by a participle or participial phrase appear more often, as do the gerund phrase, the adverbial infinitive, and the compound or coordinate predicate.

At this age children frame hypotheses and envision their consequences. This involves using complex sentences with subordinate clauses of concession. Auxiliary verbs such as *might, could,* and *should* appear more frequently. Adverbial clauses occurred twice as frequently in the speech of twelve-year-olds as in kindergartners in O'Donnell's research.

Children's Maturing Linguistic Orientation to the World

While the overall growth patterns of schoolchildren (grades K–6) is noted in Table 2.3, the continuum of linguistic development for children is shown in four important ways.[7] Boys and girls first change in their *processing of experience,* moving from physical exploration of a concrete world to the mental discovery of abstract ideas. In an effort to receive ideas, young children depend upon active manipulation of the items in their environment. The raw material of their language comes from limited personal experience with their world. All of the ideas that children can communicate are related in terms of the concrete.

Table 2.3.
Growth Patterns of Schoolchildren K–6.

Grades K–2	Grades 3–4	Grades 5–6
The Child	*The Child*	*The Child*
Is only beginning to acquire the ability to verbalize and thus his or her real "domain" is still that of action and manipulation; develops spontaneous language as a means of self-expression and as a means of responding to others.	Begins to construct concepts and relationships about a variety of subjects; is constantly experimenting, and attempting to expand knowledge of the world around him or her; interests of boys and girls tend to diverge at this age.	Strives for independence from adults, is critical and challenging in family situations; selects heroes from outside of family and immediate circle.
Develops from egocentricity in kindergarten and grade 1 to curiosity about the world outside of himself or herself in grade 2; has short attention span.	Develops noticeable change in social attitudes; loses egocentricity and exclusive dependence upon parents, and is capable of effective collaboration with the group; desires peer approval and acceptance.	Strives to establish and maintain a role in the peer group; develops feelings of camaraderie and justice in relationships with peers.
Enjoys imaginative experiences of all kinds, since at this stage the child endows the physical world with life and intentions corresponding to his or her own.	Widens attention span, is capable of individual concentration when working alone; increases skill in independent reading.	Grows rapidly in physical development, girls at a greater rate than boys; understands and accepts the sex role.
Builds concepts through a variety of thought-provoking experiences; begins to develop humor.	Begins to develop moral feelings, to distinguish between right and wrong, and to acquire a sense of justice.	Gains in concentration and begins to think logically and form concepts; is able to pursue one subject intensively.
Needs warm relationships with adults since the child's first moral values stem from the will of parents and other persons he or she respects.	Needs relaxation and relief from tension at this period of rapid growth, change and adjustment to social situations.	Expands his or her concept of the community to include the world, while still seeking his or her own identity and understanding of self.
Desires to conform to the demands of school and society by acquiring independent reading skills.	Increases awareness of and expands interest in others.	Begins to acquire concepts of time and place and understand the sequence of past events.

Source: Adapted from *The School Library Media Center—Grades K–9* (New York: The New York City Board of Education, 1975).

Pupils in the middle grades move beyond the concrete as soon as their basic ideas become very familiar to them. When these ideas do become commonplace, they can be understood in semiabstract form in pictures or models that represent experience. Also, boys and girls continue to encounter new ideas at this age, particularly concepts that are more abstract (such as courage), through observing active, concrete examples. As children move beyond mere identification of each concrete referent, relationships between the basic ideas become important to them. It is then that children begin efforts to make relationships distinct. Since they are unaware of more explicit words at this stage, they frequently relate two ideas with "and."

Older boys and girls begin to explore an idea without concrete examples by merely "thinking about" it, as long as their previous experience has provided them with an adequate base. Having learned to establish simple relationships among items and ideas, children can begin to abstract more complex relationships. They can explore the future (which exists only in language) and can even create relationships between opposite concepts which are quite abstract (such as love and hate). Nevertheless, whenever an idea is brand new or highly abstract, older pupils must still build a concrete base in an effort to reach total understanding. As they communicate with others, they now include both the overall generalization as well as appropriate supporting detail. They do so whether speaking or writing their thoughts.

The second important way in which maturing children change linguistically is found in their *processing of environment*. Although initially egocentric, boys and girls develop the capacity to be objective and to evaluate experience outside themselves. Young children cannot conceive of an experience being anything other than what they perceive it to be because they can express only one point of view. Therefore they find it unnecessary to set the stage for communication. They present the facts as they see them and assume that listeners can share that context. When children receive ideas from others, they merely translate them into a familiar setting.

Pupils in the middle grades become less egocentric. They begin to realize that there is more than one way to interpret an experience and start to appreciate observations of reality expressed by their peers. As a result, they are challenged to make their own ideas more explicit. They begin to look for supportive detail in both personal expression and reception of ideas. No longer can they assume that their context of communication is understood by classmates.

Older children usually grow in the capacity to be objective. They appreciate that there are many points of view about any event, that they can assume a variety of roles, and that they can begin to correctly interpret differing opinions. They are much more selective and cautious in choosing details to communicate because these details present a point of view that may be challenged by peers, teachers, parents, or other adults.

A third element of linguistic change in children relates to the *time and space* nature of their experience. While young children are concerned with the here and now of their world, older boys and girls can express other times and places. Young children can only experience what is happening now because they are egocentric and dependent upon the concrete. In the time dimension their experiences remain specific. Most of their early efforts at communication are in narrative form, coming forth as loosely related series of events.

Pupils in the middle grades become proficient in expressing events more objectively. They can use pictures to recall experiences related to their present tasks and accumulate personal experiences from the recent past to enhance the present. Through vicarious identification they can even take advantage of the experiences of others by relating differing opinions to their own. This developing capacity may lead children into an abundance of detail. They may have difficulty in selecting only those points that concern a specific idea. For example, children's oral and written compositions may contain too many topics.

Older pupils have more experiences to relate—events from the past, present, and future set in many different contexts. They can cope with unfamiliar concepts as long as they can bring some personal experiences to bear on these concepts. In regard to expressing ideas that relate direct and secondary experiences, boys and girls are apt to focus on a few selected themes on which they can elaborate. They have much to relate and must carefully choose the most significant matters.

A fourth important way in which maturing children change linguistically is concerned with their *affective interpretation of reality*. Young children have only a personal way of viewing the world; their intake and expression of experience are pervaded by their feelings. Although pupils in the middle grades also view their experiences in strongly personal ways, they can understand and express the opinions of their peers. Older children develop the capacity to be more objective. Their perceptions of the world are built upon broader experiences and have greater impact involving numerous points of view. Provided that older children have been able to maintain positive self-images, they will bring personal views to the reception of unfamiliar ideas. Thus they will be able to express themselves clearly to classmates and concerned adults.

How Children Think, According to Piaget

The Swiss psychologist, Jean Piaget, views intellectual growth in children as a matter of sequential stages. These stages in the development of a child's capacity to use increasingly difficult thought operations are clearly defined. They are generally regulated by wide age spans and follow in an ordered sequence. A new stage will not be successfully undertaken until the previous stage has been properly attained. As children modify and add new experiences to those previously absorbed, new abilities evolve from the old. Although the sequence in which the stages appear are the same for all children, such factors as motivation, environment, native intelligence, and diversity of experience may retard or hasten the process of intellectual growth.

The sequence of stages described by Piaget begins with the *sensorimotor period* (birth to age two years). The first stage of interest to elementary teach-

During the preoperational period, children's growth in ability to relate language symbols and objects is found in their efforts to draw and make graphic representations. (Photo courtesy of the Ocean View School District, Huntington Beach, California.)

ers, however, is the *preoperational period* (ages two to seven years). This period is divided into the *egocentric* phase, which lasts until about age four, and into the *intuitive* phase. In the egocentric or preconceptual phase symbols are constructed in which boys and girls imitate and represent what they see through language and action. In the intuitive phase children extend and combine their action-images and correct their intuitive impressions of reality. During the preoperational period boys and girls are continually seeking information, asking questions, and acquiring new concepts. The relationship between language and concepts may be strengthened through puppetry, creative drama, and imaginative play. Additional growth in the ability to relate language symbols and objects may be found in children's initial efforts to draw and make graphic representations.

The next stage of intellectual development is the *concrete operations period* (ages seven to eleven/twelve years) when children lose much of their egocentricity. They become less dependent on either immediate perceptual cues or on actions as their thinking becomes "decentered." In this period boys and girls accept ideas other than their own as they communicate with their peers. They are now able to do mentally what they previously had to act out. Their internalized thinking operations help classifying, ordering in series, numbering, grouping, and subgrouping of action-images. This is a period of avid reading.

The fourth and final stage is generally beyond the immediate concern of most elementary school teachers. It is the *formal operations period* (ages eleven/twelve years to age fifteen years and beyond) when children advance to the solution of complex problems through reasoning. Their thinking is flexible and they perceive many possibilities, including those beyond any actual situation. They are no longer bound to the concrete but can think with symbols.

Principles of Development

Several principles from Piaget's theory can provide a basis for both curriculum construction and teacher roles in the elementary school:

1. While the acquisition of language is closely related to the growth of the thought process, both competencies do not necessarily develop at the same rate. A dominant factor in stimulating language growth is a specific set of environmental conditions. Thought processes, on the other hand, develop more slowly and are affected by a much wider (and more accessible) variety of environmental factors. A teacher should provide activities for children which are commensurate with their ability to understand rather than to articulate; otherwise the teacher will be deceived in attributing to the more verbal children mental growth that is beyond their years. The teacher must not assume that because a child can utter the word, he or she knows the concept. Language alone is not the answer. Nor does language training by itself lead to intellectual development.

2. Children's thought and language patterns differ from those of adults. A child must attain each level of thought development alone and the child does so through interaction with his or her world. While boys and girls may be helped to move to a higher level of thinking through proper experiences, they will not benefit from verbal explanations that are extraneous to their ways of thinking. The imposition of intellectual growth by means of formal instruction is not possible.

3. Learning is an active process and children learn best from concrete activities. There is intrinsic motivation in this type of learning which stems from children's innate curiosity about their world and the rewards that can be reaped by satisfying that curiosity through knowledge. When learning is physically and mentally active, thought is the internalization of that action.

   Young learners especially must be able to actively manipulate and explore varied materials and equipment in their environment so that they may construct their own knowledge. They are capable of intuitive learning when they have some part in purposeful activities both in and out of the classroom.

4. Though there is a fixed sequence in development, each child proceeds at his or her own rate. Knowledge of the developmental stages in children's thinking can help teachers become aware of the limitations as well as the possi-

bilities at each stage. Still, each boy and girl is different and should not be forced to learn material for which he or she is not ready.

While all children are not at the same place at the same time, all of them enjoy the same kinds of materials at the same stage of maturity. Therefore, differences in ability do not constitute a major factor in determining and providing for the listening, reading, and viewing interests of boys and girls. However, there are differences in the rates at which children pass through the various stages and in the number and complexity of book and nonbook materials that they choose.

5. Children learn from social experiences with their peers and with adults. In addition to learning by interacting with their physical environment, boys and girls learn by sharing experiences and discussing reactions and viewpoints with others. As they grow older, they lose their egocentricity. They have their opinions challenged; they encounter new ideas; and gradually they reshape and reconstruct their knowledge.

Bingham-Newman and Saunders warn teachers to listen *to* an answer, not *for* an answer, because children's answers can provide excellent information about children's thinking.[8] The unexpected answers can be used advantageously as another starting point. By accepting pupils' egocentric replies, teachers encourage young learners to be intellectually honest rather than to be looking, listening, or waiting for the right answer to be provided.

Within every heterogeneous classroom there are wide variations in the children's physical and emotional health and in their out-of-school experiences. The children are highly individual persons, shaped and influenced by the environment in which they have developed. The teacher's most challenging responsibility is to provide a program that meets children where they are, recognizes their potential, capitalizes upon their strengths, and moves them along at a pace consonant with their ability. The teacher recognizes individual variations in ability to understand and speak standard English; ability to observe and listen; ability to deal with abstraction; size and appropriateness of vocabulary; number and accuracy of concepts acquired; and in desire and ability to verbalize experiences.

Providing for Individual Differences

Since children learn at different rates, they require different materials, experiences, and instructional techniques; a single group activity often affects each member differently. The following section describes various types of learners and offers suggestions for adapting instruction and material to their needs.

Some Children	**The Teacher**
Use patterns of language that represent a dialect unlike the standard English classroom dialect.	Accepts each child's nonstandard dialect for communication purposes. Offers additional instruction in standard English.

Some Children	The Teacher
Have speech patterns that result in poor communication with teacher or classmates.	Assists each child in the speaker-audience situation. Plans program designed to improve pronunciation and intonation. Uses tape recorder for children to record and play back their own voices in different situations.
Are learning English as a second language, having had little or no practice with the structure, sound system, and vocabulary of the English language.	Supplements the class program with additional instruction and practice in English (see chapter 14).
Find their vocabulary inadequate, unfamiliar, or inappropriate in school situations.	Plans activities to develop concepts and related vocabulary. Checks constantly on word meaning. Replaces vulgarisms with acceptable expressions.
Use actions, gestures, facial expressions, and noises rather than words to communicate.	Encourages children to use oral language to make known their wishes and needs, or to describe actions, by letting them hear repeatedly what they are expected to say.
Lack confidence in their ability to learn.	Develops assurance by providing activities, materials, and assignments that promote successful learning.
Learn and work at a slower pace than others in the group. Need to take smaller learning steps.	Adapts instruction to individual and group needs. Introduces new concepts slowly, allowing time for understanding. Allows sufficient work time.
Have limited experience with school-type materials—pictures, books, educational toys, and games. Are insecure in handling and responding to them.	Provides abundance of intellectually stimulating materials and time to peruse and enjoy them. Gives careful direction in the handling and use of those materials.
Are less confident in school situations than in out-of-school situations.	Builds confidence so that the children can expect positive reactions and rewards from adults when they complete a task, ask questions, or explore ways of finding answers. Communicates to the children, by word or manner, any recognition of their progress, no matter how slight it may be.

Some Children	The Teacher
Require special support strengthened by the interest and cooperation of the school and the home.	Reports frequently and formally to the children and their parents. Plans regular parent-teacher conferences, providing a translator when necessary, and includes the children on appropriate occasions.
Lose interest in sustained "talking" by the teacher or other adults.	Tries to watch his or her own "talking" time. Encourages dialog with children. Intersperses verbal instruction with gestures, visuals, and realia. Provides children with interesting events to discuss; limits "listening time."
Listen actively when a physical response or game element is present, or when there is a visual focal point of attention.	Uses listening games that call for action rather than verbal response. Involves listeners in activities such as refrains, pantomime, and rhythms. Makes provision for interaction (teacher-pupil, pupil-pupil), noting how each child feels and responds.
Find it easier to discuss and evaluate incidents that are presented through dramatization rather than through verbalization.	Allows the children to act out incidents with projective devices that promote free speech. Uses realia, pictures, stories, filmstrips, and firsthand experiences as the basis for conversations and discussions.
Are shy in revealing personal fantasies and the realm of their imagination.	Involves the children in creating additional incidents for familiar story and TV characters or in creating imaginary characters and incidents. Encourages children to select media for interpretation.
Have a limited range of the concepts and vocabulary useful in school. Are not accustomed to looking for similarities that help them to classify objects.	Checks frequently on each child's understanding of common, everyday words and provides experiences to develop better understanding. Plans activities involving classifying, labeling, and discussing objects. Uses verbal experiences to deepen understandings.
Are limited in ability to draw inferences or to generalize on the basis of related experiences.	Offers activities through which he or she can guide children to arrive at generalizations and draw inferences.

Some Children	The Teacher
Lack interest in standards and study. Work without goals or an organized system.	Gives close supervision to development of work-study habits, setting sensible standards and requiring children to meet them.
Are not inclined to review experiences and to see the relationship between what happened today and yesterday.	Increases the number of experiences designed to stimulate recall and to relate the past to the present and the future.
Find it difficult to relate to unfamiliar adults or to confide in them.	Finds opportunities to establish a one-to-one relationship with every child. Comments positively on each child's personal appearance and performance. Encourages each child to talk with him or her about individual interests and problems.
Tend to rely on physical skill and courage to bolster self-image and to meet problems.	Shows the children that discussion is a better way of solving problems than name-calling and physical force.
Are happiest and most confident when they are permitted to engage in physical activities.	Provides ample time for physical expression—running, jumping, skipping, dancing, balancing, and playing singing games. Praises gross motor skills.

A student with individual interests, this boy has been encouraged by his teacher to share his hobby with the class. (Photo courtesy of Emil Fray.)

Some Children	The Teacher
Can accept responsibility and enjoy the importance of being asked to share in classroom duties.	Rotates duties and assignments. Discusses need for monitors. Stresses individual responsibility for class pride in room appearance.
Are accustomed to considerable freedom of movement and self-determined and self-directed play activities. Are ingenious in devising materials and games.	Praises independence of action and thought. Encourages creative use of time and equipment.
Pursue individual interests of academic value—collecting rocks or reading about dinosaurs.	Challenges children to continue and extend their interests. Helps them to plan ways of sharing their hobbies with the class.
Approach problem solving creatively and use materials and equipment imaginatively.	Praises original ideas and solutions. Provides the materials and equipment with which to work out problems.
Learn rapidly. Read at levels considerably beyond those of the majority of the group.	Provides special activities beyond the usual group assignments. Sees that books and other printed materials cover a sufficiently wide reading range. Offers nonprinted resources.
Can handle abstract ideas. Are able to generalize and hypothesize.	Poses problems, questions, and situations that require children to select, relate, and evaluate ideas and to make generalizations.

Efforts must be made to incorporate language into all the school activities of retarded children. The teacher/clinician should begin by using each child's own language system, especially when the pupil is acquiring a new skill. Then the teacher should work to expand the children's language by giving pupils a correct model to follow.

Developmentally, the foundation for language is based upon children learning to *respond to the stimuli* in the environment. Next, they must *organize the stimuli* into a structure that is purposeful for them. Finally, children must *react to the stimuli* overtly in relation to their responses and organization; this reaction elicits verbal and physical communication. Figure 2.1 shows these three divisions of language growth and the sequential stages within each which help children progress in language skills and concepts. In Table 2.4 each stage is described and a sample visual activity and a sample auditory activity which promote each sequential stage are presented.

Fostering Language Development among the Mentally Retarded

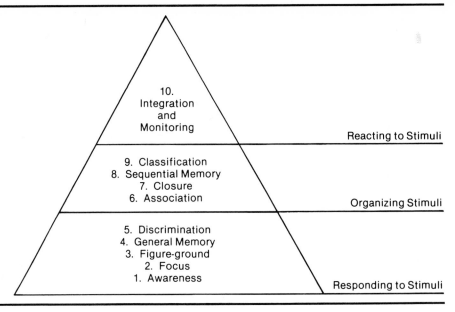

Figure 2.1.
Foundation for
Language Growth.

10.
Integration
and
Monitoring

Reacting to Stimuli

9. Classification
8. Sequential Memory
7. Closure
6. Association

Organizing Stimuli

5. Discrimination
4. General Memory
3. Figure-ground
2. Focus
1. Awareness

Responding to Stimuli

Source: *Language Is Living* (Madison: Wisconsin Department of Public Instruction, 1976), p. vi.

Evaluation of Pupils' Progress in Language Development

Two formal tests for assessing early language usage among normal and handicapped children are the *Utah Test of Language Development* (revised edition) and the *Verbal Language Development Scale.*[9] The first is an instrument of fifty-one items that measures the expressive and receptive language skills of children ages 1.5 to 14.5; about one-half of the test items are related to the preschool age. An individual, untimed assessment, the *Utah Test of Language Development* can generally be completed in less than one hour. It is published by Communication Research Associates (Salt Lake City, Utah 84111) and has been fairly well received critically.

The *Verbal Language Development Scale* has received similar reviews. It consists of fifty items designed to be individually administered to children ages 1 month to 16 years, although 70 percent of the items relate to the preschool age (5.5 years and below). An expansion of the verbal portion of the *Vineland Social Maturity Scale,* it was revised in 1971. The test requires approximately thirty minutes to administer. It is published by American Guidance Service (Circle Pines, Minnesota 55014).

Besides these two published tools, there are some research instruments which are not available commercially but which may be ordered on microfilm (for a fee) from ERIC Document Reproduction Service.[10] Only those for the preschool age range (birth to kindergarten), primary age range (grades one to three), and intermediate age range (grades four to six) are listed here by title, author, date of construction, purpose, and ordering information.

Table 2.4.

Foundational Stages for Language Growth—Descriptions and Sample Activities

Foundational Stage and Definition	Auditory Activity	Visual Activity
Awareness Auditory: An individual's recognition that a sound has started, stopped, and/or changed. Visual: An individual's recognition that an image has appeared, disappeared, and/or changed.	Materials: Large objects in the classroom such as books, blocks, tambourines, etc. Technique: Produce sudden noise beyond immediate visual field and yet loud enough to attract child's attention auditorily. Watch for any reaction (head jerk, blinking of eyes, head turn, startle reflex, or a sudden stillness) from a very active child.	Materials: Large soft objects in the classroom such as foam balls, balloons, fleece balls, pillows Technique: Stand directly in front of child. Toss toward child. If objects touch the child, the soft quality will not hurt and the tactile stimulation will add to an awareness reaction. Any reaction such as eye blinking, flinching, verbal utterance, moving away, etc., would be acceptable.
Focus Auditory: The ability to locate a sound source in relation to the listener. Visual: The ability to locate an image in relation to the individual or the ability to localize in a distinct visual form.	Materials: Large objects in the classroom such as books, tambourines, bells, etc. Technique: Produce noise with object next to child's ear. Watch for reaction of head turning. If child does not turn head, do so for him or her. Reward appropriately.	Materials: Large toy or object Technique: Sit in front of child. Pick up large object and have the child focus on it. Move it around, left-right, high-low, and make sure he or she follows it. After a while, substitute small object for large.
Figure-Ground Auditory: The ability to distinguish foreground and background noise and to separate them meaningfully or the ability to pick out a specific sound from a background of other sounds. Visual: The ability to distinguish foreground and background image and to separate them meaningfully or the ability to pick out a specific image from a background of other images.	Materials: Record player Technique: Play soothing music softly in background. At first, just call child's name to get him or her to look at you. Then try simple commands. Slowly increase the background. Then change the background to chaotic noises, softly at first and then slowly louder. If child can perform commands despite noise, some appropriate reward is suggested since this will motivate the child.	Materials: Large objects in room Technique: Place two or three very different objects in a cleared area. Ask child to point to, go to, or bring you one of the objects. Reward appropriately. Note: Slowly add more objects to ones already there and slowly make them more similar in size and appearance.

The Child   37

Table 2.4 (cont.)

Foundational Stage and Definition	Auditory Activity	Visual Activity
General Memory Auditory: The ability to retain and recall general auditory information. Visual: The ability to retain and recall general visual information.	In order for a child to proceed to discrimination ability, the child has to remember the sound he or she has focused on in order to discriminate it from another or previous sounds. This idea is built on an expanding continuum. The child must increase his or her memory ability along with the increasingly more difficult language development. Thus, included in every activity is a memory factor aimed at developing the specific skill being worked on while at the same time increasing language ability. Note: This stage contains no specific activities because it was found that memory as defined was involved with most other activities contained in the other stages.	
Discrimination Auditory: The detection of differences in sounds. Visual: The detection of differences in shapes (visual images).	Materials: Two bells, two wooden blocks, two alarm clocks Technique: Place a bell, a wood block, and an alarm clock on table before child. Have a matching set out of child's visual field. Play one item. Child must reach for object with the corresponding sound.	Materials: Fruit (actual) Technique: Have the child actually examine real fruit from different angles and distances.
Association Auditory: The ability to relate stored auditory experiences so meaningful communication is achieved. Visual: The ability to relate stored visual experiences in order to interpret visual symbols, objects, or cues.	Materials: Objects in room Technique: The teacher names a sound like *m-m-m-m*. The children must search the room until they can name an object that begins with that sound. Later, the object that comes to mind does not have to be in the room.	Materials: Objects or pictures of objects (e.g., pencils, shoes, wagons, eggs, purses, nails, dolls, persons, umbrellas, etc.) Technique: Show the child one of the objects. Have the child point to and tell you (in sentences) the parts of the object while he or she is looking at it.
Closure Auditory: The auditory ability necessary to fill in gaps in what is heard so as to obtain correct and meaningful information from the auditory stimuli. Visual: The ability to complete an image, symbol, or cue even when the complete stimuli is not seen.	Materials: Animal picture cards Technique: Say, "I see a mon(*key*)," and show the picture card. Work on 2 or 3 pictures at a time.	Materials: Flannel board, half circles, quarter circles Technique: Assemble three-quarters of circle; have child complete.

Table 2.4 (cont.)

Foundational Stage and Definition	Auditory Activity	Visual Activity
Sequential Memory Auditory: The ability to recall in correct sequence and detail prior auditory information. Visual: The ability to recall in correct sequence and detail prior visual experiences.	Materials: Buzzer board, pencils Technique: Produce a pattern of long and short sounds and pauses. Child repeats pattern using the same materials.	Materials: Pictures of animals, toys, people Technique: Child studies one row of pictures, and after the pictures are removed, names the subjects pictured in their proper order.
Classification Auditory: The ability to sort and store incoming auditory signals. Visual: The ability to sort incoming visual stimuli into appropriate groups.	Materials: None Technique: Name three or four categories. Then describe something you are thinking of—"I am thinking of something with four legs. It is made of wood, has a cushion on it, and you sit on it." The child must name the category to which it belongs (e.g., furniture, animals, vehicles).	Materials: The classroom and all the objects in it; pencil and paper Technique: Have the child go around the room listing the objects according to the classification of what each is made of (e.g., wood, metal, plastic, glass, rubber, fiberglass, etc.).

Integration and Monitoring Verbal communication aided by emotion, gesture, and forethought.	**Practicing Proper Total Communication** **(Listening, Respecting What Is Said, and Speaking Sensibly)**

Rationale: Music involves reaction of the emotions of the entire body. These emotions can then be channeled for verbal expression.

Materials: Records or tapes of music that evoke different types of emotion

Technique: Students listen to music and move the way they feel.

Variations: Have children listen and describe how they feel.

Rationale: In this activity, awareness of instructions and memory are expanded.

Materials: Everyday objects

Technique: Give the students a series of instructions to follow. For example: take off your boots, open the door, step inside. Start with only a few simple, familiar directions. When they are receiving instructions correctly, make the instructions more difficult and rapid. Repeat what you ask if necessary. As the activity matures, you should be less willing to repeat.

Source: *Language Is Living* (Madison: Wisconsin Department of Public Instruction, 1976).

Preschool	*Elicited Imitation,* Dan Slobin and Charles Welsh, 1967, to discover the child's underlying linguistic competence, ED 012 892 and ED 051 881.
	Imitation-Comprehension-Production Test (ICP), Colin Fraser, Ursula Bellugi, and Roger Brown, 1963, to determine whether, as language develops, particular utterances or features of an utterance are generally understood before the same utterances or features are produced, ED 097 717.
Preschool/Primary	*Berko's Test of Morphology,* Jean Berko, 1958, to describe the evolution of the child's ability to apply morphological rules to new words by asking the child to inflect, to derive, to compound, and to analyze compound words, ED 097 716.
	Noun Plural Development Test, Stephen Koziol, Jr., 1970, to assess the ability to produce and recognize selected regular and irregular noun plural forms, ED 091 718.
Primary	*Linguistic Structures Repetition Test,* Carol Fisher, 1972, to measure the acquisition of syntactic structures in kindergarten, first-, and second-grade pupils, ED 091 746.
	The Test of Cognition, Estelle Fryburg, 1972, to evaluate a child's expressive and receptive language ability, ED 091 766.
Preschool, Primary, Intermediate	*Acquisition of Syntax Experiments,* Carol Chomsky, 1969, to study systematically the acquisition of complex syntactic structures in children between the ages of five and ten by testing their ability to interpret sentences exhibiting the structures under scrutiny, ED 045 626.
Intermediate	*K-Ratio Index,* K. H. Calvert, 1971, to measure the syntactic maturity of oral speech, ED 091 722.
	Linguistic Ability Measurement Program (LAT), Lester Golub and Wayne Frederick, 1970, to test linguistic structures in the English language, ED 040 401.
	Schema for Testing Language Arts Concept Attainment, Lester Golub et al., 1971, to test achievement of basic English language arts concepts appropriate to and generally taught at the fourth grade level, ED 068 960.
	Semantic Differential Scales for Use with Inner-City Pupils, Thomas McNamara, James Ayrer, and Irvin Farber, 1972, to provide a quantified estimate of the extent of meaning of a concept held by a respondent, using language patterns familiar to the respondent, ED 064 374.
	A Test of Sentence Meaning (ATSM), Albert Marcus 1968, to measure the level of understanding of literal meaning attained by pupils in grades five through eight by means of syntactic clues within written standard English sentences, ED 091 734.

1. Can the teacher help a child learn to process environment or experience? If so, how?
2. Why are social experiences so critical to the intellectual growth of children?
3. As an aide or teacher, how can you adapt phases of the language arts program to pupils who (a) use gestures or noises to communicate; or (b) have a limited range of concepts and vocabulary useful for school; or (c) lack interest in work and study?
4. Why must a teacher working with a retarded child begin with the child's own language system?

1. Tape the speech of one kindergartner, one second grader, and one fourth grader for three minutes each. Analyze each recording to determine the average number of words per communication unit.
2. Collect ten narrative replies by children. Then choose the three longest and most detailed replies and describe what kind of information they furnish about the thinking of elementary pupils.
3. Develop one auditory activity and one visual activity to develop the stage of general memory.
4. Watch an educational television show for young children. List the language skills it develops and describe how that development occurs.

Biehler, R. F. 1976. *Child Development: An Introduction.* New York: Houghton Mifflin.

Elkind, D. 1978. *A Sympathetic Understanding of the Child: Birth to Sixteen.* Boston: Allyn and Bacon, Inc.

Hallahan, D. P., and Kauffman, J. M. 1978. *Exceptional Children: Introduction to Special Education.* Englewood Cliffs, New Jersey: Prentice-Hall.

Hammill, D. D., and Bartel, N. R. 1978. *Teaching Children with Learning and Behavior Problems.* 2d ed. Boston: Allyn and Bacon, Inc.

Leitch, S. M. 1977. *A Child Learns to Speak: A Guide for Parents and Teachers.* Springfield, Illinois: Charles C Thomas Publisher.

Pflaum-Connor, S. 1978. *The Development of Language and Reading in Young Children.* 2d ed. Columbus, Ohio: Charles E. Merrill Publishing Co.

Robeck, M. 1978. *Infants and Children: Their Development and Learning.* New York: McGraw-Hill.

Smart, M. S., and Smart, R. C. 1977. *Children: Development and Relationships.* New York: Macmillan.

White, B. L. et al. 1978. *Experience and Environment: Major Influences in the Development of the Young Child.* Volume II. Englewood Cliffs, New Jersey: Prentice-Hall.

Yawkey, T. D., and Aronin, E. L. 1976. "Premises on Child Development: A Boon to the Elementary School. *Elementary School Journal* 77: 33–41.

The English Language 3

The varieties of phonemes and morphemes

The four basic sentence patterns most generally used in the elementary school

The difference between a regional dialect and a social dialect

Factors explaining why the English language is constantly changing

The English language is an arbitrary system relating sounds and meanings. Someone is described as "knowing" the language when he or she understands the sounds used in that language, the basic units of meaning, and the rules combining sounds and meanings to form sentences. A person is then said to have command of the language's phonological, morphological, syntactic, and semantic systems.

Phonology

Each language has its own set of vocal sounds (*phones*). As children grow into productive members of the speech community, they develop only those phones which they find useful in communicating. The study of phones is called *phonetics*.

Of the many phones in the English language, only a relatively small number differ significantly from each other. Those that do differ are called *phonemes* or minimal contrastive elements. While English is generally said to possess forty-five phonemes, there is actually little agreement as to the number of phonemes in the American English language. The reported totals range from thirty-five to forty-seven because there are different classification schemes and because sounds which are significant in one dialect may be less so in another. The study of phonemes or distinctive sounds that make up a language is called *phonology*. When phonemes appear in textual matter, the symbol for a phoneme appears between slanted bars: / /.

There are both segmental phonemes and nonsegmental (or suprasegmental) phonemes. The first group of thirty-three includes consonants, vowels, and semivowels (or phonemes that function either as consonants or as parts of diphthongs like /w/ and /y/) and constitutes the sequential elements, with some overlapping and gliding, of syllables, words, and sentences. The second group of twelve includes phonemes of stress, pitch, and juncture which occur simultaneously with the segmental phonemes or separate them, and which are often considered together under the heading of *intonation*. The briefest utterance in English will have at least two segmental phonemes and three suprasegmental phonemes.

Combinations of suprasegmental phonemes are responsible for the rhythm and cadence of a language. Their function is similar to that of punctuation in writing although punctuation and intonation are not in exact correspondence. Intonation patterns are divided into stress, pitch, and juncture.

Stress refers to the relative degree of intensity of loudness of different syllables in a sentence, and there are four stress phonemes in speaking which can be quite simply indicated for purposes of discussion as: primary (the strongest stress (/); secondary stress (\); tertiary stress (∧); and weak (slight) stress (⌣). One-syllable words, when pronounced alone, usually have the strongest, or primary, stress, for example, *féet, ádd, íf*. Words of two or more syllables have varying patterns of stress, as in *ínvălĭd* or *ìnválĭd* and *mágnĕt* or *màgnétîc*. Phrases may vary in stress according to the meaning expressed, as in *lóud speàkĕr* or *loùd speákĕr*. Sentences, too, have varying patterns of stress, depending upon the meaning intended, for example, *Jóhn bought three books; John boúght three books; John bought thrée books;* or *John bought three bóoks*.

Pitch refers to the ups and downs, or tunes, in a stream of speech. Although many changes in pitch do not affect meaning, there are some that do. Differences in pitch distinguish between statements and questions in English. A way of picturing this difference might be as follows: *John bought ⌐three books?* or *John⌐ bought three ⌐books*. A statement has a falling pitch contour, while a question has a rising pitch contour. There are four significant pitch phonemes in English, designated from lowest to highest as low, normal, high, and highest and numbered from one to four. The basic pitch of a person's voice, regardless of whether the person is a man or woman, is marked as pitch two.

The term *juncture* refers to the ways a speaker of English makes the transition from one phoneme to the next. There are four juncture phonemes and all are relevant to the teaching of spelling. Open or internal juncture (+) is the vocal signal that usually divides words from each other; it is the slight retarding of the flow of sound that distinguishes *ice cream* and *I scream*. The three terminal junctures are the vocal signals that generally divide sequences of words into constructions: (a) falling or fade-fall terminal (↘) ordinarily ends statements, commands, and some questions; (b) rising or fade-rise terminal (↗) usually ends questions that are intended to express surprise, doubt, regret, or other emotion; and (c) sustained or level terminal (→) marks the divisions between certain constructions within a sentence.

When pupils listen carefully to someone speaking his or her native language, they will notice that while the speaker always uses certain phonemes in certain places, the same phoneme is not always pronounced in exactly the same way each time. The speaker's different pronunciations of the same phoneme, however, are of a kind that indicate clearly to someone familiar with the language which phoneme is being used. Most native speakers do not realize that they make these differences in sounds and a student of the language is free to use any one of the pronunciations in such cases. In describing a language it can be stated that such variations are *allophones* or two (or more) forms of the same phoneme.

Morphology

Any linguistic utterance is a sequence of individually meaningless phonemes as well as a sequence of meaningful morphemes. The sentence *The cat chased the birds* consists of vowels and consonants (segmental phonemes) spoken at varied *pitches* with different degrees of *stress*. It is simultaneously a string of the following *morphemes:* {the}, {cat}, {chase}, {-d}, {the}, {bird}, {z}.

Morphemes are larger building stones which cannot be defined as precisely as phonemes. While phonemes only distinguish between meanings without adding to or changing them, morphemes are units of discourse that carry meaning. In the words *big* and *bag,* for example, there is a contrast in sounds

Fourth graders listen to a taped lesson on prefixes and suffixes with the assistance of a parent volunteer. (Courtesy of the Fountain Valley School District, Fountain Valley, California.)

by which one word is distinguished from the other, but the sounds responsible for the distinction do not in themselves carry any meaning and are, therefore, phonemes. In the words *bag* and *bags,* however, the sound that has been added causes a change in meaning and such a sound is termed a morpheme. One morpheme may contain one phoneme or several phonemes. Linguists write the symbol for a morpheme between braces: { }.

Morphemes are the smallest units of speech that have identifiable meanings of their own. They are not necessarily identical with syllables or words. The major morpheme classes in English are *bases* and *affixes*. Most bases (or roots) stand alone as words and so are described as *free* morphemes. Affixes never stand alone; they are always attached to bases, either before them as prefixes or after them as suffixes, and so are called *bound* morphemes. The study of morphemes or units of meaning is known as *morphology*.

Affixes are either derivational or inflectional. All prefixes are derivational affixes but suffixes may be either derivational or inflectional. In English no new inflectional affixes have been added for 700 years although derivational affixes are added routinely as needed, such as the recent prefixes {mini}, {midi}, and {maxi}. Derivational affixes help in evolving new words whose grammatical forms differ from the words to which the affixes are attached. Inflectional affixes cause words to which they are attached to change their grammatical meanings.

Just as phonemes have allophones, morphemes have *allomorphs* or positional variants; for example, the prefixal morpheme *in* has four allomorphs: *in-* (inactive), *il-* (illogical), *im-* (immodest), and *ir* (irrelevant).

Syntax

Morphemes cannot be arranged one after another in any elective order. Instead, for each language there are combinations in which morphemes can be put together in an utterance. Such combinations are known as constructions, and *syntax* is the study of these constructions. Syntax deals with word order and the relationships between word order and meaning; for example, the words *the* and *cat* can be grouped together in the construction, *the cat,* but not *cat the.* As mentioned earlier, most syntactic structures are used by even the youngest children.

The largest English construction is the sentence. Children therefore should have considerable experience in changing sentences about; in modifying and rearranging the information that sentences provide; and in exploring relationships among the various kinds of sentences. During the elementary years basic sentence patterns can be taught inductively and largely without emphasis on terminology. All theories of grammar recognize that English sentence patterns have two main parts: the subject and predicate (according to traditional grammar) or the noun phrase and the verb phrase (according to transformational generative grammar). Although linguists do not agree as to the number of patterns to be considered basic, these four sentence patterns are the ones most generally used in the elementary school, with the first two types accounting for 85 percent of the sentences found in the speech uttered by children:

Pattern I. *N¹ V.* Noun (or pronoun) and (intransitive) verb.
Example: *Birds sang.*
   Subject/predicate

Pattern II. *N¹ V N².* Noun (or pronoun), (transitive) verb, and noun
   (or pronoun).
Example: *Mother bought cookies.*
   Subject/predicate/object
(Can be transformed to passive voice.)

Pattern III. *N¹ L V N¹.* Noun (or pronoun), linking verb, and noun
   (or pronoun).
Example: *Mother is a teacher.*
   Subject/predicate/predicate noun
(Can be an equation pattern since nouns or pronouns can exchange
places.)

Pattern IV. *N¹ L V Aj.* Noun (or pronoun), linking verb, and
   adjective.
Example: *Summer is hot.*
   Subject/predicate/predicate adjective[1]

Semantics

The study of the role of language in human life is called *semantics*. It explains how language is used to persuade, to control behavior, to transmit information, to create and express social cohesion, and to express thoughts and feelings.[2]

Children today must understand certain concepts about the content of language since they are constantly exposed to the pervasive effects of the mass media. They must comprehend propaganda and persuasion techniques. They must learn to distinguish between what is actually reported, what is inferred from the report, and what judgment has been formed. They must recognize varying degrees of abstraction and generality in words. They must realize the importance of context and how words or sentences lifted out of context can distort meaning. They must understand that words possess an affective content as well as an informational one and that the attitudes of writers and speakers can frequently be discerned by studying the words which they use. Magazine and newspaper advertisements are readily accessible sources that children can use for examination and analysis of how language may be manipulated.

Usage and Dialect

Language must be suited to the context in which it is used. The notion that there is only one "correct" way to express an idea is both linguistically naive and counterproductive, states Malmstrom; and wise language arts teachers encourage students to observe usage variety in literature and to experiment with language choice in composition.[3]

There are at least seven interlocking dimensions of modern English usage. The first is *socioeconomic-educational* and involves the spectrum of usage extending from standard to nonstandard English and reflecting the speaker's education and/or socioeconomic status. The second is *stylistic* and involves the distinction between usage at formal ceremonies, for example, and that at a backyard picnic. The third dimension is *sex-based* and concerns the spectrum of usage extending from the obscenities deemed rough and masculine to the gentle expressions considered to be very feminine. The fourth viewpoint is *methodological;* this involves the choice between writing and speech and the distinction between the punctuation of writing and the intonation of speech. The fifth dimension is *historical;* for example, it concerns the differences between Chaucer's usage and present-day usage. The sixth viewpoint is *occupational* and involves the unique vocabulary and phraseology of each job speciality. The seventh dimension is *geographic* and relates to the phenomenon that English usage possesses international, national, regional, and local dialects.[4] All seven of these dimensions interact, thereby creating the total situation of modern usage. Dimensions involved in a speaker's ability to understand and to produce appropriate styles of language as part of his or her broader ability to communicate can be illustrated by the acronym SPEAKING:

<u>S</u>etting:	When and where the speech act occurs affects variables such as volume. In some places no speech is allowed at times.
<u>P</u>articipants:	Sex, kinship, age, occupation, social class, or education may make a difference.
<u>E</u>nds:	The purpose of the speech act matters: Is it a request, warning, demand, query, or statement of fact?
<u>A</u>ct sequence:	Sometimes this refers to the prescribed form a speech act can take when it is controlled by the culture. At other times it refers to what can be talked about during the speech act.
<u>K</u>ey:	Identical words may express various moods, tones, or manners. The signal may be nonverbal or it can be conveyed by intonation, word choice, or other linguistic convention.
<u>I</u>nstrumentalities:	Different verbal codes may be chosen. A bilingual may choose between languages and a monolingual among regional or social dialects. The choice is generally an unconscious one and may indicate humor, distance, respect, intimacy, or insolence.
<u>N</u>orms:	Norms of interpretation and interaction during a speech act include taking turns in the conversation (if proper in the speaker's culture), knowing polite greeting forms, and other "linguistic manners" (including, for example, appropriate topics for dinner conversations).
<u>G</u>enres:	Certain speech acts may be categorized in formal structures, such as proverbs, riddles, editorials, myths, poems, or prayers.[5]

A change in one or more of these speech components of the social context may signal that some different linguistic rules should be used.

Some people mistakenly assume that *dialect* refers to corrupted, inadequate, or incorrect speech. Actually the term implies no value judgment. It refers merely to a habitual variety of usage or to a distinct variation in how a language is spoken. Dialects are fully formed systems. Every language has dialects and its native speakers use several dialects to meet the many needs of daily life.

Speakers of a particular dialect form a *speech community* which reflects the members' life styles or professional, national, family, or ethnic backgrounds. Certain common features mark the speech of the members, however these features may be defined. Nevertheless, no two members of a particular community ever speak alike because each person's speech is unique. This individualized speech or individual dialect is termed an *idiolect*.

One of the principal types of dialect is *regional* or geographical dialect used by speakers living in the same area. In the United States no single regional dialect is the accepted standard for the country. Instead, each area has its own standard which represents the dialect of its educated residents. In 1930, linguistic geographers (or dialectologists) led by Hans Kurath identified three major dialect areas on the Eastern Seaboard—the Northern, the Midland, and the Southern—as they began their work on the *Linguistic Atlas of the United States*. Incidentally, this monumental project is still unfinished, although publication is anticipated in another 25 years.

The Northern region includes the New England states and New York, extending northward from a line that starts on the northern edges of New Jersey and Pennsylvania and cuts through central Ohio, Indiana, and Illinois.

The Southern region extends southward from a line that begins in Delaware and then turns sharply southwest, following the Blue Ridge Mountains into the Carolinas. This is surprisingly the most heterogeneous dialect area.

The Midland region covers approximately the area between the two borders previously described.

Within the three major dialect regions there are a number of subregional variations in language. The New England coastal region, for instance, is plainly different from the rest of the Northern dialect area.

Regional dialects differ from each other in phonological, vocabulary, and syntactic or grammatical features. An example of the first difference is the "intrusive *r*" that appears in *Washington* and *wash* among residents of Indiana and Missouri. Vocabulary variety may be proved by the many synonyms for the word *relatives,* including *folks, people, kinfolk, folkses, homefolks,* and *kinnery.* Finally, a grammatical difference is the preference for *he don't* rather than *he doesn't* among residents in North Carolina. Americans generally are said to be puzzled by pronunciation differences, delighted by vocabulary differences, and repelled by grammatical differences.

On the whole, however, the speakers of American English have an advantage over those who speak the dialects of languages in most other countries where social and geographic mobility has been more limited for long periods of time. In the United States no functional block in communication normally intrudes between native speakers.

Regional dialects make interesting study. Some of the current English textbook series used in elementary schools contain material on regional dialect differences.

Social Dialect

Residents of the same geographical region do not all sound alike. The variations in their speech include differences in sounds, words, expressions, and sentence patterns. Such differences within a single regional speech community often correlate with social variables of occupation, isolation, education, and the resulting social status in the community. Speech variants used by one socially identifiable group of speakers comprise the second major type of dialect known as a *sociolect* or social dialect. Studies by sociologists and linguists— or *sociolinguists*—have increasingly focused on this kind of dialect since the 1960s.

Sociolects are generally divided into two broad classes: standard and nonstandard dialects. The first class is used by persons who are usually well-educated, well-traveled members of occupations ranking at the middle-to-high socioeconomic levels. They interact with other standard dialect speakers in social and job settings and read nationally disseminated journals and books. Speakers of a nonstandard dialect, on the other hand, are generally persons with a limited education and mobility who interact with others with the same background.

Children also reflect a nonstandard or standard social dialect in their speech. Although this dialect is hardly the result of occupation or formal educational background, it is the social dialect used by the children's parents, neighbors, and friends. If boys and girls mature in a language-learning environment filled with standard dialect speakers, they are likely to speak a standard dialect. Similarly, if children are surrounded by nonstandard dialect speakers, they will typically speak a nonstandard dialect. An oral language rating form which teachers can use with pupils who speak a nonstandard English dialect is found in Figure 3.1.

Upon entering school however, children who speak a nonstandard dialect are no longer limited to speaking that one dialect for the rest of their lives. In school they learn a second and alternative dialect—the standard dialect—and gradually become able to shift from one dialect to the other depending upon the setting and the situation. They retain the right to use their own first and nonstandard dialect in speech and writing. Furthermore, they gain an equal right to acquire a second and standard dialect for the same communicative purposes.

Black English

One nonstandard English dialect has received special attention in recent years from the sociolinguists. It is that dialect spoken in the urban ghettos of major cities in the United States. Since most inner-city residents are black people of relatively low socioeconomic and educational levels, the dialect they speak is

Figure 3.1. Oral Language Rating Form for Use with Children Who Speak a Nonstandard English Dialect.

Oral Language Rating	Dialect Interference	5	4	3	2	1
		Never	Almost Never	Sometimes	Usually	Almost Always

School _____ Date _____

Name _____

Grade _____ Teacher _____

	5 Never	4 Almost Never	3 Sometimes	2 Usually	1 Almost Always
Pronunciation: Distinguishes between *then* and *den; they* and *day; both* and *boat; thin* and *tin;* and *thin* and *sin.*	___	___	___	___	___
Comparison: Uses the correct form of comparison such as *bigger, biggest; more beautiful,* and *most beautiful* rather than *more bigger; beautifuller* and *beautifullest.*	___	___	___	___	___
Double Negative: Uses negative expressions, such as *don't have any* rather than *don't have none.*	___	___	___	___	___
Plurals: Distinguishes between regular and irregular plurals (i.e., says *feet* and not *foots*). Pronounces the *s*-ending of regular plurals correctly (i.e., boot*s* /s/, hors*es* /iz/, dog*s* /z/).	___	___	___	___	___
Past Tense: Uses the appropriate past forms of irregular verbs rather than participle forms (uses appropriate *I ate* instead of *I et*). Uses the appropriate past forms of irregular verbs rather than inappropriate forms with the regular *-ed* ending of past form (i.e., *I drank* instead of *I drinked* my milk).	___	___	___	___	___
Past Participles: Uses the appropriate participle form (i.e., *cut* rather than *cuted,* or *brought* rather than *brung*).	___	___	___	___	___
Pronouns: Uses appropriate pronoun form.	___	___	___	___	___
Uses of Do: Uses appropriate forms of *DO* in questions, answers, and in negative statements.	___	___	___	___	___
Uses of Be: Uses, rather than omits, appropriate forms of *BE.*	___	___	___	___	___
Uses of Have: Uses, rather than omits, appropriate forms of *HAVE.*	___	___	___	___	___
Subject-Verb Agreement: Uses correct verb form when he or she is used as subject. Verb form has appropriate ending sound (i.e., *he takes* /s/, *he watches* /iz/, *he wears* /z/, rather than uninflected or simple forms (i.e., *he take, he watch, he wear*).	___	___	___	___	___

Source: *Michigan Oral Language Series* (New York: ACTFL, 1969).

frequently referred to as Black English although, of course, not all black people use it. Middle-class teachers (white or black) assigned to work in innercity schools must understand some of the distinctions of this dialect, its effect on reading problems, and some of the techniques for teaching standard English as an alternative.

That Black English and standard English elicit emotional reactions even among young listeners was concluded by Rosenthal after her interviews with 136 monolingual preschoolers (between the ages of 3:0 and 5:11) living in the metropolitan Washington, D.C. area. Socioeconomic and linguistic evaluations made by the preschool children were higher for the standard English speakers than for the Black English speakers.[6] Language awareness begins as early as age 3, and children form their attitudes toward standard and Black English before entering first grade. Therefore, as children acquire the linguistic system of language with their mastery of its syntax, apparently they also are acquiring sociolinguistic perceptions that are part of the socialization process.

Insofar as reading performance is concerned, black dialect has minimal, if any, effects on black children's reading achievement, according to the ERIC Clearinghouse on Reading and Communication Skills.[7] Black dialect speakers have no more difficulty with the oral comprehension of standard English material than do standard English speakers. There is also minimal support for the theory that nonstandard dialect interferes with the reading of materials written in standard English. There are no significant differences between reading performances when speakers of nonstandard dialects read materials written in their own dialects or those written in standard English.

A study of black first graders in the inner city of New York concluded that its data did not support the general use of dialect readers for beginning reading instruction.[8] Reading and language development programs based on the expectation that urban ghetto children have no usable language applicable for school instruction should also be questioned. If, in the course of oral reading, pupils sometimes recode standard English structures into dialect equivalents, teachers should accept such an oral recoding because the procedure is likely to be an effective instructional strategy and not a reading error. Children who read *she goes to school* as *she go to school* are completing a linguistic translation from standard to nonstandard English and revealing their comprehension of the underlying meaning of the sentence.

Although Black English is linguistically more similar to standard English than different from it, there are some distinctions in pronunciation and grammar. The most significant sound feature in Black English is the simplification of consonant clusters at ends of words: if a word ends with two consonant sounds, the last one is apt to be omitted. Consequently, the standard-English-speaking teacher will misinterpret the Black English speech of the child who says: (1) *las* for *last;* (2) *contes* for *contest;* and (3) *sof* for *soft.* Other misinterpretations may result because of the (1) absence or weakness of the *r* and *l* sounds so that a child may say *cat* for *carrot* and *rea* for *real;* (2) weakening of the final consonant so that a child may say *frien* for *friend* and *bea* for *beat;* and (3) omission of the final *s* so that a child may say *Sam book* for *Sam's book, he sing* for *he sings,* and *my sister* for *my sisters.*

Grammatical differences exist too. There is the unique use of *be* to describe intermittent events and some special forms of the verbs *do* and *have.* Other features such as the pronominal apposition (*my mother, she*) and the double negative (*he didn't get no cookies* and *you're never not gonna find us*) are common in nonstandard forms of many dialects besides Black English.

In summary then, according to Williams, Hopper, and Natalicio, what appears to an untrained listener as a deep-seated distinction between standard English and Black English is upon closer examination only a small set of differences in a sea of similarities between the language forms used by black and white children.[9] In other words, *some* black boys and girls *occasionally* use a relatively *small* number of uniquely Black English features in their speech. And these features are alternate forms of communication which are intelligible, logical, and consistent.

For those teachers who still wish to put into effect a program for teaching standard English as a second dialect (SESD), here are some sample contrasting drill-type activities used by elementary public school teachers in New York City. These are suggested for oral work only, may be taped, and can be used for periods lasting ten to fifteen minutes.

1. Discrimination Drill: focuses attention on sentences or on words that contrast standard with nonstandard endings.
   a. Teacher says *He likes milk* and *He like milk.* The pupil responds *different.*
   b. Teacher says *with* and *with.* The pupil responds *same.*
   c. Teacher says *bof* and *both.* The pupil responds *different.*
   d. Teacher says *Jack plays games* and *Jack plays games.* The pupil responds *same.*

2. Translation Drill: elicits the translation of sentences or words from nonstandard to standard dialect or vice versa.
   a. Teacher says *He likes milk.* The pupil responds *He like milk.*
   b. Teacher says *then.* The pupil responds *den.*
   c. Teacher says *Crystal bake cookies.* The pupil responds *Crystal bakes cookies.*
   d. Teacher says *mof.* The pupil responds *mouth.*

3. Response Drill: elicits contradiction of a standard or nonstandard statement with an appropriate response in the same dialect.
   a. Teacher says *Your mother work at the store.* The pupil responds *No, she don't.*
   b. Teacher says *John picks me up at eight.* The pupil responds *No, he doesn't.*[10]

Language History

The study of the development of the words in a single language as well as of the changes in the relationships among those words is termed *language history*. The reason for including it in the curriculum is to show that language is constantly changing, that the change affects word meanings, and that the change also affects the way that people string words together into units of meaning.

Three factors help explain the change. First, there is *normal growth* or routine progress as ideas and inventions develop and are absorbed into the language. Second, there is *human mobility* occurring whenever people move to new locations and new situations. And finally there is the *importation of foreign words and expressions* when speakers and writers of different languages meet and exchange words.

The application of the history of the English language to the teaching of English is largely unexplored although it is a potent source of interest to students at all levels of growth in the use of English. It remains probably the chief means by which a truly linguistic attitude toward English can be developed and maintained in the classroom.

In structure, the teacher should know the reasons for, and be able to explain to pupils, such matters as the variety of forms of the verb *to be;* the similar forms of certain adjectives and adverbs as *fast, slow,* and *loud;* the several ways of forming the plural of nouns; and other peculiarities of the English language.

Some of these details can be introduced to the language curriculum as early as the middle grades, along with the history of English words and their meanings. Several textbook series have sections labelled variously as "Working with Words," "Where Words Come From," or "Words Are Interesting" which involve etymology. Consequently, third graders learn, for instance, that the word *hello* was once spelled *holla* and that it came from the French and means the same as "Hey, there." Fourth graders must match Modern English words (such as *heaven, eastward, right,* and *live*) with the Anglo-Saxon words from which they came (namely, *heafonum, easteweardre, riht,* and *libban*) and then discuss why, in their opinion, the pairs of words look and sound so differently. Fifth graders are asked to determine why the land formation known as a delta is named after the fourth letter of the Greek alphabet. And sixth graders are first told that pioneers borrowed many words from the Indians, such as *tomahawk* (which comes from the Indian word *tamahaken,* or something to cut with); then the pupils must consult the dictionary to check the meanings of other words borrowed from the Indian language, including *wampum, wigwam, moccasin,* and *powwow.*

Historical Development

Many languages appear to be related. For instance, some English words sound and look much like words having identical meanings in other languages. The English word for *mother,* for example, is *mère* in French, *Mutter* in German, and *moder* in Norwegian. The English word for *family* is *famille* in French, *Familie* in both German and Norwegian, and *fameel* in Persian. Linguistic study of the origins of language have shown that such similarities exist because these languages all developed from one early language spoken by people called Indo-Europeans.

Originally, these people lived together somewhere on the land mass which today is Europe and the Near East. As their culture grew, however, they began migrating to various corners of the continent. One such group settled in northern Europe and became the Germanic branch of the original Indo-European language family, whose descendants presently cover nearly the entire world.

Between 600 and 400 B.C., a tribe of Indo-Europeans called Celts crossed the English Channel and conquered the island of Britain. About a century after Gaul had fallen to Caesar, Britain too was annexed to Rome; then after the Romans withdrew early in the fifth century, the British Celts were invaded and conquered by the Germanic tribes of Angles, Saxons, and Jutes from the eastern coast of the North Sea. The English language is generally dated from this last conquest. By the beginning of the seventh century, the language called Anglo-Saxon, or Old English, emerged as the language of the island and took its place among the modern tongues of Europe.

Old English was a highly inflected language, as were its Germanic progenitors. It carried distinctive endings for four forms of the verb, for case in nouns and adjectives, for number in several parts of speech, and for person, number, and case in pronouns. Its phonology resembled that of modern German rather than that of Modern English.

Although English in the seventh century did include some Latin after Britain's conversion to Christianity, the vocabulary was predominantly Germanic (and even today it has been stated that half of the words on any one page of English are Anglo-Saxon in origin). It changed markedly, however, with the influence of Norman French from William the Conqueror's conquest of England in 1066 until the end of the Hundred Years' War in 1453. Little wonder that Chaucer's fourteenth-century vocabulary looks very different from King Alfred's ninth-century one since so many of Chaucer's words were borrowed from the French. The period of Middle English, during which *Canterbury Tales* was written, extended from approximately 1100 to the Renaissance.

Shakespeare was a writer of Modern English. Although the dates are highly arbitrary, Modern English is the language from 1500 on. The language of each of the two early major periods—Old and Middle—differs so much from the type of English used today that one must study it almost as a foreign language in order to understand it at all. Over the centuries a vast simplification of the language has evolved, with the pattern of deteriorating inflections being felt everywhere.

For the last thousand years the English language has borrowed words greedily from other languages. Through invasion and exploration the English came in contact with the ideas, items, and ways of peoples of continental Europe and many other lands. Their language grew and changed. In recent times, however, through the apparent dominance of English-speaking peoples in everything from sports to science, other languages have borrowed words from Modern English.

A special strand of Modern English is American English which, from the seventeenth century on, began to run a separate course. Emigrants from certain regions in England usually settled together in their new homeland, with the result that the English dialects they spoke were transplanted to particular areas along the Atlantic coast. People who came from southern England settled in New England and spoke with a broad *a* and softened terminal *r* as in *father* and a softened or abandoned *r* before consonants as in *lard*. Those who came from northern England settled mainly in Pennsylvania or moved to the North Central States. The third dialect area extended from Chesapeake Bay south and reflected the dialect of southeastern England.

As pioneer society in the New World was in constant flux, there was a cross-fertilization of dialects and the eventual development of an American English that is related to the most noticeable features of the cultural history, institutional growth, and physical environment of the American people. The language has borrowed words from the American Indians (e.g., *chipmunk, moose, pecan, squash,* and *tamarack*); the French (e.g., *cent, chowder, depot, dime,* and *pumpkin*); the Spanish (e.g., *alfalfa, burro, palomino, rodeo,* and *stampede*); the Dutch (e.g., *boss, cookie, Santa Claus, sleigh,* and *waffle*); and the Germans (e.g., *delicatessen, noodle, pinochle, semester,* and *seminar*). It also has frequently altered word function (e.g., from noun to adjective or verb) and demonstrated a fondness for compound formations (e.g., twenty words have *stage* as a first element), word blends (e.g., *cablegram* for *cable telegram*), and the creation of mouth-filling terms (such as *gobbledygook*).

While some differences between British and American English exist in vocabulary and pronunciation, the similarities between the two languages far outweigh the differences. In the critical area of grammatical structure and syntax, the difference is negligible.

Generalizations Regarding Language History

Children need to know something of the history of the English language in order to interpret information about derivations as provided in the dictionary. The historical context furnished to help them interpret A.S. (Anglo-Saxon), M.E. (Middle English), O.F. (Old French), and L. (Latin) should lead the pupils to four important generalizations:

- English is basically Anglo-Saxon.
- English became a simpler language after the Norman Conquest and one that is more dependent upon word order to express relationships.
- English vocabulary has been enriched by extensive borrowing from other languages, particularly Latin and French.
- The assimilation of borrowed words was made possible by the ease with which English endings could be given to them.

Teaching Activities in Language History

The English language is dynamic and changing. Elementary language arts instruction should reflect this reality. An intermediate teacher can help children develop a better understanding of the history of their language when he or she chooses to:

1. Make bulletin boards or wall charts showing the similarities among many words in the Indo-European language family. If these are also discussed with the class, the pupils will generalize that many languages evolved from a common ancestor.

2. Use library or media center references to motivate the class to investigate the civilizations of the Indo-European culture and subsequently report on its research.

3. Tell the story of the migrations to the British Isles of the Germanic branch of the Indo-European culture. Perhaps the students will hypothesize concerning the reasons for such migrations.

4. Show transparencies of English writing during the Old English and Middle English periods. A discussion of the characteristics of some of the strange letter formations and unusual spellings may lead the class to generalize that language indeed changes.

5. Select at random a 100-word sample of Modern English writing and have the class look up in a reputable dictionary the origin of each word. Results can then be tabulated to indicate the percentage of English words borrowed from other languages and the percentage which are American in origin. Using such data, the pupils may generalize regarding the effect that other languages have had in changing the English language.

6. Lead children to investigate the pronunciation of geographically isolated American people, such as the hill people of North Carolina (who pronounce *boil* as *bile* and *drop* as *drap*). The class may then hypothesize concerning the evolution of a language.

7. During the social studies unit on Discovery and Exploration, have pupils list words which explorers may have brought back from trips to alien lands. The dictionary can be consulted to see if the words suggested did truly originate from those lands. (The same procedure can later be used during the unit on The Settlement of America and the words that varied ethnic groups contributed to American English.)

8. Display books investigating etymology, such as Asimov's *Words on the Map* (Houghton, 1962), the Epsteins' *First Book of Words* (Watts, 1954), the Lairds' *The Tree of Language* (World, 1957), Ludovici's *The Origins of Language* (Putnam, 1965), Ogg's *The 26 Letters* (Crowell, 1971), and Rogers' *Painted Rock to Printed Page* (Lippincott, 1960). If you first read sections of each book aloud to the boys and girls, you can help them understand the vitality of the English language.

The teacher may also wish to examine these books by Charles Earle Funk for amusing and interesting stories of the strange histories of some common English expressions: *Heavens to Betsy and Other Curious Sayings* (Harper & Row, 1955), *A Hog on Ice and Other Curious Expressions* (Harper & Row, 1948), *Horsefeathers and Other Curious Words* (Harper & Row, 1958), and *Thereby Hangs a Tale: Stories of Curious Word Origins* (Harper & Row, 1950).

Discussion Questions

1. How and why should intermediate students study semantics?
2. Why is it so important that each child's dialect receive the approval of the teacher?
3. What is the role of the dictionary in an elementary unit on language history?
4. How can an understanding of phonology and morphology help the reading teacher?

Suggested Projects

1. Tape the speech of three children who were born in different parts of the country. Then analyze the recordings for distinct sound features.
2. Determine how many morphemes are contained in the first paragraph of the lead story on the first page of the local newspaper. Which ones are free morphemes and which are bound?
3. Compile a list of children's stories that use nonstandard English dialects.
4. Examine a current language arts series to see which generalizations about the history of the English language are presented to elementary students.
5. Set up the learning center on etymology shown in Figure 3.2.

Related Readings

Blatt, G. T. 1978. "Playing with Language." *Reading Teacher* 31: 487–93.

Bryen, D. N. et al. 1978. *Variant English: An Introduction to Language Variation.* Columbus, Ohio: Charles E. Merrill Publishing Co.

Dieterich, D., ed., 1976. *Teaching about Doublespeak.* Urbana, Illinois: National Council of Teachers of English.

Granger, R. C. 1976. "The Nonstandard Speaking Child: Myths: Past and Present." *Young Children* 31: 478–85.

Groff, P. 1978. "Children's Spelling of Features of Black English. *Research in the Teaching of English* 12: 21–28.

Nilsen, D. L., and Nilsen, A. P. 1978. *Language Play: An Introduction to Linguistics.* Rowley, Massachusetts: Newbury House Publishers.

Noyce, R. M., and Wyatt, F. R. 1978. "Children's Books for Language Exploration." *Language Arts* 55: 297–301.

Reed, C. E. 1977. *Dialects of American English.* Rev. ed. Amherst: University of Massachusetts Press.

Rigg, P. 1978. "Dialect and/in/for Reading." *Language Arts* 55: 285–90.

Spolsky, B. 1978. *Educational Linguistics: An Introduction.* Rowley, Massachusetts: Newbury House Publishers.

Figure 3.2. Language Arts Learning Center: Etymology.

TYPE OF CENTER:	Etymology	**TIME:** 20–30 minutes
GRADE LEVEL:	Upper 3–5	**NUMBER OF STUDENTS:** 1

INSTRUCTIONAL OBJECTIVE: (1) The student should demonstrate an interest in the origin and history of words, and (2) the student should be able to demonstrate knowledge of dictionary skills in the process of locating word origins.

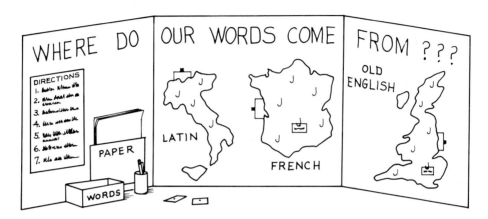

MATERIALS: 3-sided cardboard display (covered with contact paper, maps, and other characteristic pictures of the languages used) box for the words, answer sheet, paper, pencils, word tags, folder for finished work, instruction sheet, dictionary and other reference books.

DIRECTIONS TO STUDENTS:
1. Select three words from the word box.
2. Using the dictionary or other reference book, find the origin of each word.
3. Place each word on the word map of the country from which the word came.
4. Check your answers by pulling the tags out from each country.
5. Now take a piece of paper and choose a word whose history you would like to find.
6. Use the books provided to write a brief history of the word.
7. Place the history in the folder on the back of the center.

EVALUATION: The student should be able to evaluate how well he or she can use the dictionary by how many he or she gets correct. The brief history will give the teacher knowledge on the student's use of the dictionary and other reference materials as well as his or her development of writing skills. The teacher should select a few of the histories each day to read to the class.

SUGGESTED WORDS TO USE: (Choose words for your class's level and ability.)

Old English: daisy, free, neighbor, food, barn, house, mouth, cloth, madman, belief, fiendish, guess, riddle, alike, talk

Latin: imitate, amusing, ambulance, arrive, fee, fool, infant, pencil, record, humor, antique, standard, adore, conversation

French: matinee, brunette, alarm, bank, butcher, escape, mail, tailor, sheep, harvest, shepherd, furniture, beef, polecat

Grammar 4

Why children should study grammar

The major kinds of grammar presented in elementary classrooms today

The influence of Latin on traditional English grammar

Distinctions between *kernels* and *transforms*

The grammar of English refers to the system or organization underlying the total language. Various lengthy and well-written theoretical explanations of this system have developed over the years. While some of their terminology and elements are similar, the emphases usually differ. In historical order the three systems used in the teaching of grammar in elementary schools today are traditional, structural, and transformational-generative. Each will be discussed later in this chapter.

Some school districts select one grammar over the others, and some elementary textbook series are equally dedicated. Other districts and texts prefer to present an eclectic grammar which combines elements freely from all three types. They believe that the way to assist students in using language more effectively is not necessarily through a study of any one theory of the nature of English grammar; instead, they believe that there are significant components to be derived from all three grammars. Consequently, these generalizations are worthy of a place in the elementary curriculum:

- The emphasis in grammar teaching should be on how language works to convey meaning.
- The study of basic sentence patterns should be central to the beginning study of grammar because it can help students become more conscious of the subject-predicate relationship and the rhythm of the sentence. Work with the complete subject and the complete predicate should be part of the instruction when treating basic relationships within the sentence.
- The study of sentences should include the four major word classes (i.e., nouns, verbs, adjectives, and adverbs) and their inflection as well as the most useful classes of structure words and their use.
- The basic sentence patterns may be compounded, subordinated, and transformed. Work in grammar therefore should give much practice

in compounding, subordinating, and modifying. It should also include substituting structures within the basic sentence patterns and transforming the patterns themselves.

- Grammatically essential sentence elements tend to be fixed, and grammatically less essential elements tend to be movable. All children should have considerable experience in changing sentences about and in rearranging and changing the information conveyed by the sentences.[1]

Roles of Grammar Study

Grammar study has a role in today's education of children in the middle grades, according to the Wisconsin Department of Public Education which has delineated three functions of grammar study. First, as an immediate function, such study can be helpful to the writing program. Certain types of syntactic study and experiences can produce more syntactically fluent writers according to recent and respected research (Mellon, 1969; O'Hare, 1973). Second, as a long-range function, grammar study is the most accessible avenue to the structure of language and can probably help people understand themselves a little better. Finally, as an aesthetic function, the content of grammar is a theoretical human construct and so can help people define their human uniqueness.[2] Eliminating grammar study could be another step in the conversion of education to mere training.

The varied instructional objectives in elementary school grammar are listed in Table 4.1.

Major Kinds of English Grammar

English grammar as it is known today did not exist until the seventeenth century. Although grammar was an important part of the school curriculum before that time, the grammar taught in the schools was Latin, not English. English was, after all, only the language of the common folk.

Currently there are three different and undiluted grammars prominently presented in elementary classrooms in the United States—traditional, structural, and transformational-generative. A fourth kind, the so-called eclectic grammar, draws from all three and presumably uses the best elements of each. It is as yet uncharted, however, and varies from district to district and from publishing house to publishing house.

Traditional Grammar

Since Latin was for centuries considered by scholars to be the perfect language, traditional grammar is a classification of English based partly on resemblances, real and supposed, to Latin. Originating in England during the seventeenth and eighteenth centuries, it was written by grammarians whose goal was to prescribe usage, establishing "rules" for speakers and writers to follow.

Refined in this century, traditional grammar accurately emphasizes the subject-predicate nature of the English sentence and the fact that function

Table 4.1.
Instructional Objectives in Elementary School Grammar.

Instructional Objective	Grades to Introduce (X) or to Review (R) the Objective					
	1	2	3	4	5	6
Understand that meaning in an English sentence is conveyed through the order in which words are put together.	X	X	R	R	R	R
Understand the classification process as a means of coming to understand language.	X	X	R	R	R	R
Understand the concept of subject and predicate in a sentence.		X	R			
Recognize the noun in the subject and the verb in the predicate.			X	R		
Understand that nouns have both a singular and a plural form.			X	R		
Understand the difference between a statement (declarative sentence) and a question.			X	R		
Note the relationship between sentences (and meanings) and pitch in declarative statements and questions.			X	R		
Understand the inflectional and positional clues for recognizing and classifying nouns.				X	R	R
Know the difference between common and proper nouns.				X	R	
Understand the inflectional and positional clues for recognizing and classifying verbs.				X	R	R
Understand the principle of noun-verb sentence pattern.				X	R	
Understand positional clues for recognizing and classifying adjectives.				X	R	R
Understand the inflectional clues for identifying and classifying adjectives.					X	R
Understand the use of intensifiers or qualifiers with adjectives.					X	R
Understand the ordered sequence of adjectives when several precede the noun.						X
Understand that a sentence is a basic pattern with modifiers added.						X
Understand the inflectional and positional clues for identifying adverbs.						X
Know that adverbs can be classified in categories of manner, time, and place.						X

Source: Bloomington Public Schools. *Language Arts Curriculum Guides K–6.* (Bloomington, Minnesota: Bloomington Public Schools, 1971).

within the sentence is the ultimate determinant of word classification. It is primarily interested in syntax and it is always presented to pupils through the deductive method.

Traditional grammar, however, makes little attempt to discover how people learn languages. It fails to distinguish adequately between content words and function words in English sentences. It demands memorization of eight parts of speech (nouns, verbs, adjectives, adverbs, pronouns, prepositions, conjunctions, and interjections) whose inconclusive definitions often mix levels (e.g., the definition of a noun tells what it is, but the definition of an adjective tells what it does). It divides unnatural sentences into categories named by the parts of speech showing the relationships of each to the others. It uses a form of diagramming which does not help many children to see the basic building blocks of each sentence clearly. It fails to describe its operations with any consistency. It deals with exceptions, making the pupil unaware of the major grammatical patterns in the language. Finally, it has little impact on composition and tends to ignore English as a spoken language. Many, but not all, traditional grammarians are prescriptive, operating from the false assumption that there is a standard English grammar which is changeless and permanent, and that the school's task is to develop competence in understanding the elements of that grammar.

Traditional grammar is concerned with the knowledge of eight parts of speech and an understanding of such terms as *case, number, tense, mood, agreement, comparison,* and *paradigms.* It mandates the ability to define and recognize structural elements of sentences (such as subjects, predicates, complements and modifiers of all types) and the ability to recognize sentence faults that are associated with predication, pronoun reference, parallelism, placement of modifiers, and tense sequence. It classifies sentences both by purpose (declarative, interrogative, and exclamatory) and by form (simple, compound, complex, and compound-complex). It considers the word as the most important element of communication. And since traditional grammar deals primarily with the written forms of language, it tends to explain only what happens when language is used formally by educated people.

Even with good teaching, traditional grammar suffers from the efforts of early scholars to fit English (a Germanic language) into the preferred Latin mold. One major example concerns *nouns.* Every Latin noun has a different spelling depending on its case—nominative, genitive, dative, accusative, and ablative—or its relation to other elements in the sentence. In English, however, none of the properties of case matter except those of the genitive (or possessive) case because the relationship of nouns to other sentence elements is established by word order.

A second major example concerns *verbs.* The six tenses of traditional grammar—present, past, future, present perfect, past perfect, and future perfect—tally exactly with the Latin. Yet English can be regarded as having only two true tenses (the simple past and the simple present) that are ordinarily represented by single words spelled differently. Tense in English verbs then is more often a property of inflection rather than of time, for other elements in the construction may show time functions too. Latin, on the other hand, expresses time only by variations in the forms of the root word. Little wonder that the attempts to fit English into Latin patterns have resulted in confusion.

A descriptive grammar developed in the United States in the 1930s by Charles Fries, George Trager, Henry Lee Smith, and others, structural grammar began as a study of the structure of English. Instead of prescribing how people should talk (as traditional grammar does), it is concerned with how people do talk today. It analyzes the living spoken language to ascertain the basic structure of English sentences, the intonation patterns signaling meaning, and the words which operate as signs to indicate parts of speech. It believes that grammar is essentially a description of speech sounds and of sound combinations, and that language goes from form to meaning. It also finds that any structure generally accepted by a given speech community is correct for that community: there is no "ideal" language.

Structural Grammar

The structuralists have developed a technique for classifying words into parts of speech that is sometimes referred to as the slot-and-substitution method. The best way to understand this technique is to look at a few examples:

- A noun is a word like *bicycle* in *The (bicycle) is old.*
- A verb is a word like *see* in *I can (see) it.*
- An adjective is a word like *sad* in *She is very (sad).*

Sometimes called Class I, Class II, Class III, and Class IV, there are four word-form classes among the words with lexical meaning (i.e., nouns, verbs, adjectives, and adverbs). All other words are called structure words, of which there are fifteen to seventeen groups. The English language is broken into four subdivisions:

1. *Intonation* or melody, whose elements are levels of pitch, degrees of stress, and junctures. The oral approach to teaching punctuation is one of the by-products of a knowledge of intonation.
2. *Sentence patterns,* including especially:

   Pattern 1 (NV, noun and verb) which is the simplest structure and most basic pattern of the English language; for example, (a) *Men run;* (b) *Children are running.* Two variants are NVA (noun, verb, adjective) and NVAd (noun, verb, adverb); for example, (a) *The door seemed shut;* (b) *Bob plays well.*

   Pattern 2 (NVN, noun, verb, and noun complement) which is one of the most common sentence patterns in American English; for example, (a) *Children eat candy;* (b) *Bob drinks milk.*

   Pattern 3 (NVNN, noun, verb, noun, noun); for example, (a) *Ann calls her dog Chip;* (b) *Bob gives his cat milk.* A fairly common variant is NVNA; for example, *He painted the boat blue.*

Pattern 4 (NLvN, NLvA, and NLvAd, or noun, linking verb, and noun, adjective, or adverb); for example, (a) *Rover is a dog;* (b) *Boys are rough;* (c) *Bob is here.*

Once the children have mastered these basic patterns they are ready for practice in expanding sentence patterns through such techniques as *compounding* (or adding subjects, predicates, and/or objects), *modification* (or adding adjectives, adverbs, determiners, intensifiers, prepositional phrases, participial phrases, and dependent clauses), and *subordination* (with relative clauses modifying noun headwords, or with clause modifiers after the noun headword). Examples of these three techniques include, respectively: (a) *Birds and bees fly;* (b) *The three tall boys were brothers;* (c) *The girl who was in my class went to Japan.*

3. *Structure words* or function words, showing primarily the grammatical and syntactical relationships within sentence patterns. They number about 300, and are used with greater frequency than all other words in the language. Relatively lacking in meaning or content, they are often the most difficult for pupils to learn in reading. Although they are never taught in isolation, the most important structure words are noun markers (including articles, cardinal numbers, and possessive pronouns), verb markers (including modals as well as forms of *be, do,* and *have*), clause markers (including conjunctions and sentence pattern connectors), phrase markers (or the prepositions of traditional grammar), and question markers (or words that begin questions or introduce inverted sentence patterns).

4. *Word-form changes* which have two main divisions. There are the inflectional endings of the four word classes. There are also the derivational prefixes and suffixes that modify the meanings of words, or convert words from one form class to another.[3]

In structural grammar the study of syntax becomes essentially a problem of determining the regularities in the arrangements of form-classes. Constructions have no specific content but comprise a series of "slots" into which particular kinds of material, including form-classes, can be fitted. Each slot must contain a specific kind of material because if it does not do so, the result either belongs to another construction or is not accepted as meaningful by the speakers of the language. A sample construction can be diagrammed as follows:

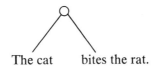

The cat   bites the rat.

Here the little circle represents the construction, and the lines running from it lead to the *constituents* of the construction. There are both *immediate* constituents and *ultimate* constituents. In this example the major subwholes, or largest parts of the construction, are the immediate constituents (or ICs for short): *The cat* and *bites the rat*. The ultimate constituents, which are its individual morphemes, are: {The}, {cat}, {bite}, {-s}, {the}, {rat}.

The structuralists stress oral communication and believe that written language is only a repetition of spoken language. Their goal is to describe and catalog all the observable features of language.

Transformational-Generative Grammar

Developed in the United States since the mid-twentieth century by Noam Chomsky, the third major kind of grammar is generally known as *transformational-generative*. It has, however, also been labelled generative transform, generative-transformational, and, simply, transformational grammar.

This grammar provides patterns for the analysis of existing sentences just as structural grammar does, but it also has rules for producing new sentences. Its proponents assert that if preschool children with limited experience can generate thousands of new sentences based on the early sentence structures they have learned, there must be an underlying process that can be explained and taught.

The basic assumptions of this kind of grammar are that a language is a set of sentences and that a grammar is a series of rules which describe as simply as possible how all the sentences in the language can be formed. In terms of goals, this grammar seeks to explain the nature and function of language.

The term "transformational" refers to the division of American English sentences into two classifications: basic sentences or *kernels* with subjects and predicates and their variations or *transforms*. The formula for a basic sentence may be written as follows: S → NP + VP (a sentence consists of a noun phrase plus a verb phrase). It can also be diagrammed as follows:

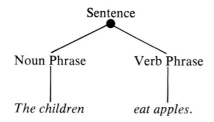

Unlike the diagram in traditional grammar, this "tree" diagram begins with the rules or directions for rewriting rather than representing an arbitrary division of an existing group of words (sentence) into its component parts.

Kernels

There are four to ten or more basic types of kernels or kernel sentences, depending upon the linguist questioned. Each such sentence is affirmative (not negative) and each is a statement (not a question). Each kernel is in the active voice and always begins with the subject. Finally, a kernel contains only a single predication and that follows the subject. Essential to the basic kernel are the terms *noun phrase* and *verb phrase.*

Four groups of words or kinds of words function as a subject in a kernel: (a) determiner + common noun (*The boy* walked the dog); (b) proper noun (*Mr. Black* is a teacher); (c) personal pronoun (*They* ran home); and (d) indefinite pronoun (*Everyone* seemed hungry). Each of these kinds of subjects is called a noun phrase even though it may be a single word. A noun phrase is the name for a structure but not for a word class, *noun* being an example of a word class.

All linguists agree that there are at least two kinds of nouns: countable (or regular) and uncountable (or mass). The former literally can be counted (*one girl, two girls*), but the latter cannot (*one furniture, two furnitures*) in any ordinary sense.

In a kernel the first word of the predicate is usually a verb or a form of the word *be—am, is, are, was,* or *were.* The word *be* and its forms do not behave the way verbs do, so *be* is not called a verb but is considered in a class by itself which makes it possible to simplify the treatment of syntax. Every predicate of a kernel must contain either *be* or a verb. If it contains a form of *be,* something else must follow as in *He is a sailor.* If the predicate contains a verb, the verb may or may not be followed by something else as in *They look sick.* Verbs may also be followed by other words such as adverbials of manner, place, time, or frequency.

The verb phrase is probably most clearly understood if these sentences are noted:

> The girl works quickly.
> The girl is working quickly.
> The girl has worked quickly.
> The girl will work quickly.
> The girl has been working quickly.
> The girl may be working quickly.
> The girl could have worked quickly.
> The girl must have been working quickly.

A variety and a flexibility of material may appear within a verb phrase. It may simply be characterized as containing an auxiliary (including past or present tense) and a main verb; other tenses are handled as combinations of auxiliary parts. In the previous example sentences, *could, may, will,* and *must* are called modals and operate as important auxiliaries; remaining modals are *can, shall, might, would,* and *should.* In changing from present to perfect, *have* is inserted between the present and the main verb.

All English verbs in the present tense have two forms: the simple form (*see, walk*) that goes with the plural subject, and the *s* form (*sees, walks*) that goes with the singular subject. Verbs, however, are not considered singular or plural but merely correspond in form to the requirements of the subject. In transformational-generative grammar there are only two tenses—the past and the present—which are always shown by the first word in the predicate and which, of course, are not the same as time.

Any sentence that is not a kernel is a transform or transformation, and most sentences that people use are transformations. The base of any transformation is the kernel (or kernels) out of which it is formed. There are both *single-base* and *double-base* transformations.

Single-base transformations concern one kernel sentence. Among the most common are the interrogative, the negative, the passive, the command, the expletive (or "there" transform), and the indirect object transformations. One of the simplest is the *yes-no transform*. In order to form a yes or no question, elements are transposed and the final punctuation in written language is changed:

The girl is pretty. (kernel)
Is the girl pretty? (transform)

Double-base transformations involve the combination of two or more kernels into a single, more complex sentence. The two most common types are *coordinating transforms* and the more numerous *subordinating transforms*. In the latter group the most frequently used is the *relative clause*. Always beginning with a relative pronoun or relative adverb, it actually replaces the subject of the inserted or embedded kernel:

My friend has a brown dog. (kernel)
The brown dog can do tricks. (kernel)
My friend has a brown dog that can do tricks. (transform)

Exercises A through D[4] (see pages 71–74) are inductive exercises (designed for students in the middle grades) which involve either single-base or double-base transformations. In them the symbol $\Rightarrow$ indicates that this is a transformation rule and is read as "is rewritten as."

Instructional Activities

Table 4.1 lists instructional objectives for a modern grammar program in the elementary school. Sample activities promoting such objectives are described in this section by grade level.[5]

Grade One

1. Children use word cards to demonstrate logical placement, with each card containing a single word. (Example: Mary ride can Mike with). If cards are punched in one corner, they can be fastened as soon as correct order is established. If cards are not punched, children can arrange the cards on the chalk tray or on the desk to see how many different sentences can be made from these few words.
2. Children arrange the words in each section according to the size of the object named, smallest to largest:

A		B		C		D	
mouse	2	tadpole	2	wasp	1	banana	2
mountain	5	tent	5	wagon	4	balloon	3
match	1	tack	1	world	6	barn	6
moon	6	top	3	weed	2	bug	1
moccasin	3	tree	6	waterfall	5	boy	4
mule	4	trumpet	4	watermelon	3	blanket	5

(The answers are indicated according to the numbers following the words.)

3. Children listen to a poem entitled "First Things First" (Leland B. Jacobs, *Happiness Hill,* Artists and Writers Press, Inc., 1960), which introduces the concept that common, everyday items can be ordered. Then the class names things not in the poem which also come before other things. (Example: "First the hammer and then the ouch.")
4. Children complete a worksheet which contains four large section boxes entitled Things to Ride On, Things Made of Glass, Tools, and Vegetables by drawing, writing, or cutting and pasting from magazines the items for each category box. (Other categories may be substituted.)

Grade Two

1. Children take everything out of their desks and classify the items by laying them in piles on top of the desks. A discussion follows regarding the classifications the children have developed; for example, colors, shapes, sizes. In classrooms without desks, the teacher fills a large sack with numerous items and asks one child to classify the items; the teacher then writes the child's classification on the board, puts the items back into the sack, and asks if another child can classify them in a different way.
2. Each group of children receives individual word cards comprising a possible sentence. Then the members come to the front of the room and arrange themselves into a sentence. (Examples: |a| |Mary| |little| |had| |lamb| and |to| |her| |day| |He| |one| |followed| |school|.)
3. Children are shown pictures of objects with two definite parts which can be easily named; for example, frying pan (handle and pan), book (pages and covers). Then they are given sentences written on slips of paper which must be cut apart into the subject and the predicate. (Example: |The lions| |run fast|.)
4. Children must match from a chalkboard or on a worksheet five subjects and five predicates correctly, all related to the same story or unit.

Grade Three

1. The teacher prepares sets of subject cards and sets of predicate cards. Then each child chooses one card from each set and reads aloud his or her complete sentence; the child may also be asked to identify the subject or the predicate. (Humorous sentences may result in some instances; for example, |The boy| |barked|.)

Part A

GIVEN:

1. The boy is my friend. ⇒ Is the boy my friend?
2. I can go. ⇒ Can I go?
3. Mary has left. ⇒ Has Mary left?

MATERIAL:

1. The orange bat is my friend. ⇒
2. Pete was a little grey squirrel. ⇒
3. Louise has hit the fat cat. ⇒
4. Some of the boys will leave. ⇒
5. The group of children can stay. ⇒

DIRECTIONS:

Change each of the above sentences in MATERIAL to questions that a listener can answer with either "yes" or "no."

CONCLUSION:

1. What did you do to the word order when you made questions out of the sentences?
2. What kind of word now comes first after you have a question?

APPLICATION:

1. Make up three sentences like those in MATERIAL.
2. Change them into questions which can be answered with "yes" or "no."

Part B

GIVEN:

1. The child hit the ball. ⇒ Did the child hit the ball?
2. A worm ate the apple. ⇒ Did a worm eat the apple?

MATERIAL:

1. A small goat swallowed a can. ⇒
2. The perfume smelled like roses. ⇒
3. The poodle swam across the pool. ⇒
4. A fimply snirple uggled an orf. ⇒

DIRECTIONS:

Change the above sentences into questions which can be answered with "yes" or "no."

CONCLUSION:

1. What new word was added?
2. What happened to the verb?

APPLICATION:

1. Make up three sentences like those in MATERIAL.
2. Change them into questions which can be answered with "yes" or "no."

Part A

GIVEN:

1. a) Children play.
   b) Children work. ⇒ Children play and work.

2. a) Children play.
   b) Children work. ⇒ Either children play or children work.

MATERIAL:

1. a) I like cake.
   b) I like ice cream. ⇒

2. a) The boys have a hot rod.
   b) The boys have a club. ⇒

3. a) You leave.
   b) You stay. ⇒

DIRECTIONS:

Join sentences "a" and "b" in each group in MATERIAL.

CONCLUSION:

How did you know which sentence group to use "either-or" with?

APPLICATION:

Write a short paragraph using "and" and "either-or" in the writing.

Part B

GIVEN:

1. a) Mary stayed.
   b) He left. ⇒ Mary stayed but he left.

2. a) John did not laugh.
   b) *John* did not smile. ⇒ John did not laugh, nor did *he* smile.

MATERIAL:

1. a) The pilot flew the plane.
   b) The mechanic stayed on the ground. ⇒

2. a) It had quit raining.
   b) The road was still wet. ⇒

3. a) Joe didn't come to class.
   b) *Joe* didn't stay home. ⇒

4. a) The wind didn't blow.
   b) The rains didn't come. ⇒

DIRECTIONS:

Join sentences "a" and "b" in each group in MATERIAL. Use "but" for two of the groups. Use "nor" for the other two. Drop the italicized word.

CONCLUSION:

1. What happens to the word order of sentence "b" when you use "nor"?
2. How did you know when to use "nor"?

APPLICATION:

1. Write three sentences using "nor."
2. Write three sentences using "but."

Part A

GIVEN:

1. The boy hit the ball.
2. The boy is my friend.

⇒ The boy who is my friend hit the ball.

MATERIAL:

1. The girl was very noisy.
2. The girl had long pigtails. ⇒
3. The lady quickly left the room.
4. The lady was the oldest. ⇒

DIRECTIONS:

1. In sentence no. 2 in MATERIAL change *the girl* to *who*. Now place sentence no. 2 between *girl* and *was* in sentence no. 1. Write the new sentence.
2. In sentence no. 4 change *the lady* to *who*. Now place sentence no. 4 between *lady* and *quickly* in sentence no. 3. Write the new sentence.

CONCLUSION:

What can you do with two sentences that have the same first part?

APPLICATION:

Make up three sentences that look like the two you made in DIRECTIONS.

Part B

GIVEN:

1. The dog ate the bone.
2. The dog had fleas.

⇒ The dog which had fleas ate the bone.

MATERIAL:

1. The little cat was pretty.
2. The little cat had a sore paw. ⇒
3. A bird hopped merrily.
4. A bird was eating a worm. ⇒

DIRECTIONS:

1. In sentence no. 2 in MATERIAL change *the little cat* to *which*. Now place the sentence between *the little cat* and *was* in sentence no. 1.
2. In sentence no. 4 change *a bird* to *that*. Now place sentence no. 4 between *a bird* and *hopped* in sentence no. 3.

CONCLUSION:

Compare these new sentences with those made in PART A. In PART A you used *who*. In this part you used *which* and *that*. Why? (Clue: Look at the nouns in these sentences and compare them with those in PART A. How are they different?)

APPLICATION:

Make up three sentences that look like the two you made in DIRECTIONS.

Exercise D
The Negative Transformation

GIVEN:
1. The dog is in the yard. ⇒ The dog is not in the yard.
2. His father owns a car. ⇒ His father does not own a car.

MATERIAL:
1. The bird was in a bush. ⇒
2. I am a new student. ⇒
3. A freeple is a furple. ⇒
4. A snirkle uggled a smiffle. ⇒
5. A green dog bit a pink postman. ⇒

DIRECTIONS:
Change the sentences in MATERIAL so that *not* will be in each.

CONCLUSION:
1. Where is *not* added in sentences like nos. 1–3?
2. What other changes must be made in sentences like nos. 4–5?

APPLICATION:
Make up four sentences using the word *not*. Two of the four sentences should include the word *did*. Now write these four sentences without the *not*.

2. Children bring magazine or newspaper pictures from home or draw some pictures in class. Then each child tells which nouns depicted in his or her picture are singular and which are plural. Some pictures may even be arranged on the bulletin board according to the two classifications.
3. The teacher prepares a list of singular nouns and a list of related plural nouns. Then the children write or tell a sentence, matching a singular noun (e.g., *library*) to a plural noun (e.g., *books*).
4. The children divide into groups to develop three declarative sentences relevant to a science or social studies unit. These are written on the chalkboard. Then the groups are disbanded and each child changes the declarative sentences of his or her group into three questions and writes them down on a workpaper.

Grade Four

1. Children circle all the noun determiners in a group of sentences. (Example: (The) girls went to (that) zoo.
2. Children choose the appropriate noun-verb agreement in each pair of sentences. (Example: *Seals eat fish. Seals eats fish.*).
3. Children collect several news article headlines using the noun-verb sentence pattern. They then identify the nouns and verbs in the collected headlines.
4. The children classify the following adjectives into three columns headed Color, Size, and Number: *green, fat, yellow, three, small, twelve, blue, tiny, large, six, short, white, slim, fifteen, slender, brown, dozen, red, tall, thin, purple, black, blonde, little, thousand, huge, orange, gigantic, seventy, tan, pink.*

Grade Five

1. The teacher prepares a set of sentences, each of which contains one blank. The children plan suitable intensifiers or qualifiers for the blanks. (Example: *His model was _____ colorful than mine.*)

One of the instructional activities in a modern grammar program requires the children to locate the nouns and noun determiners which appear in a supplementary reader. (Photo courtesy of the Fountain Valley School District, Fountain Valley, California.)

2. The children circle the verbs in a set of sentences prepared by the teacher. (Example: *The rabbit* (*ran*) *fast.*)
3. Children match the words from a column of common nouns with corresponding words from a column of proper nouns and make a statement about the difference between each. (Example: A *city* is any city. *Chicago* is a certain city.)
4. Children list as many events as possible by fitting verbs in the blank(s) of a set of sentences prepared by the teacher. (Example: *People* _____ *their homes.*)

Grade Six

1. Children rearrange sets of words into meaningful sequences to determine the order of modification words before a noun. (Example: *giant nine peas the* and *small frosted cakes our birthday.*)
2. Each child writes a simple five-line verse by using one noun (the subject) in the first line, two adjectives in the second line, three verbs in the third, an adverb in the fourth, and the subject and an adjective modifying it in the fifth line:

    Ghosts,
    Scary, wispy
    Glide, float, drift
    Slowly,
    Pale ghosts.

3. Each child makes up ten jumbled sentences. Then each exchanges sentences with a partner who must rearrange every sentence into meaningful order. (Limits restricting the number of words per sentence are suggested.)
4. Children classify the following words into groups and then make a generalization about each group: *Monday, Baltimore, Thursday, Easter, March, New Year's, Michigan, Christmas, Thanksgiving, September, Idaho, January, Minneapolis, Wyoming, May, Friday, Florida, Alaska, Pittsburgh, Veteran's Day, Atlanta, Boston.*

Evaluation of Pupils' Progress

Presently there is no separate standardized test for elementary school grammar that is both current and recommended.[6] Some well-rated achievement test batteries, however, do include a section on grammar.

Intermediate teachers in one school—or even an entire district—may prefer to develop an instrument to meet the needs of their own pupils. Such a tool should be readily administered and graded. It could then be used either as a diagnostic test at the beginning of the academic year or as an achievement test at the end of that year. A sample evaluative instrument of this category that might be administered during the fifth or sixth grade is found in Figure 4.1.

Discussion Questions

1. How can teachers make grammar a lively subject that will interest children?
2. Do you see any similarities among the three major kinds of grammar? What differences exist among them?
3. If you were assigned to a school which is planning to introduce transformational-generative grammar next semester, how would you prepare the parents for the new grammar in an effort to solicit their support?
4. Should boys and girls earn a separate letter grade for achievement in grammar? If not, how do you propose to evaluate them?

Suggested Projects

1. If you do not live in an area which uses state-adopted texts for elementary school grammar, discover which English grammar (if any) is being presented in a school where you have visited or are observing.
2. Select one instructional objective in elementary school grammar for either a primary or an intermediate grade. Then develop a teaching strategy for that objective.
3. Design a learning game to teach some aspect of grammar (e.g., the concept of subject and predicate). Try it with a group of children and then refine it.
4. Report to your peers about one of the more recently developed grammars, i.e., tagmemic grammar or stratificational grammar.
5. Examine one primary level book and one intermediate level book in a single current language arts text series for their grammar content, e.g., American Book Company's *Patterns of Language* (1977), Harcourt Brace

Figure 4.1. Grammar
Test for the
Intermediate Grades.

Grammar Diagnostic Test or Achievement Test

Grade 6

1. Classification

   A. Cross out the word that does not belong in each grouping.
      1) Asia, Africa, Texas, Europe
      2) gorillas, bears, alligators, cats
      3) tall, warm, short, skinny
      4) apples, lemons, limes, grapefruit
      5) apron, doll, hat, raincoat

   B. Explain your choices in Section A.

   C. Since the following words can be classified into two groups, decide
      what classification to use and put each word into the right
      classification: (*To the Teacher:* Classification is Nouns-Verbs)
      1) bed
      2) ran
      3) went
      4) broke
      5) submarine
      6) satellite
      7) glass
      8) answered
      9) surfers
      10) football
      11) write
      12) speak
      13) screamed
      14) door
      15) letter
      16) creaked
      17) wind
      18) Bob
      19) Denver
      20) built

2. Unscramble the following sentences:
   1) In sentences appear words in order.
   2) Stalled in traffic the car was.
   3) Off the light turn.
   4) Ran the boys to the park.
   5) On our block tag play the children.
   6) To me them please send.
   7) The city light many lamps.

3. Write the plural form of the following words:
   1) leaf
   2) dog
   3) car
   4) potato
   5) baby
   6) decoy
   7) boy
   8) fly
   9) dish
   10) horse
   11) lunch
   12) dress
   13) box
   14) buzz
   15) flag
   16) lamb
   17) number
   18) hatch
   19) month
   20) key

Figure 4.1 (cont.)   4. Underline the noun determiner(s) in each of the following sentences:
1) Please teach me a song.
2) An overcoat may be necessary in winter.
3) Many houses were hit.
4) We saw several children.
5) Each girl chose wisely.
6) Both children ran home.
7) There were few people at the game.
8) The dress fit every girl there.
9) Jack threw the ball.

5. Noun identification

A. Complete each sentence by adding a noun.
1) The _____ felt very warm.
2) _____ left for school early.
3) I wanted to go to the _____.
4) The boy ate two _____.
5) Children ask many _____.

B. Explain in your own words what a noun is. Give examples.

6. Put the following nouns in the proper column: bob, Bob, carol, Carol, mountain, Rocky Mountains, capitol, State Capitol.

Common Noun	**Proper Noun**

7. Verb identification

A. Underline the verbs in each sentence.
1) He wanted the ball.
2) The girl baked a cake.
3) The car runs well.
4) She skates with skill.
5) I was dancing beautifully.
6) Swimming turns me on!
7) The letter was well written.
8) He has spoken to them.

B. Explain in your own words what a verb is. Give examples.

8. Noun-verb agreement

A. Complete each sentence by filling in one noun *or* one verb.
1) The boy _____ down the road.

Jovanovich's *Language for Daily Use* (1978), or Houghton Mifflin's *Language for Meaning* (1978). Evaluate the content and the activities presented.
6. Set up the learning center on grammar shown in Figure 4.2.

2) The children _____ home.
3) _____ will go alone.
4) The _____ turned over.
5) Several people _____.

B. Write ten sentences with the noun-verb pattern.

9. Identify the subject in each sentence by underlining it once; identify the predicate in each sentence by underlining it twice.
   1) The boy was swinging.
   2) Judy bought a doll.
   3) He is laughing.
   4) The crowd roared.
   5) Charlie has gone.
   6) Charlie will go.
   7) These stories should be read silently.
   8) The gold has been found.
   9) The boys were given help.

10. Adjective identification
    A. Underline the adjectives in the following sentences. Explain in your own words what an adjective is.
       1) The tall boy hit his head on the door.
       2) I want the yellow car on the table.
       3) She has a pretty dress!
       4) They sent a written invitation.
       5) The broken bottle cut his foot.

    B. Use the words in the following list as adjectives in sentences.
       broken   nine
       born   oak
       alley   small
       school   smart

    C. Categorize (classify) the following list of adjectives:
       blue   several
       three   yellow
       few   round
       large   silver
       beautiful   green
       dark   straight
       square   tiny
       red   eight

Source: Adapted from *Language Arts Curriculum Guides K–6* (Bloomington, Minnesota: Bloomington Public Schools, 1971).

Related Readings

De Boysson-Bardies, B. 1977. "On Children's Interpretation of Negation." *Journal of Experimental Child Psychology* 23: 117–27.
Ehri, L. C., and Ammon, P. R. 1974. "Children's Comprehension of Comparative Sentence Transformations." *Child Development* 45: 512–16.

Figure 4.2. Language Arts Learning Center: Grammar.

TYPE OF CENTER: Grammar   TIME: 25–35 minutes
GRADE LEVEL: 3–4   NUMBER OF CHILDREN: 1 (maybe 2)

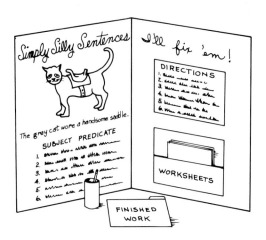

INSTRUCTIONAL
OBJECTIVE: The student will be able to rewrite sentences using subjects and predicates given, and
                    completing the sentences correctly.

MATERIALS: A center display, a folder for finished work, worksheets, and pencils.

DIRECTIONS   1. Look at the sentences on the left side of the center.
TO STUDENTS: 2. Rearrange the predicate part of each sentence so that it makes sense.
                    3. Write your name and the corrected sentences on the top half of the worksheet.
                    4. Check your sentences using the key on the back of this center.
                    5. Finish the worksheet by following the directions.
                    6. Place the finished worksheet in the folder marked "Finished."

EVALUATION: Children check their sentences with key. They may exchange worksheets to check
                    each other's work. The teacher reviews the sheets to determine any needs.

Elgin, S. H. 1975. *A Primer of Transformational Grammar for Rank Beginners.*
    Urbana, Illinois: National Council of Teachers of English.
Golub, L. S. 1975. "English Syntax of Black, White, Indian, and Spanish-American
    Children." *Elementary School Journal* 75: 323–34.
Landes, J. E. 1975. "Speech Addressed to Children: Issues and Characteristics of
    Parental Input." *Language Learning* 25: 355–79.
Meade, R. A., and Haynes, E. F. 1975. "The Extent of Learning of
    Transformational Grammar in One School System." *Research in the Teaching
    of English* 9: 184–91.
Quirk, R., and Greenbaum, S. 1973. *A Concise Grammar of Contemporary English.*
    New York: Harcourt Brace.

SILLY SENTENCES:

The gray cat	wore a handsome saddle.
The brilliant stars	rode around the ring in a tiny car.
Black Beauty	cheered as they won.
The funny clown	glistened in the sky.
The happy boys	howled at the moon.
The hound dog	chased the tiny mouse.

SAMPLE
WORKSHEET

(Top half of worksheet should be reserved for children's revision of sentences on display center.)

NAME: _____

I. Draw lines to connect the right subject and predicate.

1. The old man
2. The fluffy kitten
3. A huge red ball
4. This leaf
5. Jim

A. played basketball last Tuesday.
B. bounced off the wall.
C. walked with a cane.
D. licked up the milk on the floor.
E. turned yellow when autumn came.

II. Write your own predicates to complete the sentences below:

Subject	Predicate (write your own)
1. Mary Silvers	_____
2. My favorite TV star	_____
3. Many circus clowns	_____
4. White chocolate candy	_____
5. His grandfather's brother	_____

III. Write your own subjects to begin the sentences below:

Subject (write your own)	Predicate
1. _____	comes from outer space!
2. _____	struck me in the face with a pie.
3. _____	only flies at night.
4. _____	can run the mile in four minutes.
5. _____	grows in gardens.

Source: From *Language Arts Learning Centers and Activities* by Angela Reeke and James Laffey. Copyright 1979 by Goodyear Publishing Company. Reprinted by permission.

Reeves, H. R. 1975. "Modern Grammar Enhances Writing Skills." *Language Arts* 52: 1035–39.

Townsend, B. 1977. "Sentence Blocks." *Teacher* 94: 63–64.

Western, R. 1978. "Grammar and Composition: Why People Disagree about Their Relation to Each Other." *Elementary School Journal* 78: 284–89.

Spelling 5

The alphabetic orthography used in the United States

Young children and invented spelling

The two major areas which make English spelling highly systematic

How teachers can individualize spelling instruction

All modern natural languages have been and continue to be primarily aural-oral communication systems. Over the centuries, of course, a few of them have added a writing system as a secondary means of communication for the transmission of messages over space and time. Such a writing system, or *orthography,* is only a substitute for the oral language, however. Demanding that its users be facile with both visual skills and listening-speaking skills, it is predicated upon the structural characteristics of oral language. Its symbols graphically represent the phonology, morphology, and syntax of speech, with the influence of each of these components dependent upon the nature of the written form of the language.

Three broad kinds of writing systems can be noted. In their usually accepted order of historical development, they are *pictographic, ideographic,* and *alphabetic.* In pictographic or picture writing the visual symbol is directly related to the visual appearance of its referent: the written word for *cow* simulates an actual cow. (Aztecs and early American Indians are among the groups that have used pictographs.) In ideographic writing the visual symbol is related arbitrarily but directly to the "idea" of a cow: the symbol itself means *cow* and may bear little or no resemblance to animals that look like cows or to words that sound like *cow.* (China and Japan still have ideographic writing systems although there is some concern that the systems may become extinct due to the demands of typesetters and typists.) In alphabetic writing the visual symbol is directly related to the sound of the name of its referent: the written word for *cow* resembles the spoken word and not the appearance of a live cow. An alphabetic system (like that first developed by the Greeks) relies mainly on the phonological components while an ideographic system depends primarily upon the morphological and syntactical components. Most contemporary orthographies are based on the alphabetic system due to its economy and flexibility.

Spelling and Reading

Each writing system is concerned with the transmission of information from one person to another. Such an act demands an ability on the part of the recipients to decode (read). Therefore, all users of an alphabetic system must acquire two closely related processes: (1) the mastery of the graphic symbols needed to set forth speech in writing (*encoding* or spelling) and (2) the ability to translate printed or written graphemes into the oral forms which they represent (*decoding* or reading).

Since the American-English orthography suffers from a lack of an exact one-to-one correspondence between phoneme and grapheme, there are major differences between encoding and decoding.

In reading children start with a word that is seen; in spelling they see nothing whatsoever. Therefore, the context and/or picture that will assist them in reading will be of no help to them in spelling. In spelling they end with what they begin with in reading; that is, they conclude with the visual symbol.

In reading children respond to the symbol(s) and must decide which of several different sounds for the same letter or combination of letters they should use. In spelling they hear a sound (or group of sounds) that they either utter or think, and they must then decide what letter or groups of letters will properly convey that sound (or groups of sounds) to someone else reading what they have written.

Reading requires solely a mental response (except for oral reading). However, spelling demands a muscular response as well, for letters must be written to represent the sounds which children hear in their minds. As good spellers, children respond automatically to such mental sound stimuli. As good readers, their response is dependent upon the meaning the words have for them.

Due then to these several distinctions that exist between encoding and decoding, it is decidedly unwise to teach spelling *through* reading.[1] Such a practice may adversely influence perceptual patterns in word recognition and comprehension abilities among certain children during the reading act. It may also interfere with the thought-getting process by focusing attention on the letters in, rather than the meanings of, words.

It is better to teach spelling *with the help of* reading. Reading and spelling may enrich each other as a common vocabulary based on what pupils need to write and on what they are reading. In this respect, the language-experience approach to reading produces significantly better spellers than the basal reader approach, both on lists of regular and irregular words and in written composition, according to a study of twenty-one first-grade classrooms in Delaware.[2] Although the children (and their teachers) using each approach were matched evenly, the pupils in the basal reader classes found the phonologically irregular words of American English orthography somewhat more difficult than the phonologically regular words, whereas the language-experience classes did not. The latter classes were the group that integrated listening, speaking, and writing in a broad-based reading program.

Reading also supports spelling through the pronunciation of words subvocally or audibly and through the use of phonics in sounding out words or word parts.

In an alphabetic orthography the spelling act involves the sensory mechanisms of *speech, audition,* and *vision.* The importance of the first two cannot be overlooked in any consideration of spelling processes, according to a questionnaire survey of late intermediate pupils. This survey revealed that the most effective technique for teaching spelling to slower learners involves pronunciation of the spelling words by students and teacher.[3]

Reinforcing the aural-oral process is *visual memory* of the spelling of phonemes and of whole words. When children have spelled a word through their knowledge of phoneme-grapheme correspondences, they can check the success of their encoding efforts by comparing the word with a visual memory of the same word as they have seen it in a correctly spelled model (such as in a basal reader or a dictionary). In fact, for some learners the visual processes represent the chief means by which spelling is mastered.

The fourth mechanism involved in learning to spell is that of *haptics.* In writing a word, a pupil calls into play the sense of touch and the motor mechanisms (muscles of the hand and arm that guide the writing act). While spelling ability generally is not truly dependent upon haptical experiences, nevertheless *haptical memory,* which is so fundamental to typewriting, aids in the act of spelling when combined with oral, auditory, and visual recollections of words.

All four mechanisms come into play in the study of each spelling word, as outlined in Figure 5.1.

Besides sensory memories and motor responses, spelling ability is also related to the development of concepts about the orthography. Children can acquire these concepts deductively or inductively. The former method, whereby the learner is first told the concept and then asked to locate verifying examples of it, has an important place in the modern spelling program. It expedites the learning process. Excessive reliance on the *deductive method,* however, may result in a child's inability to apply a concept in practical settings.

How to Study a Spelling Word

1. Say the word. Listen to the sounds in it.

2. Look at the word. Notice which letters are used to stand for the sounds in the word.

3. Write the word. Say the word to yourself as you write it. Do not look at the copy.

4. Proof the word. Check the word against the copy to see if it is spelled correctly.

5. Identify the error. Determine which part of the word, if any, has been misspelled.

6. Restudy the word. Study again any word you have misspelled, repeating the steps from the beginning.

Figure 5.1. How to Study a Spelling Word.

The better approach is the *inductive method,* which encourages the learner to induce significant spelling concepts and then to apply them. Concept development is an ongoing process, and good spellers learn to internalize the underlying relationships governing the writing system.

Invented Spelling or Early Spelling

Since an alphabetic orthography is essentially a matter of encoding the phonemes into the graphemes (or letters of the alphabet), the ideal writing system would always use one grapheme to represent each phoneme. Young children who invent their own spelling soon realize that the twenty-six letters of the English alphabet are not enough to spell all the words which they wish to write because English has more than twenty-six phonemes. Upon making this discovery, the children either ask parents, teachers, or other adults how to spell the missing sounds or they invent their own nonstandard spelling. They organize and classify the sounds they hear and do not use graphemes frivolously.

During recent years work with preschoolers, kindergartners, and early primary pupils has shown that there is an apparent analogy between learning to spell and learning to speak.[4] Children learning to speak constantly mispronounce words, omit words, or improperly order words. Nobody actually teaches them to speak; they learn about their language as they listen and talk. In a similar way, boys and girls learn to spell by writing, and later, by reading. They misspell many words when they first write, but given enough opportunities over a prolonged period of time, they will learn to spell. If young children are corrected constantly as they try to talk, they will soon hesitate to speak for fear of correction. Likewise, if young children are corrected constantly as they try to spell, they will become thwarted for fear of correction.

Language acquisition is a creative feat of the first magnitude and all children are creative when it comes to acquiring their own language. This additional aspect of language processing—innovative spelling—is not confined to just a few boys and girls. Instead, linguists recognize that children generally are able to spell on their own. The teacher or other adult, however, must give the children the idea that they *can* spell. He or she must also recognize "correctness" (by taking cues from the children and from a few phonetic perceptions—not from standard spelling) and must learn to respond to nonstandard spelling appropriately.

The particular circumstances of the first writing will vary with the child, depending upon his or her own timing and the situation in which the need arises. What remains constant is the expectation that children will figure it out for themselves when the time comes. The activity must develop as an expressive one and not degenerate into a form of exercise. The function of the teacher should be to give boys and girls access to spelling but not to require it of them. How much writing they will eventually produce, if any, depends on their interest.

An analogy to painting and drawing is useful. A teacher of young children makes paints and paper available to them and encourages them. The teacher still leaves it up to the children, however, to decide when, how, and what they will paint. Early spelling should be treated in much the same way. If a teacher encourages spelling once it starts, welcomes and values the spelling, and transmits a feeling to the children that they are doing something exciting and useful, some children will go ahead and make progress.

Cramer describes how one teacher helped a first grader approximate the spelling of a word needed for a written composition. The child, Jenny, thought she was not able to spell *hospital*. The teacher, Mrs. Nicholas, told Jenny to spell it as well as she could, writing as much of the word as possible. When Jenny insisted that she didn't know any part of the word, the teacher-pupil dialogue proceeded in this manner:

> Mrs. Nicholas: Yes, you do, Jenny. How do you think *hospital* begins? (*Mrs. Nicholas pronounced* hospital *distinctly emphasizing the first part slightly. She avoided distorting the pronunciation.*)
> Jenny (*tentatively*): h-s.
> Mrs. Nicholas: Good! Write down the *hs*. What do you hear next in *hospital*? (*Again Mrs. Nicholas pronounced* hospital *distinctly, but this time she emphasized the second part slightly.*)
> Jenny (*still tentatively*): p-t.
> Mrs. Nicholas: Very good! Write down the *pt*. Now, what do you hear last in *hospital*? (*While pronouncing the word* hospital *for the last time Mrs. Nicholas emphasized the last part slightly.*)
> Jenny (*with some assurance*): l.
> Mrs. Nicholas: Yes, Jenny, *h-s-p-t-l* is a fine way to spell *hospital*. There is another way to spell the word, but for now I want you to spell all words you don't know just as we did *hospital*.[5]

Overcoming the spelling barrier in this fashion elicits at least three important results: (1) children can more freely express their thoughts in written form since they can quickly transfer words from their speaking vocabulary to their written vocabulary; (2) children can meaningfully practice word-recognition skills presented in their reading programs; and (3) children can learn to spell faster and better when they are encouraged to test the rules which govern English spelling.

Boys and girls do not proceed as spellers randomly or by rote. Instead there is "a hierarchy of articulatory features" at work.[6] Observed in the early writing of young pupils are these spelling strategies:

Strategies and Stages of Invented Spelling

1. The use of single letters to represent the sound of the full letter name (*hol* for *hole,* and *ppl* for *people*).
2. The omission of nasal sounds before consonants (*plat* for *plant* and *sic* for *sink*).
3. The use of *t* to render /t/ in the past tense form of certain verbs (*likt* for *liked* and *lookt* for *looked*).
4. The omission of the vowel when the syllable has a vowel-like consonant such as *l, m, n,* and *r* (*brd* for *bird* and *opn* for *open*).

5. The use of *d* to render the flap phoneme for *t* between vowels (*prede* for *pretty* and *bodm* for *bottom*).
6. The use of a rather advanced set of linguistic rules for deciding which vowel letter to use when children have not yet learned the spelling of the short vowel sounds (*fel* for *feel* and *fill*).

Stages of early spelling evolve systematically, regardless of the geographical location of the children or the instruction they receive. The various stages seem to form a sequence for spelling development. The most elementary stage involves writing the first letter or phoneme of each word or syllable (*F* for *Friday* or *tb* for *toybox*). During the next stage the children add the final phoneme of the word or syllable while they continue to omit the short vowel sounds (*hl* for *hill* and *rt* for *rabbit*). During the second stage vowels that "say their names" may appear too (*te* for *tea* and *bot* for *boat*).

In the third stage children begin to separate short vowel sounds from surrounding consonants and try to represent them in spelling. Although Read predicted that children would use consistent nonstandard spellings for short vowel sounds, Paul observed that when her kindergartners wished to spell a short vowel sound they seemed to give equal value to the vowels that were formed similarly in the mouth and to use them interchangeably.[7] They always chose some vowel letter to stand for a vowel sound even before there had been any formal teaching of vowel sounds.

During the fourth stage spelling moves closer to standard forms as children read. Some digraphs appear and sight vocabulary (such as *house, saw,* and *was*) is spelled correctly. Stories become longer.

It is important to note at this point that none of the children studied had any difficulty in switching to standard spelling. If spelling is regarded as based on a set of implicit rules about sound-to-symbol correspondences and morphological principles, then the developing child can be described as modifying those rules readily as he or she acquires new information about standard spelling.[8] Research has shown that words misspelled in early writing are later spelled correctly. Progressions made by one first grader in learning to spell *elephant,* for example, were reported as follows: *ift* (October), *elfnt* (December), *elefnt* (February), and *elephent* (May).[9] Kindergartners often spell one word several different ways in the same story, attacking each word as a new problem. As soon as they learn the standard orthography for a word, however, they will spontaneously substitute it for their own.

The English Alphabetic Orthography

Ideally, an alphabetic orthography would always use one grapheme to represent each phoneme. A spoken language that used thirty different phonemes, for example, would also use exactly thirty different graphemes. Some languages such as Hawaiian, Turkish, Spanish, and Finnish come close to attaining the ideal orthography. Their native speakers find it easy to spell nearly any word they know how to pronounce and equally simple to pronounce nearly any word they see spelled. Apparently, all that the schoolchildren in these language communities have to do to become successful spellers is to memorize the comparatively few graphemes involved and their matching phonemic references, and later learn to write the graphemes in the same sequence in which the phonemes are arranged.

No alphabetic orthography however has an ideal and consistent "fit" between its phonemes and its graphemes. American English, for example, has approximately forty-five phonemes in its sound system and only twenty-six graphemes in its writing system. The discrepancies between English pronunciation and English spelling have been considered by linguists who have determined that several factors are responsible:

1. There have been historical accidents of printers' preferences or lexicographers' errors. For example, the earliest English books were printed by the Dutch who mistakenly spelled English words by analogy with Latin roots.
2. English vocabulary includes many *loanwords* from foreign languages which preserve the graphic conventions found in the native language. For example, the French *eau* appears in *bureau* and *tableau*.
3. The pronunciation of English words has changed without corresponding graphic changes so that words which were once distinct in pronunciation are now homophonous. For example, there is *knight* and *night*.
4. The spelling of English words tends to ignore changes in sound, particularly when vowel changes result from a shift of stress. Related words may look more alike than they sound. For example, there is *crime* and *criminal*.
5. The current pronunciations of words are not at all distinctly represented in writing. For example, there is *machine*.

The discrepancies between pronunciation and spelling are found in roots, prefixes, and suffixes. One grapheme may represent more than one phoneme while one phoneme may be represented by more than one grapheme. In all there are about 2,000 ways to spell the phonemes of English. Both consonant and vowel phonemes together with their symbols and common spellings are shown in Figure 5.2.

Despite its frequently touted discrepancies, *English spelling is highly systematic and essentially alphabetic*. More than a decade ago, Paul and Jean Hanna and their colleagues at Stanford University proved through computer analysis of more than 17,000 common words that English spelling is a usually reliable set of phoneme-grapheme correspondences. A few years later, transformational-generative grammarians Noam Chomsky and Morris Halle concluded that English spelling is a very reliable system based not only on phoneme-grapheme correspondences but on morphological principles of English as well.[10] The sound-to-spelling correspondences are generally predictive of the spellings of individual base morphemes while derived words are generally spelled according to morphological principles. These two groups include:

Figure 5.2. English Sounds: Their Symbols and Common Spellings.	**Symbol**	**Example**	**Symbol**	**Example**
	Consonant Sounds		*Vowel Sounds*	
	/b/	boy	/æ/	bat
	/č/	chair	/ɛ/	bet
	/d/	do	/ɪ/	bit
	/f/	fat	/a/	pot
	/g/	go	/ʌ/	but
	/h/	hit	/ʊ/	put
	/ǰ/	jet	/e/	bait
	/k/	kiss	/i/	beet
	/l/	let	/o/	boat
	/m/	man	/u/	boot
	/n/	no	/yu/	cute
	/ŋ/	sing	/ɔ/	bought
	/p/	pan	/ay/	bite
	/r/	rat	/ow/	bout
	/s/	sit	/oy/	boy
	/š/	ship	/ə/	around, chicken
	/t/	to		(frequently varies
	/θ/	thin		with /ɪ/)
	/ð/	then	/E/	the first vowel
	/v/	van		sound in Terry,
	/w/	wet		Harry, Mary
	/y/	yet		
	/z/	zoo		
	/ž/	azure		

Source: Adapted from Paula Russell, *An Outline of English Spelling* (Los Alamitos, Ca.: SWRL Educational Research and Development, 1975).

- *Monosyllabic, monomorphemic words.* Spelling is based on the relationships of individual sounds and letters; that is, phoneme-grapheme correspondences.
- *Polysyllabic, monomorphemic words.* Spelling of the *stressed* syllable is based on rules of phoneme-grapheme correspondence. Spelling of the *unstressed* syllable is arbitrary but choices are limited.
- *Compounds.* Morphemes are spelled independently according to phoneme-grapheme correspondences. No changes in either component result from combining them.
- *Prefixed words.* The base morpheme is spelled according to phoneme-grapheme correspondences. Prefixes vary only in vowel pronunciation,

not in vowel spelling; their spelling is governed by morphemic identity rather than by sound.

- *Suffixed words.* These words are governed by the same spelling principles as those governing prefixed words with three additional complexities: (1) some suffixes are homophones but ordinarily homophonous pairs have different functions (e.g., *-ess* is a feminine nominalizer but *-ous* is an adjectival suffix); (2) suffixes often cause stress changes in base morphemes in which case affix-aided spelling is of predictive value (e.g., spelling the *o* in *ignorance* on the basis of /o/ in *ignore*); and (3) special processes are involved in combining base and suffix (e.g., *tie* is changed to *ty* in *tying*).
- *Foreign words.* Some sets of foreign words, particularly those from Greek and French, have spelling patterns that deviate from normal rules of correspondence. Such words frequently have stylistic traits of identification. For example, there is the Greek *ch* spelling for /k/ and the French *ch* spelling for /š/, with the Greek words being scholarly or technical (as in *choreography* and *architect*) and the French words having connotations of prestige or luxury (as in *chauffeur* and *chalet*).[11]

There are of course spellings that do not belong in either group but these are relatively few. The ideal in teaching spelling, claims Brengelman, should be to keep to a minimum the amount of brute memorizing which is expected of children and to enable them to apply the whole set of general rules which relate the language competence they have already acquired to the task of writing.[12] It is clear that to spell English successfully one must have a high degree of sensitivity to both the phonological and the morphological structure of words. Pupils must be permitted to discover the relationships between that structure and English spelling by using materials which have been carefully prepared or properly selected by their teacher.

Good spellers, children and adults alike, are characterized by Carol Chomsky as recognizing that related words are spelled alike even though they are pronounced differently.[13] Such spellers seem to rely on an underlying picture of the words that is independent of the words' varying pronunciations. They internalize the underlying relationships among words. When good spellers encounter a troublesome word, they automatically utilize the idea that while related words may vary a good deal in their pronunciation, their spelling usually remains the same. Once the connection is clear between the new troublesome word and other related words, correct spelling is automatic.

To help children develop the habit of seeking such connections, the linguistically oriented teacher may use one of these exercises:

1. Give the children Column A of words with a /ə/ vowel omitted. Ask them to think of related words that give distinct clues to the spelling (Column B). (The clues turn out to be the same ones which preschoolers use in their invented spelling.)

A	B
pres__dent	preside
janit__r	janitorial
maj__r	majority
comp__rable	compare
ind__stry	industrial

2. Give the children only Column B from exercise 1 and ask them to think of other forms of the words. See if they notice how vowel sounds shift around.

3. Help the children guess the proper consonant when two or more seem possible. In Column C the spelling is ambiguous. In Column D the related word gives the key to the correct choice.

C	D
gradual (d̲, j̲)	gra̲d̲e
nation (t̲, s̲h̲)	na̲t̲ive
medicine (c̲, s̲)	medi̲c̲al
racial (t̲, c̲, s̲h̲)	ra̲c̲e
criticize (c̲, s̲)	criti̲c̲al

4. Help the children to observe silent consonants by giving them Column E and asking them to think of related words in which the silent consonants are pronounced (Column F).

E	F
bom̲b̲	bom̲b̲ard
sof̲t̲en	sof̲t̲
mus̲c̲le	mus̲c̲ular
si̲g̲n	si̲g̲nal
condem̲n̲	condem̲n̲ation

5. Give the children only Column F and ask them to think of related words in which the underlined consonants become silent.

6. Give the children only Column E and ask them to name the silent consonants.

7. Help the children learn consonant alternations which occur in the pronunciation of words and are reflected in the orthography too. Since the *t-c* alternation is fairly common, give the children Column G and ask them to determine the missing consonants in Column H.

G	H
pira̲t̲e	pira__y
democra̲t̲ic	democra__y
presen̲t̲	presen__e
residen̲t̲	residen__e
luna̲t̲ic	luna__y[14]

Teachers must understand why even spellers who understand the underlying interrelationship among words sometimes make mistakes. The specific kinds of errors made by a child are related to his or her level of spelling achievement, according to a study involving 2,329 suburban pupils in grades two to six. Children in the upper third of the distribution of total scores on the spelling lists tended to misspell a word in *essentially the same way* while those in the lower third had the highest incidence of "bizarre" spellings as shown, for example, in the sixth graders' spelling of *lying:*

Upper Third	Middle Third	Lower Third
lieing	lyning	leing
	lyeing	liing
	leying	lauting
	laying	laing
	liying	lyeing
	lieing	leying
		laying
		liying
		lieing[15]

There are those, of course, who argue that many spelling mistakes reflect exceptional creativity or overall ability and that spelling errors are not a fair measure of intelligence. They point out that a highly intelligent person may be too busy thinking about ideas and developing new theories to be concerned with the mechanics of putting words down on paper.[16]

Opposing them are researchers who have concluded that although individual children may revert to primitive strategies when confronted with unfamiliar low-frequency words, children on the whole seldom make random errors in spelling.[17] A study of pupils in grades one through four in various Michigan schools showed only three types of errors in spelling vowels: (1) the use of a letter-name strategy (as in *gat* for *gate*) which accounted for 68 percent of all errors; (2) the addition of an incorrect vowel after a correct vowel (as in *hait* for *hat*) which accounted for 25 percent of errors; and (3) the incorrect substitution of one short vowel for another (as in *spick* for *speck*) which accounted for 7 percent of all errors. Beers, Beers, and Grant stress that teachers must not become upset when children repeatedly make the same type of errors because the errors are not necessarily caused by "not listening" or "not trying." They may be due, instead, to the length of the children's overall development and exposure to words. Recurring errors do not indicate that children will not or cannot spell correctly at a later time.[18]

Since English spelling is highly systematic, children need to see and be able to use the systematic nature of the spelling system in order to become effective spellers. There are phonological and morphological principles or generalizations governing the system.

Spelling Generalizations

The ability to generalize in spelling, while not 100 percent infallible, is still a positive factor in spelling ability, according to the results of a comparative study of the spelling achievement of more than twelve hundred elementary school children in Scotland and the United States.[19] The Scottish pupils who had been introduced to their words in spelling groups according to phonetic or structural similarities outspelled at all three age levels (seven, eleven, fourteen) their American counterparts who had learned their words around interest units. The study which used standardized (American) tests concluded that (1) ability to apply phonetic generalizations is a valuable asset in spelling; (2) such ability can be improved through direct instruction; and (3) children in the average or low-average IQ ranges profit most from direct instruction in generalizations. Better spellers, representing to a great degree the higher intelligence-quotient ranges of the school population, will tend to make such generalizations with or without direct instruction.

An examination was recently made of a well-known list of forty-five phonic generalizations in order to determine the extent of applicability of each to a composite vocabulary of nearly 5,500 words, drawn from six spelling programs for grades two to six.[20] The following generalizations (including one word in parentheses that is an example of a conforming word) were 80 to 100 percent applicable:

1. When *ght* is seen in a word, *gh* is silent. (light)
2. When a word begins with *kn,* the *k* is silent. (knee)
3. When a word begins with *wr,* the *w* is silent. (wreck)
4. When two of the same consonants are side by side, only one is heard. (blizzard)
5. When a word ends in *ck,* it has the same last sound as in *look.* (truck)
6. When *c* and *h* are next to each other, they make only one sound. (torch)
7. *Ch* is usually pronounced as it is in *kitchen, catch,* and *chair,* not like *sh.* (merchant)
8. When *c* is followed by *e* or *i,* the sound of *s* is likely to be heard. (cease)
9. When *c* is followed by *o* or *a,* the sound of *k* is likely to be heard. (vacant)
10. The letter *g* often has a sound similar to that of *j* in *jump* when it precedes the letter *i* or *e.* (age)
11. When *a* is followed by *r* and final *e,* we expect to hear the sound heard in *care.* (share)
12. When *y* is the final letter of a word, it usually has a vowel sound. (cozy)
13. The *r* gives the preceding vowel a sound that is neither long nor short. (orbit)
14. Words having double *e* usually have a long *e* sound. (teeth)
15. When there is one *e* in a word that ends in a consonant, the *e* usually has a short sound. (zest)
16. In *ay,* the *y* is silent and gives *a* its long sound. (display)
17. When *tion* is the final syllable in a word, it is unaccented. (election)
18. When *ture* is the final syllable in a word, it is unaccented. (venture)

19. When the last syllable is the sound *r*, it is unaccented. (under)
20. In most two-syllable words, the first syllable is unaccented. (quarter)
21. If *a*, *in*, *re*, *ex*, *de*, or *be* is the first syllable in a word, it is usually unaccented. (decide)
22. In most two syllable words that end in a consonant followed by *y*, the first syllable is accented and the last is unaccented. (candy)
23. If the first vowel sound in a word is followed by two consonants, the first syllable usually ends with the first of two consonants. (fattest)
24. If the first vowel sound in a word is followed by a single consonant, that consonant usually begins the second syllable. (eagle)
25. When the first vowel element in a word is followed by *th*, *ch*, or *sh*, these symbols are not broken when the word is divided into syllables and may go with either the first or second syllable. (feathers)

Among prefixed and suffixed words, the *bases* are spelled according to the rules of phoneme-grapheme correspondence. Generalizations concerning the spelling of the *affixes* however include these among many:

1. The following nine vowel-ending prefixes are simply conjoined to bases with no double consonant ever resulting at the prefix-base boundary: *a-*, *be-*, *e-*, *de-*, *re-*, *se-*, *pre-*, *pro-*, and *to-*.
2. The following nine consonant-ending prefixes are linked to the base without a spelling change, which sometimes results in a doubled consonant at the prefix-base boundary: *al-*, *for-*, *un-*, *trans-*, *mis-*, *non-*, *super-*, *sur-*, and *per-*.
3. The following ten consonant-ending prefixes assimilate to the first base consonant: *ex-*, *dis-*, *en-*, *in-*, *con-*, *syn-*, *inter-*, *sub-*, *ob-*, and *ad-*. Consonant pronunciation variations are represented in spelling and consonant doubling occurs at the morpheme boundary if the last consonant of the prefix is the same as the first consonant of the base.
4. The base final *c* (/k/) changes to *ck* (/k/) before a suffix beginning with *i* or *e*, as in *picknicking* and *mimicked*.
5. If a base ends in *ie*, the *e* is dropped before a suffix beginning with *e*, as in *tied*. The *ie* changes to *y* before a suffix beginning with *i*, as in *tying*.
6. If a base ends in *ue*, the *e* is dropped before any suffix, as in *rescuing*, *argument*, and *truly*.[21]

In order to plan an effective spelling program, the teacher must understand the importance of phonological and morphological relationships as well as the significance of oral and written language. Furthermore, the teacher must know the backgrounds, needs, and potential of the children.

As to the most effective learning method for introducing words to children, it has been found to be the *whole word* rather than the *hard spot* or individual letters.[22] And given a choice between presenting words in context or via a list, the teacher should present words *in context*. Also, the teacher should use

Individualizing Spelling Instruction

the distributed practice system, whereby students receive a portion of the spelling words each day, according to research conducted in Kansas and Connecticut.[23] This system is superior to the prevailing practice of giving students all the words at the beginning of the week. Daily quizzes are helpful too.

As to the optimum grade for beginning formal spelling instruction, recent research studies are not in agreement. One national survey of nearly 3,000 children in twenty-two states in grades three through eight showed that after grade four no spelling instruction is almost as effective as formal instruction.[24] These findings were in general agreement with another survey of more than 2,000 children in grades two through six which concluded that many pupils had achieved a "skill in spelling" as early as the third or fourth grade and that tracking them through the sequences of the available spelling programs may not be a worthwhile utilization of their time or energy.[25]

On the other hand, arguing for a delay in formal spelling instruction are researchers involved in a Michigan study of approximately 200 children in grades one through four. They believe that formal instruction may not be appropriate until children have had ample time to develop an understanding of word-attack principles. They state that it is more important to give pupils a chance to explore words in their writing and their reading rather than to have them write lists of spelling words.[26]

Traditional Approach

Since 1900 many spelling series have followed a five-day pattern which ordinarily begins on Monday. The weekly word list or unit is introduced, and *every student in the classroom receives an identical list*. The next day the words are used in sentences. Usually on Wednesday what is erroneously termed a "pretest" is given to see how many words each child already knows. Subsequently, pupils are urged to study only those words which they have misspelled or totally omitted from the test. Enrichment practice exercises are often supplied for Thursday's work. A final weekly test is administered on Friday. Every week spelling instruction in thousands of elementary school classrooms follows this traditional pattern or one that is remarkably similar.

Some children admittedly benefit from such instruction and there are certain values to this kind of large-group or whole-class approach. The word lists are graded for each school year, with lists getting consecutively more difficult, and inexperienced teachers find them time-savers. Generalizations are introduced on a near-weekly basis and periodically reviewed. Practicing the unfamiliar words on the first day can be a handwriting exercise at the same time that children are learning to spell. On Tuesdays and Thursdays the pupils also work on other language arts projects during their spelling-handwriting practice.

While some boys and girls do profit from such a rigid format, many others do not because the program stresses the need to achieve a perfect test score. It develops short-term memory, and memorization hardly demonstrates either the usefulness of the words or their relationship to the child's original ability to spell them. A spelling program for the whole class, which consists of lists of words selected in a manner other than individual, cannot possibly satisfy every child's writing requirements for that week. It fails to emphasize the need to communicate effectively and accurately and therefore also fails to help children understand that language is a tool.

Finally, the traditional approach ignores research which has shown that among more than 2,000 children in grades two through six many pupils already know how to spell a substantial number of the words included in the spelling textbook program at each grade level. Furthermore, the average child in this suburban sample also seemed able to spell a substantial number of words designated for the level one grade *above* his or her present grade placement. The researcher concluded that qualitative differences exist in spelling that may require a greater degree of individualization than that located in the neatly compartmentalized study procedures available in many spelling programs.[27]

Each pupil needs to work with a word list that is different—either totally or slightly—from that of every other child in the classroom at any given time. Consequently some teachers have chosen to deviate from the traditional approach.

Four approaches use a basic spelling list that is in some manner and to some degree individualized to meet more of the needs of the participating students. The first of these can be labelled the *Commercial-List-Individualized-for-One-Elementary-School Approach*. It involves duplicating the total list of words taught in grades two to six for a particular commercial series. When children begin a formal spelling program, a copy of this list is placed in their spelling folders and the folders move upward through the grades with them. The list of basic words is arranged in columns of increasing difficulty, and each semester every pupil is assigned words from only those columns that are on his or her spelling level; that is, a fifth grader who is spelling on a third-grade level would be assigned third-grade words rather than words on a fifth-grade spelling level. To further individualize the word list, words that each child finds difficult to spell in any subject are added to his or her list.

Recalling Yee's study of more than 2,800 elementary school children that proved the benefits of pretesting,[28] a flexible pretesting system follows the assignment of individual spelling lists. Pupils are allowed to take pretests on clusters of words from their lists whenever they have mastered the preceding group of words. The lock-step weekly pretest, given to all members of the class at one time, is replaced by a more flexible scheme, involving student pairs giving out words to each other. After the pretest, the children mark those words they spelled correctly on the basic lists in their folders and then become involved in activities that will enable them to learn the words they missed. Final tests are also flexibly administered and allow the children to mark the words they have finally learned on their basic lists.

Learning to spell a list of basic words is only one phase of the spelling program. Children are also expected to master many spelling generalizations

Combined Individualized-Group Approaches

Paraprofessional aides play a key role in an individualized spelling program. (Photo courtesy of the Fountain Valley School District, Fountain Valley, California.)

so that they may be able to spell words they have never studied. This is an important phase and so pretests are also given on generalizations.

The well-organized spelling folders are a vital part of this program since they constitute the core from which planning is done for varied activities. They contain several different kinds of information, including analyses of errors made in spelling, progress charts, and samples of spelling in written work.

The second approach can be termed the *Commercial-List-Individualized-for-One-Elementary-Classroom Approach*. Every Monday the group pretest is given, using the weekly list, before the children have seen the week's words. The pupils immediately correct their own pretests in order to determine which words they can eliminate from the list and which words they must study. Thus, the children's individual word lists begin with the weekly spelling words that they missed on the pretest; to this they add words which they had missed during the previous week's writing and which they had entered into a small spelling notebook. Finally, a few difficult Bonus Words are posted on the chalkboard for any pupil to study who wishes extra credit. In this approach, Tuesdays are devoted to textbook exercises involving generalizations, Wednesdays to practice on individual lists, and Thursdays to specially prepared enrichment lessons. On Fridays the final tests are administered on an individualized basis, with two children of matching ability in spelling testing one another as partners.

The third plan can be termed the *Noncommercial-List-Individualized-for-One-Elementary-District Approach*. Unlike the textbook list used in other approaches, the spelling list used here is a district list, based on difficulty and frequency counts compiled from children's creative writing in grades two to six for a single school year. The five-day plan is used, with a pretest on Monday for each week's words before the pupils begin studying. Wednesday's lesson covers a retest of the words missed on Monday, and there is a final retest on Friday. Tuesdays and Thursdays are devoted to additional experiences in written language: writing, revising, and the teaching of proofreading skills. Teachers using this approach report a great increase in interest in spelling correctly. They believe that this approach puts spelling in proper perspective, for there is no point in learning to spell orally or in learning to spell words that one is not going to use in writing.

The fourth approach can be labelled the *Noncommercial-List-Individualized-for-One-Elementary-Classroom Approach*. This plan involves only two school days, coupled with home study and spelling review during free class time. Every Monday morning the students suggest twenty-five new words from several different sources including misspelled words from their writings, words they use in daily conversation without being certain of the proper spellings, and words they encounter in independent reading. The only criterion for adding a word to the class list is the frequency with which pupils will use the word in their future writings. (Should the teacher believe that a suggested word is not worth memorizing, he or she asks the class how many members have ever had to write the word.) Once the class agrees on the twenty-five words, the list is duplicated by the teacher for the week's study.

On Monday afternoons a pretest is given, and children immediately correct their own papers in order to determine which words they must study that week. On Fridays the class takes a second test to see how much improvement has taken place. The students keep scorecards on which they enter both Monday's and Friday's test scores. They compete only with themselves and come to accept improvement, as opposed to perfection, as the most important goal in learning to spell.

Individualized Approach

In Oregon some of the teachers have stopped using spelling workbooks, texts, or lists.[29] They are using instead a so-called language-experience approach to spelling which bases the teaching of spelling on a single device: each child has a personal "spelling dictionary." This dictionary is simply a loose-leaf notebook, with alphabetical dividers, in which students record words they need to know how to spell in the course of all of their writing experiences in school. The same notebook can be used year after year because the pages can be changed and updated as necessary. Once a class has been introduced to individualized spelling dictionaries, it is important to get children into the habit of using their dictionaries whenever they are involved with writing activities in any area of the curriculum. As a pupil is writing and needs to use a word he or she cannot spell, the pupil can ask the teacher or look up the word in a published dictionary. The pupil then promptly records it in his or her spelling notebook. Should the pupil need to use that word again later and is still unsure of the correct spelling, he or she need only refer back to the spelling dictionary.

An improvement in spelling has been noted with this approach, along with a new enthusiasm for reading and writing.

Proofreading

An area closely linked to individualized spelling instruction is individualized checking or proofreading. This area relates to the problem of transfer in spelling which has long been a concern to teachers who wonder why children often spell words correctly on a test and yet misspell the same words later in their written work. The reason most often presented for this enigma is the failure to develop a *spelling consciousness* in students, and solutions to the problem of transfer usually involve some aspect of proofreading written work. It is therefore crucial to help children acquire early in their school years the responsibility for correcting improperly spelled words themselves, preferably right after completing a written assignment.

Since many current spelling text series contain a variety of language arts skills, they often include exercises for proofreading. Pupils in level three, for example, find exercises in their spelling workbooks which state:

1. The following sentences have misspellings. Write the sentences correctly.

   Sam likes to draw a funny face on every purpel baloon.

   Next Saturday summer vacation will be all most over.

   In Apirl the showers keep the city streets nice and kleen.

2. There are 10 misspellings in the following paragraph. Write the paragraph correctly.

   On Teusday our art teacher gave us a choise betwen making a blew or brown auto out of newspaper. We made an awfull lot of niose. We engoyed puting the shapes together with glew. We through all the scraps into the wastebasket.[30]

Students in level five find more advanced proofreading exercises such as the following:

1. Correct the spelling errors and finish the story.

   A spider made a dandey web of spun silver. It covered one of the jungel paths. Travelers could go no father than the web. When a lion got cought in the web one day, he said to the spider, "What can you do to a terible lion like me? Lissen a minite, my freind. If you help me out of this pikel, I will rewerd you."

2. Proofread June's sentences for mistakes in spelling and capitalization.

   we got these blew grapes from iowa. mrs tufts got grape stains on her new sute. she told jim to share the frut with andy.

3. Proofread Chris's letter for mistakes in spelling, capitalization, and punctuation.

   Dere Mom and dad?

   Hear we are in the muntains Our bus from home was lait so the giude hired a jeepe. Wow, what a ride[31]

   love chris

Instructional Activities for Spelling

Activities to facilitate the learning of spelling words may be used in conjunction with any of the approaches to spelling instruction discussed earlier in this chapter. The traditional whole-class or large-group approach as well as some of the combined individualized-group approaches demand the use of activities on at least one of the middle days of the five-day plan. The exercises described in this section may involve individuals, pairs of students, or small groups, as well as, occasionally, the entire class. They focus attention on the spelling process and stress practice of correct rather than incorrect spellings. Some are particularly appropriate for younger or slower spellers while others may meet the needs of most spellers throughout the elementary grades.

Drawing Charades

Simple pictures of Words Under Attack are drawn on the chalkboard or on worksheets. Children write the correct word under each picture.

Examining Pocket Words

The teacher prepares a chart with twenty-six pockets, one for each letter of the alphabet. Then the teacher places individual cards of Words Under Attack in the pocket chart, according to the first letter of the word. Students may remove the cards, examine them, and return them to the chart. Sometimes the chart may hold all the word cards for a semester, a month, or a unit.

Fishing

Children draw pictures of Words Under Attack on construction paper cutouts of fish. The fish are placed in a bowl with paper clips attached to them. The pupils "catch" the fish with a magnet at the end of a short fishing pole. They then write on the chalkboard or on paper the words pictured on the fish that they caught.

Pasting Spots

Each child makes a large heavy cardboard giraffe and paints it yellow. Then the child cuts out a quantity of circles from brown construction paper to simulate spots. As the child learns to spell correctly a word missed on the pretest, he or she writes the word on one circle and pastes it on the giraffe. Hopefully, the teacher will provide a grooved piece of wood or some other device to help the giraffe stand up so that the spelling spots are prominently displayed.

Preparing Anagrams	The teacher or the children make cutout letters of the alphabet, with several lowercase and several uppercase forms of each one. The letters are placed in a box on a corner table. During free time, one pupil or a pair of children may go to the table to form various Words Under Attack. Either the teacher or student partner can readily check the correct spellings.
Solving a Rebus	On the chalkboard or worksheets, there are sentences for completion which use picture clues for Words Under Attack such as: *I found some eggs in the*

_____

Spacing Out	The teacher prepares a paragraph which includes many or all of the Words Under Attack. Then the teacher copies it on the chalkboard or on worksheets, purposely leaving no space between words but punctuating and capitalizing the sentences properly. The children must draw lines between the connected words to make sense out of the paragraph.
Talking about Taped Lessons	Children listen to a taped spelling lesson lasting fifteen to twenty minutes. Then they participate in a five-minute discussion period, during which their teacher answers any questions regarding the taped lesson. Incidentally, a study was completed in which the spelling achievement of fourth-grade boys after eight such taped lessons substantially exceeded that of identical subjects who had participated instead in a lecture-discussion approach.[32]
Towering a Word	A pupil writes one Word Under Attack vertically, either on the chalkboard or on writing paper. He or she then tries to use each letter of that word in a new word and may even attempt to form the new words into a sentence or question like this:

$$Can$$
$$TOm$$
$$Run$$
$$toDay$$

Using Tiny Flash Cards	After a pretest, the child writes all the words he or she has missed on small rectangles of colored construction paper. The child then uses these as flash cards, working with a partner. Upon attaining mastery of the words, the pupil may paste the flash cards in a special notebook or on an individual chart.
Writing Jingles	Children can establish the correct spelling of a Word Under Attack by writing jingles using the word in rhyme. Sometimes they learn not only to spell that word but also other words in the same phonogram (or graphemic base), as in this couplet:

> Give your hungry kids a break,
> Buy them pounds of sirloin steak.

Games can help facilitate learning and offer additional practice in spelling. Certain criteria, however, should be observed regarding selection and use of games. First, most games should be planned for individual players, pairs of students, or small groups of children. Secondly, games should stress correct spellings and avoid incorrect ones as much as possible. Thirdly, games should be selected which maximize the involvement of each pupil in a learning experience. Finally, since spelling is chiefly relevant to writing, spelling games should involve written work and not oral exercises. The learning games presented here require minimal teacher preparation with maximum pupil participation.

Learning Games for Spelling

Add-On

1. The teacher reviews with the players a list of words relevant to generalizations recently studied. A scorekeeper is selected. Teams are chosen and assigned chalkboard space far apart from each other.
2. The teacher pronounces a word and has the first member on each team go to the board and write the first letter of the word. As soon as the player is finished, he or she hands the chalk to the second member of the team, urging this player to "add-on."
3. The second member then writes the second letter, and the round continues until one team completes the word.
4. The team finishing first in each round scores one point. Points are subtracted, however, for any illegible or incorrect letters.
5. The team with the most points wins Add-On.

Countdown

1. The teacher prepares to dictate spelling words relevant to a chosen generalization. A scorekeeper is selected. Teams are chosen and are assigned chalkboard space far apart from each other.
2. The first player on each team stands at the board, listening to the word the teacher reads. The player then tries to complete writing that word by the time the teacher finishes a "countdown" from ten to one. The teacher can either count softly or indicate the count with his or her fingers.
3. Each team scores a point every time a player completes writing the dictated word correctly by the time the teacher counts down to one.
4. Individual winners are all the players who beat the countdown. The winning team or teams of Countdown are those with the most points.

Erase and Spell

1. Three players stand at their desks, each holding an eraser and a piece of chalk. A fourth student is chosen as scorekeeper.
2. The teacher writes on the board a list of words relevant to a certain generalization, for example, *now, brown, prow, sow, cow, how, owl, chow.*
3. When the teacher asks, "Who can find, erase, and rewrite the word *sow?*", the first player to walk to the board, complete the chore successfully, and return to his or her desk scores one point.
4. The round continues until all the words have been erased at least once. The winner of Erase and Spell is the player with the most points.

5. Variation: The teacher may give a brief definition instead, e.g., "Who can find, erase and rewrite the word which means a pig?"

Leave-Out
1. The teacher writes on the board a word relevant to a current generalization, omitting the vowels of a word (e.g., *m ssp ll*).
2. At their seats the players write the word completely and correctly (i.e., *misspell*) on paper.
3. The teacher selects a player to write his or her answer on the board. If the player's response is correct, he or she may then put a vowel-less word on the board for the rest of the class to solve. If the player's response is incorrect, another player has a turn.
4. The winners of Leave-Out are all the players who solved the incomplete words correctly either at the board or at their seats.

Missing Relay
1. The teacher writes on the chalkboard identical lists of words and each word has one missing letter. There are as many words in each list as there are players on the team assigned to that list, and the words all relate to certain generalizations.
2. At a signal the first player on each team goes to the board and writes in the missing letter in one word on the team's list. As soon as the first player finishes, the second player on the same team attempts to complete a different word.
3. The first team to complete all its words correctly wins Missing Relay.

Spelling Bingo
1. Each player folds a sheet of paper into sixteen squares.
2. The teacher writes on the chalkboard sixteen different words relevant to a particular generalization. The players copy the sixteen words on their papers, putting only one into a square and determining the locations by themselves.
3. The teacher erases the board and proceeds to call out the words, one at a time. The players put dry beans or discs on the appropriate squares.
4. When a player has a row or diagonal filled, he or she calls out, "Spelling Bingo!" and reads the words aloud. The player's classmates and teacher help check the bingo.

Take a Chance
1. Words relevant to a particular generalization are written on separate slips, folded, and placed in a box.
2. One at a time, the players draw a slip but do not look at it. Each player hands the slip to the teacher or to "It" who pronounces the word for the player to write on the chalkboard.
3. If the word is spelled correctly, the teacher or It keeps the slip. If the word is misspelled, the player keeps the slip.
4. Players who have no slips at the end of the round are the winners of Take a Chance.

1. The teacher prepares a list of words relevant to certain generalizations and reviews these with the future "touchdown" makers. The teacher then draws on the chalkboard a large diagram of a football field, indicating the goal lines and the 10-to-50-yard lines.
2. Two teams are chosen (Teams A and B), who in turn each select a team captain. The captains determine which goalpost each team will defend and choose a team color. A scorekeeper is selected to continually note the teams' positions on the field with chalks representing team colors.
3. On the chalkboard, outside the diagram but near the goalpost it is defending, each team is assigned space in which to write the words the teacher will dictate.
4. The teacher begins the game by reading one word at a time to Team A, whose players in turn write the words in the space allocated. Each word correctly spelled advances the team ten yards, as duly noted by the scorekeeper. If no misspellings occur, a touchdown is scored by Team A after ten words or one hundred yards.
5. However, if Team A misspells a word on their own 30-yard line, for example, Team B has its turn and can score a touchdown by running only thirty yards or spelling three words correctly. Should Team A misspell a word on Team B's 30-yard line, then Team B can score a touchdown by running seventy yards or spelling seven words correctly.
6. The team with the most touchdowns within a designated period of time wins Touchdown.

1. Two teams are established (Teams A and B) and their players make out individual name tags which are collected facedown and separated into two piles.
2. The teacher calls out a spelling word relevant to the generalizations of the present or past week. Players on both teams write the word on paper at their seats.
3. The teacher selects a name tag from Team A's pile and calls upon the owner to copy his or her word on the board for the class to see. If the player can do so correctly, Team A gets a point; if the player fails, a tag from Team B is picked.
4. With each new word during Write or Wrong, all tags are returned to their proper pile so that every player has an equal opportunity to be chosen for any one word.

Learning-Disabled Spellers

Successful spellers must almost simultaneously reauditorize, revisualize, and produce kinesthetically, all with accurate sequencing. They must first be able to analyze auditory constructs, or the words as pronounced, into their ordered component parts. Then they must have the ability to summon up the word parts' appropriate visual representations in correct sequence. Finally, successful spellers must be able to reproduce the words synthesized in written form.

In almost every classroom there is at least one learning-disabled speller who is deficient in one or more of the basic processes needed for the spelling task. If these spellers also have memory- and motor-sequencing problems, their efforts to learn to spell are further hampered because they will be unable to recall how the various letters are formed.

Ordinarily, when one modality is weak the others take over in an effort to compensate. The problem area thus goes relatively unnoticed and the modalities continue to function in integrated fashion, mutually reinforcing each other. In the learning disabled, however, there is likely to be mutual interference instead of integration. Thus these pupils become less efficient in receiving and processing information as well as less efficient in monitoring their expressions.

Techniques for Improvement

The best approach for aiding learning-disabled spellers depends on how many deficient areas are involved. Children whose auditory competencies are reasonably intact but who suffer from poor visual memory can at least be expected to spell phonetically and to develop a visual memory bank for some of the phonologically irregular words. Their other misspellings may remain identifiable but highly phonetic. On the other hand, pupils whose spatial and visual skills are fairly intact may learn to spell through these strengths, recalling many sight words readily. Gradual development of their phonic tools may even make them adequate spellers. In regard to both of these groups of children, the job of bridging the auditory and visual areas must proceed from the area of strength.

A third group of children has neither visual nor auditory competencies and their spelling is often bizarre. Haptic methods are suggested as a start in dealing with these children's deficiencies. Partoll recommends a typing program which is patterned and linguistic to help bypass the motoric problems which may also be present.[33] Such a method can introduce both visual and auditory skills and provide for their development to an almost automatic level.

For the problem spellers, ordering of tasks to limit the confusing number of generalizations is considered essential. Introducing and solidifying one sound-to-symbol set of relationships at a time is deemed crucial. Phonic skills must be taught simultaneously in a relatively fixed order in early reading and spelling, and they must be reinforced by writing. Later the irregular word families are introduced, and still later, the roots and affixes.

Routes and approaches to help disabled spellers vary according to age and grade level. In the primary grades the need is to solidify associations of sounds-to-letters and of sound patterns to letter patterns. In the middle grades teaching strategies must be directed to the obvious and specific deficits displayed. Reference to the checklist in Figure 5.3 can help distinguish the auditorily-poor speller from the one who is visually-poor: error items 1–13 are primarily of auditory and intersensory integration nature; items 14–18 concern visual-spatial and visual-memory areas; item 19 suggests need for a learning

Severe Spelling Problems

Figure 5.3. Analysis Checklist of Severe Spelling Problems Among Learning-Disabled Children.

Put initials of child next to errors that he or she consistently makes.

_____ 1. Consonant sounds used incorrectly (specify letters missed)
_____ 2. Vowel sounds not known (specify letters missed)
_____ 3. Sounds added at beginning of words (e.g., a blend given when single consonant required)
_____ 4. Sounds omitted at beginning of words
_____ 5. Omission of middle syllables
_____ 6. Omission of middle sounds
_____ 7. Extraneous syllables added
_____ 8. Extraneous letters added
_____ 9. Endings omitted
_____10. Incorrect endings substituted (*ing* for *en* or for *ed*)
_____11. Reversals of whole words
_____12. Auditory confusion of *m/n* or *th/f/v* or *b/p* or other similar sounds
_____13. Missequencing of sounds or syllables (transposals like *from* to *form*)
_____14. Revisualization of very common sight words poor (e.g., *one, night, said*)
_____15. Spells, erases, tries again, etc. to no avail
_____16. Reversals of letter shapes *b/d* or *p/q* or *u/n* or *m/w* (specify)
_____17. Spelling phonetic with poor visual recall of word appearance
_____18. Spelling laborious, letter by letter
_____19. Spelling so bizarre that it bears no resemblance to original; even the pupil frequently cannot read his own

Observe also (additional hazards to problem spellers):

_____20. Spatial placement on line erratic
_____21. Spacing between letters and words erratic
_____22. Poor writing and letter formation, immature eye-hand coordination
_____23. Mixing of upper and lower case letters
_____24. Inability to recall how to form either case for some letters
_____25. Temporal disorientation: slowness in learning time, general scheduling, grasping the sequence of events in the day and those usually known to his contemporaries
_____26. Difficulty in concept formation; not able to generalize and transfer readily, to abstract "the rules and the tools"

Source: Adapted from *Academic Therapy* 11(1976): 344.

disabilities evaluation; items 20–24 concern kinesthetic memory and sequencing; and items 25–26 cover two broad and general areas of importance.

By the fifth and sixth grades learning-disabled spellers who are intellectually able can attach meaning and appropriate spelling to Latin and other bases and affixes. They can learn some polysyllabic, phonetically regular words too. Many sight words can be introduced; mnemonic devices are often useful; and a small number of "discovered" generalizations can help. Most children at this level have completed the transition from manuscript to cursive writing and thereby reduced the visual-spatial and kinesthetic demands in spelling. Any one of a number of different lists of common words, as discussed in the next chapter, can be adopted for use with intermediate spellers in an effort to enable them to develop a minimal memory bank of important but irregularly spelled words. A teacher can pass the list along to the next grade with notations on the progress that the disabled spellers have made.

One basic approach which has proved successful for children with learning disabilities in both the primary and intermediate grades is the visual configuration method that is color-coded.[34] The necessary materials include one-inch wooden cubes (orange and blue), felt-tip pens (orange and blue), ruled newsprint with cardboard backer, and 5 inch by 12 inch tagboard ruled in one-inch intervals. The children are told that (1) all vowels are made with orange cubes and all consonants with blue cubes; (2) tall letters are three cubes high; (3) the letter *t* is two cubes high; (4) the manuscript letters *g, j, p,* and *q* are two cubes long with lower portions hanging below the solid lines; and (5) the letter *y* is either orange or blue (depending on its use as a vowel or consonant) and is slightly tilted from right to left. The pupils are introduced to the concept of visual configuration by spelling familiar words with the cubes and letting classmates figure out the words. The words are then written with the pens with the color code remaining the same. The action of changing pens for the vowels and consonants impresses letter sequencing on the writer's mind. Each time a new word is introduced there is practice with the cubes and the pens for the first two or three days. Even certain phonics generalizations can be incorporated into this visual configuration method; for example, syllabication can be taught by leaving extra space between the cube groups.

Evaluation of Pupils' Progress

Evaluation in spelling goes on informally and continually in written composition assignments and instructional spelling sessions. It occurs, too, more formally and less frequently during periodic tests.

Teacher's Evaluation of Pupils

The wise teacher provides for both weekly and monthly testing of the pupil's mastery of his or her word list and its underlying generalization(s). Such testing, particularly when followed by brief teacher-pupil conferences, can contribute to a growing sense of spelling achievement. Every pupil is encouraged to reflect upon personal growth as the teacher reviews his or her spelling record. Such individual guidance is essential to effective teaching and learning of spelling.

Appraisal of the overall growth of the class in spelling should also be made periodically, though on an informal basis, by observing the following:

- Can the pupils use correct spelling in functional writing?
- Do they locate their own misspelled words?
- Are the pupils consulting individual word lists?
- Do they demonstrate the ability to apply generalizations?
- Is each pupil increasing his or her spelling proficiency?

Students can participate in the process of evaluating their spelling growth in several ways. First, they can correct their own spelling tests. This useful procedure is made even more effective when the children *hear* the teacher read the correct spelling while they *see* each word spelled correctly on a specially prepared overlay.[35]

Secondly, students can keep individual progress charts. They can note either the number of words missed, as shown in Figure 5.4, or the number of words correctly spelled (multiplied by a given number to provide a point-score), as shown in Figure 5.5. In either case, dots are entered on the simple graphs and connected periodically.

Finally, pupils can maintain lists of words that they continue to misspell during composition work or in other subject areas. Such a Personal Spelling Demons list for an intermediate student might contain the following words:

Figure 5.4. Self-Evaluation Progress Chart, Form A.

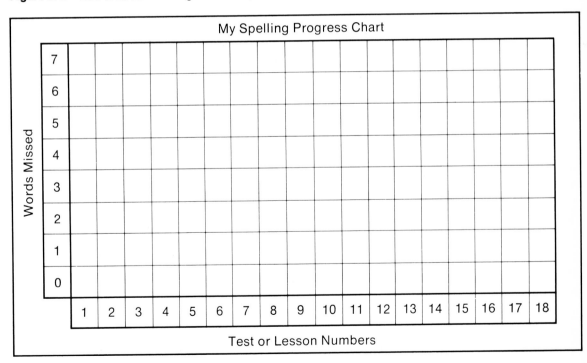

Figure 5.5. Self-Evaluation Progress Chart, Form B.

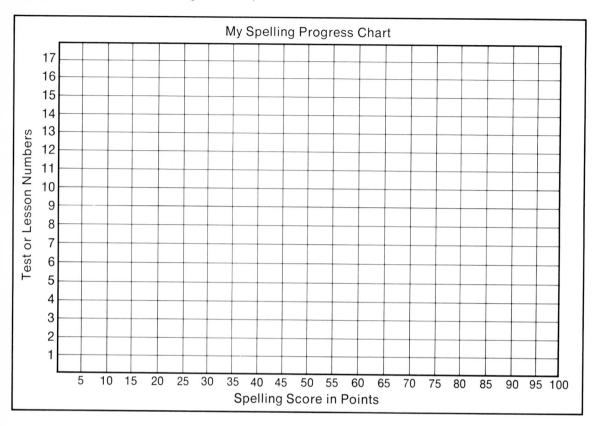

money	cousin	business	vegetable
forty	knowledge	review	argument
courtesy	difference	valuable	naturally
often	seize	height	whose
although	anxious	separate	amateur
changeable	occasion	against	mischievous
ninety	persuade	necessary	trouble
straight	receive	calendar	sandwich
hospital	acquaintance	disappear	plaid
absence	sincere	familiar	misspell

Standardized Achievement Tests Besides the class tests frequently administered, there are formal standardized tests available which are given infrequently and are purported to inform teachers where their pupils stand in relation to other pupils in the local school system and across the nation. Some of these spelling instruments are:

1. *Kansas Elementary Spelling Test* (grade 3) and *Kansas Intermediate*

Spelling Test (grades 4–6). Testing time: fifteen to twenty minutes. Publisher: Data Processing and Educational Measurement Center, Kansas State Teachers College, Emporia, Kansas 66801.

2. *Spelling Test: National Achievement Tests* (grades 3–4, 5–8). Testing time: twenty-five minutes. Publisher: Psychometric Affiliates, Munster, Indiana 46321.

Other standardized spelling tests are those found as subtests of such reputable achievement test batteries as the *Iowa Tests of Basic Skills* (from the Houghton Mifflin Company of Boston) and the *Metropolitan Achievement Tests* (from Harcourt Brace Jovanovich, Inc. of New York City). Standardized achievement tests do not constitute the best means of evaluating spelling instruction, however, because they cannot measure the growth that has taken place in learning in a particular situation. After all, words used in any spelling test should be the meaningful and useful words taught and learned in the spelling lessons of a particular group of children.

Discussion Questions

1. Why is invented spelling such an important area?
2. Can you detect any similarities between spelling and reading? What differences exist between them?
3. Describe the multisensory mechanisms involved in learning to spell.
4. How can a teacher help the intermediate student who is able to spell words presented during a test but misspells those same words a short time later in a written composition?
5. In the modern elementary classroom how should the pupils' progress in spelling be evaluated?

Suggested Projects

1. Ask one kindergarten teacher for examples of invented spelling.
2. Make a chart that could be displayed permanently in the classroom which shows How to Study a Word.
3. Obtain some compositions written by fourth graders and list the words most frequently misspelled in them. Can you conclude anything as to common types of spelling errors?
4. Use one of the learning games described in this chapter with a group of third-grade pupils. Then report to your peers about the group's reactions.
5. Investigate some of the alternative forms to traditional orthography such as those designed by Sir James Pitman and George Bernard Shaw. Do you believe that one of these forms would help resolve the spelling problems of some children?
6. Examine two current editions of commercial spelling programs for level five and compare the kinds of activities suggested for children of high ability and those of low ability. Which of the two programs would you prefer for your classroom?
7. Set up the learning center on spelling shown in Figure 5.6.

Figure 5.6. Language Arts Learning Center: Spelling.

TYPE OF CENTER: Spelling	TIME: 20 minutes
GRADE LEVEL: 4–7	NUMBER OF STUDENTS: 2 or 3

INSTRUCTIONAL OBJECTIVE: The student will review a number of spelling words.

MATERIALS: Paper and pencils for the students, timer, dictionary, folder for finished papers, letters of the alphabet cut from construction paper and placed on the display board.

DIRECTIONS TO STUDENTS:
1. Take a sheet of paper and a pencil. Write your name in the top righthand corner.
2. Set the timer at 30 minutes.
3. Start with the letter A. Think of a word beginning with A and write it on your paper.
4. Continue with the entire alphabet—26 in all—writing words for each letter.
5. Be sure to spell all your words correctly. If you need help with your spelling, consult a dictionary.
6. When the timer rings, turn it off and stop writing.
7. Count how many words you have completed. Clock the time and write it on your paper. Try to increase the number of words the next time you come to the center.
8. Place your finished paper in the folder labeled "FINISHED PAPERS."

EVALUATION: The teacher will evaluate a student's spelling ability and vocabulary facility.

Source: From *Language Arts Learning Centers and Activities* by Angela Reeke and James Laffey. Copyright 1979 by Goodyear Publishing Company. Reprinted with permission.

Related Readings

Cabán, J. et al. 1978. "Mental Imagery As an Approach to Spelling Instruction." *Journal of Experimental Education* 46: 15–21.

Camp, B. W., and Dolcourt, J. L. 1977. "Reading and Spelling in Good and Poor Readers." *Journal of Learning Disabilities* 10: 300–307.

Groff, P. 1976. "Why There Has Been No Spelling Reform." *Elementary School Journal* 76: 331–37.

Hillerich, R. L. 1976. *Spelling: An Element in Written Expression.* Columbus, Ohio: Charles E. Merrill Publishing.

Maxim, G. W. 1975. "Set the Spelling Scene in a Center." *Teacher* 93: 42–44.

Rowell, C. G. 1975. "Don't Throw Away Those Spelling Test Papers . . . Yet!" *Elementary English* 52: 253–57.

Santa, C. M. 1976–77. "Spelling Patterns and the Development of Flexible Word Recognition Strategies." *Reading Research Quarterly* 12: 125–44.

Schell, L. M. 1975. "B+ in Composition: C— in Spelling." *Elementary English* 52: 239–42.

Schofer, G. 1977. "Teachers Should Be Dictators." *Language Arts* 54: 401–402.

Zutell, J. 1978. "Some Psycholinguistic Perspectives on Children's Spelling." *Language Arts* 55: 844–50.

Vocabulary 6

General vocabularies that each child possesses

Factors that influence vocabulary growth

Guidelines for a curriculum in vocabulary development

The three major independent techniques for learning English vocabulary

Due to the verbal nature of most classroom activities, knowledge of words and ability to use words fluently are essential to academic success. The achieving pupil invariably possesses the best and largest word collection.

The relation of vocabulary to reading performance is high. In fact Chomsky has suggested that one of the best ways to teach reading may very well be by enriching children's vocabularies so that they may construct for themselves the deeper representation of sounds which correspond so closely to the orthographic forms.[1]

Classroom teachers then should be vitally interested in establishing a systematic approach to vocabulary development. They should seize every opportunity to awaken the children to the joy of hearing, repeating, and understanding new words. The boys and girls in turn are faced with a twofold task. First, they must learn as many as possible of the thousands of words or symbols that their culture has assigned to various objects, sensations, and processes. Then they must be able to recall the object, sensation, or process when the naming word is mentioned.

As children begin to acquire a vocabulary, the words they learn will have meaning if each word is linked with something the children have actually experienced through their senses. Vocabulary development is generally understood to be the result of the combined study of concepts and of symbols. Only experience can provide the mind with the concepts for which the spoken or visual symbols must be located as needs arise. Children cannot and do not acquire a large vocabulary by accumulating a stock of words as symbols for definitions apart from concepts.

Growth in Word Meaning

As boys and girls acquire experiences and learn to regard the environment in various ways, their ability to attach meaning to words changes and grows. Four ways in which this growth develops have been identified.

First, children are able to see and label *an increasing number of critical properties* of events, objects, persons, and actions. Young boys or girls are solely concerned with the physical attributes of size, color, and texture. More experienced children, however, can describe an object or condition in terms of other physical attributes as well. Similarly there is growth in the connotative meanings that boys or girls attach to a person or an object. Initially they may have only been able to experience anger or happiness but later they experience many other reactions as well to events or people. As their experience broadens they are able to identify more functional attributes and more aesthetic qualities of objects and actions.

Second, children acquire *a more precise label* for any critical property as they begin to differentiate shades of meaning. Young boys or girls experience everything so simply that they only need words for either end of the meaning spectrum: *rough/smooth, happy/sad, round/square.* More experienced children differentiate the extremes of meaning and try to qualify their words. Still later, pupils acquire standard labels or create their own metaphors for clear meaning.

Third, children's words become *more generalized words;* a single word may be applied to more objects, in more contexts, from more physical points of view, and in more time frames. *Pencils* are no longer just yellow and wooden, for example. Instead, they can be purple or green, dull or sharp, thin or oversized. They may be used in school or at home, in the car or at the library media center. They may be mechanical pencils, drawing pencils, grease pencils.

Fourth, while children are differentiating and generalizing their experiences, they are building *a supply of expressions* relating to any one element of meaning. Young boys or girls have only one way to describe a certain color. More experienced pupils retain their original expressions but simultaneously collect new expressions. They thereby become better able to communicate personally and to understand the speech and writing of others.

In an effort to examine these aspects of growth in word meaning, children at four different maturity levels were asked to define or describe the word *horse.* The responses revealed that *boys and girls at every level tend to observe and label a common property of size.* The children's answers were categorized by properties, connotations, synonyms, class names and contexts, and these are enumerated in Figure 6.1.

Figure 6.1.
Children's Meanings
for *Horse.*

Properties

Level a black one
1 hair
legs   -ride it   -walk

Level big, high
2 brown, white
long tails, 4 feet, whiskery things on their necks
walk, run, gallop
ride 'em
(*demonstrates noise*)

Level 3
kinda big, some are little
brown, white, spotted, kinda blonde
some have short tails, usually long though, manes
trot, gallop, some do fancy steps
work, pull things, ride 'em
makes a sort of snorting noise (*demonstrates*)

Level 4
big compared to ponies, small compared to elephants;
tall—measure height in hands—about 4 hands high
many colour combinations; colour often indicates what *kind*
of horse it is
manes (sometimes braided); hooves-shod;
walk, gallop, trot, canter, fight with teeth and hooves
used for work, entertainment, transportation

Connotations

Level 1
nice

Level 2
scary
neat
yech
stinks
nice

Level 3
sometimes scary
nice if they just stand still!
the ones I've seen are friendly

Level 4
can be mean if mistreated
brave (like Black Beauty)
depends on what kind of horse it is

Synonyms

Level 1
horsie

| Level 2 | horse | colt |
| | | pony |

Level 3	horse	pony
		colt
		Shetland

Level 4	horse, "cheval," nag	
	plough horse, beast of burden	pony
	stallion	mare

Figure 6.1 (Cont.)

Class Names

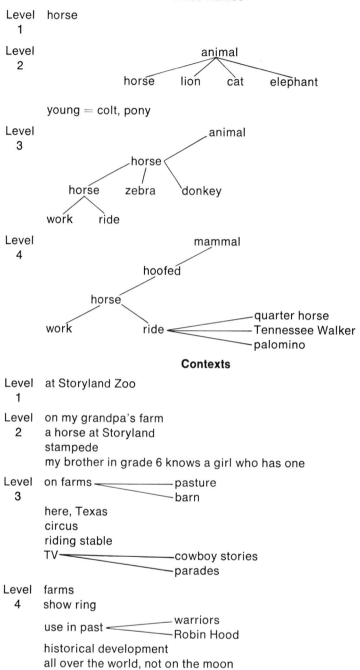

Level 1   horse

Level 2
```
              animal
       ┌────────┼────────┐
    horse   lion   cat   elephant
```

young = colt, pony

Level 3
```
                     animal
               horse
        ┌────────┼────────┐
     horse    zebra    donkey
   ┌──┴──┐
 work   ride
```

Level 4
```
                          mammal
                    hoofed
               horse
        ┌────────┴────────┐
     work              ride ──── quarter horse
                            ──── Tennessee Walker
                            ──── palomino
```

Contexts

Level 1   at Storyland Zoo

Level 2   on my grandpa's farm
          a horse at Storyland
          stampede
          my brother in grade 6 knows a girl who has one

Level 3   on farms ──────── pasture
                     ──────── barn
          here, Texas
          circus
          riding stable
          TV ──────── cowboy stories
             ──────── parades

Level 4   farms
          show ring

          use in past ──── warriors
                      ──── Robin Hood
          historical development
          all over the world, not on the moon

Source: *Elementary Language Arts Handbook* (Edmonton: Alberta Department of Education, 1973), pp. 19–21.

Each child has at least four general and related vocabularies with which the elementary teacher must work. Two of them—the listening and reading vocabularies—are receptive and emphasize understanding. Speaking and writing vocabularies, however, refer to use and are expressive. All four vocabularies develop continuously, albeit at different rates, into adulthood.

The *listening or hearing vocabulary* refers to all the words that children recognize and understand when they hear them in an oral context. It is the first vocabulary to develop during the language acquisition stage and is also the one that continues to grow most rapidly during the elementary school years. It remains substantially larger than a pupil's visual vocabulary until the age of ten, at which time the size difference diminishes.

The teacher must realize that the listening child may comprehend one meaning of a word or one shade of meaning and yet be wholly ignorant of the other denotations. In addition, the teacher must recognize that the size of a primary child's listening vocabulary ordinarily will not affect the reading progress experienced by the pupil until the third grade.

The *speaking vocabulary* includes all the words that children use in everyday speech. It forms the basis for the development of the reading and writing vocabularies, and it is at the oral/aural level that vocabulary development generally takes place in the classroom. The recommendation has been made that

Types of Vocabularies

pupils should possess sizable speaking vocabularies in a language before they begin reading lessons in that language whether it be their first or second tongue.

The *reading vocabulary* consists of all the words that children recognize and understand in print or in writing. When boys and girls enter school, their reading vocabularies are generally limited to their names and the few words they have learned to recognize from billboards, television, and food container labels. It is during reading instruction that children build their word banks. By the time they reach reading maturity in the upper grades their reading vocabularies overtake and surpass their oral/aural vocabularies. The more pupils read, the more their reading vocabularies grow.

All the words that children recognize and understand when they hear the words in an oral context constitute their listening vocabulary. (Photo courtesy of the Oceanview School District, Huntington Beach, California.)

Reported to lag perpetually behind the other three vocabularies is the *writing vocabulary*. It is the last to develop and includes only the words that children can use in written compositions. It is closely tied to spelling instruction. Pupils' writing vocabularies reportedly overlap more than 90 percent with their speaking vocabularies. Moreover, writing vocabularies are generally nonexistent when children begin school.

Planned instruction in any one area of vocabulary tends to result in improvement in all four areas. They are interrelated and uniformly based on conceptual development.

There are many specific factors which significantly affect the development of vocabulary in children. While some of them are beyond the domain of the teacher, others can be influenced by his or her planning. **Factors Influencing Vocabulary Growth**

The first factor is the *socioeconomic status of the child's family*. Johnson and Barrett's survey of word recognition among 210 primary children revealed that boys and girls from schools that served families of upper socioeconomic status did better than children from schools that served families of lower socioeconomic status.[2] While the age at which significant differences first appear in vocabulary performance among boys and girls of varying socioeconomic groups has not been firmly set, some studies do indicate that these differences have been established by age three.

Nevertheless, an excellent environment alone cannot assure a wide vocabulary for children who are not alert and able to learn. Since there is a high correlation between vocabulary and *intelligence,* what children gain from their environment is conditioned by their native capacities to learn. Retarded readers have a limited writing vocabulary and possess a listening vocabulary that is larger than their reading vocabulary. Bright children, on the other hand, remember their experiences with greater clarity; they can abstract and generalize words and terms that are beyond those of pupils of limited mental ability.

The *age or grade level* of the child is an important factor too. The older the child, the more words he or she knows. Eighth graders commonly recognize four to six times as many words as first graders. Even second graders outperform first graders, according to two separate vocabulary surveys.[3] Children in grade two recognized 90 percent of the 306 words presented; children in grade one, 64 percent.

The factor of *motivation* is always crucial. Dale and O'Rourke believe that motivated individuals can increase their working vocabularies by 10 percent.[4] Such an increase will result, in part, from bringing into sharper focus those words, those parts of words, and those expressions whose meanings are presently fuzzy. The teacher can help motivate students into moving some of their words/word phrases out of a so-called twilight zone into their working vocabularies.

Such *instruction and guidance in the use of words* is vital. Besides teachers, children's parents, grandparents, and other interested adults—at home and in the community—can and should take the time to explain unfamiliar vocabulary to boys and girls. Conversing with someone like the mail carrier, for instance, can help children enrich and refine their use of words.

The *continued and regular listening to storybooks* is a critical factor. Vocabulary appears to be learned best by young children in a context of emotional and intellectual meaning. Pupils, especially those who are slow academically, find it difficult to deal with words in isolation. Reading aloud to boys and girls, however, has resulted in increasing their knowledge of words as well as the quality of their vocabularies.

Another contributing factor covers the *personal interests* that the child has developed. Boys and girls engrossed in sports or science readily acquire the specialized vocabulary that their avocation demands. Interest centers in the classroom which are properly planned and frequently changed can stimulate word study too.

Sex differences have also been noted in all types of vocabularies. Girls develop larger speaking vocabularies prior to school entrance and they soon exceed elementary school boys in reading vocabularies. These differences, however, level off as the pupils enter adolescence.

Television viewing is yet another factor. It offers simultaneous visual-auditory presentation of vocabulary. It promotes concept building and offers experience with standard English, allowing many pupils to increase both their speaking and reading vocabularies. However, the teacher must stress *selective television viewing* if he or she wishes to insure that the medium will make a useful contribution to the vocabulary growth of the children.

The *social organizations* to which boys and girls belong make a difference in their vocabularies. If they regularly attend a synagogue or church, for example, they are more likely to be acquainted with Biblical terms than if they did not attend.

The final factor is *locale* and this is growing less significant under the influence of the mass media. Still, there are words dealing with coal mining or condominiums that are not commonplace to everyone in the nation.

Guidelines for a Curriculum in Vocabulary Development

Based upon research studies and classroom experience, the following principles are suggested for promoting vocabulary growth among elementary school pupils.

Developing a vocabulary requires understanding of the meanings and concepts which underlie words. Concepts may be expanded both by differentiation and by generalization. Children learn to group lemons and limes under *fruit*. They also learn to separate *cats* into Angora, Manx, and Persian. Boys and girls with learning difficulties or bilingual backgrounds find it hard to recognize different meanings of a single word such as *big*.

Vocabulary development is closely related to general maturation and varied interaction with a stimulating environment. Teachers generally cannot expect adequate vocabularies in immature, impoverished, or handicapped children. Although heredity sets the limits of possible development, the child with an IQ slightly below normal who is growing up in an environment favorable to language development is likely to have a better vocabulary than the child with an IQ slightly above normal who is being reared in relatively sterile surroundings.

The vocabulary of the home and home community greatly affects the school program in vocabulary development. Not only have children learned to listen and speak long before they enter kindergarten, but even after they have been enrolled in school, they continue to spend many hours listening and talking at home and in their neighborhoods. Little wonder that if the type of vocabulary that the boys and girls hear and use outside of school is inadequate, it will partly offset the teacher's efforts to help them improve their stock of words. In this delicate area of home-school relations (sometimes affected by bussing problems) it is critical that care be taken so that children do not develop feelings of inadequacy about their families or communities due to matters of vocabulary.

A planned and systematic approach to vocabulary instruction yields greater gains than incidental instruction, and a variety of instructional methods seems to be more beneficial than any single method. (Photo courtesy of the Fountain Valley School District, Fountain Valley, California.)

Not only does planned vocabulary instruction yield greater gains than incidental or unorganized instruction but a variety of instructional methods appears to be more effective than any single method. Wide reading or listening alone will not guarantee vocabulary growth. Yet either or both skills bring children in contact with new words once they have become sensitive to contextual and structural analyses. Word games may be useful in heightening motivation, but their use is probably as an accessory rather than as a primary instructional device. The two major groups of useful methods for fostering vocabulary development are labelled *independent* and *dependent*. Each is described later in the chapter.

Children must become aware of their need to improve their personal vocabularies independently. School success depends heavily upon the size and utility of a child's stock of words. As a pupil is usually aware of only about half of the words that he or she cannot define, a vocabulary building program is a service program. It is valuable in its own right as well as for its contribution to curricular areas and to the child's personal development.

In the lower grades growth in the pupil's meaning vocabulary is obtained chiefly through oral methods. The words that boys and girls encounter in primary reading books are chosen partly from concepts that have meaning for those children. Therefore, it is in these grades that much emphasis must be placed on vocabulary improvement through oral communication. The issue is critical in view of the fact that the absolute scale of vocabulary development and the longitudinal studies of educational achievement indicate that approximately 50 percent of general achievement at grade twelve has been reached by the end of grade three.

As children progress into the upper grades they have more opportunity to improve their vocabularies through printed words. On the whole, however, it is an oral/aural program that furnishes elementary school children with greater word power.

The dictionary is a valuable tool for extending vocabularies. Although the proper use of the dictionary is introduced in grade one, some pupils never seem to grasp the importance of the dictionary or develop the habit of using one. The teacher should therefore informally evaluate the dictionary competencies of the class and periodically schedule group lessons in the use of the dictionary. Also the teacher should insist that each child have access to a dictionary appropriate to his or her reading and maturity levels.

Vocabulary development must grow out of experiences that are real to the learner. A teacher cannot overlook the need for carefully structured experiences. For primary children especially, firsthand experiences are the best and often the only source of conceptual development. The teacher must recognize that pupils at any level who lag behind their peers in vocabulary growth do not need additional *written* work. Instead they will profit from nonprint media and direct experiences.

Comprehension is an integral part of word knowledge. Comprehension was recently defined as the relating of new experiences to the already known.[5]

This definition is especially appropriate for the comprehension of words. Students with enriched backgrounds of experience bring more to the vocabulary which they hear or read.

Vocabulary improvement requires periodic use of the new words by the teacher and by the pupils in conversation and discussion as well as in printed material. There must be adequate opportunities to use the new vocabulary in order to classify and reinforce word meanings. Only when a child has made a word his or her own has that word been mastered. The process does take time and rapid gains in vocabulary occur less frequently than in comprehension or rate of reading.

Sometimes children who have acquired words in their reading vocabularies fail to use them in their speech. It may be that they do not know how to pronounce those words properly and they need to be reminded of still another use of the dictionary.

Teaching English Vocabulary: Methodology

The foundations of vocabulary development are laid in the home during the preschool years. The school builds upon those foundations. It introduces new words to children during each curricular activity. It also teaches them how to develop their word power independently both in and out of school.

The process of vocabulary building involves sensory perception of an object (or the attributes of an object) or perception of the relationships of objects with one another. As each new perception is added to the earlier ones, the composite is then associated with familiar words or with new words spoken or written by other people.

Teachers must recognize that the more pupils learn about a given vocabulary concept, the broader and deeper their understanding of that concept becomes. O'Rourke terms this the BVD strategy for enlarging children's word stock; i.e., the broader (B) the knowledge of synonyms for the vocabulary (V) concept of *old,* the deeper (D) the knowledge of the basic concept.[6] Conversely, the deeper the children's understanding of the concept of *old,* the broader their knowledge of suitable synonyms.

Another useful strategy in vocabulary instruction is *elaboration,* especially extended elaboration. Elaboration (or the embedding of information within verbal contexts) facilitates learning because it provides stronger relations between two or more words or concepts learned together in a single context. It may appear even where only a single simple sentence is used. However, recent research findings suggest that extended elaborations (e.g., paragraphs) have even more impressive effects than simple sentences.[7]

Elaborations involving story themes (e.g., myths and fables) have been used effectively to develop and interrelate new vocabulary words for children from preschool through the sixth grade. Such elaborations were also used successfully over a four-week period with 107 educable mentally retarded pupils, ages eight to eleven, whose overall mean IQ was 74.4. This group was taught five vocabulary words per taped lesson which was presented while the children followed in their picture books. The pictures were simple, easy to understand, and introduced only a single context or relation. This combination of pictorially presented elaborations and audiotape descriptions appears to be an excellent instructional package for vocabulary development, state Taylor, Thurlow, and Turnure.[8]

Besides audio and visual experiences there are many other ways to help children acquire word knowledge and proficiency. As yet there is insufficient evidence to indicate which methods of vocabulary instruction work best at the different grade levels or with pupils of varying degrees of ability. However, there are two broad headings of techniques for the development of vocabulary in the classroom: the *independent* and the *dependent*. Whether a particular method falls into one category or the other depends primarily upon the amount of teacher/adult follow-up that is required once the child has learned the technique.

Independent Techniques

As soon as the teacher has introduced a child to any one of these three major techniques, the boy or girl may unlock the meaning of many unknown words by using knowledge of familiar words. The three techniques are *external context-clue methods* of word attack, *mastery of affixes,* and *mastery of roots.* The last two may also be grouped together as morphological or internal context-clue methods.

External Context Clues

By using such clues a child can frequently figure out the meaning of a strange word without using the dictionary. Therefore, the teacher must demonstrate the various kinds of external context clues so that the child will be aware of their availability. The teacher can (a) construct several sentences to illustrate each kind of clue; (b) point out random context clues in paragraphs the pupil may be reading; or (c) present sentences which typify three or four kinds of clues and let the pupil explain which kind each sentence represents. Dale and O'Rourke have delineated the following kinds of external clues (together with illustrative sentences) which students can learn to recognize:

1. *Formal definition* or expressing the meaning of a word in a direct statement. *Example:* A phoneme is one of a group of distinct sounds that comprise the words of the English language.
2. *Definition by example* or defining a word by example alone or further clarifying a formal definition. *Example:* An example of a phoneme is the *f* in *fan* or the *n* in *fan.*
3. *Definition by description* or listing the physical characteristics of the object representing the word. *Example:* An orange is a reddish-yellow, round, juicy fruit. (A definition by description often does not distinguish one word from others in its class. It does, however, distinguish among classes.)
4. *Definition by comparison* or stretching the meanings of words creatively even to the extent of sometimes using similes or metaphors. *Example:* The map of Italy is shaped like a boot.

5. *Definition by contrast* or telling the reader what the word is not. *Example:* A tomato is not a vegetable. (The effectiveness of this context clue depends heavily on the reader's experience.)

6. *Defining by synonym* or providing a short similar word that is closer to common usage than the original word. *Example:* Bondage is slavery.

7. *Defining by antonym* or providing a short, opposite word often used to show the extreme of an object or idea. *Example:* She was willing but he was loath to walk to the stadium.

8. *Definition by apposition* or placing a clarifying word or phrase next to another noun or pronoun. *Example:* Jute, the plant, grows in India.

9. *Definition by origin* or providing a setting in which the word was first used. *Example:* Samuel Maverick was a Texan whose cattle were unbranded wanderers.[9]

Most context clues demand some degree of inferential thinking. The reader should gradually learn to use the sense of the sentence or the surrounding sentences as an aid in identifying the probable meaning of a difficult word.

Current language arts texts for the elementary school sometimes contain exercises to help pupils learn about context clues. Those that do may begin as early as the primary levels.

While most boys and girls accept the importance of context, some of them do not understand *morphology* and how words also derive meaning from their component parts. To introduce this valuable generalization, the teacher must start with a familiar word, break it into meaningful parts, and then transfer the meaning of these parts to new words. The teacher should move stepwise from known words (*triangle* or *good*) to unknown words (*tricolor* or *goodness*). Children will then be able to infer the meaning of a difficult word if (a) they know the meaning of the *bound morpheme* or prefix/suffix used to form the word, and (b) realize that meanings of mastered prefixes and suffixes can be transferred from one word to another.

Mastery of Affixes (or Bound Morphemes)

The value of such mastery can be quickly shown by an examination of Edward Thorndike's list of the 20,000 most common words in the English language. Five thousand words or 25 percent of those listed have prefixes. Of this group 82 percent use one of these fourteen prefixes: *ab* (away from), *ad* (toward or to), *be* (overly or on all sides), *com, con, co* (together or with), *de* (downward, reversal, or from), *dis* (apart from, not, opposite), *en* (in, into, or to cover), *ex* (former or out of), *in* (not or into), *pre* (before), *pro* (for, before, or in favor of), *re* (again or restore), *sub* (beneath or under), and *un* (not or the opposite of).

Common suffixes that children should learn in an effort to develop their vocabularies independently include: *able, ble, ible* (can be done or inclined to), *al, ial* (relating to), *fy* (make or form into), *ic* or *ical* (in the nature of), *ism* (system or state of), *ist* (person who), *less* (without), *let* (small), *ment* (concrete result, process, or state of), *ness* (quality or condition of), *ory* (place where), and *ward* or *wards* (course or direction).

Current language arts texts for the elementary school contain exercises to help pupils learn about affixes. They generally introduce suffixes by level three and prefixes by level four, although some begin one level earlier. Spelling text series also include material on affixes.

Mastery of Roots

Unlike affixes, which are bound morphemes, most roots are free morphemes. Still, mastery of roots or base words will also help children attack new words which may come up outside the classroom. With a knowledge of base words, children will be able to unlock dozens of words by transferring the meaning of a single root to other words.

During a beginning lesson, for instance, the students could be asked to underline the common element in the following words: *telephone, microphone, saxophone, earphone, phonics*. They could discuss the meaning of *phon* (sound) and then write other words they know that contain the same root. They might even make up new words.

Common roots which the children can learn include: *cap* (head), *cav* (hollow), *circ* (ring), *dent* (tooth), *form* (shape), *geo* (earth), *gram* (letter), *mari* (sea), *min* (small), *mov* (move), *scrib* or *script* (write), and *vis* (see).

Most current language arts texts for the elementary school do not contain exercises to help boys and girls learn about the roots of words. Such exercises, however, are included in various spelling text series presently available.

Dependent Techniques

Dependent techniques do not teach for transfer. Instead, the child studies one word at a time and learns it only under the close supervision of the teacher or paraprofessional aide. Still the techniques are organized and any systematic approach to vocabulary growth is preferable to incidental or unorganized learning. The two dependent techniques are *mastery of a word list* and *dictionary/glossary study*.

Mastery of a Word List

The teacher assigns, weekly or monthly, a specific number of whole words from lists suggested in children's texts or from word counts developed by educators or psychologists. Ten basic word lists include those by Robert Hillerich (1974); William Durr (1973); Albert J. Harris and Milton Jacobson (1972); John B. Carroll, Peter Davies, and Barry Richmond (1971); Dale D. Johnson (1971); Henry Kucera and W. Nelson Francis (1967); Edward Fry (1960); Henry D. Rinsland (1945); Edward Thorndike and Irving Lorge (1944); and Edward W. Dolch (1939).

Mastery of such basic word lists readily meets demands for behavioral objectives and classroom accountability. The children may be quickly assessed by means of a short test on the number of words they have learned from all those assigned. Teachers may also choose to use lists of words introduced during science or social studies units.

Such study is sometimes linked with mastery of a word list. The teacher may ask the children to look up one or more words from their list in the dictionary so that they become familiar with the meaning of the assigned word or words.

At other times a new word may appear in the current events lesson, math assignment, or basal reader. The children locate this word in their dictionaries or glossaries at the teacher's suggestion. Later they may find that the new word reappears in a follow-up activity planned by the teacher.

Of course the dictionary is more than a book of word meanings, and proper use of the dictionary is an important skill. Locating one or two unrelated words in the dictionary, however, does not lead to substantial vocabulary growth. The children learn only those exact words which their teacher has assigned and which they must use in a written exercise or test.

Further discussion about dictionary skills can be found in Chapter Thirteen.

**Instructional
Activities**

Vocabulary building requires attention. Every day at least a few minutes should be taken for discussion of words used or needed for the communication of ideas. This is the only way that precise meanings can be learned. Teachers must understand that when a word is introduced too quickly or too casually, pupils often receive only a vague impression of its definition.

Some of the following instructional activities appeal especially to children with learning disabilities or to younger pupils. Others will interest gifted pupils at all levels or intermediate students. Finally, there are activities that are suggested for all elementary classes, primary and intermediate alike.

1. Listing things needed to (a) bake cookies; (b) build a tree house; (c) go camping; (d) set the table; or (e) go to school on a rainy day.
2. Giving more than one meaning for such words as *run, pipe, can, shell, ice, bark, sheet, park, slip, call, date, yarn, strike, spring, roll, light, fall, cut, check,* and *charge.*
3. Making interesting beginnings for these endings:
   ". . . slipped down the icy slope"
   ". . . struggled wildly"
   ". . . called for help"
   ". . . huddled in the cave"
4. Constructing definitions from handling such objects as a *locket, darning needle, abacus,* or *avocado.*
5. Illustrating such mathematical and geographical terms as *plateau, diagonal, perpendicular,* and *plain.*
6. Constructing a simple crossword puzzle that uses a series of related words, for example, *airplane, pilot, fly, sky, hangar.*
7. Drawing a pear (pair) tree and adding pears. On each pear should be written a word and its homophone.
8. Describing scenes on picture postcards.

9. Making a sound-train by painting and lettering shoe boxes, and filling them with realia whose names begin or end with the letters shown.
10. Keeping a list of unfamiliar words which appear in newspaper headlines during one week.
11. Discovering colorful words in travel brochures or in newspaper travel advertisements.
12. Examining the *Reader's Digest* section entitled "It Pays to Increase Your Word Power."
13. Listing "moody" words that make readers/listeners feel angry or keep them in suspense.
14. Collecting job words about computer technicians or anthropologists.
15. Reading juvenile magazines such as *Cricket, Children's Digest, Highlights for Children,* and *Ebony, Jr.*[10]
16. Describing one food item (*pickles*) according to the five senses (*green, crunchy, sour, slippery, brined*).
17. Discovering how three acronyms (e.g., *radar*) have developed.
18. Collecting "loaded" words gleaned from speeches made by political candidates at election times.
19. Preparing menus based on a single food specialty such as desserts or sandwiches.
20. Writing or listing reduplications (*helter-skelter, lickety-split, wishy-washy*).
21. Discussing environmental sounds.
22. Keeping word folders after study trips, such as "Visiting a Greenhouse" or "Going to the Planetarium."
23. Consulting Greet, Jenkins, and Schiller's *In Other Words: A Beginning Thesaurus* (Scott, Foresman, 1969) to locate five synonyms each for *break, go, jump, push, say,* and *send.*
24. Charting specialized words for such pastimes as tennis, bowling, fishing, or stamp collecting.
25. Promoting alliterative phrases (*ferocious flea, courteous crocodile*) that are humorous.
26. Making an illustrated dictionary relating to a special project which incorporates magazine pictures or personal drawings.
27. Using an opaque projector to display pictures of people or animals that plainly describe adjectives such as *grim, impatient, excited,* or *amazed.*
28. Creating names of imaginary animals by combining names of zoo or farm animals (*kangarooster, elephanteater*).
29. Drawing a favorite baked food such as chocolate cake and then writing all of the recipe ingredients of that food underneath the picture.
30. Adding up words instead of numbers (e.g., *high speed* plus *careless driving* equals *a highway accident*).
31. Creating a mysterious art gallery on a large bulletin board by posting several exciting and colored pictures (clipped from magazines) which have each been covered by sheets of numbered construction paper. A small

rectangle is cut out of each numbered sheet so that one segment of each picture becomes visible. The caption above the gallery reads: "Can you solve the mystery of the hidden pictures?" Children can relate their guesses orally or on paper.

32. Writing words to reveal their meanings (e.g., *fat* would be drawn or written with plump thick letters *f, a,* and *t* while *flag* could have a flag drawn in place of the *f*).

33. Developing an alphabet of words originating from famous names (e.g., *pasteurization* from Louis Pasteur). The list might begin with *America* (Amerigo Vespucci), *Braille* printing (Louis Braille), *Celsius* thermometer (Anders Celsius), and *diesel* engine (Rudolph Diesel).

34. Rewriting familiar proverbs or creating new ones.

35. Researching the origin of a space-age word like *capsule* or *lunar.*

36. Perusing from the library table one of the following:
    Asimov, Isaac. *Words from History* (Houghton, 1968).
    Fadiman, Clifton. *Wally the Wordworm* (Macmillan, 1964)
    Ferguson, Charles. *The Abecedarian Book* (Little, Brown, 1964)
    Kohn, Bernice. *What a Funny Thing to Say* (Dial, 1974)
    Merriam, Eve. *A Gaggle of Geese* (Knopf, 1960)
    O'Neill, Mary. *Words, Words, Words* (Doubleday, 1966)
    Rand, Ann and Paul. *Sparkle and Spin* (Harcourt, 1957)
    Reid, Alastair. *Ounce, Dice, Trice* (Little, Brown, 1958)
    Tremain, Ruthven. *Fooling Around with Words* (Greenwillow, 1976).

37. Examining some of the specialized vocabulary found in scout manuals.

38. Miming *outrage, delight, terror* and other emotional reactions.

39. Listing items (*nylon, vinyl*) composed wholly or partly of synthetics.

40. Playing commercial word games such as Junior Scrabble, Concentration, Spill and Spell, or Password.

41. Charting words which first surfaced during the past decade (e.g., *Watergate*).

42. Developing fresh similes (*fragile as a new pencil point*) or collecting familiar ones (*nose like a cherry*).

43. Listening to newscasters to elicit five current terms.

44. Expressing one action word (*lag* or *leap*) graphically through one of the art media.

45. Listing some of the specialized vocabulary used by sportscasters or found on the sports pages.

46. Identifying some of the photographs found in Loss's *What Is It?* (Doubleday, 1974) which employ macrophotography effectively.

47. Writing word puns after perusing Basil's *Nailheads and Potato Eyes* (Morrow, 1976).

48. Charting antonyms for five common words much like Richard Hefter does in *Yes and No: A Book of Opposites* (Larousse, 1975).

49. Drawing some amusing and confusing figures of speech such as *fork in the road* and *his foot in his mouth*.
50. Listing some one-word palindromes (*nun, rotor, Otto*) or words that can be read backwards and forwards with the same result.

Learning Games

Regardless of their academic level, children enjoy playing an instructional game. Most of these group games require little, if any, special preparation.

Break-Down

1. The teacher writes a long word on the chalkboard (e.g., *hippopotamus*).
2. At their desks, the players write as many smaller words as they can from any arrangement of the letters contained in the board word.
3. The winner, the player with the most words correctly written, is allowed to put a new word on the board for the class to use.
4. Suggestions: Seasonal words such as *pumpkin* or *valentine* are appropriate and interesting to break-down. Gifted classes enjoy sesquipedalian words (or long words) to break down such as *pneumonoultramicroscopicsilico-volcanoconiosis* with forty-five letters.

Classified Information

1. The teacher writes the name of a category (e.g., *sports*) on the board.
2. The players write at their seats as many words as they can recall that fit that category (e.g., *boxing, tennis, baseball, soccer*).
3. One point is awarded for each word correctly listed. (The teacher may also award an extra point for each item correctly spelled.)
4. The winner is the player with the highest number of points. The winner may choose the next category (e.g., *trees*) of Classified Information.

Dash-Dillers

1. The teacher writes on the board a short sentence, using only the first letter of each word and a dash for the rest of the word, (e.g., *M— b— c— f— t— p—*).
2. At their seats, the players try to complete the sentence by writing in their versions of the letters needed to complete each word, (e.g., *Mother baked cookies for ten people.*)
3. The winners of Dash-Dillers are the pupils whose sentences are not only reasonable, but comply with the board arrangement (even though the final sentences may not be ones the teacher had in mind).

Definition

1. Each player receives a portion of a newspaper and then circles five published words which he or she can define but believes will be difficult or impossible for others to define.
2. The teacher chooses a player to read one of his or her words. Should one of the other players be able to give an acceptable definition, then that player in turn reads a word for the class to define.
3. The winners are all pupils who announced words for which only they could furnish a satisfactory definition.

1. The teacher writes on the chalkboard a sentence containing two or three nouns but no adjectives (e.g., *Children are eating apples and oranges.*)
2. The players rewrite the sentences, using one or more uncommon adjectives before each noun.
3. The winners of Descripto are the players who chose unique but appropriate adjectives not selected by the rest of the class.

Descripto

1. The teacher writes an incomplete sentence on the chalkboard (e.g., *Sam lives in a _____*).
2. Each player copies the sentence and completes it with the most original word he or she knows.
3. The winners are the players with suitable words that no one else has chosen. They may help to write the next incomplete sentence that requires a fill-in word.

Fill-In

1. The teacher writes a pupil's name on the chalkboard vertically like this:

   J
   A
   M
   E
   S
2. The players copy the name on their papers exactly as it appears on the board.
3. They use each letter of the name as the first letter of a word to be completed on the paper.
4. The winner is the first player who has used all the letters correctly. This player's name heads the next round of Name-O.
5. Variation: The winner is the first player who has used all the letters correctly and formed a sentence out of the words.

Name-O

1. The teacher distributes a portion of a newspaper (advertisements and articles) to each player, who is then asked to circle with a crayon or colored pencil any three affixes.
2. At a signal from their teacher, all children who have completed the task stand at their seats. Every pupil who can give the meaning of the printers' words that he or she has circled is a winner.
3. Variation: The game may be repeated for root words, depending upon the interest and maturity of the group.

Printers' Words

1. The teacher, or a child chosen as "It," draws one card from the word box or one entry from a word notebook.
2. "It" then describes the word drawn; for example, "The word has two syllables; it begins with *Q* and means to shake or tremble. What's the riddle word?"
3. The other players try to write the riddle word at their seats.

Riddle Word

4. "It" now says the riddle word (*quiver*) and also writes it correctly on the board.
5. Players award themselves one point if they guessed the word correctly. They get one additional point if they spelled the riddle word correctly.
6. The winners are the players with the highest number of points after a designated number of rounds.

Sentence Relay

1. The pupils are divided equally into teams.
2. The first player on each team writes any word he or she chooses on the chalkboard. The second player on the same team adds another word toward building a sentence placing it either before or after the first player's word. Each pupil receives a turn. But if a player cannot add a suitable word, the player forfeits his or her turn and the next team begins to build a sentence.
3. The team with the longest sentence after every player has had at least one turn wins Sentence Relay.

Stretcher

1. The teacher writes a short word on the chalkboard (e.g., *pin*).
2. The players, at their seats or at the board, then write as many words as they can by adding one or more letters before or after the chosen word (e.g., *spin, pint, spinning, pints*).
3. The winner of Stretcher is the player with the longest list of words correctly written when the round has been completed.
4. Suggestion: The teacher may wish to use a simple kitchen timer to stop a round after only thirty to forty seconds if the group of players is mature.

String of Words

1. The teacher writes a word on the chalkboard (e.g., *chair*).
2. The players, at their seats or at the board, then each write a word starting with the last letter of the chosen word (e.g., *run*).
3. Within a time limit of one to three minutes each player must compile a string of words, starting each word with the last letter of the preceding word.
4. The winner is the player with the longest string of words correctly written when the round has been completed.

Substitute

1. The teacher writes a one-syllable word on the chalkboard (e.g., *bid*).
2. The players, at their seats or at the board, then write as many words as they can by substituting one or more vowels for the original vowel (e.g., *bad, booed, bead, bud*).
3. The winner of Substitute is the player with the longest list of words correctly written when the round has been completed.
4. Variation: Teams may be chosen and then provided with individual dictionaries.

Tic-Tac-Toe

1. Two pupils compete, each in turn, either at the chalkboard or using a sheet of writing paper.

2. The object is to write correctly three words, in a line or diagonally, which contain a common element such as an affix, phonogram (graphemic base), or root word. For example, if the first player wrote words all in capital letters and the second player wrote words in small letters, the Tic-Tac-Toe board might look like this after three turns:

SEND		erased
	erase	
LEND	eraser	TEND

The first player could write in *MEND* (or any word containing the phonogram *end*) in the first column and so win Tic-Tac-Toe with a completed vertical line.
3. Variation: Teams of three to four members each may be chosen with the game played only at the chalkboard.

Evaluation of Pupils' Progress

To assist in the planning of a program of vocabulary building, the teacher needs measured insight into the progress made by individual pupils in their acquisition of broad listening, speaking, reading, and writing vocabularies.

Numerous standardized reading and reading-readiness tests contain sections on vocabulary and so do various standardized achievement batteries including the *Comprehensive Tests of Basic Skills* (CTB/McGraw-Hill, 1973), the *Metropolitan Achievement Tests* (Harcourt Brace Jovanovich, 1978), and the *SRA Achievement Series* (Science Research Associates, 1978).

A teacher may also choose to devise his or her own tests. There are four major ways of testing vocabulary, according to Dale and O'Rourke: (1) *identification,* whereby pupils respond orally or in writing by identifying a word according to its use or definition; (2) *multiple-choice,* whereby the students choose the correct definition of the tested word from three or possibly four meanings; (3) *matching* (which is really another form of multiple-choice), whereby the tested words, roots, or prefixes are presented in one column and the matching definitions are listed out of order in another column; and (4) *checking,* whereby the pupils check the words they know or don't know although they may also be required to define the words they have checked.[11]

Within these four groups the teacher can employ a variety of techniques to test vocabulary. Hopefully, with middle-grade or intermediate children the teacher will often choose self-tests which allow individual students to make an inventory of their stock of words to determine its strengths and weaknesses. Words contained in an easy-to-hard sequence in a sample self-inventory checklist (relevant to a fourth-grade unit on nutrition) might each be marked with a simple ✔ (to indicate knowledge of the word) or ○ (to indicate lack of such knowledge):

____ nutrition	____ strength
____ diet	____ calories
____ muscle	____ calcium
____ vitamin	____ cholesterol
____ protein	____ carbohydrate
____ energy	____ thiamine

The most important evaluation of vocabulary growth, however, is that which looks to the performance of the pupil in all the other areas of instruction. Proper measurement of word recognition and understanding is best seen in the light of evaluation of the pupil's progress in the total process of education.

Discussion Questions

1. Why is it necessary to see vocabulary development as conceptual development?
2. Which of the factors affecting vocabulary growth may be influenced by teacher planning?
3. When should the teacher ask a student to look up the meaning of a word in the dictionary?
4. With what kinds of exceptional children would some of the independent methods for teaching vocabulary be especially successful?

Suggested Projects

1. Design a learning game that could be used to teach vocabulary to kindergarten pupils. Then try it out with a small group of school beginners.
2. Examine and evaluate two of the following commercial word games listed by the International Reading Association: *Picture Dominoes* (Childcraft), *Phonetic Quizmo* (Milton Bradley Company), *Scrabble* (Selchow and Righter), *Match* (Garrard Publishing Company), and *Judy's Match-Ettes* (Judy Company).
3. Discover how antonyms are presented to second graders in two current language arts series: *Language for Meaning:* Level Purple (Houghton Mifflin, 1978) and *Language for Daily Use:* Level Blue (Harcourt Brace Jovanovich, 1978).
4. Compare the presentations on roots in various language texts for children at the intermediate levels. Are any of them appropriate for pupils with learning disabilities or for gifted pupils?
5. Develop an animal crossword puzzle appropriate for either upper primary or intermediate boys and girls. Possible clues could include: the official bird of the United States, a baby cow, the king of beasts, etc.
6. Set up the learning center on vocabulary shown in Figure 6.2.

Figure 6.2. Language Arts Learning Center: Vocabulary Building.

TYPE OF CENTER:	Morphology—Vocabulary Building	TIME: 15–20 minutes
GRADE LEVEL:	4 and up	NUMBER OF STUDENTS: 1
INSTRUCTIONAL OBJECTIVE:	For children to experiment and learn new words by adding prefixes and suffixes to root words.	

MATERIALS:

Learning center (made of pegboard and hinged together); hooks to hang the cards; three boxes and a variety of cards with one prefix, root word, or suffix printed neatly on each; envelope for finished papers; and paper and pencils for children to use.

DIRECTIONS TO STUDENTS:

1. Choose a root word from the ROOT WORD box.
2. Using the hooks, hang your root word in the middle of the center.
3. Build as many words as you can by hanging a prefix or suffix beside your root word.
4. Can you build a word with both a prefix and a suffix?
5. Write down on your paper the words you have made.
6. You can check your answers on the back of the learning center.
7. Then deposit your paper in the finished papers' envelope. (Don't forget to put your name on your paper.)
8. For extra practice, choose another root word and build some more words.

EVALUATION:

The children can check themselves, and learn new words by seeing words they didn't build. The teacher will check the words the children have made, and later go over these words with the class. These words can then be added to the weekly spelling list. This center can also be turned into a game involving more children by having the children race to see who can get the most words. The pegboard learning center has endless possibilities, as the teacher can make cards that could combine into compound words. The children could also study the formation of plurals by using this method.

Figure 6.2 (cont.)

Suggested Common Prefixes		Suggested Common Suffixes		Suggested Common Root Words	
a	intra	able	ine	cover	visit
ab	mis	acy	ious	act	connect
ad	multl	al	ise	alter	check
ante	non	ance	ize	agree	finish
at	ob	ant	ish	direct	clean
bi	per	ary	ism	fill	load
con	poly	er	ist	flex	set
contra	post	ate	ity	form	polite
de	pre	ation	ive	graph	create
dif	pro	cle	less	late	pick
dis	re	ee	like	phone	count
ex	semi	ent	ly	place	like
extra	sub	er	ment	read	active
ig	sum	ette	ness		
in	super	fold	or		
ir	ultra	ful	ous		
inter	un	fy	ship		
		hood	tude		
		ible	ward		
		ile	y		

Source: From *Language Arts Learning Centers and Activities* by Angela Reeke and James Laffey. Copyright 1979 by Goodyear Publishing Company. Reprinted by permission.

Related Readings

Davis, V. S., and Davis, W. Q. 1976. "Vocational Vocabulary." *Teacher* 94: 100–102.

Dixon, G. T. 1977. "Investigating Words in the Primary Grades." *Language Arts* 54: 418–22.

Fillmer, H. T. 1977. "A Generative Vocabulary Program for Grades 4–6." *Elementary School Journal* 78: 53–58.

Hargis, G.; Gickling, E.; and Mahmoud, C. 1975. "The Effectiveness of TV in Teaching Sight Words to Students with Learning Disabilities." *Journal of Learning Disabilities* 8: 37–39, 44–46.

Johns, J. L.; Edmond, R. M.; and Mavrogenes, N. 1977. "The Dolch Basic Sight Vocabulary: A Replication and Validation Study." *Elementary School Journal* 78: 31–37.

Johnson, D. D., and Pearson, P. D. 1978. *Teaching Reading Vocabulary*. New York: Holt, Rinehart and Winston.

Sheehan, D. S., and Marcus, M. 1977. "The Effects of Teacher Race and Student Race on Vocabulary and Mathematics Achievement." *Journal of Educational Research* 70: 123–126.

Stewart, D. M., and Hamilton, M. L. 1976. "Imitation as a Learning Strategy in the Acquisition of Vocabulary." *Journal of Experimental Child Psychology* 21: 380–92.

Stotsky, S. L. 1978. "Teaching Prefixes in the Elementary School." *Elementary School Journal* 78: 278–83.

Vaughan, S., and Mountain, L. 1977. "Vocabulary Scavenger Hunts." *Teacher* 94: 75–77.

Listening 7

How listening relates to other language arts

Factors that affect listening ability

The type of listening that occupies the major part of the school day

Why critical listening is so important today

Listening is the newest and the oldest of the language arts. Although reading and writing are the more recently developed of the communication skills in human societies, they have been more readily accepted as legitimate subjects of school instruction than have the older skills of listening and speaking. Since the establishment of compulsory education in many countries in the nineteenth century, elementary schools have traditionally been concerned with providing training in the skills of literacy and, to some extent, of speaking. Any listening skills that the pupils acquired came incidentally in the course of studying other subjects or were learned indirectly at home. Today, however, interest in the teaching of listening appears to be gaining the momentum of a movement because the idea that everyone who can hear knows how to listen has finally been discredited.

Fundamental Queries about the Listening Program

Listening can be taught and students who receive listening instruction evidence significant improvement in listening ability (in contrast to those who do not receive such instruction) regardless of the grade level tested. Still, some confusion remains among teachers concerning the goals and overall importance of the listening program, the relationship of listening to the other language arts, and other basic aspects of this challenging curricular area.

What Is Listening?

The simplest definition states that listening is the process by which spoken language is converted to meaning in the mind.[1] Listening involves giving active and conscious attention to sounds of auditory expression for the purpose of gaining some meaning from them. A child who really listens may be expected to make some reaction to the sounds. Linguistically, it is a learned receptive skill, a personal, often private absorption of ideas and attitudes expressed through oral language. Listening differs from hearing, which is a physiological function and does not involve interpretation.

Among some authorities there has been disagreement as to whether or not the word "listening" should be restricted to the process of directing attention to spoken sounds. Consequently, in an effort to refine the terminology, it was proposed over a decade ago that "auding" should be employed as the more comprehensive label to include all three aspects—hearing, listening, and understanding spoken language. The proposed distinction between listening and auding is only useful semantically. Verbal communication is carried on primarily so that others may comprehend the information transmitted, and therefore listening implies comprehension of the material heard.

Why Is Listening Important?

Listening occupies the baseline position in the quadratic context of the language arts. Progress in reading, speaking, and writing is directly governed by listening ability. It is quantitatively the most important of the four arts since nearly half of the adult working day and more than half of the child's classroom activity time are spent in listening. A major means of learning and recall, particularly for poor readers, listening is essential to success in the phonetic analysis of words and the ability to discriminate among sounds and to identify initial and final sounds. Listening is also a critical part of today's culture in the United States where approximately 70 percent of the people reside in nonrural areas causing person-to-person relationships to typify modern lives. Moreover, the knowledge explosion since the mid century has demanded the processing of greater amounts of information through listening.

Listening constitutes one of the most rapidly expanding leisure-time activities in present-day society and is the mainstay of two popular and pervasive communications media: radio and television. According to the latest census each child and adult in this country has more than one radio available to him or her, and in 96 percent of the households, the use of one or more television sets as well.

During the early school years most instruction takes place through oral language. Even after a child begins reading, listening remains the more effective tool for gaining information until the sixth- or seventh-grade level. It directs attention to details and their synthesis, and therefore develops thinking skills.

Listening is a basis for the good human relationships that are considered to be among the most important educational goals. It influences value formation. It results in greater emotional responses and changes in attitude than other language arts. Finally, according to the Florida State Department of Education, listening constitutes the threefold problem of today's generation that must decide: what to listen to, how to strengthen listening ability, and how to listen appreciatively and critically.

How Is Listening Related to the Other Language Arts?

Listening belongs in the comparative context of language processing which includes the major skills of transmission and reception. Consequently, improving listening is likely to affect other language arts.

The relationship between the receptive skill of listening and the expressive skill of writing was explored in research on children with normal hearing and those with impaired hearing. Children able to hear were found to use more complex types of language structure and more concise composition, thereby reflecting a higher degree of maturity in writing expression than that of children who were deaf or who had partial hearing. Comprehension of meaning in writing is dependent upon the base of comprehension in listening. Furthermore, while composing ideas in written form, some children speak and listen internally as they record.

Research has established a positive statistical correlation between listening and speaking. Not only are speech patterns learned largely through listening to other persons speak, but, in turn, the growth of the listener function in an individual probably plays an important role in the ultimate development of his or her skill as a speaker in being able to order verbal behavior. (No wonder, then, that the child born into a large, overcrowded, noisy household often learns "practiced inattention.")

Both listening and reading are phases of language serving as major avenues for the acquisition of information. Both are a complex of related skill components and the same postulated higher mental processes seem to underlie the two of them (although the evidence indicates that each receptive skill may contain verbal factors individually unique). Both flourish in a relaxed environment where the ideas and vocabulary are at least partially familiar to the receivers. And both use signals such as intonation and pauses in oral language and their corresponding punctuation marks.

In listening, however, the rate is determined by the speaker; the ideas usually are presented but once; the listener loses a portion of the content whenever his or her attention lapses; and the listener's evaluation of that content is often influenced by the speaker's use of gestures or voice inflections. Communication through reading, on the other hand, is less personal and may include visual aids; the reader proceeds at his or her own rate and may reread the material as often as needed to gain the information; and printed ideas are more likely to be expressed in well-organized fashion.

Is There a Learning Hierarchy of General Listening Skills?

A sequential program in listening skills is equally as important as a sequential program in reading skills. Because most children are not accomplished listeners, a developmental listening improvement program is needed in many schools. An instructional hierarchy of general listening skills or objectives for such a program should include at least two entering or prerequisite skills and several behavioral objectives, according to Lundsteen.[2] Since the prerequisites continue to be reinforced as the hierarchy progresses, they may be initially possessed by the pupil at a relatively low degree. The prerequisite skills are—

distinguishing hearing from listening, and
demonstrating two-way listener-speaker responsibility.

The other pupil behaviors then follow, to be practiced and evaluated; namely—

selecting facts and details,
recalling and identifying sequential order,
selecting the main idea,
summarizing,
relating one idea to another, and
making inferences.

A more detailed sequence of listening skills in sighted as well as visually handicapped children has been compiled by Weaver and Rutherford.[3] It includes sections on auditory discrimination skills, listening comprehension skills, and environmental skills. Environmental skills involve the identification and interpretation of sounds from the environment, excluding verbal sounds, which play an important role in the orientation and mobility skills of visually handicapped (VH) people. In this hierarchy of listening skills, discrepancies in the time when certain skills are apt to occur in sighted and visually handicapped persons are indicated by (VH+):

Discrimination Skills

Kindergarten—Grade 3:
Learning that sounds differ in intensity (VH+), pitch (VH+), pattern and duration.
Recognizing the differences in initial consonants auditorily.
Recognizing the differences in final consonants auditorily.
Recognizing the differences in medial sounds auditorily.
Recognizing the discrete words within a sentence.
Recognizing the sequence of words within a sentence.
Identifying the accented words within a sentence.
Identifying the number of syllables within a word.
Identifying the accented syllable within a word.
Changing the accent from one syllable to another.
Recognizing the initial and final consonant sounds.
Recognizing the short vowel sounds.
Recognizing the long vowel sounds.
Recognizing rhyming words.
Recognizing and discriminating among word endings.
Discriminating among the temporal order of sounds within words.

Comprehension Skills

Kindergarten—Grade 3:
Recognizing verbal absurdities.
Associating spoken words with pictures or miniature objects (VH+).
Associating auditory cues with motor responses.
Using new words learned by listening.
Using context to predict words in a sentence.

Relating new information to past experiences.
Identifying the main ideas of a simple story.
Sequencing details correctly.
Listening for specific information.
Following travel directions (VH+).

Grade 4—Grade 6:
Following the directions in making things.
Recognizing associations and relationships.
Drawing inferences and conclusions.
Interpreting the feelings of the characters.
Generalizing from details.
Distinguishing between true and false statements.
Distinguishing between relevant and irrelevant statements.
Comparing and contrasting.
Evaluating critically.

Environmental Skills

Kindergarten—Grade 3:
Learning that sounds differ in intensity (VH+), pitch (VH+), pattern, and
duration.
Learning the concept of distance in relation to sound localization and movement (VH+).

Grade 4—Grade 6:
Identifying sounds in the environment at certain times of the day and evaluat-
ing them in terms of orientation and mobility (VH+).
Promoting growth of echo perception and spatial orientation (VH+).

Which Factors Influence Listening?

There are at least a dozen factors which affect the listening processes in general as well as the teaching of listening in particular. Negatively, some of them
could also be listed as possible causes for specific listening deficiencies.

The highest correlate of listening ability is *intelligence,* especially verbal
intelligence. This positive relationship is demonstrated even among handicapped children. It is commonly assumed that the direction of the relationship is from intelligence to listening but it is interesting to conjecture whether
the opposite might not be true. Children who for one reason or another never
learned to listen live in self-made cells, isolated from the world about them and
cut off from the stimulating influences that contribute to optimum development
of intellect.

A second factor is *hearing sense,* for during the hearing process the ear
receives and modifies speech sounds in the form of speech waves. Pupils must
be able to receive the sounds accurately in ordinary situations involving some
background noise. Approximately 11 percent of schoolchildren have reduced
hearing (with reduced hearing defined as a loss of at least twenty decibels in
one ear).

Another factor is the *family*. Children in small families generally obtain higher listening scores than those in large families. Pupils coming from smaller, television-viewing families are better listeners than those of larger, television-viewing families.

Although evidence concerning the possibility of a relationship between listening and family size is not yet conclusive, it has been speculated that the heightened noise and confusion in a large group leads to the development of a protective insulation, or a nonlistening attitude that children transfer to the classroom. Socially and economically, good listeners tend to come from middle- and upper-middle-class homes, while poor listeners come from lower- and lower-middle-class homes. Middle children (those who have older *and* younger brothers and sisters) are no better listeners than the oldest or the youngest children in the family. More good listeners than poor listeners, however, are first-born or only children.

In the area of *personality and social development,* good listeners are better adjusted than poor listeners. They are indicated to be more participating, ready to try new things, and more emotionally stable and free from nervous symptoms. They are chosen significantly more often than poor listeners as work partners and play companions. Their teachers too seem to be aware of the differences for they rate poor listeners as lower in such traits as willingness to work, vigor, ability to get a task done, cheerfulness, and participation in class and playground activities.

Listening achievement increases with the *chronological age and grade level* of its owners. This factor holds true even when the rate of presentation is increased and speech is compressed. Older, intermediate-grade boys and girls always comprehend more by listening than do their younger, primary-age friends who, in turn, surpass kindergarten and preschool pupils.

A sixth factor is a *structured program*. Listening skill and listening performance can be and have been improved by instruction. Even at the first-grade level children profit from a structured listening program.

Another factor is *cognition,* for listening is affected by the thinking skills that allow the pupils to index, make comparisons, note sequence, react by forming sensory images, draw inferences, abstract main ideas, categorize, recognize relationships, and use appreciation. Thinking skills used during listening are quite similar to those employed during reading, and consequently, training in these skills through listening activities produces a gain in both listening and reading.

The extent to which meaning is associated depends initially on the listeners' *experiential background*. Words are more easily apprehended when they form a part of predictable and meaningful speech. Pupils who come to school with a broad background of experiences can apprehend each word to which they listen and will, therefore, enjoy listening to their teachers and peers.

A ninth factor is *television viewing*. Children who watch commercial television are better listeners than those who do not. The amount of time spent in watching television, however, has no effect on listening. Children who watch for only two hours a day or less are not better listeners than those who watch four or more hours a day.

Once the listening pupil has identified a sound or recognized a sound sequence as a familiar word, then the *presentation* variables of mode and rate must be considered. Primary children listening to a storytelling program across three modes of presentation, for instance, had their highest comprehension performance for videotape and lowest for audio cassette.[4] Also, comprehension has generally increased as the rate of presentation increases, and speeds of 228 to 328 words per minute seem more efficient for children's learning and retention than the normal speaking rate of 178 words per minute.[5]

Recognition of voices is the eleventh factor. The differentiation that is made between the voices of other persons depends on the period during which the threshold becomes lower and lower and allows the hearer to be increasingly confident in his or her recognition of the speaker. Children find it easiest to listen to a single voice. They can also comprehend a conversation or recitation that involves several voices, but in one setting. They do not perceive, however, a situation in which several persons are talking without being in the same place, or a situation in which voices are added from the outside either to comment on a scene or to produce some psychological or moral effect. Interestingly, it does not matter to pupils who use Black English whether speakers use standard English or nonstandard dialect because all are comprehended equally by primary children.[6]

Finally children have the best opportunity to improve their listening ability in a *supportive classroom environment.*

Such an environment is flexible. Children learn to communicate best when they have the chance to practice in small groups first, and later in increasingly large groups. Furniture which allows freedom of movement from one type of organization to another is desirable.

Such an environment has opportunities for interaction. When listeners are active in the communication process, their level of personal involvement reaches its highest peak. The amount of interaction possible often depends upon the group structure, for while only minimum response is possible in a whole-class discussion with a questioning teacher and answering children, maximum interaction can occur when children work in pairs for problem solving or oral reading. Pupils need practice in communicating in groups of various sizes and for many different purposes.

Such an environment stimulates speaking and listening. Children will communicate about those activities and objects which they encounter in their classroom. When the room has ample materials and interest centers, pupils are stimulated to improve the quality and increase the quantity of their oral language.

Such an environment is physically comfortable. The noise level is tolerable, and legitimate noise distractions are acknowledged by the teacher. When a loud thud from the next room or a sudden thunderstorm startles the children, a wise teacher will spend a moment or two discussing the cause of the distraction before returning quietly to the regular lesson. Such discussions have proven more effective than admonitions.

How Can the Teacher Help the Hard of Hearing Listen Better?

The elementary teacher today will generally enroll two or more children with reduced hearing each year. Since the teacher is concerned with developing listening skill in the hard-of-hearing pupils, he or she will make sure to:

1. *Seat them carefully*. Place them from six to ten feet from the area where teaching is centered. Permit them to move their seats if the teaching center moves to another part of the room. Permit them to turn around to hear their classmates speak. Make sure that each pupil's better ear is toward the source of significant sounds and not toward the windows or hallway.
2. *Speak properly*. Avoid using loud tones, exaggerated mouth movements, or too many gestures. Avoid talking when walking about the room or when facing the chalkboard. Avoid placing hands or books in front of the face while speaking. Avoid using homophones (such as *road-rode*) which look alike on the lips. Use clear enunciation. Check frequently and informally to make sure that the handicapped children comprehend the discussion.
3. *Assist them casually*. Write new words on the chalkboard, since names of people and places are difficult for them to understand. Ask other children to help them get the correct assignment. Provide special help in such language activities as spelling and reading where sounds have unusual importance. Explain special events such as field trips well in advance. Repeat instructions as often as needed.
4. *Watch their physical condition*. Prevent further hearing loss by noting respiratory infections and other ailments. Prevent undue fatigue from the strain of seeing and listening intently by providing alternating periods of physical activity and inactivity in the day's planning.
5. *Encourage participation*. Allow extracurricular activities, especially vocal music. Help them discover abilities and talents by guiding them into activities where they can achieve their share of success.

Instructional Activities

Like all language skills, listening demands responsible and systematic teaching and practice. Without the guidance of a teacher and the reinforcement of parents, children are unlikely to attain the facility required by the impact of listening competence upon contemporary society.

While listening is a receptive language art, it is also an active process, entailing thinking and interpretation on the part of the listeners. They question, accept, reject, enjoy, or dislike some, if not all, of what they hear. At the same time, they are called upon to recall what they have heard or read earlier in the same area in order to evaluate more accurately the present information.

Although as many as twenty-five different kinds of listening have been identified (ranging from accurate and active to responsible and selective), basically there are only three types of listening: *appreciative, attentive,* and *critical.* They differ primarily in the degree of concentration demanded, with appreciative listeners being considerably less tense than critical listeners. It must be pointed out, however, that all listening demands interpretation and consequently some degree of concentration. Listening is not merely hearing; therefore, when two or more distractions are present, during a radio broadcast for example, children only hear the presentation on the radio. They cannot listen to it until the number of distractions is reduced and they give conscious attention to the performer or performance. Listening is more than a physiological reaction and it demands more than passive participation.

Appreciative Listening

Appreciative listening is the ability to listen for enjoyment and creative response. It is less concentrated than either attentive or critical listening, and the hearer is therefore more relaxed. Children may listen to musical recordings, to radio and television programs, and to concerts. They may listen to shadow plays, puppet shows, roll movies, sound filmstrips, and taped dramatizations. They may also simply listen to enjoy pleasant sounds, indoors or outdoors, such as a cricket's chirp or a canary's song.

Boys and girls may fingerpaint or draw designs to music or use chalk or clay to express ideas inspired by a recording of Tchaikovsky's *Nutcracker* Suite; Dvořák's *Slavonic Dances;* Grieg's *Peer Gynt* Suite; Rossini's *William Tell* Overture; or Gershwin's *Rhapsody in Blue.*

They can paint their responses to poems they have heard, including Morley's "Animal Crackers" and "Song for a Little House"; Field's "The Sugar Plum Tree" and "Wynken, Blynken and Nod"; Stevenson's "My Shadow" and "Block City"; and Behn's "The Kite" and "Hallowe'en."

Children can divide themselves into small literary committees, each selecting one of its members to read aloud to the others. The child's audience listens, with books closed, to poems rich in imagery or poems that evoke excitement, contentment, or drowsiness. Sometimes the reader selects stories that have a dominant mood such as three of those by Hans Christian Andersen so that the audience can sense sadness-triumph-surprise for "The Ugly Duckling," sadness-pity for "The Little Match Girl," and the exaggeration-arrogance of "The Princess and the Pea."

Choral reading provides for participation as well as for appreciative listening. At times as many as six to ten pupils can recite while the rest of the class listens. Suggestions for simple choral activities are given in Chapter 11.

Watching performances of a children's theater group also involves appreciative listening. The theater provides enjoyment and expression, allowing the young audience to identify with the onstage characters and actions. Listeners are sometimes subtly exposed to learning about cultures of other lands as well.

Storytelling also offers children the opportunity to learn to listen appreciatively to their teacher, media center specialist, or their peers. They can tell

This young pupil is engaged in appreciative listening, which is less concentrated than attentive listening. (Photo courtesy of National Education Association Publishing, Joe Di Dio.)

round-robin chain stories in which each participant carries on from where the preceding speaker stopped. They can tell, extemporaneously, an original ending to a classic story that they have heard.

Kindergartners and early primary pupils are generally interested in finger plays, which are excellent devices to foster appreciative listening. Sometimes a child can even be encouraged to develop his or her own finger play to share with classmates. Younger children also often enjoy interpreting music with simple rhythm instruments, while older pupils can select background music for an original class story or a poem located in a basal reader.

Finally, children may compile a picture book of sounds with separate sections devoted to sounds at home, sounds of the city (or country), sounds in the classroom, and sounds on the playground. Younger pupils may wish to include only pictures while older children can write an accompanying text.

Attentive Listening

Attentive listening demands that the attention of the listener be focused on one person or on one electronic medium so that the listener can purposefully respond either orally or in written fashion. It may or may not involve a two-way conversation or discussion, for in some cases it is strictly a one-way communication process. The listener, however, must think carefully about the telephone conversation, radio broadcast, recording, telecast, play, lecture, or classroom announcement.

Attentive listening concerns the ability to respond to directions and explanations. In the primary grades children may be sent on errands throughout the building after they have received exact directions as to how to get to the nurse's, the custodian's, and the principal's offices, or how to locate the sixth-grade classroom. They should have many opportunities to recall the directions given for their safety regarding standards for fire drills, playground behavior, and cafeteria decorum. They can explain to newcomers how a particular classroom routine is handled that requires three or four steps in sequence: for instance, how to care for paintbrushes, how to line up for morning recess, or how to be a book monitor. Individual pupils can give directions for reaching their own homes or the nearest public library; the class can later evaluate the clarity of these directions. In the intermediate grades one group of pupils may explain the steps in a science experiment, while a second group follows the directions as stated, and a third group evaluates both procedures. In another instance, the teacher can read the instructions for making a salt and flour map, and let the children retell the steps in order.

This kind of listening, which occupies a greater part of the school day than either appreciative or critical listening, also includes the ability to recognize and respond to grapheme-phoneme relationships, to rhyming, to onomatopoeia and alliteration, and to gross sounds (by identifying, duplicating, or classifying them). It involves as well the ability to retell in sequence what has been heard, to recognize specific details in a story told on tape, and to note similes, metaphors, and other figurative language in poems read orally. Therefore primary children can, for example, do these attentive listening activities:

1. Sit quietly outdoors and name the sounds around them.
2. Classify sounds according to intensity and pitch or by the specific object with which each is linked.
3. Choose pairs of rhyming words out of three-word and four-word series of mixed words.
4. Supply single words to complete rhyming couplets.
5. Name three other words that begin with the same initial consonant blend as the chalkboard word which the teacher has just pronounced.

Fourth, fifth, and sixth graders develop attentive listening habits when they are given an opportunity, for example, to:

1. Answer specific questions about an article on Australia which the teacher has just read aloud.
2. Note the metaphors after listening to Rachel Field's "Roads."
3. Identify the triple blends (such as *scr* and *spl*) in lists of words which have been taped.
4. Listen to two stories, and then compare them to determine their similarities.
5. Discuss the alliterative unit in tongue twisters recited by their classmates.

Critical Listening   Critical listening is the most complex kind of listening to teach or to learn. It implies the use of a highly conscious standard or criterion for evaluating spoken material while comprehending. It is this advanced degree of evaluation or reflection about what is heard that is crucial and intricate. A continuum of the goals or skills involved in lessons in critical listening in the elementary school should include teaching the children how to do the following:

1. Distinguish fact from fantasy, according to explicit criteria.
2. Distinguish relevant statements from irrelevant ones and evaluate them.
3. Distinguish well-supported statements from opinion/judgment and evaluate them.
4. Evaluate the qualifications of a speaker.
5. Detect and evaluate the bias, emotional slant, or lack of objectivity of a speaker.
6. Recognize and evaluate the effects of devices the speaker may use to influence the listener, such as propaganda, voice intonation, or music.
7. Evaluate the validity and adequacy of the central theme or point of view of a performer or performance.

Primary children are capable of critical listening. For example, a day after telling the class the story of "The Three Bears," the teacher can read them McCloskey's *Blueberries for Sal* and then ask them to give evidence of why yesterday's tale was fantasy or make-believe and today's story is real. Another day, the teacher can pose a series of questions, some of which are meaningful and some of which are not; the child responding must determine in each instance whether the question is nonsense (Why is the grass red?) or whether the question is reasonable (If chickens are birds, why can't they fly?).

Intermediate pupils can listen to recordings of talks or conversations by unidentified persons and then decide whether the speakers showed prejudice or used loaded words during the presentations. On another occasion they can listen to a selection containing instructions for making paper snowflakes, for instance, but containing, as well, some extraneous information. The class, omitting all irrelevant data, must then make the snowflakes.

That both late primary and intermediate pupils can be helped to develop critical listening has been substantiated by research involving two hundred children, ages eight to ten, in Maryland.[7] The boys and girls, both white and black, were given sixteen lessons to help them become aware of propaganda employed by commercial advertisers in their television programs. It was concluded that children can be made conscious of commercial propaganda emanating from television. Furthermore, they can successfully transfer their new critical listening skill to other disciplines as they begin to recognize propaganda in reading, in conversations with teachers and peers, and in newspaper and magazine advertising.

Learning activities that promote each of the three basic types of listening are listed in Table 7.1 (pages 152–53). The behavioral objective as well as the suggested grade level for each instructional activity also are included.

Some of the skills essential to the development of good listening among boys and girls can be reviewed through a variety of purposeful games. All of the games outlined in this section are instructional group games which can be adapted by the teacher to meet the needs of a particular classroom of children. Few of the fifteen games described herein require special materials.

Airplanes Fly

1. The teacher is the first leader, and the pupils are seated (or standing) far enough apart to move their arms freely.
2. The teacher describes a flying object or animal; and if the statement is true (e.g., "Airplanes fly"), the pupils wave their arms. Should the statement be false (e.g., "The chalkboard flies"), the pupils must keep their arms still.
3. Any pupil who moves his or her arms when the statement made by the teacher-leader is false is dropped from the game.
4. The pupil who remains in the game the longest wins the first round and becomes the next leader.
5. Variations: (a) Fish Swim; (b) Frogs Jump; and (c) Dogs Run.

Bartholomew Cubbins Has Lost a Hat

1. Flash cards of consecutive numerals from 1–35 (when there are thirty-five pupils in the room) are distributed to the players so that each pupil holds a card with a different numeral and each player knows the range of numerals in the classroom.
2. "It" stands in front of the room while the others remain at their seats, and opens the dialog: "Bartholomew Cubbins has lost a hat. Do you have it, Number 6?" The player holding the numeral 6 card promptly stands and says, "Who, sir? Me, sir?" before "It" repeats the line, "Bartholomew Cubbins has lost a hat." "It" replies, "Yes, sir, you, sir," and Number 6 insists, "No, sir." Then "It" demands, "Then who, sir?" Number 6 retorts, "Number 13, sir."
3. The player holding the numeral 13 card must stand quickly and repeat, "Who, sir? Me, sir?" before "It" repeats the line, "Bartholomew Cubbins has lost a hat." Should "It" have time to repeat the line, Number 13 is out of the game and must forfeit his or her numeral card.
4. The game continues quickly until each player has had a turn or until the period is over.
5. Suggestions: (a) The class may be numbered consecutively, beginning with any number and going up to 500 or 1000, to stress a review of higher numbers; (b) Instead of numerals, names may be used either at the start of the semester or during the week that new pupils have joined the group; (c) If the teacher will secretly designate the guilty party earlier in the day, this pupil can admit taking the hat when his or her number is called during the game, and the game can end with a flourish.

Bouncing Ball

1. The pupils are seated with their eyes closed.
2. The teacher, as "It," bounces a rubber ball or tennis ball a number of times at random.

Table 7.1.
Sample Instructional Activities in Elementary School Listening.

Type of Listening	Grade Level	Behavioral Objective	Learning Activity and/or Teaching Strategy
Appreciative	K, 1, 2	The children will listen to music chosen by the teacher and describe how it makes them feel.	The teacher will play a musical selection via record, piano, or tape while the children listen. The children will then respond by describing how the music makes them feel (sad, happy) through pictures or words.
Appreciative	3–4	After the teacher reads or tells a given story, the children will be able to interpret the mood of that story.	The children will listen to the story which the teacher has chosen to read or tell. They will then be able to state whether the story has made them angry, sad, or happy.
Appreciative	5–6	After listening to a literary selection, the pupils will determine the attitude of the writer (or speaker) by discussing the selection with their peers.	The teacher will read Carl Sandburg's "Chicago" which denotes approval, joy, and ambition.
Attentive	K, 1, 2	After listening to a story, the children will arrange pictures related to that story in the proper sequential order.	The teacher will choose any story which has a definite beginning, middle, and end; and then prepare pictures illustrating actions in each part of the story. Later, the children will arrange four or five pictures in sequence.
Attentive	3–4	After listening to a given story, the children will be able to recall five details of the story.	The teacher will read or tell a story to the class and then ask five questions concerning what had happened in the story.

3. The players listen and count the number of bounces silently.
4. "It" calls on one player who responds, "You bounced the ball . . . times." If the player's response is correct, he or she is allowed to have the next turn to be "It." If the player's response is incorrect, another player has a turn to give the proper number of bounces.
5. The winner of Bouncing Ball is the pupil who is "It" the longest.
6. Variation: The ball may be bounced three times, then a pause, and then bounced four times more. The player responds, "You bounced the ball three and four times," or "Three and four are seven."

Type of Listening	Grade Level	Behavioral Objective	Learning Activity and/or Teaching Strategy
Attentive	5–6	The pupils will listen to a passage which explains how to do something. They will take notes and later complete the assignment correctly.	The teacher will read orally the instructions for making a papier-mâché animal. After listening to the instructions, the pupils will outline the steps involved and then make the animal.
Critical	K, 1, 2	After listening to a story in which there is conversation and/or actions which reveal the emotions of the characters, the children will deduce how the characters feel by citing examples of their conversation and/or actions.	The teacher will read a story with conversation and/or action which reveals feelings. The children will evaluate orally the conversation and/or actions of the story characters in order to determine their feelings.
Critical	3–4	After a classmate talks on an assigned topic, the group will discuss the presence of both fact and opinion in the speech and whether or not the facts were substantiated and the opinions qualified.	A pupil is assigned to speak on "Pollution of the Streams and Rivers in Our State." Classmates listen to the speech and criticize it for substantiating facts and qualified opinions.
Critical	5–6	Given a passage which propagandizes, the pupils will orally identify examples of slanted, loaded words and varied propaganda techniques.	The teacher will locate newspaper advertisements for a particular product and the pupils will be able to identify orally examples of such propaganda techniques as plain folks, glittering generalities, testimonials, and band wagon.

Cross Out Relay

1. Before the game the teacher writes on the left half of the chalkboard fifty or more numerals with which the class is familiar, presenting them in a mixed or inconsecutive order. Then on the right half of the board the teacher repeats the process, using the same numerals but in a different mixed order.
2. Two teams are chosen and stand facing the class, *not* the numbered board. The player on each team who is nearest to the board receives a piece of chalk.
3. The teacher calls out one number at a time, and a player from each team

must quickly cross out that numeral on the board and pass the chalk to the next player.

4. Any player who does not cross out the proper numeral must return to the board, erase his or her mistake, and rewrite the numeral.

5. The team which has the smaller amount of numerals left after a designated time is declared the winner of the Cross Out Relay.

Fruit Basket

1. "It" stands holding a basket with various fruits (or pictures of various fruits on individual pieces of paper). Other players are seated in a circle or in two parallel lines, but there are no extra chairs.

2. "It" studies the contents of the "fruit basket" and then passes the basket to each player, who is allowed to remove one piece of fruit.

3. When the players are ready, "It" stands at the end of the double line or in the center of the circle and begins the dialog:

It:	Good day, my friends.
Group:	Good day, It, how are you?
It:	I am hungry.
Group:	Do you like fruit?
It:	Yes, I like fruit very much.
Group:	Which fruit would you like?
It:	I would like—grapes and bananas.

4. As "It" says, "I would like—grapes and bananas," the two players holding those fruits must change places while "It" tries to sit in one of their empty chairs.

5. The player without a chair is "It" next, and the game continues.

6. Variations: (a) Animal Basket; (b) Vegetable Basket; (c) Laundry Basket (clothing); (d) School Basket.

I Am Packing a Bag

1. The pupils are seated at their tables or desks.

2. The first child chosen as "It" says, "I am packing a bag and will put something in it that begins with . . . (and names a single consonant sound) *b*."

3. Then the other players who can supply a needed word raise their hands.

4. "It" calls on one player who correctly says "book," "bear," or "bicycle." That second player now becomes "It" and chooses the next and different sound.

5. Suggestions: (a) A large paper bag, book bag, or zipper notebook binder makes an effective prop for It; (b) With older children, this game may be played with teams and scoring of points as each player says a different word with the same initial sound; (c) Initial blends may be used on occasion.

Jump Up

1. The teacher reads or tells a story. It may be an original tale, an old folk tale, or a simple anecdote.

2. Each player is then assigned to be a character or object in the story.

3. The teacher now retells the whole story except that this time each player must jump up (or stand up, in a crowded classroom) every time his or her character or object is mentioned.

4. The players with superior listening comprehension are all declared the winners.
5. Variation: As the players jump up, each must make a sound characteristic of his or her role.

1. Chairs are arranged in one, two, three, or more rows, depending upon the number of pupils playing. Seats and backs are faced alternately along the row, and the total number of chairs is always one less than the number of players.
2. The teacher plays the piano or uses taped music as the players march around the chairs.
3. When the teacher stops the music suddenly, each player must scramble for a chair. The only child left standing must remove one chair from the area; this child is out until the next game.
4. The round continues until there is only one chair left. Its occupant is the winner of Musical Chairs.
5. Variation: Large cutouts are taped to the floor at various points in a circle and the players march around the circle, stepping on each cutout as they come to it. When the music stops, any pupil whose foot or feet are on a cutout is eliminated from that round.

1. The pupils are seated at their desks or at their tables.
2. With a drumstick, the teacher beats out on a drum or table top a certain number of syllables.
3. The pupils listen for the number of syllables in their first name, and later, in their first and last names.
4. When a child believes that his or her name has been tapped out, the child stands and claps as many times as there are syllables in his or her name.
5. All pupils who succeed in recognizing the number of syllables in their names in any one round are declared the winners of that round.
6. Suggestions: (a) The teacher may select a child to beat the drumstick; (b) Older children may sound out the names of songs or the first lines of familiar poems or song lyrics.

1. The teacher is Sally (or Sam) during the first round and stands in front of the room. The pupils stand at their seats.
2. When Sally precedes a command with "Sally says" (e.g., Sally says "Touch your toes"), each pupil performs the command with Sally. If Sally does not precede a command with "Sally says," the pupils must ignore the command no matter what Sally does, or be dropped from the round.
3. A pupil who is out of the first round sits down and the last pupil standing becomes Sally (or Sam) during the second round.
4. Suggestions: (a) Sally (or Sam) should work quickly and always perform her (or his) own commands; (b) Actions and clothes can be stressed as well as parts of the body.

Secret Color

1. All pupils are seated in a circle except "It" who stands inside the circle.
2. The players seated are each assigned a secret color by the teacher. The teacher whispers the secret color individually to each boy or girl and may assign the same secret color to more than one player at once.
3. "It" begins to call out color names at random. As soon as "It" mentions one of the secret colors assigned during that round, the players given that color must promptly leave the circle and move clockwise around the outside. They may hop, skip, or walk, but all must follow the identical action of the first player that leaves.
4. "It" also leaves the circle and imitating the action of the moving players tries to tag the players one at a time.
5. The last player to be tagged becomes "It" for the next round.
6. Suggestions: (a) The total number of different secret colors assigned should depend upon the maturity of the group; four colors are adequate for kindergarten and early primary children; (b) When the game is played outdoors, "It" and the other players have the option of running around the circle.

Shopping Cart

1. The teacher needs pictures of foods available at the market.
2. One player is chosen as "It"; the other players sit in a large circle with no empty chairs and hold up pictures which are visible to "It."
3. "It" walks around the circle, saying, "I went to the market and in my shopping cart I put some . . . and some . . . (etc.)," naming different foods which he or she sees pictured. The players holding those pictures leave their chairs and follow "It" around the circle.
4. When "It" decides to stop shopping, he or she says, "My shopping cart fell over." Then "It" and the players following "It" must find empty seats.
5. The player left standing becomes "It" for the next round of Shopping Cart.

This Is My Shirt

1. The players line up in a row. One player is "It."
2. "It" walks up and down in front of the line. Suddenly "It" touches a part of his or her clothing (or body) and deliberately misidentifies it (e.g., "This is my shirt," while touching a shoe), and points to one of the players.
3. The player addressed promptly replies in the reverse ("This is my shoe," while touching his or her shirt).
4. The first player that "It" can trap becomes "It" in the next round.

Utellem

1. The pupils are seated at their desks or tables.
2. The teacher as the first "Director" chooses one volunteer player to follow directions which are given all at once and demand the performance of several actions within the classroom. For instance, the teacher may say, "Walk to the chalkboard. Draw a circle. Then draw a square inside the circle. Write the word 'dog' inside the square. Run to your seat and sit down."
3. If the player successfully follows all the directions, he or she becomes the second Director.
4. The Director who retains the post the longest wins the Utellem game.

5. Suggestions: (a) The directions must be given slowly and clearly; (b) The teacher may need to help the succeeding Directors decide if the directions have been followed properly; (c) The directions may relate to some current classroom unit such as New York Geography; and the Director could say, "Draw a map of New York. Locate Albany. Locate Buffalo. Label the Hudson River."

Verbal Tennis

1. Two teams of players face each other seated in rows or across tables.
2. The teacher or leader announces a word like *feed* which is made up of a phonogram (or graphemic base) preceded by a consonant.
3. The first player on the first team must say a word that rhymes with *feed* like . . . *seed.*
4. The first player on the second team then says a third word that rhymes with both *feed* and *seed* like . . . *need.*
5. Verbal Tennis continues back and forth between the two teams until the players have given all the words they know using the same phonogram or until the teacher supplies a word with a different phonogram preceded by a consonant like . . . *get.*
6. The team with the greater number of correct words recognized or points earned wins Verbal Tennis.
7. Suggestion: Homophones (e.g., *bead* with *feed* and *seed*) are acceptable among primary and middle-grade pupils.

Evaluation of Pupils' and Teachers' Progress

Richards claims that the education profession is still without a first-rate instrument for the measurement of listening skill.[8] Nevertheless, there are two standardized tests useful for assessing abilities basic to listening, and both can be employed with primary and middle-grade pupils.

The first is the *Illinois Test of Psycholinguistic Abilities,* published by the University of Illinois at Urbana. It is an individual test for use with children between the ages of two and ten. Of the twelve subtests of the ITPA battery, the four that are relevant to listening are Auditory Reception, Auditory Association, Auditory Sequential Memory, and Auditory Closure.

The second is the *Wepman Auditory Discrimination Test,* published by Language Research Associates of Chicago. It is an individual test orally administered to children between the ages of four and nine. It assesses the ability to discriminate changes in frequency, intensity, or pattern of auditory stimuli. Upon being presented key words in pairs, the child is asked whether each two words sound the same or different. The test takes five to ten minutes to administer. Two forms are available.

There are also two standardized instruments for measuring listening comprehension in the elementary classroom. The first is the *STEP (Sequential Tests of Educational Progress)* Listening Test, published by Educational Testing Service of Princeton, New Jersey, and available in two alternate forms for each of four levels (including Level Four for grades four to six). It is based upon oral presentation by the teacher, and its eighty-four option items are reported to measure plain-sense comprehension, interpretation, and evaluation-application. Since the pupils have copies of both the questions and the four options, the STEP test has been criticized for: (a) achievement may be largely a matter of verbal comprehension and not uniquely associated with listening as a distinct skill; and (b) many of the printed items may be answered by pupils who have not heard the oral materials. It is a group test.

A second instrument is the listening test contained in the *Cooperative Primary Tests,* also published by Educational Testing Service. There are alternate forms available for children in grades 1.5 to 2.5 and in grades 2.5 to 3.0. The teacher reads words, sentences, stories, expositions, and poems; and the children demonstrate their comprehension by marking the appropriate pictures. Listening in this group test includes more than receiving the spoken word; it includes identifying associated or illustrative instances, recalling elements, interpreting the ideas presented, and drawing inferences. The test takes about thirty-five minutes to administer and has generally been accepted critically.

Another standardized instrument, which has been revised recently, is designed to provide a comparison of children's listening and reading abilities. Published by Harcourt Brace Jovanovich, the *Durrell Listening-Reading Series* seeks to assess both vocabulary and sentence comprehension at three levels, two primary (grades one and two) and one intermediate (grades three to six). The optional responses are all administered orally so that pupils do no reading to confound the scoring. This is a group test.

Informal Evaluation

Formal tests are hardly a substitute for informal tests, and in the evaluation of listening, both kinds of measuring devices should be developed and used. Informal techniques are more appropriate for specific classroom situations in order to evaluate objectives which have been established for individual programs.

The alert teacher will discover numerous opportunities to determine the extent of listening progress displayed in her or his classroom as the children plan units of work, make announcements, present reports, or read stories aloud. The teacher can evaluate the listening skills of small groups of children by asking: Can they follow directions? Can they identify main ideas, supporting details, or a sequence of events? Can they distinguish between fancy and realism, between opinion and fact, between statements and questions? Have they been developing a meaningful listening vocabulary? Do they listen attentively and courteously? Can they make critical or value judgments about what is heard? Do they listen for enjoyment and aesthetic appreciation? Can they identify with a character and his or her problems?

As children mature and learn, they become more aware of the characteristics of good listeners and of their own strengths and weaknesses relative to those standards. Fourth, fifth, and sixth graders are better qualified to listen than six-years-olds and are also more capable of evaluating their own listening according to a checklist such as that shown in Figure 7.1.

Intermediate Pupil's Self-Evaluation Checklist in Listening

Figure 7.1. Listening Checklist for an Intermediate Student.

Physical Aids

	Always	Sometimes	Never
1. Do I clear my desk of all unnecessary articles?			
2. Do I have everything out of my hands except when writing?			
3. Do I watch the speaker for helpful facial expressions and gestures?			
4. Do I make sure that I am not a distraction?			

Attitude

5. Do I practice all rules of courtesy?			
6. Do I shut out all distractions?			
7. Do I listen with an open mind?			
8. Do I withhold final evaluation until comprehension is complete?			
9. Do I actively engage in listening?			

Content

10. Do I understand the purposes and goals for this listening experience?			
11. Do I understand the kind of listening to use for this listening experience?			
12. Do I screen the material for what I need?			
13. Do I concentrate on what the speaker is saying?			
14. Do I listen for main ideas first and details second?			
15. Do I take notes when they will be of use to me?			
16. Do I use past knowledge to give meaning to the current listening experience?			
17. Do I ask questions at the appropriate time?			

The teacher's role in informally evaluating listening in the classroom is not complete until the teacher has evaluated his or her own listening abilities and program as outlined in Figure 7.2. Realizing that listening *can* be taught, the teacher plans carefully and then displays the same unfailing interest and courtesy in listening to the oral contributions of the pupils that they are expected to show to him or her and to each other. Children who observe their teacher sorting papers or taking roll while they are talking to him or her can hardly be expected to develop into attentive listeners.

Discussion Questions

1. Why is the teaching of listening so frequently neglected?
2. Which factors that affect listening fall within the domain of the teacher?
3. How can elementary teachers improve the listening ability of those children who are hard of hearing?
4. How could a school evaluate children's listening? Would a letter grade ever be warranted?

Suggested Projects

1. Plan a listening lesson for intermediate pupils which involves critical listening.
2. Try to arrange an experiment involving the physical conditions in one elementary classroom and their effect on children's listening.
3. Develop six learning experiences in attentive listening and six more in appreciative listening for a grade level of your choice.
4. Spend one hour each in the kindergarten, second-grade, and fifth-grade classrooms. Record the amount of time the students spent listening and the amount of time the teacher listened. Do older children have as many opportunities to listen as younger pupils do?
5. Examine two current language text series for one intermediate grade level to see how listening skills are being presented. Compare, for example, the material in *Language for Meaning* (Houghton Mifflin, 1978) with that of *Language for Daily Use* (Harcourt Brace Jovanovich, 1978). Which do you prefer and why?
6. Set up the learning center for listening shown in Figure 7.3.

Classroom Teacher's Self-Evaluation Checklist in Listening

Figure 7.2. Listening Checklist for a Classroom Teacher.

	Always	Sometimes	Never
1. Do I pursue a program in which listening skills are consistently developed?	_____	_____	_____
2. Do I prepare for the listening activities to be presented?	_____	_____	_____
3. Do I initiate activities to which the pupils want to listen?	_____	_____	_____
4. Do I create an emotional climate for good listening?	_____	_____	_____
5. Do I create a physical climate for good listening?	_____	_____	_____
6. Do I realize that the attention span of pupils is limited?	_____	_____	_____
7. Do I realize that the concentration span of pupils is limited?	_____	_____	_____
8. Do I help the pupils to develop an appreciation and awareness of sounds?	_____	_____	_____
9. Do I help the pupils to establish purposes for each listening activity?	_____	_____	_____
10. Do I listen to each pupil during the school day?	_____	_____	_____
11. Do I encourage the pupils to listen to each other?	_____	_____	_____
12. Do I use changes in pitch, loudness, and rate in my classroom voice?	_____	_____	_____
13. Do I secure the attention of the group before beginning to speak?	_____	_____	_____
14. Do I give attention to unfamiliar vocabulary?	_____	_____	_____
15. Do I help pupils recall related experiences which may aid their understanding?	_____	_____	_____
16. Do I pose questions that promote careful listening?	_____	_____	_____
17. Do I try not to repeat my presentations or directions?	_____	_____	_____
18. Do I express appreciation for what each child says?	_____	_____	_____
19. Do I promote good listening by not talking too much myself?	_____	_____	_____
20. Do I make myself available for listening and teach listening in every subject area?	_____	_____	_____

Figure 7.3. Language Arts Learning Center: Listening in the Intermediate Grades.

TYPE OF CENTER: Listening   TIME: 15–20 minutes

GRADE LEVEL: Intermediate   NUMBER OF STUDENTS: 1 or more

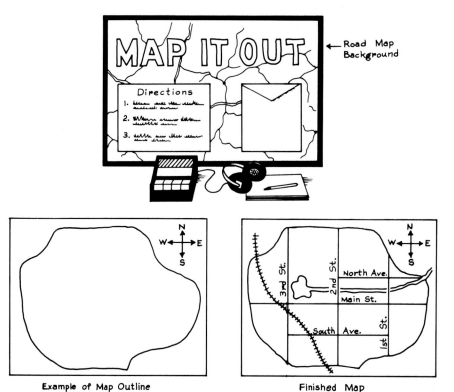

Example of Map Outline   Finished Map

Related Readings

Devine, T. 1978. "Listening: What Do We Know after Fifty Years of Research and Theorizing?" *Journal of Reading* 21: 296–304.

Faber, C. 1976. *On Listening.* Pacific Palisades, California: Perseus Press.

Faix, T. 1975. "Listening as a Human Relations Act." *Elementary English* 52: 409–13.

Halley, R. D. 1975. "Some Suggestions for the Teaching of Listening." *Speech Teacher* 24: 386–89.

Larson, G., and Petersen, B. 1978. "Does Noise Limit the Learning of Young Listeners?" *Elementary School Journal* 78: 264–65.

Mendelson, A. 1976. "Listener." *Young Children* 31: 184–86.

O'Donnell, H. 1975. "Are You Listening? Are You Listening?" ERIC/RCS Report. *Language Arts* 52: 1080–84.

Rubin, D. 1977. "Listening: An Essential Skill." *AV Instruction* 22: 31–32.

INSTRUCTIONAL OBJECTIVE:	The student should be able to draw a map accurately by following precise oral directions.
MATERIALS:	Outlines of city, pencils, tape recorder, listening center with earphones, work folder.
DIRECTIONS: (WRITTEN)	1. Have teacher explain how to use the tape recorder. 2. Get pencil and outline of city from table. 3. Turn on the tape recorder.
DIRECTIONS: (ORAL)	Today you are going to draw a map. Listen carefully to the directions. After you hear each instruction, turn off the tape recorder while you draw that part of the map. If you are ready, we will begin. 1. Put Main Street through the center of the city running east and west. Label it. Stop. 2. First Street runs north and south near the east edge of the city. Put it on your map and label it. Stop. 3. Third Street runs north and south near the west edge of the city. Put it on your map and label it. Stop. 4. Put Second Street where you would expect to see it. Label it. Stop. 5. North Avenue is north of Main Street. It starts at Second Street and runs out the east side of the city. Draw it on your map and label it. Stop. 6. South Avenue runs between First Street and Third Street. Put it on the side of Main Street where you think its name shows it would go. Label it. Stop. 7. Put a small lake near the northeast corner of Third Street and Main Street. Stop. 8. Be careful now! A river goes from the lake, flows northeast, passes under Second Street and First Street, and runs out the northeast corner of the city. Show the river on your map. Stop. 9. Now show a railroad. The railroad comes into the northwest corner of the city. It crosses Main Street and goes out the south edge of the city. Stop. 10. You have now completed your map. Put your finished drawing in the folder, and turn off the tape recorder.
EVALUATION:	The teacher will assess the student's work by checking his or her finished map drawing. From this, the teacher will be able to determine whether the child needs more practice in listening activities.

Source: From *Language Arts Learning Centers and Activities* by Angela Reeke and James Laffey. Copyright 1979 by Goodyear Publishing Company. Reprinted by permission.

Schneeberg, H. 1977. "Listening While Reading: A Four-Year Study." *Reading Teacher* 30: 625–35.

Stammer, J. D. 1977. "Target: The Basics of Listening." *Language Arts* 54: 661–64.

Tutolo, D. J. 1977. "A Cognitive Approach to Teaching Listening." *Language Arts* 54: 262–65.

Speaking 8

The three major components of the speech curriculum in today's elementary
    school

The most important domain of the language arts

Puppets that children can make

Speech disorders that teachers should refer to clinicians

The child's control of the features of language proceeds along a continuum of
mastering the highly predictable and productive features toward the mastering
of less common forms with limited distribution. Speech skills necessary for
effective oral communication must therefore be taught through a developmental process, with learning opportunities offered in varied areas of the
curriculum.

Speech habits formed in the preschool years will vary greatly with the
individual child. The teacher who is cognizant of the variations will modify
the program accordingly. The wise teacher is aware that competence in spoken
language constitutes the basis for competence in reading and in written composition.

Investigations completed during the past decade among pupils from kindergarten through grade seven show that children speak more words in each
succeeding year, produce more communication units, and increase the average number of words in those units. The fastest spurts in development of oral
expression appear to occur in the time spans between kindergarten and the
end of first grade and between the end of fifth grade and the end of seventh
grade.

These studies in speech found no evidence of linguistic superiority of girls
over boys at comparable ages. (Possibly changes in social, cultural, and educational environments have reduced differential behavior of the sexes.) There
is, however, a frequently recurring pattern of boys at the extreme ends of a
number of measures: boys in the high-ability group excel the girls in the same
group, while the boys in the low-ability group are the least proficient of all
pupils observed.

Whether these children are academically advantaged or not, their language patterns are largely established by the time they reach school age. Still

every person who has contact with the children from the day they enter kindergarten influences their speaking patterns.

In turn, the children's patterns and other speech characteristics affect the expectations that teachers have of the elementary pupils. Two recent studies—one in the Midwest and one in Texas—involved black, white, and Mexican-American students of middle- and low-income families.[1] The investigations found that teachers tended to evaluate children's speech samples in terms of two relatively global dimensions. One was confidence-eagerness and was found to be related to a child's fluency, lack of hesitations, and tendency to participate actively in a linguistic interview. The second was labeled ethnicity-nonstandardness and was a reflection primarily of the degree of nonstandard English found in a child's speech.

Consequently, any teachers introduced under school busing to a child whose native language or nonstandard English dialect is unfamiliar to them must be certain that their attitudes will affect the pupil's progress in the school environment positively. They must be aware, as discussed earlier in chapter 3 that all dialects are fully formed language systems. They also must recognize that the speech education program developed and maintained by the school needs the active support of the home and community.

Such a speech curriculum should incorporate three major components:

Speech improvement for all children, planned by the classroom teacher in every grade in order to present specific lessons in articulation and other skills.

Speech arts for all children, planned by the classroom teacher in every grade in order to present applications of specific skills.

Speech correction for the few handicapped children in every grade, who suffer from disorders of articulation, fluency, voice, or delayed speech and require the services of a clinician, who relies in turn on the follow-up activities of the classroom teacher between visits. In districts that do not employ clinicians or therapists, the teacher has sole responsibility for speech correction work.

To create an effective oral language program the teacher must consider several notable factors. First, since students learn to speak by speaking, *the environment of the classroom* should resemble that of a communication center and allow pupils to translate their thoughts into words for questioning, comparing, contrasting, reporting, evaluating, and summarizing. Yet that center cannot deteriorate into a classroom of unorganized confusion where students ignore the social amenities needed for interaction. Second, *the role of the teacher* must be that of listener, facilitator, and participant in learning. Third, *the role of the student* must be an active role, whether it be in small groups, whole-class groups, or with a partner. Fourth, skills and activities using *the components of oral language* should be those emphasizing vocabulary, syntax, fluency, intonation, and articulation. Finally, language is *a communication tool* and therefore it should be used for re-presenting the meaning of experiences.[2]

Speech Improvement

Helping children to speak well is a major objective of the language arts program. In light of current educational philosophy it is apparent that the classroom teacher is responsible for attaining that objective.

The fact that children come to school knowing, with varying degrees of effectiveness, how to speak, should not mislead the teacher into believing that no instruction is needed. As a matter of fact, it is only through the disciplined correlation of the factors of language, thought, voice, and action that effective oral communication can be achieved.

Since the development of speech depends upon physical and psychological development, it is to be hoped that each child will have normal organs of speech and hearing and the security of a psychologically comfortable environment. When some pupils lack these assets, it becomes the teacher's responsibility to assist the children in making the adjustments necessary for effective speech.

Through such various speech arts as will be presented later in this chapter, children learn the values of pleasant audible speech, clear articulation, attentive and discriminating listening, and the correct use of stress, phrasing, and intonation. The program of speech in action, however, may not provide sufficient instruction and practice in proper posture, breathing habits, and control of the speech organs. Nor may it pinpoint minor speech faults that must be corrected. Specific instruction in speech skills, therefore, is critical and constitutes that integral part of the language arts curriculum which is known as speech improvement. It is concerned with building positive attitudes and attempts to meet the speaking needs of all children in the classroom.

Such a program does not require the services of a speech clinician but can be implemented successfully by the classroom teacher. Several school districts in New Jersey, for example, reported that young children showed a marked decrease in articulation errors and displayed improved auditory discrimination as a result of a thirteen-week program of daily fifteen-minute lessons.[3] The first week was spent on generalized listening to environmental sounds and on introducing listening for a particular sound at the beginning, middle, or end of a word. The work of the remaining twelve weeks was progressive in difficulty; it was divided into two-week segments during which one particular sound was heard, identified, discriminated, and reinforced in a variety of contexts. (The six sounds studied in this fashion were *k, f, s, r, l,* and *th*). Commercially available speech-improvement stories and picture cards were incorporated in the lessons and given to the teachers along with the syllabus of complete lesson plans for each day of the thirteen-week period.

A sample plan covering one of the final lessons on the *k* sound ran this way:

Eighth Day: Articulation and Difficult Discrimination—
Further Reinforcement

The teacher says:

1. Let me see how sharp your ears are. Do you think you all know the crowing sound of *k* now? We'll see. I'm going to say two words, like *key/tea.* Where did you hear the crowing sound of *k?* In the first *key* or in the second *tea?* Now here are some more pairs of words. Tell me where the *k* is. Is it in the first or second word? Listen to both words and then answer "first" or "second"—*call/tall, tan/can, pearl/curl, cop/top.*

2. Here are some words with *k* at the end. Listen to both words and then answer "first" or "second" . . . . . *sick/sit, back/bat, like/light, lock/lot, oat/oak.* (Exaggerate the sounds, but no more than you have to.)

3. Who likes riddles? I'm thinking of something beginning with *k*
   . . . and it's yellow and I like to eat it on the cob (*corn*).
   . . . and it's soft, furry and says "Meow" (*kitty* or *cat*).
   . . . and it's a long orange vegetable. Rabbits like it too (*carrot*).
   . . . and we ride in it and get driven to many places (*car*).
   . . . and soup comes in it and all kinds of other foods too (*can*).

4. I'm thinking of something with a *k* in the middle
   . . . and it's something that lives at the zoo, climbs trees, and does very funny tricks (*monkey*).
   . . . and it's something I have on my coat that I put paper or money or important things into (*pocket*).
   . . . and it's orange and I make a jack-o'-lantern out of it at Halloween (*pumpkin*).
   . . . and it's something I eat for Thanksgiving dinner (*turkey*).

5. I'm thinking of something with a *k* at the end
   . . . and it's white and we drink it (*milk*).
   . . . and it's the sound a clock makes (*ticktock*).
   . . . and it's the thing we wash our hands in (*sink*).
   . . . and it's what you put on your foot before you put on your shoe (*sock*).
   . . . and it's what I am if I have to stay in bed and can't go to school (*sick*).

6. Who wants to make some riddles for us to guess? (The children will not be able to do this if they are left entirely on their own. However, if you give them one of the picture cards containing a *k* sound and let them describe the picture, it should go fairly well.)

A new dimension of interest in speech improvement lessons such as this one has resulted from research studies showing significant relationships between defective articulation and auditory discrimination, and between reading retardation and auditory discrimination.

The sound system of English can create problems in the sequence of speech development in children with respect to six areas. The first of these is *reversals,* for a child may say *alunimum* for *aluminum* due to immaturity, inadequate learning, or cerebral damage; some of the words commonly reversed appear in Table 8.1. Another problem area is *consonant blends,* for either the nervous system or the muscular system of the child may not be sufficiently mature to master two or three consonants bound together such as *str.* While the ability to discriminate among sounds develops at a different rate in different people,

Table 8.1.
The 100 Most Frequently Mispronounced of the Commonly Used Words.

1. aluminum	35. gather	69. recognize
2. American	36. genuine	70. regularly
3. apron	37. geography	71. rinse
4. arctic	38. get	72. roof
5. asked	39. government	73. room
6. athlete	40. height	74. sandwich
7. battery	41. hundred	75. secretary
8. because	42. iron	76. sink
9. booths	43. Italian	77. smile
10. bury	44. keg	78. soot
11. bushel	45. larynx	79. spoil
12. can't	46. length	80. squash
13. catch	47. library	81. statistics
14. cavalry	48. Massachusetts	82. such
15. cement	49. material	83. sure
16. child	50. men	84. surprise
17. children	51. Michigan	85. ten
18. chimney	52. milk	86. tired
19. column	53. nuclear	87. tournament
20. could you	54. onion	88. towel
21. cushion	55. orange	89. tower
22. dandelion	56. our	90. veteran
23. davenport	57. particularly	91. vision
24. deaf	58. party	92. vowel
25. Detroit	59. peony	93. wash
26. diphtheria	60. percolate	94. wheelbarrow
27. eggs	61. perspiration	95. where
28. escape	62. picture	96. wiener
29. film	63. police	97. wouldn't
30. finally	64. power	98. wrestle
31. fire	65. pumpkin	99. years
32. fish	66. push	100. your
33. fists	67. put	
34. flower	68. radish	

Source: Alan W. Huckleberry and Edward S. Strother. *Speech Education for the Elementary Teacher* (Boston: Allyn & Bacon, Inc., 1973), p. 307. Reprinted with the permission of the publisher.

an eight-year-old child who says *wabbit* for *rabbit* is showing vestiges of *baby talk,* which is another area of difficulty.

Then there is *voice pitch* which is related to general body tension, inadequate loudness, outdoor yelling, heredity of vocal apparatus, or a change of voice. There is also *voice loudness* which may involve discriminational, psychological, physical, or environmental causative factors. The final problem area is *mispronunciations* which, in part at least, may be resolved by the teacher's model pronunciation of all words and especially those found in Table 8.1.

Testing and Recording Speaking Patterns

In order to plan lessons well and use time wisely, the teacher must be cognizant of the specific speech faults that prevail among the boys and girls. The teacher can observe during several short periods of class activity the habitual patterns employed by the pupils and then record these impressions quickly and accurately with *yes* or *no* answers on individual profile sheets. Taping the activities may sometimes help the teacher form conclusions in doubtful cases. Such profile sheets can be used later for referrals to speech clinicians or for consultations with parents, administrators, or other teachers. A typical profile sheet is shown in Figure 8.1.

Skills

When a school program begins with the kindergarten classes and is subsequently developed throughout the grades, the students, upon completion of the sixth grade, have the ability to *modulate their voices* to reflect feeling, mood, and meaning. They can *speak in clear and pleasing tones,* giving attention to intonation and tonal quality. They are able to *use their teeth, lips, and tongues to give precise enunciation* to beginning sounds, middle sounds, and ending sounds. Finally they can *pace their speech* in order to obtain and maintain sustained listening.

Ability to Modulate the Voice

In both the primary and the intermediate grades the ability to modulate the voice may be developed and improved through a variety of learning experiences. Younger children can dramatize stories in which the characters feel strong emotions, such as the animals in *The Three Little Pigs, The Three Billy Goats Gruff,* and *The Three Bears,* or stories that demand a variety of voices such as *Jack and the Beanstalk* and *Hansel and Gretel.* They can listen to poems such as Stevenson's "The Wind" and discuss how the refrain should sound.

Their teacher can exhibit visuals of busy children and allow each pupil to select one picture as a basis for an impromptu oral composition. The teacher may also display chalkboard sentences that express happiness, surprise, or fear, such as "What a good time we had!" and "Stay away from the fire" and encourage the pupils to practice saying these sentences aloud, preferably using a tape recorder. Sometimes the teacher may read or tell a story to the class and then have the children evaluate his or her reading or telling in terms of feeling, mood, and meaning.

Older pupils can participate in choral reading of poems with story contrast, such as Poe's "Bells," or poems with pictures or sounds, such as Ben-

Profile of General Speech Faults

Figure 8.1. Sample Profile Sheet for Recording General Speech Faults of Elementary Pupils.

Child's Name _____ **Date** _____

1. Attitude toward Speaking Situations _____
   a. Does the child enjoy speaking situations? _____
   b. Does he apparently avoid speaking situations? _____
   c. Is he reluctant to speak in group situations? _____
   d. Does he participate actively? _____

2. Rate and Fluency
   a. Is the child's speech too rapid? _____
   b. Is the child's speech too slow? _____
   c. Is his phrasing poor? _____
   d. Is his speech hesitant? _____
   e. Is his vocabulary limited? _____
   f. Is he able to organize his thoughts? _____

3. Voice
   a. Is his voice loud? _____
   b. Is his voice nasal? _____
   c. Is his voice hoarse? _____
   d. Is his voice monotonous? _____
   e. Is his voice inaudible? _____
   f. Is the pitch abnormally high? _____
   g. Is the pitch abnormally low? _____

4. Articulation and Pronunciation
   a. Does he distort sounds? _____
   b. Does he substitute one sound for another? _____
   c. Does he omit sounds? _____
   d. Does he mispronounce? _____

Source: Adapted from *Handbook for Language Arts: Grades Three and Four* (New York: Board of Education of the City of New York, 1969–1970), p. 310.

nett's "Motor Cars" or Reeves' "The Sea." Their teacher can have them recite or read statements that can show both annoyance and pleasure, such as "Who left this box here?" and "Is this for me?" Also, the teacher can encourage the children to suggest words that describe a pleasant voice, such as one that is soft or musical, as well as words that characterize an unpleasant voice, such as one that is gruff or whining. Finally, the teacher and the pupils can prepare and tell two brief stories, each ending with the same sentence but showing a different feeling; for example, "He dropped the letter into the fire."

Young children can develop and improve the ability to speak clearly in pleasing tones through dramatic play activities planned in conjunction with a unit on The Home. They can recite or read sentences such as "It is snowing" and

Ability to Speak in Clear and Pleasing Tones

"Come here" with different inflections. They may listen to tapes or records of appropriate stories and orchestral selections for changes in volume and pitch. Later they can tape short selections by themselves from their basals in order to determine how to improve tonal quality.

A primary teacher can read poems to the class and discuss how intonation must change with meaning. The teacher may encourage the children to read chorally "The Three Little Kittens" as he or she points out the sounds that help make the Mother Goose rhyme a favorite with listeners. Also, the teacher can introduce the class to different kinds of bells and let the pupils imitate the bells for the purpose of distinguishing between the tone and the pitch of the telephone, the doorbell, and the alarm clock.

Children in the intermediate grades can help list criteria for pleasing speech such as "Speak slowly" and "Use the lips and tongue to make clear speech sounds." They can use a teletrainer kit that is available from the telephone company to schools at no cost in many parts of the country, and then chart standards for pleasant telephone conversations.

Their teacher can help the class participate in the oral reading of poems from books such as Smaridge's *Only Silly People Waste* (Abingdon, 1976), listening for distinct beginnings and endings of words. The teacher can ask each child to present a one-minute talk on a topic like "Noise Pollution in the School" or to spin a one-minute tale from such a beginning phrase as "One dark and rainy night . . ." Finally, the teacher and the pupils can discuss how pitch and stress are used during telecasts or broadcasts of sports events or news reports of tragedies.

Ability to Use Teeth, Lips, and Tongue For Proper Articulation

To practice proper articulation, boys and girls in kindergarten and the primary grades can recite those nursery rhymes, including "Sing a Song of Sixpence" and "Baa, Baa, Black Sheep," that feature the consonant sounds of *s, b,* and *p.* They can hold a piece of tissue paper before their mouths, trying to keep it vibrating as long as possible while they sound out certain consonant digraphs such as *sh* and *th.* They can also practice the *wh* digraph by pretending to blow out a lighted candle or asking, "Why did you whisper that there is a whale under the wharf?" The children can create and recite sentences with alliteration, such as "Paul Pipwick prefers pumpkin pie" or sentences that contain tongue twisters, such as "Many mothers make money mending mittens." Finally, with the help of their teacher, they can compile a list of word pairs that begin or end with the following letters: *d* and *t, p* and *b,* or *th* and *t.*

Pupils in the intermediate grades should continue to do oral exercises with rhyming words and tongue twisters. They can work in teams to pronounce such word pairs as *pin/pen, which/witch,* or *breathe/breed.* They can divide polysyllabic words, learning to enunciate distinctly the sequence of sounds in words like *chronological* and *arithmetical.* They can listen for the often-forgotten syllable in words like *family, geography,* or *poem.* Lastly, they can compile lists of words using the consonant sounds of *l, r,* and *z,* and the digraph *ch.*

While young children are hearing and reciting tongue twisters, they can be shown how the difficulties in pronouncing and understanding the sayings increase with the tempo of the recitation. They can listen to poems with definite rhythms such as Lindsay's "The Mysterious Cat," and discuss how rhythm affects pace. They can discover by rereading some of the sections in their basals how oral pacing is related to the subject matter of a narrative.

Older boys and girls can contrast two poems such as Stevenson's "Windy Nights" and Moore's "Snowy Morning" in order to establish the relationship between mood and pacing. They can make announcements over the public address system and later play back their presentations so that they may evaluate the pace they exhibited and discuss the differences between the delivery of an excited speaker and that of a calm one. Finally, the class can take turns giving directions relevant to artificial respiration or other first aid, for example, in order to demonstrate the importance of clarity and variety of pace in instances of emergency instructions.

Evaluation

Two formal tests that measure articulation have been well received critically.[4] Examining a specimen set of either of these standardized instruments may aid the teacher in evaluating some pupils:

1. *Goldman-Fristoe Test of Articulation* (for ages two and up). Published by American Guidance Services, Inc., Circle Pines, Minnesota 55014. An individual test which takes ten to fifteen minutes to administer.
2. *Templin-Darley Tests of Articulation* (for ages three and up). Published by the Bureau of Educational Research and Services, Ohio State University, Columbus, Ohio 43210. Individual tests. The screening test requires five to fifteen minutes for administration, and the total diagnostic test requires twenty to forty minutes.

Self-evaluation by the teacher and by the child by means of a checklist (Figures 8.2 and 8.3) has proved worthwhile, although the teacher can also appraise the speech of each pupil from time to time (Figure 8.4). (See pages 174–76 for Figures 8.2, 8.3, and 8.4.) A comparison of the teacher's rating with the pupil's appraisal often leads to a better understanding of exhibited weaknesses and strengths, especially when the suggestions are specific enough to point the way to growth. Generalities such as *interesting* or *good* offer little enlightenment or practical assistance. Records of evaluations should be kept up-to-date on individual cards or in separate folders in order to provide a basis for diagnosis and deliberation.

Speech Arts

Learning to communicate through speech demands frequent opportunities for oral language skills. Through the speech arts program, favorable attitudes may be established by the pupils toward good speech and toward themselves as speakers. Desirable social relationships may be fostered to meet the needs

Figure 8.2. Sample Checklist for Teacher's Self-Evaluation in Speech.

Classroom Teacher's Self-Evaluation Checklist of His or Her Role in Speech

	Always	Sometimes	Never
1. Do I provide a good speech example?	_____	_____	_____
2. Do the children in my class feel socially and emotionally secure when they talk to each other and to me?	_____	_____	_____
3. Do I keep records of my children in order to chart improvement in speech over a period of time?	_____	_____	_____
4. Do I maintain separate standards for each group of children since I recognize their differences in readiness to learn?	_____	_____	_____
5. Do I provide ample time for the children to hear the correct production of sounds in a variety of activities?	_____	_____	_____
6. Do the parents know that I am working on improving children's speech, and do they understand and approve of the methods I use?	_____	_____	_____
7. Do I consciously integrate speech activities with the rest of the school program?	_____	_____	_____
8. Do I encourage the whole group to participate in the speech improvement activity so that no one is singled out for individual correction?	_____	_____	_____
9. Do I give praise for good speech by the children?	_____	_____	_____
10. Do I promptly refer children with speech disorders to the speech clinician and do I then follow his or her recommendations closely?	_____	_____	_____

Intermediate Pupil's Self-Evaluation Checklist in Speech

	Yes	No
1. Is my voice pleasant to hear?	_____	_____
2. Is my voice too loud or too soft?	_____	_____
3. Is my voice too high or too low?	_____	_____
4. Do I use a variety of inflections?	_____	_____
5. Do I speak too slowly or too fast?	_____	_____
6. Do I speak distinctly?	_____	_____
7. Do I use a varied vocabulary?	_____	_____
8. Do I use appropriate language for each speaking situation?	_____	_____
9. Do I explain myself well so others can understand my ideas?	_____	_____
10. Do I remember to wait for my turn to speak?	_____	_____

Figure 8.3. Sample Checklist for Pupil's Self-Evaluation in Speech.

Classroom Teacher's Evaluation of Pupil's Speech

Pupil's Name _____ **Date** _____

(The teacher should check the vocal difficulties below each speech technique that is rated *average* or *unsatisfactory*.)

Tempo   Very Good_____ Average_____ Unsatisfactory_____

_____ Too fast

_____ Too slow

_____ Unvarying, monotonous

_____ Poor phrasing; irregular rhythm of speaking

_____ Hesitations

Loudness   Very Good_____ Average_____ Unsatisfactory_____

_____ Too loud

_____ Too weak

_____ Lack of variety

_____ Force overused as a form of emphasis

Figure 8.4. Sample Form for Teacher's Evaluation of Pupil's Speech.

Figure 8.4 (cont.)   **Pitch**   Very Good_____ Average_____ Unsatisfactory_____

_____ General level too high

_____ General level too low

_____ Lack of variety

_____ Fixed pattern monotonously repeated

_____ Lack of relationship between pitch changes and meaning

_____ Exaggerated pitch changes

Quality   Very Good_____ Average_____ Unsatisfactory_____

_____ Nasal

_____ Hoarse

_____ Breathy

_____ Throaty and guttural

_____ Strained and harsh

_____ Flat

_____ Thin and weak

Articulation   Very Good_____ Average_____ Unsatisfactory_____

Consonants: _____ Slurred over or omitted

                 _____ Specific sounds defective

Vowels: _____ Improperly formed

_____ General diction careless or slovenly

---

of individuals and groups. Progressive speech development may be stressed through a variety of beginning and advanced kinds of speaking situations. Pleasant voices may be encouraged in order to promote an effective and natural manner. Practical standards of speech may be determined and maintained mutually by the pupils and their teacher. Realistic situations and experiences may be presented for applying speech improvement exercises.

The speech arts include primarily: giving talks, conversing, discussing, debating, following parliamentary procedure, interviewing, participating in social courtesies, and using puppets, as well as engaging in choral reading, storytelling, and creative drama. The last three arts listed will be discussed later in chapters 11 and 12. The other eight speech arts are presented herewith, with Table 8.2 listing instructional activities which involve each of them.

Table 8.2.

Sample Instructional Activities in Elementary School Speech Arts.

Kind of Speech Art	Grade Level	Learning Activity and/or Teaching Strategy
Conversing	K–6	Six pupils participate in a (directed) conversation about children's television shows available on Saturday mornings.
Debating	5–6	Two boys and two girls debate the proposition that no four-legged pets should be allowed in apartments.
Discussing	3–6	All the pupils engage in a round-table discussion about the responsibilities involved in being left alone at home.
Following parliamentary procedure	5–6	All the students are involved in various committees that must report back to the class regarding the year-end picnic at a nearby park.
Giving directions	1–3	The child has just encountered someone from an unidentified flying object on the school playground and must direct this being to the principal's office.
Interviewing	4–6	Two students interview a neighborhood woman who weaves small rugs and sells them to a New York gift shop.
Making announcements	2–4	Two Brownie Scouts announce, completely but concisely, a forthcoming event: the annual cooky sale.
Making introductions	2–6	The child picks a friend to be the New Boy in the Class; then "during recess" he first introduces himself to him and later introduces the boy to other classmates.
Reporting	1–3	The child informally reports to the class what the members of his or her family like to eat and don't like to eat.
Telephoning	5–6	Using a coin telephone, the child receives from the information operator the telephone number of the Washington, D.C. office of his or her senator.
Using puppets	K–3	Three children use hand puppets to stage a play describing the downfall of Lazy Louey who refused to brush his teeth.

(The objective of each activity is to assist the learner in communicating thought and feeling with voice/body.)

Talks

Oral language ability must be viewed as the most important domain of the language arts, states Klein.[5] School settings being rarely conducive to talk, however, it is up to the teacher to transform the classroom atmosphere, at least metamorphically, into a variety of settings with a variety of audiences with different genuine purposes and subjects available for potential talkers. If the teacher can accomplish this task, most of the effort to motivate talkers will be unnecessary because the environment itself will stimulate.

Talks center about four basic purposes: to inform, to describe, to persuade, or to entertain. Although several kinds of talks are included in this segment of the language arts, the majority of them fall under either one of two categories: reporting or announcing-explaining-directing.

Reporting

In the lower grades there is *informal reporting*. The teacher begins by sharing with the class some anecdotes, incidents, and descriptions from his or her own life in order to extend the children's experiences. The teacher then encourages the pupils to report on news that they think important by helping them to understand which incidents are appropriate for sharing with the class and which are better suited for relating to him or her alone. After listening attentively to the reports the pupils share with their classmates and assisting with sequence, relevancy, and length, the teacher asks the listeners for constructive comments or questions. Also, the teacher compliments each speaker on some aspect of his or her report, calling attention to choice descriptive or action words, sentence patterns, or speech skills. The teacher explains the cues Who? Where? What? Why? When? How? and lists them on a chart. Sometimes informal reactions to particular films or television programs can be elicited, as the teacher points out qualities that make certain productions worthwhile.

In turn, the children begin to develop a sensitivity to suitable topics for informal reporting and to gain confidence in their ability to share ideas with others. In their role as listeners, they pay close attention and ask questions truly related to the reports presented. In their role as reporters, they try to remember to speak audibly, look at their audience, realize that the opening sentence must be an attention-getter, and keep to the topic.

Since children are less self-conscious when they become absorbed in *showing and telling* about an object, especially one that bears a personal significance for its owner, their oral reports are likely to be longer, livelier, and less rambling. Young pupils find it easier to share facts and experiences while they are showing objects which can be held in the hand and admired by the class—an arrowhead, a frog, or a seashell. Teachers may choose to vary this type of activity in several ways, but the basic experience remains valuable for developing body control, a sense of audience, and an ability to elaborate on a topic the speaker knows well.

Although some districts feel that by the middle of first grade, most children have outgrown the need for holding an object as a supportive measure, there are other schools where seventh graders still show-and-tell, though on a more sophisticated level. Students in one New Jersey school, for example, are invited to select an afternoon to "demonstrate and elaborate," using multi-media aids if they wish. Such talks are generally made up of two parts: first, the informal showing of the photographs, lucky coins, birds' nests or other objects; and then, a report on close-up photography, superstitions, nest-building and feeding habits of different birds, or some other topic closely allied to the object presented.[6]

Planned or *formal reporting* is common in the intermediate grades where students are taught to organize, outline, and use reference materials. Besides being a good listening exercise for the audience, such reporting provides an opportunity to build on skills in the selection and collection of material and the organization and presentation of the report. The children can be shown how to delimit the scope of their talks and how to choose pertinent material quickly by using the index and by scanning and skimming. They can learn to take notes relevant to the major ideas, to keep a record of the books used, and to organize their material into a logical order by making an outline of the main points to be stressed. Finally, class members can be shown how to give reports extemporaneously without obvious reference to their papers. Some children may wish to use visual aids to enhance their presentations.

Topics for talks may be assigned by the teacher or determined by the children in cooperation with their teacher. The range of topics suitable for reporting include weather reports, school news, committee reports, and student council reports. Special subject reports for social studies, science, or current events could focus on the sport of hang gliding, on plants and music, on drinking water from the sea, or on the black widow spider.

Primary teachers can encourage informal reporting by sharing with the class some anecdotes and objects from their own travels. (Photo courtesy of Jon Jacobson.)

The skills and abilities necessary for making announcements and for giving directions and explanations are similar to those in reporting. The verbal message should be brief, exact, and complete, answering the questions Who? What? When? Where? and sometimes How? and Why? It should be arranged in suitable order and presented enthusiastically so that listeners will become convinced that the matter is worthy of their time and attention.

Announcements may be made about the safety patrol, community events, ball games, scout meetings, lost-and-found articles, and exhibitions. In schools which have public-address systems, the students can make announcements about the PTA meeting. In classrooms they can use puppets to announce a forthcoming classroom drama. Boys and girls can listen to commercial television or radio and list the many kinds of announcements heard in one hour. Their teacher can invite a local radio announcer to talk to the class about his or her job and the preparations necessary before going on the air. The teacher and the children can tape a series of announcements and then play back the material in order to evaluate it in terms of sufficiency and relevancy of information.

Explanations may be offered about a variety of topics ranging from the operation of a battery-operated toy to the passage of vessels through a canal. Children may give *directions* for playing handball, for building bird houses, for setting up experiments, and for planting radish seeds. Sometimes, however, talks giving directions are really *speeches of demonstration,* useful for elementary school classes because there is a visible crutch to supply meaning to the listeners if and when the speaker stops momentarily. Since demonstrations involve processes, they reinforce the need for orderly sequence. Pupils often use them in social studies or science.

Evaluation of Talks

The teacher can evaluate the class progress in giving talks by asking these questions about the pupils:

- Are they becoming better able to discriminate between significant and insignificant information in planning their talks?
- Are they describing details more accurately?
- Are they developing the habit of observing sequence?
- Are they learning to face an audience with reasonable confidence and to speak up clearly?
- Are they incorporating properly the use of visuals in their presentations?

Conversation and Dialogue

In current language arts texts for both primary and intermediate grades *conversation* is included as a speech activity. Conversation is an informal and spontaneous experience where the stress is primarily on the development of social skills. It contributes to the child's ability to make friends, to acquire self-confidence, and to speak easily and well. Conversation may be stimulated by sharing such uncommon experiences as hiking in the mountains, riding in

These kindergarten children have yet another opportunity to enjoy an informal dialogue. (Photo courtesy of Jean-Claude Lejeune.)

the desert, visiting a national park, and exploring a cave. It also develops from ordinary activities that pupils can relate, including washing the dog, shopping for new clothes, watching a ball game, and playing a musical instrument.

To encourage conversation the teacher again has the responsibility to create the proper environment. It must be stimulating and ever-changing. At the same time, however, the teacher must also provide a relaxed classroom atmosphere with wholesome teacher-pupil and pupil-pupil relationships that make every child feel secure and accepted.

Social conversations can take place during free periods or during ongoing activities in the classroom or on the playground. A small group of children may assemble around a learning center or bulletin board indoors or in the swings area or on the softball diamond outdoors. Their informal sharing of reactions in a small group makes it possible for children to respond freely, each in his or her own way. Even timid pupils are encouraged to enter into a small circle of participants.

When there are only two pupils instead of several, such a language experience can be termed a *dialogue*. Dialogue offers a combination of human closeness and immediacy of feedback that is appealing to children. Informal kinds of dialogue activity include the preparation by two pupils of a project, research assignment, or skit. More formal activity can develop questioning skills or inferences, as in the following examples from Klein:

1. The first child has a specific sense experience which he must then narrate to his partner. She in turn must select the correct olfactory, visual, auditory or tactile cue from a group of three or four such cues. She questions carefully.
2. The first child is shown how to make or do something, e.g., fit a part into a machine. The second child in the meantime has been given the necessary materials for the project. Now the first child must explain to his partner how to complete or do the job with the materials provided.[7]

Evaluation of Conversations

After some conversational experiences the children, with the help of their teacher, could ask themselves:

- Was our subject an interesting one? Did we keep to the subject?
- Were we careful listeners? How did we show we were interested in our classmates' ideas?
- Did everyone in our group have a turn to talk? If someone didn't have a turn, how can we invite him or her to talk the next time?
- Could we hear each speaker?
- Did someone use an "unusual" word in today's conversation?
- Since conversations often include something that is said only for fun, was anything said that made us smile or chuckle?

Discussion

Like conversation, discussion uses oral language in a small-group setting. Unlike conversation, however, its purpose concerns problem solving, critical thinking, and decision making. Sticking to the topic is a critical quality of a good discussion for the goal is to reach a conclusion. Conversations, on the other hand, generally meander from topic to topic, rarely probing for any in-depth coverage or final resolution.

The stress in discussion is on leadership skills, and in this regard, Wilcox's work with fifth and sixth graders from a low-income area is helpful. She studied the participation of students in classroom discussion under three different conditions: leadership by the teacher, leadership by an untrained student, and leadership by a student who had been given training on how to encourage active participation on the part of all the group members. Six classes were involved and the analysis of forty-five discussion sessions showed that group members led by students had a significantly higher rate of participation than the group members led by teachers. Also, the groups led by trained students displayed a different kind of participation (with more divergent and analytic acts) than groups led by teachers.[8]

Kinds of topics most appropriate for beginning discussion call for listing or enumeration ("How many different ways does an animal get food?" or "How can you tell what will cost a dollar and what will cost a dime?") which in turn leads to comparison topics by making the category either one of similarities or one of differences ("In what ways are cars and airplanes alike?" or "What are the differences between dogs and cats?"). A third kind of topic calls for chronology—planning an action or telling how something is made ("How can John get his bicycle back?" "How will we raise money to buy a record player for the classroom?" or "How should we go about building a miniature mission?").

One practical aspect for promoting good discussions involves seating arrangements. Greater and more effective interaction is promoted by face-to-face grouping patterns. There are both single-circle and double-circle arrangements. The *large single circle* of participants guided by a teacher or student leader often promotes one, two, or more *small single-circle spin-off groups*. These small groups meet for special interests or needs and later share their results with the large parent group. The *double-circle* or fishbowl arrangement involves an outer circle of listeners and an inner circle of talkers. Sometimes a variation of this pattern occurs when one or two empty chairs are added to the inner circle, thereby permitting one or two listeners to join the discussion briefly in order to raise a question or answer a query.

Other forms of discussion procedure include the round-table discussion, the panel discussion, and the buzz group. The *round-table discussion* generally involves between three and eight pupils. There is a moderator who guides the group, introduces the members, presents the problem (e.g., eliminating playground litter), and keeps the discussion moving. It can be used in the middle and upper grades by having one group discuss a problem before the rest of the class or by dividing the class into several small discussion groups that function without an audience.

The *panel discussion* is much like the round-table discussion but there are also some important differences. First, the procedure is more formal, usually opening with a short statement by each discussant. Second, there is a greater responsibility on the part of the panel members to prepare themselves for each panelist is considered to be a knowledgeable "expert" on the topic (e.g., nominating and electing the vice-president of the United States). Finally, panels are more audience-oriented than round tables with some provision being made for questions or participation by the observers at the end of the panel's presentation.

Buzz groups solicit suggestions, reactions, or comments to problems informally. There may or may not be leaders designated and conclusions reached. Still they are helpful in clarifying ideas and getting pupils to participate who might otherwise be reluctant or fearful. Since such brainstorming can readily get out of hand, however, standards must be established or reviewed before each buzz session.

Following a discussion the teacher and class might find it useful to evaluate the participants and the leader separately: Evaluation of
Discussion

Rating Scale

Did the discussion leader—	Did each participant—
1. State the problem or question correctly and in a manner that the class members could understand?	1. Understand the problem and keep in mind the purpose of the discussion?
2. Summarize important points brought out along the way?	2. Contribute his or her share of information and consider contrary ideas?
3. Skillfully keep the discussion progressing?	3. Listen attentively and critically?
4. Give a good summary and conclusion at the end of the discussion session?	4. Have an acceptable attitude toward suggestions?

The children could also evaluate their own roles by asking themselves silently:

- Did I participate today?
- Did I participate too much?
- How did I treat my classmates whose ideas differed from mine?
- Did I encourage someone who is very shy to add his or her ideas to the discussion? How?
- Was I able to ask questions which helped others to think?
- Did I make my point promptly?[9]

Debating

Debating can be successfully used with intermediate children who are well informed and good speakers. It provides them, explains Blake, with basic experience in democratic procedure and in disciplined evaluation and judgment on issues for which more than one solution is equally good.[10]

Debate is the presentation of arguments between two teams (often consisting of two members each) who represent positions in opposition to each other on a single issue. That issue or debate subject is termed the proposition, and it is stated briefly and affirmatively; for example, Resolved: Students shall be allowed to buy candy and soft drinks in the school cafeteria. The affirmative team supports the proposition; the negative team attacks it.

In a classic debate the constructive speeches by both sides appear first, followed by the rebuttal speeches by both sides which attack the opposing arguments. The order for four debaters, for example, would be as follows:

1. first affirmative—constructive speech
2. first negative—constructive speech
3. second affirmative—constructive speech
4. second negative—constructive speech
5. first negative—rebuttal speech
6. first affirmative—rebuttal speech

7. second negative—rebuttal speech
8. second affirmative—rebuttal speech

In this manner the affirmative team speaks first and last, and each debater presents one constructive speech, prepared in advance, as well as one rebuttal speech. The latter is more of an impromptu address, in which the speaker differs with the arguments and information of the opposing side while defending the arguments and information of his or her side.

The debate has a chairperson to introduce the topic and the team members to the audience, a timekeeper (elementary debates average thirty minutes), and judges to determine which side debated best and so won the debate. Often the judges include all the members of the class who are not debating.

Elementary school debates can be informally evaluated by asking:

Evaluation of Debating

- Was the proposition a significant issue?
- Were the constructive speeches carefully prepared?
- Could all the speakers be heard?
- Was sufficient time available for the contest?
- Was the judgment fairly determined?

Following Parliamentary Procedure

Parliamentary procedure is used universally wherever organized groups exist in order to help them carry on activities in an orderly and democratic manner. Like several other speech activities, parliamentary procedure is learned best by participation, and the elementary school is an ideal place to begin to practice the proper way to conduct a meeting. Activities that call for group decisions and require a presiding officer should be conducted within the framework of parliamentary procedure. Adaptation and informal use of many of the procedures in *Robert's Rules of Order Newly Revised* can be appreciated by pupils as early as the fifth grade, and some can be taught or incorporated as early as third grade. Even a first grader can be taught to raise his or her hand and not speak until recognized by the teacher.

The purposes of parliamentary procedures are fivefold. First, rules of order are meant to keep order where commotion and disorder are likely to occur. Second, rules of order are meant to keep things in proper sequence; sometimes known as rules of preference, they are also known as rules of precedence. Third, parliamentary procedure is intended to either delay or expedite action, depending upon the wishes of the group. Fourth, parliamentary procedure is designed so that the majority, sooner or later, will always win if there is a vote. Finally, parliamentary procedure protects the rights of the minority, and the chief right of the minority is that it might someday become the majority.[11]

In every grade the parliamentarian is the classroom teacher. Both the children and the parliamentarian must become familiar with five segments of procedure: *motions* ("I move that our class visit the Museum of Natural History to see the dinosaur exhibit."); *resolutions* ("Resolved that we thank the room parents for the Halloween party they gave us."); *amendments* ("I move to amend the motion about visiting the Museum of Natural History by adding the words 'on Saturday, March 14.' "); referral to *committees* problem topics that arise during class meeting ("I move to refer the motion about visiting the Museum of Natural History to a committee of three pupils appointed by our chairperson. I believe the committee should tell us its recommendation by Friday afternoon."); and *voting* on either an idea or a motion ("Would someone make a motion about how many classes we should invite to see our Christmas program?"). The sixth segment of parliamentary procedure—*the table of precedence of motions*—need only be understood in the elementary school by the parliamentarian.

When an intermediate teacher believes that students are ready to be organized as a club, he or she may act as chairperson until the club or class president has been elected. The president then asks for nominations for the remaining officers. After nominations have been closed, voting is done by the raising of hands or the marking of ballots. Later, after several meetings have been held, the officers and the other students in the room will probably conclude that much time could be saved if standard parliamentary procedures were used in conducting the meetings. It is then that the teacher quietly introduces some of these rules of order:

Calling the meeting to order: "The meeting of the _____ class (or club) will please come to order."

Reading of the minutes: "Will the secretary please read the minutes of the last meeting?"

Approving or correcting the minutes: "Are there any corrections or additions?"

Announcing the result: "The minutes are approved as read." (or) "The minutes are approved as corrected."

Asking for reports of committees: "We will now have a report of the _____ committee."

Approving reports of committees: "Is there any discussion of the report?" "The report is accepted."

Asking for announcements: "Are there any announcements to be made at this time?"

Asking about unfinished business: "Is there any unfinished business?"

Asking about new business: "Is there any new business to be brought up?"

Turning the program over to the program chairperson: "I shall now turn the meeting over to the program chairperson."

Ending the meeting: "If there is no further business, the meeting stands adjourned." Usually the chairperson ends the meeting but during the meeting any member can make a motion to adjourn at any time (provided the motion does not interrupt another speaker); once the motion has been seconded, the chairperson immediately calls for a vote.

As more club meetings are held, occasions will arise when points need clarification. Questions such as these could be used for additional discussion: (a) Why are the regular rules of order called parliamentary procedure? (b) How is a motion made? (c) What does the president say before a vote is taken? (d) When is it not necessary to address the chair? (e) When is it not necessary to rise? (f) How can you politely disagree with a classmate's proposal? and (g) How do club members show respect for authority.[12]

The teacher-parliamentarian will note the pupils' gradual development in the areas of social skills and speech skills. Critical points from both of these skills are incorporated into the criteria which children typically formulate—with the help of their teacher—for evaluating club meetings:

Evaluation of Club Meetings

- Are we following the rules of parliamentary procedure?
- Are the meetings worthwhile? Do they move smoothly?
- Are members courteous to one another? Do they show respect to the officers?
- Do members use well-planned sentences when presenting items of business? Do they speak convincingly?
- Are the club activities run by a minority or majority of the members?

Interviewing

Since the interview is one of the principal methods employed in obtaining first-hand information, the ability to conduct interviews should be a speech activity presented to children from their kindergarten year through the sixth grade.

Cowe distinguishes between informal and formal interviewing, explaining that the latter involves preplanning and the formulation of questions in advance by the group or individual pupil. She describes a kindergarten child who brought some wooden animals to show her classmates during the sharing period. The girl's presentation became more lucid as her friends *informally interviewed* her, inquiring casually (one at a time) about the origin, cost, and production of the animals. On the other hand, the anticipated visit to the kindergarten class by a room mother familiar with the Japanese New Year prompted a different and more formal sort of questioning. Queries developed by the group were first recorded on the chalkboard by the teacher and then copied by her on separate sheets of paper. Once each sheet had been distributed to the boy or girl who had developed the question, the interview began. Each child read his or her question independently or with some assistance and the resource visitor responded. A total of ten questions and answers comprised the *formal interview*.[13]

Young pupils can also use dramatic play for interviews between a child and a parent, a child and a teacher, and a child and the school principal. Later, after they have all interviewed each other, primary pupils can go out in small teams with a list of prepared questions to use in interviewing the media specialist, the cafeteria manager, the custodian, and other school workers. Their teacher may wish to help them develop another set of questions before inviting a police officer, fire fighter, or other community worker to visit the classroom for an interview. Slowly, the teacher and the children will begin to use the tape recorder as they conduct interviews.

Older classes can set up interviewing criteria and techniques and list these on charts. The pupils can interview foreign exchange students as well as parents or teachers who have recently visited other countries. Some of them can interview classroom committees that are preparing to report on a science project, or they can role play in social studies imaginary interviews between such personages as Sacagawea and Meriwether Lewis or William Clark. They can interview the principal for the school paper. They can dramatize a "Meet the Press" type of interview or conduct telephone interviews with persons in charge of local places of historical interest. Gradually they will become adept at using the tape recorder for self-evaluation of interviewing techniques.

Evaluation of Interviewing

After a make-believe interview conducted in class, the teacher and children should ask each other:

- Did the interviewer maintain a natural, easy posture?
- Was his or her voice audible?
- Did the interviewer get the information he or she wanted?
- Was the interviewer courteous?
- Did the interviewee help the interviewer?
- Was the interviewee in a hurry?
- Was the interview concluded properly?

Participating in Social Courtesies

The fundamentals of social conventions should be initially presented in the primary grades and then amplified in the intermediate grades. Telephone etiquette, informal introductions, proper table manners, and politeness toward others should be stressed early in the child's school life. Since most social conventions are accompanied by polite speech, teaching the proper conduct in a variety of situations is a responsibility of the language arts program.

Merely knowing what they are to do without experiencing a sufficient number of occasions to practice the social behaviors tends to make pupils self-conscious rather than secure. Consequently, opportunities to let the children use the newly learned courtesies must be furnished routinely. Confidence and social understandings grow best through realistic social experiences throughout the school year at every grade level.

The critical factor in the program is the teacher because courtesy is indeed contagious. The climate that the teacher creates in the classroom must be accepting and encouraging, helping the pupils to learn the pleasant and polite thing to do. Social behavior is learned chiefly by imitation. Knowledge about everyday courtesies contributes to the children's sense of security and orderliness.

Planned lessons about correct social behavior and thoughtfulness toward others will hopefully elicit the following generalizations:

- Social courtesies are genuine expressions of respect and regard for other persons.
- Basic good manners provide the individual with poise and personal satisfaction.
- The customs of good manners vary from place to place and change from time to time.
- Basic good manners depend upon honesty, tact, and common sense.

Social Skills and Attitudes

Included in this segment of speech activities is the development of courtesy in the classroom, courtesy in the school, and courtesy in the community. The first involves accepting personal responsibility for the completion of certain tasks and showing consideration for fellow members by adjusting one's personal desires for the common good. It also suggests ways of working together, solving group problems, and being a proper host or guest.

The second category—courtesy in the school—teaches consideration for the rights and property of others on the playground and in the halls, auditorium, and media center. It stresses thoughtfulness of others and respect toward teachers, administrators, and other staff personnel. It shows pupils how to be well mannered during assembly programs and lunch periods.

Courtesy in the community—the final group of social skills and attitudes—emphasizes awareness that good manners should be used wherever one happens to be. It teaches children to avoid conduct that might attract unfavorable attention to themselves when they are in the synagogue or church, in the neighborhood theater, in a public restaurant, or at the local supermarket.

Numerous occasions arising naturally both inside and outside the school demand the proper use of social skills by the young child: introducing a parent to the teacher during the first parent conference of the semester; acting as room host for an open house; ushering at an assembly program; winning a school award and accepting congratulations sincerely and simply; apologizing to the school secretary/nurse for being late in returning a medical slip; cordially accepting an invitation to a birthday celebration and then, awakening with a cold on the day of the party, telephoning excuses for not being able to attend; thanking neighbors while collecting papers during a scout drive; taking a telephone message for another family member; meeting a distant cousin who has just arrived from Australia; telephoning a friend about a homework assignment. In each of these instances, the child presumably reacts with poise and courtesy.

Introductions

Of the two areas of social courtesies that are especially studied in the elementary school, the first is the making and acknowledging of introductions. Boys and girls learn to introduce themselves to a new person or a new group by giving their names and stating something about themselves. When they are introducing a newcomer to others, they should remember to say something interesting about the new person or suggest a topic of conversation.

Children learn to handle introductions through role-playing sessions, especially if both correct and exaggeratedly incorrect procedures can be observed. Tape recordings of such activities may also prove helpful for later evaluation of the greetings and conversational topics selected. Since it is not sufficient for the pupils to merely memorize the correct wording and manner for making and acknowledging introductions, they should be allowed ample practice time before the class to demonstrate such situations as:

How Mike introduces his friend Dick Stern to
    James Thomas, a classmate
    Dr. Charles Kellogg, his uncle
    Kathleen Merritt, his sister
How Betty introduces her friend, Patty Ishizu, to
    Celeste Vodola, a classmate
    Ms. Amy Howard, her aunt
    Nick Hogan, her cousin
How Joanne introduces her mother, Mrs. Johnson, to
    Mr. John Miles, the principal
    Mrs. Janet Cohen, her teacher
    Joe Jordan, her girlfriend's brother

Older children can discuss practical criteria for making and receiving introductions. They also can prepare a chart illustrating proper techniques.

Telephoning

The second area of social courtesies suitable for study by young children is the use of the telephone. Conversing by telephone has become increasingly important in daily living, with the United States ranking first among the countries of the world served by telephone. There are approximately 125 million telephones in the country today, or about one telephone for every two persons. Although the public makes three kinds of telephone calls—local, long distance, and overseas—approximately 95 percent of the calls in the United States are local calls, which children can receive and place routinely. Pupils therefore should learn how to make and answer a telephone call, how to take messages, and why it is important to speak clearly and courteously.

To become familiar with the proper way of using the telephone, older children can be introduced to the teletrainer distributed by the local telephone company. The teletrainer is a relatively simple device, usually consisting of two telephones attached by approximately thirty-five feet of cord to an amplifying unit. The cord allows the phones to be passed around the room and since there are two phones, a typical conversation can take place. The amplifier permits the class to hear the conversation. The teacher has the added advantage of being able to control volume of voice with a special switch on the back of the amplifying unit as well as being able to control telephone rings, busy signals, and dial tone. The students who are speaking on either of the two telephones can hear themselves over the amplifier as well as through their individual phone units as they act out situations involving social, business, or emergency reasons for telephoning. They may call to obtain a dental appointment, to order ice cream for a class party, to wish their grandmother a happy birthday, to report a fire, or to obtain the new number of a former classmate who recently moved.

Primary children can learn to name the parts of the telephone and to recognize the dial tone, the busy signal, and the ordinary ringing sound. They can practice taking messages, learning to listen carefully for details, and repeating the message before writing it down. They can be made aware that there are different instrument models. Their teacher can help them develop an illustrated chart on telephone courtesy.

Older pupils can become proficient in using a telephone directory, including the classified section. They can determine the area codes of nearby towns as well as those of the major metropolitan centers such as Chicago (312), San Francisco (415), New York (212), Boston (617), New Orleans (504), and Los Angeles (213). They can prepare a class directory of pupils' names and telephone numbers. They can learn the proper way to handle wrong numbers that have been dialed by mistake either by themselves or by someone else. They can practice making long-distance calls, either by dialing direct or with operator assistance, to places within the United States or to foreign countries. Their teacher may plan a field trip to the local telephone building or invite a resource person from the telephone company to visit the class.

Intermediate grade pupils may wish to research and discuss such questions as: (a) Do all telephones need wires? (b) How does the weather affect the work of the telephone repairperson? (c) Why is the telegraph still used when it is so convenient to make a telephone call? (d) How would a picture phone (a telephone with a TV screen) operate? (e) How does the transmission of sound in a string-and-can telephone differ from the transmission of electricity in a real telephone? (f) How does the push-button type of telephone differ from the dial type? (g) Is it merely an inconvenience to be without a telephone?

Finally, older and younger boys and girls alike must be reminded not to reveal to a stranger on the telephone that they are home alone. Any and all information concerning their parents' whereabouts also should not be mentioned. Any child who is in doubt as to how much to tell on the telephone should remember to ask only for the stranger's name, telephone number, and brief message.

Pupil participation in evaluating how others use the telephone is probably the most effective way to promote good telephone usage. Among the more important criteria to be considered in rating a telephone conversation are these:

Evaluation of Telephone Conversation

- Did both parties listen as well as talk?
- Was identification of the caller made early in the conversation?
- Was the purpose of the call achieved to the satisfaction of both parties?
- Was the conversation courteous?
- Was the message clear?
- Did both parties use pleasant speaking tones?
- Was the call concluded politely and promptly?

Using Puppets

Acting through the medium of dolls is termed puppetry and it has existed as an entertaining and educative medium since the days of ancient China and Egypt. When the dolls are operated by strings, they are called marionettes and are suitable for manipulation by adolescents or adults. When they are worked directly by hand, the dolls are appropriate for manipulation by children and are called puppets. Elementary school language arts programs should be concerned with lessons involving puppets only.

The teacher should realize that puppetry is especially helpful for both shy and overaggressive pupils because puppeteers are generally hidden from their audience and so lose themselves in their characterizations. The attention of the audience is channeled away from the puppeteers to the puppets they are operating. In this fashion, the timid children lose some of their self-consciousness and the highly extroverted pupils become more restrained. Children suffering from such speech handicaps as defective articulation, stuttering, or loudness also benefit from repeated roles as puppeteers. They are motivated to practice correct speech patterns so that their puppets' conversations can be understood.

At any grade level beginning puppetry should revolve around the fun of using the puppets, and a wise teacher keeps a supply of inexpensive puppets available for this purpose. Later, after the children have become acquainted with puppetry and have learned to enjoy manipulating the figures, the teacher can assist them in making their own puppets. Even kindergarten children are capable of making and manipulating simple stick and hand puppets.

Steps in Classroom Puppetry

In preparing to give a show, it is first necessary to select a story which is suitable for the age of the puppeteers and their audience. The story should have numerous short lines, with no more than three characters performing simultaneously. It must be fast moving to sustain the attention of the viewers.

Next, the class must choose puppets that can best tell the story and begin to imagine how each puppet should look and act. While some groups will wish to make puppets of their own at this point, others may still prefer to use puppets from the teacher's supply or to bring puppets that have been made at camp, scout meetings, or summer recreational centers.

Thirdly, the boys and girls should discuss the dialog and try out different tonal qualities in order to match the voices with the characters. With children who are timid or inexperienced, this step will take a longer period of time than with fluent and resourceful pupils. Written scripts, however, are not necessary.

Fourthly, the puppeteers should set up the stage and manipulate the puppets. They must decide how to hold the figures and how to enter or exit from the stage. Manipulating puppets is not an easy chore and the job becomes even more difficult when lines are added to the actions.

The class is now ready to present the puppet show for a useful experience in creative action. Background scenery may be screened through the opaque projector. Sound effects, miniature portable properties, and music may also be added for variation and interest.

Finally the children and their teacher evaluate the performance. Suggestions for improving the manipulation of the puppets and the voices of the puppeteers are in order.

Since there should not be too many characters in a puppet show staged by or for elementary school pupils, the teacher may wish to encourage the class to write its own script. If the children should choose to do that, they have to realize that (1) all action must take place in the present; (2) each section must arise naturally from the preceding section; (3) the plot has to be brief and simple with a definite beginning, middle, and end; and (4) the characters must be faced with a problem whose solution brings conflict to the action of the play.

Suggested Stories for Puppetry

Sometimes, however, the teacher may find that the boys and girls prefer to adapt a literary story they have heard or read. Folk tales such as "The Story of the Three Little Pigs," "Snow White and the Seven Dwarfs," "Henny Penny," "Tom Tit Tot," "The Bremen Town Musicians," "The Three Billy Goat Gruff," "Gudbrand on the Hill-side," and "The Pancake" have simple plots that can be easily adapted for puppetry.

Other stories that lend themselves to interpretation include Lionni's *Alexander the Wind-up Mouse* (Pantheon, 1969) and *Frederick* (Pantheon, 1967), Hutchins' *Rosie's Walk* (Macmillan, 1968), Kipling's *The Elephant's Child* (Walker, 1970), and Travers' *Mary Poppins* (Harcourt, 1934).

Young children are capable of constructing a large variety of puppets, and their teachers can find simple directions for making puppets in books by Shari Lewis (1977), Lis Paludan (1975), Goldie Chernoff (1971), Eleanor Boylan (1970), M. C. Green and B. R. Targett (1969), and others. There are four major groups of puppets that boys and girls can fashion.

Puppets That Children Can Make

There are *push or table puppets* which are the easiest of all to operate and are recommended especially for early puppet dramatization. These small figures stand on their own. When a child wants such a puppet to perform in a moment of play, he or she will lift it by its head or push it along to its next position. This frees the puppeteer to concentrate on his or her oral expression. Children can readily use watercolors or construction paper to transform into a stationary puppet such a commonplace item as a bottle, can, block of wood, paper cone, water glass, balloon, or cup. They may also bring from home two-dimensional plastic man-like or animal-like figures to help in the development of stories about favorite poems or stories.

Another group includes the familiar *hand puppets,* which fit somewhat like gloves. The most common variety is worked by two fingers and the thumb. The pointer finger is projected into the neck while the fourth and little fingers remain in the palm of the hand. The heads of hand puppets may be made from a wide selection of commonplace and inexpensive materials, like fruits and vegetables, stuffed socks, rubber or styrofoam balls, stuffed napkins, papier-mâché, or small boxes. After the head is finished, the operator's hand is readily covered with a piece of colored fabric about the size of a man's handkerchief;

then rubber bands are slipped over the fingers to help define the arms, and the head is put into position.

Probably the simplest type of hand puppet from the standpoint of materials and construction is the paper-bag puppet. A sturdy bag such as a lunch sack is placed flat on the desk and colored with crayons. When it is time for a performance, the bag is slipped over the entire hand without making allowance for puppet arms. The children must remember, however, that the mouth opening always falls on the fold of the bag so that the underside of the flap is the inside of the mouth. For the advanced type of paper-bag puppet the head is stuffed with torn newspapers or paper toweling to create a three-dimensional effect.

Another kind of hand puppet is the finger puppet which usually slips over an individual finger. Properly cut, a finger puppet can also slip up onto the second knuckles of two fingers so that the puppet walks. Finger puppets can be made from rolled cylinders of construction paper, from toilet-paper rolls, or even from mittens. Face and body features can be added with crayons, marking pens, or other materials.

A third and large category of puppets is composed of the *stick puppets,* which consist of pictures, drawings, objects, or push puppets attached to sticks. Each is animated by moving the stick up and down or from side to side. Types of sticks include tongue depressors, yardsticks, pencils, broomsticks, dowel sticks, and narrow plywood. Hand-puppet heads may also be mounted on sticks for quick puppetry.

When a stick puppet has two sticks instead of the usual one, it is known technically as a rod puppet. The second stick or rod is attached to a jointed arm or head. Operators of such puppets must be capable of using both their hands skillfully as they simultaneously deliver their lines. Consequently, rod puppeteers are generally mature sixth graders.

The fourth and final group of puppets useful in the elementary curriculum are the *shadow puppets.* An extension of the stick puppets, they are distinct, flat figures that have been cut from stiff paper or tagboard and may be jointed or unjointed. When placed between a bright light (such as that from a slide projector or a 200-watt bulb) and a translucent screen and provided with sticks for manipulation, they cast clear shadows. Most shadow puppets are black and white, although colored effects may be obtained by means of colored cellophane placed over the light source or through the use of a colored bulb. Another method of projecting shadow puppets is to hold them flat on the "stage" of an overhead projector.

While facial expressions are obviously invisible on shadow puppets, they are critical to push, hand, and stick puppets. The teacher must therefore impress upon the students the importance of building character into the faces of the puppets they construct and decorate. Incidentally, the teacher should also stress the importance of saving all remnant pieces of items that could be used in future puppet-making projects. Such leftover bits can go into a large cardboard box for the production of so-called "junk-box puppets."[14]

The stage and the staging for a puppet show should be as uncomplicated as possible. Elaborate preparations are beyond the scope of young children. There is a variety of temporary stages which the pupils can make quickly as well as some more permanent stages whose construction requires the assistance of parents and/or teachers.

At least four temporary stages are readily and inexpensively assembled. The first is a *table stage*. When a rectangular table is placed on its side with the top part facing the audience, a large piece of cloth is strung as a curtain around the sides and front of the stage and the puppeteers crouch behind the curtain in order to operate the puppets from below. If two tables are available, one can be turned on its side on top of the other; then the front and sides of the bottom table can be wrapped with butcher paper or with cloth to hide the puppeteers from the audience. A bookcase or portable chalkboard properly covered also provides a good stage surface.

The second type of temporary stage is a *box stage*. A large cardboard appliance box is used and the upper half of its front is cut back so that the puppeteers can enter from the rear. The box is then painted and some type of anchor applied to prevent the box from tipping over. Should a smaller grocery carton be available, the back of the carton is completely removed and the front is cut to give the effect of a curtain drape. After the box has been painted, a table is covered with a sheet or blanket and the back edge of the carton is placed along the back edge of the table; the puppeteers then kneel behind the table and are hidden from view. Even a shoe box can become the stage for puppets of suitable size.

The *doorway stage* is a third kind of temporary stage. A single drape, sheet, or blanket is fastened to a rod or is thumbtacked across an open doorway so that it reaches the floor. It is attached at a point one inch above the heads of the puppeteers so the players can remain completely hidden, even when they stretch their arms to show their puppets. When a pair of drapes or sheets can be found, the shorter one is hung so that it falls from the top of the doorway and leaves a twenty-to-thirty-inch opening, and the second one is hung down to the floor. The puppeteers reach up to work the figures in the opening.

A fourth stage is a *chair stage*. A board may be placed across the top of two chairs placed back to back and a blanket draped over the board. Should an overstuffed chair be available, the puppeteer can kneel on its seat and manipulate the puppets so that they are visible to an audience facing the back of the chair.

There are at least three kinds of more permanent stages that take longer to construct and are more costly to assemble. The first of these is a *wooden stage,* and some teachers like to have one wooden theatre in the room for use throughout the year. It is built of plywood or wallboard and can include curtains and floodlights as well as backdrops that are fastened to the theatre by a rod for easy changes. The height of the stage opening from the floor will depend on whether the puppeteers sit or stand as they use the figures.

Some teachers may desire a wooden stage that rests on a table. They should realize that it is possible to build a basic frame of two upright one-by-eight-inch planks, putting one plank at each end of the table and then attaching four angle brackets to each plank. The frame can even be moved to tables of different thicknesses by adjusting the angles with a screwdriver. Brown wrapping paper is taped to the edge of the table to hide the feet of the participating pupils, and the stage has both a scenic curtain and a concealing curtain.

Other arrangements evolve from a wooden box of suitable size. For instance, one of the wider sides can be removed and sawed into about half lengthwise, with one of the two pieces nailed under the box to form a shelf that extends a few inches; then a piece of tagboard is attached to the front of the stage to give the effect of a curtain. In another instance, the bottom side can be knocked out; then the box is placed on its side and stick legs are nailed to each of the four corners. Finally, cloth is draped and tacked around the sticks.

A second stage is a *screen stage* which uses a three-fold screen. An opening is made into the upper part of the middle section, and the puppeteers operate their figures from a sitting position below the level of the bottom of that opening. The two side sections of the screen are perpendicular to the middle section in order to hide the puppeteers. A curtain can be drawn across the open part of the theatre.

The *tray stage* is especially portable, but useful to only one puppeteer at a time. It is made from the shallow top cover of a cardboard box which has been painted. Two holes which are large enough to accommodate the hands of the puppeteer are cut into the box cover. A large piece of ribbon or string is then attached to each of four corners of the box top. The puppeteer carries the tray around his or her neck, making sure the cover stays parallel to the floor, and the puppets are ready to perform on their tiny stage.

Properties for both the permanent and temporary stages should be few and restricted to essentials, with all other items painted on the inside of the stage or on the backdrop. The scenery should be suggestive rather than realistic, with careful attention paid to the matter of size in relation to the height of the puppets. It is paramount that the figures and not the background dominate any puppet stage.

| Evaluation of Puppetry | The teacher can readily evaluate the progress of the boys and girls in using puppets by asking: |

The teacher can readily evaluate the progress of the boys and girls in using puppets by asking:

- Do the children show increasing ability in handling puppets?
- Are their overall speech patterns becoming consistent in speaking for a particular puppet?
- Can they make up adventures for an inanimate figure?
- Does the use of puppets stimulate interest in developing sentence sequence?
- Is there increasing variety and quality in creative puppet dialog?
- Are the children whose speech sounds are sometimes defective, distorted, or omitted, gaining incentive to improve their speech?

A national study based on a random demographic sample of about 40,000 school pupils showed that 12 percent have moderate communicative disorders.[15] In 1974 the state of New Mexico published the results of its own survey which identified almost 8 percent of its school-age population as being speech impaired. And neither of these figures includes incidence of communicative disorders among the learning disabled, physically handicapped, emotionally disturbed or mentally retarded, which would surely raise the percentages considerably. Although estimates do vary, the largest single group of handicapped children in the nation's schools, claims the U.S. Office of Education, are those with speech disorders.

Speech is defective, according to Van Riper, when it deviates so far from the speech of other people that it calls attention to itself, interferes with communication, or causes its possessor to be maladjusted.[16] Briefly, it is conspicuous, unintelligible, or unpleasant.

Byrne and Shervanian have developed criteria for evaluating the level of an individual's communication skill based on social acceptability:

1. Does the individual function with adequate linguistic skill in his or her own speech community? (If the answer is yes, then go on to evaluative question 2.)
2. Does the individual function with adequate linguistic skill outside his or her own speech community? (Again, if the answer is yes, go on to evaluative question 3.)
3. Are there any minor differences in the speech patterns of the individual that contribute to social differences that in turn lead to social devaluation or reduction of status? (If the answer is no, the individual's communication can be rated as adequate or possibly superior.)[17]

Should a child be unable to function linguistically in his or her own community, the chances are slight that he or she will be able to do so outside that community, such as in a school situation.

Consequently, it is important that elementary teachers be able to identify speech disorders and refer speech-handicapped children. Studies have shown that the percentage of accurate referrals tends to rise as the severity of the disorder increases. Teachers are most accurate in referring stutterers (or children suffering from dysfluency) because interruptions in speech fluency and the accompanying mannerisms tend to interfere with the communication process to a greater extent than do most other speech disorders. Teachers are least accurate in referring children with voice disorders because such disorders often do not affect speech intelligibility.

Teachers must have a tolerant attitude toward the speech-defective children in their classrooms. If they say nothing, they are indicating that the children's speech is not noticeably objectionable. This creates the most favorable environment for the speech-handicapped pupils whose peers then accept them readily. On the other hand, the teacher who demands unusually high standards of speech behavior, with little tolerance for individual deficiencies, tends to generate reduced acceptance of the speech-defective children by their class-mates.

In a school district with an adequate number of speech therapists, the elementary teacher can and should work closely with the clinicians in helping speech-handicapped children gain intelligible speech. He or she can help these pupils develop a sense of carry-over in their speech correction activities from the speech class to the regular classroom and can quietly urge the children to focus attention daily on the sound or sounds which the therapist is presenting. Through teacher-and-speech-correctionist conferences, the teacher can provide information regarding the strengths and weaknesses of the children referred from his or her classroom. Finally, the teacher can report to the therapist any progress the children are making, and together they can plan an approach for speech reeducation which will hopefully provide maximum success for the pupils.

In school districts with relatively few speech therapists the classroom teacher can include speech correction in lesson plans by employing one of these practices:

1. A weekly speech period plan which sets aside a specific period of time every week for concentration on the skills of speech
2. An adaptive instruction plan which schedules remedial speech lessons during periods when other pupils are engaged in reasonably self-directed study

The elementary teacher will ordinarily encounter one or more of the four common groups of speech deficits in the classroom: disorders of articulation, disorders of voice, disorders of fluency, and language disorders/delayed language. The teacher will want to do whatever possible to help the pupils with speech problems by assisting those with minor cases and referring those with more serious disorders to speech clinicians. Some children will, of course, have deficiencies in more than one dimension of speech.

Disorders of Articulation

Speech surveys in the public schools have indicated that most children with speech problems fall into the category of speech disorders classified as problems of articulation. As many as 80 percent of all speech problems found in the elementary classroom will concern those pupils who cannot make certain phonetic sounds either within blends with other phonetic sounds or in isolation.[18] The largest proportion of these problems occurs in the population of grades one through three, and the incidence decreases continuously through grade six. Children who have difficulty in articulation are not able to produce consistently and effortlessly the accepted sound patterns of speech. Instead, they may form some sounds poorly (making distortion errors), leave some sounds out completely (making omission errors), add sounds in either the medial or final position of words (making addition errors), or exchange one sound for another (making substitution errors), as they find that there are some sounds, such as *s, r, th, l,* and *z,* that seem to be harder to learn than others. Of the four categories, the predominant type of misarticulation—at least among primary children—is simple substitution, according to a three-year survey of Caucasian pupils in a Chicago suburb.[19]

Articulation problems are classified as *organic* when they erupt from abnormalities of the organs or systems of speech and as *functional* when they are deemed to represent abnormal behavior developmental patterns related to faulty learning. Organic causes include (1) central nervous system pathologies (such as multiple sclerosis and cerebral palsy); (2) structural anomalies of the organs of articulation (including cleft palate and dental abnormalities); (3) reduced hearing levels due to a pathology of the end organ of hearing (such as a loss resulting from measles or viral diseases); and (4) emotional disorders. Functional impairments that may or may not be of organic origin, are linked to such factors as motor skills, oral sensation, auditory discrimination, intelligence, mental age, and socioeconomic status within an overall context of *faulty learning*. Stimulability and consistency of correct sound production in a variety of acoustic situations are also involved in functional articulation disorders.

The Office of Child Development of the U.S. Department of Health, Education, and Welfare offers these suggestions to the parents and teachers of children with disorders of articulation:

1. Let speech be fun by letting the children know that you like to hear them talk and that you like to talk to them by playing games with sounds and words and by telling them stories and reading aloud to them.
2. Build up their feelings of success about speech by letting them use the few words or phrases that they have been practicing at times when the words are easy for them and by praising them for trying to talk.
3. Help them to learn new speech skills through imitation and ear training by choosing sounds or words that fit in with daily activities and by showing them how those sounds are made.

Disorders of Voice

Speech is made up of tones and noises, and in articulation, noises are added and tones are modified. Sometimes, however, the tones themselves may be defective, varying too far from the norm to be deemed acceptable. There may be impairment of the tones, partial loss or (rarely) complete loss. Among 40,000 school pupils surveyed nationally, 3.1 percent had extreme voice deviations.

Such deviations are associated with faulty pitch, loudness, or quality of voice or with the absence of vocalization. *Physical* determinants are three-fold: (1) structural defects in the larynx (resulting in breathiness, huskiness or hoarseness); (2) damage or maldevelopment in the central or peripheral nerves innervating the larynx (resulting in pitch, loudness, and quality disorders); and (3) hearing loss necessary for monitoring feedback control of voice production (resulting in speech that is too loud or too soft for conversation). Accountable for functional voice disorders are the factors of faulty training or poor adjustment to the environment.

The Office of Child Development suggests that parents and teachers of children with disorders of voice: (a) refer children for medical examinations; (b) help them to relax by easing tensions and pressures in the environment; (c) give them a chance to talk without interruption so that they need not strain their voices; (d) help the children find a pitch level that is comfortable for them, changing the pitch of their own adult voices if necessary since the children may imitate them; and (e) discuss "voice rests" with a speech specialist, for the children's problems may be serious enough to require a period of silence.

Disorders of Fluency

A frequent disruption in the relative continuity or fluency of speech is known as *stuttering*. It is marked with repetitions and prolongations of syllables and sounds and by hesitancies in the utterance of syllables, sounds, and words. Sometimes there are interjections of unneeded sounds as well as associated lip, eye, or head movements.

The problem of stuttering typically appears between the ages of three and five, after the child has begun to make great strides toward fluency. Boys are much more likely than girls to become stutterers—by a ratio of three or four to one—and twins of both sexes seem to stutter more than other persons. No matter what language is spoken, about 1 percent of the population in Western countries has a stuttering disorder.

In the elementary school the grades with the greatest number of stutterers are the second grade followed by the fifth grade. Teachers and parents, however, should realize that many children who are diagnosed as stutterers recover spontaneously.

It has been suggested that stuttering is a learned response, a behavior that stutterers have acquired in order to avoid stuttering. Stutterers generally anticipate when they are going to stutter, recognizing for example the certain words (known as Jonah words) that usually give them trouble in ordinary conversation. In an effort to avoid an episode, they increase the tension in the speech mechanism and thereby disrupt their breathing patterns. Stutterers may be fluent when talking to themselves, to animals, or to those in a lower status position (younger children, for instance). On the other hand, they are apt to stutter on the telephone or when talking to an indifferent audience.

The onset of stuttering is insidous, making it hard for teachers or parents to pinpoint it. Furthermore, although stuttering has had a comparatively long history and there has been more research in this area of speech disorders than in any other, no one yet knows what causes it. Faulty learning appears to be an important factor however.

Though many people have feelings of pity and embarrassment toward stutterers, current trends to mainstream handicapped children may have some positive effects on changing attitudes. One study showed that elementary school boys did not differentiate (in ranking social position) between classmates who stuttered and those who were fluent speakers.[20] The pupils were aware of the defect but simply evaluated stutterers as poorer speakers than peers who did not stutter.

The classroom teacher, in an effort to help stuttering children, should attempt to:

1. Create an environment which encourages talking.
2. Offer positive feedback.
3. Provide a selection of individualized learning activities (e.g., learning centers or student contracts).
4. Encourage participation in creative drama.
5. Help them develop realistically positive opinions of themselves.
6. Make talking enjoyable and rewarding.
7. Encourage participation in a variety of school activities.

Teachers and parents alike must understand that any environment which pressures children beyond their tolerance levels can and does contribute to speech dysfluency.

Language Disorders/Delayed Language

Language disorders of children represent departures from an orderly sequence in learning the language code. Delayed language, on the other hand, infers that the orderly sequence was followed but language development is not appropriate to the chronological age of the user. Both are major causes of learning disabilities.[21]

Children with language disorders suffer from poor auditory discrimination, poor auditory sequencing, and defects of auditory memory. They have difficulty either with receptive language or with expressive language. They are divided into the hearing-impaired, the neurologically-impaired, and the environmentally-deprived. They show a peak of development well below their chronological age; e.g., at age five they may still be using incorrect pronouns. Some of them use syntactic structures that differ from those of children of their age group in terms of complexity, variety, and correctness. There are also morphological problems; e.g., all inflections are omitted. Pupils may not have learned the rule for contractions.

Children whose language is delayed know the rules consistent with their level of development. They are learning the grammar in an orderly sequence but they are doing so at a slower pace than other children in their age group. They use the proper inflections for regular plurals and regular past tense verbs, for example, but they overgeneralize those endings to other plurals and verbs. They can also use the simple affirmative-declarative sentences with some transformations but are incapable of the advanced degree of embeddings and coordination that they should be using.

There is then a distinction between the two groups. One either does not have a set of rules or has such a set and applies it incorrectly. The other group knows the rules consistent with its level of development but has not learned to apply the rules correctly in all instances.

To help these children it has been recommended that teachers continue to:

1. Be sensitive to individual needs, providing a program that is relevant to current social, economic, and cultural patterns of speech-retarded children.

2. Create a pleasant and stimulating atmosphere in which learning can occur.
3. Offer an individually determined curriculum, incorporating the children's weaknesses and strengths.
4. Encourage the children to want to talk and to talk more clearly.
5. Teach them new sounds and then put the new sounds together to make whole words.

Evaluation of Pupils' Progress

In the critical field of speech arts, evaluative techniques vary among the numerous facets of the skill. As a consequence, methods of evaluation have been described at the conclusion of the discussion of each facet. The reader may wish to review these techniques briefly at this point.

Discussion Questions

1. How would you propose to resolve some of the problems created by the sound system of English during the sequence of speech development in children?
2. Show-and-tell should be a purposeful speech art. What guidelines might help the primary teacher who uses this activity?
3. Why is puppetry enjoyed by so many children?
4. How can the classroom teacher help children afflicted with any one of the speech defects?

Suggested Projects

1. Examine some of the free materials available from the telephone company. Plan a lesson involving their use.
2. Make a puppet that a third grader could construct and manipulate as well as an adult does. Then assemble a temporary stage and demonstrate how that puppet moves and talks.
3. Interview the speech clinician in a local school. Learn what types of speech problems are encountered and what kinds of remedial procedures are used.
4. Plan a beginning lesson in parliamentary procedure for fifth graders. Rewrite some of *Robert's Rules of Order Newly Revised*.
5. Begin a card file of common situations involving speech arts. Arrange cards by major headings such as interviewing.
6. Set up the learning center on speech shown in Figure 8.5.

Related Readings

Anastasiow, N., and Hanes, M. 1976. *Language Patterns of Poverty Children*. Springfield, Illinois: Charles C Thomas, Publisher.

Bloom, L., and Lahey, M. 1977. *Language Development and Language Disorders*. New York: John Wiley and Sons.

Brown, M. E. 1977. "A Practical Approach to Analyzing Children's Talk in the Classroom." *Language Arts* 54: 506–510.

Currell, D. 1975. *The Complete Book of Puppetry*. Boston: Plays, Inc.

Johnson, G. F. et al. 1978. "Multidays: Multidimensional Approach for the Young Stutterers." *Language, Speech, and Hearing Services in Schools* 9: 129–32.

Jonas, G. 1977. *Stuttering*. New York: Farrar, Strauss and Giroux.

McClanahan, T. 1978. "Puppet Fever." *School Arts* 77: 10–13.

Figure 8.5. Language Arts Learning Center: Speech Improvement in the Kindergarten.

TYPE OF CENTER: Literature	TIME: Unlimited
GRADE LEVEL: Kindergarten	NUMBER OF STUDENTS: 1–5

INSTRUCTIONAL OBJECTIVE: Listening to a tape of well-known Mother Goose Rhymes, the children will be able to repeat them along with the tape.

MATERIALS: Mother Goose characters, Mother Goose books or sheets, a cassette tape recorder and earphones.

DIRECTIONS: (To Teacher)
Demonstrate the use of the tape recorder. It should be ready to play with only the push of a button.

SUGGESTED SCRIPT: Hello! I am Mother Goose. If you listen carefully you will hear me say rhymes about some of my children. If you know a rhyme, say it with me. Let's begin with Mistress Mary who is on the center before you. Are you ready?

Mistress Mary quite contrary, etc.

Now look at the second character on the center. Do you recognize him? Let's say the rhyme together:

Humpty Dumpty, etc.

(Other rhymes can be added to the tape and the children referred to pages in the Mother Goose book for the pictures and rhymes or to individual sheets with the rhymes and pictures.

EVALUATION: The teacher will note if the children enjoy the tapes and repeat the rhymes as recorded. The teacher may work with groups asking what rhymes were enjoyed and suggest acting out these.

Source: From *Language Arts Learning Centers and Activities* by Angela Reeke and James Laffey. Copyright 1979 by Goodyear Publishing Company. Reprinted by permission.

Skinner, P. H., and Shelton, R. L. 1978. *Speech, Language, and Hearing: Normal Processes and Disorders.* Reading, Mass.: Addison-Wesley Publishing Co.

Tough, J. 1977. *The Development of Meaning: A Study of Children's Use of Language.* New York: Halsted Press.

Trosky, O. S., and Wood, C. 1976. "Discussion: A Chance for Everyone." *Elementary School Journal* 76: 296–301.

Handwriting 9

The primary goal of handwriting instruction

Signs of handwriting readiness

Why manuscript writing is taught first

Typewriting in the elementary school

The modern handwriting program in the elementary school incorporates numerous research findings as it stresses the following principles.

Handwriting is primarily a tool of communication. It is a means to an end. Handwriting is a human skill and an individual tool whose ultimate purpose is to facilitate effective communication of ideas and feelings in written form. Consequently, from the beginning of instruction the pupils must write material that is meaningful and important to them. They should have regular help in writing specific alphabetic letters or groups of letters, followed by ample opportunity to practice under supervision.

Children who write for a valid reason and not just as a mechanical task (and even copying from the chalkboard or book can be made purposeful) accept the importance of handwriting. They recognize that if their writing is so illegible that what they have written cannot be read, their attempts at communication have failed. Teachers must therefore always strive to present a good model of handwriting for the pupils or else the teachers' personal inadequacies will be promptly imitated by the children. Yet teachers' handwriting is reportedly less legible today than it was in the past since there is less time available in today's teacher-education courses for future teachers to learn to handwrite legibly.[1]

Handwriting is part of the integrated program of language arts. It extends into all written work, and attention to it throughout the school day is necessary to achieve the best development in the writing skills. Although special handwriting periods are necessary to attain and maintain the desired efficiency levels, instruction and practice provided during these periods must incorporate the needs of children in practical writing situations related to their reading, spelling, or social studies.

Writing is linguistic expression, and studies have shown positive correlations between abilities in the various language arts although the extent to which

A child must learn to recognize handwriting as an individual tool of expression that serves important needs in writing letters, stories, and reports. (Photo courtesy of Jean-Claude Lejeune.)

these correlations increase or decrease as pupils mature is a matter not clearly established. Many of the interrelationships present are likely due to the presence of common elements in each facet, as well as to the fact that an experience which affects one cannot be isolated from the others. Genuine interrelated learning would seem to result best from an instructional program that teaches all of the language arts in a communication framework, while recognizing the need for directing teaching attention to specific skills.

Handwriting is an individual production which is influenced by physical, mental, and emotional factors. The development of handwriting skill is closely related to the total growth and development of the individual, and while some children learn to write easily and quickly, others will find handwriting a more laborious task. Teachers who recognize that children's growth patterns are not identical will not insist that every child meet the same standard of achievement. Instead, they will allow each pupil to develop his or her own optimum rate of writing and level of writing pressure, and encourage handwriting practices which are adjusted to individual differences in motor control. These teachers will allow an individual show of readiness to precede each step in the writing process. They will also insist gently that each child develop his or her own style of handwriting—within limits of legibility and speed.

Since the motor control that plays such a large part in learning to write neatly is not highly correlated with intelligence or scholastic achievement, high skill in handwriting may be possible for many children who do not have widespread academic success. It can serve them as a much-needed source of feelings of adequacy and thereby aid development of a sense of industry.

Handwriting lessons for both slow and fast learners in the intermediate grades should emphasize individualized practice on only those letters which have proven troublesome. Otherwise, the children will lack a strong incentive to improve their writing skills.

Legibility is the primary goal in teaching handwriting. Plain and simple legibility rather than beauty of style is the goal of teaching handwriting today. Legibility has been defined as the ease with which something can be read. The first essential of legibility is correct letter formation; the second, proper spacing of letters and words.

Since the primary purpose of handwriting instruction is to help the learner acquire the ability to produce legible handwriting with economy of time and effort, the classroom teacher will be interested in an investigation completed in Wisconsin of 588 handwriting samples written by fourth-, fifth-, and sixth-grade children.[2] The investigation concluded that there is a relationship between legibility and size (with the more legible sample being the larger writing) and between legibility and slant uniformity (with the more legible sample having a more uniform slant). Both boys and girls improved their legibility as they moved from the fourth grade to the sixth grade; simultaneously they also wrote smaller and showed an increase in size uniformity. Girls wrote better than boys.

Speed (without loss of legibility) is the secondary goal in teaching handwriting. The speed of handwriting is a flexible, relative, and highly individual matter, as is any other facet of the writing act, and receives emphasis only after certain standards of legibility have been attained. Since no end is served by making letters, words, and sentences rapidly but illegibly, attention to speed is not only useless but harmful until letter formation is spontaneously good.

Although speed is never a factor in the early grades, from grade three through grade six there is a consistent increase in the speed of writing in both manuscript and cursive styles.

Pupils become aware of the fact early in their schooling that there may be a difference in legibility when handwriting is done for their own use and/or under the pressure of speed, and when handwriting is done for others and/or without pressure of time. In the fourth, fifth, and sixth grades girls write more rapidly than boys and left-handed and right-handed writers show no significant difference in writing speed. Furthermore, in these grades fast writing is associated with higher pressure and greater force variability. If a student is forced to write faster than his or her usual comfortable rate, then the legibility of his or her handwriting will almost certainly deteriorate because the motor set is disturbed and variation in application of force is likewise increased.

While a tool subject such as handwriting should be done as efficiently as possible, writing speed may be stepped up only to the point where a reasonable degree of legibility can be maintained.

Well-planned lessons develop proficiency in handwriting. Handwriting is definitely a skill and improves with proper systematic instruction rather than with a program which leaves learning to chance. Most schools teaching handwriting, therefore, offer it five times a week in the primary grades and three times a week in the higher grades. Class periods average ten to twenty minutes at all grade levels, with shorter periods of carefully planned lessons being more effective than longer periods of random practice. In England recently, research revealed the extent of handwriting activity reported by 936 schools sampled for their six- and nine-year-old pupils. Twelve percent of the younger children and 21 percent of the older ones had *no* time allocated for handwriting. In most schools with both age groups, class-based work occupied at best thirty minutes a week and only 20 percent of the pupils were encouraged to practice handwriting during their free time, with again a limit of thirty minutes per week.[3]

Copying is more effective than faded tracing in promoting correct letter formation behavior.[4] And the rhythmic count, incidentally, is ineffective as a teaching procedure because research reveals that rhythmic pattern or timing does not exist in handwriting.

The greatest single factor in determining the nature of the instructional program in handwriting in a given school is the commercial system of handwriting instruction that is used. Seventy-five to 80 percent of all school systems in the nation rely on a commercial system as the basis for their programs of handwriting instruction. While there have been reported to be at least twenty-six different systems that are regarded by their users as appropriate for instruction in handwriting (and more teachers use manuals for the instruction of manuscript than those who use them to teach cursive writing), only sixteen are complete programs specifically intended for handwriting instruction, and, of these, four are used by a majority of the schools. More than half the states have requirements for the institution of handwriting programs at the local level and adopt or approve textbook series for that purpose; these states have approved sixteen different commercial systems. Since the various handwriting programs show considerable divergence in letter forms, sequence in the introduction of letters, and recommended teaching practices, the classroom teacher using a commercial system should be thoroughly familiar with the guides, alphabet cards, and all other materials furnished by that system in order to plan lessons properly and supervise handwriting activities carefully.

One such popular, commercially prepared system was compared recently to a program using a planned series of lessons presented through educational television. In a study involving more than 2,500 third graders in Virginia, it was concluded, after approximately one semester, that the teaching of transitional cursive handwriting by means of television was better than the method traditionally used in elementary classrooms, according to scores attained on the Freeman Cursive Handwriting Scale, Grade 3.[5]

Each pupil must develop correct posture, correct hand movement, and proper position of writing paper and handwriting tools. Good posture and position in writing influence the ease and quality of performance and are essential to the general health of the child. To further facilitate instruction, handwriting tools must be suited to the developmental characteristics of children at each grade level.

One of the most important physical factors affecting the individual handwriter is the matter of the table or desk and his or her position with respect to it. The table or desk should be of a height comfortable for the pupil with a writing surface that is smooth and flat. It should be positioned, if at all possible, so that the light falls over the child's left shoulder if he or she is right-handed (or over the right shoulder if the child is left-handed). The child should face the table or desk squarely, leaning slightly forward, hips touching the back of the seat, both feet flat on the floor. Both arms should rest on the writing surface at equal distances from the body but elbows should be off the surface to permit free arm movement.

Proper positioning of the writing paper is another important factor in preparing to write comfortably and well. For manuscript writing, the right-handed student places the paper on the desk or table squarely in front of him or her, with the left or writing edge of the paper even with the midsection of the body; the left-handed child tilts the paper up and toward the right so that the lower-right corner is slightly to the left of the body's midsection. During cursive writing, the right-handed student tilts the paper toward the left so that the lower edge of the writing surface and the lower edge of the paper form a thirty-degree angle; the left-handed pupil tilts the paper toward the right (about thirty-five to forty-five degrees) so that the lower-right corner of the paper points either toward the body's midsection or to the right of the midsection. Whatever the handedness, the nonwriting hand should be on the paper, shifting it to keep the writing area clearly visible to the pupil.

Each pupil must develop the ability to evaluate his or her own handwriting. Establishment of self-defined goals in writing creates improved penmanship and seems to result in a higher aspiration level. Progress in handwriting may be determined in terms of legibility or product readability, ease of the writing act, and speed.

Self-evaluation is especially important since relatively few teachers at present make use of handwriting scales.

Writing Readiness

A structured readiness program that meets each child's special abilities and needs is as essential to the successful beginning of writing as it is to a successful start in reading or mathematics. Such a readiness program for young writers should be based on the following:

1. Development of the intricate muscular control and hand-eye coordination necessary for beginning writing.
2. Development of the spoken language upon which the writing must be based.
3. Appreciation and understanding of the value and special uses of writing as a means of communication and expression.

Many years ago Maria Montessori, after extensive experimental work with young children, stated that learning to write demands both intelligence and an efficient motor mechanism. Children acquire mental readiness through experiences that reveal the value of handwriting and promote interest in learning to write. They attain motor readiness through activities that enable them to learn to hold the writing tools and to perform the simple movements required.

Some of the experiences that prepare for handwriting are acquired informally during preschool years as children engage in play and in the ongoing activities of the home. Generally children who participate with other children and use their hands continuously develop the types of motor control and visual discrimination that are needed for initial writing activities. Should they come from homes where little or no writing ever occurs, their preparation for learning to write is largely motor and sensory. Should they be reared in homes where writing is commonplace, they come to school more or less familiar with the writing act and may even be keenly interested in learning to write. Due to wide differences in rates of development, children from each kind of home environment will vary greatly in their readiness for writing when they start school.

Some of the activities in the regular school program can be utilized for the development of writing readiness, and the teacher should plan whole-class, small-group, and individual activities in which each child has repeated opportunities to manipulate many of the following materials:

primary crayons and paper
primary pencils and paper
chalk
scissors, both left- and right-handed
clay and plasticine
rulers
sewing cards
weaving looms
beads and string
snap blocks and Tinker Toys
sandpaper letters
woodworking tools
rhythm instruments
templates
finger paint
brushes and easel paper
Montessori dressing forms: snapping frame, zipper frame, shoe-lacing
    frame, large-button frame, and bow-tying frame

Children develop motor control through the use of games, building blocks, and modelling clay. With their teacher's help they also become acquainted with some of the materials used in writing, as they crayon, cut paper, and work at the easel. Consequently, handwriting may well emerge as an art form in the children's life experiences.

The kindergarten or first-grade teacher is aware of the importance of writing readiness. The teacher tells or reads stories and poems, encouraging the children to comment freely on them in order to stimulate their desire for self-expression. He or she writes the names of the pupils on labels which adhere to lockers, books, sweaters, or lunch boxes. As the children observe, the teacher writes their dictated captions for pictures and experience charts as well as their dictated messages to ailing classmates. The teacher also involves the children in discussions or observations of writing situations which arise directly from their personal experiences: party invitations, thank-you notes, and weight-and-height records. Finally, the teacher presents in story form some of the drawing exercises described in Figure 9.1 which the children can readily perform on the chalkboard or on unlined newsprint.

The teacher does not, however, present formal writing instruction to young children until they have displayed numerous signs of readiness. One of these is *an interest in writing and a desire to write.* As the children observe the teacher writing in a meaningful way, their desire to do the writing themselves begins to grow. They soon sense a personal need to communicate in writing and enjoy learning to write their names.

A second sign is *adequate visual acuity and ability to make visual discriminations.* For writing, children must have sufficient acuity to recognize what is to be written and to be able to see what they have written. Besides the necessary eyesight, they should be able to recognize differentiating features of letters and words, and to make mental notes of the differences in the visual image on the retina. They must be able to detect likenesses and differences in symbols, objects, and pictures.

Still another evidence of readiness is *an understanding of the concept of left-to-right progression.* Before starting to write or to read, children need to know the meaning of the terms, *left* and *right.* While some pupils may begin school with a clear understanding of the differences between the terms, other pupils must gradually begin to comprehend them through teacher-planned psychomotor activities such as Looby-Loo and the Hokey-Pokey which call for the use of a particular hand or foot. Other activities recommended to help children master the bodily concept of left-to-right orientation involve:

1. Drawing green "go" and red "stop" signs on the chalkboard and then providing the children with colored chalk to draw the left-to-right horizontal lines between the signs. Later a simulation game can be played with toy cars being "driven" along the lines from "go" to "stop."
2. Creating a dramatic play setting for fire fighting and then providing the boys and girls with toy fire trucks/engines to move from the fire station at the left to the "fire" area at the right.[6]

A fourth critical sign of writing readiness is *adequate muscular coordination.* When pupils start school, they use their arm and leg muscles fairly well, but skill in the use of wrist and finger muscles comes slowly. Before they can develop skill in writing, they must be able to hold the chalk or crayon without

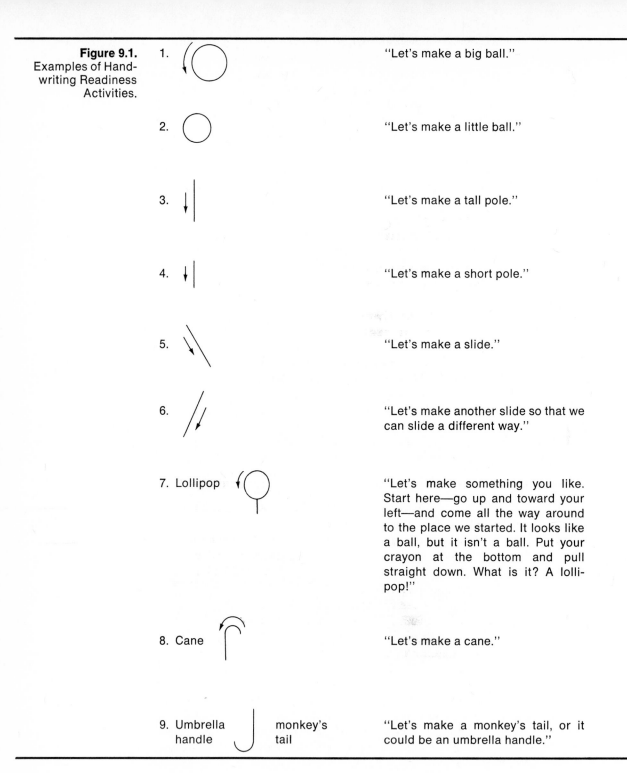

Figure 9.1. Examples of Handwriting Readiness Activities.

1. "Let's make a big ball."

2. "Let's make a little ball."

3. "Let's make a tall pole."

4. "Let's make a short pole."

5. "Let's make a slide."

6. "Let's make another slide so that we can slide a different way."

7. Lollipop "Let's make something you like. Start here—go up and toward your left—and come all the way around to the place we started. It looks like a ball, but it isn't a ball. Put your crayon at the bottom and pull straight down. What is it? A lollipop!"

8. Cane "Let's make a cane."

9. Umbrella handle / monkey's tail "Let's make a monkey's tail, or it could be an umbrella handle."

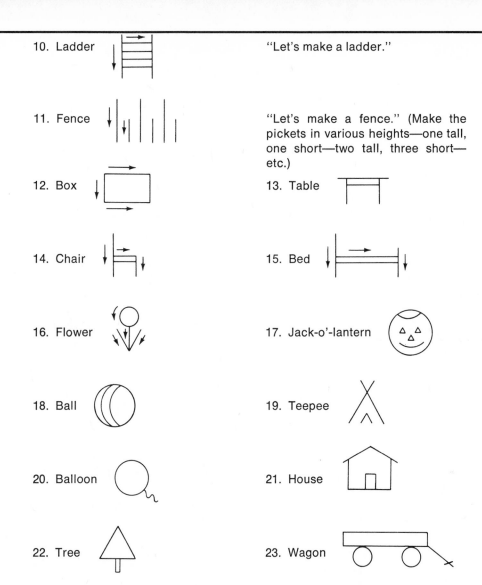

10. Ladder   "Let's make a ladder."

11. Fence   "Let's make a fence." (Make the pickets in various heights—one tall, one short—two tall, three short—etc.)

12. Box

13. Table

14. Chair

15. Bed

16. Flower

17. Jack-o'-lantern

18. Ball

19. Teepee

20. Balloon

21. House

22. Tree

23. Wagon

Each of these activities should be presented in a story form or in such a way that the children can associate the stroke to be made with a familiar experience.

For example: If the children are making the circle ◯, the teacher could say, "There is something that we like to play with."

noticeable strain and to make the finger muscles respond so that they can copy simple geometric or letterlike characters. Cursive writing is consequently deferred, since it demands a finer muscular coordination than is required for manuscript.

Should children lack the ability to control their muscles in a manner necessary to produce legible handwriting or overexert themselves in order to achieve the muscular coordination needed for writing, they may develop an antagonistic attitude or even a fear toward all writing activities. In many schools boys and girls are encouraged to use oversized pencils, chalk, or crayons for the initial writing experience so that they can make marks without having to cramp their fingers.

Another physical sign which may affect readiness for writing is *proper bone development of the arm*. X-rays have shown that some six-year-olds have only cartilage in their wrists in place of the bone which will develop later. To subject these children to formal writing before their hands have developed properly could result in subsequent complications, yet teachers lack facilities to determine such anatomical readiness.

A sixth sign of writing readiness is *hand preference*. Most authors agree that considerable instability of manual preferences exists before school age in most children. Although hand preference may appear as early as the first year of life, the frequency of strong predominating left-handedness or right-handedness increases with age.[7] Using data from a follow-up study of a small group of children over three years of age, Sinclair reported that hand preference usually seems stable after the age of five (as does foot and eye preference), but ear preference shows variation up to the age of seven.[8] A teacher should be aware that if young children have not firmly determined a hand preference by the time they start school, they should be encouraged to participate in activities leading to left-handedness if they are left-eyed or activities leading to right-handedness if they are right-eyed. Numerous instances of mixed laterality (especially involving the eye and hand) have been associated with reading and learning disabilities as well as with autonomic disturbances.

Another significant sign of readiness for writing is *social and emotional maturity*. The children need an attention span that will permit them to pay heed to one activity long enough to participate successfully in the various learning tasks required in the program. They must be able to follow simple directions whether these instructions are given in a group situation or individually. And they need self-confidence to attempt this new venture of handwriting.

An eighth sign is *language maturity*. When pupils verbalize satisfactorily, their oral experiences provide meaningful vocabularies for the first writing experiences. As they participate in discussion in the social studies and science areas, their vocabularies are further amplified. They enjoy listening to stories as well as composing and sending written messages, and they should have many opportunities to dictate stories, poems, reports, plans, ideas, and funny or frightening incidents. The teacher, when writing for the pupils, is not only introducing them to writing and reading, but is also helping to bridge a gap between oral language and written language and between oral language and reading. Consequently, young pupils need to write through the teacher about themselves and their friends.

Finally, though of less importance than all other signs of writing readiness, there is evidence of *a school writing program suitable for the children's level of maturity*. Research has shown that such a program is more effective if it uses the letters of the alphabet as its content and if it emphasizes formational procedures.[9]

Manuscript writing is a twentieth-century development which began in London, England, in the early years of the century as an easier method of teaching and learning the art of writing, and was introduced into the schools of Boston and New York in 1921. Soon it was accepted by hundreds of American public schools and today is part of the curriculum in nearly every primary grade in the country.

Basic Handwriting Skill: Manuscript

Manuscript or print-handwriting, written with only three basic strokes, is the fundamental handwriting tool because it is easy to learn and easy to teach. Its legibility produces early, deep, and widespread pupil satisfaction; and its clarity creates emotional security. It is similar to the kind of drawing with which the pupils are acquainted. It can be written with little physical strain and allows the children to rest between strokes if necessary. Since each letter is separate, it makes few demands on muscle coordination so that even a child with poor muscular control can produce readable results. It calls for few eye movements, making it easier on the eyes of all young children and especially on those with visual difficulties. It is less tiring and, therefore, can be employed for longer periods of time. It can be written rapidly without loss of legibility (and hence is even favored by business concerns).

Since manuscript writing resembles the print found in most primary reading materials, it aids beginning reading. Only one alphabet needs to be mastered for both reading and handwriting: as pupils read, they write; and as they write, they read. Because the pupils write more, and therefore come into contact with more words, manuscript writing benefits spelling. It improves the quality and increases the quantity of written composition. Also, it promotes self-correction as children can readily compare their own letters with commercially printed ones. Manuscript writing has a clear and pleasing appearance on charts, booklet covers, and art work.

Finally, manuscript writing can be learned easily by non-English speaking children, slow learners, and physically handicapped pupils. It is as useful with illiterate children as it is with illiterate adults. A manuscript written signature is considered legal at most banks (if it is the regular signature of the writer). And it has even been recommended that manuscript handwriting replace cursive handwriting as the style used by all teachers for classroom work since the superior legibility of manuscript writing is indisputable.[10]

Chalkboard Writing

As several children show numerous signs of writing readiness, the first-grade teacher gathers them into a group and instructs the members at the chalkboard. The children are taught to face the chalkboard, standing comfortably, though back far enough to enable a good arm movement and adequate visualizing of letters and words. They are shown how to hold an eraser in one hand, and in the other hand, a half-length piece of chalk about one inch from the writing end (between the thumb and first and second fingers). They are told to hold the elbow close to the body, writing directly in line with the center of the body.

The teacher makes certain that the chalkboard is at the correct height so the children's writing is at or near eye level, and that guidelines are semi-permanently ruled on the board to help children gauge the size, shape, spacing, and linear evenness of their writing.

Chalkboard writing for young children is especially valuable because it gives them an opportunity to use their large muscles to write on a broad surface without the restrictions they find in writing on paper.

When a group of children is ready for its first writing experience, the teacher plans instruction at a time when the members are not fatigued or shaky after vigorous exercise. The teacher supervises each pupil carefully so that correct habits are established and that the focus is centered on correctly formed letters and numerals.

Paper Writing

Following the experience of writing at the chalkboard, writing activities with crayons and unruled newsprint should precede the introduction of pencils and lined paper. The teacher may guide the making of simple figures that incorporate the basic strokes used in manuscript writing. Large free movements, left-to-right direction, and a feeling of form and space should be stressed. Special black crayons are provided by some districts for these initial writing experiences.

Usually the first writing which boys and girls wish to complete is the writing of their names. The purpose is significant and readily achieved. They repeat the writing often, whenever they must sign drawings or paintings, label personal possessions, or mark worksheets. Many teachers prepare individual name cards in manuscript writing so that every child has a guide to keep on his or her desk for reference at all times.

Beginning writers must be cautioned to hold a thick crayon or pencil (with large, soft lead) between the thumb and the first two fingers, about an inch above its point. The first finger rests on the top of the crayon/pencil, and the end of the bent thumb is placed against the instrument to hold it high in the hand near the large knuckle. The last two fingers touch the paper.

Incidentally, lined paper for beginning manuscript experience has 1¾″ spacing or ruling, but the spaces narrow to ⅞″, to ¾″, to ½″, and finally to ⅜″ ruling as the pupils advance in age and writing skill. It has usually been recommended that children write on properly ruled paper with colored baselines and midlines so they can attain legibility and writing satisfaction. Recent research, however, has concluded that the width of the writing space (whether

½″ or 1″) has no differential effect on the quality of beginning handwriting. Neither does paper with writing spaces with closed ends.[11]

Once children have learned how to write the manuscript alphabet, they must learn how to use it. While the major emphasis during the scheduled handwriting period, particularly at the beginning of the school year, is on learning the skill, some stress during that period and during instructional sessions for other school subjects should be placed on the use of that skill.

When handwriting is taught in relation to situations that demand it, the boys and girls begin to recognize writing as a tool of expression that serves their needs. There should then always be a balance between a reasonable degree of skill and a utilitarian situation. Overemphasis on skill without practical use results in a fine tool of questionable value, while too much emphasis on use without practice sessions results in inferior ways of holding the writing instrument and in careless productions.

Guiding Rules

In teaching the manuscript letters shown in Figure 9.2, the lowercase and uppercase (or capital) letters should be presented together, one or two letters at a time. Children can then begin writing words and short sentences. Letters that are similar should be introduced together, such as *o* and *c, v* and *w,* and *m* and *n.*

The letters of the manuscript alphabet vary widely in difficulty. The ten easiest letters for first-grade children are *l, o, L, O, H, D, i, v, I,* and *X;* the most difficult letters are *q, g, p, y, j, m, k, U, a,* and *G.* Uppercase letters are generally easier than lowercase letters for the children to write.

The classroom teacher should always emphasize through his or her board, chart, and paper writing the significance of these four areas of the manuscript style:

Letter Formation

This has been termed the core of the writing program and beginning writers are more concerned with letter formation than with any other aspect of legibility.

All letters are made with circles and straight lines. All vertical and all slant lines start at the top. Vertical lines of a letter are formed before the horizontal lines, and movements go from left to right. Strokes within a letter are made separately, and though combined strokes are not continuous, they touch each other.

Circles or parts of circles which are made counterclockwise begin at the two-o'clock position and proceed to the left. However, circles or parts of circles which are made clockwise begin at the ten-o'clock position and proceed to the right.

Size and Proportion

Maximum letters extend the full space from headline to baseline and include all uppercase letters and the "tall" lowercase letters. All other lowercase letters (except *t*) extend from the baseline to the midline. The lowercase *t* is the only intermediate letter in manuscript writing and extends from the baseline to halfway between the midline and the headline.

Figure 9.2.
Manuscript Hand-
writing Alphabet.

Spacing

Pupils should space words four fingers apart for chalkboard writing, two fingers for newsprint, one finger for first attempts on ruled paper, and finally, the width of an *o* when the size of their writing has been reduced.

Circular letters (such as *a, b,* and *d*) are placed closely together, while vertical letters (such as *i* and *l*) are placed farther apart. Spacing is considered by many to be the most difficult element in manuscript writing.

Alignment

All letters must rest on the baseline. There should also be an evenness of the letters along their tops with letters of the same size having even heights.

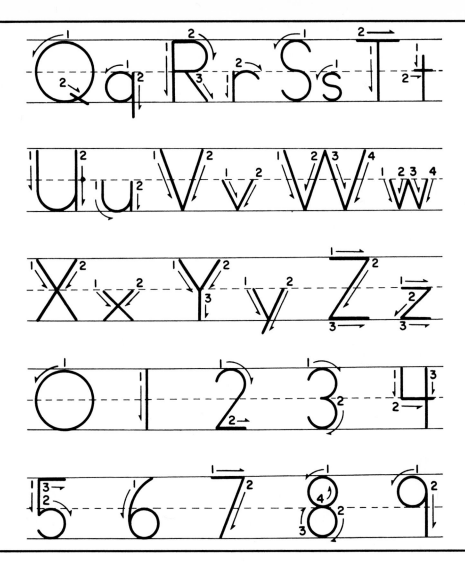

In an effective handwriting program the teacher should develop many purposes for which the children need to write so that instruction in manuscript writing does not become merely an exercise period set aside for meaningless and tiresome drill.

Primary pupils can be encouraged to label exhibits and displays in the classroom. With mechanical grease pencils or ballpoint pens, even first graders can make posters, booklets, and flashcards. They can prepare daily school cafeteria menus for the bulletin board, keep weather reports, and send letters to parents about school events. Children can write poems, stories, invitations,

Functional Use of Manuscript Skills

letters of thanks, and simple autobiographies. On the chalkboard they can copy the daily program and other announcements, including local news events.

Teachers must realize that writing lessons aim toward the eventual achievement of one or more specific objectives: writing ability, knowledge of letter names, awareness that letters represent sounds, understanding of initial sounds, knowledge of letter-sound associations, awareness that words are comprised of letters, and an awareness that the writing (spelling) of a word is related to its pronunciation.[12]

First Addition: Cursive Writing

Nearly 70 percent of the public, private, and laboratory schools in the United States introduce cursive (or running) writing between the first half of the second grade and the first half of the fourth grade. Research has shown that the time of transition does not affect grade-to-grade progress nor is it as important as the nature of the instructional program. Still, it is a factor influencing children's handwriting performance: late transition is associated with rapid writing, while early transition is associated with legible handwriting.

Cursive writing is not faster, easier, or more legible, but it is the socially accepted form of handwriting. Since children and parents alike believe that manuscript writing is associated with the primary grades, cursive writing is added to the fundamental skill of handwriting because it carries wide social acceptance and prestige. Adult females, for example, use cursive writing to a considerably greater extent than adult males because they consider it less childish and more businesslike.

Transitional Stage

An intermediate step, commonly effected in the second grade, is the use of slant print. Some mature first-grade pupils begin to slant manuscript writing of their own volition during the last half of the school year, and many second graders shortly follow suit.

Slant print, which dates back to the Middle Ages, is advantageous for pupils because it is a natural way of writing with greater freedom of movement. It improves the vision, hand position, arm leverage, and body position of the writer.

It is also advantageous for teachers because slant print makes successful cursive instruction much easier, and as a handwriting style, it is in harmony with the cursive script as it is being learned. Of the four performance tasks involved in cursive writing, three also occur in slant print: habitually turning the paper on the desk; keeping the nonwriting hand out of the way at the top of the page for easy paper shifting; and slanting the product. Slant-print is especially helpful for left-handed writers because it makes possible the prevention of position failure.

At least one national commercial handwriting system is presently using slant print *instead of* manuscript for beginning writers to ease the later transition to cursive.

Pupils arrive at the threshold of advanced writing readiness at varying times, and chronological age or grade placement does not constitute a reliable index. A teacher must adapt instruction readily, for a homogeneous group of fast learners may display readiness for cursive writing months before a low-cluster group. Consequently, a teacher plans flexibly and prepares large-group manuscript lessons or slant-print lessons as well as small-group cursive lesson plans. Second-, third-, and fourth-grade teachers are constantly noting individual signs of readiness for cursive handwriting among their students.

A group can be successfully introduced to the cursive style when most of its members can be described as:

1. Children who can read writing. A pronounced relationship exists between the ability to read manuscript and cursive style writing. Pupils who have developed adequate skill in reading manuscript style will likely require little instructional emphasis on reading cursive style, while those who have experienced difficulty in learning to read manuscript will need substantial attention. One aspect of this attention may well be to postpone the addition of cursive writing until suitable growth has been made in reading manuscript writing. Another possibility is to precede the introduction of cursive writing with the reading of material written in the cursive style.
2. Children who have attained adequate physical development so there is muscular coordination of the arm, hand, and fingers.
3. Children who have had a sufficiently long experience in manuscript writing to use it properly and skillfully.
4. Children who can write all the letters of the manuscript alphabet from memory.
5. Children who can copy a selection in manuscript at a rate varying from twenty to forty-five letters per minute.
6. Children who have the ability to reduce the size of their manuscript letters.
7. Children who are unconsciously starting to join manuscript or slant-print letters.
8. Children who want to write in the cursive style.

Comparison to Manuscript

The most important difference between cursive and manuscript writing—and the fourth performance task involved in cursive writing—is sliding laterally to join letters. Cursive writers lift their pens or pencils from the paper upon completion of each word. Manuscript writers lift their writing tools after each letter, for they may combine separate letters but do not connect them to make words.

The basic shapes used in cursive writing are slant strokes, connecting strokes, and ovals. In manuscript writing the basic shapes are straight lines and circles.

The letters *i* and *j* are dotted and the letter *t* is crossed after the entire word has been written in cursive style. In manuscript writing, the dotting and crossing occur immediately after the letters are formed.

The uppercase letters in the cursive alphabet always differ considerably from the lowercase letters; but 30 percent of the manuscript alphabet is much the same for lowercase and uppercase letters—*c, o, p, s, v, w, x, z.*

In cursive writing, the spacing between letters is controlled by the slant and manner of making connective strokes. In manuscript writing, where the letters are bunched to form words, the space between the letters is controlled by the shape of the letter.

Cursive letters shown in Figure 9.3 differ from book print. Manuscript letters closely resemble such print, and during the past decade, books using slant print have become available in the United States.

Figure 9.3. Cursive Handwriting Alphabet.

The classroom teacher should constantly stress through both presentations and public writing efforts the importance of these six areas of the cursive style:

All the cursive letters, regardless of the commercial handwriting system used, are comprised of overcurves and undercurves which originate from the oval and are combined with slant strokes of other curves. They represent natural movements of the relaxed arm, wrist, hand, and fingers; and considerable legibility and speed can be attained when finger movements are not exaggerated or overused. There are *loop letters* (such as *j* and *p*) whose upstrokes must curve and whose downstrokes must be straight. There are *retraced letters* (such

as *m* and *n*) which must not become loops. There are *rounded turn letters* (such as *x, y,* and *z*) which must not be pointed. There are *closed letters* (such as *a* and *d*) which must not overlap.

When either the overcurve or the undercurve is made hastily, however, it tends to become merely a straight stroke and consequently difficult to read. When the overcurve is made straight:

a becomes *u*	*n* becomes *u*
d becomes *il*	*o* becomes *u*
g becomes *y* or *ij*	*v* becomes *u*
m becomes *w*	*y* becomes *ij*

When the undercurve becomes straight, *e* becomes *i* and the *r* and *s* become overcurves. Practicing the two curves at the top and bottom of a well-formed oval will help eliminate undesired straightness and reduce the number of handwriting illegibilities shown in Figure 9.4.

The teacher should realize that the most difficult letter, according to a survey of 1,000 sixth graders, is the letter *r*.[13] Its malformations account for 12 percent of all illegibilities. Other letters that pupils frequently malform are *h, i, k, p,* and *z.*

Figure 9.4. The Most Difficult Cursive Letters and Numerals. (These constitute half of all the handwriting illegibilities.)

		Wrong	Right			Wrong	Right
1.	a like o	*o*	*a*	10.	n like u	*u*	*n*
2.	a like u	*u*	*a*	11.	o like a	*a*	*o*
3.	a like ci	*a*	*a*	12.	r like i	*i*	*r*
4.	b like li	*b*	*b*	13.	r like n	*n*	*r*
5.	d like cl	*d*	*d*	14.	t like l	*t*	*t*
6.	e closed	*e*	*e*	15.	t with cross above	*t*	*t*
7.	h like li	*h*	*h*	A.	5 like 3	*5*	*5*
8.	i like e with no dot	*e*	*i*	B.	6 like 0	*0*	*6*
9.	m like w	*w*	*m*	C.	7 like 9	*7*	*7*

Source: Adapted from California State Series *Handwriting Made Easy,* Part III. Sacramento: State Department of Education, 1963.

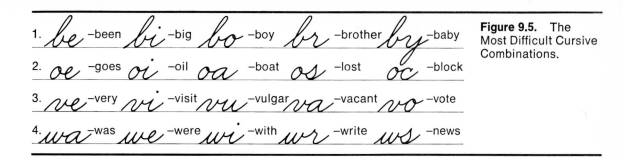

Figure 9.5. The Most Difficult Cursive Combinations.

Joining the cursive letters is unique to the style and is as important as forming the letters. The four letters which give the most trouble in joining are *b, o, v,* and *w,* for they connect the next letter at the top and not on the line. These difficult combinations of overcurves and undercurves are listed in Figure 9.5. By the sixth grade, after all lowercase joinings have been mastered and all uppercase letters separately perfected, the teacher may introduce joinings of uppercase to lowercase letters. There are seventeen uppercase letters which have a natural joining finish and so should be taught as joinable capitals. The remaining letters—*D, F, L, O, P, Q, T, V,* and *W*—do not readily permit joining, due to their final evolvement from roman print.

Joining

All twenty-six uppercase letters are of maximum height. All lowerloop letters (whether uppercase or lowercase) take a full descender space below the baseline. All upperloop letters extend a full space from the baseline to the headline.

Size and Proportion

The downstrokes or slant strokes of the letters slant uniformly and in the same direction. Cursive writing which has a consistent, forward slant is easier to read than writing which slants too much or is irregular. A slant between sixty degrees and seventy degrees is regarded as the most acceptable.

Slant

Between each letter there is an even distribution of sufficient blank space. Between each word there is the space of one letter.

Spacing

Every letter rests on a baseline, whether that line is real or imaginary.

Alignment

Meaningless drill can quickly dull children's desires to improve their handwriting techniques. The wise teacher, however, builds a program that encourages all pupils to write primarily to communicate ideas and feelings. Writers thereby attain satisfaction as well as fluency.

    Middle- and upper-grade children can use cursive handwriting in preparing stories, verse, dialogs, book reports, and invitations. They can take notes, make outlines, keep vocabulary lists, and plan the school newspaper. They can keep minutes of club meetings. They can compile a class directory. Pupils can write letters to government offices or to private firms asking for information or

Functional Use of Cursive Skills

arranging study trips. They can write up interviews with resource speakers or class visitors. As committee members, they can participate in developing a unit of work in science or social studies.

Through these and other everyday experiences, children are made aware of the many purposes for acquiring handwriting skills.

Second Addition: Typewriting

After boys and girls have achieved a comfortable degree of success in cursive writing while continuing to maintain their skill in manuscript writing, they are ready to make a further addition to their handwriting capability by learning to typewrite. Their progress in typing is generally in direct proportion to their physical and emotional maturity, although the mechanics of fingering are reasonably easy for even early intermediate grade pupils to acquire.

A national survey by the Educational Research Service of the NEA revealed that a limited number of elementary school children are already learning typewriting. Twelve percent of the school systems (with a minimal enrollment of 12,000 pupils) responding to the study have typewriting instruction in the elementary school, and these schools are located in all geographical areas of the nation from Texas to Michigan and from Connecticut to California. Larger districts offer such instruction in grades five and six, while smaller districts with fewer than 25,000 pupils provide experimental classes in typewriting for younger children.

Why Is Typewriting Being Taught?

Typewriting skill is a value in and of itself. It has become a desirable tool of written communication, useful personally as well as vocationally. It is also an educational tool.

Typewriting should be considered not so much as a new field of learning but as an instrument which increases the efficiency of learning and of expression in basic knowledge, particularly in the language arts. Consequently, it cannot be taught to children as an isolated skill for the sake of the skill itself. Instead, typewriting should be taught as a tool which makes spelling, reading, written composition, and other curricular areas more interesting.

Since such instruction contributes to nearly all of the major goals of education, the opportunity to acquire proficiency in typewriting should be made available to more and more pupils. Specifically, the typewriter can aid children in virtually every area of the upper elementary curriculum. It creates a need to spell more words, provides clearer word images, and improves composition skills. It aids in the production of both individual and committee booklets and written reports as well as labels and legends for posters, maps, bulletin boards, and displays. Teaching children to typewrite helps them clarify margins, line spacings, paragraphing, hyphenating, bibliographies and outlines, spacing between words, vertical and horizontal centering, and addressing of envelopes and postal cards. The production of class newspapers, book reports, letters, and notes is simultaneously increased.

Furthermore, the affective, cognitive, and psychomotor values engendered through the use of the typewriter may prove more important over a period of time than the fact that children are also learning the first rudiments of keyboard literacy.

Instructions found in junior-high and senior-high textbooks for teaching beginning typewriting, such as A. Lloyd and R. Krevolin's *You Learn to Type* (Gregg Division of McGraw Hill Book Company, 1966), can be used with upper-grade elementary children. The teacher, however, may wish to simplify textbook directions, due to the vocabulary limitations, interests, and needs of pupils at this level. Or the teacher may choose to use one of the typewriting books especially designed for younger pupils such as *Introductory Typewriting* by D. D. Lessenberry et al. (South-Western Publishing Company, 1975) or Edward Fry's *Typing Course for Children* (Dreier Educational Systems, 1969). A sample lesson from one elementary school typewriting book is found in Figure 9.6.

The method presented in elementary school typewriting classes is touch-typing. The course content includes presentation of the keyboard, manipulation of other parts of the machine, completion of correspondence and report forms, and understanding simple tabulation. The elementary classroom or language arts teacher usually conducts the typing class. This teacher is sometimes assisted by a paraprofessional aide or monitor and occasionally by instructional records and music. Class periods run twenty to sixty minutes during the regular semester with younger students attending the shorter sessions once or twice a week. Older children attend on a daily or near-daily basis for longer periods of time.

The skill can be mastered by pupils in a relatively short time. Thirty hours of class instruction produce sufficient skill to enable most pupils to use typing in their home and school work. Second, third, and fourth graders in Del Mar, California master the touch system in three to four months. Fifth and sixth graders in Jackson, Mississippi take between twelve and eighteen weeks to master it. Incidentally, these same Jackson fifth graders reach a typing speed of forty words per minute by the end of their first year in the program.

Children can learn with either a manual or an electric typewriter, and with either an office or a portable machine. There has been no appreciable difference noted between skill development by a learner on the manual model and a learner on the electric typewriter. However, at least one writer—Petit-clerc—insists that every typewriter must be portable electric: *portable* so that any child can pick up the machine and carry it to a secluded spot to type alone if he or she so desires; and *electric* because young fingers fatigue when working on manual machines.[14]

Typewriting can be taught without the addition of any special furniture or equipment other than the machines themselves, although adjustable desks are helpful. Few elementary schools, however, can equal the typing lab in one

Figure 9.6. Sample Lesson in Elementary School Typewriting.

Lesson 2: Learning "E"

Now that we have learned the home key fingers, we are ready to learn the letter "E."

Type "E" with the "D" finger. After typing the letter E, the D finger returns to home base again.

Practice:

    ded ded ded ded ded ded ded ded

    eee eee eee eee eee eee eee eee

    fff eee lll fell fell fell fell

Have fun typing the hockey game. See how many goals you can score!

ded ded dea dea deal
ded ded dea dea deal
see a seed; see a seed

see a sled; see a sled
sell a sled; sell a sled
see a lad; see a sad dad

G O A L ! !

Directions: Type the practice drill you see on the hockey field. Each time you complete the drill you score a goal. How many goals can you score?

Source: Mary Ellen Switzer, *Typing Fun* (Santa Barbara, Ca.: The Learning Works, 1979). Reprinted with permission.

Mississippi school which is furnished with thirty IBM Selectric typewriters with multiple listening stations and audio-belt recording machines.[15]

One state which believes in extending access to typewriting to all public school students from kindergarten through grade twelve is Hawaii. During one recent year, for example, almost 50,000 children, ages five to ten, on six Hawaiian islands, used the electric typewriter to develop keyboard literacy.

The Primary Typewriting Program of Hawaii

The Primary Typewriting Program is one part of the language skills segment of the Hawaii English Program. Early in the language skills curriculum, the pupils learn to write cursive or manuscript and to type because both typewriting and handwriting are regarded as means of purposeful communication. The program has produced a series of ten typewriting books which allow each child to learn correct keyboard fingering, typing techniques, and format through self-instructional picture cues and exercises.

Individual typewriting stations and learning centers, with one machine for thirty children, are provided in the nongraded K–3 classes throughout the state. In grades four to six one machine is planned for every fifteen children. Classroom teachers generally work with only the first few learners (who then tutor their peers in the lessons they have completed) except for monitoring and checking progress of all learners periodically.

The nearly 1,500 primary teachers involved in the program have confirmed several reasons for including typewriting as an essential part of the language skills. First, it stimulates children's motivation to learn to use the graphic symbols of the English language. Second, typewriting supports the development of the children's reading ability. It also offers boys and girls an alternative mode of writing so that they can use the typewriter for their stories, songs, poems, and letters. Fourth, it supports the development of the children's handwriting ability. And finally, typewriting helps the children become independent learners and promotes individualization because it is self-pacing.

Since 1926 when the first group of six-year-olds used a typewriter at the Horace Mann School in New York City, more than 900 studies have been made that deal in total or in part with typing in the classroom. Conclusions reached in surveys and research studies completed in the middle and upper elementary grades in recent years emphasize the following:

Summary of Recent Research Findings

1. The use of the typewriter has a significant positive effect on both handwriting quality and handwriting speed.
2. Pupils learn to type at rates which exceed their handwriting rates by as much as two or three times in most cases.
3. The use of the typewriter has a positive effect on the study skills achievement of pupils. It also increases productivity of written composition to a marked degree and improves the "eye sweep" in oral and silent reading.
4. The typewriter can be used as the basis for a multisensory and multidisciplinary approach to the teaching of reading to children of average or above-average intelligence who have learning disabilities.

5. There is a positive correlation between a pupil's IQ and his or her typewriting ability, and between his or her motor dexterity and mental age.[16]

6. Fifth- and sixth-grade pupils can accomplish more in typing than high school students taught by the same instructor in the same amount of class time. Fourth-grade pupils learn to type on the electric portable with less instruction than adults.

7. There is the same wide range of physical development among elementary school typing students as with high school and adult students.

8. Left to their own devices, children do not learn to operate the machine with any degree of skill. They need teacher direction if they are to achieve superior typing techniques.

9. Reactions of the parents to the typewriter are those of approval of its use in elementary classes as a valuable education tool. Parents often display an almost "for granted" attitude toward the introduction of the machine.

10. Reactions of the pupils to the use of the typewriter are those of enthusiastic acceptance. They use the machine for written work in preference to handwriting. They come to school early for extra practice or ask to type at noon. They produce reports on the typewriter which are about 3.3 times longer than similar reports written in longhand by nontypists. And they use the machines to answer examination questions in the areas of English and social studies whenever they can.

Providing for Children with Special Needs

Schools must develop, to some degree, ways of individualizing instruction in handwriting because individualization is indirectly related to the whole area of self-evaluation, motivation, and pupil interest. Although the entire class is presently taught at one time in the majority of schools across the nation, projects have already verified the utility of meeting individual differences in handwriting needs.[17]

Research involving third and fourth graders in an urban elementary school, for example, revealed after nine weeks of daily instruction that individualized approaches to teaching handwriting produce greater increases in legibility than the formal group approach, and that individualization is most effective before the pupils' handwriting habits have been fairly well established —probably before the fourth grade. The children were randomly assigned to one of three instructional programs: the formal group, the formal-individualized group, and the individualized-diagnostic group. The last-named group made no use of commercially prepared materials. However, its teachers helped each pupil focus on a limited number of his or her own errors and malformations at the beginning of each instructional sequence; allowed each pupil to practice as he or she completed writing tasks of his or her own choosing; and systematically encouraged all pupils to develop the habit of continuously evaluating their own handwriting.

A transitional step between complete individualization of instruction and the whole-class approach occurred in one New York State district where a supervisor, using an overhead projector, made *group* presentations of proper manuscript and cursive writing to 150 intermediate students at least once each month. Then, during the follow-up by classroom teachers, all malformed letters that the pupils made on any written assignment were carefully noted next to their owners' names on a Handwriting Record Chart posted on the bulletin board. Finally, twice weekly, there were *individualized* activities on the particular handwriting problems facing each pupil.

In one northern Illinois community another project for individualizing instruction was undertaken, with fifth graders being scheduled for daily twenty-minute periods. During two such sessions a week a teacher directed the whole group, stressing such essential skills as spacing and baseline alignment, and using the overhead projector or the chalkboard. Two other periods a week were devoted to individual diagnosis and practice, with the activities centered on each child analyzing and evaluating his or her own work and then practicing in those areas where there was room for improvement. Finally, small-group instruction took place once a week in order to resolve self-diagnosed handwriting problems. During these sessions children in groups of three to eight could choose to use specially prepared tapes, have their papers examined by a classmate, work with the teacher, or participate in other activities which they deemed helpful. Incidentally, the groups remained totally flexible and were never based on terms of good, average, or poor penmanship.

Every teacher must realistically view a handwriting program not so much in terms of meeting the broad needs of one whole-class group as in terms of satisfying individual pupils with varying demands who may sometimes be grouped together temporarily to overcome a common failing. In any heterogeneous classroom there are numerous children who encounter occasional difficulty in letter formation, uniform slant, or in proper alignment, and they need to be united only until the purpose for establishing the group has been attained. There are also a few other pupils with less common and more permanent characteristics for whom the teacher must plan special handwriting instruction. This group may include—

educable mentally retarded children
children with learning disabilities
emotionally disturbed children
young children learning English as a second language
left-handed children

Educable Mentally Retarded Children

Mentally retarded children score significantly better on handwriting quality than do children in regular classes, but they do not score as well on handwriting speed as the others do. For slow-learning children, handwriting should particularly develop out of meaningful experiences correlated with other curricular areas. They must have a definite writing purpose, individually determined and practical. Before these boys and girls do any extensive work in handwriting, they need to read with some degree of understanding and use a basic sight vocabulary. It is not necessary that they add cursive writing.

Research regarding the teaching of handwriting to the brain-injured, educable mentally retarded (with IQ scores ranging from fifty to eighty-nine) has concluded that the best approach appears to be the kinesthetic one. Activities can correlate with the physical education program and many hours may be devoted to large and small muscle play. Care should be taken to provide a placid, happy, nonrestricted yet orderly classroom atmosphere. Relaxation training by means of an audio-taped program is effective in enhancing the quality of handwriting produced by these children who sometimes try too hard to write and use too much energy in the process.[18]

Children with Learning Disabilities

Major problem areas in handwriting have been identified as visual-perception-input, visual-spatial relationships, visual-motor ability, and short-term visual recall.[19] For learning-disabled children there may be a deficit in one or more areas while the others are at a normal developmental stage. For example, a learning-disabled pupil can have good short-term visual recall and still have inadequate visual-spatial relationships. A checklist of possible handwriting difficulties possessed by a learning-disabled child is shown in Figure 9.7.

Visual-perception-input means the ability to perceive a configuration. Children who do not perceive a shape correctly put the motor response in the wrong place and thus their writing consists of twisted letters, inconsistently reversed letters, and letters slanted diagonally toward the line. Remediation for visual-perception-input difficulty starts with the use of cardboard form boards to help the children visually recognize like and unlike shapes. They are given one of the form boards and a variety of cutout shapes and parquetry blocks to place on that board; later they can sort the blocks and shapes into piles together with shaped templates. Along with this exercise the children can also match shapes to form designs or pictures. Finally, the pupils advance to learning the actual letter shapes visually and kinesthetically by using sandpaper, clay or playdough, crayons, tagboard, and writing paper.

Visual-spatial relationships develop from the ability of children to relate themselves to space, and thus, to relate two objects in space to each other. Children with a weakness in this area of handwriting have difficulty just placing letters on the line, organizing the letters on the paper, and positioning the spaces properly. Also, they often produce a disproportion in the size of the letters. For remediation in the visual-spatial area, heavy dark lines or colored lines can be drawn or printed on writing paper to visually accentuate the spatial orientation of the letters. Another technique is to color the three writing spaces blue, green, and brown and then to designate the letters as being "placed in the sky," "placed on the grass," or "placed under the ground." Finally, such lines are gradually lightened until children can properly place the letters without guide lines.

Pupils experiencing difficulty in *visual-motor ability* produce lines of writing that are either very heavy or very light. They will often take an unusually

Checklist of Handwriting Difficulties of a Learning-Disabled Child

Directions: Have the child copy *exactly* at least three lines of writing either from the chalkboard or from another sheet of paper. The handwriting sample should not exceed eighteen letters and/or spaces per line.

Handwriting Clue	Writer's Difficulty			
	Visual-Perception Input	*Visual-Spatial Ability*	*Visual-Motor Ability*	*Visual Recall*
Constantly reversed letters*	x			
Constantly twisted letters*	x			
Parts of letters not connected	x			
Shape of letters distorted	x			
Upside-down letters*	x			
Letters not on the line		x		
Unequal spacing of letters		x		
Unequal size of letters		x		
Heavy use of the pencil			x	
Light use of the pencil			x	
Pencil held in fist grip			x	
Tense grip while writing			x	
Wavering lines			x	
Deterioration of letter shape as repeated across line			x	
Letters copied out of sequence				x
Letters omitted or words omitted				x

* A constant occurrence, not just an occasional learning error.
Source: Adapted from *Correcting Handwriting Problems* (Lexington, Massachusetts: Public Schools, 1974), p. 18.

long time to execute one letter or to complete one writing lesson. Although they have been taught how to hold a pencil properly, they either hold it so tensely that they make holes in the paper or so lightly that their letters can be barely seen. Such children will try to make numerous erasures since they realize that they are not making the letter shapes properly. Remediation begins at the chalkboard: a pupil is given a piece of chalk in each hand and told to draw parallel lines, then large squares, and finally large circles with both hands while simultaneously saying the directions of his or her movements. Then the pupil gradually traces pictures, traces letters, and finally writes letters with crayons.

The fourth area involves visual imagery, and a problem in *short-term visual recall* occurs when children encounter difficulty in transferring something from one paper to another or from the chalkboard to their papers. Letters or entire words may be omitted or letters may be copied out of sequence. Remediation requires teaching visual sequencing by matching a group of manipulative objects with a row of pictures of the same objects; the same process can also be used with parquetry blocks. To help children copy items in proper sequence, a cardboard strip the width of three writing spaces can be used when copying from another sheet of paper. The cardboard strip is drawn along the line of print that is being copied, exposing only one letter at a time. Gradually, as a child's skill improves, more letters can be uncovered at once until the strip is unnecessary.

Emotionally Disturbed Children

Pupils who resist handwriting and handwriting instruction may be suffering from such problems as undue pressure from home or school, poor adult-child rapport, sibling rivalry, poor acceptance by their peers, a broken-home environment, or other emotional disturbances. The teacher must be especially aware of basic personality needs, providing constant reassurance and understanding to these children. The teacher is advised to overlook inadequate handwriting or unusual tensions until he or she fully comprehends the background of each writer. Only to the extent that problems in the teaching of handwriting are viewed in relation to the children's total problems can the teacher hope to improve the pupils' handwriting in regard to legibility and speed.

Since emotionally disturbed children tend to tire easily, they need shorter, more frequent periods of writing practice than other pupils. They should continue to do all written work in manuscript until such time as their cursive writing becomes legible.

Young Children Learning English as a Second Language

Mastering the mechanics of handwriting is the same for these children as for English-speaking children at this early stage of schooling. Since they are unlikely to know the names of the letters in English, however, they should be given special help by having them say the name of each letter as they learn to form it during handwriting lessons. The use of alphabet books and picture dictionaries reinforces this learning.

The one form of individual differences that appears most frequently during handwriting instruction and thus receives the greatest attention is left-handedness. This phenomenon (ranging from moderately to strongly left-handed) is found in approximately 10 percent of the population, and its incidence has remained relatively unchanged from *Australopithecus* through the Egyptians of 2500 B.C. to the present.[20]

Teachers must realize that while evidence for a genetic base for handedness remains positive, no direct link has been established. The development of preferred handedness can also be markedly affected by such factors as cultural and social pressures, family preference, educational practices, specific brain damage, and the prevalence of certain types of devices more suitable for one hand than the other. That some cultures even today simply forbid the use of the left hand for writing is exemplified by the many European countries where all pupils learn to write with the right hand.

American teachers are urged to identify the nature of each young child's handedness and direct him or her to write accordingly in order to avoid having the pupil develop a writing pattern solely on the basis of chance. Consistency in the use of one writing hand is important from early beginnings. If either the left or right hand is used without strain, it is perfectly safe to encourage use of that hand. Children who shift readily from one hand to the other, however, should be encouraged to use the right hand.

It is also important that teachers are aware that recent research has revealed that there is no difference in intellectual and cognitive performance between left- and right-handed elementary pupils. Hardyck, Petrinovich, and Goldman took intellectual and performance measures on the total school population, grades one through six, in a medium-size California community with a large black and Oriental citizenry. The pupils were tested on three measures of handedness and one measure of eyedness, and no relationships of any kind were discovered. The researchers then went on to compare their results against thirty-three studies concerned with possible deficits associated with left-handedness including areas such as reading ability, intelligence, perceptual performance, mental retardation, and emotional instability. Still there was no difference in intellectual or cognitive performance that could be attributed to any deficit linked to handedness.[21]

Measures of handedness and eyedness can be individually administered by kindergarten and first-grade teachers in an effort to assess the preferences of their pupils. Such informal tests involve materials which are familiar to the children and adapted to their age and development. Teachers should repeat each stage of a test a sufficient number of times to detect the dominant hand and should remember never to hand the materials to the children. Tests that teachers can make and administer include the following.

The teacher cuts assorted colored papers about the size of playing cards and shuffles them. He or she places a pile (of at least twenty) of these cards where

Sorting Colored Cards

the child can reach them and then tells the child to get the cards and sort them according to the colors. The teacher observes which hand the pupil uses in picking up the cards and in sorting them.

Bouncing a Ball	The child picks up a ball and then bounces it ten times on the floor, catching it on each rebound. As only one hand can be used during the entire perform-ance, the pupil's preference can be readily noted.
Slicing and Eating an Apple	Given a quarter of a pared apple, the child picks up a knife and is asked to slice the apple in five pieces. The child then picks up each piece with a fork. The teacher notes which hand held the knife and fork.
Screwing Caps on Jars	Several empty jars with removable lids are placed on the table. The child is asked to put the lids on the jars and close them tightly. (Sometimes changing from jar to jar may encourage a change in hand preference.)
Threading a Needle	On the table is a piece of sturdy thread and a large needle. The child is asked to thread the needle.
Putting a Puzzle Together	On the table are the large pieces of a puzzle. The child is asked to assemble the puzzle.
Cutting Pictures	On the table is an old magazine and a small pair of regular (right-handed) scissors. The child is asked to cut out a picture. The left-handed child will have more difficulty than the right-handed one, and a repeat test with the other hand will show whether or not there is a preferred hand.
Cutting Paper	On the table are a small pair of regular (right-handed) scissors and three pieces of paper of different colors. The child is asked to use the scissors in order to cut three strips from a sheet of paper of one color. The process is re-peated with each of the other two sheets because a change in the color of paper may influence a change of hand.

In addition to testing for handedness, teachers may wish to administer in-formal tests to determine eyedness, repeating each enough times to reveal the dominant eye. Individual tests to show which eye is used for sighting when both of a pupil's eyes are fixed on a common point include the following:

Simple Tube Test	On the table is a long mailing tube and an object which the pupil has not seen before in the classroom. He is asked to look at the object through the tube and describe it. He will use his preferred eye to sight the object.
Advanced Tube Test	The pupil holds a long mailing tube about six inches from both eyes and looks through it at a distant object in the room, keeping both eyes open. Then her right eye is covered, and if she continues to see the object, she is left-eyed. But

if the object has apparently moved when she looks at it and she does not see the object, she is right-eyed. Then her left eye is covered, and if she continues to see the object, she is right-eyed. But if the object has apparently moved when she looks at it and she does not see the object, she is left-eyed.

Hole-in-Card Test

In the center of a card or sheet of stiff paper, the teacher cuts a hole about an inch in diameter. The pupil holds the card in both hands, with his arms stretched out in front of him, and is asked to sight, with both eyes open, a distant object through the hole. Then one eye is covered and if he reports that he can still see the object, it is obvious that the dominant or preferred eye is the uncovered eye. If he cannot see the object, it is apparent that the dominant eye is covered. The teacher should have the pupil try the test from different positions as a single trial may not be sufficient.

Aiming Test

The pupil sights a distant object with both eyes open, and then brings up her hands and points to the object. Then she closes or covers her left eye, and if she finds her fingers still in line with the object, she is right-eyed. She is left-eyed, however, if her fingers have apparently moved out of line. When she closes or covers the right eye, she is left-eyed if she finds her fingers still in line with the object, or she is right-eyed if her fingers have apparently moved out of line.

With proper instruction there is no significant difference in the handwriting performance of left-handed and right-handed pupils. Consequently, teachers must be careful to guide left-handed writers by encouraging them to do the following:

1. Use the chalkboard often and for extended periods of time. Left-handed pupils are especially comfortable if they can stand at the right end of the chalkboard. They need two spaces—one in which to stand and one in which to write.
2. Sit at the left side of a desk or table that is somewhat below average in height (so that they may look over the top of the writing hand to the point of the writing instrument). If possible, left-handed pupils should be seated so the light comes over their right shoulders.
3. Tilt their papers to the right as much as a thirty-five to forty-five degree angle to improve both vision and arm leverage. Then they should keep the left hand below the base line. In this way the slant of the paper and the hand position can help them to see what they write. (When they cannot see the line of writing, they are tempted to twist the hand to the left to peer under it, thereby developing a hooked or cramped position.)
4. Use a writing tool that does not smudge, such as a pencil with a hard lead or a ball-point pen with an extended tip.
5. Hold back about one and one-half inches on the writing tool so that they can see over or around the writing hand. (A rubber band or a thin strip of

masking tape can be put around the instrument at the point where it should be grasped.) They should hold the tool lightly and grasp it so that the top points to the window or wall at the left.

6. Learn first the four manuscript letters that begin with a stroke to the left since these develop muscular control most readily: *a, d, g,* and *o.* Then, develop coordination in the forward motion from left to right by practicing the manuscript letters *b, e, f, i, l, r, t, u,* and *w.*

7. Pull all downstrokes toward the left elbow.

8. Realize that they can use the manuscript style indefinitely if they find that it is easier to write.

For instructional purposes left-handed students should be separated from right-handed students. This is especially important for left-handers since if they interpret directions as demonstrated by the teacher in the normal teaching method, they will write in reverse. By producing such mirror writing they are correctly interpreting directions given only visually or given in the directionality of the right-handed students. Consequently, the teacher must demonstrate techniques to the left-handed pupils separately.[22]

Evaluation of Pupils' Progress

Young children are graded for handwriting in about 70 percent of the American and Canadian schools, according to a survey published recently.[23] Hopefully such evaluation of handwriting progress occurs individually or on a small-group basis. The teacher who recognizes that children's growth patterns are not identical will not insist that every child in the grade meet the same standards of handwriting achievement. Some children may make appreciable progress in handwriting skill during the year and yet not write as well as pupils who have average ability for the grade; to try to force such slow learners to meet a kind of standardized norm would not only be unfair to them but would probably promote apathy or even outright resentment. Children who exhibit very little improvement, as well as those who show unusual growth, may both be progressing consistently with their current rate of overall development.

Since the chief aims of the handwriting program are legibility and speed, evaluation of each pupil's progress in handwriting demands that those two factors be measured objectively. The best form of evaluation, and the only one that has a genuine meaning for the child, occurs when he or she and the teacher set up goals for the improvement of personal writing skill. Class or group discussion on the qualities of good writing and the ways of discovering and correcting weaknesses should precede the time of personal examination and goal setting. Evaluation then becomes a day-to-day technique as well as a long-term device for handwriting growth.

Speed and Legibility in Handwriting

Speed of the measurement of rate of handwriting may be expressed in either letters per second or, more commonly, in letters per minute. The score is obtained by counting the total number of letters written by the pupil and then

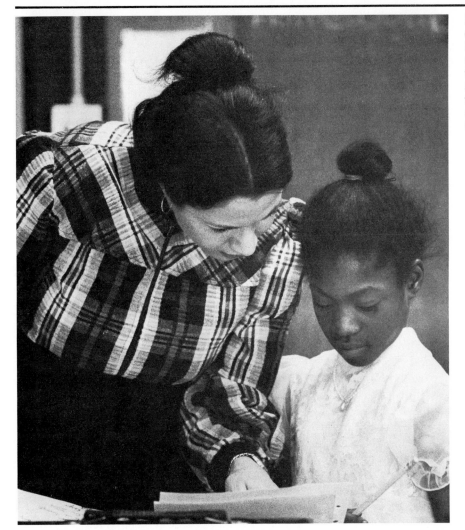

dividing this number by the number of minutes allowed for the writing or, less commonly, dividing this by the number of seconds allowed for the writing. Beginners in either style write more slowly than advanced pupils.

The average speed for manuscript writing in the second grade is about thirty letters per minute. The standard speed for cursive writing in the fifth grade is about sixty letters per minute. Speed is readily and informally measured by having pupils write for a specific period a selection from materials with which they have had sufficient time to become familiar.

Legibility in handwriting usually involves line quality, alignment, spacing, size and proportion, and slant. These facets may be informally measured among manuscript and cursive writers in the following ways.

Line Quality	This refers to the smoothness, color, and thickness of the pencil or pen line. Is the writing too heavy or too light? Is there a mixture of heavy and light, thick and fine writing? Are there any wavering lines?
Alignment	Compare the evenness of the tops of all the maximum letters, of all the minimum letters, and of all the intermediate letters. Then, with a ruler, draw a line touching the base of as many of the letters as possible. Is this line the same as the baseline?
Spacing	In manuscript, is the widest space between the straight line letters? Is the second widest space between a circle and a straight line letter? Is the least amount of space between two circle letters? Does the spacing between words equal one lowercase *o*? Does spacing between sentences, for margins, and for indentations equal two lowercase *o*s? Is spacing uniform throughout the writing? In cursive, is there enough spacing between letters within a word so that each letter appears legible by itself? Does spacing between sentences equal one uppercase *O*? Does spacing between paragraphs equal two uppercase *O*s? Is spacing uniform throughout the writing?
Size and Proportion	For manuscript and cursive writing, lines may be drawn along the tops of letters to see if they are uniformly written as suggested in the particular handwriting program. In manuscript, are uppercase letters and the tall lowercase letters a full space high? Do all other letters except the lowercase *t* extend from the baseline only to the midline? In cursive, there are two proportions used (primary and adult) with the change from primary to adult proportion usually occurring at the fifth-grade level. In primary proportion, are the minimum letters one-half the size of maximum letters? Are the intermediate letters midway between minimum and maximum letters in size? Do the uppercase letters, the maximum letters, and the lowercase *b, f, h, k,* and *l* touch the headline?
Slant	In manuscript writing, are all the letters straight up and down? In cursive writing, regularity of slant is readily determined by drawing straight lines through the slant strokes of the letters. If the lines are at different angles, the slant is irregular, but if the lines are parallel, the slant is uniform and the writing legible. All cursive letters slant whether they are uppercase or lowercase.

Evaluation of each child's progress in handwriting skill should occur regularly. It can easily be accomplished with the use of one or more of the following means: an individual folder, an individual chart, or an individual scale. The teacher may also wish to keep a small box of four-by-six-inch file cards, listing each pupil's strengths and weaknesses in the handwriting area; such a box is helpful during parent conferences and should always be available for pupil examination.

The pupils file handwritten or typed compositions into their folders weekly, dating each example of their work throughout the year. When the folders are begun at the start of the school year and maintained with regular additions, the children can quickly see their own progress and detect areas where improvement is needed. The content of the folder may include papers prepared in other curricular areas such as social studies or science. The teacher and the pupils can use the folders in setting up mutually defined goals.

An Individual Folder

In their notebooks the pupils keep a chart which has been adapted for manuscript, cursive writing, or typewriting. They can use it to indicate progressive levels of achievement, thereby evaluating their own writing performances and in turn establishing new goals with the aid of the teacher. A sample chart for cursive writing is shown in Figure 9.8.

An Individual Chart

The pupils can make handwriting scales from specimens of their own writing. They begin by collecting several of their papers over a period of some three or four weeks and then (a) cut a few lines at random from each paper; (b) date each sample and arrange them all in order of quality (not date); and (c) paste them on a large sheet of paper, putting the best specimen at the top. Such a scale should be made each semester for an accurate indication of steady or erratic progress. They will aid the teacher in conferences with pupils regarding proper letter formations and other critical aspects of writing skill.

An Individual Scale

Besides individual scales, some school systems have developed their own scales; and commercial handwriting scales are also available. Although only one-third of the schools in the nation use some sort of scale in evaluating children's handwriting, the four most commonly used scales account for 95 percent of those that are employed in instructional programs. Besides the locally developed school scales, the other three are commercial scales: the Freeman Scale, the West Scale, and the Ayres Scale. The Freeman Scale was first developed in 1912 and last revised in 1959; the West Scale (known as the American Handwriting Scale) first appeared in 1927 and was revised in 1951; and the Ayres Scale, developed in 1912, was revised in 1915. The use of a scale to evaluate handwriting is often tied to the use of a corresponding commercial system.

Although scales for evaluating the quality of pupil handwriting were among the first standardized measuring instruments to be used in American schools, they are not in current use generally. Their reliability is either not given or only moderate. All material used for writing is copied and/or memorized by the writer. There is no assurance that the total nature of the range of the handwriting quality of a given population of children has been explored. The scales predominantly measure only cursive writing, and right-handed writing is mixed with left-handed writing in a single scale. Teachers are generally unfamiliar with scales and inconsistent in using them; once given experience in their use, however, teachers are then able to evaluate the handwriting of their pupils more consistently and accurately.

Figure 9.8.   Self-Evaluation Chart for Cursive Writing.

Clues to Improvement in Handwriting (for pupil self-evaluation)

Name _____ Grade _____ School Year _____

	Oct.	Dec.	Feb.	Apr.	May
I. Rate the quality of your handwriting:					
Excellent (1), Good (2), Average (3), Fair (4), Poor (5)					
Neatness	___	___	___	___	___
Arrangement (margins, indentations)	___	___	___	___	___
Legibility	___	___	___	___	___

II. Locate the trouble spots in your handwriting:
Check (✔) one or two areas in which you need special practice.

	Oct.	Dec.	Feb.	Apr.	May
Slant: Do all your letters lean the same way, and are your down strokes really straight?	___	___	___	___	___
Space: Are the spaces between letters and words uniform?	___	___	___	___	___
Size and Proportion (Adult): Are your tall letters (*l, h, k, b, f*) about three times as tall as the small letters; the middle-sized letters (*t, d, p*) twice the height of small letters; and the descender letters one-half space below the baseline?	___	___	___	___	___
Alignment: Are all tall letters evenly tall; all small letters evenly small; and all letters resting on the baseline?	___	___	___	___	___
Line Quality: Are the thickness and color of the line about the same throughout the page?	___	___	___	___	___
Ending Strokes: Are the endings without fancy curves and long enough to guide the spacing between words?	___	___	___	___	___
Letter Formation:					
1. Are the loops open and equal in size?	___	___	___	___	___
2. Are the hump letters *m, n, h, v, y, z, x* rounded?	___	___	___	___	___
3. Are the letters *o, d, a, s, g, p, q, f* closed?	___	___	___	___	___
4. Have you made long retraces in letters *t, d, p?*	___	___	___	___	___
5. Are your uppercase letters well-formed and legible?	___	___	___	___	___
Formation of Numerals:					
1. Do you use the correct form?	___	___	___	___	___
2. Do you use the correct slant?	___	___	___	___	___
3. Are the numerals halfway between the headline and the baseline?	___	___	___	___	___

1. How can you determine when a young child is ready to learn handwriting?
2. Why is manuscript the fundamental handwriting tool?
3. What specific practices would you use to teach a left-handed pupil to write?
4. Should everyone be able to type in a highly industrial nation such as the United States? If so, should typewriting instruction be offered in every elementary school? Would it be feasible?

1. Examine some of the more commonly used resources which accompany any one commercial system of handwriting. Then, if possible, compare several different systems (including Zaner-Bloser, Noble and Noble, and Peterson), noting similarities and differences in philosophy, equipment used, and evaluative techniques.
2. Administer to a five- or six-year-old child one informal test for handedness and one for eyedness. Report your results to your peers.
3. Plan an introductory lesson in cursive writing for a group of third-grade boys and girls.
4. Save the next dozen handwritten envelopes which come to you through the mail. Then determine which ones are the most legible and what specific factors comprise legibility.
5. Evaluate your own handwriting, whether it be manuscript or cursive. Could it serve as a model for young learners?
6. Collect handwriting samples from five elementary school children. Then confer (or describe how you would confer) with each in order to help the pupil improve his or her writing.
7. Set up the learning center on handwriting shown in Figure 9.9.

Bevensee, S. E. 1977. "Hands on Handwriting." *Teacher* 95: 26–27.
Cothran, A., and Mason, G. E. 1978. "The Typewriter: Time-Tested Tool for Teaching Reading and Writing." *Elementary School Journal* 78: 171–73.
Hall, M., et al. 1976. "Writing Before Grade One: A Study of Early Writers." *Language Arts* 53: 582–85.
Hanson, I. W. 1976. "Teaching Remedial Handwriting." *Language Arts* 53: 428–31.
Lebrun, Y., and Van de Craen, P. 1975. "Developmental Writing Disorders and Their Prevention." *Journal of Special Education* 9: 201–7.
Mendoza, M. A., et al. 1978. "Circles and Tape: An Easy Teacher-Implemented Way to Teach Fundamental Writing Skills." *Teaching Exceptional Children* 10: 48–50.
Sorensen, M. R. 1977. "Write On! Creative Handwriting in the Classroom." *Language Arts* 54: 294–96.
Søvik, N. 1976. "Effects of Different Principles of Instruction in Children's Copying Performances." *Journal of Experimental Education* 45: 38–45.
Westbrooks, L. K. 1976. "Prescription for Ailing Penmanship." *Teacher* 94: 100–106.
Western, R. D. 1977. "Case Against Cursive Script." *Elementary School Journal* 78: 1–3.

Figure 9.9. Language Arts Learning Center: Handwriting.

TYPE OF CENTER: Handwriting

GRADE LEVEL: 3

TIME: 15–20 minutes

NUMBER OF STUDENTS:
One at a time

INSTRUCTIONAL OBJECTIVE:
The student will obtain good handwriting by choosing six letters and practicing them with precision and speed.

MATERIALS:
Table, heavy board for making the female kangaroo,* piece of wood with a thin slit in the middle to support the kangaroo, burlap to cover the kangaroo, yarn to outline her body, accessories for her eyes and nose, sign (poster board), squares with letters from construction paper, folder for finished papers, directions.

DIRECTIONS TO STUDENTS:
1. Put your pencil and paper down on the table.
2. Stick your hand into the kangaroo's pouch and pick out six squares.
3. Sit down at the table and practice writing the six letters. Do this as quickly as you can but with neatness too. Write each letter six times.
4. Look at your writing and check it with the letters on the squares to see if you have done them correctly.
5. Put your paper in the folder and drop the squares into the pouch.

EVALUATION:
The student checks his or her writing with the writing on the squares. The teacher checks all papers in the folder to determine handwriting faults and/or improvement.

* The teacher can use both sides of the kangaroo, having letters in one pouch and words in the other pouch. Primary grades can use this learning center for manuscript letters and words.
Source: From *Language Arts Learning Centers and Activities* by Angela Reeke and James Laffey. Copyright 1979 by Goodyear Publishing Company. Reprinted by permission.

Written Composition 10

Factors that affect children's writing performance

The five distinct stages of writing through which most children progress

Major aspects of the curriculum in written composition

The best and only way to evaluate children's written compositions

Since pupils need to communicate to others their ideas and reactions in a permanent form, written language must be an integral part of the school program. While written composition may be used less than oral composition in everyday life, this does not mean that written communication should be accorded less attention in teachers' planning. Instead, written composition should require additional instruction because writing is more difficult. It involves expressing ideas thoughtfully and precisely without the aid of facial expression, tone, or gesture. In fact, the more significant the idea and the greater the conviction, the more difficult the writing becomes.

The first requisite for effective writing is the creation of ideas formulated from the experiences the children have had—or are presently having—with a real or imaginary world. It is therefore important that teachers understand creativity and their role in stimulating creative effort in the classroom.

Creativity: The Foundation of Composition

English educators during the past decade have directed significant attention to the development of creativity in students. They are aware that there now exists scientific evidence that creativity is not a free-wheeling, amorphous quality which operates as part of an unorthodox personality, but that it is an identifiable part of the intellect which (with its attendant skills) can be measured and taught. A survey of 142 experiments designed to provide information about the teachability of creativity revealed that the most successful approaches seem to be those that involve both emotional and cognitive functioning, supply adequate structure and motivation, and give opportunities for practice, involvement, and interaction with teachers and other students.[1]

Creativity as a subject presents a problem in definition. Behaviorists in creativity research describe as creative that which produces something unique either to the individual or to society or to both. Some data support the theory that divergent thinkers are more creative than other types of thinkers and that indeed the terms *divergent thinking* and *creativity* are largely synonymous.

Creative people are those who rely less on the aspects of memory and cognition (which are most often measured by IQ tests) and so may sometimes be labelled as less intelligent. They approach learning situations in nonstandardized ways and appear offbeat or inferior at times in their thinking. They are not highly success-oriented. What they are, however, is curious, original, self-directing, sensitive, secure, flexible, persistent, humorous, and productive. They need to meet challenges and to attempt difficult and dangerous tasks, just as they need to give themselves completely to a task and to become fully absorbed in it.

A school climate that is most favorable to the development of creative attitudes and abilities is one that, according to Torrance, provides not only for periods of non-evaluated practice or learning but also provides opportunities —and even credit—for self-initiated learning.[2] Children are supplied with a model of self-determined exploration when learning is to some extent based on individual projects involving personal research in the media center. They need a responsive environment—rather than merely a stimulating one—that will lead to the controlled kind of freedom so necessary for productive, creative behavior.

The characteristics of their teacher are important too. Although not all the teacher's traits for producing creative endeavor in children have yet been determined, it is known that he or she must be resourceful in adapting to student leads and be pupil-centered. The teacher should be respectful of unusual questions or unusual ideas that the children propose and always indicate to the pupils that their thoughts have value. Ideally, the teacher should be knowledgeable and democratic by design, rather than merely cheerful and friendly. Moreover, he or she should perform as a facilitator of an atmosphere conducive to the individual thought of learners.

In addition, it is likely that creative efforts are stimulated by the teacher's confidence in the children's abilities to think adventurously and in new directions, which in turn will determine the children's estimation of themselves and their talents. A necessary condition of creativeness appears to be a certain self-confidence and particularly an absence of anxiety of nonconformist responses.[3] Constant availability of varied media is also beneficial.

Factors identified as the most inhibitive to creative expression include: (1) discouragement of fantasy and imagination; (2) tests based on detailed memorization; (3) stereotyped sex roles; and (4) social expectation, including peer censure. The last named is especially important since international studies of children and their written imaginative compositions have revealed that American children show the greatest concern for peer censure.

What all this means to the teacher of writing is reasonably clear. The ideas of students must be valued first for their quality. Correctness of expression has to take second place. Children rated on standardized tests as less intelligent must be regarded as having creative potential just as those rated as most intelligent are. Finally, the teacher must tolerate occasionally unorthodox reactions among the pupils and keep an open mind.

Numerous factors affect children's writing.[4] Late research studies have established the positive importance of the factors which are discussed in this section.

1. *Intellectual capacity.* Pupils who are superior in verbal ability are also superior in composition writing, producing more words per minute and per paper. IQ scores are significantly related to writing accomplishments. In a heterogeneous sample of 300 children ages 7.0 to 9.11 the able group showed an advantage of nearly three years in written language development.

2. *Reading achievement.* Children who read well also write well, while those who read poorly write poorly too. In low-income, urban neighborhoods even first graders reveal a high correlation between reading and written composition, while sixth graders who rank illiterate or primitive in writing read below their chronological age. Finally, as the students' level of reading comprehension increases, so does the number of compound and complex sentences they can write.

3. *Grade level/chronological age.* Advances in grade/age correlate positively with increasing length of written sentences and of T-units (i.e., terminable units—main clauses together with all phrases and clauses syntactically related). On the other hand, the difference between the performance of the low-achieving groups and the national performance in expressive writing increases at each successive age level.

4. *Sex.* Girls write more than boys. On measures of complexity, boys and girls score at generally the same levels; on most measures of quantity, however, girls score significantly higher than boys. Girls also tend to write compositions which are judged to be of high quality.

   Seven-year-old boys write more about the so-called secondary territory or the metropolitan areas beyond the home and school, while seven-year-old girls write more about the primary territory related to the home and school. Girls stress more prethinking and organizational qualities and feelings in characterizations than do boys. Primary boys are more concerned than primary girls with the importance of spacing, formation of letters, and neatness.

5. *Oral language proficiency.* Children who are rated superior or above average in their use of oral language are also rated above average in writing. Those below average in oral expression rate the same in written language.

6. *Type of writing tool.* Story-writing performance is significantly better with ball-point or felt pens than it is with standard (adult-size) pencils, whether the writers are primary or intermediate children. Furthermore, the pupils write more when offered a green writing pen than they do with red, blue, or black pens. Also, the novelty of writing with pens does not wear off after repeated exposure.

7. *Special training program.* A program emphasizing many experiences in writing and a focus on clarity and interest in writing (rather than on mechanical correctness) results in a greater number of words per T-unit, greater sophistication in language control—and fewer mechanical mistakes.

8. *Structured literature program.* The type of program described in the next chapter provides a balance between fiction and nonfiction, between prose and poetry, and between the traditional and the modern. The ability of children to write often depends upon their ability to hear/read good books. They and their teacher should set aside time to share favorite volumes with each other.

9. *Classroom environment.* Results of writing done in informal environments demonstrate that pupils do not need supervision in order to write. Informal environments also seem to favor boys in that they write more than girls do in such environments, whether the writing is assigned or unassigned. Formal environments, on the other hand, seem to be more favorable to girls in that they write to greater length and more frequently than do boys in these types of environments, whether the writing is assigned or not. Finally, an environment that requires large amounts of assigned writing inhibits the content, range, and amount of writing done by elementary school children.

    Teachers must be sensitive to establishing a relaxed classroom climate in which divergent thinking is encouraged. Each member of the class —and his or her work—should be respected. In order to encourage dialogue and foster sensory awareness, learning centers should be maintained.

10. *Handedness.* Left-handers outperform right-handers on both verbal and nonverbal tests. They should therefore have a clear advantage because ability is a powerful determinant of writing development. However, since their output is identical with that of right-handed children, Harpin suggests that teachers make special provision for left-handers and offer them direct help.[5] Otherwise the physical difficulty of writing may take an abnormal share of the left-handed child's attention and so restrict the freedom to experiment syntactically.

11. *Socioeconomic background.* The proportions of good expressive papers written by students whose parents have post-high school education and by students who live in relatively affluent communities are greater than the proportion for children of the poorly educated and children who live in relatively impoverished areas. Pupils in the top socioeconomic groups are more fluent in their writing and use a greater variety of words than pupils in the lower levels. In every measure of language studied, the child writers in the upper levels, socially and economically, show an advantage over those in the lower levels; this is true even among children of only average intelligence. Pupils from low-metro schools do not routinely produce unique written creations; very often their stories are stereotypic, descriptive, and not very imaginative.

12. *Length of writing time.* The longer the time the children are permitted to write, the better the quality of their written expression. They should therefore be allowed to choose how long they wish to write during any one period. Even middle-grade pupils profit from a prolonged time span of as much as 225 minutes for writing.

13. *Instruction in modern grammar.* Boys and girls receiving instruction in structural grammar or transformational-generative grammar—whether formally or informally—are producing longer and more syntactic structures of greater complexity than students taught the older, traditional grammar.

14. *Lack of integration of writing and reading tasks.* The practice of assigning reading-related writing tasks may in the long run detract from the development of positive attitudes toward reading among intermediate pupils. Over a number of assignments the less positive attitudes that pupils have toward writing tasks may transfer to the closely associated reading activities and reduce the positive attitudes toward reading. If a major objective of the teacher's planning is the development of positive responses toward reading, then the assignment of related writing activities becomes a questionable procedure.

   Good readers and poor readers alike enjoy reading a story significantly more than they enjoy writing about it. And there is no evidence that integrating writing and reading enhances enjoyment of the reading.

15. *Teacher attitude.* A receptive and encouraging attitude on the part of the teacher is crucial. Children whose teachers stress originality of expression develop more ideas, write more words, and make fewer mechanical errors.

   The matter of teacher criticism of completed compositions, however, has not been resolved. There is no significant difference between the effects of negative reaction as opposed to positive criticism by teachers of children's writing. Either type of criticism may apparently be used since each gets similar results.

The curriculum for written expression for the elementary grades is concerned with two major aspects. There is the *content* or the ideas which the children wish to relate. There are also the processes or *skills* through which those ideas may be communicated. Both phases are expedited when teachers underscore their planning with the principles enumerated in this section.

Guidelines for the Teaching of Written Composition

1. *Children must recognize the significance of writing, in their own lives and in the lives of others.* Through daily contact with labels, direction sheets, maps, menus, coupons, charts, bulletin boards, and newspapers, pupils can be taught to sense the importance of writing—in the home, school, and community. Studies of such famous writings as historical documents of the past and present offer another dimension to older children's recognition of the role of written composition in society.

Such writing sensitivity is intensified when the elementary teacher helps the boys and girls to think of themselves as recorders of classroom activities and school events.

2. *Children must have a variety of experiences and interests about which to write.* Firsthand happenings at home or school, on the playground or at a nearby park, on a study trip or at a club meeting, are all useful means of input. So are vicarious experiences through the media of selected books, magazines, films, or television programs. Finally, hobbies and sports, from stamp collecting to soccer, furnish material for written compositions too. Input, however, can and must be continued during the year through the ongoing classroom activities and learning centers provided by the teacher in the areas of science, social studies, reading, arts and crafts, and health.

3. *Children must communicate orally before they can express themselves in written form.* Speaking and listening habits profoundly influence pupils' abilities to write. Until they can express themselves clearly through oral means, they generally are not ready to compose their thoughts in written form. This is true of both school beginners and upper primary children.

   Suggested activities for developing oral communication skills include puppetry, story dramatization, reporting, dramatic play, interviewing, and discussion.

4. *Children must enjoy a satisfying and supportive classroom environment.* In a pressure-free atmosphere pupils believe that their values, encounters, and feelings are important enough to share with each other. If they are thereby encouraged to talk freely about these experiences and beliefs, they are more apt to be able to use their oral contributions as a basis for their writing.

5. *Children must realize that a writer always communicates with someone when he or she writes.* The subject or subjects being addressed by a writer comprise the "audience." Writer attitude as well as writing style and language are all dependent upon the nature of this "audience."

   The framework in elementary school composition published by the Wisconsin Department of Public Instruction treats audience in three different senses—Me-as-Audience, Personal You-as-Audience, and Unknown You-as-Audience.[6] Each of these is removed somewhat from the other in psychological distance, passing from inner-person or self-as-audience to an unknown audience which may be geographically many miles away, or at least, some audience about whom the writer knows very little.

6. *Children must hear and read literature in order to write well.* Next to direct experience, the reading which children do is usually their most important source of new words and ideas. Since carefully chosen literature presented effectively can do much to stimulate good writing, a teacher should plan many types of literary experiences, including storytelling and choral reading. Scheduled browsing in the school media center or classroom library is also helpful.

   Gay enumerates five specific ways in which students' writing abilities will be enhanced when the teacher reads aloud from quality literary works every day for at least twenty minutes. First, their vocabularies will increase both in comprehension and in word count. Second, their abilities to distinguish among subtle differences in word meaning will improve. Third, their sentence structures will become more effective and more complex. Fourth, they will gain a sense of writing form and organization: e.g., their compositions will have proper introductions and conclusions. Fifth, they will gain a reason or rationale for writing after hearing the rhythm of standard speech and the pattern of literary prose.[7]

7. *Children must understand that the composing process actually consists of two activities: writing and rewriting.* This two-step operation demands a balance of creativity and craftsmanship, according to Gebhardt. He warns that teachers must foster creativity in order to avoid squelching the originality and enthusiasm of pupils and to do justice to the humanizing power of language. Yet teachers must also foster discipline in order to remain true to the essential craft behind language and to prepare children for a demanding world.[8]

8. *Children must appreciate that vocabulary is a major element contributing to effective writing.* Students can be taught to refer to a variety of sources in which they can locate the words they need, including appropriately graded dictionaries, word boxes, basal readers, spelling books, and special chalkboard or chart lists. To improve their written communication they must also learn to select expressive words, employ synonyms and antonyms, and become acquainted with a beginning thesaurus.

9. *Children must become actively involved in evaluating their own writing.* Through writing conferences with their teacher, pupils acquire the ability to occasionally revise and to routinely edit their own work. As they complete some compositions, they may decide to *revise the contents* in order to make the compositions more interesting to readers. As they finish all written work, however, they *proofread or edit* it in order to make meanings clearer to readers. Occasionally a pupil may even copy a composition for the sake of neatness if the composition has been revised/edited extensively.

10. *Children must be encouraged but not forced to share their writing with others.* Since writing implies communication, compositions may be read aloud in the classroom or posted in the halls. They may be delivered to parents or published in local newspapers or national journals. On the other hand, compositions may be quietly placed in children's language folders or the teacher's file and never displayed at all. While the teacher can and should guide pupils to share their writing with peers and parents, it is the children themselves who must finally choose to accept or decline publicity about their written compositions.

   For pupils who are eager to share their writing with a wide audience, there are more than a dozen national children's magazines ranging alphabetically from *American Girl* and *Boys' Life* to *Weewish Tree* and *Young*

World that publish the creative efforts of elementary school pupils. Competition is keen and delays in notification of the acceptance or rejection of submitted material are common. Still, each of the magazines accepts two or more of the following: poems, riddles, book reviews, jokes, letters, stories, puzzles, recipes, photographs, comic strips, drawings, and articles. All work must be original and accompanied in most instances by a signed statement regarding originality. Occasionally a magazine will pay a small sum for work accepted.

Stages of Writing Compositions

Elementary school teachers guide children in the primary and intermediate grades through five distinct stages of writing which are discussed in this section. Boys and girls pass through the stages at different rates, remaining at some levels for months and possibly skipping others entirely.

Group Dictation to the Teacher

Children in the early grades do not have the spelling and handwriting skills necessary for independent writing. Their language is largely oral, and therefore the beginnings of written expression occur as the pupils orally share their ideas and feelings with others.

Their first writing is done by dictating to the teacher who acts as a secretary. While recording the children's dictation, the teacher guides them into appropriate wording and organization of ideas and informally calls their attention to the mechanical aspects of capitalization and punctuation. They in turn begin to develop readiness for later learning of the structural elements of language and become conscious of the need for orderly sequence.

Pupils enjoy hearing their teacher read back from the chalkboard or chart what they have said, and should be allowed numerous opportunities to dictate compositions and to hear these compositions read aloud. An audience, after all, is part of the cycle of communication so that even when a group record is made, that product deserves to be heard by its writers.

The boys and girls at this stage are capable of dictating couplets, questions, plans, letters, reports, stories, titles, captions, jingles, conversations, and greeting card messages. After they have cooperatively dictated several of these types of written expression, the teacher may demonstrate how to proofread before preparing the final copy on chart paper or the chalkboard.

Group dictation activities contribute to children's learning. The materials produced can be used as reading matter for the class. Boys and girls learn to work together as a result of participation in such group projects. And children begin to sense that writing is not a contrived process, but a routine activity. They are constantly experiencing, pondering, and recording ideas in interest-centered classrooms.

(Group dictation techniques should be familiar to all elementary teachers although such procedures are obviously used more in the primary than in the intermediate grades.)

Dictated cooperative writing provides a springboard for individual dictation. Children enjoy seeing their own words neatly written or typed on a page. They perceive that their words may be reread at a later time and shared with their classmates and that the spoken word has its counterpart on the written page. Primary children who have repeatedly felt the satisfaction of joining their classmates in a writing experience are easily encouraged by their teacher to begin individual dictation.

Sometimes such dictation is a natural outgrowth of the show-and-tell period when children take turns in exhibiting and explaining realia that are personally interesting. These vocal situations offer the opportunity to compile ideas and to gain immediate satisfaction from communication with an audience. The teacher may write down the experiences that some of the children describe in order to interest other pupils to participate.

Individual dictation demands that the teacher plan some self-directed activities for the pupils while he or she works with one child at a time. Looking at picture books, reading alone or with a friend, painting or crayoning pictures, modeling clay, or playing number games are examples of activities that need minimal adult supervision after the children have performed them repeatedly and know where the materials are and how to care for them. Once the teacher has discovered which quiet learning exercises work best with this roomful of children, he or she can set aside short uninterrupted dictation periods ranging from five to ten minutes for work alone with one pupil. Pupils look forward to these times of private conversation with their teacher.

Once a child has begun dictating, the teacher must avoid interrupting so as not to block the flow of ideas and original expressions. The teacher can of course quietly change gross errors in nonstandard English ("I seen") while recording the child's version. When the child has finished dictating a story, he or she may wish to illustrate the story and later staple the picture to the story.

With the writers' permission, dictated compositions—whether poetry or prose—can be subsequently compiled and placed on the library table for the entire class to enjoy again and again.

Group Dictation to the Teacher with Individual Copying

As soon as children can read for themselves the stories, verse, and observations which they have been dictating collectively or individually to the teacher—and as soon as they are receiving systematic instruction in handwriting as well—most are ready to copy a dictated composition of approximately one paragraph.

Purpose, however, should be the key to any copying that the children do of cooperatively dictated material. If only one letter or one list is needed for the entire class, there is no reason why every pupil must make a copy of that letter or list. But if each child's parents need a separate invitation to the PTA spaghetti supper or if each pupil is responsible for a brief list of fire hazards to look for in his or her home, then each child should copy the note or memo that has been determined and dictated by the group. Each child should also proofread his or her writing slowly and efficiently.

Independent Writing with Much Teacher Help

A teacher can assist beginning writers toward greater independence by helping them plan a sequence of ideas for compositions. During the oral discussion preceding the written assignment, the teacher enters on the chalkboard a simple outline of the proposed letter or report. The teacher may also write down any specialized vocabulary which is needed.

Throughout the grades, and especially with groups learning English as a second language, the teacher may encourage beginning writers first to draw pictures of their stories or experiences and then to discuss the pictures with their classmates (or teacher) before attempting to write down any thoughts. Some school districts even supply writing paper that has been especially designed for this purpose, for primary teachers particularly have observed that the visual medium may help children progress from a phonemic to a graphemic expression of ideas.

The teacher may also hold group discussions with those pupils who have difficulty translating ideas into written words, and may recommend the use of a tape recorder to some of the students.

Independent Writing with Little Teacher Help

Although dictated writing may continue through the intermediate grades, most pupils are able to write a couple of sentences independently by the time they complete the first grade, and by the third grade they can write a well-structured paragraph. Children make better progress in their development of independent writing ability when their teacher is supportive of their efforts and the classroom climate is open and free.

They vary individually in their writing skills just as they do in their reading skills. Consequently, there are those first graders who can write lengthy letters readily and independently, and then there are those sixth graders who still need assistance in order to complete a single brief paragraph. Teachers should therefore continue to plan their writing activities carefully at any grade level.

Major Aspects of Written Communication: Content

The aspects of written expression have been described as the content—or the *what*—and the skills—or the *how*. Valid distinctions exist between these two important areas. However, an effective teacher will not ignore the fresh viewpoint or novel description contained in student writing while pointing out the need for such mechanics as handwriting, capitalization, and spelling. Content is critical; the mechanics are subordinate and need only express the content accurately and quickly.

The Content of Writing: An Art

Most pupils need assistance in working with the ideas they wish to communicate. Since ideas remain the substance of all written expression, the ability to work with them is a fundamental one.

The content of ideas embodied in written composition is nevertheless varied. First, there is writing that is an expression of personal view—a feeling, belief, or preference. Then there is writing that is sheer imagination. A third type encompasses accurate reflections of events, persons, procedures, or objects. A fourth conceptualizes relationships existing in the world—similarities, differences, or classifications. The final category includes writing projects, explanatory designs, or schemes, which extend beyond observable data but are yet consistent with these data.[9]

In order for children to explore in writing many of these different kinds of content, they must of course first be able to work with many different kinds of ideas:

A. *Expression of personal view*. Content that denotes opinions, judgments, preferences, or personal feelings.
   1. *Opinion*—a personal belief or point of view not necessarily in accord with fact.
   2. *Judgment*—an expression of the justifiability, consistency, importance, effectiveness, or overall worth of a person, event, outcome, object, invention or design; the judgment is supported by reference to clearly defined criteria.
   3. *Preference*—a liking or disliking for someone or something; it may be supported with reasons.
   4. *Feelings*—an outpouring of personal, emotional feelings of either a positive or negative nature; an emotional reaction to an event, person, or object.
B. *Imagination*. Content that involves the fabrication of speeches, descriptions, persons, and/or plots that go beyond real and/or actual occurrences.
   1. *Inventive speech*—a monolog, dialog, or conversation that does not purport to be a record of actual oral communication which has taken place.
   2. *Inventive description*—description of an item that does not exist; a description that departs from fact.
   3. *Person*—a character devised by a writer, based not completely on an individual who exists or who has existed.
   4. *Plot*—a sequence of concocted events.
C. *Reflection of the world*. Content that purports to represent accurately objects, persons, events, materials, and observable procedures read and heard.
   1. *Report of a happening*—a factual account of an event that tells, for instance, who was involved, where it happened, when it happened, what happened, under what conditions it happened, what materials were associated with the happening, and how long it lasted.
   2. *Procedures*—a systematic accounting of how to do something, how to go somewhere, how to act.
   3. *Description*—a factual enumeration of the attributes of a person, an object, or some material, including such properties as shape, size,

smell, color, taste, texture, motion, quality, temperature, weight, shadow, reflection or conduction of light and sound.

4. *Retelling of something heard or read*—a recounting in one's own language of a report, story, generalization, description, plan, or direction that has been expressed by some other person.

5. *Summary of perceptions*—a summary statement of a more complete description, report, recounting, paper.

D. *Conception of relationships existing in the world.* Content that identifies interrelationships among elements perceived.

1. *Contrast*—a statement indicating that two or more elements differ in a particular attribute.

2. *Comparison*—a statement indicating that two or more elements share a common attribute.

3. *Classification analysis*—an indication that an element belongs to a previously defined set or category.

4. *Sequential analysis*—an indication that an element sequentially comes first, another second, another third.

5. *Qualitative analysis*—an indication of which elements are in a lower or higher position in a hierarchy, which elements are more complex than other elements, which are closer and which are more distant, which are smaller and which are bigger.

6. *Explanation*—an indication of why something happened.

   a. Explanation in terms of cause-and-effect—an explanation connecting two events, one of which has a causal relationship with the other.

   b. Explanation in terms of interlocking generalizations—an explanation of a happening by reference to a series of known generalizations.

   c. Explanation in terms of supporting principles—an indication that certain data are supported by a known principle, that an event can be explained by reference to a known generalization.

   d. Explanation in terms of rational intent—an indication that something was done or is being done to serve a human purpose.

E. *Projection of explanatory schema and designs.* Content that projects original ideas, going beyond observable data but consonant with these data.

1. *Hypothesis*—an educated prediction or guess that is founded on the study of data, and that forms the basis for future action.

2. *Conceptual schemes*—generalizations founded on analysis of several related events that can be used to explain these events; also, a complex system of generalizations; theories.

3. *Designs*—schemes for classifying data, for taking action, for putting things together; plans.

   a. Plan for action—an original procedure for doing something; a projected new way for carrying on an activity.

b. Pattern—plans for construction of an original device.
c. Classification scheme—a new organizational system through which elements can be categorized.
d. Taxonomy—a new organizational system through which elements can be categorized in a hierarchy.

The skills or mechanics of writing include spelling, handwriting, capitalization and punctuation, and paragraphing and sentence sense. Young children begin to appreciate the proper use of these tools when they realize that these tools can help them express their thoughts more clearly and thereby aid their readers. To help children gain this realization, teachers should encourage children to edit their work.

In the early grades most editing is done in conference with the teacher. Since many beginning compositions are relatively brief, a great deal can be accomplished in a short period. By the third grade pupils are capable of greater self-reliance and can be introduced systematically to techniques of editing that they can gradually apply on their own. By the fourth grade many children can function as independent editors, provided that they have had a lengthy introduction to corrective procedures. Some groups even adopt a few professional proofreading marks:

∧	Insert a word, punctuation mark, or sentence.	Christmas is here∧
≡	Capitalize.	He is mr. Mason.
/	Don't capitalize.	She moved to the State of Washington.
	Delete a word, punctuation mark, or sentence.	I can can go home.
¶	Start a new paragraph.	. . . my aunt. The horse ran away . . .

Child writers should compose knowing that their work may possibly need editing. If they write on every other line and leave broad margins, they may later insert, delete, or correct material without problems of space. To help them identify choppy sentences or letters and words omitted unintentionally, they can read their poems or reports aloud to classmates or to a tape recorder. Such listening or oral proofreading aids self-editing, according to researchers who found that a quantity of syntactic deviations can thus be eliminated from children's written sentences. Many omissions of the subject, the verb *be,* tense markers, articles, expletives, and capital letters can be detected and corrected. Most extraneous and redundant words can be deleted.[10]

Mechanical skills are never introduced all at once or taught in isolation. Neither are they stressed to the point where they curb the creativity of pupils, and cause a loss of interest in writing. Nevertheless, mechanical skills are considered to be a legitimate extension of the written form of speech, and children can gradually become independent editors.

Spelling

There is no question, states Margaret Peters, that the behavior of the teacher determines, more than any other single factor, whether children learn or do not learn to spell.[11] The teacher's behavior or attitude toward spelling may also influence the children's attitude toward writing and the wise teacher cannot permit spelling handicaps to stifle pupils' ability to communicate. The teacher's positive attitude toward the importance of spelling in relation to good communication will encourage personal responsibility for spelling and still promote good writing.

Each child needs to know what to do independently upon discovering a word that he or she cannot spell while writing. The teacher, to avoid breaking the writer's train of thought or interrupting work with other boys and girls, may advise the pupil with a spelling problem to leave a space on his or her paper temporarily (writing in only the initial letter or syllable of the troublesome word). The teacher can then help the pupil later. Or better yet, the teacher may do the following:

1. Place topic words on reference charts for copying as needed. Most classrooms have various kinds of classification charts, showing word lists that grow out of the units of study.
2. Compile a chalkboard list of class-dictated words to be used when needed.
3. Obtain appropriate dictionaries, preferably one for each pupil. Such books should list single-entry words in alphabetical order and supply some classification pages.
4. Encourage children to consult a familiar reader or storybook which contains the word they need to spell.
5. Promote the construction of individual notebooks, dictionaries, or word boxes.
6. Permit spelling the word according to structural or phonetic analysis, with the understanding that the child can correct the word later if he or she misspells it.
7. Allow the pupil with a spelling problem to receive aid from a classmate.

Handwriting

Interrelated with spelling is handwriting, for each depends on the other for communication. When letters are correctly proportioned and words are properly spaced, the composition is more readily understood.

The real issue is not the form of the handwriting but its legibility. Although the primary pupil ordinarily uses manuscript and the intermediate pupil employs cursive writing or the typewriter, each boy or girl should be encouraged to compose in whichever form he or she feels comfortable. Nevertheless, since some types of writing always require the use of manuscript, the teacher will wish to help every child develop or maintain skill in that form of penmanship.

Children tend to use too many marks of punctuation and too many capital letters rather than too few. The responsibility of the teacher is often as much a matter of showing the boys and girls when not to insert capital letters and punctuation marks as it is a matter of teaching them when to use these conventions meaningfully.

Primary and intermediate pupils alike possess individual writing needs, and it is these needs that usually determine what is to be taught in the areas of punctuation and capitalization at each level of development. The successful teacher offers specialized drill tailored to the specific demands of the class and consequently does not routinely use workbook exercises in either of these skills. Occasionally the teacher does employ an opaque projector or the chalkboard to promote group discussion and correction of an unidentified paper, with special attention to the elements of capitalization and punctuation.

Elementary school children are able to understand that punctuation marks help translate speech into writing. And the teacher can point out how, through the use of punctuation, a writer can convey meaning to readers without benefit of the help which a speaker has—gestures, pitch, stress, juncture, and facial expressions.

Capitalization and Punctuation

Children can be helped early to understand and to write good sentences. Even in the beginning primary years when children are dictating stories, they can gradually discover that a sentence may tell something, ask a question, express strong feeling, or give a command. As sentence skill develops, they can move from the one-sentence composition to the two- and three-sentence compositions. Finally children learn that a group of sentences (or even occasionally a single sentence) that tells about one idea is called a paragraph, and older pupils begin to write expository paragraphs with a topic sentence.

As pupils attempt to write complex sentences and experiment with new forms of expression, the run-on sentence, the choppy sentence, and the excessive use of the *and* connective appear more frequently in children's writing. While such difficulties cannot be quickly eliminated, the teacher may wish to schedule individualized or small-group practice in (1) understanding the sentence itself as well as sentence intonation patterns and sentence building; (2) adjusting run-on sentences through sentence connectors, conjunctions, separation, or subordination; and (3) combining short sentences and using connectives other than *and* to add variety to sentences.

Paragraphing and Sentence Sense

School beginners love to talk, to read, and to write. Early in the intermediate grades, however, children often lose some of their spontaneity and enthusiasm, especially in the area of composition. This period then is the appropriate time to introduce concepts basic to written communication—style, invention, and arrangement/order—in lessons designed to treat aspects of each of these three. After a cycle of lessons such as those that follow, the children are asked to use what they have learned by writing one or two stories or poems.[12]

Lessons in the Fundamental Concepts of Composition

Written Composition   259

**Basic Lesson
in Style**

Style refers to the special way a writer uses language. The students are introduced in this lesson to the idea that compositions are directed toward an audience.

A. The teacher and children discuss what is an audience.
   1. The teacher asks a series of questions designed to evoke such terms as *reader* and *viewer:* Are all movies alike? How do they differ? Are some more interesting to you than others? What are some of the terms that we call the people who watch a movie and decide whether or not it is interesting? (The same series is repeated, discussing books instead of movies.)
   2. Once the term *audience* has been discovered (or introduced by the teacher if necessary), the teacher asks questions to help the students discover that a professional writer composes for an audience.
B. The teacher and children discuss why all writers must always be aware of who is going to read their paragraphs, stories, or poems.
   1. The teacher asks questions designed to elicit the differences between books written for first graders and those written for intermediate pupils.
   2. In order to help students generalize about differences between audiences, the teacher reproduces a short excerpt from an informational book (or encyclopedia) written for intermediate pupils, and an excerpt from an informational book (or encyclopedia) written for adults. In both instances the teacher reads the excerpts aloud as the students follow their own copies, and then asks a series of questions to help the class discover the obvious differences: Which example has the longer paragraphs? Which tends to have shorter sentences? Do you know the definitions of the following words in the second excerpt (e.g., *aberrant, quadruped, dentition, diminutive* in an article about dinosaurs)? Following the discussion, most students are able to generalize that the first excerpt is easier to read due to its structure and vocabulary and that it has been written for younger readers.
   3. The teacher and the children now study two other excerpts, preferably contrasting a definition found in a basal reader glossary with a definition of the same word found in a collegiate dictionary and copied on the chalkboard. The students continue to generalize regarding the responsibility of the writer toward his or her audience.
C. The children plan to rewrite and critique a two-minute version of a folktale for a group of first-grade pupils.
   1. The students ask a series of questions regarding the first graders as a potential audience: What will interest them most? For how long will they remain attentive? Would a picture (or two) help hold their attention during the presentation?
   2. Each of the students receives a copy of the old Norse folktale about

"The Husband Who Was to Mind the House" and follows along as the teacher reads the tale aloud. She then asks the students to consider the first graders as an audience and to write out and illustrate a two-minute version of the folktale. They must complete the reading before the younger children become restless, and they must be certain to include all the pertinent details in a style the audience can understand.

3. When the writing is completed, the students meet in small groups to read in turn what each has written (and drawn) and evaluate it in terms of the following questions: Are the sentences clear enough for first graders to follow? Will this version hold the interest of the audience? Will the picture (or pictures) help the audience understand the story? If any folktale does not meet all these criteria, the group helps that writer determine how to make his or her tale more comprehensible to a young audience. In other words, the students receive immediate feedback from their peers who have struggled with the same task.

D. The children, with the cooperation of several primary teachers, read their folktales aloud to small groups of first-grade pupils. They thereby receive additional feedback from a meeting with the actual audience.

Later lessons explore other aspects of the concept of style.

Invention refers to a writer's imaginative selection and exploration of content. The students are introduced in this lesson to the idea that authors must draw upon their own experiences and learn how to use those experiences well. **Basic Lesson in Invention**

A. The teacher and children discuss ways in which a writer might begin a story or a poem.
1. The teacher asks a series of questions regarding the opening sentence of an imaginary story—*When I woke up, all of the lawns had turned bright purple:* Would thinking of questions your readers might wish answered help you write your story? Would asking questions about only the opening sentence help you write? If you cannot tell everything about purple grass, is it wiser to concentrate on relating just one description or fact? Would questions about the cause or effect of this phenomenon help you write your story?
B. The teacher and children discuss from the chalkboard the following paragraph entitled "The Watch": *My father owned a watch. It was old but it was kind of handsome. Some strange-looking scratches were on the back. His boss wanted it.*
1. The students are asked to determine what readers might want to know that the story did not tell them. Such questions as "Where did your father get his watch?" and "What kind of scratches?" may be

suggested. Then each student writes two other questions that would aid readers.

C. The children are shown a picture illustrating three (or more) different objects and are asked how the three objects might serve as an idea for a story that would interest other students in the class.

1. The teacher suggests that a few questions be posed about one separate item. Next, questions are posed which include two items. Finally, questions are asked which include all of the items in the picture.

2. Each student selects those questions which he or she believes would make an interesting story for classmates to hear/read.

D. The children write and critique stories about the picture of the objects.

1. Using questions previously evaluated as stimulating, each student writes his or her own story.

2. When the writing is completed, the students meet in small groups to read in turn what each has written and evaluate it in terms of its interest to the audience. If any story does not meet this criterion, the group helps the writer determine how to make his or her story more interesting.

Later lessons explore other aspects of the concept of invention.

Basic Lesson in Order or Arrangement

Order refers to a writer's arrangement of material so that it will make sense to his or her audience. The main thrust of this lesson is to help students realize that authors must always be concerned with whether or not their readers can follow what has been written.

A. The teacher and children discuss what happens when sentences in a story or the frames in a comic strip are not in logical order.

1. The students are given a comic strip in which the frames have been disarranged. They are asked whether they can read the confused version or prefer to rearrange the frames first so that the strip makes sense and is more fun to read.

2. Each student rearranges the frames and compares the arrangement with those of classmates.

B. The teacher and children discuss the concept of time order or chronological order.

1. On the chalkboard the students arrange a series of historical events centered about the famous ride of Paul Revere in 1775.

2. On the chalkboard the students practice rearranging a straight chronological narrative (from a basal reader or a children's magazine) in which half of the sentences are not in sequence.

C. The teacher and children examine a well-written paragraph in their science book which gives instructions for an experiment or tells readers how to perform in sequence some activity (e.g., preserving the shape and color of flowers), and discuss that paragraph.

1. The students decide upon a good title for the paragraph that would also aid readers.
2. They determine what words the writer used to help readers know what to do first and what to do next. They think of additional words that might be helpful in keeping order straight.

D. The children write and critique original explanations about how to perform some activity.
   1. Students are reminded to keep the sequence of steps in order and to give the readers enough information so that they will be able to do the job themselves. Students also recall how asking questions helped them in an earlier lesson in invention.
   2. Each student discovers his or her own topic for composition or else selects one from a posted list (e.g., making popcorn, toasting marshmallows, flying kites, planting a vegetable garden, etc.). The boys and girls then write their compositions.
   3. When the writing is completed, the students meet in small groups to read in turn what each has written and to ask a series of questions about each paper: Has the writer included everything the reader needs to know? Are the directions in order so that the reader knows what to do first, next, and so on? Will the writing hold the interest of the reader? Has the writer paid attention to spelling and punctuation? If any paper does not satisfactorily answer all the questions, the group helps the writer make the necessary improvements.

Later lessons explore other aspects of the concept of order/arrangement.

School Stimuli for Writing

Children clearly do not leap at the opportunity to do creative writing, concluded Smith and Hansen after their recent study of 464 fourth graders in Madison, Wisconsin. The pupils as a whole enjoyed reading a story significantly more than they enjoyed writing about it, regardless of whether the writing task was creative or noncreative, assigned by the teacher or self-selected. Furthermore, the good readers did not respond any more positively to the writing task than did the poor readers.[13]

The problem of motivating written composition remains acute. Today's children are more accustomed to electronic devices that stress the spoken word over the written word. Still, writing in the elementary grades can be spurred on through a variety of stimuli. Approximately seventy of these stimulating situations are explored in this section. Additional activities are described briefly in Table 10.1.

Grocery Labels

Fourth graders became concerned with consumer education. Each child brought in one colorful label from a grocery item and *wrote a short television commercial* describing the product honestly. Some of the thirty-second commercials proved humorous.

Table 10.1.

Instructional Activities in Elementary School Written Composition.

Instructional Objective	Grade Level	Learning Activity and/or Teaching Strategy
Understands the relationship between speech and writing.	K	Class cooperatively dictates to the teacher the directions for responding properly to a fire drill.
	1	The teacher brings in a hand eggbeater and a sponge for squeezing water into a tin pie pan. Then he or she asks the children to dictate what the eggbeater and the sponge may be saying as they are being used.
Comprehends the relative permanence of writing.	1	Children individually prepare picture scrapbooks to share with classmates. They paint, draw, or cut out pictures and then paste them on heavier paper. Finally they label the pictures.
Understands that people write to influence the behavior or convictions of others.	4	Each child writes a pro or con argument on littering.
	5	Each child designs a commercial for a billboard.
	6	The debate teams write out their opinions and facts before the oral presentation. Resolved: Christmas has become too commercial.
Understands that people write to record information clearly and accurately.	2	Upon returning from a field trip to the science museum, each child writes a description of his or her favorite item and reads it aloud to a small group. The group must guess the identity of the object; whoever guesses correctly becomes the next reader.
	3	Each child keeps an individual diary for one week. At the end of each day the child writes one or two sentences about the day's happenings.
	4	Students record observations of the behavior of mealworms as seen under a microscope.
	5	Each student prepares a brief bibliography on American presidents. Bibliographies are exchanged and the receivers must check the library shelves to determine accuracy of the documentation.
	6	Class makes a time line tracing the development of the growth of democracy from ancient times to 1776.
Understands that people write to respond to a verbal or written stimulus.	2	Children clip coupons from newspapers or magazines and complete the forms correctly, pretending to be ordering merchandise.
	3	Children write friendly letters to the room mothers after the St. Valentine's Day party.
	4	Children individually write a definition of a common object (such as a balloon) by naming and classifying it properly and by giving one identifying characteristic.
	5	Each student chooses a topic sentence about a special interest/sport/hobby and proceeds to write a paragraph using details to expand that sentence.
	6	Class lists several transitional words and phrases that keep time order straight in a paragraph or story and that keep the relationships clear between ideas (e.g., *if, when, then, while, because, first*).

Instructional Objective	Grade Level	Learning Activity and/or Teaching Strategy
Applies mechanical skills (i.e., punctuation, capitalization, spelling, and handwriting) to all writing.	1	Children take turns erasing capitalization errors and correcting the errors with colored chalk in a dictated experience chart story written on the chalkboard.
	2	The teacher displays one concrete item and has each child write a sentence about it. The sentences are collected and read aloud to the class (with the owners' permission), which must decide which sentences are complete sentences.
	3	Some children are chosen to be question marks; others, exclamation marks; and the rest are periods. The teacher reads aloud a class summary of a field trip, which includes all three marks. After a question, the question marks stand up, and so on.
	4	Children are given written instructions (for a science experiment) which have no periods. The class places periods in the correct places.
	5	Each child writes a paragraph summary about a film the class recently viewed, purposely misspelling five words. The children exchange papers, and each then proofreads the new paragraph carefully for proper spelling.
	6	Portions of editorials which the pupils have written are projected on a screen (with owners' names deleted). The class must evaluate the handwriting—slant, size, shape, spacing, and alignment.
Organizes expository writing logically and clearly.	6	Children bring to class copies of their favorite comic strips and list details which happen in each frame.
Understands that people write to express, both for themselves and others, their ideas, opinions, and insights.	1	Class cooperatively writes "Fun at a Picnic" (via the teacher and the chalkboard) just to a certain point, at which time the children individually conclude the story.
	2	Children are given a worksheet entitled "This Is How I Feel." The children individually write a sentence or two about what makes them glad and what makes them sad. On the back, they choose one other emotion to discuss in writing.
	3	Children are given the middle sentence of a story. They must write one sentence which shows what may have happened before and also write one sentence which shows what may have happened after.
	4	Children write a legend about an event or a figure in state or local history.
	5	Class writes three original sentences containing metaphors and copies them on the chalkboard, underlining the words that constitute the metaphor in each. Then each child writes a poem in metaphoric language.
	6	Each student personifies (or gives human qualities to) an inanimate object such as a baseball, a pencil, an apple, or a paper clip, and writes a story about it.

Christmas/Birthday Gifts	During December when the newspapers were filled with advertisements of gift items for boys and girls, the fifth-grade teacher collected many pages of such advertisements. Each child chose one or two pages and *wrote a math story problem* involving some of the games, clothes, books, or other gift items. The following day the problems were exchanged and solved.
Choral Reading	After the first graders had learned "If I Were King" by A. A. Milne, their teacher asked, "What would you do if you were king (or school principal) for just one day?" Following a prolonged discussion the children were eager to *write tercets*. One imaginative pupil preferred to be a giraffe for just one day.
Weather Conditions	The winter that their state was experiencing record snowstorms the sixth graders became interested in meteorology. They studied about the weather and *kept weather logs* for two weeks. Each daily log consisted of two sections: one for observations and one for actual weather measurements (temperature, humidity, barometric pressure, wind, and precipitation).
Color Posters	The second-grade teacher read aloud Rosetti's "Color" and Orlean's "Paints" and then created a picture-color poster with the help of the children. There were three word columns: color words, movement or action words, and describing words. The group then *wrote five-line cinquains* about a chosen color, first cooperatively and then individually. The cinquains were later mounted on sheets of construction paper that matched the color titles of the cinquains.
High School Sports	Some of the boys and girls in the third-and-fourth-grade combination class had brothers on the high school football team. The class was invited to see the game one Friday evening. The following Monday the children decided to *write new cheers* for the team.
Recorded Sounds	Fifth graders listened to *The Sounds Around Us* (Scott, Foresman and Co.) and *wrote unrhymed verse* about the visual and auditory images that the album created for them.
Kitchen Timer	After the third-grade teacher had read John Holt's *What Do I Do Monday?* (Dutton, 1970), he introduced writing marathons in his classroom. There was considerable discussion before each marathon, and then a kitchen timer was set. Each child had to *write continuously about any idea for five minutes*. There was no prescribed amount or speed of writing. Proofreading occurred after the timer rang.
Library Media Center Budget	The gifted sixth graders had read and discussed several novels. Then they learned that the school board had found it necessary to reduce the budget for the book collection at the media center. They decided to *write individual full-length books*. The writing process ran from November to April. The rest of the spring was devoted to copying the texts on unlined, margined paper with

blue or black ink and to binding the books with the help of the art teacher. Most of the children wrote fiction. All of the books were placed in the library media center and permitted to circulate.

The fifth graders were provided with cameras and film. They took photographs of flowers, friends, trees, the kindergarten swing set, and the school building. Later each *wrote a lengthy poetic composition made up of several couplets* describing the subject of the picture or an impression/reaction to that subject.

Cameras

The sixth graders had glued to small individual cardboard sheets various objects such as steel wool, velvet, cotton balls, nylon, sandpaper, bits of fur, redwood bark fragments, long nails, and a sponge. The sheets were then placed into a large covered box which had a slot on top. After the children had carefully handled each object without seeing it they proceeded to *write jingles* consisting of a succession of sounds or a repeated phrase.

Buried Treasure

As the night for group parent conferences approached, the kindergarten children painted pictures about springtime. They then *dictated labels* for their paintings which were put on display both in the corridor and in the classroom.

Parents' Night

The third graders had been invited to perform some of the classroom experiments they had done with magnets at the school science fair. To assure a successful learning experience, their teacher urged that any pupil or group of pupils that had volunteered to do an experiment at the fair should *write down the steps of the selected experiment.*

Science Fair

Attending the local high school one year was an exchange student from Mexico. The sixth-grade teacher invited him to her classroom and the young man enjoyed talking to the boys and girls. He arranged to get names of Mexican children who wished to correspond with their northern neighbors and who had studied English in school. The sixth graders were soon busy, as they started to *write friendly letters* to their foreign pen pals and to exchange inexpensive souvenirs.

Foreign Exchange Student

The fourth graders watched a film called *The Glob Family* (Learning Corporation), whose sound track contains no narration. Then they were divided into committees in order to *write a film narrative.* The short film was subsequently rerun several times until each committee's composition had been read aloud as an accompaniment.

Film

The kindergarten teacher distributed many colored construction paper shapes. The pupils arranged and pasted the shapes into pictures on manila paper. Those who wished were allowed to *dictate couplets* about their pictures into the tape recorder. The following day the children were asked to turn their pictures upside down or sideways and to discuss their new ideas or create a different couplet.

Shapes

Puppet Theater	The third graders first constructed hand puppets based on the tale of *The Three Billy Goats Gruff,* and then they built a puppet theater out of a bicycle carton. When they began to *write scripts,* they decided to record them. Thus the puppet operators could concentrate on manipulating the puppets while the tape recording supplied the voices.
Unfinished Sentences	A lengthy list of unfinished sentences was posted on the board. Each pair of fourth-grade boys and girls chose one of the sentences to complete. Then each member of a pair tried to *write as many different endings to the same sentence* as possible. If one partner wrote more endings than the other, he or she was allowed to copy this list on the board.
Interclass Debate	The fifth graders in Room 15 were getting ready for a debate on the United Nations with their peers in Room 16. In order to be able to verify statements made by their team during the debate, the pupils in Room 15 *prepared a bibliography* listing all books (and the significant page numbers).
School Campaign	After a teller from the First National Bank had explained to the middle and intermediate grades how each pupil was welcome to participate in the school savings plan, he distributed deposit cards and enrollment slips. Children interested in the plan were asked to *complete the printed forms* carefully after discussing the matter at home.
Filmstrip	After the second graders had seen the silent filmstrip *Out, Out, Out!* (Miller-Brody) which had no captions, they wanted to make a filmstrip of their own from sheets of wrapping paper. Later, although they proceeded to keep their filmstrip silent, they chose to *write appropriate captions* for each picture frame.
Book Jacket	The fifth-grade teacher pinned on the bulletin board many colorful book jackets with the caption "What's It All About?" after removing all the blurbs. Since he had succeeded in selecting book titles which were unfamiliar to a majority of the pupils, the short *book review* each student prepared (based on his or her favorite book jacket) proved enjoyable to read as well as to write.
Animated Cartoon	The first-grade class had seen the series of Disney's "I'm No Fool" safety cartoons and had discussed various safety precautions. Their teacher then offered them some short jingles about traffic safety, and asked the boys and girls if these reminded them in any way of Mother Goose rhymes. With her encouragement, the children began to *write contemporary nursery rhymes* about safety involving familiar characters. One result began: Jack and Jill stepped off the curb.
School-Made Products	The first-grade class was planning to make gingerbread men in conjunction with their economics unit. The pupils wanted to try to sell some of their prod-

ucts in order to raise money for the class library. They chose to cooperatively *dictate an announcement* about the gingerbread sale which could be read to other primary classrooms.

The YMCA had arranged to hold swimming classes for both beginners and advanced students of elementary school age. As teachers discussed the formation of the classes with the children, they urged the boys and girls to talk over the matter at home. Three days later each interested child was given time to *complete an application* for admission to the swimming class.

Community Sports

When six-year-old Stephanie got the mumps, her classmates told their teacher that they wished to *dictate a get-well message* to their friend. The group letter was accompanied by many funny pictures which the children drew to cheer up Stephanie.

Sick Classmate

Intermediate children enjoy listening to some of the music written by Leroy Anderson, Ferde Grofé, Peter Tchaikovsky, and others. Against such a background they can *write, collectively or individually, an original ballad* based on the current scene. Any incident having dramatic, relevant, and contemporary interest can be fashioned into a ballad whose lines are organized into a quatrain, or into a quatrain plus a refrain.

Recorded or Taped Music

The fourth graders listened intently to their principal after he had stopped by one morning to review appropriate behavior on the school bus. He encouraged them to *take notes* during his visit so that the whole class might later recall the salient points of the discussion.

Principal's Visit

Primary children made animals from discarded gift boxes and scrap materials including yarn, velvet, feathers, colored cord, and egg cartons. The following day each pupil was asked to *write an original definition* for his or her "wild thing." Some even wished to *develop new name words* for their creations.

Wild Things

The first-grade teacher placed a silver gravy boat on her desk one morning as she told the children her favorite poem about three wishes and read them the story of "Aladdin and His Wonderful Lamp." Each pupil was then allowed to rub the "magic lamp" three times before drawing his or her wishes. Later the teacher stopped at each table so that each child could *individually dictate a story* about his or her wishing picture.

Magic Object

When the school nurse visited the fifth grade she reviewed the importance of good nutrition and the daily need for the basic food groups. Then she suggested that each pupil *complete a chart* of the kinds of food he or she should eat for balanced breakfasts, lunches, and dinners for one week.

Nurse's Visit

Assembly Program	Each month the PTA program chairperson selected a different grade to supply the entertainment for the all-school meeting. When it came time for the second graders to perform, their teacher suggested they *write invitations* to each of their families to attend the Thanksgiving concert they had planned.
Community Campaign	During National Safety Week, the boys and girls in the third grade decided to *make a list* of all the precautions each was taking regarding pedestrian safety. The lists were later discussed informally with the school crossing guard.
Visitor	A professional music instructor visited the school where many of his students were enrolled and presented two violin concerts in the auditorium. The first-grade teacher whose class had attended the morning performance encouraged her pupils to *write notes of appreciation* to the school visitor to let him know how much they had enjoyed the concert.
Collages	The sixth-grade students (some individually, some in small committees) created collages by using newspaper or magazine pictures, colored construction paper, printed labels, paste, and tempera. Each collage had a theme, such as "Freedom" or "Busyness." Later, the pupils decided to *write dramatic paragraphs* about their collages.

A visit from a professional wood carver and artist stimulated these first graders to write him notes of appreciation. (Photo courtesy of the *Daily News Tribune,* Fullerton, California.)

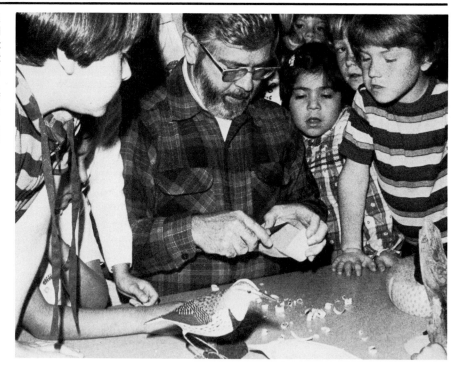

During the early part of October, the boys and girls in the fourth grade each chose to *keep a personal journal* (as might have been written by Columbus in the final days of his first voyage to the New World) or to *keep a logbook* of the *Niña,* the *Pinta,* or the *Santa María* (as written by the first mate of each vessel during the fall of 1492). The final entry in either the journal or the logbook was dated October 12.

Patriotic Holiday

Over several days, the second-grade teacher sometimes read and sometimes recited numerous poems about mail carriers, fire fighters, and other community workers. After discussing the poems with their teacher, the children decided to *write riddles* about the community helpers that had been described. The riddles were later placed in a folder on the library table for all to read and attempt to solve.

Poetry Presented by the Teacher

The sixth-grade teacher distributed some reproductions of famous paintings on four-by-six-inch postcards. She encouraged pupils to look at the reproductions carefully and to keep a favorite. The students later studied the lives of the artists of their favorite paintings before *preparing biographical sketches* to read to their classmates.

Art Reproductions

In the midst of their unit on Japan, the fourth-grade class became interested in *writing haiku, senryu, and tanka.* After the initial drafts had been completed, large sheets of wrapping paper were spread around the room and the nine-year-olds copied their poems with large vigorous strokes of their paintbrushes or thick-tipped felt pens.

Social Studies Unit

When two second graders reported during the same week that their pet cats had had litters, they and their classmates decided to *write a classified ad* of twelve words or less in which they would try to find good homes for the new kittens. The ad was later posted—in excellent manuscript—on the news board at the local market.

Free Kittens

The third graders enjoyed watching "The Electric Company" program. After several weeks of such viewing, the pupils were able to *write short reviews* of the program, advising their family members as to whether or not some of them would enjoy watching the show at home.

Telecasts

The sixth-grade class was responsible for writing, duplicating, and distributing the *Commonwealth Register* each month. Some of the boys and girls especially enjoyed *writing editorials* on such diverse topics as dress codes, longer lunch hours, detention periods, and spanking.

School Newspaper

Fourth graders took a short trip to collect (with permission) such items from nature as leaves, twigs, rocks, worms, feathers, insects, and bits of wood. They brought their collections back to the classroom where they chose the most in-

Nature Specimens

teresting specimens for further examination. Each child was then asked to *write a description* of a favorite (unnamed) specimen. Later, papers were exchanged, and sketches were drawn in accordance with the written description. Finally, comparisons were made among the items, the written descriptions, and the sketches.

School Camp

The sixth graders at Lakewood Elementary spent five days camping in the mountains with their teachers. Since five pupils in the grade had been unable to attend the activities, the teachers asked the campers to *write a summary* of the week's experiences to share with their parents as well as the absentees.

Party Invitation

Veronica, whose family had just recently arrived in Newton, invited all the girls in her first-grade class to a Halloween party. However, none of them was familiar with the new area where Veronica lived. So the teacher worked with the girls to help them *write down the directions* to Veronica's house.

Science Unit

As a result of their unit on sound, the fifth-grade class became interested in sound effects developed by radio stations. After each pupil who wanted to *write a radio commercial* about his or her favorite food had completed the assignment, the convincing—and sometimes comical—commercials were taped and appropriate sound effects added.

Nonsense Titles

The teacher posted on the chalk tray a variety of nonsense titles, including "How to Catch a Snapperdinck" and "The Day I Met a Rhinoraffoose." Each second grader selected one such caption to illustrate. Later the children were able to *write original fanciful stories* about their drawings and captions. Children who preferred to develop their own titles rather than use the teacher's stock were encouraged to do so.

Flannelboard Figures

Each reading group in the second grade chose its favorite basal story. The children then made felt figures of all the characters in that story. Finally they decided to *write new story endings* and present them on the flannelboard to the other groups.

Books for Beginning Readers

Fifth graders were permitted to *write original realistic stories for younger readers*. Working individually or in pairs, they had to be careful to choose subjects that would interest six-year-olds and had to develop a beginning-level vocabulary list. After the best stories—as rated by the class—had been copied in manuscript, the pages were carefully stapled and the books delivered to the first-grade pupils.

Study Trip

The second graders had visited the zoo on Monday. On Tuesday some children expressed a desire to learn more about the little-known animals they had seen, such as the llama. Other pupils wondered how the big bears, lions, and elephants were captured and brought to the zoo. The teacher encouraged each child or group of children to use the library media center in order to *make a report, gathering data from nonverbal sources,* about the animals in which there was special interest.

The sixth graders brought to class various items they had made at home, ranging from vases and pot holders to kites and model airplanes. As these objects began to collect on the display table, the class nicknamed them their Make-It Collection. Each pupil was able to *write an explanation* giving the steps for making or assembling his or her item.

Homemade Objects

For securing the largest number of PTA members, the fifth-grade class earned a new wall map of the United States. Each child chose one state for an in-depth study and began to *write business letters for information* to the major chambers of commerce in that state. The replies, accompanied by some free materials, arrived within two months.

New Wall Map

After school one day the teacher pasted large paper footprints on the floor and the walls of the classroom. The next morning the first graders were delighted to *dictate an experience chart story* about their strange visitors.

Mysterious Footprints

When school opened in the fall, the third graders each brought some snapshots from home showing summer outdoor activities in which they had participated. After some discussion, the class voted to *write limericks.*

Snapshots from Home

Sixth graders were shown pictures of the star-nosed mole, the flamingo, some jellyfish, a pelican, a gar fish, and one gnu. Then each pupil was encouraged to *write appropriate similies and metaphors* involving these animals.

Pictures of Unusual Animals

Second graders discussed the significance of numbers in everyday life. They noted that four, for example, is the number of walls in a room, the number of seasons, the number of petals on the dogwood flower, and the number of directions on the compass. Then each boy and girl chose one number and prepared to *write a quatrain* about the number.

Numbers

In the fifth grade there were three story boxes. In the first were some slips with the names of the seasons; in the second, slips with the names of places; and in the third, slips with the names of actions. Each pupil drew one slip from each box (e.g., *summer, Pacific Ocean, sailing*) and then proceeded to *write a personal expository paragraph* incorporating the words on the three slips. The children stapled or pinned the story-box slips to their completed paragraphs.

Story-Box Slips

The kindergarten class planned to bake cookies to serve to visitors for open house festivities. After each child had participated in purchasing, measuring, or mixing/shaping the ingredients, the group *dictated the recipe* for the teacher to post on a chart near the serving table. The cafeteria was happy to cooperate in the venture by handling the oven chores.

Open House

Nature Study	The third graders acquired some rabbits, guinea pigs, mice, and goldfish. On a lined sheet of writing paper, the teacher wrote the first two entries of a journal about the animals, and pinned it to the bulletin board. Then each child was encouraged to keep a *written observational record* of the activities of his or her favorite animal at school or a pet at home.
Burning Issues	Pencils, rulers, and crayons kept disappearing from the second-grade classroom. In order to *make a written report* on the situation, the children got busy *gathering data from verbal sources* in small and large groups, hoping to find a solution to their common problem.
Prose Read Aloud by the Teacher	To launch a unit on myth writing, the teacher read aloud to her fifth-grade class from the D'Aulaires' *Book of Myths* (Doubleday, 1960). The adventures of Prometheus, Pandora, Orion, and other gods were used to encourage each boy and girl to *write an original myth* offering a convincing explanation of a natural phenomenon to a primitive group of people.
Newspaper Headlines	The sixth-grade teacher cut out intriguing headlines from daily newspapers and pasted each on a sheet of lined writing paper. The papers were turned face-down on the teacher's desk and each pupil chose one sheet on which to *write a news story* that fit the headline. (On another occasion the teacher provided the original newspaper articles so pupils could compare their stories with the published accounts.)
Class Walk	In a school located close to a lake, the first-grade teacher suggested one morning that the children put on their coats and walk over to see the waves on the lake. The lake was especially choppy that day and the pupils commented excitedly about the waves. Back in the classroom the teacher asked each child to write one sentence describing how the waves made him or her feel. The papers were collected and assembled into group *free verse*.
Special School Event	The fourth-grade teacher had been placed in charge of faculty participation in the forthcoming school carnival. He invited his students to publicize the carnival by creating comic-strip advertisements for distribution around the school. Committees were chosen, and each included at least one artist, one idea person, and one pupil who could *write comic strip dialog*.
Pupils' Birthdays	About one week before any member of the third-grade class celebrated a birthday, classmates prepared interview questions about the celebrant's family, pets, toys, favorite sports, or scouting. Later, each pupil had to *write up the interview* that took place on the festive occasion. Children whose birthdays occurred in the summer or on weekends were allowed to choose alternate days for their interviews.

After several weeks of construction work, the first graders were ready to participate in dramatic play concerning transportation. Still they needed such captions as Hangar and Garage to place on their sets. With the help of their teacher, they were able to *dictate and copy signs* that aided their activity.

Dramatic Play

The fifth- and sixth-grade pupils were eligible to join the Safety Patrol, whose members served as crossing guards for the children coming to and leaving school. The patrol meetings were held once a week, and their adviser selected a different secretary each month to *write up the club minutes.*

School Club

Fifth graders created three-dimensional figures of fabulous beasts and monsters. They provided these nightmarish figures with original names. Then they began to *write character sketches* or stories about the creatures.

Clay Figures

Pupils in the third grade each brought from home an inexpensive, inanimate, but carefully wrapped personal possession. The packages (with the owners' initials carefully hidden) were prominently displayed on the library table for most of the morning. Just before the noon recess, every child was allowed to *write a detailed guess* of the contents of a package other than his or her own.

Wrapped Secrets

Composition written by pupils aged five to twelve encompass a multitude of forms, ranging from the long-established prosaic paragraph to the relatively new, seven-lined diamond-shaped poem known as diamanté. Such written products may be quite brief, consisting of merely seventeen syllables of imagery in nature (in the form of haiku or senryu poetry). On the other hand, they may become fairly lengthy, expanding to several pages of expository prose relating to a plant-growth experiment. Some written communications may follow a predesigned structure; others may be arranged freely and extemporaneously.

    In all instances, however, what truly matters is that the composition represents a boy's or girl's approach to life—straightforward, honest, inquisitive, observant. It is a reflection of the discoveries that a child makes in his or her day-to-day progress. Essentially, it displays a child's awareness. Each composition included in this section meets these standards.[14]

Samples of Children's Written Composition

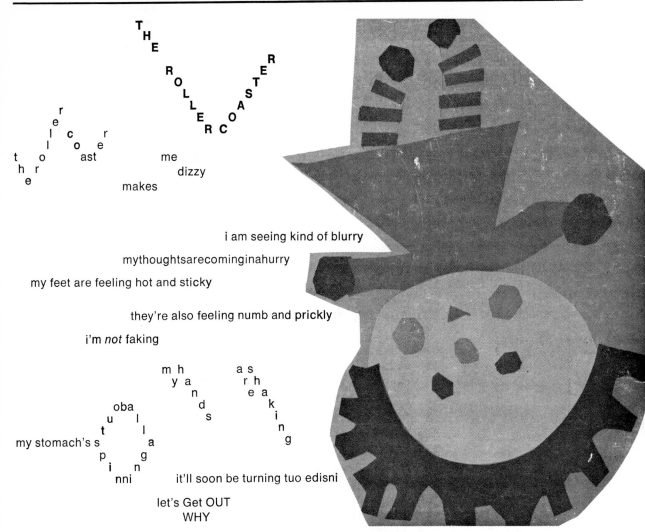

THE ROLLERCOASTER

the rollercoaster makes me dizzy

i am seeing kind of blurry

mythoughtsarecominginahurry

my feet are feeling hot and sticky

they're also feeling numb and **prickly**

i'm *not* faking

my stomach's spinningallaboutmyhandsareshaking

it'll soon be turning tuo edisni

let's Get OUT
WHY

BeCause I'm

ScArEd!

Janine
Written in Grade 6

Glen Canyon

Dramatic shapes
Emerge from mysterious canyons.
Eerie calls
Blow through the glens
Beauty glimmers
On cathedral ceilings.
Light seeps
Through the vast number of openings.
Mysterious forms
Dance along the sun-covered rocks.
Ancient writings
Cover the red sandstone walls.
All of the fascination
We once felt
Is gone forever.

Rita
Grade 6, age 12

Some Days

Some days the sky is bright and gay; and some days it's so angry that it cries. Some days it breathes hard. It blows and blows. Some days it only has one eye open, and that's the sun.

Laura
Written in Grade 1

A Day in Winter

It was a freezing, windy, snowy January day; but inside it was cozy with the fire snapping. My mother was baking molasses cookies which you could smell right through the oven door.

The snow was drifting like leaves from a tree in autumn. I felt sad because I couldn't go out and play, but it was fun watching the snow fall lightly from the sky.

My brother and father were out cutting wood for the fire. The dog was sleeping calmly in front of the fireplace, dreaming. I had nothing to do but watch the snow fall heedlessly, but I think that's a good way to spend a snowy day.

Susan
Written in Grade 4

The Man in the Boat

Once there was a little boat. A man was in it. He was sailing along. Sundown came. Then night came. It started to rain. The sea grew rough; the man went inside.

He got close to the rocks. He thought he was going to crash. Day came; the sea slowed down. The sun came out.

Billy
Written in Kindergarten

Dear Elders,

Please try to listen to what I have to say. Let me, please, tell you of my opinion. You may speak out when I am done; and if you listen and you think my opinions are valid, you may think differently than you do now.

The clothes I wear are different from yours. But is my outward appearance that important? Won't you look further? My hair is long, hanging loose; sometimes it's messy after I've played too hard and my cheeks are flushed, but need that close up our relationship? Sometimes I think differently than you—is that why I'm the foolish younger generation?

Sincerely,

Melinda
Written in Grade 6

My name is Don M. I live on a small dairy farm. It's a lot of work.

We milk the cows twice a day and have to make sure they have hay and water all the time. A cow drinks about 35 gallons of water a day. That's a lot. It's my responsibility to make sure their water tub stays filled. They drink out of an old bathtub. I fill it twice a day or three times when it's hot.

There should always be hay in the feeder, so the cows can eat it whenever they want. A cow has to spend a lot of time eating and chewing. First, she eats very fast, getting as much hay down her as she can. That hay goes into her first stomach or rumen. Then she lays down and just like a burp, a wad of food comes back up to her mouth so she can chew it. This is called chewing the cud or ruminating. A cow spends about eight hours a day just chewing her cud. A cow has four stomachs in all. She needs her complex stomach system in order to digest grass and hay and get food value out of them. Her fourth stomach is like ours, the other three are extra, just for digesting this roughage.

Don
Age 11

Just Before I Sneeze

There's a tingle
And a twitch,
A switch
And a tickle—
Until I just can't resist,
  And then
    And then
      And then
I sneeze.

Simone
Written in Grade 6

There was a young man from
  Orum
Who bought some new pants
  and he wore 'em.
He stooped and he sneezed;
He wiggled his knees;
And he knew right where he
  had tore 'em.

Jeff
Written in Grade 6

There once was a boy named
  Mitch,
Who always sang off pitch.
He started to squeak;
It was very unique.
That poor little boy named
  Mitch!

Maureen
Written in Grade 4

There was a young Frenchman
  of Cault
Who had but one little fault;
  He liked to rob banks
  To steal all their francs,
Until one day he got locked in
  a vault.

Paul
Written in Grade 6

Bam, Bam, Bam

Bam, bam, bam
Goes the steel wrecking ball;
Slam, slam, slam
Against a concrete wall.

It's raining bricks and wood
In my neighborhood;
Zam goes a chimney,
Zowie goes a door.

Bam, bam, bam
Goes the steel wrecking ball,
Changing it all,
Changing it all.

Eugene
Written in Grade 4

The Can Opener

A crackly monster
All white to be seen,
He chomps all my can lids.
He is meant to be mean.

He chews them and chews them
Till they are all gone.
He chews them and chews them
From midnight till dawn.

Then he gives me my cans
Without any lids.
I ask him (so softly)
Not to like kids.

Marie
Written in Grade 6

The Two Ghosts

There once were two ghosts
  sitting on a wall.
One of them was short and the
  other was tall.

Then they heard someone
  coming up the stairs.
They got all sorts of scares.

Then the one near the steeple
Said, "Do you believe in
  people?"

Cheryl
Written in Grade 4

Animals

Sometimes a horse won't eat
his oats.
A champion chicken won't
lay.
Sometimes a birdie chirps off
key just cause it isn't his
day.

Mike
Grade 6

The Rise and Fall of a Tree

From seed to seedling,
From seedling to tree,
The majestic fir
Rises high above me.

The tree falls to the ground,
Felled by thougtless men,
While the litle seed starts
The cycle again.

David
Written in Grade 6

"Quack" went the duck in the spring——————.

"Ee-ah" went the donkey in the spring——————.

"Oink" went the pig in the spring ——————.

An-i-mals feel like singing in the spring.

Quack, oink, ee-ah; quack, oink, ee-ah.

Leland
Written in Grade 1

Kites

Zooming and swirling,
Kites go.
Dipping and twirling,
Kites flow.
Diving and whirling,
Kites blow
On a windy day.

Karen
Written in Grade 1

The Bear

The bear
Is
Just
A
Big
Bunch
Of
Hair.

Ellie
Written in Grade 4

Round is the center of a flower
so the petals will stay on.

Carol
Written in Grade 1

Turtle

Below the shell and
Above the plastron,
A little creature lurks.

Ben
Written in Grade 4

My Tree

My tree is an old tree. Its arms are tired from holding many leaves. Its feet are resting under the cool ground. See my tree go back and forth with the rocking-chair wind.

Tami
Written in Grade 3

Haiku

Please, little cricket,
Turn off your loud volumed
    sound.
The trees are sleeping.

Wayne
Written in Grade 5

Why the Platypus Is So Mixed Up

When God was done creating the world, he had some leftover parts. He had a giant chimney, the skin of a beaver, the bill of a duck, and two pairs of geese feet.

Well, he thought and planned and pondered and finally thought of something to do with the giant chimney. He would stick it down in the United States and call it Chimney Rock!

Now he had gotten rid of the chimney, but what about the other things? Well, God thought and thought and at last came up with something. He would make it into an animal! It would be a little bit strange but so what?

So he mixed them together and came up with the duck-billed platypus. Poor creature!

Carol
Written in Grade 5

The Frog

Once there was a big frog. He lived with his mother and father near a pond under a rock.

He liked to sit on the rock in the sun. He would sit very still and wait for bugs and ants to come by. Then quick as a flash, his tongue would zip out and he would have some lunch.

After a lunch of bugs and ants, he would sometimes hop, hop, hop down to the pond to get a drink of water. Then he would hop right back to his rock to rest in the sun some more.

Some days while he was resting, he would sing, "Ga-rump, ga-rump, ga-rump." He thought he sang very pretty, but some of the other animals at the pond didn't think so!

After so much singing, he was always thirsty; so he would hop, hop, hop down to the pond for a drink. One day as he was drinking, he fell into the pond!

He went down, down, down into the deepest part of the pond. When he was almost to the bottom, he saw a whale. Before he could think what to do, he saw two whales! And they were coming right after him.

The poor frog went straight to the bottom of the pond as fast as he could. He knew that he had to get to the muddy bottom.

But, oh, worse than the whales, two sharks were coming after him now! He could see that they wanted to stick him with their sharp teeth and have him for their lunch.

Poor frog! He was so scared. He dug down deep, deep into the mud at the bottom of the pond. He was trying to hide.

The frog hid in the mud for a long, long time. When he finally peeked out, the sharks were gone; but he could see the whales still waiting for him. They seemed bigger than ever! He got very frightened.

The frog thought of a plan. He pretended to be dead. The whales didn't want a dead frog for dinner, so they swam away.

As soon as the whales were gone, the frog went back to his rock by the little pond. He decided that he would NEVER go back to the deep water again.

Todd
Written in Grade 1

The Sad Worm

The sad worm is trying to climb up the tree to get the apple, but he couldn't climb up the tree.	It is a sunny day and the sad worm is trying to get in his hole, but he can't find it.	The sad worm climbs up the tree and finds his hole in the tree, then he changes into being happy.

John Wilde

The Highwayman

As he came, his clothes looked as if they were fighting the wind; his horse's hooves sounded like a blacksmith hitting an anvil. The white foam poured from the horse's mouth mixing with the dust behind him. His breath acted as a shield against the harsh wind. The ground rumbled and shook as he passed. The man's pants were torn like a rag, his velvet cape flashed in the moonlight, and his green beret clung against him. His sword was glittering, and his spurs shone like lanterns. I heard something so I turned to see what it was, but it was only a chipmunk caressing a nut; but when I turned back, the highwayman was gone; but the trail of dust was there.

Eric
Written in Grade 5

If I were a pair of shoes,
I'd walk to the sundown.

Angela
Written in Grade 1

A poet's time
Flies by in rhyme.

Debbie
Written in Grade 3

At the Beach

We like the beach.
We make sand castles
And find starfish
While the sea talks to us.

Brian
Written in Grade 1

Ocean waves—here they come
And back they go,
Fighting a battle that
Will never end.
They go crashing on the rocks,
Crashing on the shore,
Crashing on me.

Steven
Written in Grade 3

Fog

Fog is like a blanket
Someone dropped from the sky.
It covers the earth with a
Cold and damp stillness
When you walk by.

Tammy
Written in Grade 6

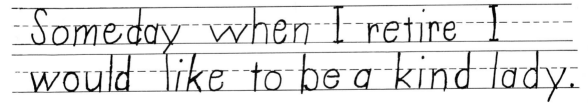

Someday when I retire I would like to be a kind lady.

Brenda
Written in Grade 1

Sally

Sally was picking flowers. It started to rain. She started going into the tent. Then it started getting sunny again so she took a nap. Then she ran and skipped and walked.

Renee
Written in Kindergarten

City

Fast, busy

Rushing, moving, hurrying

Streets, buildings, trees, fields

Yielding, rolling, harvesting

Quiet, free

Country

Martin
Written in Grade 6

Man

Strong, brave

Working, helping, loving

Rough, tough, soft, smooth

Cooking, loving, caring

Feminine, delicate

Woman

Lynda
Written in Grade 4

Cat

Quiet, gentle

Rolling, playing, climbing

Yarn, mice, shoes, bones

Running, digging, jumping

Noisy, rough

Dog

Lori
Written in Grade 6

This Story Is about Mississippi

Mississippi is my home. My papa has a wagon. My papa has a mule and my papa has dogs. My papa has some hens, too. But he does not have little pigs.

Mississippi is my home, the best of all for watermelon. The watermelon is good. All of it is good. I like one watermelon a day.

My house is white at Mississippi. I like to go to the pond with my big brother and sister. Mississippi is a good home to go to sometimes. And I like Mississippi all of my life. I like to eat and play in Mississippi.

For a long time I have been here in San Diego. But I like San Diego a little bit. San Diego is a good place, too, for fun and to play and to go to this school. San Diego is my home. Forever and ever it will be my home. But I like Mississippi best of all, all of my life.

Virgil
Written in Grade 1

Fall Is Here

As I ran across a branch, I saw a winding road. There was a barn and a tall tree with colorful leaves. There must be houses nearby, for I could see mailboxes. I was right; the trees with colorful leaves did have acorns, but would the owner chase me away?

Dusk was falling, and I must collect my acorns before night falls. So back to my nest—a trunk of a tree! Perhaps I'll be braver tomorrow.

Tim
Written in Grade 5

The Cat and the Mouse

It was a stormy day. It was lightning outside. It was raining outside. The cat and the mouse were outside. The cat saw the mouse. The mouse was drowning. The mouse said, "Help! Help!" The cat picked the mouse up. He took him onto some dry land. The cat was getting ready to eat the mouse. The mouse got away. He looked at the cat and said, "Thank you but I don't like you chasing me or eating me."

Daren
Written in Grade 1

Most teachers reportedly use excitement buzzers when they evaluate composition. They find a misspelled word and go *buzz! buzz!* Or they get excited about a faulty comma—*buzz! buzz!* The poor students, confronted by teachers who use excitement buzzers, write home runs, so to speak, only to discover later that their teachers were excited that time around by stolen bases. The students soon give up in despair.

Such close grading or correcting of pupil compositions indicates that a premium has been placed upon skills rather than upon content. It reveals what the teacher considers most valuable. What it may also show is that the teacher lacks the ability to evaluate the higher cognitive processes expressed in the poetry or prose.

Concerning the effects of negative versus positive criticism of children's compositions by teachers, research studies reported during the past decade indicate that teachers may use either type of criticism since both kinds get similar positive results.[15]

Other research has shown that it may be best to eliminate teacher evaluation completely. Positive correlations have been found between creativity and teachers' use of the technique of rewarding children by personal interest in their ideas rather than by evaluation. And Torrance concluded that unevaluated practice compared with evaluated practice is followed by a more creative performance in similar tasks requiring creative thinking.[16] Unfortunately, by the fourth grade, pupils are apparently so accustomed to being evaluated constantly that instructions freeing them from the threat of evaluation have little effect.

In the noncritical environment so important for creative thought, teachers throughout the modern school cease to function as chief evaluators. Instead, the primary writing program is structured so that children gradually begin to function as their own editors (in the area of mechanical skills) and their own revisionists (in the area of content). By the intermediate grades most of the pupils can handle these responsibilities independently. By and large the teacher in each classroom serves as a supportive resource person who helps the students acquire the specific language skills as well as the technical skills they will need to serve as their own editors. The teacher also introduces the children to a self-check list, similar to the one shown in Figure 10.1, or helps them develop such a list cooperatively.

The foundation of any program in which students learn to revise their own work is the teacher-pupil conference. It is regularly scheduled as often as every five or ten days. Each child keeps a writing folder of all work in progress (and may even choose to designate some papers as first drafts and others as final drafts) and brings this folder to the conference. The teacher works with the child at his or her own level by attempting to identify the child's composition weaknesses in much the same fashion as he or she tries to diagnose the child's reading difficulties. With one child it may be difficulty in sequencing. With another, it may be paragraph unity. The teacher also helps every pupil

Figure 10.1. Self-Check Writing List for Children.

Checking My Writing

1) Is it clear?
   Does my writing make sense to me?
   Will others understand it?
   Do all sentences and words make sense?

2) Is it suitable?
   Who will my audience be?
   Did I write in a way that they will understand?
   Did I choose the best words?

3) Is it complete?
   Does my topic sentence say everything it needs to?
   Does it say too much?
   Have I said all I need to say about my subject in order for the audience to
      understand and enjoy it?

4) Is it well-designed?
   Do all of my sentences deal with the main idea?
   Are there any unnecssary sentences or words?
   Are my sentences in proper order?

Source: *Composition in the Language Arts, Grades 1–8: An Instructional Framework* (Madison: Wisconsin Department of Public Instruction, 1976), p. 38.

develop an individualized editing guide which is posted on the inside of the writing folder to aid in proofreading.

While reviewing a pupil's composition during a conference, the teacher should take special note of the basic idea the child is trying to express with written symbols. The teacher should also consider these questions: Does this child communicate his or her thoughts? Does the child have a purpose for writing? Does the child have sufficient background from either real or vicarious experiences to deal properly with this topic? Does the choice of words contribute to the intended message? Is there a variety of sentence patterns? What conventions of spelling, capitalization, and punctuation are used successfully? Does the child apparently enjoy writing even though it demands close attention, effort, and thought?

Not all written work needs review or revision, however. Thus the conference can sometimes develop into a guided discussion period during which the student begins to see and feel elements and events previously unrecognized in his or her environment. The student needs the time to hear himself or herself express ideas and offer opinions. The listening teacher benefits as well. The teacher learns more about what interests the child and how he or she thinks.

It has been suggested that when boys and girls are involved in individual conferences beginning in the primary grades and are led to discover strengths and weaknesses in their own communication, *they* soon begin to tell the teacher what is needed to make their writing a stronger communication.[17]

Recently, Williams visited elementary school writing classes in three countries and found that the most important difference among them lay in the methods the teachers used to give pupils feedback about writing efforts. While teachers in the United States seemed prone to think that evaluating children's work and having the children make corrections somehow inhibits their creativity, teachers in England and Canada had no compunctions about making evaluations. In both these countries, in open settings, there was individual conferencing during which the children read their compositions aloud so that they could discover for themselves areas for improvement. The teacher would ask each pupil, "How can you make me understand better what you mean?" Subsequently, when the child would offer solutions, the teacher would either accept them or respond with more guiding questions.[18]

Graded Appraisal

The teacher-pupil conference is still a rarity in the area of evaluation of written products. One survey of teachers from urban and suburban systems in Pennsylvania, New Jersey, and Florida showed that none of the two hundred teachers questioned held such conferences. Instead, 78 percent of these intermediate teachers used letter grades, or letter grades and comments, to evaluate children's compositions, probably because evaluation was required for the report cards.[19]

Should a school district demand that written compositions be assigned letter grades, the faculty may wish to develop a cooperative grading system using local goals. The basis for this system can come from the results of a writing-sample test administered to a group of pupils in each elementary grade

During the personalized writing conference the teacher can help each child become his or her own editor and revisionist. (Photo courtesy of the Ocean View School District, Huntington Beach, California.)

who represent the full range of student abilities. The pupils are provided with a topic sentence or a trio of words and told to write as much as they wish (developing the topic or using the vocabulary) in a specified time period. Later, grade-level chairpersons meet with the language arts coordinator to analyze the papers with enough specificity so that it will become possible to describe the typical strengths and weaknesses of student-written papers at each grade level. Standards are established and papers ranked on a five-point scale for separate criteria, including ideas, organization, originality/flavor, vocabulary, and mechanical skills. Finally, results are compiled and distributed throughout the school district.

Such an attempt at standardizing district-wide evaluation of written composition should prove worthwhile. Elementary teachers, according to research, are relatively inconsistent in their concepts of what constitutes good and poor children's writing, due to their differing criteria.[20] An obvious initial step to improve their evaluative efforts is to ascertain collectively the goals and grading standards of the schools' writing program.

Presumably such an attempt at graded appraisal will keep in mind the results of a late study on the effect of handwriting quality on elementary teachers' evaluations of children's written compositions.[21] The forty-five full-time teachers and thirty-six student teachers, grades one to five, in a southwestern city consistently gave higher scores to papers with good handwriting than to papers with poor handwriting *regardless of the quality of content*. Teachers should be aware of the possible overemphasis of the handwriting factor as they strive for fairness and objectivity in evaluating written compositions of primary and intermediate pupils.

Standardized Tests   Teachers may be asked to examine (or administer) nationally standardized instruments for written language.

Certain achievement batteries such as the *Comprehensive Tests of Basic Skills* (published by McGraw-Hill Book Company, New York 10020) include a section for language, with one subtest for expression and one for mechanics. In the CTBS (which is available for grades 2.5–4, 4–6, and 6–8) the expression subtest requires the student to add correct words and phrases to incomplete sentences, to replace underlined parts of sentences in a poem or story, and to recognize errors and usage. This battery has received good reviews critically.[22]

A relatively new diagnostic instrument for appraising normal and abnormal development of written language is the *Picture Story Language Test* (published by Grune and Stratton, Incorporated, New York 10003). The children are presented with a picture about which they are asked to write a story. From these written stories, scales are developed to measure length (productivity), correctness of expression (syntax), and to attempt to measure content or meaning of the sentence (abstract-concrete). The test, which is intended for children ages seven to seventeen, runs twenty to thirty minutes. It has received mixed reviews.[23]

Teachers may also be interested in consulting some research instruments which are not available commercially but may be ordered on microfilm (for a fee) from ERIC Document Reproduction Service.[24] Only those for the primary age range (grades one to three) and/or the intermediate age range (grades four to six) are listed here by title, author, date of construction, purpose, and ordering information:

Intermediate Only

- *Syntactic Maturity Test for Narrative Writing* (SMTNW), Fritz Dauterman, 1969, to measure syntactic fluency or maturity in narrative writing. (ED 091 757)
- *E.T.S. Composition Evaluation Scales* (CES), Paul Diederich, John French, and Sydell Carlton, 1961, to evaluate the quality of written compositions. (ED 091 750)
- *Transformational Analysis of Compositions* (TAC), Mary Dupuis, 1972, to analyze and describe the transformational operations in sentences in written compositions. (ED 091 747)
- *Sager Writing Scale* (CWRS), Carol Sager, 1973, to assess the quality of pieces of creative writing. (ED 091 723)

Primary and Intermediate

- *Indexes of Syntactic Maturity* (Dixon-Hunt-Christensen), Edward Dixon, 1970, to measure growth in syntactic fluency. (ED 091 748)
- *Glazer Narrative Composition Scale* (GNCS), Joan Glazer, 1971, to assess the quality of children's narrative compositions. (ED 091 763)
- *Factors of Syntactic Fluency* (Hunt-Mellon), John Mellon, 1969, to measure growth in syntactic fluency. (ED 018 405)
- *Syntactic Maturity Test* (SMT), Roy O'Donnell and Kellogg W. Hunt, 1970, to measure the written syntactic maturity of writers from grade four to adulthood. (ED number unlisted)
- *Schroeder Composition Scale* (SCS), Thomas Schroeder, 1973, to describe the writing behaviors of elementary and junior high children. (ED 091 760)
- *Literary Rating Scale* (LRS), Eileen Tway, 1969, to assess the quality of children's fictional stories. (ED 091 726)

1. Describe the kind of teacher who is most likely to produce creative effort in children.
2. Which four of the factors affecting the writing performance of children do you perceive as being the most important?
3. How could it prove helpful to the composition program to have the pupils guided by a teacher who is also a writer?
4. How do you plan to evaluate children's written expression?

1. Encourage a six-year-old (who lives in your home or attends a school where you visit) to dictate a report of a personal experience to you; then share that report with your peers.
2. Collect several compositions written by children in a particular grade or age bracket. Note the variations in content and mechanics. Determine the creativity of each.
3. Plan a middle-grade bulletin board which will encourage self-editing of written work.
4. Examine three national children's magazines which publish original prose or poetry by elementary school boys and girls.
5. If poetry is talking to one's self, share a collection of unrhymed poetry with intermediate children in order to show them that their own writing need not rhyme to be poetry.
6. Begin a picture file which will aid your composition program. On the back of each picture, place a typed label describing how you would introduce or use that picture with young writers.
7. Set up the learning centers on written composition shown in Figures 10.2 and 10.3.

**Related
Readings**

Day, B. D., and Swetenburg, J. 1978. "Where Children 'Write to Read.' " *Childhood Education* 54: 229–33.

Harris, M. M. 1976. "The Limerick Center." *Language Arts* 53: 663–65.

Hyman, R. B. 1978. "Creativity in Open and Traditional Classrooms." *Elementary School Journal* 78: 266–74.

Kohl, H. 1978. "Writing: Revisions and Corrections." *Teacher* 95: 14–16.

Larson, R. L. 1975. *Children and Writing in the Elementary School.* New York: Oxford University Press.

Lundsteen, S. W., ed. 1976. *Help for the Teacher of Written Composition: K-9.* Urbana, Illinois: National Council of Teachers of English.

Meisterheim, M. 1977. "Rx for Helping Johnny Write Better." *Elementary School Journal* 78: 5–8.

Rothenburg, A., and Hansman, C., eds. 1976. *The Creativity Question.* Durham, North Carolina: Duke University Press.

Schwartz, M. 1977. "Rewriting or Recopying: What Are We Teaching?" *Language Arts* 54: 756–59.

Tripp, J. G. 1978. "The Positive Approach: Response-Evaluation of Children's Writing." *Language Arts* 55: 358–61, 408.

Figure 10.2. Language Arts Learning Center: Written Composition.

TYPE OF CENTER:	Creative Writing	TIME:	20–30 minutes
GRADE LEVEL:	2–3	NUMBER OF CHILDREN:	2

INSTRUCTIONAL OBJECTIVE: Children will use their imaginations and write down what they think the animals might be thinking or saying.

MATERIALS: Supply of pictures of animals, paper and pencil, folder for finished papers, directions.

DIRECTIONS TO STUDENTS:
1. Think about each of these animals and what they might say about the world today and how human beings treat them.
2. Using your imagination, write your ideas on the paper.
3. Proofread what you have written.
4. When you have finished your paper, place it in the folder on the back of the learning center.

EVALUATION: The teacher will read the papers looking for originality; later the students may read their own papers aloud to the class or mount them on a bulletin board.

Source: From *Language Arts Learning Centers and Activities* by Angela Reeke and James Laffey. Copyright 1979 by Goodyear Publishing Company. Reprinted by permission.

Figure 10.3. Language Arts Learning Center: Written Composition.

TYPE OF CENTER: Creative Writing   TIME: Varies
                          Using Visual Stimuli

GRADE LEVEL: 4–7   NUMBER OF CHILDREN: 1

INSTRUCTIONAL   Student will demonstrate the ability to create a story by using visual stimulation.
OBJECTIVE:

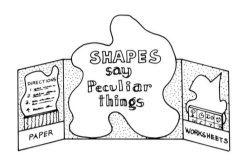

MATERIALS: Paper, worksheets, directions, folder for finished work (on back of center).

DIRECTIONS   1. Take a copy of the worksheet and one sheet of writing paper.
TO STUDENTS: 2. Choose one of the twelve shapes.
                        3. Write a descriptive story about it. Tell what you think it is, how it makes you feel,
                           and why.
                        4. When you have finished, place the worksheet back in its folder, and place your
                           finished work in the folder behind the center.

EVALUATION: The teacher and writer should determine how much imagination the student showed
                      when describing the shape. How well did the student use descriptive vocabulary?

Source: From *Language Arts Learning Centers and Activities* by Angela Reeke and James
Laffey. Copyright 1979 by Goodyear Publishing Company. Reprinted by permission.

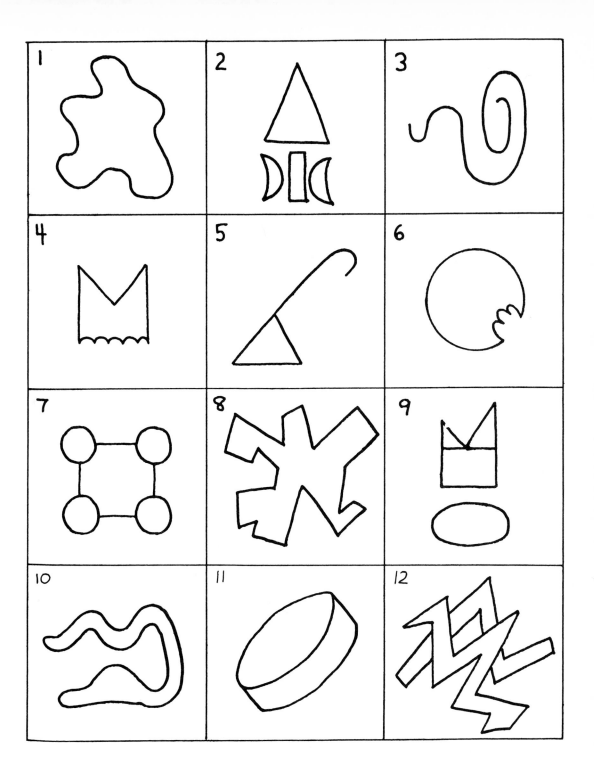

Children's Literature

11

The emergence of children's literature

The single most important differentiating factor in reading preferences among children

Titles among the perennial best sellers in the children's book market

Two ways in which the teacher can use bibliotherapy

Literature provides the best opportunity in the school curriculum for boys and girls to examine the values by which people live and to test for themselves the codes of conduct derived from various value systems.[1] It helps children determine those values and relate them to their own standards. It also helps children discern what has perplexed people in the past and what these people have done about it. By understanding and evaluating the experiences of life as described in literature, the boys and girls become better able to integrate vicarious experiences with their own daily lives. In the process they also become more sensitive to the needs of others and to their own needs.

Books written especially for children are a relatively recent kind of literature, first emerging as a significant category in the eighteenth century. From Anglo-Saxon times until the early 1700s, children's books were inseparably linked with educational or moral purposes, and children who read fiction at all read easy adult works (romances and fables). The change from uncensored adult literature for children to a literature written specifically for a child audience developed from the change which had occurred in the social pattern of Western life. As the life of adults became separated from the life of children and increased in technological complexity, children began to read a literature radically different from that of adults.

The first book especially designed for children's entertainment and quite apart from a schoolbook was published in England in 1744 by John Newbery. Entitled *A Little Pretty Pocketbook,* it was sold with a ball for boys and a pincushion for girls, and consisted mostly of games. A major shift in literature slowly followed, and by the mid-nineteenth century Hans Christian Andersen, Louisa May Alcott, Charles Kingsley, and dozens of other talented authors were producing many kinds of juvenile entertainment, surprisingly similar to that being done for children today.

Modern authors of children's literature are aware that their writing cannot involve the same criteria of literary excellence as adult literature does. Most children have a more limited range of language experience and understandable experience (in both kinds and amounts) than many adults. Most children are also limited in their ability to attend to experiences over lengths of time, as compared to adults, and cannot normally manipulate as many elements at once, as most older persons can. Finally, they are less inclined than their elders to concern themselves with what may happen in the future.

While the children's first exposure to literature is Mother Goose and other rhymes and stories, children should gradually experience every type and form of literature in a school program that is comprehensive and sequentially plotted throughout the elementary grades. Such a program not only strengthens the developmental reading curriculum but contributes in a significant way to the attainment of several other objectives of elementary education:

- The school aims to meet the needs of individual pupils—and literature is widely diversified.
- The school aims to provide a learning program which will utilize the natural interests of its pupils—and literature appeals to all age groups.
- The school aims to provide socially satisfying experiences for its children and to develop in its pupils a wider social understanding—and good stories and pleasing verse are enjoyed more when they are shared with others.
- The school aims to give each child self-insight—and books introduced in childhood can sometimes bring about a profound change in one's outlook on life.
- The school aims to give each pupil a knowledge and appreciation of his or her cultural heritage—and literature is the means whereby much of that heritage is preserved and perpetuated.
- The school aims to stimulate and foster creative expression—and book experiences are an exciting springboard to art, drama, and other expressionistic activities.

Yet, teaching literature should not be considered synonymous with teaching reading. Neither should it be thought to be the same as the library media skills program, though both reading and the library media center support a literature program. It is not even the same as free reading, whereby pupils have a chance to choose their own books, read them during school time, and perhaps share them with their peers or the teacher. Should free reading turn into guided reading and parents/teachers/media specialists help pupils choose books, it still does not replace a literature class.

Literature as a subject in the elementary school deserves a special period to itself and should appear as such on the class schedule. Children can then regularly hear/read and understand writings of quality both from the past and the present.

A properly structured literature program provides a balance among the numerous elements relevant to this segment of the language arts. A balance is needed between fiction and nonfiction, between prose and poetry, between realism and fantasy, and between the classics and contemporary works. Such a balanced offering that could actively strengthen and expand the pupils' skills in language and composition as well as in literature might be charted as shown in Table 11.1.

Objectives/
Functions,
Satisfactions,
and Trends

Literature teaching means that elementary classes receive a planned program of activities designed to achieve certain general objectives:

1. To help pupils realize that literature is for entertainment and can be enjoyed throughout their entire lives
2. To acquaint children with their literary heritage
3. To help pupils understand what constitutes literature and—hopefully—to persuade them to prefer the best
4. To help children evaluate their own reading and extend beyond what is to what can be
5. To help pupils in their growing up and in their understanding of humanity in general[2]

For schools that prefer to follow behavioral objectives for the teaching of literature, Peterson has listed ten major headings. Under the *cognitive domain,* the children will know literary forms; they will know, analyze, and evaluate the theme and supporting details, the plot, the characterization, the setting, the literary and artistic style; and they will know and evaluate the physical format. Under the *affective domain,* the children will enjoy hearing selections read, will enjoy reading independently, and will enjoy sharing literature experiences.[3]

The school literature program should be structured to attain certain objectives because literature itself performs particular functions. It provides both pleasure and understanding. It shows human motives for what they are, inviting the readers/hearers to identify with or react to fictional characters. Literature provides a form for experience, placing relevant episodes into coherent sequence and thereby showing life's unity or meaning. Literature reveals life's fragmentation as well, sorting the world out into segments that can be identified and examined. It helps focus on essentials, permitting readers/hearers to experience with different intensity but with new understanding the parts of life they have known. Literature reveals how both the institutions of society and nature itself affect human life. Finally, literature leads or entices the readers/hearers into meeting a writer-creator whose medium (words) they know, whose subject (human nature) they live with; and whose vision (life's meaning) they hope to understand.[4]

Children are eager to know about innumerable subjects and literature can satisfy their curiosities. Boys and girls exhibit and share:

■ An inward-looking *curiosity about themselves,* and a book like LeShan's *What Makes Me Feel This Way?* (Macmillan, 1972) responds to this concern.

Table 11.1.

Planning Guide for a Literature Program in the Elementary School
(Recommended Sample Selections from *Adventuring with Books* [NCTE, 1977])

Suggested Age Level	Animal Stories	Historical Fiction	Folk-Fairy Tales	Other Lands/Peoples
5–6	(1) *Stubborn Bear* (Little, 1970) (2) *Hector Penguin* (McGraw, 1973)	(1) *Aaron and the Green Mountain Boys* (Coward, 1972) (2) *On the Day Peter Stuyvesant Sailed into Town* (Harper, 1971)	(1) *The Princess and Froggie* (Farrar, 1975) (2) *Little Sister and the Month Brothers* (Seabury, 1976)	(1) *Zaire: A Week in Joseph's World* (Macmillan, 1973) (2) *Buccaneers* (Golden Press, 1975)
7	(1) *Detective Mole* (Lothrop, 1976) (2) *The Mule Who Refused to Budge* (Crown, 1975)	(1) *King George's Head Was Made of Lead* (Coward, 1974) (2) *This Time, Tempe Wick?* (Coward, 1974)	(1) *Seven at One Blow* (Parents, 1972) (2) *The Tale of the Magic Bread* (Scroll, 1970)	(1) *Turkey: A Week in Samil's World* (Macmillan, 1973) (2) *Salima Lives in Kashmir* (Macmillan, 1971)
8	(1) *Elephant in Trouble* (Troll, 1970) (2) *The Crocodile in the Tree* (Knopf, 1973)	(1) *The Drinking Gourd* (Harper, 1970) (2) *Pocahontas and the Strangers* (Crowell, 1971)	(1) *The White Cat* (Bradbury, 1975) (2) *Jack and the Beanstalk* (Walck, 1975)	(1) *Book of Cities* (Random, 1975) (2) *Lito the Sunshine Boy* (Four Winds, 1975)
9	(1) *The Easter Cat* (Macmillan, 1971) (2) *A Dog and a Half* (Nelson, 1971)	(1) *Where's Florrie?* (Lothrop, 1976) (2) *Up the Hill* (Doubleday, 1970)	(1) *The Three Toymakers* (Nelson, 1971) (2) *Are All the Giants Dead?* (Harcourt, 1975)	(1) *Eskimos* (Watts, 1973) (2) *Looking at France* (Lippincott, 1970)
10	(1) *Panther* (Houghton, 1973) (2) *The Death of a Wombat* (Scribner, 1972)	(1) *Two If by Sea* (Random, 1970) (2) *Gettysburg: Tad Lincoln's Story* (Windmill, 1976)	(1) *Sorcerers and Spells* (Dutton, 1973) (2) *Favorite Fairy Tales Told in India* (Little, 1973)	(1) *Children of Hong Kong* (Childrens, 1975) (2) *Welcome to England* (Childrens, 1974)
11	(1) *Silver Wolf* (Atheneum, 1973) (2) *Trumpeter: The Story of a Swan* (Holiday, 1973)	(1) *Zia* (Houghton, 1976) (2) *A House on Liberty Street* (Atheneum, 1973)	(1) *The Donkey Prince* (Simon, 1970) (2) *Witches, Wit and a Werewolf* (Lippincott, 1971)	(1) *Europe for Young Travelers* (Bobbs, 1972) (2) *Iran* (Watts, 1972)

Source: *Adventuring with Books* (Urbana, Illinois: National Council of Teachers of English, 1977). Each book listed in the guide has met two criteria: It has "a high potential interest for young readers of the designated age level," and it reflects "a significant degree of literary merit in general and with respect to the particular category in which it might be classified."

Realistic Stories	Fables, Myths, and Legends	Fantasy	Biography	Informational Books	Poetry/Rhyme
(1) *Sabrina* (Dial, 1971) (2) *One to Teeter-Totter* (Whitman, 1973)	(1) *The Woman with the Eggs* (Crown, 1974) (2) *Tuhurahura and the Whale* (Parents, 1971)	(1) *The Aminal* (Abingdon, 1972) (2) *The Giant Jam Sandwich* (Houghton, 1973)	(1) *Jacques Cousteau* (Putnam, 1976) (2) *Walt Frazier* (Harcourt, 1975)	(1) *Farming Around the World* (Scribner, 1970) (2) *Have You Seen Boats?* (Addison, 1971)	(1) *All for Fall* (Parents, 1974) (2) *Big Sister Tells Me I'm Black* (Holt, 1976)
(1) *Good Lemonade* (Watts, 1976) (2) *Tony's Hard Work Day* (Harper, 1972)	(1) *Why the Wind God Wept* (Doubleday, 1972) (2) *The Seventh Mandarin* (Seabury, 1970)	(1) *Mr. Gumpy's Motor Car* (Crowell, 1976) (2) *Elephant Girl* (Morrow, 1976)	(1) *Ringling Brothers* (Crowell, 1971) (2) *Elizabeth Blackwell* (Garrard, 1975)	(1) *What Can She Be? A Musician* (Lothrop, 1975) (2) *A Building on Your Street* (Holiday, 1973)	(1) *Alligator Pie* (Houghton, 1975) (2) *Crickety-Cricket* (Harper, 1973)
(1) *Sleep Out* (Seabury, 1973) (2) *I'm Moving* (Abingdon, 1974)	(1) *The Song That Sings Itself* (Bobbs, 1972) (2) *Wizards and Wampum: Legends of the Iroquois* (Abelard, 1972)	(1) *The Parade* (Watts, 1975) (2) *Elvira Everything* (Harper, 1970)	(1) *John Muir* (Crowell, 1973) (2) *Henry Hudson* (Watts, 1974)	(1) *What Is Bowling?* (Atheneum, 1975) (2) *Football Players Do Amazing Things* (Random, 1975)	(1) *Feathered Ones and Furry* (Crowell, 1971) (2) *4-Way Stop* (Atheneum, 1976)
(1) *Willy* (Doubleday, 1971) (2) *Matt's Grandfather* (Putnam, 1972)	(1) *Why the Corn Is Red* (Abingdon, 1973) (2) *The Path to Snowbird Mountain: Cherokee Legends* (Farrar, 1972)	(1) *Mat Pit and the Tunnel Tenants* (Lippincott, 1972) (2) *Runaway Ralph* (Morrow, 1970)	(1) *Maria Tall-chief* (Crowell, 1970) (2) *The Boy Who Drew Sheep* (Atheneum, 1973)	(1) *Lighthouses* (Houghton, 1971) (2) *The Amazing Stethoscope* (Messner, 1971)	(1) *Amelia Mixed the Mustard* (Scribner, 1975) (2) *Poetry of Earth* (Scribner, 1972)
(1) *The Preacher's Kid* (Watts, 1975) (2) *Shoeshine Girl* (Crowell, 1975)	(1) *Animal Tales* (Doubleday, 1970) (2) *Raven-Who-Sets-Things Right* (Harper, 1975)	(1) *The Magical Cupboard* (Atheneum, 1976) (2) *A Near Thing for Captain Najork* (Atheneum, 1976)	(1) *Mr. Whittier* (Viking, 1974) (2) *The Fighting Apache* (Morrow, 1975)	(1) *Careers in Sports* (Lothrop, 1975) (2) *Basic Hockey Strategy* (Doubleday, 1976)	(1) *Rainbow Writing* (Atheneum, 1976) (2) *As I Walked Out One Evening* (Greenwillow, 1976)
(1) *What Are We Going to Do, Michael?* (Watts, 1973) (2) *And Then Mom Joined the Army* (Abingdon, 1976)	(1) *The Story of Persephone* (Morrow, 1973) (2) *The Treasure of the Mule-teer and Other Spanish Tales* (Doubleday, 1974)	(1) *The Snake Horn* (Atheneum, 1973) (2) *The Kingdom and the Cave* (Doubleday, 1974)	(1) *The Dark Eagle* (Macmillan, 1976) (2) *William Bradford of Plymouth Colony* (Watts, 1974)	(1) *Be a Winner in Tennis* (Morrow, 1975) (2) *Eating Places* (Morrow, 1975)	(1) *America Is Not All Traffic Lights* (Little, 1976) (2) *The Enduring Beast* (Doubleday, 1972)

- A *curiosity about the natural world,* and Hawkinson's *Let Me Take You on a Trail* (Whitman, 1972) helps them appreciate their environment.
- A *curiosity about people and places,* and writers like Allan Carpenter, Jean Fritz, and Ronald Syme help young readers discover facts about various American states, historical Americans, and famed explorers, respectively.
- A *curiosity about machines and how they work,* which is satisfied by a book like Halacy's *What Makes a Computer Work?* (Little, 1973).
- A *curiosity about facts and proofs of facts,* and so a popular book is the *Guinness Book of World Records,* revised annually by the Sterling Publishing Company of New York City.
- A *curiosity about the ideals by which men live,* which leads children to ponder Black's *The First Book of Ethics* (Watts, 1975).
- A *curiosity about the social world* and how to get along in society, which is satisfied by books like Hoke's *Etiquette, Your Ticket to Good Times* (Watts, 1970) and Meeks and Bagwell's *Families Live Together* (Follett, 1969).
- A practical and energetic *curiosity about creative experiences,* and writers like Bernice Wells Carlson, Joseph Leeming, and James Seidelman help children have fun with arts and crafts.
- A *curiosity about the world of make-believe,* and books about science fiction written by John Christopher are welcomed.
- A *curiosity about the unknown world,* which is satisfied by books explaining haunted houses or dreams, for example, as written by Larry Kettelkamp.[5]

Contemporary Trends

Books published since 1970 offer a splendidly diversified reading fare for boys and girls, according to Cianciolo, who has identified some of the modern trends.[6] *Most* of the current writers for young readers have restated rather than abandoned the cultural traditions and so traditional literary forms are still very much present. Still there are three forms of iconoclastic novels that have been created for the juvenile reader: existentialist or activist novels like Tate's *Ben and Annie* (Doubleday, 1974); impressionist novels like Blume's *Are You There, God? It's Me, Margaret* (Bradbury, 1970); and antirealistic or surrealistic novels like Wersba's *Amanda, Dreaming* (Atheneum, 1973). The contemporary authors of literature for children do not sentimentalize childhood but presume that boys and girls have basically the same emotions as adults although children's emotions are less complex. Children are reading this new literature with enthusiasm and pleasure.

Other trends in literature have been recognized too. There are many more picture books and those books that are profusely illustrated but not truly "picture books" per se have been offered to readers of all ages, not just to preschool and primary children. Then there are books displaying various art styles, with some artists creating sophisticated drawings or paintings as carefully as if the illustrations were intended for exhibition in an art gallery.

Another noticeable trend since 1970 has been the increasing number of children's novels about World War II and the Great Depression as well as many antiwar books. Also, an antiestablishment theme of disillusionment is now being reflected in some of the literature written for children. In addition, books are currently available about physical, mental and emotional disorders and handicaps, as well as books concerned with the plight of the elderly and the addiction of the young to drugs or alcohol. Finally, the advancement of technology has made available for young readers some excellent foreign literary selections in translation.

Children's Literary Interests

Since the beginning of the century, over three hundred studies on children's literary interests or reading preferences have been completed. The most important differentiating factor in reading preference, according to recent studies, is *sex*. As early as the first grade, there is a sex-based divergence in the interests that children have in the books that they read or are read to them. Although there are some books that appeal to both boys and girls, children most often name as their favorite book characters those that are of their own sex.

Research reported in this decade reached several important conclusions. First, all children prefer to watch (television) rather than read; low socioeconomic middle-grade pupils, however, are especially addicted and particularly to cartoon-like fantasy. Second, interest patterns of black readers resemble those of the general population. Third, book titles that excite inner-city children resemble titles that interest suburban readers. Fourth, fiction rates high, especially humorous fiction. Fifth, primary children in all three grades like realistic and fantasy characters, but while first graders place animal stories on top, third graders rate them at the bottom.[7]

Other recent studies regarding children's preferences in literature reveal that:

1. Intermediate girls read more recreational books than intermediate boys.
2. Better readers select books by known authors more often than poor readers.
3. Informational selections have an appeal for primary pupils.
4. Passages written in nonstandard dialect do not elicit as favorable a response toward the character as passages written in standard English.
5. Both boys and girls are more likely to have suitable reading fare if they are permitted to do much of their own choosing. Boys especially make their book choices according to interest appeal.
6. Children's reading tastes have largely crystallized by the fifth grade.

Although obviously children's literary tastes cannot be strictly categorized any more than adults' can, there are certain general areas of interest common to the different age levels.

Five- and Six-Year-Olds	These children enjoy picture books, especially those which stress reassurance and achievement. Thus they delight in such stories as Hoban's *A Bargain for Frances* (Harper, 1970) and Bemelmans' *Madeline in London* (Viking, 1961), each of which belongs to a series published in modern times. However, the young pupils also like tales written in another century and currently available in well-illustrated editions, including *The Traveling Musicians* and *The Three Little Pigs,* because these beloved old stories represent familiarity and emphasize independent accomplishment.

Books which extend and reinforce the developing concepts of this age group include Hoban's *Over, Under, and Through* (Macmillan, 1973) and *Push-Pull, Empty-Full* (Macmillan, 1972), and Brown's *The Important Book* (Harper, 1949). Other books these children enjoy are those about everyday experiences of pets, people, and playthings in the immediate environment, such as Cohen's *Will I Have a Friend?* (Macmillan, 1967) and Keats' *Peter's Chair* (Harper, 1967).

Seven-, Eight-, and Nine-Year-Olds	Children at this age are beginning to read for themselves and yet are not always able to match their reading competence with their interests. The teacher can help by providing many easy-to-read books with mature content, such as Butterworth's *The Enormous Egg* (Little, 1956) and Selden's *The Cricket in Times Square* (Farrar, 1960). The teacher can also help by reading aloud other stories that may be beyond the pupils' reading skill but not beyond their enjoyment level, such as Bulla's *White Bird* (Crowell, 1966) and Peare's *The Helen Keller Story* (Crowell, 1959).

This age group enjoys fantasy, such as Dahl's *James and the Giant Peach* (Knopf, 1961), as well as a realistic story like Burchardt's *Project Cat* (Watts, 1966).

Children's interest in fairy tales peaks at the age of seven or eight, gradually declining to a point of disinterest by the age of ten or eleven.[8] Boys and girls enjoy Andersen's *The Little Match Girl* (Houghton, 1968) and *The Nightingale* (Harper, 1965) as well as the Grimm Brothers' *The Seven Ravens* (Harcourt, 1963) and *The Sleeping Beauty* (Scroll Press, 1967).

In these years the children's curiosity is boundless, both for informational books and simple biography and for fiction. The boys and girls can become absorbed in stories of present-day life in regions of America other than their own, as well as in modern life outside the United States. They show concern as well with historical fiction of this country and that of other lands.

Throughout this age period, children can become interested in many kinds of reading categories if only the school district will provide them with an ample supply of well-selected, sturdy books and if only the classroom teacher will become familiar with the many fine juvenile books that are available.

Ten- and Eleven-Year-Olds	These boys and girls have experienced more of the world in which they live so their interests are broader. They turn therefore toward informational books

which will help satisfy or develop their curiosities. Popular subjects include biographies of famous historical figures, fanciful and imaginative selections in a more sophisticated context, and tall tales/folklore/legends with underlying humor. The growing maturity of fifth and sixth graders is evident as they select reading material with a fast-moving plot such as mysteries and adventure stories. Due to their increasing self-awareness of the struggle of life itself, they want to read and need to read stories and poems reflecting problems encountered by people like themselves, such as Clymer's *My Brother Stevie* (Holt, 1967), Mann's *My Dad Lives in a Downtown Hotel* (Doubleday, 1973), Rodgers' *Freaky Friday* (Harper, 1972) and Wersba's *The Dream Watcher* (Atheneum, 1968).

By the fifth grade the independent reading skills of some pupils may lag behind their owners' social maturity. For this group of readers the teacher will wish to supply books which transcend grade barriers and skill levels, such as Adamson's *Elsa* (Pantheon, 1963) and Morey's *Gentle Ben* (Dutton, 1965). Books written by Clyde Bulla in areas of both historical fiction and (contemporary) realistic fiction are easy reading but still command the respect of older boys and girls.

In mid-November 1977 the *New York Times Book Review* reported rankings of children's best sellers based on sales figures revealed by 420 of the principal juvenile book outlets throughout the country. The sample of stores was drawn so that it represented both geographic distribution and bookstore sizes. Respondents were asked to provide sales figures for best-selling titles in three categories: hardcover editions published in 1976–1977, paperback editions published in 1976–77, and perennial favorites or books published before 1976. The *Times* listed the top fifteen titles in each group. **Juvenile Best Sellers**

The hardback best sellers were:

1. Charles Schulz's *Charlie Brown's Super Book of Questions and Answers* (Random)
2. Carolyn Keene's *The Strange Message in Parchment* (Nancy Drew #4) (Grosset)
3. Franklin W. Dixon's *The Jungle Pyramid* (Hardy Boys #56) (Grosset)
4. Walt Disney Productions' *The Rescuers* (Random)
5. Shel Silverstein's *The Missing Piece* (Harper)
6. Gyo Fujikawa's *Oh, What a Busy Day!* (Grosset)
7. *Richard Scarry's Busiest People Ever* (Random)
8. Margaret Musgrove's *Ashanti to Zulu* (Dial)
9. Arnold Lobel's *Frog and Toad All Year* (Harper)
10. Jay Williams's *Everyone Knows What a Dragon Looks Like* (Four Winds)
11. Mitsumasa Anno's *Anno's Counting Book* (Crowell)
12. William Steig's *Abel's Island* (Farrar)
13. Richard Adams's *The Tyger Voyage* (Knopf)
14. Jill Krementz's *A Very Young Dancer* (Knopf)
15. William Steig's *The Amazing Bone* (Farrar)

For the same period the paperback best sellers were, in order:

1. Judy Dunn's *Little Duck* (Random)
2. Judy Dunn's *Little Lamb* (Random)
3. Judith Viorst's *Alexander and the Terrible, Horrible, No Good, Very Bad Day* (Atheneum)
4. Judy Blume's *Tales of a Fourth Grade Nothing* (Dell)
5. Jane Watson's *Dinosaurs* (Golden)
6. Charles Schulz' *The Charlie Brown Dictionary* (Scholastic)
7. George Jonsen's *Favorite Tales of Monsters and Trolls* (Random)
8. Fred Gwynne's *A Chocolate Moose for Dinner* (Dutton/Windmill)
9. Wallace Tripp's *Granfa' Grig Had a Pig* (Little)
10. Jack Kent's *There's No Such Thing as a Dragon* (Golden)
11. Harry McNaught's *Baby Animals* (Random)
12. Jan Pfloog's *Kittens Are Like That* (Random)
13. Linda Allison's *Blood and Guts* (Little)
14. Judith Viorst's *My Mama Says There Aren't Any Zombies, Ghosts, Vampires, Creatures, Demons, Monsters, Fiends, Goblins, or Things* (Atheneum)
15. Wanda Gág's *Millions of Cats* (Coward)

All published before 1976, the perennial best sellers in the children's book market were:

1. Shel Silverstein's *The Giving Tree* (Harper)
2. *Richard Scarry's Best Word Book Ever* (Golden)
3. E. B. White's *Charlotte's Web* (Harper)
4. Dorothy Kunhardt's *Pat the Bunny* (Golden)
5. Margery Williams's *The Velveteen Rabbit* (Doubleday)
6. Watty Piper's *The Little Engine That Could* (Platt)
7. Shel Silverstein's *Where the Sidewalk Ends* (Harper)
8. Franklin W. Dixon's *The Tower Treasure* (Hardy Boys #1) (Grosset)
9. Carolyn Keene's *The Secret of the Old Clock* (Nancy Drew #1) (Grosset)
10. Laura Ingalls Wilder's *Little House on the Prairie* (Harper)
11. Maurice Sendak's *Where the Wild Things Are* (Harper)
12. Beatrix Potter's *The Tale of Peter Rabbit* (Warne)
13. Dr. Seuss's *Green Eggs and Ham* (Random)
14. A. A. Milne's *Winnie-the-Pooh* (Dutton)
15. Margaret Wise Brown's *Goodnight Moon* (Harper)

The lists are significant only to the extent that they reveal the broad range of children's literary interests. Included are fantasy, fairy tales, serial fiction, and picture dictionaries. Some books first appeared more than fifty years ago and still remain children's favorites. There are books listed whose characters were expressly created for one volume, but in other instances the characters have appeared in many more books by the same publisher. Also, some of the popular titles have formed the bases for commercial television series or full-length commercial films/cartoons.

Television in particular and other informational-recreational media generally have broadened the reading interests of the elementary age group. To meet these interests a wide variety of books is being made available for children to read, hear, and watch.

Until approximately 1960 the volume of literature for children was relatively small, averaging less than 1,000 juvenile titles published per year. Then came federal funding for the support of library materials. As a result, 2,895 titles were published in 1965, 2,640 titles in 1970, and 2,235 titles in 1975.[9]

Since 1919 when Macmillan established the first children's department in a publishing house in the United States (and probably in the world), the children's book market has become a twentieth-century phenomenon. More than fifty publishing houses are now engaged in printing children's books; there are now nearly 30,000 juvenile titles available, and the production and distribution of juvenile books comprises a big business market of $150 million. There are even best-selling children's authors such as E. B. White whose *Stuart Little* and *Charlotte's Web* together have sold more than two million copies in hardcover editions, with *Charlotte's Web* alone selling more than three million copies in paperback.[10]

Despite the deluge of children's books, discriminating selection of a fine book for a specific class or pupil cannot yet be computerized. It still requires a knowledge of the interests, reading ability, and maturity level of that class or child, coupled with a knowledge of the best books to meet those interests and abilities.

The classroom teacher who has personally enjoyed some of the finest children's books can speak convincingly when introducing those books to the boys and girls. Children need to know a little of what each book is about, and a brief preview—or sales talk—concerning a particular volume helps them gain this information. These days children can receive satisfaction from a variety of readily accessible media, including television and motion pictures, and so the satisfaction a well-written book can bring must be explored in every classroom. This demands a personal knowledge by the teacher of many books in order that he or she may convey some of the excitement, wonder, and beauty of the printed page to young listeners and readers.

To learn more about new books and recent editions of older books, the teacher can consult such periodicals as *Language Arts* and *School Library Journal* (each published eight times a year), *Horn Book Magazine* (issued bimonthly), and *Childhood Education* (issued six times a year); or such basic book sources as:

> *Adventuring with Books* (National Council of Teachers of English, 1977)
> *Children's Books Too Good to Miss* (University Press Book Service, 1971)
> *Children's Catalog* (H. W. Wilson, 1971, and its annual supplements)
> *Good and Inexpensive Books for Children* (Association for Childhood Education, 1972)

Growing Up with Books (R. R. Bowker, 1975; revised annually)
Growing Up with Paperbacks (R. R. Bowker, 1975; revised biennially)
Guide to Non-Sexist Children's Books (Academy Press, 1976)
Paperback Books for Children (Citation Press, 1972)
Reference Books for Elementary and Junior High School Libraries
    (Scarecrow Press, 1972)
Reading Ladders for Human Relations (American Council on
    Education, 1972)
Young People's Literature in Series: Fiction (Libraries Unlimited, 1973)

In the spring and fall (usually May and November), large metropolitan newspapers such as the *New York Times* and the *Chicago Tribune* publish special children's book sections that provide brief reviews of new books; most public libraries carry at least one of these journals. Publishers such as Atheneum, Viking, Dell, and Scholastic, which specialize in children's books, furnish catalogs to schools or to teachers interested in learning about new books to share with their pupils. Teachers can also keep in mind the many award-winning books for children, especially the Caldecott Medal and Newbery Medal winners recognized since 1938 and 1922, respectively; a list of these titles is contained in Appendix 3.

With the ever increasing number of juvenile books from which to choose, the classroom teacher must be aware of certain criteria to help her identify a quality book for children, whether it be fiction, fact, or biography, and whether it has words or is wordless.

Fiction

Although the pupils' reading will not be limited to stories, they will remain the first and enduring favorite of the boys and girls. Good stories possess six strong elements.

Plot

Children are most interested in the action or plot of the story. In a well-written book the action is plausible and credible, developing naturally from the behavior and decisions of the characters, and is not dependent upon coincidence or contrivance. A story must have a beginning, a middle, and an ending. Children prefer an orderly sequence of events and generally lack the maturity to understand flashbacks. A well-plotted book for the intermediate grades is Griffiths' *The Wild Heart* (Doubleday, 1963).

Setting

The setting is the time and place of the action. It may be in the past, the present, or the future. The story may take place in a specific locale, or the setting may be deliberately vague to convey the feeling of all large cities or rural communities. It should, however, be clear, believable, and, in the case of historical fiction, authentic.

Both the time and the place should affect the action, the characters, and the theme. Younger readers can quickly grasp the setting of Monjo's *The Secret of the Sachem's Tree* (Coward, 1972) and Skorpen's *Old Arthur* (Harper,

1972). Older readers understand the setting of Steele's *The Perilous Road* (Harcourt, 1958) and Hunt's *Across Five Aprils* (Follett, 1964).

A good book needs a worthy theme which provides a dimension of the story beyond the action of the plot. It may be the acceptance of self or others, the overcoming of fear or prejudice, or simply growing up. The theme of a book reveals the author's purpose in writing the story. **Theme**

In a well-written book the theme avoids moralizing and yet effectively evolves from the events in the story and unifies them. Such a book is Ward's *The Biggest Bear* (Houghton, 1952), which younger children especially enjoy.

The personalities (animal or human) portrayed in children's books must be convincing and lifelike, displaying realistic strengths and weaknesses, and must be consistent in their portrayal. While not every character in a well-constructed story will change, there is frequent personality development as happenings occur and problems are solved. Too, characters should speak and behave in accordance with their culture, age, and educational experience. **Characterization**

Books with sound characterizations for primary children include Lindgren's *Pippi Longstocking* (Viking, 1950) and Caudill's *Did You Carry the Flag Today, Charley?* (Holt, 1966). Two for intermediate grade pupils are Alcott's *Little Women* (Crowell, 1955) and De Angeli's *The Door in the Wall* (Doubleday, 1949).

The style of writing in a book is the manner in which the author has selected and arranged words in presenting the story. A quality book possesses a style which respects children as intelligent individuals with rights and interests of their own. Children resent books whose style is patronizing or overly sentimental, or contains too much description or material for contemplation. Some pupils prefer books not written in the first person. **Style**

Primary grade children like to listen to Tresselt's *White Snow, Bright Snow* (Lothrop, 1956) and McCloskey's *Time of Wonder* (Viking, 1957). Intermediate grade pupils appreciate the contemporary dialogue in many of the books by E. L. Konigsburg.

Technological improvements in printing and picture reproduction are making possible attractive books for young readers. Although no book should ever be selected on the basis of format alone, matters of illustration, typography, binding, spacing, and paper quality cannot be wholly ignored when books are chosen for classroom use with elementary school boys and girls. Such books must represent the combined efforts of the best editors, illustrators, authors, book designers, and printers. **Format**

Young children appreciate Wildsmith's *The Little Wood Duck* (Watts, 1973) and Lionni's *Swimmy* (Pantheon, 1963). Older pupils are sensitive to Burton's *Life Story* (Houghton, 1962) and Jarrell's *The Animal Family* (Pantheon, 1965).

Informational Books

The best informational books, according to Sutherland and Arbuthnot, are written by people who not only know their subjects well but write about them imaginatively, with an understanding of the needs and limitations of their audiences.[11] Accuracy, currency, organization and scope, and format are important. So are the author's competence and responsibility to distinguish between fact and theory/opinion. Finally, informational books must be interestingly written, with vocabulary geared to the reading ability of the children. Younger pupils enjoy Bendick's *Names, Sets, and Numbers* (Watts, 1971) and Holling's *Paddle-to-the-Sea* (Houghton, 1941). Older children like to read the Gidals' *My Village in Ghana* (Pantheon, 1970) and McClung's *Thor: Last of the Sperm Whales* (Morrow, 1971).

Biography

There are three kinds of biography presented in children's literature. The first is authentic biography that is a well-documented and researched account of a person's life. It corresponds to adult biography and often includes photographs. Any conversations that are described include only those statements that are actually known to have been made by the subject. Outstanding examples are Meigs' *Invincible Louisa* (Little, 1961), McNeer's *America's Abraham Lincoln* (Houghton, 1957), and McKown's *The World of Mary Cassatt* (Crowell, 1972).

The second kind is fictionalized biography. Though grounded in thorough research, it allows the author more freedom to dramatize certain events and personalize the subject. The author may invent dialog, but the conversations are usually based upon actual facts taken from journals and diaries of the period. Fictionalized biography makes use of the narrative approach and is the generally accepted form for juvenile books. Recommended examples are Felton's *Mumbet, The Story of Elizabeth Freeman* (Dodd, 1970) and Judson's *Abraham Lincoln, Friend of the People* (Follett, 1950).

Biographical fiction is the third kind of children's biography. It consists entirely of imagined conversation and reconstructed action. Outstanding examples include Robert Lawson's amusing *Ben and Me* (Little, 1939) and *Mr. Revere and I* (Little, 1953).

In all well-written biographies the young readers enjoy a style that is vigorous and a narrative that is fast moving. The research material never detracts from the absorbing account of the life of the subject.

Wordless Picture Books

During the past decade books without words have appeared from reputable publishers. They are useful for reading readiness activities and stimulate language development. Since their interpretation depends solely on the pictures, it is crucial that the immediate action of each picture as well as the cumulative sequence of action in all the pictures be distinctly portrayed and readily understood.

Larrick conducted an informal survey concerning wordless picture books among elementary classroom teachers and children in three Pennsylvania towns. Kindergarten teachers used wordless books with small groups of pupils who later role played or produced their own "surprise books" (using personal drawings or magazine photos). Primary children also responded more creatively to such follow-up activities as the taping of stories when a wordless book was introduced to a very small group or even on a one-to-one basis. Finally, those sixth graders who were poor readers thought that a wordless book would be "a good starter" for young readers because it challenges the imagination, resembles a silent movie, gives the readers more to ponder, and allows them to experience feelings which they must then put into words. For themselves, however, the sixth graders agreed that they preferred books with words since "you've got to learn to read sometime and we need words at our age." Popular authors of wordless books in the survey were Aliki, Martha Alexander, Edward Ardizzone, Eric Carle, Tana Hoban, Pat Hutchins, and Mercer Mayer, with Mayer rated the top favorite.[12]

Wordless picture books cover varied subjects. There are wordless animal stories like Fromm's *Muffel and Plums* (Macmillan, 1973), Hamberger's *The Lazy Dog* (Four Winds, 1971), Mayer's *Frog Goes to Dinner* (Dial, 1974), and Winter's *The Bear and the Fly* (Crown, 1976). There are realistic stories, including Lisker's *Lost* (Harcourt, 1975) and Ardizzone's *The Wrong Side of the Bed* (Doubleday, 1970). There are more subtle books like Hogrogian's *Apples* (Macmillan, 1972) and Krahn's *A Flying Saucer Full of Spaghetti* (Dutton, 1970). And there are informational, wordless books including the Maris' *The Apple and the Moth* (Pantheon, 1970), Simmons' *Family* (McKay, 1970), Koren's *Behind the Wheel* (Holt, 1972), and Reiss' *Shapes* (Bradbury, 1974).

One of the longest wordless books is Ward's *The Silver Pony* (Houghton, 1973) which has some 80 pictures and appeals especially to middle-graders.

Since children are entitled to hear satisfying poetry as well as fine prose, their teacher should be cognizant of three important elements in good poetry:

Poetry: Literary Work in Metrical Form

1. *Singing quality.* Some poems have as much melody as does music, for the rhythm and the arrangement of the lines are suggestive of the mood of the poem. There is movement as well. De la Mare's "Silver" and McCord's "Song of the Train" have pronounced melody and movement.
2. *Distinguished diction.* The words and phrases must be carefully chosen and rich in sensory and associated meanings. Both strong and delicate words are interwoven in Meigs' "Silver Ships" and Cane's "Snow Toward Evening."
3. *Significant content.* Poems should appeal to the intellect as well as to the emotion; therefore, even poems of a few lines need a well-defined theme. Fields' "Taxis" and Frost's "Dandelions" provide new meanings to the pupils' everyday experiences.

In selecting a poem for children, the teacher must consider their background and age level, their needs, their previous experience with poetry, and the modern setting in which they live. The teacher should begin where the children are. For preschool and kindergarten pupils, the rhymes in *The Mother Goose Book* (Random, 1976) represent a strong and pleasant beginning. If primary children have not heard much poetry, the teacher can start with some of the traditional rhymes for games and tongue-twisters found in Lee's *Alligator Pie* (Houghton, 1975) as well as more modern poems such as Tippett's *Crickety-Cricket* (Harper, 1973). Older boys and girls who have not yet been introduced to poetry may be reached through narrative or humorous poems, such as Noyes' *The Highwayman* (Prentice-Hall, 1969) and Bodecker's *Let's Marry Said the Cherry and Other Nonsense Poems* (Atheneum, 1974), respectively. The teacher can use country or folk music as a prelude to poetry with pupils in all grades. With older students the teacher may wish to develop an introductory unit centered about a poet to whom pupils can relate, such as Rod McKuen, and initiate the unit with tapes of his songs and poems.

The poetry presented should have relevance for today's child. It should be appropriate in theme and mood to the maturity of the group. It should not be didactic or filled with archaic vocabulary. Neither should it be coy, nostalgic, or sarcastic. Finally, it should generally be true poetry and not always merely verse, since verse—or "poetry in petticoats" to Elizabeth Coatsworth—provides only a background of readiness for the acceptance and presentation of real poetry.

The teaching of poetry can follow no set pattern. Unless the teacher enjoys poetry, the students will not respond enthusiastically. The teacher's personal choice of poetry guides pupils in building their own individual yardsticks. Therefore, the teacher's personal definition of poetry will determine how far he or she will carry the children into the realm of poetry.

Forms of Poetry for Children

One of the literary understandings to develop in elementary school literature is knowledge of types of poetry. These understandings grow gradually, so the wise teacher will provide balance in the selection of poetic forms as children exhibit readiness for them. There are several major forms.

Most of the poetry written for children is *lyric* poetry. It is usually descriptive or personal, with no prescribed length or structure except that it be melodic and music-making. Many of the poems of Robert Louis Stevenson, Christina Rossetti, Eleanor Farjeon, Elizabeth Coatsworth, Sara Teasdale, Eve Merriam, and Harry Behn have this singing quality and can therefore be termed lyrical.

One of the best ways to capture pupil interest in poetry is to present a variety of *narrative* poems. Each of these so-called story poems relates a particular episode/event or tells a long tale. Seven- and eight-year-olds enjoy the long narrative verses of the many books by Dr. Seuss. Older children respond to Longfellow's *Paul Revere's Ride* (Crowell, 1963) and Whittier's *Barbara Frietchie* (Crowell, 1965), both editions having been illustrated by Paul Galdone. Classical narrative poems include Browning's *The Pied Piper of Hamelin* (Scroll Press, 1970) and Moore's *The Night Before Christmas* (Rand, 1976) which have wide appeal. Narrative poems may appear as lyrics, sonnets, or free verse.

A special type of narrative poem that has been adapted for singing and that contains repetition, rhythm, and a refrain is a *ballad*. With the growing popularity of folk singing in recent years there has been renewed interest in the ballad form. There are both literary ballads with recognized authors and popular ballads with no known authors. Children in the middle grades will enjoy popular ballads like "The Raggle Taggle Gypsies," "Get Up and Bar the Door," and "Robin Hood and the Widow's Sons." Literary ballads appropriate for use with children include Benét's *The Ballad of William Sycamore (1790–1871)* (Little, 1972), and Cary's "A Legend of the Northland."

Children enjoy *limericks,* a nonsense form of five-lined verse. The first and second lines rhyme, as do the third and fourth lines, but the fifth line generally ends in a surprising or humorous statement. Contrary to popular belief, Edward Lear did not originate the limerick; he did however do much to popularize it, and pupils listen eagerly to many of the limericks in his *The Complete Nonsense Book* (Dodd, 1958). Middle-grade children also find Smith's *Typewriter Town* (Dutton, 1960) challenging because it combines limericks with pictures made by using the typewriter.

Pupils who have the opportunity to hear *free verse* are relieved to discover that all poetry does not rhyme. Free verse sounds much like other poetry when read aloud, but often looks different on the printed page. Sandburg's "Fog" and Hughes' "April Rain Song" are popular examples of the effective use of free verse which depends upon cadence or rhythm for its poetic form.

Some children enjoy hearing—and others enjoy writing—a Japanese verse form of three lines called *haiku*. Containing a total of only seventeen syllables, the first and third lines of the haiku have five syllables each, and the middle line has seven. Nearly every haiku may be divided into two parts: first a simple description that refers to a season; and second, a statement of feeling or mood. The teacher may wish to share with the class two volumes of haiku translated by Harry Behn and entitled *Cricket Songs: Japanese Haiku* (Harcourt, 1964) and *More Cricket Songs* (Harcourt, 1971).

Other old Japanese poetic forms are *senryu* and *tanka*. The first is identical to haiku, with seventeen syllables in three lines, except that it may deal with any topic; it is named after the poet who originated the form. Tanka is identical to haiku for its initial three lines, but adds two more lines of seven syllables each, for a total of thirty-one syllables; it usually completes a thought or tells a story. Elementary children may wish to hear or read some Japanese poetry compiled by Virginia Baron, *The Seasons of Time: Tanka Poetry of Ancient Japan* (Dial, 1968), and by Richard Lewis, *There Are Two Lives: Poems by Children of Japan* (Simon, 1970).

Unlike the sex-based differences in preference which they have for prose literature, boys and girls of similar capacities and experiences like the same kinds

Children's Preferences

of poems. Children from grades kindergarten through sixth grade like poetry that contains humor, action, rollicking rhythm, a story line, and a minimum of description. They reject poems that are sentimental or subtle. They prefer narrative poems or contemporary poetry which has meaning for their lives.

In a four-state school survey, Terry found that boys and girls in grades four to six like poems that rhyme and that include words used for acoustic effects. Limericks were among the best-liked poems for they contain many of the elements popular with children. On the other hand, haiku poems were strongly rejected because they are too short, lack rhyme, and are difficult to understand. Terry's overall findings suggest that children's preferences in poetry have not changed in at least twenty years.[13]

What may be even more significant is the conclusion reached in a national survey of 1,401 elementary students in urban, suburban, and rural schools with varied socioeconomic backgrounds: *two out of three pupils like poetry.* Urban students like poetry more than either the suburban or rural pupils, indicating that teachers in urban areas may be reading poetry aloud more frequently than their colleagues in other areas.[14]

Boys and girls in most of the elementary grades find nothing peculiar, boring, or silly about poetry because so many of the experiences of the children and their language are related to poetic experiences and language. Elements that are shared by both young pupils and poets, such as love of concrete imagery, use of accentuated rhythm, and indulgence in playfulness, work positively for the interest that children have for poetry—at least through grade four. And fifth and sixth graders, whose teacher possesses a realistic concept of poetry and couples pupils and poems as subtly as pupils and prose, will also continue their initial enthusiasm for poetry, although interest in poetry begins to wane as students mature.

Boys and girls in the primary grades enjoy a wide variety of verse and poetry. They respond readily to nonsense and humor, ballads and narrative poetry, poems about animals, automobiles, and trains, and poetry that deals with daily activities. A sampling of the kinds of poetry and verse that they enjoy includes:

Austin's "Texas Trains and Trails"
Baruch's "Automobile Mechanics"
Bennett's "A Modern Dragon"
Brown's "Jonathan Bing"
Burnham's "The Barnyard"
Carroll's "You Are Old, Father William"
De la Mare's "Quack"
De la Mare's "Tired Tim"
Durston's "The Hippopotamus"
Field's "The Duel"
Herford's "The Elf and the Dormouse"
Lear's "The Owl and the Pussy-Cat"

Le Cron's "Little Charlie Chipmunk"
Lindsay's "The Little Turtle"
Lindsay's "The Mysterious Cat"
Meigs' "The Pirate Don Durk of Dowdee"
Nash's "The Tale of Custard the Dragon"
Rands's "Godfrey Gordon Gustavus Gore"
Richards' "Eletelephony"
Richards' "The Monkeys and the Crocodile"
Richards' "Mrs. Shipkin and Mrs. Wobblechin"
Riley's "The Raggedy Man"
Tippett's " 'Sh' "

Children in the intermediate grades like poems which are related to their interests and experiences, poems that are humorous, and poems with strength of rhythm and rhyme. They will accept narrative verse that has action and excitement, such as Thayer's "Casey at the Bat," and may be exposed to some serious poems such as the Benets' "Nancy Hanks." They enjoy popular ballads that are not too difficult to read, including the traditional ones like "Get Up and Bar the Door." They like the element of mystery in Stevenson's "Windy Nights."

Intermediate and younger pupils alike who live in urban areas find these poetry compilations appealing:

Adoff's *City in All Directions* (Macmillan, 1969)
Bontemps' *Hold Fast to Dreams* (Follett, 1969)
Fufuka's *My Daddy Is a Cool Dude* (Dial, 1975)
Langstaffs' *Shimmy Shimmy Coke-Ca-Pop!* (Doubleday, 1973)
Larrick's *On City Streets* (Evans, 1969)
Lewis' *The Park* (Simon and Schuster, 1968)
Merriam's *The Inner-City Mother Goose* (Simon and Schuster, 1969)
Ridlon's *That Was Summer* (Follett, 1969)

Lastly, the teacher should be aware of the results of a national poll of approximately 5000 children in classrooms across the country for top selections among recently published poetry volumes. The seven finalists, according to a joint committee of the Children's Book Council and the International Reading Association, were: Bodecker's *Hurry, Hurry, Mary Dear* (Atheneum, 1976); Caudill's *Wind, Sand and Sky* (Dutton, 1975); Plath's *The Bed Book* (Harper, 1972); Prelutsky's *Nightmares: Poems to Trouble Your Sleep* (Greenwillow, 1976); Tripp's *Granfa' Grig Had a Pig and Other Rhymes Without Reason from Mother Goose* (Little, 1972); Wallace's *Witch Poems* (Holiday, 1976); and Worth's *More Small Poems* (Farrar, 1976).[15]

Children should hear poems—and poems were written to be read aloud—published earlier in this century as well as those printed for them in the eighteenth and nineteenth centuries. And teachers can readily locate such poems in the

Modern Poetry for Children

fine anthologies compiled by May Hill Arbuthnot, Edward Blishen, Helen Ferris, Nancy Larrick, Elizabeth Sechrist, and Louis Untermeyer.

However, elementary pupils are also entitled to listen to poetry/verse written or compiled more recently. The recommended publications listed here are marked (E) for easy reading for younger children or (J) for juvenile books for intermediate pupils. The teacher should, of course, examine each volume to determine its suitability for a particular group of students.

(E)   Abisch and Kapian's *Sweet Betsy from Pike* (McCall, 1970)
(J)   Adams' *Poetry of Earth* (Scribner, 1972)
(J)   Adoff's *Black Out Loud* (Macmillan, 1970)
(J)   Adoff's *It Is the Poem Singing into Your Eyes* (Harper, 1971)
(J)   Allen's *Poems from Africa* (Crowell, 1973)
(J)   Allen's *The Whispering Wind* (Doubleday, 1972)
(J)   Atwood's *Haiku, The Mood of Verse* (Scribner, 1971)
(E)   Clifton's *Everett Anderson's Christmas Coming* (Holt, 1971)
(E)   Clifton's *Some of the Days of Everett Anderson* (Holt, 1970)
(J)   Cole's *Oh, How Silly* (Viking, 1970)
(J)   Cole's *Oh, That's Ridiculous* (Viking, 1972)
(E)   Fisher's *Feathered Ones and Furry* (Crowell, 1971)
(J)   Froman's *Street Poems* (McCall, 1971)
(E)   Hopkins' *Me! A Book of Poems* (Seabury, 1970)
(E)   Hopkins' *This Street's for Me* (Crown, 1970)
(E)   Kuskin's *Any Me I Want to Be* (Harper, 1972)
(J)   Larrick's *I Heard a Scream in the Streets* (Evans, 1970)
(E)   Lenski's *City Poems* (Walck, 1971)
(E)   Livingston's *Listen, Children, Listen* (Harcourt, 1972)
(J)   Livingston's *The Malibu and Other Poems* (Atheneum, 1972)
(J)   Livingston's *Speak Roughly to Your Little Boy* (Harcourt, 1971)
(J)   McCord's *For Me to Say: Rhymes of the Never Was and Always Is* (Little, 1970)
(J)   Merriam's *Finding A Poem* (Atheneum, 1970)
(E–J)   O'Neill's *Winds* (Doubleday, 1971)
(J)   Plotz' *The Marvelous Light* (Crowell, 1970)
(J)   Rasmussen's *Beyond the High Hills: A Book of Eskimo Poems* (World, 1971)
(E)   Solbert's *32 Feet of Insides* (Pantheon, 1970)
(E)   Stoutenburg's *A Cat Is* (Watts, 1971)
(E)   Wilbur's *Opposites* (Harcourt, 1973)
(J)   Worth's *Small Poems* (Farrar, 1972)

Bibliotherapy— or Books That Help Children to Cope

As children grow and develop, they encounter a multitude of problems stemming from sibling relationships, family mobility, hospital confinement, parental separation, physical handicaps, or other sources. Some of their concerns arise chiefly within themselves, while others evolve from outside events that affect the boys and girls: John's parents are getting a divorce; Jennifer is fat and awkward; Doris is the first Oriental in the school; and seven-year-old Chris has already lived in eight different states.

To help these children attain some degree of understanding of their personal difficulties, there are books that can be used to enable the reader or listener to accept problems in a wholesome manner. Books for precisely such mental hygiene comprise *bibliotherapy* and provide a source of insight and relief from the varied pressures that young readers face during the ups and downs of normal development. Bibliotherapy may help boys and girls relieve conscious problems in a controlled manner and gain information about the psychology and physiology of human behavior. What it cannot do, however, is to provide therapy through literature for those who have emotional or mental illnesses and are in need of clinical treatment.

Once defined as a process of dynamic interaction between literature and the personality of the reader (which may be utilized for personality assessment, adjustment and growth), bibliotherapy may generally be used by the teacher in

Some of the problems associated with starting school may be resolved for this child through therapeutic bibliotherapy. (Photo courtesy of Charles Campbell.)

two ways. With *therapeutic* bibliotherapy the teacher may attempt to solve children's actual problems by presenting similar experiences vicariously through books. By recognizing their problems and possible solutions in literature, the children presumably gain new insight and are then able to take a step toward resolving their personal difficulties. On the other hand, the teacher who employs *preventive* bibliotherapy believes that pupils will be better able to make satisfactory adjustments to some trying situations in the future provided that they have met similar problems in stories which they presently read or hear. In a sense, preventive bibliotherapy is analogous to an inoculation to prevent a contagious disease. It contributes to understanding and compassion as it offers children attitudes and standards of behavior that will help them to adjust to some or most of the personal difficulties they will encounter.

Selecting and Using Books to Help Pupils Cope

Books designed to help change social and emotional behavior among nonclinical cases should still exemplify good literature. Their content must be worthwhile and their style respectful to children. Racial, religious, or nationality groups must each be pictured with accuracy and dignity. In short, any book selected for bibliotherapy should be a book that boys and girls today want to read.

The teacher may choose to use a particular book either with a large-group guidance session, a small-group session, or in an individual conference. The large session is especially suited for preventive bibliotherapy where each member can benefit from exposure to the book. The small-group session, much like a group reading lesson, is appropriate for therapeutic bibliotherapy where several children all have a common problem. Individual conferences may incorporate preventive bibliotherapy when the teacher has been made aware of a forthcoming change in a child's life, e.g., that seven-year-old Rhonda will be leaving California for upstate New York before the end of the term. An unforeseen occasion may also demand therapeutic bibliotherapy, e.g., when Mike's grandfather suddenly dies. In preparation for either the personal conference or the group session the teacher is advised to maintain a supply of index cards, each containing the title and subject matter of a useful book available in the school library media center.[16]

After either the individual conference or the group guidance sessions, the teacher must assign follow-up activities. Younger children can be challenged through such projective devices as drawing, painting, puppetry, or dramatic play. Older pupils, however, often wish to retell what happened in the story itself and explore the results of certain behaviors or feelings before reaching a generalization about the consequences of certain conditions or traumas. With both age groups follow-up activities are important, for without them no significant amount of behavioral change can occur.

Selected Books Useful in Bibliotherapy

Of the books included in the following list, those marked with an *E* are picture books or easy books planned especially for the primary grades, while juvenile books marked with a *J* are intended for intermediate-grade children. In either case the teacher will wish to personally examine each book to determine its appropriateness and utility for the individual child's or group's needs.

A. Exceptionality: Adjustment to Physical or Mental Handicaps
Blindness
    (J)   Heide's *Sound of Sunshine, Sound of Rain* (Parents, 1970)
Cerebral Palsy
    (J)   Little's *Mine for Keeps* (Little, 1962)
Deafness
    (E)   Levine's *Lisa and Her Soundless World* (Behavioral Publications, 1974)
Diabetes
    (J)   Branfield's *Why Me?* (Harper, 1973)
Lameness
    (J)   Armer's *Screwball* (Collins & World, 1963)
Learning Disability
    (E)   Lasker's *He's My Brother* (Whitman, 1974)
Mental Retardation
    (E/J)   Klein's *The Blue Rose* (Hill, 1974)
Paraplegia (in Wheelchair)
    (J)   Savitz' *Fly, Wheels, Fly* (Day, 1970)
Rheumatic Fever
    (J)   Lenski's *Corn-Farm Boy* (Lippincott, 1954)
Stuttering
    (J)   Lee's *The Skating Rink* (Seabury, 1969)
B. Adjustment to New Environment
Boarding School
    (J)   Carlson's *Luvvy and the Girls* (Harper, 1971)
    (J)   Nordstrom's *The Secret Language* (Harper, 1960)
Camp
    (J)   Hodges' *The Hatching of Joshua Cobb* (Ariel, 1967)
    (J)   Stolz' *A Wonderful, Terrible Time* (Harper, 1967)
Entering School
    (E)   Adelson's *All Ready for School* (McKay, 1957)
    (J)   Cleary's *Ramona the Pest* (Morrow, 1968)
Foster Home
    (J)   L'Engle's *Meet the Austins* (Vanguard, 1960)
    (J)   Floyd's *Second-Hand Family* (Bobbs, 1965)
Hospital
    (E)   Collier's *Danny Goes to the Hospital* (Grosset, 1970)
    (E)   Weber's *Elizabeth Gets Well* (Crowell, 1969)
Integrated School
    (E)   Ormsby's *Twenty-One Children Plus Ten* (Lippincott, 1971)
    (J)   Carlson's *The Empty Schoolhouse* (Harper, 1965)
New Country
    (J)   Little's *From Anna* (Harper, 1972)
    (J)   Norris' *A Feast of Light* (Knopf, 1967)
New Home
    (E)   Zolotow's *A Tiger Called Thomas* (Lothrop, 1963)
    (J)   Wallace's *Toby* (Doubleday, 1971)

C. Family Relationships

Adopted Child

    (E)   Caines' *Abby* (Harper, 1973)

    (J)   Bradbury's *Laurie* (Ives Washburn, 1965)

Siblings

    (E)   Bonsall's *The Day I Had to Play with My Sister* (Harper, 1972)

    (J)   Blume's *Tales of a Fourth Grade Nothing* (Dutton, 1972)

New Baby

    (E)   Arnstein's *Billy and Our New Baby* (Behavioral Publications, 1973)

    (E)   Alexander's *Nobody Asked Me If I Wanted a Baby Sister* (Dial, 1971)

Grandparents

    (E)   Behrens' *Soo Ling Finds a Way* (Childrens Press, 1965)

    (J)   Howard's *The Ostrich Chase* (Holt, 1974)

Stepmothers

    (J)   Alcock's *Duffy* (Lothrop, 1972)

    (J)   Sherburne's *Girl in the Mirror* (Morrow, 1966)

Stepfathers

    (J)   Huston's *Ollie's Go-Kart* (Seabury, 1971)

    (J)   Platt's *Chloris and the Creeps* (Chilton, 1973)

Stepbrothers/Stepsisters

    (J)   Daringer's *Stepsister Sally* (Harcourt, 1952)

    (J)   Willard's *Storm from the West* (Harcourt, 1963)

Twins

    (E)   Cleary's *The Real Hole* (Morrow, 1960)

    (J)   Cleary's *Mitch and Amy* (Morrow, 1967)

Great-Grandparents

    (J)   Bulla's *The Sugar Pear Tree* (Crowell, 1960)

    (J)   Carlson's *Marchers for the Dream* (Harper, 1969)

D. Personal Traits

Courage

    (E)   De Paola's *Andy (That's My Name)* (Prentice, 1973)

    (J)   Turkle's *The Fiddler of High Lonesome* (Viking, 1968)

Egocentrism

    (J)   Burch's *Simon and the Game of Chance* (Viking, 1970)

    (J)   Tunis' *Highpockets* (Morrow, 1948)

Greed

    (E)   Duvoisin's *Petunia, I Love You* (Knopf, 1965)

    (E)   Kimishima's *Lum Fu and the Golden Mountain* (Parents, 1971)

Height: Short

    (E)   Schlein's *Billy, the Littlest One* (Whitman, 1966)

    (J)   Lee's *It's a Mile from Here to Glory* (Little, 1972)

Height: Tall

    (E)   Krasilovsky's *The Very Tall Little Girl* (Doubleday, 1969)

    (J)   Christopher's *Johnny Long Legs* (Little, 1970)

Honesty

    (E)   Matsuno's *A Pair of Red Clogs* (Collins & World, 1960)

    (J)   Little's *One to Grow On* (Little, 1969)

Loneliness
- (E) Coatsworth's *Lonely Maria* (Pantheon, 1960)
- (J) Rolerson's *A Boy Called Plum* (Dodd, 1974)

Shyness
- (E) Krasilovsky's *The Shy Little Girl* (Houghton, 1960)
- (J) Nathan's *The Shy One* (Random, 1966)

Weight
- (J) Du Bois' *Porko von Popbutton* (Harper, 1969)
- (J) Solot's *100 Hamburgers: The Getting Thin Book* (Lothrop, 1972)[17]

Learning to accept and respect the diverse cultures in our pluralistic society—another phase of bibliotherapy—involves more than recognition of differences in family custom, diet, and language pattern, according to the Committee on Reading Ladders for Human Relations of the National Council of Teachers of English. Literature which goes beyond a mere acknowledgment of difference to an appreciation of the richness of cultural distinctions leads to sensitivity and feelings of empathy. It also allows the reader or listener to span the barriers of race, color, and religion which keep people apart.

Minority-Americans in Modern Children's Literature

Carefully planned literary experiences that expose children to books other than those of the dominant culture can help them realize that:

1. No one cultural group has a corner on imagination, creativity, poetic quality, or philosophic outlook. Each has made important contributions to the total culture of the country and the world.
2. People belonging to ethnic groups other than the pupils' are real people with feelings, emotions, and needs similar to theirs.
3. Other cultures have ways of looking at life and expressing ideas which can expand the pupils' own understandings. Therefore, pupils who judge other cultures in terms of their own lose the opportunity to broaden their bases of choice in developing values and modifying their life-styles.
4. While in other cultures people may have different value systems, individuals in all cultures can and must live together in harmony.[18]

Sample selections in each category listed here appear either in the new edition of *Adventuring with Books* (National Council of Teachers of English, 1977) or in the fifth edition of the *Reading Ladders for Human Relations* (American Council on Education, 1972). Books preceded by (*E*) are easy books particularly appropriate for younger children, while those preceded by (*J*) are more truly books for intermediate pupils.

A. Black Americans
- (E) Clifton's *Everett Anderson's Friend* (Holt, 1976)
- (J) Greene's *Philip Hall Likes Me, I Reckon Maybe* (Dial, 1974)
- (J) Jackson and Landau's *Black in America* (Messner, 1974)
- (E) Keats' *Goggles!* (Macmillan, 1969)
- (E) Molarsky's *Song of the Empty Bottles* (Walck, 1968)

(J)   Steptoe's *Stevie* (Harper, 1969)

(J)   Williamson and Ford's *Walk On!* (Viking, 1972)

B. Chinese-Americans

(E)   Anderson's *Charley Yee's New Year* (Follett, 1970)

(J)   Dowdells' *The Chinese Helped Build America* (Messner, 1972)

(E)   Keating's *Mister Chu* (Macmillan, 1965)

(E)   Molnar's *Sherman: A Chinese-American Child Tells His Story* (Watts, 1973)

(J)   Niemeyer's *The Moon Guitar* (Watts, 1969)

(J)   Sung's *The Chinese in America* (Macmillan, 1972)

(E)   Wright's *A Sky Full of Dragons* (Steck, 1969)

C. American Indians

(E)   Benchley's *Small Wolf* (Harper, 1972)

(J)   Clymer's *The Spider, the Cave, and the Pottery Bowl* (Atheneum, 1971)

(J)   Lampman's *The Potlatch Family* (Atheneum, 1976)

(E)   Mills' *Annie and the Old One* (Little, 1971)

(J)   Momaday's *Owl in the Cedar Tree* (Northland, 1975)

(E)   Perrine's *Nannabah's Friend* (Houghton, 1970)

(J)   Sneve's *High Elk's Treasure* (Holiday, 1972)

D. Japanese-Americans

(J)   Haugaard's *Myeko's Gift* (Abelard, 1966)

(E)   Hawkinson's *Dance, Dance, Amy-Chan!* (Whitman, 1964)

(J)   Means' *The Moved-Outers* (Houghton, 1945)

(E)   Politi's *Mieko* (Golden Gate, 1969)

(J)   Uchida's *Journey to Topaz* (Scribner, 1971)

(J)   Uchida's *Samurai of Gold Hill* (Scribner, 1972)

(E)   Yashima's *Umbrella* (Viking, 1958)

E. American Jews

(J)   Cone's *A Promise Is a Promise* (Houghton, 1964)

(E)   Hirsh's *Ben Goes into Business* (Holiday, 1973)

(J)   Konigsburg's *About the B'Nai Bagels* (Atheneum, 1969)

(J)   Kurtis' *The Jews Helped Build America* (Messner, 1970)

(J)   Meltzer's *Remember the Days: A Short History of the Jewish American* (Doubleday, 1974)

(J)   Neville's *Berries Goodman* (Harper, 1965)

(J)   Rose's *There Is a Season* (Follett, 1967)

F. Mexican-Americans

(J)   Bonham's *Viva Chicano* (Dutton, 1970)

(J)   Fitchs' *Soy Chicano, I Am Mexican-American* (Creative Ed., 1971)

(J)   Greene's *Manuel, Young Mexican-American* (Lantern, 1969)

(J)   Lampman's *Go Up the Road* (Atheneum, 1972)

(E)   Politi's *Juanita* (Scribner, 1948)

(E)   Politi's *Pedro, the Angel of Olvera Street* (Scribner, 1946)

(J)   Smith's *Josie's Handful of Quietness* (Abingdon, 1975)

G. Puerto-Rican Americans

(J)   Anderson's *Just the Two of Them* (Atheneum, 1974)

(J)   Bailey's *José* (Houghton, 1969)

(E)   Belpre's *Santiago* (Warne, 1969)

(E)   Bouchard's *The Boy Who Wouldn't Talk* (Doubleday, 1969)

(J)   Brahs' *An Album of Puerto Ricans in the United States* (Watts, 1973)
(E)   Thomas' *Mira! Mira!* (Lippincott, 1970)
(J)   Weiner's *They Call Me Jack* (Pantheon, 1973)

Literature can be shared in a variety of meaningful ways in which children enjoy taking part and which grow naturally from the love of books. Such learning experiences furnish an avenue through which children can relate their personal feelings and develop their creative potential. These experiences also provide exposure to new media and new ways of thinking about books while they simultaneously build appreciations and develop standards in literature.

Instructional Activities in Literature

The activities that teachers can plan with or for their pupils should meet varying ability levels. Some are primarily *motivational* activities and others are especially *interpretive* experiences and the division between the two groups is not always clear-cut; often an interpretive or culminating activity for one pupil will serve as a motivating literary experience for another child. While the teacher serves as the primary force bringing literature into the classroom to motivate children's reading, he or she also guides and assists the readers when they wish to share their books with one another. Aware that each book which is read need not be followed by some kind of report or interpretive exercise, the teacher is not disturbed when some children (notably the higher achievers) prefer to continue reading rather than to participate in creative expression.

Nearly sixty selected motivational and interpretive activities that have been used successfully in elementary classrooms are described as follows:

The story is the heart of any storytelling experience. Consequently, the teacher-storyteller should develop a familiarity with different kinds of story collections by spending some time reading in the children's room of the public library. When the teacher has located a promising tale he or she should consider: Is the story one that personally excites me? Is it a story that I wish to share with others? Is it a story that *I* can tell? Is it a tale that lends itself to telling (or should it be read aloud instead)? Is it a tale that will appeal to the age group of the listeners? Is the length of the tale correct for the attention span of the audience for which it is intended?

Motivational Experiences

Storytelling

Storytelling is not difficult and child audiences generally are highly appreciative. Busy teachers must therefore discount the notably tough requirements from the traditional writers on storytelling which call for long hours in preparation and exceptional efforts at concentration, memorization, overlearning of stories, and considerable speech work.[19]

Instead, once the teacher-storyteller has chosen a tale and prepared adequately, he or she needs only to establish an effective setting for the narration before proceeding with the performance. Successful storytelling does demand an informal and relaxed atmosphere in which every child can see and hear the teller without strain. It also demands that the modern teacher-storyteller perform with as much dramatization as possible—including gestures, body movements, facial expressions, and voice changes—for the child audience is truly television-minded.

When the story is over, there is often no follow-up planned by the teacher, for the simple responses of the children are adequate. Trite remarks such as "Wasn't that a nice story?" add nothing to the story hour, although questions prompting insight into cultural similarities or into social values may seem in order after certain kinds of tales.

A recent two-year study involving 298 intermediate pupils concluded that children exposed to storytelling make significant gains in library usage and interest in literature as well as in reading ability, positive self-concepts, creativity, and empathy. During the investigation the children participated for a twenty-eight-week period each year at public library branches representing a cross section of a metropolitan area. Librarians served as storytellers and generally told two folktales and four or five poems during the half-hour story time. A discussion followed each session only if the children responded with comments on the ending(s), the character(s), or events.[20]

By setting an example as a storyteller, the librarian or teacher can inspire children to try storytelling themselves. Some may wish to tell stories to their peers, while others will desire to entertain younger pupils. Children and teacher alike will find many good tales for the storyteller in such collections from the *Best Books for Children* (1972) as:

Arnott's *African Myths and Legends* (Walck, 1963)
Courlander's *The King's Drum* (Harcourt, 1962)
Grimms' *Grimms' Fairy Tales* (Follett, 1968)
Hughes' *How the Whale Became* (Atheneum, 1964)
Leach's *How the People Sang the Mountains Up* (Viking, 1967)
MacManus' *Hibernian Nights* (Macmillan, 1963)
Mehdevi's *Bungling Pedro and Other Majorcan Tales* (Knopf, 1970)
Sinclair-Stevenson's *A Parade of Princes* (Norton, 1966)
Tashjian's *Three Apples Fell from Heaven* (Little, 1971)

Story Reading

While many stories may either be told or read aloud to the children, there are two broad categories of stories which can never be told but must always be read. The first covers picture books because their illustrations are an integral part of the story, as shown in Keats' *A Letter for Amy* (Harper, 1968) and Graham's *Benjy's Dog* (Harper, 1973). The second includes stories whose charm lies in their language, due to either (a) the marked use of dialect as exemplified in Nic Leodhas' *Heather and Broom* (Holt, 1960) and Lenski's *Strawberry Girl* (Lippincott, 1945) or (b) the strong individualistic style of the author as in Kipling's *Just So Stories* (Doubleday, 1952), and Seuss' *Horton Hears a Who* (Random House, 1954).

For reading aloud to boys and girls, teachers should look for materials which they know and genuinely like and which they believe the pupils are not apt to read themselves. Some of the older Newbery Medal Books, for example,

are considered dull by the standards of today's children until the teacher reads them aloud to the group.

Story reading is an important and pleasurable experience for the children from all socioeconomic levels. For younger pupils, it is also a precursor to success in learning to read, for such children, after only two semesters of daily presentations, score significant increases in vocabulary, word knowledge and reading comprehension in contrast to children denied the opportunity to hear good stories. With intermediate boys and girls, listening to stories helps them significantly to understand or draw inferences from selections of good literature. Yet only 60 percent of the teachers in the middle grades read aloud to their pupils, according to a national survey of nearly six hundred teachers.[21]

Nevertheless, older pupils like to hear their teacher read to them from Supraner's *Think About It, You Might Learn Something* (Houghton, 1973) or Lewis' *The Lion, the Witch and the Wardrobe* (Macmillan, 1950). Primary children enjoy hearing Thurber's *The Great Quillow* (Harcourt, 1944) or Travers' *Mary Poppins From A to Z* (Harcourt, 1962). Some elementary pupils enjoy reading stories to their classmates or to younger children in the neighborhood or school.

The teacher may plan a listening period for playing some of the better commercial recordings of dramatizations or readings of such children's stories as Andersen's *The Emperor's New Clothes* (Random, 1971) or Carroll's *Alice's Adventures in Wonderland* (Macmillan, 1956). Poets like Robert Frost and

Listening to Records and Cassette Tapes

John Ciardi have also read from their own works for children, and such presentations have been carefully recorded for classroom use. Some school districts carry a collection of such materials. Others prefer that their teachers borrow the records or cassette tapes from the public library or make their own tapes, either alone or with the assistance of interested pupils.

Attending Children's Theatre Productions

The teacher may occasionally see an announcement in the daily paper concerning the production of a children's theatre group that will be presented locally. Classroom discussions of the book on which the production will be based may then be planned. Paul Galdone's *Puss In Boots* (Seabury, 1976) is one of the tales often dramatized by professional or college groups for child audiences.

Often the admission prices for such productions are substantially reduced for young pupils. In some districts, school buses are used to transport the children to the theatre, particularly on Saturdays.

Watching Telecasts

The teacher should check the listings in the weekly television guides in order to suggest or assign the pupils to watch a suitable production of a story like Lawson's *Rabbit Hill* (Viking, 1944) that is done with taste and fidelity.

Opening a Private Children's Library

Some pupils may be interested in following the example of two boys in Wellesley, Massachusetts, who each organized a library in one room of his home. The Great Library and the Kid's Library stock tapes, records, and magazines in addition to books which have been donated or purchased at rummage sales. Dues-paying members of either library receive an official monthly publication entitled *The Bookworm* in one case and *Book Life* in the other. The children's librarian of the Wellesley Hills Public Library has supported the boys' efforts, as would other public librarians or school media specialists.

Attending Book Fairs

During the annual Public Schools Week or National Book Week, some schools schedule book fairs where all the grades are invited to display their creative reactions to certain children's books. The fairs are generally held in the school library media center and may involve commercial exhibits and films.

In other schools the teachers prefer to plan book fairs within their own classrooms, holding these on a bimonthly basis and encouraging children to participate in the planning. Parents are often invited to the fairs so they may have the opportunity to discover more about the school reading and literature program and to learn how they may assist the classroom library.

Watching Filmstrips

The class may sometimes enjoy listening to the teacher (or one of the members) read aloud from Turkle's *Obadiah the Bold* (Viking, 1965) as the filmstrip is run silently. On other occasions the boys and girls may wish to watch and hear one of the many acclaimed sound strips of children's stories issued by such studios as Weston Woods. Many filmstrip-cassette and filmstrip-record combinations are listed in Appendix 4.

Some basal reading series for the middle and intermediate grades include excerpts from such books as Cleary's *Henry Huggins* (Morrow, 1950) and Wilder's *Little House in the Big Woods* (Harper, 1953). Children are more eager to read the complete story after they have enjoyed discussing an introductory selection.

Reading in a Basal Series

Children can copy their favorite literary passages on slips of paper and place the signed slips into a large envelope which hangs by the classroom door (portal). Then, as the boys and girls are lined up for dismissal near that door—and a few minutes remain before the bell—a child can be chosen to reach into the envelope and draw out one of the selections. The pupil who copied the passage is pleased to hear his or her choice read aloud. In the meantime, classmates become acquainted with still another good book, like Skorpen's *Old Arthur* (Harper, 1972).

Writing Portal Passages

Publishers of children's books often supply free or inexpensive bookmarks, maps, illustrations suitable for framing, buttons, brochures, photographs, and other display materials, sometimes in quantity lots. Such offers are described in *The Calendar,* issued quarterly by the Children's Book Council, Inc., 67 Irving Place, New York 10003, and are directed to all its members. The Council invites teachers to join its ranks at a onetime charge of three dollars.

Examining Free or Inexpensive Materials from Publishers

An Author's Afternoon is an exciting event during which children hear an author discuss his or her life and books. The Children's Book Council, Inc., offers speakers' lists of authors and illustrators who are willing to speak to various groups—sometimes for fees and sometimes for the payment of transportation costs alone; the lists are compiled by states and available for the price of a large self-addressed stamped envelope. Publishing houses, local libraries, and educational organizations can also help the children in arranging an Author's Afternoon.

Planning an Author's Afternoon

Bulletin boards can announce new books or book events, display unusual book illustrations, and encourage imaginative writing in the classroom. Some boards point up authors like E. L. Konigsburg or Roald Dahl. Others stress categories like sports stories or tall tales. An interesting addition is a pegboard which holds books and other three-dimensional objects.

Making Bulletin Board Displays

Background for in-depth understanding of many units in social studies and a few units in science can be furnished through broader use of literature. A primary unit on transportation, for example, helps develop familiarity with Gramatky's *Little Toot on the Mississippi* (Putnam, 1973) and Woolley's *I Like Trains* (Harper, 1965). An intermediate unit on the exploration and settlement of the American Northwest encourages reading of *Of Courage Undaunted* (Viking, 1951) and *Marcus and Narcissa Whitman* (Viking, 1953), both of which were written by James Daugherty.

Studying Assigned Units

Attending Storytelling Workshops	In schools with media centers and professional media specialists, a series of storytelling workshops may be held under the supervision of the specialist. Interested pupils from the middle and intermediate grades are invited to attend in order to learn how to tell folktales and other stories to kindergarten and primary children.
	In schools without library media centers, the children's librarian from the nearest public library may schedule the workshops, which help introduce good stories and good storytelling techniques to older boys and girls.
	While some schools prefer to hold the workshops during National Book Week, nearly any time during the academic year that is convenient for the librarian is appropriate for the children.
Using Community Resources	Primary classes that visit the harbor during a study trip return to school with a special desire to read Ardizzone's *Little Tim and the Brave Sea Captain* (Walck, 1955). Classes in districts whose budgets do not allow for many trips away from the school building may be privileged to hear resource speakers from the community, who visit schools to make presentations to the students and thereby elicit interest in books like Clymer's *The Big Pile of Dirt* (Holt, 1968).
Reviewing Books for Publication	School newspapers and magazines often have a column for book reviews, and children throughout the building can be encouraged to write reviews of new and old favorites in order to inform their friends of books they have personally enjoyed.
	Older pupils may even review books for readers outside the immediate school-community. In one elementary school in Austin, Texas, for example, the book editor of the local newspaper came to discuss book reviewing with the more advanced members of the sixth grade. She provided a number of new books for them to review, and subsequently all their reviews were published in the book section of the Sunday edition. Since then, reviewing new books for the paper has become a regular activity at the school.
Meeting Book Characters in Person	Children can dress up as their favorite book characters and tell about themselves and their experiences. Sometimes they may even be invited to parade through a neighboring classroom and introduce briefly the characters they are representing.
	Pupils who like to read realistic stories of the here and now, like Conford's *Felicia the Critic* (Little, 1973), find it easy to borrow appropriate costumes for the characters they want to be in the parade.
Joining a Book Club	Some boys and girls become interested in literature through membership in a book club which is geared to their age bracket. Sponsors of book clubs for elementary school children include:

Junior Literary Guild, 245 Park Avenue, New York 10017 (ages three to sixteen). Hardcover selections. Six age groups.

Parents' Magazine's Read Aloud and Easy Reading Program, 52 Vanderbilt Avenue, New York 10017 (ages three to eight)

Scholastic Book Services, 50 West 44 Street, New York 10036. Paperback reprints and originals.
  (1) See-Saw Book Program (kindergarten and grade one)
  (2) Lucky Book Club (grades two to three)
  (3) Arrow Book Club (grades four to six)

Xerox Education Publications, 245 Long Hill Road, Middletown, Connecticut 06457
  (1) I Can Read Book Club (ages three to eight). Hardcover selections from Harper & Row's *I Can Read* Series.
  (2) Paperback Book Clubs.
    (a) Buddy Books Paperback Book Club (kindergarten and grade one)
    (b) Goodtime Books Paperback Book Club (grades two to three)
    (c) Discovering Books Paperback Book Club (grades four to six)
  (3) Weekly Reader Children's Book Clubs (ages five to eleven). Hardcover selections from all children's book publishers. Three age groups: primary (5–7), intermediate (8–9), and senior (10–11).

Keeping a Computerized Date with a Book

Before the date is set, the child completes a personal date application (including name, age, hobbies, favorite television program, etc.) which is then posted in the room. When a classmate spots a book in the media center that he or she believes the applicant would enjoy, the book is recommended and a computerized date set.

Reading and Writing Newspaper Headlines

A provocative headline such as "U.N. Ambassador Receives Penguin Support" might be tacked on the bulletin board and children encouraged to guess which book is represented; the answer, of course, is Freeman's *Penguins, Of All People!* (Viking, 1971). Older pupils can develop their own headlines to intrigue their classmates.

Keeping an Author's Birthday Calendar

The primary teacher can post a large monthly birthday calendar and mark it with pictures of authors whose prose or poetry the class has enjoyed hearing and reading. In the intermediate grades the calendar can include a list of the author's books as well. Such calendars are more stimulating to young readers if pupils' names are also listed, especially when a class member was born on the same day of the year as a favorite writer-illustrator like Maurice Sendak (June 10).

Playing Charades and Other Games	Some children, singly or in small groups, can act out the names of books while their friends try to identify the correct titles. Others will enjoy matching book-jacket pictures with their corresponding titles. Still other pupils can take turns unscrambling the names of authors or story characters out of jumbled letters fastened to a magnetic board.
Working in the School Media Center or Classroom Library	Boys and girls can help with the charging out and returning of books. They can prepare magazines and books for circulation. They can repair torn pages, make catalog cards, and shelve books. They can set up attractive displays and exhibits. All of these activities which involve the handling of books and magazines stimulate interest in the contents of the materials.
Watching Films	A class that can observe on the screen the famed doughnuts episode from McCloskey's *Homer Price* (Viking, 1943) is generally anxious to read the entire story. Watching a full-length film of a book like the Cleavers' *Where the Lilies Bloom* (Lippincott, 1969) will also entice children to examine the published story.
Interpretive Activities Using Story Dramatization	Children who have heard or read Galdone's *The Three Billy Goats Gruff* (Seabury, 1973) or Slobodkina's *Caps for Sale* (Young Scott, 1947) are quickly prompted into participating in story dramatization. Any properties that are needed can be readily improvised by the players.
Singing	The class may be interested in singing some of the poems written by Robert Louis Stevenson that have been set to music; several series of elementary music books carry songs based on his poems from *A Child's Garden of Verses* (Watts, 1966). Another favorite poem that has been set to music is the lengthy *The Night Before Christmas* (Rand, 1976) written by Clement Moore.
Making Puppets and Holding Puppet Shows	Children of every grade level can construct puppets of their favorite book characters, using a variety of materials ranging from paper bags to soda straws. Some groups may even prefer to hold puppet shows based on Pearce's *Beauty and the Beast* (Crowell, 1972) or Galdone's *The Little Red Hen* (Seabury, 1973).
Filing Instant Reactions	In an attempt to avoid overstructured book reporting, children can be encouraged to dictate or write on index cards their brief and spontaneous reactions to books they have read, such as Lester's *To Be a Slave* (Dial, 1968). The cards are placed in a small box on the library table and shared by both teacher and class.
Making Collages	Boys and girls, individually or in groups, can prepare a collage depicting a favorite scene from a book like Monjo's *The Secret of the Sachem's Tree* (Coward, 1972) which they have heard or read. On a background of a large piece

of brown wrapping paper or burlap is attached an assortment of materials to represent the characters and objects. The finished collage may later be displayed if its producers approve.

Children can cut out of remnant pieces of flannel or felt the animals, persons, or objects described in a book such as Rose's *How Does A Czar Eat Potatoes?* (Lothrop, 1973) which the group has enjoyed. Sometimes the pupils will wish to decorate the pieces or to back tiny lightweight realia with flannel. Finally, they are ready to share their book adventure by means of a flannelboard.

Using Flannel or Felt Characters

Although the framework of the three-dimensional design is made of wire or wood, the pendants or suspended objects on the mobile are made from a wide collection of materials which the pupils can bring from home. The class may prefer to restrict the pendants to represent the characters or events from a single story (like Seuss' *If I Ran the Zoo,* Random House, 1950) or to confine them to the stories of a single author (as Paula Fox).

Constructing Mobiles

Sometimes it is the teacher that supplies the materials for the mobile-making project. First the students make a list of important quotations, incidents, words, or characters from a book recently heard or read. Then they are given some index cards, glue, thread, and scissors. The cards are cut into different shapes, e.g., squares for quotations. The students copy each item on their list on a different card. Finally, they hang the card shapes one below the other in proper vertical sequence.

Children can use clay to model their favorite characters or scenes. Later, after the clay has been fired, painted, and glazed, the models are displayed before a backing made of a folded piece of cardboard on which the pupils can write the words best describing their representations. The text may be copied from a book such as Cleary's *Ribsy* (Morrow, 1964) or created by the children.

Modeling Clay

Both nursery rhymes (as in De Forest's *The Prancing Pony,* Walker, 1968) and counting poems (as Tudor's *1 Is One,* Walck, 1956) lend themselves to adaptation to finger plays. Kindergarten and first-grade children enjoy creating rhymes for such activities.

Creating Finger Plays

When they use a super 8-mm camera with a built-in viewfinder, children can be taught quickly how to take movies. The teacher can borrow a camera from a staff member or from one of the room parents, and if the school lacks indoor lighting equipment, the pupils can paint scenery on large sheets of heavy cardboard and film all scenes outdoors. The major expenses incurred in this activity, therefore, lie in the cost of film and film development.

Making Films

Many of the folktales that the teacher reads aloud or tells to the class—such as Galdone's *The Gingerbread Boy* (Seabury, 1975)—are suitable for an elementary class project in filmmaking.

Designing Book Jackets	Boys and girls can design their own book jackets and display them next to the original ones issued by the publishers. Inside the jacket may be written or dictated a synopsis of a book, like Kishida's *The Lion and the Bird's Nest* (Crowell, 1973). A biographical sketch of the author can be substituted for the synopsis if adequate reference books are available and the boy or girl is skilled in using them.
Making Transparencies	In schools where overhead projectors are readily available, pupils can make transparencies of drawings of selected characters or scenes from books that they have enjoyed reading. Once the drawings are completed, the book (like Binzen's *Miguel's Mountain,* Coward, 1968) can be read aloud, wholly or in part, as the transparencies are projected on the screen.
Producing Shadow Boxes	Large shallow boxes can be quickly converted into shadow boxes when the box fronts have been removed; the remaining frames are then painted and hung on the wall. In them the children can display three-dimensional objects that are essential to the plot of a favorite story like Estes' *The Witch Family* (Harcourt, 1960). The boxes can also be prepared to represent the settings for a story like Handforth's *Mei Li* (Doubleday, 1938).
Making Dioramas	Children can build dioramas of several scenes from a book like Estes' *The Coat-Hanger Christmas Tree* (Atheneum, 1973). Similar to shadow boxes in construction, dioramas can be made simply from cartons, or made more elaborately from wood and heavy cardboard. When the teacher helps the boys and girls to see the relationships between the available materials and the mood or scene they are trying to depict, children find more creative ways of making dioramas realistic and attractive.
Constructing Box Theaters	Dioramas with some sort of movement added are box theaters. They can be adapted to finger puppets and used for Colver and Graff's *The Wayfarer's Tree* (Dutton, 1973) when the pupils or teacher wish to depict a scene or story without too much preparation. Larger box theaters can be used with hand puppets.
Drawing Maps	Maps can be made of individual states, countries, continents, or of the entire world. On them are sketched or marked the birthplaces of authors like May Justus, the settings of favorite books like Taylor's *All-of-a-Kind Family Downtown* (Follett, 1972), or the travels of a character like Chakoh in Baker's *Walk the World's Rim* (Harper, 1965). Where fictitious places are key points in books, the class members may create original maps, as for Baum's *The Wizard of Oz* (Reilly and Lee, 1963).

While some children may prefer to make small individual desk maps, others will wish to work together on a huge wall map.

Some young readers, particularly those with speech handicaps, enjoy sharing with their peers scenes from a book like Haywood's *Eddie's Valuable Property* (Morrow, 1975). The pantomimes they present are short, lasting five minutes or less.

Presenting
Pantomime Skits

Children enjoy panel discussions during which they informally explore a popular topic. One group of ten children considered the books written by Carol Brink, all of which had been read by two or more panel members and subsequently discussed:

Participating in
Panel Discussions

> How is *Caddie Woodlawn* different from the author's later books?
> What is a classic?
> Do you think these books by Brink might become classics?

Another group of intermediate grade pupils that had read biographies of David Livingston, Harriet Tubman, Clara Barton, Martin Luther King, Albert Schweitzer, and Jane Addams centered their panel discussion on the theme of humanitarianism.

With the aid of room mothers, the teacher can arrange an unusual Halloween or end-of-the-semester party. Each pupil, at home or during an earlier school art period, makes a hat to help depict a well-known story character and then wears the hat to the Mad Hatter's Party.

Attending a Mad
Hatter's Party

When a group or the entire class has completed a book like Udry's *The Moon Jumpers* (Harper, 1959), the boys and girls may like to create a rhythmical interpretation of the story. Their teacher may either compose music for the dance or use a recorded accompaniment. More than one series of basic movements may be possible, and the audience can then select the dance interpretation that it prefers.

Creating Rhythms
and Dances

Scenes from a well-liked story such as Goodall's *Jacko* (Harcourt, 1972) can be painted or crayoned on a long sheet of shelf paper. Then the sheet is rolled up on two dowels inserted through the holes in the back of a puppet stage. As the movie rolls slowly along, a pupil reads the matching excerpt from the book.

Making Roll Movies

Brightly colored murals involving tempera paint, construction paper, and colored chalk may develop from the reading of a single book like George's *Julie of the Wolves* (Harper, 1972). They may also represent the composite of many books on a single unit like "The Zoo."

Painting Murals

Posters of every size and sort can be created by readers who wish to inform others of a pleasant book such as Ness' *Sam, Bangs, & Moonshine* (Holt, 1966). When they are three-dimensional, posters add special interest to book exhibits.

Making Posters

With the help of their teacher, the boys are planning a poster for the library media center which will describe their favorite book. (Photo courtesy of the Fullerton Elementary School District, Fullerton, California.)

Dressing Character Dolls

A child who has read a story such as Estes' *The Hundred Dresses* (Harcourt, 1944) may want to show classmates how some of the characters in the story looked. Should the teacher have a stock of small inexpensive dolls available from a variety store as well as a supply of colorful remnants donated by room mothers, the child may easily sew the clothes to dress the book characters. At other times, a group of children enjoys making paper clothes for a sturdy paper doll character.

Writing Classified Ads

A student can write a "Lost and Found" ad for a person, object, or pet from a story, such as Schneider's *Uncle Harry* (Macmillan, 1972). He or she may also wish to write an ad for the "Jobs Wanted" or "Help Wanted" column after reading a book like Varga's *Circus Cannonball* (Morrow, 1975).

Preparing Rebus Reviews

Primary pupils especially enjoy preparing a rebus review of a book like Viorst's *Alexander and the Terrible, Horrible, No Good, Very Bad Day* (Atheneum, 1976). In place of certain portions of a sentence or paragraph, old magazine pictures are substituted. Such clippings can cover significant persons, places, objects, or actions. Some exceptional children in the upper grades enjoy writing rebus reviews too.

Pupils from six to ten can make pancakes after the group has read or heard Sawyer's *Journey Cake, Ho!* (Viking, 1953). The younger children especially will each like to make a "happy day pancake" by first forming the eyes and smile with batter, then letting it bake a while before adding the rest of the batter, and finally flipping the pancake over to see its "happy face."

Cooking and Eating

Intermediate boys and girls familiar with newspaper and magazine cartoons can draw their own cartoons to depict important situations, problems, and events from a favorite book such as Kerr's *Dinky Hocker Shoots Smack* (Harper, 1972).

Drawing Cartoons

Several children who have heard or read the same story such as Daudet's *The Mule of Avignon* (Crowell, 1973) may wish to turn it into a ballad which may later be presented either with or without a musical accompaniment. One pupil in the group begins and then points to another child to continue the ballad until all have had an opportunity to participate.

Creating Ballads

Almost any story or poem lends itself to a shadow play, which may be done in pantomime or with voices and movement. Scenes for such a play can be made by cutting simple shapes from wrapping paper or newspaper and pinning them to a sheet; then a bright light is placed behind that sheet and the pupils stand between the sheet and the light. Even shy children enjoy performing in a shadow play by acting out roles from a favorite such as Lenski's *Policeman Small* (Walck, 1962).

Performing in Shadow Plays

Quiz shows patterned after "What's My Line?" offer an opportunity for intermediate students to become acquainted in depth with book characters. Each child contestant can assume the identity of a character in a modern story such as Konigsburg's *About the B'nai Bagels* (Atheneum, 1968). For the lower grades the quiz can be kept to a simple guessing game in which the character answers only "yes" or "no" to questions regarding the identity of Mr. Small, for example, from Lenski's *The Little Farm* (Walck, 1942).

Appearing as Quiz Show Contestants

Beginning readers can cut pictures from magazines to prepare a report of a favorite story such as Hayward's *Here Comes the Bus!* (Morrow, 1963). Each picture is properly mounted and accompanied by an appropriate caption.

Preparing Picture Reports

Pupils may occasionally prepare book reports to communicate their feelings about books in purposeful, written fashion. While some children are ready to begin such reports in the middle primary years, others are not ready until the intermediate grades. There are, however, five levels of book-report writing adaptable to children's written language maturity.

Preparing Written Reports for a Reason

- Level One—The pupils record on a four-by-six-inch card the title and author, the number of pages read, and a one-sentence opinion of the book. They later arrange their cards in chronological order of books completed.
- Level Two—The pupils use a five-by-eight-inch index card to record the title and author, and to write one sentence on each of the following: the general idea of the book, the part liked best, the reasons for recommending or not recommending the book, and the place where a copy of the volume was located.
- Level Three—The pupils use the same form as at Level Two, but expand to a short paragraph each of the following points: the general idea of the book, the part liked best, and the reasons for recommending or not recommending the book. Pupils may substitute in place of one of the aforementioned points a discussion of the plot or an analysis of the characterization. In this case, however, the pupils abandon the index card for writing paper.
- Level Four—The pupils respond at length about the title and author, the type of story, its main idea or subject, its outstanding qualities or features, and their general comments or opinion. They write or use a typewriter.
- Level Five—The pupils follow the assignment for Level Four, but they also complete one or more of the following activities: a biography of the author, a discussion of the effect of the book on the reader, a different ending for the story, a commentary on the characterizations, or a comparison of books by the same author or on the same subject. They write on notebook paper or type the report.

Choral Reading: A Unique Interpretive Activity

Choral reading is sometimes called "choric interpretation," "choral speaking," or "unison speaking." All of these terms refer to a similar technique of group reading or recitation of poetry or poetic prose without music but under the direction of a leader.

Suitable for any group of elementary school children (even those with speech handicaps), regardless of their socioeconomic background, age, intelligence, or sex, choral reading is also appropriate for any class size. It is a valuable experience because it synchronizes three linguistic skills: listening, reading, and speaking. It improves the everyday speech of children. It builds positive group attitudes and offers an acceptable outlet for emotional expression. It promotes desirable personality traits and offers a socializing activity for both the shy and the forward. It develops imagination and heightens the appreciation of poetry.

To make effective use of choral reading, however, teachers must first understand the rhythm and the tempo of the poetry as well as the color and quality of the children's voices. Then, with that background in mind, they must be able to choose wisely among the five different types of arrangements that are possible:

Easiest for beginners are poems with a refrain or chorus. The teacher or pupil leader recites most of the narrative, with the class responding with the words that constitute the refrain or the repeated line(s). Typical examples of poems with refrains include:

> Abney's "The Circus Is Coming to Town"
> Lindsay's "The Mysterious Cat"
> Stevenson's "The Wind"
> Tennyson's "Bugle Song"

and (by Unknown)

Little Brown Rabbit

Leader:	Little brown rabbit went hoppity-hop,
Group:	Hoppity-hop, hoppity-hop!
Leader:	Into a garden without any stop,
Group:	Hoppity-hop, hoppity-hop!
Leader:	He ate for his supper a fresh carrot top,
Group:	Hoppity-hop, hoppity-hop!
Leader:	Then home went the rabbit without any stop,
Group:	Hoppity-hop, hoppity-hop!

Poems involving alternate speaking by two or more groups demand antiphonal choral reading that will remind some of the pupils of the responsive readings occurring during church services when the clergyman and the congregation take turns reading the lines. While, at the beginning, it is simply a question and answer session between two groups (of boys and girls or of heavy and light voices), it may culminate with older children in a verse choir grouped into three or four pitch levels. Poems that provide contrasts, parallels, or characterizations, such as many lyric poems do, are especially appropriate for antiphonal speaking. Typical examples include:

> Coatsworth's "Who Are You?"
> Farjeon's "Choosing"
> Greenaway's "Susan Blue"
> Rossetti's "Who Has Seen the Wind?"

and (as an old rhyme) for two groups:

To London Town

Group A:	Which is the way to London Town To see the king in his golden crown?
Group B:	One foot up and one foot down, That's the way to London Town.
Group A:	Which is the way to London Town To see the queen in her silken gown?
Group B:	Left! Right! Left! Right! Up and down, Soon you'll be in London Town!

This arrangement differs from the antiphonal variety only in that it engages not two, but three or more individual children or choirs. The line-a-child or line-a-choir arrangement is always popular with pupils because it possesses variety and offers the challenge of picking up lines quickly in exact tempo. Children must come in on cue, however, so early effort with this kind of choral reading should find the students standing in the order in which they present their lines. Teachers who wish to use it with younger children, however, will find it helpful to choose poems that have lines or couplets that end with semi-colons, periods, or even commas, so that the poet's thoughts are not broken up after the assignment of parts. Typical examples include:

> Browning's "Pippa's Song"
> De la Mare's "Bunch of Grapes"
> Eastwick's "Where's Mary?"

and (by Unknown), for five children or five groups of children that begin and end their reading together:

Five Little Squirrels

All:	Five little squirrels sat in a tree.
Group A:	The first one said, "What do I see?"
Group B:	The second one said, "A man with a gun."
Group C:	The third one said, "We'd better run."
Group D:	The fourth one said, "Let's hide in the shade."
Group E:	The fifth one said, "I'm not afraid."
All:	Then bang went the gun, and how they did run.

The Cumulative Arrangement

The cumulative arrangement differs from the line-a-choir arrangement in that the addition of each group to the presentation is permanent, not temporary, in order to attain a crescendo effect. It is one of the more difficult forms of choral reading because it involves the use of voice quality to achieve interpretation. The addition of voices is not simply to gain greater volume but to build, too, toward a more significant climax. An entire class can readily take part. Typical examples of poems for cumulative arrangement include:

> Lear's "The Owl and the Pussycat"
> Lindsay's "The Potatoes' Dance"
> Tippett's "Trains"

and (by Mother Goose):

The House That Jack Built

Group A:	This is the house that Jack built.
Groups A–B:	This is the malt That lay in the house that Jack built.
Groups A–C:	This is the rat, That ate the malt That lay in the house that Jack built.
Groups A–D:	This is the cat, That killed the rat, That ate the malt That lay in the house that Jack built.

Groups A–E: This is the dog,
That worried the cat,
That killed the rat,
That ate the malt
That lay in the house that Jack built.

Groups A–F: This is the cow with the crumpled horn,
That tossed the dog,
That worried the cat,
That killed the rat,
That ate the malt
That lay in the house that Jack built.

Groups A–G: This is the maiden all forlorn,
That milked the cow with the crumpled horn,
That tossed the dog,
That worried the cat,
That killed the rat,
That ate the malt
That lay in the house that Jack built.

Groups A–H: This is the man all tattered and torn,
That kissed the maiden all forlorn,
That milked the cow with the crumpled horn,
That tossed the dog,
That worried the cat,
That killed the rat,
That ate the malt
That lay in the house that Jack built.

Groups A–I: This is the priest all shaven and shorn,
That married the man all tattered and torn,
That kissed the maiden all forlorn,
That milked the cow with the crumpled horn,
That tossed the dog,
That worried the cat,
That killed the rat,
That ate the malt
That lay in the house that Jack built.

Groups A–J: This is the cock that crowed in the morn,
That waked the priest all shaven and shorn,
That married the man all tattered and torn,
That kissed the maiden all forlorn,
That milked the cow with the crumpled horn,
That tossed the dog,
That worried the cat,
That killed the rat,
That ate the malt
That lay in the house that Jack built.

Groups A–K : This is the farmer sowing his corn,
That kept the cock that crowed in the morn,
That waked the priest all shaven and shorn,
That married the man all tattered and torn,
That kissed the maiden all forlorn,
That milked the cow with the crumpled horn,
That tossed the dog,
That worried the cat,
That killed the rat,
That ate the malt
That lay in the house that Jack built.

The Unison Arrangement

Even more difficult than the cumulative variety is the unison type of choral reading with no subgrouping. An entire class or group reads or recites every line together. Only an experienced teacher-leader can skillfully direct a large number of voices speaking simultaneously.

Unison reading is unfortunately where most teachers begin choric speech, although it is the hardest of all the popular arrangements and often elicits the singsong monotony that results when inexperienced children read together. However, when the class—and the teacher—have developed considerable background in choral reading, unison arrangements become dramatically effective. Obviously they are better suited to intermediate-grade children. Young children will enjoy saying nursery rhymes and other simple verse together, but they should not be given a heavy dose of unison experience because of the problems of coordinating timing and inflection. Typical examples of poems for unison recital include:

Fyleman's "Husky Hi"
Hugo's "Good Night"
Sandburg's "Fog"

and (by Unknown) :

Weather

Whether the weather be fine,
Or whether the weather be not,
Whether the weather be cold,
Or whether the weather be hot,
We'll weather the weather,
Whatever the weather,
Whether we like it or not.

Guided Sessions

The teachers who experience little difficulty in commencing choral reading are the ones who enjoy poetry themselves and share it often with their students, who write poems on charts and display them about the room, and who encourage pupils to create their own poetry. Such class saturation of all kinds of possible selections for choral reading is a natural beginning because the children acquire an ear for rhythm, a sense of mood, and a desire to say enjoyable poems with their teacher. It can also be a successful beginning if the sessions are short, simple, and well directed. The director or teacher must set the example for the choral reading periods insofar as phrasing, tempo, diction, and emphasis are concerned; and he or she must help the pupils understand that with choral speaking, every word must be readily understood by the listeners. To make direction easier, the teacher groups the children in a standing position where all can see.

The first poems presented should be those that the class had memorized earlier. Later the group's repertoire can be increased by duplicating and distributing copies of other longer poems that the pupils have enjoyed.

After everyone is familiar with the content of the material and has had several pleasing experiences with choral reading, the children should be encouraged to suggest a variety of interpretations and executions. Sound effects may be introduced upon occasion.

Two techniques for helping groups improve their choral efforts include: (1) the use of tape recordings so that all may share in the evaluation, and (2) the appointment of a small group within the class to divorce itself from the chorus and act as a critical audience of listeners.

Finally, the teacher must learn the progressive phases through which a choral reading moves so that he or she can place the whole experience in proper perspective. The first phase is an understanding of rhythm and tempo, and its purpose is to encourage each child to sense that rhythm and tempo throughout the body. The second phase is an understanding of the color and quality of the voices which demands that the teacher also comprehend the meaning of such choral reading terms as *inflection* (the rise and fall within a phrase), *pitch level* (the change between one phrase and another), *emphasis* (pointing up of the most important word) and *intensity* (loudness and softness of the voices). And the third phase that the teacher must understand is the arrangement or orchestration of choral reading to help convey the meaning of a poem.

Appropriate Selections

Literature for choral speaking should have a story or theme that is both dramatic and simple so as to be understood promptly by an audience that hears it for the first time. It should possess a marked rhythm and express a universal sentiment. Prose suitable for group reading includes—for older children— portions of Rachel Carson's *The Sea Around Us* (Golden Press, 1958) and selections from Scott O'Dell's *Island of the Blue Dolphins* (Houghton, 1960). For younger readers there is the text from Beatrix Potter's *The Tale of Peter Rabbit* (Grossett, 1968) as well as some portions of Robert McCloskey's *Time of Wonder* (Viking, 1957).

Whether the selection is prose or poetry, it must not only meet the teacher's criteria for literature and fulfill a specific objective in the day's planning but also win the pupils' interest and involvement as well. Children prefer selections that contain humor, repetition, surprise, action—and brevity.

Anthologies and literature textbooks are crowded with poems and pieces of poetic prose which can readily be done by a choral group. In selecting material for choric interpretation, the classroom teacher should consider: (1) the appropriateness of the subject matter as well as its treatment, for if the material can be said to represent many people speaking through the single voice of the writer, it is probably suitable for group work; (2) the richness of the rhythmic elements and tone color or sound values so that a group of voices can contribute deeply to the total effect; and (3) the author's overall method of organization in order that a vocal group can be utilized impressively.

Pitfalls

Besides the danger of mediocre material, choral reading has several other possible pitfalls to which the teacher must be alert. One of these that occurs when children speak together is the mounting volume of their voices; hence, the teacher must listen continually to the tone quality of the individuals in the choir, marking the time firmly, and keeping the voices warm and light. Another pitfall is the children's tendency to singsong their lines; consequently the teacher must focus the attention of the class on the meaning, the story, or the idea of the selection, and not upon the delivery. Still another pitfall is the lapse into cuteness or overdramatics, which makes the children believe that it is they and not their accomplishments that are being put on exhibition; hence, the teacher must discourage pantomimic action in the speaking of every poem by stressing manners, not mannerisms.

The teacher must also be certain that the class develops and maintains unity in the following areas of choral reading: articulation, pitch, inflection, and thought/feeling. Good diction and articulation must be accomplished first, and individuals who speak at various rates of speed must learn to enunciate each word clearly at the exact time in group work. Pitch will become more uniform as children develop better understanding of poetry and as they become accustomed to the voices of those around them. Due to a tendency to end sentences on an upward inflection, unity in the modulation of the voice is difficult to accomplish; speakers must first hear themselves to correct any bad habits. Finally, all participants must have the same understanding of any poem with depth of feeling and a sensitivity to words.

Evaluation

Classroom teachers can briefly rate the results of their choral reading sessions if they will ask themselves:

- Has there been an improvement in the speech and voice quality of the children?
- Do the pupils have a greater enjoyment of poetry because they have spoken it together, and are they genuinely eager for more and better poetry?
- Are the pupils developing growing powers of interpretation so that they speak their selections with understanding and vitality?
- Has the anonymity of choir work helped individual children?

- Are some of the pupils able to take over the leadership of the choir, showing a real feeling for the possibilities of the work?
- Are the children completely simple, natural, and sincere in their work?

A majority of positive answers would indicate that the teacher is doing sound and careful work.

More attention needs to be given to the evaluation of literature learning than has been done in recent decades.

Evaluation of Pupils' Progress

For the present, the teacher must continue to rely heavily on day-to-day observations of pupils to get an accurate idea of how the class and individuals in that class are reacting to experiences in literature. These questions can provide the teacher with a quick appraisal of the group's interests and enjoyments:

- Does the class look forward to the literature period?
- Does the class enter into the motivational or interpretive activities with enthusiasm?
- Is its attention span prolonged during those activities?
- Is there a high degree of group interaction?
- Does the class wish to share its literary findings with other classes or with parents?

Information regarding each pupil's growth toward the objectives of the literature program can be secured by inquiring:

- Does the student read widely in different fields?
- Does the student like to share his or her pleasure in reading?
- Does the student express the ideas he or she has gained from stories in creative writing?
- Does the student's speaking vocabulary include new words from the stories he or she has read or heard?
- Does the student's writing vocabulary include new words from the stories he or she has read or heard?
- Has the student read stories related to personal interests?
- Has the student's reading helped with personal problems?
- Does the student use a variety of art media to illustrate situations in the stories he or she has read or heard?
- Do the student's comments indicate the building of a personal philosophy that appears to be influenced by the stories he or she has read or heard?[22]

In evaluating student growth in interaction with literature, the teacher must always bear in mind—according to the California State Board of Education—that the primary goal is enjoyment and enjoyment is difficult to judge.[23]

There is presently available for the intermediate grades the *NCTE Cooperative Test of Critical Reading and Appreciation*. It takes sixty to seventy minutes to administer and may be purchased in either of two forms. Each form contains fourteen short literary selections and fifty-four option, multiple-choice questions. The first half of the test is read aloud by the administrator (partially to decrease the effect of students' reading ability on the test) while the second half is read silently by the examinee. The selections were chosen to represent as many as possible of the modes of literary expression found in imaginative prose and poetry deemed suitable for children. Since there are no norms or validity data, the use of the test is fairly well limited to criterion-referenced testing or to districts that wish to develop local norms. It can also be used informally as an aid in instruction. Bearing in mind the disadvantages of the test, which lie in interpretation, reviewers generally approve the instrument.[24]

Finally, the teacher may wish occasionally to evaluate his or her own Teaching Literature Quotient. A sample checklist to aid in determining T.L.Q. is shown in Figure 11.1.

Discussion Questions

1. How can literature contribute to the attainment of some of the objectives of elementary education?
2. When and how should a teacher employ bibliotherapy in the classroom?
3. Which motivational experiences in literature would you use comfortably with a class of slow achievers?

Figure 11.1.
Classroom Teacher's Self-Evaluation Checklist for Literature.

Classroom Teacher's Self-Evaluation Checklist for Literature

	Yes	No
1. Do I teach literature as a regular part of the curriculum?	____	____
2. Do I read to children regularly and at least once each day?	____	____
3. Do I plan for the day to include time for teaching literature?	____	____
4. Do I relate content areas of the curriculum to literature?	____	____
5. Do I use storytelling when appropriate?	____	____
6. Do I have in my classroom a variety of children's books—a changing but balanced collection?	____	____
7. Do I encourage the use of the public library?	____	____
8. Do I read children's books?	____	____
9. Do I encourage students to talk about the books they read?	____	____
10. Do I read regularly at least one publication devoted to articles about and/or reviews of children's books?	____	____
11. Do I help in the selection of children's books for my school?	____	____
12. Do the students I teach read and like to read?	____	____

Source: Adapted from the NCTE Committee on Teaching Children's Literature, "What Is Your T.L.Q.?" *Elementary English* 51 (1974): 581.

4. Why is it difficult to secure the participation of high achievers in exercises and activities involving the books they read? How can a teacher promote at least minimal creative expression among such readers?

Suggested Projects

1. Begin a collection of pictures of illustrators and/or authors of children's books.
2. Design and construct a hanging book mobile to interest children in reading biographies and informational books.
3. Make an annotated file of at least twenty book titles which you would include in a balanced literature program for the elementary grade of your choice.
4. Select ten poems suitable for choral reading. Then plan how you would use at least two of them, utilizing appropriate arrangements.
5. Compile a list of classroom activities for National Book Week.
6. Read, and later tell, a story suitable for a kindergarten class, using the flannelboard if you like. Finally, record that story on a cassette tape.
7. Set up the learning center on literature shown in Figure 11.2.

Related Readings

Baker, A. 1977. *Storytelling.* New York: R. R. Bowker Co.

Baskin, B., and Harris, K. 1977. *Notes from a Different Drummer: A Guide to Juvenile Fiction Portraying the Handicapped.* New York: R. R. Bowker Co.

Berg-Cross, L., and Berg-Cross, G. 1978. "Listening to Stories May Change Children's Social Attitudes." *Reading Teacher* 31: 659–63.

Brown, E. F. 1975. *Bibliotherapy and Its Widening Applications.* Meluchen, New Jersey: Scarecrow Press.

Cullinan, B. E., and Carmichael, C. W., eds. 1977. *Literature and Young Children.* Urbana, Illinois: National Council of Teachers of English.

Kingman, L., ed. 1978. *The Illustrator's Notebook.* Boston: The Horn Book, Inc.

Kingston, A., and Lovelace, T. 1977–78. "Sexism and Reading: A Critical Review of the Literature." *Reading Research Quarterly* 13: 133–61.

Sadker, M. P., and Sadker, D. M., eds. 1977. *Now Upon a Time: A Contemporary View of Children's Literature.* New York: Harper & Row.

Seefeldt, C. et al. 1978. "The Coming of Age in Children's Literature." *Childhood Education* 54: 123–27.

Stewig, J. W., and Sebesta, S. 1978. *Using Literature in the Elementary Classroom.* Urbana, Illinois: National Council of Teachers of English.

Figure 11.2. Language Arts Learning Center: Literature.

TYPE OF CENTER: Literature

GRADE LEVEL: 3

INSTRUCTIONAL
OBJECTIVE: Children will become motivated to read.

TIME: Unlimited (at least 30 minutes)

NUMBER OF STUDENTS: 3

MATERIALS: Several book jackets, cardboard, three or more boxes to put puzzles in, contact paper. Paste the book jackets on cardboard and cut into puzzles. Put the pieces into boxes decorated with contact paper. Set up a room art supply center and book center.

DIRECTIONS
TO STUDENTS:
1. Pick one of the boxes.
2. Put the puzzle together.
3. Read the book that your puzzle shows. The book is in the book center.
4. After you finish reading, design and make a different book jacket using the materials in the art center. Be sure to put the title and author of your book on the jacket you make.
5. Pin your jacket to the bulletin board in the book center.

EVALUATION: The teacher will note the interest in the book by observing the child, and then the teacher can look over the new book jacket that the child has designed.

Source: From *Language Arts Learning Centers and Activities* by Angela Reeke and James Laffey. Copyright 1979 by Goodyear Publishing Company. Reprinted by permission.

Children's Drama 12

Distinctions between children's theater and creative drama

The major groups of activities in creative drama

How sociodrama differs from dramatic play

Why children should first dramatically interpret some stories before attempting improvisation

Children's drama in the United States is a twentieth-century educational endeavor. It encompasses two aspects: children's theater and creative drama. Children's theater is formal and concerned primarily with the audience, while creative drama is informal and concerned chiefly with the players. Although its performances are occasionally staged in a school auditorium, children's theater is neither the curriculum responsibility nor the language art that creative drama is.

No conflict prevails between the two areas of children's drama, for both exist as an art form when given the proper guidance (creative drama) or direction (children's theater). Experiences in creative drama build appreciation for formal plays because the pupils learn about play construction as they work out their own plays with the assistance of an adult familiar with formal drama. On the other hand, children's theater provides standards for pupils' work in creative drama by helping the children to visualize and to be objective.

Ordinarily the two areas are distinct and separate. At least one attempt has been made recently, however, to combine children's theater with creative drama. Financed by a grant from the Bronx Council on the Arts, the Theater of Creative Involvement in New York was able to offer a short children's theater production and then have the adult actors serve as leaders while the children created their own plays. A total of three creative encounters was involved in each session with the inner-city boys and girls. During the first, the actors presented a professional dramatization of a story or poem such as "Little Miss Muffet," "Little Red Riding Hood," or "The Gingerbread Man." In the second, each actor or pair of actors became leaders of a small group of the spectators and assisted them in the creation of an original play. The third encounter found each group of children presenting its own play to other young spectators/ participants and to the adult actors.

Statement of Purposes

The objectives of drama/theater for students are sevenfold, according to the California State Board of Education:

1. The students will develop the "self," learning to discover themselves, express themselves, and accept themselves. They will become increasingly aware of and learn to trust their sensations, feelings, fantasies, memories, attitudes, thoughts, and values as they seek to give these entities coherent expression in theatrical form.
2. The students will communicate effectively in seeking to express something which has value and meaning to others. Because theater is a cooperative act in every phase, they will learn how to articulate their intentions with increasing clarity in many verbal and nonverbal ways and to receive with sensitivity what others have to express.
3. The students will solve problems inventively in both real and imagined situations, discovering or creating patterns of relationships among people and ideas in fantasy and fact. Whether they deal with imaginary people or real people, they will learn how to play many roles, to try on or simulate a broad range of life experiences, and to evaluate the results.
4. The students will learn from society, past and present, including the rich contributions of the multiethnic and multicultural groups which make up the American heritage.
5. The students will use critical and creative skills. The rigors of the discipline will help them to develop skills which they can apply to any area of chosen study.
6. The students will be awakened to theater as an art form. They will become more discerning, perceptive, and responsive theatergoers and viewers of other theatrical media (film and television).
7. The students will approach other art forms with insight. Theater has processes and concepts necessarily related to those of the other arts, and incorporates aspects of all of them.[1]

Children's Theater

Children's theater is the drama *for* children where the audience is the first consideration. Regardless of whether the play is being acted by adolescents or adults (or both), or whether the players are amateurs or professionals, the value of the experience to the actors must be secondary to what the experience means to the boys and girls who see the play, for the success of the project is judged by the cultural value and enjoyment that it gives to the child audience.

Children's theater is based on the traditional theater concept and is concerned with a polished production involving a stage. Lines written by professional playwrights are memorized, action is directed, and scenery and costumes are used. The director attempts to offer a finished product for public entertainment and engages the best actors available, for the goal in this area of children's drama is perfection.

Beginning with the establishment of the first significant children's theater in the United States, which was founded in a New York settlement house in 1903, the children's theater movement has always been guided by worthy objectives. During the movement's first decades of existence the theater projects, as conceived and administered primarily by social workers, boosted social welfare purposes like cultural integration and the teaching of English as a second language. Then, as the movement spread under the auspices of community-oriented organizations, universities, and professional companies, its direction changed to an emphasis on theater as an aesthetic device. Currently, therefore, the American children's theater promotes the development in boys and girls of a high standard of taste, provides them with the joy of seeing good stories come alive upon a stage, and helps them grow in the understanding and appreciation of life values from the human experiences seen on the stage.

The more than five million children who annually see the productions receive other benefits as well. Pedagogically, the theater can capitalize on each pupil's heightened motivation to indirectly inculcate ideas and facts regarding cultural patterns of thought, theatrical conventions, and the Judeo-Christian ethical code that is at the base of most Western drama. Psychologically, the theater teaches the child, through role awareness and character identification, socialization skills and personal maturation. Aesthetically, the theater is the only art form that deals with human behavior in a totally recognizable way.[2]

The national organization for the children's theater movement is presently the Children's Theatre Association (CTA), which was founded at Northwestern University in 1944 as a division of the American Educational Theatre Association. Its current membership of some two thousand adults is drawn from all kinds of professional and amateur groups, since agencies producing theatricals for children may be either community, educational, or professional organizations.

Community groups, which often present their plays in municipal auditoriums, have such varied sponsors as city recreation departments, the Junior League, and civic theaters in cities like Seattle, Nashville, Palo Alto, and Midland, Texas. *Educational institutions* (public and private) include universities, colleges, and high schools that offer plays in their own auditoriums and theaters. University activity today is centered at Northwestern, Minnesota, Kansas, UCLA, Florida State, Denver, and Washington. There are also some *professional studios and touring companies* that produce several plays a year. The commercial companies include The Children's Theatre Company and School (Minneapolis), The Traveling Playhouse, The Paper Bag Players, The Mask, and The Pocket Players, Incorporated. The noncommercial theaters for children are either attached to museums (as in Detroit and Chicago) or to adult regional companies (as in New Haven and Atlanta). Incidentally, a large contribution to children's theater since 1965 has been made through governmental financial interests both on the national and state levels under the National Foundation for the Arts and Humanities Act and under the Elementary and Secondary Education Act.

The most successful plays staged by these various groups for the child audience, stresses Goldberg, are those that maintain:

1. *Respect*—for the child's sense of wonder, naive emotionality, and physical/psychological weaknesses.
2. *Entertainment*—comprising nonverbal communication, repetition, direct address, slapstick, childish behavior in adults, romanticism, physical pleasures, suspense, and the antagonist's realization of defeat.
3. *Contemporaneity*—for children lack historical perspective and become most involved in a play when they sense its relevance to them.
4. *Action*—for theater is what is done and what is seen and not what is said: "Show it, don't tell it."
5. *Unity of organization*—or a careful adherence to whatever dramatic element it is that serves to organize and unify a particular script, such as a basic story line.
6. *Variety and rhythm*—since with their short attention spans, children like a rhythm of short and long scenes, talk and action, humor and seriousness, calm and tension.[3]

There can be no doubt that the creative drama program in the elementary school has benefited considerably from the growth in children's theater. While a quarter of a century ago only a few pioneers bothered with play production for boys and girls, today several hundred producers devote their time and energy to the development in children of an artistic appreciation for drama.

Incidentally, there is a technique known as *reader's theater* which is sometimes mistakenly described as a form of children's drama. It is in reality another form of oral reading. Scripts are used and literature ranging from short stories to poetry to plays is shared by the readers with their listeners. Unlike children's theater, reader's theater is not a polished, organized production. And unlike creative drama, reader's theater is not spontaneous and its action or physical movement is merely suggested. Larson believes that reader's theater adds a new dimension to reading class for it is *oral reading* at its best.[4]

Creative Drama

Creative drama is drama *with* children. Originated by a group of youngsters who are guided (not directed) by a teacher, it is always played with spontaneous dialog and action and is often termed *playmaking*. Participation is all-important for creative drama is not for the talented few, and the experience of the child who lacks ability is often as meaningful and as enjoyable as that of the child with marked dramatic talent. It may be created from an everyday experience, a story, a poem, a special event or holiday, or from an object or an idea. While it frequently develops from literature or the social studies, creative drama is not confined to a certain subject or time schedule but may be employed in any area of the curriculum where it can be used effectively for the sake of the pupils' social and emotional development.

Studies have shown that problem-solving ability, personality, behavior, verbal growth, and reading achievement can all be altered positively through creative dramatic activities.[5] Primary pupils in an integrated school, for example, who engaged in an eleven-week dramatic play program (developed to teach social studies) showed significant improvement in problem-solving skills and the acceptance of social responsibility; the children took part once or twice a week. Third graders who participated in a fifteen-week program of creative drama improved in both personal and social adjustment, with the boys making even greater gains than the girls; the class met forty minutes a week. Fourth graders who had met for one hour a week for fifteen weeks of creative dramatics more than doubled the rate of verbal development attained by the control group that had not participated. And advantaged and disadvantaged pupils alike gained in reading achievement and in self-concept after a fifteen-week program of reading and dramatizing stories; children from the primary and the intermediate grades dramatized self-selected stories from their basal and supplementary readers, their science and social studies texts, and from library browsing books as they met in small committees, three to five times weekly.

Teachers of the ever-increasing number of emotionally disturbed children can freely use creative drama too. Gillies has found that it (1) helps build the troubled children's sense of respect for their own ideas and consequently for themselves; (2) offers them a chance to become aware of and understand their feelings; (3) provides them with the social contacts often eliminated from their daily lives; (4) helps them experience firmness and inner control, so often lacking, in an enjoyable way; and (5) provides an opportunity for the children to be heard alone as well as in a group situation.[6]

That creative drama can bring teachers in contact with insightful clues as to the basis of pupils' emotional illness is readily understood. After all, this form of children's drama is a much more natural form of expression for all young students than is formal drama because it results from their own thoughts and feelings. All children in the group are encouraged to volunteer for all the parts, acting and, with the exception of pantomime, talking as they believe the characters they are portraying would act and talk. Pupils begin to realize that what they say and do is important to other people. They acquire the habit of thinking about what they are saying rather than memorizing a recitation, since the play is not rehearsed but develops with each presentation. The importance of creative drama, therefore, lies not in the product but in the process, and no school experience in the estimation of many teachers gives children a better opportunity to be creative than does playmaking.

The only audience, as a rule, is the part of the group not playing at the moment. Still, it is vital that there be onlookers (especially with older children) because they assist in evaluating the production while they themselves are developing an appreciation for drama. Should the creative thinking of the pupils result in a particularly good play, it may sometimes be shared with another group of children or with the parents. Such a sharing is not considered a performance, however, but rather an informal demonstration incidental to the creative experience. The players, nevertheless, are generally so fluent that should the audience be unaware that the dialog is being improvised, they might readily believe that the play has a written script.

Elementary teachers skilled in playmaking establish a physical setting and an emotional tone in the classroom that stimulate creative drama. Although they do not talk much themselves, they draw out the pupils' ideas through subtle questioning and courteous consideration of all responses. They quietly stress the importance of sense memory (or improvisations based on the five senses) and emotion memory (or improvisations based on feelings). They place emphasis on spontaneity, encouraging the children to create in their own way and to believe in themselves and their abilities. These teachers provide enrichment, as the need arises, with materials and properties, factual information, stories and verse, and audiovisual aids that help develop depth and understanding. At times when children appear unable to make suggestions necessary for the improvement of a play, thoughtful questions from teachers will elicit creative thinking among the group members.

Young children up to the age of approximately eleven or twelve years should participate in creative drama exclusively, according to the CTA Committee on Basic Concepts. Only when pupils are older and have had a background in creative drama and only after they have formed the habit of thinking through their speeches can they be counted on for a much greater degree of naturalness in children's theater roles. Pupils who are enrolled in a school that offers them a program in creative drama, will, beginning in kindergarten, enjoy during their elementary school years these five major groups of activities:

1. Pantomime
2. Dramatic play
3. Sociodrama or role-playing
4. Story dramatization: interpretation
5. Story dramatization: improvisation

Pantomime

Spontaneous expression in dramatic form is dependent upon children's security in body control and upon their freedom from embarrassment in regulating body movements. It appears reasonable then to initiate creative drama with the nonverbal pantomime.

Stated in its simplest terms, pantomime is acting without words. It can help children become prepared for story dramatization by letting them become accustomed to transmitting ideas, emotions, and actions to the audience through the medium of body motion. Confidence gained through success in pantomime automatically prepares the way for subsequent success in handling dialog. After all, psychologists claim that no less than 55 percent of the total communicated message is determined by *kinesics,* or bodily movements made by arms, hands, shoulders, and face.

Mime is an ancient and universal art form which is also a nonlinguistic means of communication common to all humanity. Perhaps this is why children enjoy it, even those who are shy and generally find oral activities distressing. It offers each child an opportunity to develop physical freedom and a feeling of self-confidence.

Participants learn to use all parts of the body to express a single action. To indicate drowsiness, for example, they can rub their eyes, stretch their arms, droop their shoulders, cover a yawn, or sit down wearily.

Children must realize that during a pantomime performance every action takes place in total silence. They can be reminded that while it is permissable to move one's lips as if talking, the lips must not form actual words. This basic tenet of pantomime is a difficult one for children to accept and follow.

Although properties are generally not allowed, a chair or table may occasionally be permitted. Should the performers be holding an imaginary object, they should practice with actual objects first. In that way, during the actual pantomime they will remember to leave space between the fingers just as if the object were actually in the hand.

The mark of an effective pantomime is that it is clearly presented so that it becomes easy to identify. Sometimes children get the mistaken impression that a pantomime has been well performed if the class is unable to decipher the activity shown. The contrary is true.

Consequently, as the pupils become more adept at their presentations, it is a wise policy for teachers to encourage them to prepare their pantomimes in advance. They must think through their movements and not rely upon impromptu actions. While it is hardly necessary for teachers to insist that all the movements to be used in a prepared pantomime be written down, it is still helpful if they know in advance just what pantomimes will be presented. Teachers may have to caution children about using good taste in their performance. Together the teacher and class can develop criteria for effective pantomimes.

Introductory Pantomime

All of the pantomime exercises during the introductory period involve gross actions only. What is being portrayed should be easily recognized by one and all.

If drama is new to both the primary teacher and the class, one starting point is a simple exercise executed in the form of a charade. The teacher asks, "If right at this moment you could do the one thing you enjoy doing most of all in the world, what would it be?"; and then as children raise their hands, the teacher adds, "Don't tell us what it is; show us!" Each child then pantomimes an activity that he or she especially enjoys, such as playing ball, helping to sail a boat, running with a dog, or riding a bicycle.

Should the group be timid or afraid of ridicule, the teacher should first set the mood verbally ("It is a snowy day") and then establish a feeling of confidence by doing the first large-movement pantomime. The teacher then asks the children to guess the situation, giving them the opportunity later to present their own interpretations of the same situation. Finally they are ready to enact some familiar actions for their classmates to decipher.

Besides charades and guessing games like "Secret" or "Who Am I?", riddles and Mother Goose rhymes are other ways to introduce pantomime to young children. One rhyme that works well is:

One, two, buckle my shoe;
Three, four, knock at the door;
Five, six, pick up sticks . . .

The teacher quickly recites the rhyme, demonstrating the actions that might accompany each part. Then he or she asks the children to present their interpretations individually as the rest of the class recites the rhyme. In a few instances the children slavishly copy the teacher's actions, but in other cases the pupils create and express their own ideas.

In teaching pantomime to intermediate grade boys and girls who have never engaged in such dramatic activities before, the teacher must always assume the lead and give an informal demonstration. The teacher can pantomime, for example, the humorous efforts to retrieve a pencil that has rolled under a heavy piece of furniture in the corner of the room. This demonstration will generally elicit other amusing pantomimes by the more extroverted pupils. Their demonstrations will, in turn, probably provoke pantomimes by shyer students.

Suggested exercises which may be effective for freeing inexperienced or withdrawn pupils to perform in front of their peers include the following pantomimes:

- Pretend to eat—an ice cream cone—a sour pickle—a freshly toasted marshmallow.
- Pretend to—nail two boards together—put on a pullover sweater—brush your teeth.
- Pretend that you are walking—on hot sand—through fallen leaves—through very deep snow.
- Pretend to throw—a baseball—a basketball—a football.

Developmental Stages

Children's pantomime is often so generalized that it communicates poorly or not at all. Yet pantomime is a skill, and good pantomime results only from thought and practice. Therefore, Stewig advises that in order to pantomime successfully, children should perform a series of steps. First, they must *particularize mentally* the actions and objects which are to be portrayed; for example, when picking up a fork, the performer must reflect upon such matters as the age/dexterity of the fork-user, the weight of the fork itself, and whether the fork is being used to eat solid or slippery food. Second, after establishing the pantomime in their minds, the children must *practice physically* again and again, until they have eliminated all actions which are not completely necessary and strengthened all those which genuinely communicate.[7]

True pantomiming however concerns more than mere mute action. It expresses vividly the participant's feelings and thought. For example, is there anyone who cannot interpret fully the facial expression and wordless actions of a boy cleaning the yard on a warm summer day while a ball game is in progress down the street? The boy sighs, looks longingly in the direction of the game, and then with a stolid face, resumes his chores with feverish haste. By his gestures and looks, he has revealed his inner reactions and wordlessly expressed, "I must finish this job so I can get back to my friends."

Consequently, once children have learned to respond to the typical large-movement pantomimes that make suitable class beginnings, it is time for pantomimes involving *action and emotion*.

The first group of these should be *short individual pantomimes* that will allow each member of the class to perform at least once during the lesson. Either a boy or girl may pretend to be—

- Biting into a sour apple
- Drinking cocoa that is too hot
- Hiking up a rocky hill
- Walking on an icy sidewalk
- Picking up a crying baby

After children have had some experience performing and watching "quickie" pantomimes, they will be encouraged to select topics for *lengthy individual pantomimes*. At this stage, they may either develop their own theme or choose to mime situations like these:

- Seeing a kindergartner who is mistreating a small cat that does not belong to her, becoming very angry, running between the girl and the cat, rescuing the frightened kitten, and finally scolding the unkind child.
- Walking down the street on the way home from school, noticing a three-year-old dart into the street after a ball just as a truck comes rapidly around the corner toward him, and reacting properly.
- Receiving a letter from favorite Aunt Kathleen with an invitation to take a trip to Florida to visit Disney World, thinking about what fun it will be, and hurrying to tell a parent the good news.

A third stage in pantomime activities is reached when children choose partners and perform *double pantomimes* such as—

- a barber cutting the hair of a wiggling boy;
- a boy scout walking an elderly person across the street;
- an indifferent student showing a poor report card to a parent;
- a bank robber holding up a frightened teller; or
- a beginning driver backing out of the garage with a nervous friend.

A variation of the double pantomime is the *mirror pantomime* where two players must harmonize their movements so as to give the impression of one person looking at his/her reflection in a full-length mirror. All actions are done in unison as the players face each other (and appear sideways to the audience). They should be of approximately the same size, though they need not be dressed alike. They should use broad gestures which are clearly visible to the audience, and make all movements with moderate speed.

After some practice with double pantomimes, the children may wish to attempt *group pantomimes* with character analysis and finer movements. Demanding the cooperation of several children, group pantomimes are especially suited for those pupils who are hesitant about giving individual performances but who still enjoy pantomime. Groups in the primary or middle grades may decide to do individual themes, variations on the same theme, or may even wish to pantomime in sequence a different scene from a complete story such as:

Anglund's *A Friend Is Someone Who Likes You* (Harcourt, 1958)
Asbjørnsen and Moe's *The Three Billy Goats Gruff* (Harcourt, 1957)
Bannon's *Scary Thing* (Houghton, 1956)
D'Aulaires' *Animals Everywhere* (Doubleday, 1954)
De Regniers' *What Can You Do with a Shoe?* (Harper, 1955)
Elkin's *The Loudest Noise in the World* (Viking, 1954)
Grimm Brothers' *The Traveling Musicians* (Harcourt, 1955)
Justus' *Little Red Rooster Learns to Crow* (Whitman, 1954)
Martin's *Little Princess Goodnight* (Holt, 1967)
Mayer's *There's a Nightmare in My Closet* (Dial, 1968)
Seuss's *The Lorax* (Random House, 1971)
Udry's *A Tree is Nice* (Harper, 1956)

Material suitable for group pantomime in the intermediate grades includes many of the fables, folktales, legends, and fantasy stories to which the pupils have been introduced during their literature periods. Readily found in several anthologies are such stories that can be pantomimed as "Pecos Bill and His Bouncing Bride," "The Emperor's New Clothes," "The Mad Hatter's Tea Party," "The Crow and the Pitcher," and "The Milkmaid and Her Pail." One successful group pantomime consists of having a student fluently read aloud a lively story as a selected cast simultaneously pantomimes the action.

Dramatic Play

Much of the knowledge children absorb is best acquired by exploration in the real world where they may freely and actively construct their vision of reality, rather than be passively instructed about it. Happily, therefore, one of the most spontaneous interests of five-, six-, and seven-year-old children is dramatic play. It involves neither plot nor sequence, just conversation and action. In their dramatic play, children reenact their own experiences, imitate the activities of adults, animals, and inanimate objects, and live in an imaginary world. They are the father, teacher, truck driver, mother, doctor, nurse, fire fighter, and scores of other characters in the home, school, and community. During the play period, children move about freely, choosing their own activities, materials, equipment, and companions as long as their selections do not interfere with the welfare of the classroom.

What the children do in this initial kind of creative drama is wholly exploratory and experimental. Although they lack the background to bring full knowledge to the situation, they are capable of conceiving ideas, planning their own dramatizations, and performing with the "dress-up" materials, playhouse, boxes, planks, or other properties that will help them produce something that provides them at least with gratification. Sometimes they may shift swiftly from one character to another, playing each role for only a few minutes. In other cases, they may continue the same role for days or weeks, becoming the person, animal, or object with which they have an impulse to identify. Children may play the part of a barking dog, a galloping pony, or a soaring airplane. Dramatic play concerns being rather than playing and incorporates feeling with action. It is fragmentary and fun.

There is no definite beginning, middle, or end. Dramatic play may start anywhere and may conclude abruptly, especially in its early stages, when a child says, "I'm finished."

Teachers should keep in mind the sequence of growth through which children **Sequence of Growth** progress in their play and recognize that there is a gradual transition from simple movement and manipulation through the following phases:

Solitary play. The child plays alone, with little or no attention to other children. Although the child may show interest in others, he or she will not play with them.

Parallel play. The child still plays independently, but alongside of other children, and he or she enters into the same types of activities that they do. There is very little conversation.

Associate play. Children playing in the playhouse may share some ideas and materials, and their activities may be similar. One child sets the table while another feeds the baby. Each plays according to individual interests.

Cooperative play. Late in the first year of school (first grade or kindergarten, depending on the school organization) a more organized type of play may appear. The play period may be lengthened and the same interest may carry over for several days. Two to five children may play together.

The teacher should also be aware that as children mature, the character of their dramatic play changes. Older children demand a higher degree of organization than younger children before beginning to play, as they assume roles and divide responsibilities. Older children also have a desire for properties that are real, while younger children are able to participate in dramatic play in which all the properties they use exist only in their imaginations. As children mature, a distinction between "work" and "play" develops: work involving the constructing, gathering, or arranging of materials for dramatic play; and play concerning the use of those materials for dramatizing an idea or a situation. Consequently, the intervals between play periods obviously lengthen as the children create the properties they need. Finally, the amount of time that is devoted to dramatic play and the place of dramatic play in the daily schedule will differ according to the maturity of the children.

Conditions and Developmental Steps

Play is the child's vehicle of growth. And teachers who have successfully guided dramatic play have discovered factors which contribute to stimulating play in the kindergarten and early grades. There must be adequate space to promote free expression, and numerous and different kinds of properties to encourage participation. Proper stimuli from both firsthand and vicarious experiences are needed before young children can play creatively. Development of the children's own ideas, not those imposed by the teacher, is always an encouraging factor. Sufficient time for children to employ previous learnings and explore additional ones is an especially significant matter in the early grades. Participation by the children in all phases of the play from problem solving to evaluation honestly furthers creative expression. Finally, there is no apparent interference or criticism on the part of the teacher.

After its beginning weeks in any classroom, dramatic play usually encompasses the following steps, according to the Shaftels:

1. There is an environment arranged by the teacher.
2. The boys and girls explore that environment and are permitted to manipulate and discuss all the materials and tools that it contains.
3. A story such as Beskow's *Pelle's New Suit* (Harper, 1929) is heard or read to further stimulate interest in the selected area.
4. The boys and girls elect to play a part of the story or improvise their own situation.
5. The first play is unguided, but carefully observed by the teacher.
6. A discussion period follows the play to clarify dissatisfactions and unexpressed needs.
7. There is a planning period for problem solving and work assignments.
8. A period of extension of experiences through research, excursions, and multimedia ensues before and beside further play.
9. Play proceeds on a higher level due to enriched experience.
10. This continuous and expanding procedure progresses on an ascending spiral.[8]

Sociodrama or Role-Playing

Sociodrama is a structured extension of dramatic play. It differs from play only in that it always involves a group situation in which a problem or controversial issue in the area of interpersonal relations is enacted and the observers evaluate the factors involved as well as the solution. It is sometimes referred to as role-playing. Children often learn to resolve problems in real life by working them out successfully in role-playing situations.

Sociodrama increases skill in communication. It aids children in understanding their own behavior and feelings as well as the behavior and feelings of others. It also helps them learn new ways of handling acceptance and rejection situations, criticism and praise, failure and success, and dilemmas involving sibling rivalry, racial tension, parent-child conflicts, shyness, and social isolation. Often its purpose is to change the attitude of a part of the audience.

Sociodrama is not to be confused with psychodrama because it concerns the use of drama as therapy for the group. Psychodrama means the use of drama as therapy for an individual and can therefore be safely used only by a psychiatrist. However, since sociodrama does focus upon a social problem in human relations, the teacher has an opportunity to diagnose the group needs of the children and evaluate their attitudes, their sensitivity to the feelings of others, and their ability to think through a problem. The child who never volunteers, the child who overreacts, the child who is highly critical of others, the child who always wants to be a participant—for these and other pupils, sociodrama indicates whether further study or specialized help might be valuable.

It is one of the most useful methods of helping pupils resolve the many social problems that arise daily. A quarrel develops on the playground because there is a shortage of equipment. The teacher arranges a sociodrama by getting the attention of all the children, discussing the setting of the "play" situation, and choosing the participants: Sean has the role of an aggressive child who will not share the equipment; Elizabeth plays a polite child who wishes to use the equipment but will not fight to get it; and Brian plays a shy pupil who is disturbed by the quarrel.

It is helpful when the situations chosen are representative of the problems of the group, and the members want to explore them. Situations in which the pupils feel misunderstood, those in which they have difficulty in making up their minds about what is right to do or say, or those that make them unhappy are all suitable for sociodrama. There should never be a feeling that there is only one right way of behaving in a given situation; instead, the same situation may be played several times in order that the children can reinterpret the factors and reach solutions that are personally satisfying. The outcomes of sociodramas should aid the participants and their audience to discover ways of behaving that will expand the present skills they possess in dealing with problems of deep personal concern. Generalizations about human relations appropriate to the age and maturity of the group involved may also be discovered.

In organizing and directing a sociodrama, teachers should choose a problem that the children cannot meet adequately or toward which they have conflicting attitudes; that problem should involve three or more participants. Teachers should take sufficient time to clarify the various roles and explain the situation—not the solution—before they ask for volunteers for the different roles. (If there are no volunteers, they should select those pupils who are neither shy nor readily upset.) Next, they can arrange the details of the situation, discuss the physical setting, and prepare the nonparticipants for their role as observers. Promptly after the first unrehearsed enactment, teachers and children should discuss the presentation and summarize how the problem was met. Then the first actors may be replaced by new ones who have different ideas of how the roles should be played, and again the enactment should be evaluated and modifications suggested. Sometimes a third version may ensue.

One of the most effective stimulants for decision making through role-playing is the unfinished problem story which presents an unresolved conflict that offers many possible endings. Some teachers choose to use the more than forty such stories written by the Shaftels concerning areas like individual integrity, group responsibility (to support and respect the individual), self-acceptance, and managing one's feelings.[9] Other teachers elect to produce their own stories, believing that they know best their own students' maturity level and interests as well as the attitudes and values to be explored with the individual group. Under the circumstances, these teacher-authors also understand more clearly the numbers and types of character parts to be included in the unfinished story.

In an effort to aid beginning teachers in the upper elementary grades who are interested in sociodrama, the Fairfield (Connecticut) schools have developed a checklist for guiding teachers during role-playing sessions involving problem stories.

Classroom Teachers Checklist for Guiding Role-Playing

Part A
1. Define the problem (Recall).
   After reading the story, allow time for the children to reflect and to make voluntary comments. Then ask: What is happening here?
   Should the children still seem to be having difficulty in moving into the situation, ask further recall questions: Who is involved? How are they affected by this situation? How is Chief Character feeling? Why is he or she feeling this way? How are Other Characters feeling? Why?
2. Delineate alternatives (Projection).
   Ask: What do you think will (not should) happen now?
   Invite ideas from the children.
   Both antisocial and socially sanctioned solutions will generally be mentioned. If only one kind of solution is offered, however, ask: Is this the only way in which such a situation usually ends? Then if still no other solution is proposed, proceed into role-playing.
3. Explore alternatives.
   If the group has offered both negative and positive proposals for solving the story dilemma, begin with a consideration of the antisocial or impulsive solutions first.
   a. Negative solutions
      (1) Choose one negative solution and hold a brief discussion.
      (2) Choose a volunteer to role-play the proposal. Ask the volunteer: Whom will you need to help you? Then assist him or her in selecting other volunteer role-players.
      (3) Set the stage for the role-playing session by asking: Where is this happening? What time of year (or day) is it? What is each of you doing?
      (4) Prepare the audience. If beginners, ask the group to evaluate, as

they watch, how realistic the role-playing is by pondering: Could this really occur? Are the persons behaving as they would in real life?

If the class is experienced in role-playing, divide the members into observer groups and ask Group I to observe for true-to-life behavior, Group II to observe how individual players feel, and Group III to consider next steps for solving the dilemma.

(5) Start the role-playing and continue it only until the acting has clearly delineated the proposed solution.

(6) Start the discussion by asking: What has been happening? How does Chief Character feel? Why does he or she behave in that way? What will happen next?

b. Interim

Decide whether it is worthwhile to continue further enactment exploring the negative solution or to go on to explore proposals offering alternative courses of behavior. Should time allow for elaborated role-playing, consult Part B.

c. Positive solutions

(1) Choose one positive solution and hold a brief discussion.

(2) Proceed as outlined under 3a—sections (2) to (6).

4. Make a decision.

a. If the group has reached some definite understanding of the alternatives explored and of the consequences that may ensue, ask: Which one of the solutions to this problem do you believe to be the best? Why? For whom is it best? Who will benefit from the solution and who will suffer? If you were (One Story Character), how would you decide? If you were (Another Story Character), how would you decide?

b. Ask: At which point in the story could a choice have been made that would have precipitated an acceptable solution?

Part B

1. Add extra steps to role-playing when time allows.

For occasions when the group may be guided into role-playing with some depth, up to three additional steps may be added to the process.

a. Extend exploration of the consequences of the proposed solution to the dilemma by suggesting another scene to be enacted. This second scene should logically be an aftermath of the proposed behavior.

b. Reverse the roles of the chief characters in the problem story. (In order to convince an individual who is unaware of the effect of his or her behavior upon others, it is often impressive to put this individual into the position of the person most seriously affected by that behavior.)

c. Seek out the implications of the proposed alternative by means of analogy. Apply the principle suggested by the alternative to other situations outside the story.[10]

Story Dramatization: Interpretation

Stories come alive, claims Bissett, when humanity jumps from the page and is examined closely by groups of children who have the advantage of acting out stories.[11] Constituting the most popular means that pupils and their teachers have to get behind the printed word, story dramatization helps develop a new dimension in understanding literature.

Children who are younger or less experienced in creative drama generally want to do stories already familiar to them and only gradually abandon stereotypes and conventions for more original creations. Briefly, this illustrates the sequence of *interpretation* and *improvisation*. In planning story dramatization with students, the teacher begins with an interpretation of the story or an accurate re-creation of the author's intent and statement. Then as the pupils mature and become more knowledgeable in dramatization, the teacher can proceed to improvisation, for that involves going beyond the basic story in an attempt to extend or expand upon the thematic material.

Developmental Steps

When the class has shown readiness for story dramatization *the teacher tells or reads a well-structured story* that possesses most or all of the following characteristics:

1. Brevity—as in one of Kipling's *Just So Stories* (Doubleday, 1952)
2. A simple, strong, dramatic conflict—as in Seuss' *The 500 Hats of Bartholomew Cubbins* (Vanguard, 1938)
3. One setting—as in Slobodkina's *Caps for Sale* (Young Scott, 1947)
4. Natural, interesting characters—as in Marcia Brown's *Stone Soup* (Scribner, 1947)
5. A simple plot that hinges on action—as in the Grimm Brothers' *The Shoemaker and the Elves* (Scribner, 1960)
6. Dialog that furthers that action—as in Du Bois' *The Three Little Pigs* (Viking, 1962)
7. A strong climax and a quick, definite ending—as in Galdone's *The Three Wishes* (McGraw, 1961)

Before reading or telling the intended story, the teacher becomes so familiar with it that he or she can reflect upon the thoughts, movements, appearances, and feelings of the characters in order to make these figures real. The teacher attempts to establish in the students' minds one version to which they can repeatedly return in the dramatization. During the recitation the teacher watches for external clues from the children that may indicate their interest and involvement. It is vital that all or most of the children like the materials which will be dramatized. The teacher may be certain that they will enjoy a story if it appeals to their emotions.

The teacher's own viewpoint about the story is also important. The teacher can hardly guide children to create successful dialog and action from literary selections concerned with values or characterizations that he or she personally finds unacceptable.

Once a story has been told, *the teacher poses questions to stimulate dis-*

Listening to the teacher tell or read a well-structured story promotes the interest of young children in creative drama. (Photo courtesy of the *Daily News Tribune,* Fullerton, California.)

cussion of sequences, characters, and setting. The children must be able to bring out in their dramatization the essential elements of the story just read. So the teacher asks the pupils carefully framed questions to point up the key actions and lines which will move the play along. In some instances more than one discussion period may be necessary to stimulate thoughts about the story plot and people, for it is wise not to pose more than five specific questions during a single discussion.

After they have carefully analyzed the story, *the children determine the characterizations and the scenes.* Whether the story requires one scene or several, the pupils will find that the playing proceeds more smoothly if they decide in advance the number of scenes and the characters who appear in each scene, and plot all these details on the chalkboard.

Characterization being principally a matter of imagination, the teacher should always stress developing a character from within. Boys and girls should try first to understand how the other person thinks and feels before they attempt to act like the person. In one New York classroom, for example, there is a "magic stage," a special space reserved for creative drama activities. Once children step onto this stage, they are encouraged to be the characters they have chosen to portray by acting like them with both their bodies and their minds. To help the boys and girls keep clear about the characters and their goals and obstacles in the story, the teacher and the class play a game called Circle of Characters, in which they take turns asking the characters on the Magic Stage various questions to help them establish who they are: Where do you live? What is your favorite color? What hobby do you have? Which animals do you like? Which foods do you prefer to eat? What is your favorite sport? What do you like to do best? How old are you? Who is your best friend?

As they follow the general outline of the story, *the children create the dialog and the dramatization.* As a consequence of the discussion periods held earlier, the boys and girls generally can speak all or nearly all of the key lines, adding other phrases to make the play their own and to round out the characters they will be portraying. For the first performance, the teacher designates a space within the room as a stage or playing area and selects five or six confident volunteers (explaining to the others that each will be given an opportunity in turn to play a role). The group of players for the initial performance is then permitted a planning conference among themselves, away from the rest of the class, in order to prepare in greater detail exactly what each member will do and how he or she will do it. This conference, serving as a brief orientation period for the players, runs about five minutes and takes place just prior to the start of the dramatization.

Once the play has begun, it must move along without interruption because to the children this step is the most important of all. The teacher should attempt to limit the performances in the lower grades to five minutes, and those in the middle and intermediate grades to fifteen minutes.

As soon as the performance has been completed, *the class promptly evaluates the presentation.* Such appraisal under the positive guidance of the teacher is a training of vital importance, according to Gillies, for all age levels, beginning in the second grade.[12] It starts with an acknowledgment of strengths: What did you see that you liked? What was good (about Cinderella's stepsisters)? Once trained to look for what is good or what they liked, children can soon reach the second level of discussion: How can we make that scene more real (or more powerful, more exciting)? What shall we change or add the next time we play it? Throughout the discussion the boys and girls should examine the action and consider the voice and diction of the actors. They can study the characterizations, using the names of the characters rather than those of the players in order to be more objective in their criticism. They can ask one another these questions:

Was the play just like the story we heard?
What was left out of the play?

Were the characters the way we had imagined them to be?
What different things could have been done?
What did we like best about the performance?

Slowly the class can be led through creative group appraisal to realize that while first dramatic attempts may appear uneven and crude, story dramatizations gradually become more convincing. Therefore, every sincere effort of each child is acceptable and praiseworthy and every child retains the right to reject or modify proposed changes in the role that he or she has undertaken.

Finally, *the children reenact the dramatization,* incorporating the constructive criticisms just discussed. Properties are still kept at a simple minimum, with no costumes necessary. Eventually, several casts are drawn up, with every child playing at least one role. Variations in actions and dialog are anticipated and appreciated during each performance.

All of the stories listed here have proved suitable for informal dramatization and can be adapted to different age groups. Readily located in most standard anthologies of children's literature, they include:

Suggested Stories

"The Ant and the Grasshopper"
"Ask Mr. Bear"
"The Blind Man and the Elephant"
"Cinderella"
"The Elves and the Shoemaker"
"The Emperor's New Clothes"
"The Fox and the Crow"
"The Kite and the Butterfly"
"The Lion and the Mouse"
"The Painted Pig"
"The Peddler and the Monkeys"
"Rapunzel"
"The Turtle Who Couldn't Stop Talking"
"The Ugly Duckling"
"The Wind and the Sun"

There are also some stories in poetic form that children and teachers may enjoy dramatizing, such as the following:

Browning's "The Pied Piper of Hamelin"
Field's "The Duel"
Follen's "Three Little Kittens"
Moore's "A Visit from St. Nicholas"

Improvisation involves going beyond the basic literary material. The children are compelled to extrapolate and enrich the material by drawing from within themselves. Their thoughts, emotions, and conclusions are based upon, but not truly found in, the poem or story in question.

Story Dramatization: Improvisation

This type of story dramatization encompasses many of the same developmental steps that were discussed earlier for the interpretation category. The major difference lies in the sort of questions that the teacher must write. Unlike the factual variety demanding strict recall, which are a significant part of interpretation, questions that are developed in preparation for an improvisation session are inferential. They require original, creative thinking.

A teacher, for example, who had told the familiar myth of King Midas to a class that had been interpreting stories for months, might pose such questions as the following as a prelude to improvisation:

1. Why do you believe the king was so greedy? What might have caused him to be that way?
2. Why was his daughter so sweet, despite the fact that she had been raised alone in the castle with her father as an example?
3. How did the king react to other people? (Remember that the story did not show him interacting with others). How did he treat his servants? The townspeople?
4. In what other ways might he have resolved his problem?[13]

These are fairly specific questions about only two characters. Other, more general questions could be asked regarding the physical, social, and psychological facets of additional characters in that or a different story.

Once the children have pondered the questions carefully, they then proceed to the final three developmental steps previously explored under Story Dramatization: Interpretation. They create the dramatization complete with dialog which in turn results in an evaluation session and a subsequent reenactment of the improvisation.

Evaluation of Pupils' Progress

Appraisal of the growth of the child in this area of the English language arts can be made on an informal and individual basis through observing to what extent he or she fulfills the following:

- Does the child participate freely and wholeheartedly in imaginative playmaking?
- Does the child find satisfaction and enjoyment in watching children's drama?
- Does the child control situations by words rather than physical force?
- Does the child share ideas and materials?
- Does the child accept and fulfill committee responsibilities?
- Does the child recall a series of episodes in sequence and distinguish between central ideas and subordinating details?
- Is the child's language expanding properly?
- Is the child able to organize stories, verse, and other media for dramatic expression?
- Has the child developed physical coordination and good posture habits?

- Has the child's voice quality and projection improved?
- Has the child increased in self-confidence and self-direction, whether working alone or before an audience?
- Has the child formed the habit of original flexible thinking?
- Has the child's problem-solving ability expanded?
- Has the child developed a respect for the creative forms that he or she has experienced and for the creative efforts that fellow classmates have demonstrated?

Discussion Questions

1. As a beginning teacher, how would you explain your creative drama program to a group of stolid parents?
2. How can a teacher interest fifth graders into doing pantomime or story dramatization if they have never attempted either one before?
3. Listening is said to improve after creative drama sessions. How can you explain this improvement?
4. Should a teacher assign a letter grade to the young performer in creative drama? How can the teacher best evaluate the child's participation in this critical area?

Suggested Projects

1. Write an unfinished problem story which could serve as the basis of a sociodrama session in the fourth grade.
2. Observe a group of pupils in kindergarten or first grade who are engaged in dramatic play. What values are apparent in this type of creative drama?
3. List the organizations in your community that are currently producing plays for children. Visit one of their performances and assess its reception by the young audience.
4. Plan a beginning pantomime lesson for primary pupils.
5. Examine one of the standard anthologies of poetry for children, such as Arbuthnot and Root's *Time for Poetry* (Scott, Foresman, 1968). List several ballads and story poems that pupils might enjoy dramatizing.
6. Set up the learning center on creative drama shown in Figure 12.1.

Related Readings

Allen, E. G., and Wright, J. P. 1978. "Just for Fun: A Creative Dramatics Learning Center." *Childhood Education* 54: 169–75.

Caldwell, B., and Yowell, R. 1977. "Action Dramatics: Language Enrichment Through Action Dramatics." *Instructor* 86: 118–19.

Lewis, G., and Fuller, R. 1977. *Storytelling Dramatization Creativity*. Dubuque, Iowa: Kendall-Hunt.

Mazor, R. 1978. "Drama As Experience." *Language Arts* 55: 328–33.

McCaslin, N., ed. 1977. *Theatre for Young Audiences*. New York: David McKay Co., Inc.

Paley, V. 1978. "The Uses of Dramatics in Kindergarten." *Elementary School Journal* 78: 319–23.

Ross, E., and Roe, B. 1977. "Creative Drama Builds Proficiency in Reading." *Reading Teacher* 30: 383–87.

Figure 12.1. Language Arts Learning Center: Creative Drama.

TYPE OF CENTER: Creative Drama   TIME: 15–20 minutes

GRADE LEVEL: 2 and 3 and up   NUMBER OF STUDENTS: 2 or 3

INSTRUCTIONAL
OBJECTIVE: The children will be able to create and act out a situation from the numbers they spin.

MATERIALS: Display board, spinning device, paper, pencil, phrases under flaps on three wheels, envelope, directions.

DIRECTIONS
TO STUDENTS: A. Take turns acting out a story by doing the following:
         1. Take the spinner out of the pocket on the back of the learning center board.
         2. Spin the spinner to get a number. Find this number on the Character Wheel. Lift the flap which is posted on this number to find a character.
         3. Spin the spinner again to find another number. Find this number on the Action Wheel. Lift the flap to find your action.

Shuman, R. B., ed. 1978. *Educational Drama for Today's Schools.* Metuchen, New
     Jersey: Scarecrow Press.
Siks, G. 1977. *Drama with Children.* New York: Harper and Row.
Stewig, J. 1976. "I Absolutely Refuse to Be An Onion." *Gifted Child Quarterly* 20:
     31–39.

4. Spin the spinner again to find another number. Find this number on the Setting Wheel. Lift the flap to find the setting.
5. Put these three together to form a sentence. Act out what the sentence says.

B. Write down your name and the act you performed on the paper provided. Put this paper in the envelope on the back of the learning center board. You may be called on in class some day to perform the task, so do a good job of acting!

EVALUATION: The teacher will observe the children acting out their situation. The teacher will also check the envelope to make sure all children have completed the activity, as well as to ask some children to perform their situations in front of the class.

Possible Characters: doctor, musician, princess or prince, firefighter, magician, good witch, man, woman, king, clown, baby, principal

Possible Actions:

Operating on a foot	Grocery shopping
Putting out a fire	Crying
Trying to roller skate	Fishing for whale
Settling an argument	Giving someone three wishes
Directing an orchestra	Refusing to laugh
Pulling a rabbit out of a hat	Fighting a dragon

Possible Settings:

In a house	In a zoo
In a hospital	In a department store
At a hotel	In a pet shop
In the kitchen	On a mountain top
In a crowded room	In a palace
In a classroom	In a forest
At the seashore	In a village
On a football field	On a rock in the sea

VARIATION: Use the same learning center but provide a prop box so that the children might have some type of costume to act out their situations.

Source: From *Language Arts Learning Centers and Activities* by Angela Reeke and James Laffey. Copyright 1979 by Goodyear Publishing Company. Reprinted by permission.

Library Media Center Skills 13

The role of the media specialist

Major library media center skills

The various types of catalog cards

The picture dictionary as a reading readiness device

In the well-planned elementary English program the school library media center is essential. The media center's program is designed to assist boys and girls to grow in their ability to find, generate, evaluate, and apply information that helps them to function effectively as individuals and to participate fully in society.[1] Nothing that children learn in school today is likely to continue to serve them so well throughout life as an interest in books and a skill in using both nonbook and book materials.

The development of such an interest and skill is primarily the responsibility of the elementary school librarian or *media specialist* (as this person is described in a recent joint statement of the American Association of School Librarians and the Association for Educational Communications and Technology). Since an educational program of excellence demands the multimedia approach to teaching and learning, the media specialist must help each student acquire and strengthen skills in reading, viewing, listening, and in communicating ideas. The specialist must also assist pupils in the development of independent study habits and must teach library research skills and the use/care of media resources.

As important as these duties may be, however, there remains an insufficient number of media professionals to handle them in elementary schools at the present time due both to budgeting problems and the relative lack of properly qualified personnel.

It is fortunate therefore that there is a direct relationship between the elementary classroom teacher's library background and reading habits and the amount and kind of library media skills and reading interests maintained by his or her students. When the teacher's library skills and reading habits are significantly high, the reading and library media skills of his or her pupils are high also. It is proposed, therefore, that elementary school children acquire library media skills from their classroom teacher (if they are in a school without a media specialist), or from a teacher-specialist team (if they attend a school that maintains a strong library media facility and staff). In this fashion pupils can eventually become independent and expert public library patrons through a comprehensive school program that encourages the love of literature and the habit of individualized reading, builds attitudes of good citizenship, develops reference and study skills, and promotes the use of nonbook materials.

Such a program may be presented to elementary school children in a variety of ways. In Concordia, California, for example, seventh graders learn library media skills through tape recordings prepared in the school from scripts written and narrated by other students; while in Islip, New York, fifth- and sixth-grade boys and girls are able to use the card catalog after two instructional sessions presented by closed-circuit television. In Phoenix, Arizona, transparencies prepared for use with an overhead projector are employed to teach library citizenship to primary children and to provide intermediate grade children with the opportunity to learn about author, title, and subject catalog cards, and to review correct ways of filling out date-due slips and circulation cards. In Charleston, Illinois, the transparencies supplement an audiovisual program consisting of two-by-two-inch color slides accompanied by taped narration. Finally, in Wayne County, Michigan, certain shelves in the library media center are specially marked with large Dewey decimal numbers and children are taught to shelve their own books; as they return the books that they have checked out, the clerk removes the transaction cards and hands the books back to the children for shelving. Since it is believed that boys and girls who cannot shelve a book also cannot locate a book on the shelf, self-shelving has become an activity that not only gives the children needed practice in handling books but also increases their opportunities to become familiar with all the areas of the library media center.

Such familiarity is important due to the many objectives of the library media center in K–8 schools, according to the New York City Board of Education:

1. To impart a lasting and genuine love of reading and an appreciation of fine literature.
2. To develop an understanding and aesthetic appreciation of aural and visual art forms.
3. To assist with programs for the development of competency in reading, listening, and viewing skills in the content areas.
4. To encourage reading, listening, and viewing as aids toward the achievement of the basic developmental tasks of children.
5. To support curriculum programs at all grade levels by providing a variety of book and nonbook materials.
6. To develop a continuity of instruction in the skillful use of school library media resources.
7. To reinforce, extend, and enrich classroom learning through planned library experiences.

8. To promote an understanding and appreciation of American institutions and ideals as well as a responsibility for supporting them.
9. To develop an understanding and appreciation of different ethnic groups and their contributions to the world.
10. To be an active participant in curriculum development, schoolwide projects and experiments, and school-related community programs.
11. To provide incentive for lifelong productive and satisfying use of libraries, museums, and other multimedia information centers.[2]

Another set of objectives for school library media center programs is in the Library Bill of Rights of the American Library Association, as shown in Figure 13.1.

Instruction in the use of the media center must be functional and preferably related directly to classroom work experiences in social studies, science, and other curricular areas. It can, however, also occur indirectly through separate units that parallel curricular units; a fourth-grade class, for example, is pursuing a unit on weather, so the media specialist may plan a unit on folklore, myths, and legends which have evolved as people have attempted to explain

Major Library Media Center Skills and Instructional Activities

---

Library Bill of Rights for School Media Programs

The American Association of School Librarians reaffirms its belief in the Library Bill of Rights of the American Library Association. To this end the Association asserts that the responsibility of the school library media center is:

To provide a comprehensive collection of instructional materials selected in compliance with basic written selection principles, and to provide maximum accessibility to these materials.

To provide materials that will support the curriculum, taking into consideration the individual's needs, and the varied interests, abilities, socioeconomic backgrounds, and maturity levels of the students served.

To provide materials for teachers and students that will encourage growth in knowledge, and that will develop literary, cultural, and aesthetic appreciation, and ethical standards.

To provide materials which reflect the ideas and beliefs of religious, social, political, historical, and ethnic groups and their contribution to the American and world heritage and culture, thereby enabling students to develop an intellectual integrity in forming judgments.

To provide a written statement, approved by the local Boards of Education, of the procedures for meeting the challenge of censorship of materials in school library media centers.

To provide qualified professional personnel to serve teachers and students.

Source: *Intellectual Freedom Manual* (Chicago: American Library Association, 1974).

Figure 13.1. A Significant Document for Elementary School Children and Their Parents and Teachers.

climatic and seasonal changes. In this way the specialist or teacher-specialist can use classroom science to motivate pupils to learn more about the realm of imaginative literature.

The instructional program should incorporate the interests, needs, and developmental tasks of the children, including activities within the pupils' understanding and ability. It should contain a sequence of growth and emphasize ten major skills.

First Skill: Understanding the Classification of Books

Since the minimal book collection in schools with 500 or fewer pupils (according to standards established by the American Association of School Librarians and AECT) contains 8,000 to 12,000 volumes, any child looking for a book needs a knowledge of the basic arrangement of books and of the Dewey Decimal System for the classification of books. Lessons that relate to call numbers and the proper placement of books on the shelf should begin by stressing the importance of careful arrangement of volumes and reviewing the division of books into fiction and nonfiction groupings. Then the lessons could proceed as follows:

Fiction and
Call Numbers

While showing flash cards with enlarged call numbers (covering both fiction and nonfiction), the teacher-specialist establishes the difference between the two categories of numbers. He or she emphasizes that a fiction call number is the initial letter or letters of an author's surname and then sends several children to get fiction books from the shelves. The children discuss the selections and justify the call numbers appearing on the book spines.

Next, the teacher tells how fiction is arranged, explaining why shelf labels are a quick way of locating the right call number, and how the library media center "landmarks" (corners, windows, pictures, and doors) will save the readers' time in finding the proper shelf label. Finally, the teacher drills on locating fiction via call numbers by showing certain flash cards and calling on the pupils to walk to the shelves to point out the books bearing the desired call numbers.

Nonfiction and
Call Numbers

The teacher-specialist randomly arranges on the chalk tray some flash cards with enlarged nonfiction call numbers, and asks the class to suggest a way to place the cards in numerical order. The children will usually respond correctly, although the teacher must be careful not to omit a card with a 000 number in the tray. Another more time-consuming way of introducing the arrangement of nonfiction is by working from the numbers on the shelf labels: pupils are carefully dispatched to each of the nonfiction shelves—except individual biography—and, one by one, they read the numbers off the shelf labels.

To establish "landmarks" in the nonfiction section of the library media center, the teacher hands out flash cards representing the major classifications to each of ten children and asks the pupils to place their cards on the top shelf of the proper section. In this way the class can easily see, for example, that the 500s are under the clock or the 800s are by the door.

Next, the teacher distributes copies of the abridged Dewey Decimal Classification System appropriate for elementary school library media centers, as exemplified in Table 13.1. The teacher explains that most libraries in the United States use the Dewey System to determine which number to use on each book, and then he or she selects a few examples from the handout sheet and has various pupils verify these numbers on the shelves. Finally, the teacher refers back to the flash cards and reminds the children that nonfiction numbers

Table 13.1.
Dewey Decimal Classification Numbers in Use in the Elementary Schools

020	Library Science	540	Chemistry	914.4	France
028	Reading	550	Geology, Rocks, etc.	914.5	Italy
030	Encyclopedias	551	Weather	914.6	Spain
070	Journalism	560	Prehistoric Life	914.7	Russia
150	Psychology, Ethics	570	Anthropology	914.8	Sweden, Norway
220	Bible	574	Wildlife	9.14.9	Other European Countries
260	Christian Church	580	Plants, Trees		
290	Myths	594	Seashore Life, Shells	915	Asia
300	Social Science	595	Insects, Worms	915.1	China
310	Almanacs	598	Birds	915.2	Japan
320	Political Science	599	Animals	915.3	Arabian Countries
323	Community Life	600	Useful Arts, Industries	915.4	India
330	Banking, Trade, Money	608	Inventions	915.5	Iran
333	Conservation	614	Health, Fire Protection, Safety	915.6	Syria
338	Commercial Establishments	620	Aviation	915.9	Other Asiatic Countries
340	Law	621	Radio, Television	916	Africa
341	United Nations	625	Highways, Roads, Bridges	917	North America
352	Police	629	Automobiles, Trucks, Machines	917.1	Canada
353	Citizenship	630	Farming, Gardening, Lumber	917.2	Mexico
355	Armed Forces	636	Domestic Animals	917.3	United States
371	Vocations	640	Food, Clothing	917.94	California
380	Transportation, Communication, Commerce	655	Printing	917.98	Alaska
383	Postal Service, Stamps	680	Handicrafts	918	South America
385	Railroads, Trains	700	Fine Arts	919	Oceania
387	Waterways, Ships	740	Drawing	919.8	Polar Regions
390	Costume	770	Photography	920	Collective Biography (Real People)
392	Families, Homes	778	Motion Pictures		
394	Holidays	780	Music	921	Biography (Individual)
395	Etiquette	790	Games, Sports	929	Flags
398	Fairy Tales, Folklore	800	Literature	930	Ancient History
400	Language	811	Poetry	940	European History
423	Dictionaries	812	Plays	940.5	World War II
425	Grammar	900	History	942	Great Britain, History
500	Science, Nature Study	910	Geography	970.1	Indians of North America
510	Mathematics	912	Atlases	973	United States, History
520	Astronomy	914	Europe	978	The West
530	Physics, Electricity, Atomic Energy	914.1	Scotland, Ireland	979.4	California, History
		914.2	England	E	Easy Book
		914.3	Germany	F	Fiction

Table 13.2.
Library of Congress Classification System

Classes A to Z			
A	General Works	L	Education
B	Philosophy, Psychology, and Religion	M	Music
		N	Fine Arts
C–D	History: General, European, African, Asiatic	P	Language and Literature
		Q	Science and Mathematics
E–F	History: United States and American	R	Medicine
		S	Agriculture
G	Geography, Anthropology, etc.	T	Engineering, Technology, etc.
H	Social Sciences (General), Economics, Sociology, etc.	U	Military Science
		V	Naval Science
J	Political Science	Z	Bibliography and Library Science
K	Law		

are composed of a first line, which indicates the subject of a book according to the Dewey System, and a second line, which—like the fiction call numbers—indicates the initial letter or letters of an author's surname. (In those few elementary schools which use the Library of Congress Classification System, as shown in Table 13.2, the teacher-specialist should use the same teaching strategies to introduce that system as have been described for the Dewey System).

Other Activities

The children may play a relay game in locating and returning books to the shelves or may straighten shelves of books that have been scrambled. They may arrange themselves in alphabetical order as if they were fiction books on the shelf or may rearrange over-sized sample book spines made of felt board. They will enjoy completing a floor plan of the library media center on which they designate the location of different classifications of books. Some pupils may wish to read and report on pertinent topics such as the Library of Congress or the life of Melvil Dewey. Others will be interested in visiting their local public library to compare its book locations and arrangements with those used in the school center.

Second Skill: Using the Card Catalog

Since the card catalog is a distinctive and important tool, children must attain an understanding of it as a complete index to all the materials in the library media center. Sample catalog cards are shown in Figures 13.3 through 13.10 (see pages 380–384).

More than one lesson may be needed to acquaint pupils with this skill. The first could relate to the cabinet itself and the use of the labels on the drawers (and include a poster-sized chart of the front of the card catalog showing the labels on each drawer, if the group of children is too large to sit directly in front of the cabinet). The teacher explains that it is through the card catalog that the pupils can learn to find independently the materials they want and that while catalogs are sometimes in book form, they are more gen-

Figure 13.2. A Popular and Useful Bookmark. (Designed by H. A. Rey for the Children's Book Council, Inc. Reprinted with permission of the Council.)

SUBJECT GROUPS

100 Philosophy

200 Religion

300 Sociology

400 Language

500 Science

600 Applied Science

700 Arts and Recreation

800 Literature

900 History

000 General Works

Curious George
wants to know about
THE DEWEY DECIMAL SYSTEM

(It may be a bit hard for him to learn but it won't be hard for YOU. Your teacher or librarian will be glad to help you.)

erally in card form in order to be kept up-to-date easily. Then the teacher calls the group's attention to the guide letters on the catalog drawers, which are a means of finding the right drawer, and demonstrates how guide cards save the reader's time. Since elementary school children almost invariably begin to inquire for materials by subject rather than author or title, the teacher now shows them a poster-sized catalog subject card and discusses what questions the card is intended to answer. Finally, as the class studies the labels on the catalog drawers, the teacher lists some subjects or topics that will require a choice between two drawers containing the same letter or that will require finding a letter not shown on the labels.

A second lesson would begin with a review of the poster-sized catalog subject card, proceed to a display of poster-sized cards showing the author and

Figure 13.3. Sample Catalog Subject Card: Fiction.

HORSES—STORIES

HEN   Henry, Marguerite.
         King of the Wind. Illustrated by
         Wesley Dennis. Rand, McNally, c1948.
         175 p. illus.
         Newbery Medal, 1949

        1. Horses—Stories   I. Title

title cards for the same book as the subject card, and culminate in a discussion with the pupils of the information contained on the three cards. The teacher then shows through the opaque projector sample author cards, title cards, and subject cards taken from the catalog in the school library and points out the publisher's name and the copyright date. He or she explains how to find titles of other books written by a favorite author and how to compare dates of books

The media specialist can help students to locate those catalog subject cards that relate to their social studies assignments or special hobbies. (Photo courtesy of National Education Publishing, Joe Di Dio.)

Figure 13.4.   Sample
Catalog Author
Card: Fiction.

```
HEN      Henry, Marguerite.
              King of the Wind. Illustrated by
         Wesley Dennis. Rand, McNally, c1948.
              175 p. illus.
              Newbery Medal, 1949.




         1. Horses—Stories      I. Title
```

Figure 13.5.   Sample
Catalog Title Card:
Fiction.

```
                   King of the Wind

HEN      Henry, Marguerite.
              King of the Wind. Illustrated by
         Wesley Dennis. Rand, McNally, c1948.
              175 p. illus.
              Newbery Medal, 1949
```

on one subject when recency of publication is an important factor. Finally, each pupil is provided with a set of questions based on the cards in one catalog drawer in the library. Since there are not enough drawers to provide one for each pupil in an average-sized class, plans are made for some of the children to read while the others work on the catalog lesson. As pupils complete the catalog assignment, they become readers, viewers, or listeners, and the drawers that they have been using are given to other members of the class.

Figure 13.6. Sample Catalog Subject Card: Nonfiction.

POETRY

821   Stevenson, Robert Louis.
STE   A Child's Garden of Verses. Illus-
         trated by Brian Wildsmith. F. Watts, c1966.

             96 p. illus.

         1. Poetry   I. Title

Figure 13.7. Sample Catalog Author Card: Nonfiction.

821   Stevenson, Robert Louis.
STE   A Child's Garden of Verses. Illus-
         trated by Brian Wildsmith. F. Watts, c1966.

             96 p. illus.

         1. Poetry   I. Title

A third lesson, especially appropriate for sixth graders, would begin with a brief review of author, title, and subject cards, and then proceed to an introduction of cross-reference cards. These "see" and "see also" cards refer the reader from one subject to another.

During other activities that lead to skill acquisition, the pupils may alphabetize sets of discarded catalog cards, demonstrate various ways that a single book may be located in the catalog, or practice locating books on the shelves

A Child's Garden of Verses

821 STE

Stevenson, Robert Louis.
A Child's Garden of Verses. Illustrated by Brian Wildsmith. F. Watts, c1966.

96 p. illus.

Figure 13.8. Sample Catalog Title Card: Nonfiction.

AA 821 STE

Stevenson, Robert Louis

A Child's Garden of Verses (audiorecording) read by Nancy Wickwire and Basil Langton. Spoken Arts SAS-3, 904.

1 phonodisc, 12 in: 33⅓ rpm.

1. Poetry I. Title

Figure 13.9. Sample Catalog Audiovisual Card: Author.

by referring to the card catalog. They may make simplified author, title, and subject cards by using the title pages of ten nonfiction books, or use prepared slips with which to practice locating book titles in the catalog. They may arrange a notebook on the use of the card catalog or find answers to specific questions by using the catalog. The children may make guide cards for some of the drawers, or may interpret the bibliographic data on a few catalog cards. Some may wish to explain how to use the catalog to classmates who had been

Figure 13.10.
Sample Catalog
Cross-Reference
Cards.

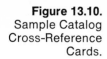

Dinosaurs

see

Animals, Extinct

Transportation

see also

Aeronautics   Railroads
Automobiles   Roads
Bridges   Ships
Cable Cars
Harbors
Motor Buses
Motor Trucks

unable to attend school on the days when the teacher-specialist initiated the study of the card catalog, while others may enjoy demonstrating the use of the catalog to the group through an impromptu skit or dialog. Older boys and girls will be interested in keeping a record of their recreational reading in the form of catalog cards, complete with guide cards, or in using the catalog to compile lists of books on unusual subjects or by favorite authors.

Incidentally, catalog cards for audiovisual materials are filed like any other cards—up to the parentheses that enclose the type of medium. The elements, arrangement, and style of the catalog cards for nonprinted materials are essentially the same as for printed matter. The library media center which uses Dewey numbers for books would use these for audiovisual materials as well. Color-coding of catalog cards for such materials or the use of symbols or abbreviations in place of fully spelled-out media designations is no longer recommended because such techniques emphasize form over content and confuse the catalog users. The AECT uses certain generic media designators (such as AA for audiorecordings, FA for filmstrips, and MA for motion pictures) in an effort to achieve standardized terminology.

Children must gradually gain an understanding of the parts of a book, the publication of books, and the technical vocabulary that relates to books. Early in the second grade the pupils learn about the parts of a book beginning with the spine ("you have a spine, too, that runs down your back") and discover that books are always kept on the shelf with the spines facing out. A few weeks later the children become acquainted with the title page when the librarian brings in several stacks of books with appealing titles, shows them the title pages of several books, and then asks each child to select one book and attempt to locate the title page. By the end of the third grade the pupils have been introduced to three items in the physical makeup of books (front and back covers, spine, and text or body of book) and two printed parts of the book (title page and table of contents).

Third Skill: Understanding the Parts of a Book

Older children become familiar with the parts of a book which precede and follow the main text: frontispiece, title page, copyright page, dedication, table of contents, list of maps—plates—illustrations, foreword, preface, acknowledgments, introduction, appendix, glossary, bibliography, index, and end papers. They may be introduced to the signature (or printed sheet containing a section of a book) and may also participate in a demonstration of the making of a signature by folding, numbering, and cutting large sheets of newsprint. Sixth graders may be taken through the steps involved in the physical production of a book from the original idea to the finished volume, may attend demonstrations on book mending, or may tour local printing plants.

All pupils may enjoy hearing a presentation by an author, printer, publisher, illustrator, or binder who can describe his or her contribution to the evolution of a book. They can make original title pages for book reports, draw book jackets of favorite books to be displayed in the library media center, or create a book individually or in cooperation with their peers. They can occasionally demonstrate the proper handling of books when new sets are distributed for classroom assignments. Sometimes they may be allowed to take apart a discarded volume in order to demonstrate the construction of a book.

Because of the nature of reference tools, children must necessarily acquire the ability to locate and use indexes. They will enjoy comparing the tables of contents to the indexes in several books, but it should be pointed out to them that while the table of contents gives the broad areas of a book's coverage, the index offers a more detailed listing of the contents of that book. A teacher-spe-

Fourth Skill: Using an Index

cialist in Clearlake Oaks, California, for example, has one of the fifth graders draw from a hat a slip of paper containing an easily located subject, such as "the moon," "Abraham Lincoln," or "bluebirds." The child then locates a book which has that subject listed in its table of contents. Presuming that the fifth grader has drawn a slip with the word "bluebirds" written on it, the discussion can soon revolve about an opaque projection of the following initial index entry:

> BLUEBIRDS, 32–48; description, 32–33;
> food, 35, 38–40; migration, 46–48;
> nests, 34, 36–37.

The teacher-specialist reminds the children that when they use the table of contents they are looking for a broad area of information such as a chapter on bluebirds generally. However, if they wish to learn more about bluebird nests in particular, how can they locate this specific information and locate it readily? A few pupils may suggest skimming through the entire chapter, but gradually the class begins to realize that using an index will make the locational task much easier.

In an attempt to help elementary teachers present the index skill, an analysis was made of 106 actual index entries in several curriculum subjects at three grade levels of representative textbooks and elementary encyclopedias. Components of index entries include the following twenty: main topic, page numbers, comma, period, semicolon, hyphen, colon, synonymous subtopic, related but not synonymous subtopic, *see, see also, illus., map, diag., pict.,* underscore, bold face, definitions, pronunciation (both phonetic and with diacritical marks), and others (chart, figure, volume). The number of components became the criterion of complexity; in other words, it was concluded that the larger the number of components the more difficult the entry. Consequently, children must be provided with experiences that will enable them to develop insights into the composite nature of the index skill.

Fifth Skill: Using Encyclopedias

Before children are abruptly plunged into certain kinds of supplementary assignments, they must attain the ability to use encyclopedias to discover information about broad topics. Since many pupils and a few teachers speak of the encyclopedia as though there were only one and it were entitled The Encyclopedia, it is better from the first to have both pupils and teachers refer to encyclopedias by their individual names.

A two-part demonstration is generally effective in teaching discrimination among sets. During the first portion, which emphasizes the number of different encyclopedias available, the children are given a week to look at various sets found in public libraries and homes and then return to class to draw up a composite list of titles. During the second portion, the children become aware of the differences among encyclopedias and the need to comprehend the arrangement and content of each set, for they must examine several identical topics in three or more different sets. An opaque projector can be used during the second part of the demonstration in order to save class time. Publishers of juvenile encyclopedias also supply printed aids for teaching the use of their particular sets.

The three juvenile encyclopedias listed by the American Library Association are *Britannica Junior* (15 vol.), *Compton's Encyclopedia* (24 vol.), and *The World Book Encyclopedia* (22 vol.).[3] All of them use the continuous-revision policy (presently followed by most of the good general encyclopedias, according to the ALA) which means that instead of publishing thoroughly revised numbered editions at spaced intervals, editorial staffs make changes with each annual printing to bring some articles up to date. In addition to the three sets already mentioned, Kister also recommends *The New Book of Knowledge* (20 vol.) and *Young Students Encyclopedia* (16 vol.).[4]

While many children learn at home about general encyclopedias, which are alphabetically arranged and discuss many subjects, they need to be introduced at school to special subject encyclopedias. These bring together related materials under broad topics in a nonalphabetical arrangement; examples include *The Book of Popular Science* (10 vol.) and *Collier's Junior Classics* (10 vol.). A few children may also be interested in learning about one-volume encyclopedias such as *The New Columbia Encyclopedia.*

Encyclopedias are not difficult to use, particularly for pupils already familiar with the card catalog. The principal teaching problems lie in the different methods of indexing (including the use of the cross-reference) and in the different spine markings. To help the children acquire facility in the use of encyclopedias, the teacher-specialist should discuss finding words alphabetically, understanding volume letter(s) or words, using an index or an index volume, and using guide words and cross-references. The teacher should be certain that pupils understand the definition of an encyclopedia and the difference between an encyclopedia and a dictionary. Moreover, the teacher should explain the importance of reading for facts, and then rewriting or retelling those facts honestly in the reader's own words. He or she should also alert older children to the significance of the date of publication and to the use of the encyclopedia for validating material in textbooks and newspapers.

A good exercise for use in beginning research work is to have the class locate pictures in an encyclopedia by using the index to look for illustrations, which are listed in italics. Pencils and paper are not needed as each pupil is asked to locate a picture of a particular person, place, animal, or item. (For example, a child who picks up the last-designated volume in most general sets must find a picture of a zebra.) While the completed task can be evaluated at a glance, the teacher must be sure to assign an interesting list of illustrations that are readily located under the proper headings.

Competence in using the encyclopedia is cumulative and involves alphabetizing, searching, reading, and acquiring-organizing information. These skills are also necessary for using the *yearbooks* which are an essential addition to most encyclopedias. They give new, detailed information on the highlights of the year and supplement the material already in the encyclopedia set. Each yearbook volume has its own index, which usually covers not only the current edition but some of the preceding yearbooks as well.

Sixth Skill: Using Dictionaries

Primary and intermediate pupils alike must possess the ability to use dictionaries to discover information about words. They will enjoy examining different dictionaries which have been set up on the library table and which range from a picture dictionary to an unabridged volume. They may compile a list of the kinds of information that can be found about most words in the dictionary or define terms that relate to dictionary usage. They may engage in contests to see how long it takes to locate a particular word in order to prove the usefulness of guide words.

In the primary grades the children should have an opportunity to become familiar with the picture dictionary. This is a suitable readiness device which generally presents words in most of the following ways: picture and caption, simple explanation of the word, the word used in a sentence, the word used in a quotation, and the word and its antonym used in a phrase.

Although the picture dictionary is less a reference book than an enrichment source (since no dictionary which most primary children can read themselves will be comprehensive enough to function as a real dictionary), picture dictionaries can be used in the classroom, library media center, and home in a variety of ways. They can teach the order of the alphabet, encourage independence in learning words, and teach the users to discover meanings and develop an interest in words through browsing. Through the picture dictionary, the children can recognize various forms of the same letter (uppercase and lowercase, cursive, and printed) and identify various words which begin with the same letter. They can also learn to spell. Should they come from a foreign language background, the picture dictionary will also help them learn English as a second language.

Among the current and better picture dictionaries are:

The Charlie Brown Dictionary (hardcover, Random House, 1973; and paperback, Scholastic, 1973)

The Weekly Reader Beginning Dictionary (trade edition, Grosset & Dunlap, 1973) which is the same as *The Ginn Beginning Dictionary* (text edition, Ginn & Co., 1973)

The Picture Dictionary for Children (Grosset & Dunlap, 1977)

Troll Talking Picture Dictionary (Troll Associates, 1974)

The Cat in the Hat Beginner Book Dictionary (Random House, 1964)

The Golden Picture Dictionary (Western Publishing, 1976)

My First Picture Dictionary (trade edition, Lothrop, Lee & Shepard, 1977; and text edition, Scott, Foresman & Co., 1977)

My Pictionary (trade edition, Lothrop, Lee & Shepard, 1970; and text edition, Scott, Foresman & Co., 1977)

The elementary schoolchild enjoys examining various dictionaries that have been placed on the library media center table.

My Second Picture Dictionary (trade edition, Lothrop, Lee & Shepard, 1971; and text edition, Scott, Foresman & Co., 1977)

The New Golden Dictionary (Western Publishing, 1972)

Storybook Dictionary or *Richard Scarry's Storybook Dictionary* (Western Publishing, 1966)

The Strawberry Picture Dictionary (Strawberry Books, 1974)

The pupils' readiness for instruction in dictionary skills should include recognizing each letter and learning its name, becoming familiar with the location of the letters in relation to each other, learning the consecutive arrangements of letters in the alphabet, and making alphabetical arrangements of words starting with a limited group of different letters.

Middle-grade children should be told about the aids contained in the dictionary for the location of words (the thumb index by letters and the guide words on each page) and the information provided by the dictionary on spelling, abbreviations and other arbitrary signs, pronunciations, definitions, proper geographical names, synonyms, antonyms, English usage, foreign words and phrases, parts of speech, quotations, and word derivation.

While each major area of the dictionary has specific skills that should be presented in the elementary grades, some of the skills are more important than others and should therefore be taught first. A majority of dictionary authorities has graded nineteen items as indispensable.[5] Should a pupil then master all of these items prior to leaving the sixth grade, the teacher can be confident that the child is well prepared in five areas of dictionary matter:

1. **Pronunciation**
   Knowing the pronunciation key being used
   Knowing that correct pronunciation is regional
   Knowing that pronunciations are usage reports

2. **Location**
   Knowing location of pronunciation keys
   Knowing alphabetical order
   Knowing how to locate idioms

3. **Meaning Selection**
   Selecting the meaning to fit the context
   Understanding status or usage labels
   Interpreting status or usage labels
   Knowing how the parts of speech are abbreviated
   Knowing each definition is numbered under different parts of speech

4. **Spelling**
   Knowing there are alternate spellings to some words
   Knowing that the basis of spelling is custom and usage
   Knowing how to locate plural spellings
   Knowing that the dictionary gives the principal point of view
   Knowing that the dictionary shows capitalization
   Knowing homographs
   Knowing that the dictionary shows syllabication of words

5. **History and Structure of the Dictionary**
   Knowing that the dictionary is a guide, not a rule book

Among the current and better dictionaries for the middle-school and upper-elementary grades are these:

American Heritage School Dictionary (Houghton Mifflin, 1972)
Macmillan School Dictionary (Macmillan, 1974)
Random House Dictionary: School Edition (Random House, 1973)
Thorndike-Barnhart Intermediate Dictionary (Doubleday, 1974)
Webster's Intermediate Dictionary (American Book, 1972)

Total entries in these volumes range from 45,000 to 65,000.

Described as strictly elementary-school dictionaries are these current and recommended titles:

The Xerox Intermediate Dictionary (trade edition, Grosset & Dunlap, 1974) which is the same as *The Ginn Intermediate Dictionary* (text edition, Ginn & Co., 1974)

Macmillan Dictionary for Children (trade edition, Macmillan, 1976) which is the same as *Macmillan Beginning Dictionary* (text edition, Macmillan, 1976)

The New Horizon Ladder Dictionary (New American Library, 1970)

Scott, Foresman Beginning Dictionary (trade edition, Doubleday, 1976; and text edition, Scott, Foresman & Co., 1976)

Webster's New Elementary Dictionary (trade edition, G. & C. Merriam Co., 1975; and text edition, American Book Co., 1975)

Total entries in these five volumes range from 9,500 to 34,000.

Elementary school children should be allowed to examine at least one unabridged dictionary in order that they may realize that that is one volume to which they can refer for quick answers to a variety of questions.

Selected activities which teachers may wish to plan with and for their classes **Activities** generally demand that each pupil have a copy of an appropriate dictionary. Less advantaged districts, however, sometimes distribute dictionaries on a one-to-three or one-to-four basis (meaning one dictionary per three or four pupils). Therefore, the sample activities briefly described here may be conducted either as whole-class or group assignments.

1. Drill: What letter comes right before *L?*

   What is the second guide word on page 172?

   On what page can you find a picture of a prehistoric animal?

   How many nouns can you find on page 212? (A small letter *n* will be printed after the word or at the end of the definitions.)

   How many pictures of birds can you find under the *K* section of the dictionary?

   See if you can find the pictures of three musical instruments. List the name of the instrument and the number of the page on which you found its picture.

2. Examine the quarters of the dictionary and list which letters are located in each quarter.

3. Look up the following words and write "yes" after the hyphenated words and "no" after those that are not hyphenated: *baseball, workman, tonguetied, overcoat,* and *takeoff.*

4. Find a homophone for each of the following: *way, ewe, be, our, cent,* and *seen.*

5. Decide which of the two spellings of the following pairs of words is the correct one: *acqueduct/aqueduct, business/busness, calendar/calander,* and *certainly/sertainly.*

6. Substitute synonyms for five words in the following sentence: *The lad with the pallid and morose countenance peered into the murky bayou.*

7. Paraphrase sentences to accommodate general meanings of specific words which are underlined (e.g., Tony looked puzzled. Tony looked as if he didn't understand.)

8. Practice opening the dictionary at a given letter, without thumbing through the pages, on a timed basis.

9. Answer yes-no questions involving words that are not in the present vocabulary of the members (e.g., Can Joan play a *duet* for the mothers' tea?)

10. Find many different meanings for such common words as *safe, husband,* or *signal.*

11. Determine the meaning of one prefix (e.g., *sub*) and then find "sub" words to fill the blanks in a list such as the following:

    A boat that travels under water   sub_____

    An underground electric railway   sub_____

12. Supply one root word and then list other members of the same family (e.g., *kind*).

13. Determine roots of words used in modern advertising (e.g., *Aqua Velva*).

14. Change phonetic spellings of certain words to the regular spellings (e.g., *fikst* to *fixed*).

15. Make up a list of words in which

    ph or *gh* sound like *f*

    ch or *ck* sound like hard *c*

    c, x, and *s* sound like *sh*

16. List the plurals of words like *alumnus, basis, index, stratus,* and *bacillus.*

17. Look up English words which have been adapted or borrowed from other languages, such as *ski, coffee, kimono, sonata,* and *waltz.* Then identify the language in which the word first appeared.

18. Tell whether each of the following is found in the air, on land, or in the water: *sturgeon, tripod, coracle,* and *obelisk.*

19. Write the words for which the following abbreviations stand: *Rev., PO, RFD, pp., dept., riv., a.m., ans.,* and *inc.*

20. Write the phrase or sentence from your dictionary that shows the correct use of the following words: *urge, noble, mellow, rummage,* and *commerce.*

21. Write the abbreviation for the word class of each of the following words: *whereas, hereby, gratis, forever, martial,* and *confident.*

22. Copy from your dictionary the following words, properly divided into syllables: *dirigible, final, nicety,* and *miraculous.*

23. List the guide words connected with each word of the current social studies lesson.

24. Extract root forms of ten words in the weekly spelling lesson (e.g., *unpaved*).

25. Indicate the syllable with the primary stress in a list of ten familiar two-syllable words (e.g., *cartoon*).

The ability to use almanacs, atlases, gazetteers, handbooks, and other special reference sources to discover geographical, historical, biographical, and statistical information becomes an increasing preoccupation of school children from the time that they are first introduced to these volumes until they gradually develop or improve their techniques for independent study. By using late issues of the *World Almanac and Book of Facts* or the *Information Please Almanac,* pupils may participate in a "scavenger hunt" by finding answers to such prepared questions as "How long is the Amazon River?" (in the *World Almanac*) and "What is the seating capacity of the Colosseum in Rome?" (in the *Information Please Almanac*). In some areas of the country where state almanacs are published, the children in California, for example, can discover where the first free public school in California was opened and what is the most widely known use of the California grape.

The pupils themselves may write questions whose answers are found in such references as an atlas ("Through what states does the Susquehanna River flow?" or "What states border Texas?"); a gazetteer ("What is the area of Zaire?" or "Where is the Isle of Man?"); the *Junior Book of Authors* and *More Junior Authors* ("Did Dr. Seuss ever work in the movies?" or "Where was Taro Yashima born?"); *Who's Who in America* ("When did Henry Ketcham create 'Dennis the Menace'?" or "From which service academy did

The ability to use atlases, gazetteers, and other general reference works is a vital library media center skill for pupils in the middle and upper grades. (Photo courtesy of National Education Association Publishing, Joe Di Dio.)

James E. Carter, Jr. graduate?"); or a handbook like Bartlett's *Familiar Quotations* ("Who wrote 'I have a little shadow that goes in and out with me . . .'?" or "What were Nathan Hale's final words?").

The boys and girls can produce a chart or table comparing various atlases or statistical reference books available in the library. They can define specialized words pertaining to gazetteers. They may even find it interesting to examine some dictionary indexes such as the *Illustrations Index,* the *Index to Children's Poetry,* and the *Index to Fairy Tales,* each of which is a separate volume. The class may also enjoy locating in an atlas the places which are mentioned on the front page of the daily newspaper.

Incidentally, for the sake of those teacher-specialists who fear that many of the children in the middle- and upper-elementary grades have not developed sufficient reading skills to be effective users of such tools as *Current Biography, Contemporary Authors,* the *Negro Almanac,* or the *Atlas of American History,* it must be mentioned that the introduction of these tools should best be left to the discretion of the media specialist or teacher-specialist. Some classes can work successfully with these resources and should be properly encouraged to do so. In other classes the introduction of these materials must be postponed until junior high school.

Eighth Skill: Organizing Printed Information and Compiling Bibliographies

As soon as children are mature enough to come to the library media center for reference work, they can begin to acquire the ability to select, organize, interpret, and evaluate information from printed material through skimming, note taking and outlining. Although any number of teaching strategies might be used to develop such research study skills, the four-stage scheme promulgated by Shores and Snoddy appears to be particularly promising. The first stage introduces the skill, clarifying its use or purpose; this could be accomplished through an expository, inquiry, or problem-solving approach. Second stage offers focused practice in a controlled situation demanding a particular skill; sometimes short drill exercises are included at this level. The third stage reinforces or reteaches the first lesson on a specific skill. The final stage of independent application involves assignments requiring the use of the newly learned skill in a content area such as social studies.[6]

Skimming occurs when pupils read at about twice their normal rate, selectively eliminating nearly one-half of the material because they are in a hurry and therefore willing to accept lowered comprehension. They may read only the topic sentence and then let their eyes drift down through the paragraph, picking up a date or a name. Their intention is to get the main thought from each paragraph, with a few specific facts. Drills useful for teaching skimming involve asking a group of pupils (all of whom are reading the same book) to see who will be the first to find a particular fact buried in a given chapter, or who will be the first to locate a subject-matter area in the index, and then report on which pages it can be found in the text; similar activities can be done with dictionaries, encyclopedias, or even telephone books. Skimming is a useful skill that can be consciously developed, although children should not consider it a substitute for other kinds of reading or for study activities.

Since there are procedures and information which elementary pupils are expected to write down for future reference, the technique of *note taking* is a critical one. Its significance as a basis for an outline, for a valuable record, or for critical evaluation of oral or written presentations must be explained to the class. Then the children can be helped to develop some group standards for note taking, including the following:

1. Read or listen first before writing down the information in your own words.
2. Write down only the important facts, rechecking for accuracy whenever possible.
3. Use underlining to indicate emphatic ideas.
4. Never record every word, except for laws, rules, and quotations.

In early grades, note taking is generally a group project culminating in an experience chart. In the middle and upper grades, however, children can be encouraged to keep individual notes (sometimes written on file cards) during a field trip or as they listen to a resource speaker, watch a film, or help prepare a committee report. Older boys and girls should also understand how to use other media for note taking in the modern school, such as transferring pictures, graphs, or diagrams to transparencies for sharing with the class.

Organizing factual material that has been collected and assimilated demands *outlining* ability. While the purpose of an outline is the more significant point for pupils to learn, some attention should also be paid to promoting an understanding of the structure of an outline. Such a form generally reflects a hierarchy of ideas or a sequence of events much like the following example:

I. A main topic demands a roman numeral.

   A. A subtopic requires indentation and a capital letter.
      1. A detail needs indentation and an arabic numeral.
         a. A subdetail must have indentation and a lowercase letter.
      2. Another detail on the same subtopic needs an arabic numeral too.

   B. Another subtopic requires a capital letter too.

II. Another main topic demands another roman numeral.

   A. Subtopic
      1. Detail
         a. Subdetail
      2. Detail
      3. Detail

   B. Subtopic
      1. Detail

C. Subtopic
    1. Detail
    2. Detail

To help beginners learn outlining, the teacher-specialist may read aloud several, short, selected paragraphs from different volumes, asking the pupils promptly after each reading to state the main topic in as few words as possible. The teacher may also deliver a well-organized but informal talk on a popular theme and then outline its major topics, using the board or overhead projector. Sometimes a common experience such as a walking trip or a carefully chosen movie may introduce the class to an outline form. Once an outline has been completed, however, the boys and girls should be reminded that it may serve as the basis for either a written or an oral report.

During their experiences with beginning research children gain a knowledge of the compilation and use of a bibliography. To help the pupils acquire this skill some schools present each sixth grader with a dittoed sheet containing bibliographical forms for books, encyclopedias, and magazines. Then different parts of each form are posted on the flannel board, and the class compares the forms to see the differences in arrangement. In other schools each intermediate pupil brings to class either one book that contains a bibliography or one list of five different books that pertain to a single hobby or sport. The class may also choose to keep a random record of all books and periodicals consulted during the preparation of a report for social studies before deciding to arrange the entries in alphabetical order for the bibliography.

Finally, the school library media center's resources and the teacher-specialist's program of teaching study and research skills must form an integral part of all levels of elementary education, according to Davies, because inquiry and independent study occupy such a strong position in the philosophy of modern education.[7]

Ninth Skill: Using and Evaluating Nonbook Media

Learning how to view and how to listen, and developing the art of perception that evaluation and appreciation of the nonbook media demand, represent two abilities that students must acquire through time, effort, and guided experiences in much the same way that they master the mechanical skills and developmental aspects of reading. Such instruction includes guidance in aiding children to turn naturally to media other than print as forms of communication; it also involves teaching them to realize when nonbook media complement printed materials and when they have no relevance to the task at hand.

While instruction in using many of these resources is being handled on an individualized basis, in one or more classroom lessons the teacher-specialist can demonstrate how to find and read quickly the table of contents (of a magazine) or the index (of a newspaper) and how to evaluate readily the pictures, physical format, and contents of the magazine or paper. The teacher may discuss the kinds of readers to whom the magazine or newspaper would appeal and the types of services that it can render for those readers. The children can bring to class a copy of one of the local papers and summarize at least three of its front-page stories into one statement each. They can examine some of the more popular juvenile magazines as well as some general adult magazines that have been recommended as interesting and informative for pupils in the intermediate grades.

Advanced students may be introduced to the *Readers' Guide to Periodical Literature,* in which over one hundred periodicals are indexed by author and subject. Once the pupils have noted the list of periodicals included and the abbreviations used for each, they should be encouraged to consult the *Readers' Guide* routinely before completing assigned reports.

The teacher-specialist should also acquaint children with vertical-file materials. These are miscellaneous items which are not individually cataloged because of poor physical durability, varied sizes, and short subject treatment. Examples include pamphlets, leaflets, clippings, and unmounted pictures printed on lightweight paper. Such materials often brighten displays in the classroom and hall, and meet the informational needs of both beginning and older readers.

Incidentally, the base collection of nonbook media for a school with 500 or fewer users (according to standards established by the AASL and the AECT) includes 50 to 175 titles of *periodicals and newspapers;* 1,500 to 2,000 *audio recordings* (tapes, cassettes, discs, and audio cards); 500 to 2,000 *filmstrips* (sound and silent); 2,000 to 6,000 *slides and transparencies;* 200 to 500 *models and sculpture reproductions;* 800 to 1,200 *graphics* (posters, art and study prints, maps and globes); 200 to 400 *specimens;* 500 to 1,000 *super 8-mm films* (silent); and access to 3,000 titles of 16-mm and super 8-mm *sound films, videotapes and television reception.*

Tenth Skill: Operating the Audiovisual Equipment

In many school library media centers primary and intermediate pupils alike are being permitted to check out the audiovisual equipment just as they do books. Anyone can learn to operate the basic equipment and children do so more rapidly than adults. Primary boys and girls in Montgomery County, Maryland, for example, learn to operate a record player, a cassette-tape recorder, a listening station, a filmstrip viewer (or previewer), an 8-mm filmloop projector, an opaque projector, a slide viewer (or previewer), an overhead projector, a filmstrip projector, and a microprojector. Intermediate children in the same county become familiar with the operation of a reel-to-reel tape recorder, a slide projector, an 8-mm or 16-mm film projector, and a videotape recorder.[8]

Step-by-step instructions for operating typical equipment found in media centers can be located in most standard audiovisual instruction texts. The teacher or media specialist can demonstrate the proper procedures on an individualized or small-group basis.

The base collection of equipment for a school with 500 or fewer users, according to standards established by the AASL and the AECT, should include:

Filmstrip equipment: ten projectors and thirty viewers

Slide and transparency equipment: six slide projectors, ten slide viewers, ten overhead projectors

16-mm and super 8-mm sound projection and video playback and reception equipment: six units (with two assigned to the media center) plus one more unit per 100 users

Super 8-mm equipment: twenty cartridge-loaded projectors, enough open-reel projectors to accommodate available films plus one more projector per 75 users

Audio equipment: thirty tape recorders and record players, one set of earphones for each audio reproduction unit plus one portable listening unit per 25 users

Opaque projectors: one per media center and one per 500 users (or one per floor in multistory building)

Microform equipment: two readers plus one reader-printer

Microprojectors: one per media center and one or more per school

Learning Experiences through the Grades

The sequence of learning should be developed from kindergarten through the sixth grade, and library media center skills that have been introduced in any one grade must be reviewed and practiced in succeeding grades.

In order that each pupil may be at ease in the school library media center an orientation session should be held for every class at the beginning of the school year before any personal borrowing is done. At this time there are two main concepts which can be brought out in discussion or summarized on the chalkboard:

- *Everyone reads and uses public libraries or school media centers to some extent* because people read for fun, for information they need for school or work, and for information on hobbies or other subjects in which they are especially interested.
- *Everyone wants to know how to get along well in a public library or school media center* so that many people can all use the facility at once, and take out the special materials that each desires.

The principal objectives of the orientation session are: (1) to present the broad range of appealing and attractive books and audiovisual materials available for curricular and personal needs; (2) to facilitate finding these materials by demonstrating their location; and (3) to provide the pupils with an opportunity to browse, examine, and try out these materials before borrowing them for classroom or home use. The atmosphere during orientation is the same as that which prevails throughout all media center activities—informal, relaxed, and warm.

Beginning Grades

The *kindergarten* class should come to the library media center at least once a month. The children can be introduced to the world of books through storytelling, through attractive displays, and through many opportunities to browse. During these visits children learn how to carry a book, how to turn its pages properly, how to replace a book on the shelf, how to place books on a book cart, and how to use book markers. They also begin to develop the habit of relying on the library as a source of information; its facilities are truly an extension of their classroom.

After listening to stories, the five-year-olds should have time to select books from the regular shelves or to sit at tables where the teacher-specialist has placed some new picture books. They can listen to story records, look at filmstrips, or handle flat pictures, models and specimens. Although the children do not check out either book or nonbook materials, they are able to observe the media aides and technicians and thus become acquainted with some of the functions of the center. It is important that kindergartners enjoy their visits to the library media center and learn to become good library citizens; for whatever activity is presented in the center's instructional program for five-year-olds, its prevailing objective is: to present an environment which will instill in the children a love of good materials and the recognition of the library media center as a friendly, helpful place to browse and to work.

Following an initial briefing in the classroom, the *first-grade* children should have a weekly opportunity to go to the center for at least thirty minutes and to check out one book at a time. The teacher-specialist will wish to informally stress the concept of library responsibility and to enumerate the qualifications for personal borrowing.

As six-year-olds listen to the teacher read or recite rhythmic prose and poetry, they continue to gain literary appreciation. As they examine more picture books, they may slowly begin to sense the relationship between illustrations and plot. They can be shown the gross differences between an encyclopedia and a dictionary, and they will begin to realize the importance of alphabetizing as they are introduced to the easy picture dictionaries. To acquaint them with simple informational books, the teacher-specialist can—

1. tell the children that books and people have names, show them books with titles that are names of people, and conclude by displaying books with other kinds of titles;
2. develop the concept that some books tell stories and some books give information;
3. show the children several books that have titles which indicate their contents; and
4. introduce and guide pupils on a restricted basis in the individual use of suitable audiovisual resources according to their ability to handle such media.

As first graders continue to use the school library media center for simple research and to develop independence in the selection of resources, they are also learning to improve their library manners and to practice proper handling of materials. Hopefully they are also discovering public library facilities and beginning to think of books in terms of possible ownership.

The *second grade* should maintain its weekly half-hour visits to the center, listening to stories and sharing reading experiences. The children can refine alphabetizing skills and enjoy simple "location" games in the library media center. They can learn the purpose of the book card and date-due slip, and recall how to sign out and return books independently. They can locate title pages, use tables of contents, read chapter titles, and find page numbers of books. The pupils will also enjoy browsing in simple dictionaries and encyclopedias, and can learn to locate and use more nonbook materials such as primary globes.

The research work done in the kindergarten and first grade is continued in the second grade with little change, as each teacher continues to help young children recognize the center as a source of information and an aid to their classroom and personal work. When second graders have completed their research, they may be asked to present their findings to their peers, thereby involving the use of multimedia resources with which they have become familiar.

Seven-year-olds can be encouraged to confer with their teacher regarding the books they are reading. They should be allowed to check out two books each week, one to read themselves and one to share with their parents in order to further home-school ties and broaden the pleasures of reading. They may also be permitted to check out one nonprinted resource if the school media collection is sufficiently large to allow second graders the privilege of borrowing cassette tapes, story records, or other nonbook items.

In the *third grade* the weekly story period may be continued (if scheduling arrangements can accommodate these older, more sophisticated media center visitors), for creative expression is stimulated with such reading-listening experiences. The children should be taught the difference between fiction and nonfiction, and where books in each of these broad classifications are found in the center. Their information-finding skills will grow as the teacher-specialist points out the table of contents in each book examined and encourages the pupils to identify the names of the title and author on both the cover and title page of every new book they read or share. Their maturing alphabetizing skills, which may even lead to the introduction of a simple card catalog, will involve alphabetizing by first, second, and third letters, and relate to shelving of fiction books. Their reporting skills and their use of the library as a research resource will continue to develop, even among boys and girls reading below grade level.

The children complete the transition from the picture dictionary to the standard beginning dictionary and start to read primary magazines. The teacher-specialist will also find them capable of grouping the books in the classroom by broad subject areas (such as sports, science, and animal stories), and capable of taking care of the shelves and tables in the school library media center and in the class library corner.

Each member of the class should be allowed to check out three books at once from any part of the library media center, and one nonbook reference because the most difficult and most important aim of third-grade library media center instruction is to encourage independent selection of materials which the children can enjoy and comprehend themselves. Their use of public library facilities should be extended, and their observation of library rules reinforced.

By the end of the third grade pupils have learned to:

Locate all kinds of books which interest them.
Use parts of books for desired information.
Consult picture and beginning dictionaries.
Use simple audiovisual materials and equipment for enjoyment and
    information.
Recognize the school media center and the public library as distinct and
    pleasant places as well as sources of information.

Instruction in the care of print and nonprint materials is reviewed briefly with the older boys and girls. It receives special emphasis only in those classes that have enrolled many transfer students. Basic research techniques are frequently mentioned. **Intermediate Grades**

By the time the children have reached the *fourth grade* they are ready to concentrate on technical skills. They can begin work with the card catalog and learn how the call numbers on the catalog cards enables readers, viewers, and listeners to find the resources on the shelves. They can analyze their textbooks as they become familiar with additional parts of a book and the purpose that each serves.

Nine-year-olds recognize the need for orderly arrangement of materials on the shelves, enjoy relay races involving location of books from clues on catalog cards, and can locate main library media center resources for guests. They show their awareness of the varied kinds of materials available in both school and public libraries by embarking on year-round use of such facilities.

At the beginning of the *fifth grade* a comparison of different standard encyclopedia sets will enable the pupils to realize how each set differs as to the number of volumes, method of indexing, location of maps, and signed articles so they may learn to evaluate the various sets in such areas as arrangement, authority, recency of publication, and accuracy of illustrations.

They learn to understand the purpose of the Dewey Decimal System and memorize the ten major divisions with key numbers. They make independent use of the card catalog to locate both book and nonbook materials needed for assignments, and enjoy filing catalog cards in classroom relay activities. They use the dictionary to find new and additional information about their spelling words or reading vocabulary.

Ten-year-olds can become familiar with award-winning books, particularly the Newbery Medal books, and may be persuaded to share some of these through oral book reports. They consult book lists and learn to distinguish among collective biography, individual biography, and fictionalized biography. They should have access to many materials dealing with the American heritage to amplify the theme of their social studies units.

In the *sixth grade* more advanced research tools should be introduced, including yearbooks of various types, the atlas, and gazetteer, and the unabridged dictionary, for the children are becoming more efficient in note taking, outlining, and making short bibliographies. They are more capable of using several reference sources independently, including nonbook materials, and can demonstrate their research findings in debates and committee reports.

The pupils begin to understand the provisions for cross-references made in different encyclopedia sets. They use the dictionary in order to trace the etymology of words and complete crossword puzzles. They are able to interpret the information contained on catalog cards for both book and nonbook materials, becoming acquainted with cross-reference cards which help them locate additional kinds of data. Finally, in their work with the Dewey Decimal System, the children begin to understand the breakdown of the ten major classifications into subclasses, and they are able to locate subheadings on the shelves, as identified by guide tabs; pupils also learn how individual biography is shelved.

The sixth graders in one Washington school keep individual reading records as an incentive to discover different types of books in the library media center. Upon completing a book, they list on a sheet of paper the title, the author's name, the publisher's name, the copyright date, the type of book it was, and the month that it was read; and then assign a number to the title. The number is then placed in one of two circles posted on the reading record: the first has divisions for various kinds of fiction (sports, folk and fairy tales, home and family, etc.) and the second has divisions for the major areas of nonfiction according to the Dewey System. In this way, the children can determine promptly which groups of books they have not yet explored and may, hopefully, remedy the imbalance with their next selections.

By the end of the sixth grade pupils have learned to:

Consult encyclopedias, atlases, gazetteers, and dictionaries.
Update information on a topic by reading periodicals, pamphlets, and newspapers.
Select and use audiovisual materials with discrimination and independence.
Obtain inspiration and stimulation from fiction, poetry, and biography.
Integrate information taken from various media and from different information sources and organize it into a sequential entity.
Explore new fields of interest through print and nonprint materials.
Work independently in the library media center due to an understanding of the classification of resources provided by the Dewey Decimal System.

Worksheets on library media center skills have been designed by some school districts for both the primary and intermediate grades. Teachers may use them for either enrichment, follow-up, or diagnostic experiences. A sample worksheet for upper primary children runs as follows:

Library Terms: author, title, title page, table of contents, illustrator, illustration

Directions: Read the sentences below and fill in the blank spaces with the correct library term.

Sentences:
1. We call the person who draws pictures for a book the _____.
2. The name of a book is called the _____.
3. The _____ is a picture found in a book.
4. The _____ is a person who writes a book.
5. We look in the _____ if we want to find the chapters in a book in page number order.
6. The author's name is found on the _____.

A sample worksheet for older children runs as follows:

Outside Guides:

A–Ba	F–Ge	L–Lo	O–P	Su–T
Be–C	Gi–H	Lu–Mi	Q–Ri	U–W
D–E	I–K	Mo–N	Ro–St	X–Z

Directions: Above is a diagram of a card catalog showing the drawers with the guide letters on them. Choose the guide letters of the drawer in which each of the following materials will be found.

Materials:
1. A book whose subject is Japan. _____
2. A book whose title is *101 Hand Puppets*. _____
3. A book whose author is Dr. Seuss. _____
4. A cassette whose title is *Many Moons*. _____
5. A book whose subject is Mexico. _____

To reinforce his or her presentations on various library media skills and to help make pupils feel at ease with books and library media center facilities, the teacher-specialist may occasionally plan to use a learning game appropriate for children of middle and intermediate grades. Ten suggested games follow, some of which may be played in either the school library media center or the classroom.

Big Stack (for the library media center only)	1. The class is divided evenly into teams or pairs, each of which receives a "big stack" of book cards that must be returned to the proper volumes on the shelves.
	2. All the players walk about the library media center busily until the teacher-specialist calls time.
	3. They then return to their seats and listen as the specialist checks the scores: one point added for correct pocketing and one point subtracted for each error.
	4. The team or pair with the highest score wins the game.

| Hidden Titles (for the library media center only) | 1. The class is divided evenly into teams. Each team receives a different paragraph or story prepared by the teacher-specialist and formulated primarily on titles of books available in the library media center; for example, |

> It was nine days to Christmas when Mei Li asked Madeline, "May I bring a friend, Cinderella, on our trip?" "Yes," said Madeline. "There's always room for one more." The girls then sailed for the little island on a boat which had to stop once to make way for ducklings. When the girls arrived, Mei Li said, "When the rooster crows, we will look for a tree to decorate for Christmas." So they each said a prayer for a child and went to sleep. Cinderella dreamed of the animals of the Bible, Mei Li dreamed of white snow, bright snow, and Madeline dreamed of Baboushka and the Three Kings...

2. The first player on each team goes to the card catalog in order to underline correctly one of the "hidden titles" appearing on the mimeographed sheet. When the player has finished checking, he or she hands the sheet to the second player.
3. When all the team players have finished checking, the last one gives the sheet to a Committee of Experts, appointed by the class president or the teacher.
4. The team that has located the greatest number of hidden titles properly within a designated time wins the game.

Hot Shelf (for the library media center only)	1. The pupil chosen to be "It" selects one card from a pile of cards of names of authors whose books are in the center.
	2. "It" must try to locate the shelf on which those books have been placed. The class is permitted to call out "Hot," "Warm," or "Cold" as "It" approaches or misses the crucial "hot shelf."
	3. When "It" has finally placed the author card on the hot shelf, he or she chooses another boy or girl to become "It."
	4. Should "It" fail to locate the hot shelf within a reasonable period of time, the teacher-specialist selects another pupil to be "It."

| Library Cart (for either the classroom or the library media center) | 1. The class is evenly divided into teams. Each team has one captain and several players who are "books." |
| | 2. Each captain is given a sheet, listing as many call numbers as there are "books" on the team. The captain assigns one call number to each "book." |

3. At a signal from the teacher-specialist, each captain tries to assemble his or her "books" in correct order for the "library shelving cart."
4. The first library cart to be arranged correctly wins the game.

Lost in Space (for the classroom only)

1. The class is divided evenly into teams whose players sit in rows.
2. The first player on each team is given a pencil and a large sheet of blank paper. At a given signal, this player must properly position on the future map any area of the school media center (e.g., the vertical files) that he or she wishes.
3. The player then quickly passes on the map to the second player, who must label a different area on the map before forwarding it to the third player.
4. The team that first completes its map correctly with no duplications has proven that it will never be "lost in space" at the media center and therefore wins the game.

Match Box (for either the classroom or the library media center)

1. The class is divided into two equal groups.
2. Each member of the first group receives a sealed slip containing a Dewey Decimal Classification System number. Each member of the second group receives a sealed slip containing the name of a subject corresponding to one of the classification numbers held by members of the first group.
3. At a signal from the teacher-specialist, all the slips are opened. The members scatter about the room, trying to match numbers and subjects. The first "match box" wins the game.

Misspell (for either the classroom or the library media center)

1. The class or group is evenly divided into teams whose members are seated in rows.
2. On the first desk (or table) in each row are placed a copy of the class dictionary, a pencil, an empty red box, and a blue box filled with slips. Each slip contains three spellings of a single word, of which only one is correct and appears in the class dictionary.
3. At a signal from the teacher-specialist, the first player on each team draws one slip from the blue box, checks the spellings in the dictionary, circles the correct spelling, and drops the slip in the red box. The first player then moves to the end of the row, all the other team members move up one desk, and the game continues.
4. The winning team has proved that it cannot "misspell" when it has been able to empty its blue box of slips first, and when its red-box entries have been checked by a class committee or the teacher-specialist.

Order Please (for the classroom only)

1. The class is evenly divided into teams.
2. On the chalkboard in front of each team is written or placed a list of authors' names which are not in alphabetical order. Each team receives a different list, and that list always contains one more name than there are players on that team.

3. At a signal from the teacher-specialist, the first player on each team walks to the board and marks with the numeral 1 the author's name which should appear in the initial position on that list. The first player then returns to his or her seat and the second player goes to the board to indicate the second name in alphabetical order with the numeral 2.
4. The first team to mark all of its authors' names properly wins the Order Please game.

Quiz in a Box (for either the classroom or the library media center)

1. A panel composed of six "experts" (preferably one pupil from each row or group of desks) is assembled in front of the class.
2. The teacher-specialist, class president, or pupil appointee serves as monitor for Quiz in a Box. He or she draws from a covered box a slip containing a prepared question or performance task for each expert, in turn. The monitor reads aloud the task (e.g., using one of the assembled reference books) or multiple-choice question. Later the monitor checks the expert's response, with the answer indicated at the bottom of the slip.
3. Should one expert make the wrong response, the next in line must attempt the same task or question.
4. The pupil expert with the highest score wins the round and becomes the next monitor for Quiz in a Box.

Shelf Fever (for the library media center only)

1. The class or group is divided into two teams.
2. The first player on each team chooses one card from a large box of cards with book titles on them. The player then uses the card catalog to find the call number of the title on the card. He or she then removes the book from the shelf and hands it to the second player on the team.
3. The second player promptly returns the book to the shelf. Then he or she touches the shoulder of the third player, who chooses a card and follows the actions of the first player.
4. The game continues until every odd-numbered player has removed his or her chosen book and every even-numbered player has reshelved a book.
5. The team which performs best within a designated period of time is the winner of Shelf Fever.

The Exceptional Child and the Library Media Center

The concept of the school library media center as the chief source of instructional materials should be extended to the service of the exceptional child.[9] Whether that pupil comes to the center alone or with regular classes, the experiences through which the media specialist guides him or her are similar to those offered to other children.

To compensate for the reading deficiencies of *the hearing handicapped,* the specialist chooses simple materials on a high interest level commensurate with the maturity development of the pupil. The visual is emphasized in an effort to provide experiences that cannot be obtained through audition—films, filmstrips with printed copies of the narrative, film loops, art and study prints, maps and globes, models and specimens. From the U.S. Office of Education have come captioned classroom films for the hard-of-hearing.

Since much of the school program is geared toward learning through vision, *the visually handicapped* must be encouraged by the media specialist to utilize all their capabilities. The specialist must provide tapes and records of stories suitable for the interests and maturity of the visually limited children (including some stories of the achievements of persons with visual handicaps), records and cassettes of music of all kinds, and aids to the reading/sharing of experiences (including magnifying glasses, blank tapes and primary typewriters). Books that the media specialist purchases for the visually limited should be printed in large, clear type (preferably 24 point) on white paper so that print and pictures stand out distinctly; they should have lines that are widely spaced with ample margins. The specialist may receive sources of materials for visually handicapped pupils from the Division of the Blind and Physically Handicapped, Library of Congress, Washington, D.C. 20540; and from the American Foundation for the Blind, Inc. (Publications Division), New York 10011.

In providing for *the mentally retarded* the media specialist recognizes that few retarded pupils have a reading ability above the fourth-grade level and that all have difficulty with abstract ideas. The specialist therefore selects magazines on arts/crafts/hobbies, simple fiction and well-illustrated information books, picture and "easy" books, combination kits of picture book/filmstrip/cassette, collections of models and prints associated with science and social studies, and games and toys. The specialist may also prepare tapes of literature which the children would enjoy but cannot read.

To meet the interests and needs of *the emotionally disturbed* the teacher or media specialist chooses print and non-print materials which are stimulating (but relatively easy) and which may be used individually to provide a necessary break from group activities. Wide use of bibliotherapy whereby disturbed pupils can identify with book characters is also recommended.

Due to the difficulty which *the physically handicapped* have in getting to the public library and to other resource places, they must often depend solely upon the school library media center. The materials collection for these children must be extensive and include many paperbacks (due to light weight), audiovisual resources (which can be easily handled), periodicals, high-interest low-vocabulary books, materials about particular disabilities, and reference collections. To provide vicarious excitement there should be a larger number of books in the fiction category than in the nonfiction. And all materials should be accessibly located so that they can be readily removed from and returned to the shelves by the children without assistance.

To satisfy the wide range of interests of *the gifted* the media specialist must provide an expanded collection of reference sources, absorbing stories with contemporary themes, a rich selection of folklore/legend/poetry, all kinds of audiovisual materials, books on arts and hobbies, and advanced print and nonprint information sources. All of these materials are needed to challenge the potential of gifted children and to develop their powers of critical thinking.

Evaluation of Pupils' Progress

There are both formal standardized and informal teacher-made written tests for evaluating library media center skills among elementary school children.

Sample items (with correct answers circled) from an achievement test on library media skills which the teacher-specialist could devise and administer to intermediate grade children are as follows:

1. There are three main types of catalog cards. Two of them are known as the author and subject cards, and the third is:
   a. the book card
   (b.) the title card
   c. the date-due card
   d. the circulation card
2. A list of subjects arranged in alphabetical order at the back of the book is called:
   a. a table of contents
   b. a title page
   c. a glossary
   (d.) an index
3. To find out how many resources your school library media center has about California, you would use:
   a. a magazine about new books
   b. the Dewey Decimal System of Classification
   (c.) the card catalog
   d. the encyclopedia
4. When you are looking at books on the shelves, the call number is found:
   (a.) on the spine of the book
   b. on the pocket
   c. on the title page
   d. on the table of contents
5. In looking up information about a person in the card catalog or encyclopedia, you would look up the person alphabetically by his or her:
   a. first name
   (b.) last name
   c. middle name
   d. initials
6. On the catalog card the call number is found at:
   (a.) the upper left-hand corner
   b. the bottom of the card
   c. the middle of the card
   d. the bottom right-hand corner

7. Cards in the card catalog which have "see" and "see also" on them are called:
   a. author cards
   b. guide cards
   c. cross-reference cards
   d. subject cards

There are also standardized study-skills tests designed to measure the ability of elementary pupils to use library catalog cards, atlases, almanacs, indexes, books, encyclopedias, maps, and graphs. Specimen sets of two well-reviewed tests may be purchased from—

1. Science Research Associates of Chicago, which publish the *SRA Achievement Series: Work-Study Skills* (Blue Level for grades 4.5 to 6.5 and Green Level for grades 6.5 to 8.5), available in two forms for each level; administration time runs from seventy to eighty minutes;
2. McGraw-Hill Book Company of New York, which publishes the *Comprehensive Tests of Basic Skills: Study Skills* (Level 1, grades 2.5 to 4.0; Level 2, grades 4.0 to 6.0, and Level 3, grades 6.0 to 8.0), available in two forms for each level; administration time runs from twenty-one to fifty minutes, depending upon the form and level.

Discussion Questions

1. How can the school media center help remedial readers?
2. Is it as important to have a well-staffed library media center in each elementary school as it is to have one in every secondary school? How can teachers persuade taxpayers to fund more such centers for young children?
3. Should an elementary school media center be open during the summer months? Should it be open on Saturdays during the regular school year?
4. How can parents assist in the media center?

Suggested Projects

1. Plan a library corner for a third-grade classroom.
2. Make a card catalog, using discarded shoe boxes for file drawers. Be sure to label each "drawer" carefully.
3. Inquire of several elementary school media specialists which teaching strategies and materials each has found to be especially useful in presenting library media skills to boys and girls.
4. Prepare a bulletin board on the Dewey Decimal System which might be used in the fifth grade.
5. Visit the children's room of the main public library in your community and determine how you as a classroom teacher could best utilize its resources.
6. Set up the learning centers on library media center skills shown in Figures 13.11 and 13.12.

Related Readings

Askov, E. N.; Kamm, K.; and Klumb, R. 1977. "Study Skill Mastery Among Elementary School Teachers." *Reading Teacher* 30: 485–88.

Figure 13.11. Language Arts Learning Center: Library Media Center Skills.

TYPE OF CENTER:	Alphabetizing Drills—Dictionary	TIME: 15–20 minutes
GRADE LEVEL:	3–5	NUMBER OF STUDENTS: Number that can work in comfort

INSTRUCTIONAL OBJECTIVE:

The students should be able to alphabetize names they see every day.

MATERIALS:

State map, list of city names on the map, pictures of students and list of students' names, dictionary, display board, directions.

DIRECTIONS TO STUDENTS:

1. Bring pencil and paper to the center.
2. Write the names of all the students in this class in alphabetical order. The list on the left will help you be sure you include everyone.
3. Look at the state map of the towns and cities given in the list on the right.
4. Write the names of the towns and cities given on the list in alphabetical order.
5. Check your answers by looking at the self-check, labeled Part A and Part B, on the back of the center.

STUDENT ASSESSMENT:

Students will compare answers with classmates.

Source: From *Language Arts Learning Centers and Activities* by Angela Reeke and James Laffey. Copyright 1979 by Goodyear Publishing Company. Reprinted by permission.

Baskin, B., and Harris, K., eds. 1976. *The Special Child in the Library*. Chicago: American Library Association.

Dresang, E. T. 1977. "There Are No Other Children: Special Children in the Library Media Center." *School Library Journal* 24: 19–23.

James, J. H. 1977. "Adapting the School Library to Early Childhood Education Programs." *Reading Improvement* 14: 248–55.

Mattleman, M. S., and Blake, H. 1977. "Study Skills: Prescriptions for Survival." *Language Arts* 54: 925–27.

Parke, B. W. 1978. "Finding Out for Themselves." *Teacher* 95: 87–88.

Prostano, E. T., and Prostano, J. S. 1977. *The School Library Media Center*. 2nd ed. Littleton, Colorado: Libraries Unlimited, Inc.

Figure 13.12. Language Arts Learning Center: Library Media Center Skills.

TYPE OF CENTER: Library Skills—Biography

GRADE LEVEL: 5–6

INSTRUCTIONAL
OBJECTIVE: The students should be able to use a biographical subject card in the card catalog to locate books, filmstrips, or records.

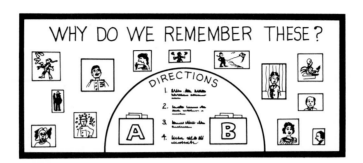

MATERIALS: Bulletin board, pictures of famous people, two boxes, pencils, index cards, card catalog.

DIRECTIONS
TO STUDENTS:
1. Find out why *five* of the people whose pictures are on display are famous. Use an index card from Box A and list your sources and page numbers.
2. Use the card catalog to find one book, filmstrip, or record about one of these men or women. List it on another index card from Box A:

    Example: 1. <u>Thomas A. Edison,</u>   <u>inventor</u>
                 (person's name)   (fame)
              Biography: <u>   </u>
                                 (media)   (title)

3. Put your name on the bottom of the cards.
4. After you have completed your research, put your finished cards in Box B.

EVALUATION: The teacher or aide will check the cards to determine if the objective has been attained.

SUGGESTED
NAMES:

Robert E. Lee	Eleanor Roosevelt	Winston Churchill
Amelia Earhart	Babe Ruth	Ralph Nader
Benjamin Franklin	Thomas Paine	Charles Dickens
John Glenn	Henry Ford	Margaret Mead
John Kennedy	Dwight D. Eisenhower	Anwar Sadat

Source: From *Language Arts Learning Centers and Activities* by Angela Reeke and James Laffey. Copyright 1979 by Goodyear Publishing Company. Reprinted by permission.

Reeves, T. C., and Atkinson, F. D. 1977. "Stimulating Creativity in the Media Center." *Audiovisual Instruction* 22: 34–35.

Wehmeyer, L. B. 1975. *The School Library Volunteer.* Littleton, Colorado: Libraries Unlimited, Inc.

Zeitz, P. 1978. "Personal Dictionaries." *Teacher* 96: 138–42.

English for Speakers of Other Languages

14

Goals of program for teaching English as a second language

Principles of the FLES method which is used to teach English to non-English speakers

The stages of reading development in the ESOL program

Kinds of writing activities in the ESOL program

Standard English is the language system that is habitually used, with some regional variations, by the majority of educated English-speaking persons in the United States. It is the level of language that facilitates communication in a highly complex and interdependent society.

Yet an estimated five million school-aged children in this country are native speakers of languages other than English, and more than four million of these are Spanish-speaking children.[1] These children have experienced a frequent lack of success in the educational institution due to their inability to understand and function in the English-speaking culture and their inability to understand and speak a form of English acceptable in the school setting. Due to this underdevelopment in oral language, the superimposing of the intricate tasks of reading and writing the English language has met in the past with phenomenal failure and its accompanying catastrophic losses in human resources.

Beginning in 1968, however, with the passage of the Bilingual Education Act (Title VII, ESEA—Elementary and Secondary Education Act), there has been a slow but dramatic shift. Millions of dollars have since been spent on *bilingual education,* defined in the legislation as education in two languages, one of which is English. Interpretations of the landmark United States Supreme Court decision of *Lau* v. *Nichols* (1974) suggest that any school division enrolling a minimum of ten to twenty students of limited English-speaking ability must consider offering a bilingual program.

In *Lau* v. *Nichols* the Court was concerned about 1,800 students in the San Francisco school system who did not speak English. The Court decided that it is discriminatory not to provide for pupils who cannot participate in instruction in which English is the language medium. It referred to the guidelines issued earlier by the Department of Health, Education, and Welfare concerning school districts that were federally funded:

413

> Where inability to speak and understand the English language excludes
> national origin-minority group children from effective participation in the
> educational program offered by a school district, the district must take
> affirmative steps to rectify the language deficiency in order to open its
> instructional program to these students. (35 Fed. Reg., 11595).

The Court explained that since basic English skills are at the very core of what public schools teach, the imposition of a requirement that before children can effectively participate in the educational program they must have already acquired those English skills is to make a mockery of public education. Children who do not understand English are certain to find their classroom experiences wholly incomprehensible and in no way meaningful.

Consequently, an integral part of any bilingual education program in the United States is English for Speakers of Other Languages (ESOL). It may however also be used as part of a monolingual program. Program goals will therefore vary in terms of the emphasis placed upon maintaining the pupils' home language and culture but the importance of teaching English as a second language is basic to both programs.

Monolingual programs are sometimes offered in schools located in ports of entry (like Washington, D.C., New York, Boston, Seattle, Los Angeles, and Chicago) that have heterogeneous enrollments. Saville-Troike cites a specific example from the District of Columbia in which one elementary school reported having sixty non-English-speaking children listed as follows: fourteen speakers of Spanish; eight French speakers; six Chinese; four Korean; three Hindi; two each Nigerian, Italian, German, Twi, Laotian, and Swiss-German; and one each Vietnamese, Hausa, Amharic, Meuda, Swedish, Russian, Czech, Dutch, Japanese, Indonesian, Ndu, Portuguese, and one other unspecified African language.[2]

The elementary school program must therefore provide a structured learning situation that will help all of these students become participating members of the classroom and the total community. Such an ESOL program recognizes the following:

1. Children enter school with good control of the sound system and structure of their native language. While their language may not meet the accepted level of usage employed by the educated adults in their culture, it is practical and functional from the children's point of view in terms of their communication needs in their own environment.
2. Non-English-speaking children bring to school a well-developed set of personal concepts that have grown out of their own experience. The teacher must not assume that the children lack an experiential base which can serve as a starting point for instruction. Nor should the teacher believe that their basic concepts are always and totally different from those of native speakers of English.
3. The range and distribution of intelligence in a group of non-English-speaking pupils are identical to those found in a similar group of English-speak-

ing pupils. Although instruments that adequately measure potential do not seem to exist today, a creditable job of evaluating pupil performance can be done through individual interviews and through the judgment of trained personnel knowledgeable about both the children and their cultures.

4. Non-English-speaking children have the same human needs as their English-speaking classmates. Their psychological needs, for example, including a positive self-image, are as intense as those of children who speak English fluently.

5. While children are learning a second tongue, their thought processes will probably continue in their first language since that is the language in which they have learned to think and in which they feel comfortable. The first language may remain their preferred language for communication in many social situations even after the children have become fluent in standard English.

Such an ESOL program incorporates four general goals for learning English as a second language. First, students must be able to carry on and understand a conversation with a native English speaker on topics of interest to persons of their peer group. Secondly, students must be able to read materials in English with comprehension, ease, and enjoyment, consistent with their level of oral proficiency. Thirdly, students must be able to write correctly, and in time creatively, in English consistent with their level of oral proficiency. And finally, students must recognize the differences between their own culture and that of their English-speaking peers, as expressed through the various arts.[3]

ESOL pupils are taught English as it is used by a native speaker in order that they may attain maximum mobility within the community. Their teacher may be a language specialist who travels within the school or district or a regular classroom teacher trained in second language methodology. At least one research study has concluded that the latter teacher is the preferred choice because he or she can readily incorporate ESOL instruction into many curricular areas throughout the day.[4]

FLES Method: Introduction

The prevailing approach to teaching a second language to these children is the FLES (Foreign Language in the Elementary School) method which shares many similarities with the audio-lingual method used at the secondary school level. Its major manifestations are the dialog approach and the story or narrative approach. It is based on the following principles:

1. *The spoken language has primacy.* Language is sound so the ear and the tongue must be trained first and the skills of listening and speaking developed before the skills of reading and writing. Any structural or vocabulary item to be learned is first presented orally. Teachers cannot afford to give only superficial attention to the oral nature of language and rush the pupils into reading and writing prematurely because language is initially speech. Listening and speaking are basic to the later stages of literacy.

2. *Words are presented in meaningful context.* Effective communication demands responses in situations simulating true life. The sounds of the foreign language are given meaning by relating them to actions and objects contained in these situations. The familiarity of a dialog or narrative setting enables children to participate in activities which are within the realm of their interests, ages, and experiences. Knowledge of language which is meaningful in everyday situations is thereby developed.

   Vocabulary is accompanied by approximate contextual equivalents, and, whenever feasible, meanings are sought in terms of the target culture. For instructional purposes, word lists are not used, and the acquisition of a large number of vocabulary items is generally deferred to a later stage of language learning. Structural patterns are presented instead of isolated words, for communication is based on such patterns.

3. *Reading and writing are of secondary importance, at least initially.* Speech, not writing, is the basis for language. For the most part, writing is no more than an incomplete and inconsistent symbolization of the communication process associated with language and many language communities in the world never develop a writing system or a subsequent need for reading.

Reading and writing skills are withheld from elementary school second language students until they have learned to hear and speak the second language. In that way reading and writing can be natural developments of the students' growth, just as they are in the students' native language. Even in bilingual programs, it is important to withhold the written language of one of the languages being taught so that students are not faced with a source of real confusion: two sets of sounds for the same symbols.

For many months elementary school pupils read and write only what they have already heard and said. Written language is not used to explain the spoken language, and the major portion of the class period is spent refining and expanding the listening and speaking skills even after reading and writing have been introduced.

4. *Basic language patterns are overlearned.* Children need a great deal of exposure to individual language patterns in a wide variety of contexts if there is to be long-term learning. By means of extensive practice, pupils can acquire a large number of semiautomatic patterns which they can use to send and receive their own messages. Certain patterns including subject-verb agreement and noun-adjective agreement should be practiced until their use is completely automatic. Only then can the pupils devote their attention to other parts of the message which require more "thinking." By overlearning certain basic sentence patterns and manipulating them in a variety of meaningful contexts, the children will be able to choose from among the patterns to produce independent speech.

5. *Grammar is caught, not taught.* By hearing and using language patterns in context, children discover the regularities (and irregularities) of the language being used. The nomenclature for parts of speech or verb tenses has no place in the second language curriculum until at least the sixth grade.

6. *There is minimal use of the pupils' native language.* Most instruction at this level can be in the second language through direct association of the words and phrases of that language with realistic situations. The process is aided through the extensive use of realia and visuals. According to a recent ten-year study of FLES in England, France, and Wales, reported by Clare Burstall et al., considerable time is saved by using the second language exclusively.[5]

7. *Speech is rendered at normal speed—the slow conversational speed of a native speaker.* In this way students will be able to understand (and be understood by) native speakers from the very onset of their instruction. Slowing speech down in an attempt to help children learn more easily merely distorts rhythms and intonations and makes later learning more difficult.

8. *Culture study is an essential part of language learning.* The anthropological concept of culture, which stresses daily social patterns of the native speakers, is a vital aspect of second language study. Children must learn to respond in realistic situations which are culturally accurate and which closely approximate contemporary life. Dialogs, games and stories should there-

fore be based on the contemporary culture of the area(s) where the language is spoken.

9. *Contrastive analysis is a tool for the teacher.* Contrastive analysis, or contrastive linguistics, compares the native tongue of the learner with the language introduced in the classroom. Such information about the differences between languages should not be presented in organized form to children. However, it is useful to the teacher in his or her planning and preparation because it points up areas of interference and unusual difficulty. A rating scale outlining some of these areas which exist between the English language and the language spoken by the majority of ESOL students—Spanish —is presented in Figure 14.1. It has been made available by the American Council on the Teaching of Foreign Languages (ACTFL) for individual evaluation of the oral language of ESOL pupils.[6]

FLES Method: Oral Skills

The classroom teacher of ESOL pupils must improve the oral English skills of those children before introducing reading and writing.

The Dialog

In order to have a basis from which the vocabulary, structures, and cultural facts can be developed into meaningful, contextual practice, a dialog is often used. A dialog is simply an exchange of conversation between two or more people about a specific topic. For use in the elementary school classroom, it usually presents or suggests only a portion of an entire episode. A well-written (or chosen) dialog can:

1. Approximate closely the real-life situations in which language operates.
2. Insure learning continuity, for items can be reviewed, expanded, and put into different contexts by their judicious inclusion in several dialogs.
3. Point up the fact that communication is the purpose of language.
4. Be geared to individual interests within the classroom, as different topics become centers of discussion.
5. Be used at all grade levels since the simple two-way conversation composed of short sentences progresses to the group conversation with longer, more complex sentence structures.
6. Help the children observe cultural implications with little or no explanation in their native language.
7. Teach culturally authentic gestures.
8. Be both informal and contemporary.
9. Have dramatic potential.

Steps in Presentation

Four stages generally comprise the presentation of the dialog to an elementary ESOL class, with the initial two including listening only and the final two concerned with both listening and speaking skills. The sequential steps are:

1. *Explanation.* The teacher describes briefly, and once only, the setting of the dialog. He or she may use visuals, puppets, or pantomime.

Figure 14.1. Oral Language Rating Scale Indicating Areas of Interference and Difficulty for Spanish-Speaking ESOL Pupils. Source: *Michigan Oral Language Series* (New York: ACTFL, 1970).

Oral Language Rating	Spanish Interference	5 Never	4 Almost Never	3 Some-times	2 Usually	1 Almost Always	0 Always

School _____ **Date** _____

Name _____

Grade _____ **Teacher** _____

Pronunciation (Sounds): Distinguishes between vowel sounds such as *sheep-ship, cut-cat, cut-cot, pool-pull,* and between consonant sounds as *sink-zinc, vote-boat, sink-think, yellow-jello, cheap-jeep.* ____ ____ ____ ____ ____ ____

Pronunciation (Clusters): Pronounces initial consonant clusters as in *school, speak, study,* and final consonant clusters as in *land, fast, old, box, act, desk, pulled, touched.* ____ ____ ____ ____ ____ ____

Pronunciation (Suprasegmentals): Pronounces sentences with appropriate rhythm, stress, pause, and pitch. ____ ____ ____ ____ ____ ____

Pronouns: Uses appropriate pronoun forms in subject position (*I, he, she,* etc.), in object position (*me, him, her,* etc.) and possessives (*my, mine; her, hers;* etc.). ____ ____ ____ ____ ____ ____

Negative: Uses *not* to express the negative after forms of *be* (*Bill is not here.*) and between auxiliary and verb in other sequences (*Bill was not talking. Bill did not talk.*). Uses singular rather than double negative. ____ ____ ____ ____ ____ ____

Noun Modifier: Uses adjectives appropriately, as in *the big dog* as opposed to *the dog big* and *Is the dog big?* as opposed to *Is big the dog?.* ____ ____ ____ ____ ____ ____

Comparison: Uses the correct form of comparison such as *bigger, biggest, more beautiful, most beautiful,* rather than *more bigger, beautifuller.* ____ ____ ____ ____ ____ ____

Present Tense: Uses the appropriate present forms of regular verbs, with subject-verb agreement when *he* or *she* is used as subject, as in *He walks,* rather than *He walk.* ____ ____ ____ ____ ____ ____

Plurals: Distinguishes between singular and plural in regular forms such as *dog-dogs, boot-boots, horse-horses,* and in irregular forms such as *foot-feet, knife-knives.* ____ ____ ____ ____ ____ ____

Past and Perfect Tenses: Uses the past forms of regular verbs as in *walk-walked, glue-glued, land-landed,* and of irregular verbs as in *go-went-gone, dig-dug, cut-cut.* ____ ____ ____ ____ ____ ____

Uses of Be: Uses appropriate forms of *be* as an auxiliary and as a verb. ____ ____ ____ ____ ____ ____

Uses of Do: Uses appropriate forms of *do* in questions, answers, and in negative statements. ____ ____ ____ ____ ____ ____

Future Tense: Uses the appropriate future forms of regular verbs as in *run-will run.* ____ ____ ____ ____ ____ ____

Possessive: Uses appropriate possessive forms as in *John's wagon.* ____ ____ ____ ____ ____ ____

2. *Modeling*. The teacher recites the memorized dialog at a natural tempo while walking among the pupils so that each may hear his or her voice at close range. As the teacher assumes different roles in the dialog, he or she may (a) point to stick figures on the chalkboard; (b) use puppets; (c) change places in the room to denote a change in parts; or (d) change distinguishing properties (hats, tools, etc.). If the teacher will not or cannot be the acoustic model, suitable tapes or records must be substituted.

In any case, the students should hear the entire dialog several times before they ever attempt to say any of the lines themselves.

3. *Imitation-repetition-memorization-internalization*. This step is the one in which the student repeats the utterance after a good model and attempts to associate it with a specific situation. What is important at this stage is a consistent quality model of each sentence, an appropriate visual configuration for each sentence, and an immediate confirmation or correction of the student's attempt at imitation. The tape-recorded native-speaker model has the advantages of authenticity, constancy, patience, and stamina.

Considerable controversy rages over the question of individual versus group repetition of new language patterns, although both camps have as their goal the polished performance of individual students. Those favoring initial group repetition believe it gives the student a sense of security to hear the responses of others. They argue that by the time a child has to respond individually, his or her confidence has been built up by the prior choruses of the whole-class, half-class, and large-group contingents.

Those in favor of individual repetition, on the other hand, maintain that young children do not need the security blanket of group repetition which adolescents often require. Furthermore, the teacher cannot distinguish pronunciation errors coming from individuals in a large group, so that by the time a student does perform alone, he or she may have practiced an error five or more times and thereby made it difficult to eradicate. Finally, correct rhythm and intonation are seldom respected in group repetition and these important aspects of the language must then be retaught or left to chance. Proponents of individual repetition recommend that group repetition be used only to break the monotony of individual repetitions.

A compromise arrangement involves smaller groups of five or six students responding chorally, since an astute teacher can generally detect individual errors in the recitation by a group of that size.

The goal of the memorization stage is for each pupil to be able to produce the correct line of the dialog when he or she hears the previous line or, preferably, when confronted with a given visual situation. Until all the children are able to do this, or at least until a high percentage of them can, it is pointless to attempt to exploit the dialog. It is not necessary, however, that each student have the dialog totally memorized. In fact, such overlearning often produces an overly automatic response which makes free conversation difficult. Dramatization of the dialog may be used as a culmination of this stage.

4. *Exploitation of the dialog.* The goal of the dialog approach is to enable students to converse freely within the limits of the vocabulary and structures they have learned. These activities are among the most useful for structure manipulation, beginning with those closely tied to the dialog situation and culminating with those concerned with the students' real lives:

a. Role-playing. The child pretends to be one of the characters in the dialog, and the teacher (or later, other students) ask him or her appropriate questions. This activity exploits the various personal forms of verbs.

b. Factual questioning. The teacher asks questions about what is happening in the dialog; e.g., Who is buying the fruit? How much does it cost?

c. Personalized questioning. Individual students are questioned about their personal preferences, using the vocabulary and structures of the dialog: What fruits do you like? What is your favorite store?, etc. Two activities which can be used effectively at this point are:

(1) Directed dialog. The teacher tells a student to ask another student a certain question (in order to provide practice in understanding indirect discourse forms). The second student either responds as he or she wishes, or uses a particular answer which the teacher specifies.

(2) Chain question. The teacher asks a student a question, the student answers, and then in turn asks another student the same question. The chain can continue up and down the rows or at random throughout the classroom. It is a good technique for working with a structure which needs considerable drill. Since it is played in a game-like atmosphere, students will not mind its repetitive nature.

d. Review questioning. It involves both factual and personalized questions but incorporates vocabulary and structures learned earlier. Students are encouraged to use more complex structures and a mixture of old and new vocabulary. In this way the linguistic stew is stirred regularly and no items are allowed to fall into disuse.

As a change of pace, students enjoy questioning the teacher. Since they need to have a good balance between asking questions and answering them, this is another way to provide it.

e. Dramatic improvisations. At first the teacher may need to suggest situations, but soon students will become adept at originating situations in which they can use known vocabulary and structure. The teacher can encourage them to do so by supplying whatever props they need. The flannelboard can be used to good advantage in this activity too.

The Narrative

A second widely used method of developing oral skills in the FLES method is via the narrative or story. Its proponents argue that it can be the basis for the entire course of study for a year or more, when purposeful activities are not restricted to a handful of talented actors but involve the entire class in listening and speaking exercises.

Usually stories are selected from traditional folktales so that students can have almost immediate comprehension of the material. Care must always be taken to insure that the chosen story presents a continuum of grammar and vocabulary items and that those items are later reused in a variety of contexts to insure their utility outside the limited setting of a single story. Their exploitation in classroom activities and their use in future narratives are critical and demand careful preplanning.

Steps in Presentation

The story approach generally proceeds through four stages dedicated to the development of oral skills:

1. *Telling the story.* There are two ways for teachers to begin and both involve the use of the pupils' native language: (a) relate the story immediately in that language, using all the gestures and props that will be needed for the English version; or (b) paraphrase the story first in the students' native language, handling and referring to all the props that will be used later.

   Next, the story is told in the English language with the use of the props. This whole procedure can be done by the teacher or else the teacher can manipulate the props accompanied by a record or tape. Then there is another telling of the story for increased practice in comprehension but decreased dependence on props.

   Finally, the story is told again by the teacher but this time with the aid of the children who voluntarily and occasionally respond during familiar places in the story, either as a group or individually.

2. *Questioning and answering.* In order to assess the pupils' overall understanding of the story, the teacher asks factual questions and the pupils respond appropriately.

3. *Working intensively on portions of the story.* After dividing the entire story into parts which can each be mastered in a single session, the teacher proceeds to tell one such part and then models the utterances for the students to imitate. To assure comprehension of the individual sentences, the teacher then uses questions, gestures, props or paraphrases—employing the pupils' native language only as a last resort—so that students are not asked to memorize something that they do not understand. By the end of the class session, the students should have nearly or completely memorized the portion of the story under study so that they are able to tell the story as the teacher manipulates the appropriate props. More adept students may even be able to simultaneously relate the segment and manipulate the props.

   At this point, the teacher may wish to exploit the vocabulary and structures incorporated in the story segment by using the various activities described earlier under the dialog approach. Or the teacher may move promptly during the following session to the next story segment, waiting until all segments have been learned before attempting a general exploitation.

4. *Working with the entire story.* After pupils have assimilated the individual portions of the story, the teacher reviews the complete story and then tells

it once again as the children furnish the lines whenever they can. This activity should be repeated several times until the pupils are virtually telling the entire story themselves.

An alternative procedure is role assignment: Have certain children give the lines for particular characters while one pupil is responsible for the strictly descriptive portions of the narrative.

FLES Method: Literacy Skills

After the language specialist or classroom teacher of ESOL pupils believes that their oral English skills are adequate, he or she can introduce reading and writing.

Stages of Reading

Learning to read consists of two distinct skills: (a) the ability to pronounce phrases and sentences with normal intonation and in response to the printed page; and (b) the ability to follow these written sequences silently with comprehension. Both these activities are included in the second language sequence, and both must be accomplished without the use of translation because translation only serves to interrupt the learner's concentration on the second language.

These Spanish-speaking children, who are listening so intently to their kindergarten teacher, belong to the large majority of ESOL pupils in the elementary school. (Photo courtesy of the Fountain Valley School District, Fountain Valley, California.)

Reading Readiness

Children who have had a sufficiently lengthy, strong, and satisfying exposure to the listening and speaking skills involved in a well-planned program should encounter no difficulties in their introduction to the graphic symbol in second language instruction. Still *it is important that ESOL pupils preparing to read must want to do so.*

It is suggested that for approximately one month preceding the addition of reading to the class period, the teacher should use one or more of these activities:

1. Bulletin board displays. Pictures, posters, and simple realia related to the unit of work under discussion can be effectively exhibited. There should be an appropriate written explanation using the vocabulary and structures already familiar to the students.
2. Chalkboard listings. The days of the week, the months of the year, names of class monitors, or titles of songs can all be listed in a corner of the board. Holidays or special school events may also be highlighted.
3. Labeling. Permanent objects in the classroom which have been discussed earlier can now be labeled with clear, uniform, fairly large phrase captions. Such items could include the clock, the windows, the teacher's desk, the door, and the chalkboard. A warning, however: Since labeling is an activity usually associated with kindergarten and first grade programs, older pupils may resent the practice.
4. Cards. Both name cards and flash cards have proven valuable to the elementary school program. Large file cards properly folded make up into name cards quickly and are especially useful to traveling language teachers who are responsible for the instruction of many different pupils. Flash cards are acceptable for drill or review purposes and can sometimes be made by the children themselves. Commercial sets of such cards, however, often require extra effort on the part of the teacher to make them totally suitable for instructional purposes.

Recognition Reading

As soon as the children have finished labeling familiar objects around the classroom, teacher-pupil reading charts can be developed and used. These charts form an important part of the language-experience approach often followed with ESOL pupils because their use furthers the concept of interrelated language skills. Pupils begin to realize that what they can think about, they can learn to talk about; what they can talk about can be written; and what is written can be read.

In selecting the language content of an ESOL/FLES reading chart, the teacher should recall four criteria:

1. The material chosen must have been heard, discussed, and said aloud earlier.
2. The structural and vocabulary items must be controlled.
3. The material must incorporate natural language.
4. The material should reflect pupil interests and be appropriate to their age level.

The teacher guides the group in developing reading charts cooperatively. Greetings, classroom routines, records, dialogs, and other situations or experiences can all be written down for reading purposes. ESOL charts range from those with highly controlled language structure to those with less controlled structure. Three examples are shown in Figure 14.2.

During the stage of recognition reading it is oral reading, first by the teacher and then by the pupils, that predominates. Most teachers prefer to use a reading chart for this purpose. Others however choose to make individual copies of familiar dialog or a short narrative for each child. And a few teachers even prepare the material on an overhead projector transparency. Then these steps occur:

In Our Room

There are 18 boys in our room.

There are 14 girls in our room.

There are 10 goldfish in our room.

There are 2 teachers in our room.

On Mondays

We stand outdoors by the flagpole on Mondays.

We salute the flag.

We sing songs.

We hear speakers.

Every Morning

Teacher: Good morning, class.

Class: Good morning, Miss Johnson.

Teacher: How are you today?

Class: Fine, thank you. How are you?

Teacher: I'm fine too. Thank you.

Figure 14.2. Sample ESOL/FLES Reading Charts Showing Controlled Language Structure.

1. The teacher and students review the material orally. If necessary, the teacher reads the entire passage at a normal speed as they listen. A tape prepared by a native speaker may supplant the teacher reading the material.
2. The teacher then distributes the individual copies or displays the prepared passages. The teacher (or the tape) reviews the passage again while the students follow silently.
3. The teacher now reads one phrase or short breath group at a time as the pupils first follow silently and then repeat chorally. It is important to choose the phrases or breath groups wisely since both oral and silent reading improve when word groups are compatible to eye span.
4. The teacher now reads one sentence at a time, which the students follow silently and then repeat chorally. It is important at this stage for the teacher to insist that appropriate rhythm and intonation patterns be observed and that the repetitions be at normal speed.
5. Individual portions of the passage, whether they be roles of a dialog or lines of a narrative, are assigned to different groups of students. Each group then reads aloud its designated part of the entire passage.
6. Individual portions of the passage are assigned to individual students, and the entire passage is read aloud one or more times.
7. Finally the teacher points to individual lines on the chart or transparency (or designates the numbers of the sentences on the students' copies) and asks for specific sentences to be read both chorally and individually. For the sake of reinforcing the initial reading skill, the teacher will also wish to engage the class in oral exercises designed to establish the sound-letter correspondences of the language, first isolating a sound within its context and then giving other examples of the sound in familiar words.

Recombination Reading

After five to ten experiences with recognition reading, the children are ready to progress to recombination reading. This consists of the presentation of a passage that contains only familiar words which have been recombined into slightly different dialogs or stories from those in which they originally appeared.

As the children read the familiar material in a fresh setting, they review both vocabulary and structures that have been previously introduced. They also receive practice in assimilating new arrangements incorporating the old material. Most important of all, the pupils experience considerable satisfaction as they discover they can read material whose exact form they have never before heard or seen.

As soon as the teacher has distributed individual copies of a narrative or dialog created with familiar structures and vocabulary, he or she can begin to build both recognition and comprehension through questioning and discussion. Then the teacher may prefer to group together words with similar sounds and develop further the area of sound-letter correspondences.

While during the stage of initial reading, it would have been misleading for the teacher to fragment sentences ahead of time and drill the class on isolated units, such drill has a place during the second stage. The teacher may use flash cards to present certain phrases, varying the order in which the cards are shown. Also, the teacher may create partial sentences using the old vocabulary and ask the pupils to complete the sentences. Or the teacher may write on the chalkboard or transparency those phrases which are giving difficulty to the class and call on pupils to read them, first chorally and then individually.

Recombination reading at first involves only known material that has been rearranged. Later, however, the teacher combines known material with new material. In general, the pupils have no problems with one new word introduced in every thirty-five to sixty running words.

Although the second stage of elementary ESOL/FLES reading demands both oral and silent reading, the emphasis is still placed on reading aloud. Though the task of recombining a restricted number of words into a new approach for beginning readers is difficult, the satisfaction of this plateau stage is enormous for both the pupils and their parents and teachers. Children no longer read from memory and so are advancing slowly toward the next level of reading development.

All pupils will find that some of the items which appear in the reading material at this stage are totally unfamiliar to them. Presumably, the new items will be distributed as evenly as possible among well-known vocabulary and sentence structure, and repeated two or three times shortly after their first appearance. Very likely too, the passage will contain as many contextual clues as possible to help the learner.

Controlled Text Reading or "Contrived" Reading

During this stage the pupils are reading with increased regularity, sometimes silently, sometimes aloud, but the emphasis is on silent reading. However, in order to stress the continued significance of the listening skill in language teaching as well as to model proper intonation and pronunciation, the teacher continues to present new material orally. One teaching technique appropriate at this stage consists of these steps:

1. Children listen, speak, and read although reading sheets or books remain out of sight.
   a. The teacher models each new word or expression in a dialog or narrative, using realia, pictures, or dramatizations, and asks for its definition or explanation. Then the teacher may ask questions which require students to use the new items in their responses. The entire process is interspersed with frequent modeling followed by group and individual repetition of the new items.
   b. The teacher writes each new structural or vocabulary item on the chalkboard and models it again. Children read each item aloud and answer an additional question or two concerning its appropriate use.
2. The teacher reads aloud the entire dialog or narrative. Questions are asked about plot, setting, or characters. Children only listen and speak as their reading materials still remain out of sight.

3. The teacher reads the selection aloud again. This time the children follow silently from their reading sheets or books.
4. Individual pupils are asked to read a few lines aloud. After each sentence or two, the teacher poses questions in an effort to determine comprehension and to stimulate discussion.
5. Once the entire selection has been reread and discussed, the teacher requests an oral summary of the material.

Follow-up activities may include written exercises, with multiple-choice, completion, and true-false questions as well as oral chart exercises with matching words and phrases on oak tagboard strips. Independent seat-work activities may involve a story or paragraph which has been prepared with large spaces between lines. Below the paragraph the teacher may reproduce (1) words which pupils will cut out and paste on the lines under matching words of the passage; or(2) paragraph sentences in garbled sequence, which pupils will cut out and paste on the lines in proper sequence.

Also activities can be found in these ESOL reading series for elementary school pupils, which generally include workbooks, tapes, and other instructional materials:

> Finkel, Lawrence S., and Krawitz, Ruth. *Learning English as a Second Language.* 3 levels. Grades 1–4. Oceana Publications, Inc., 1971.
> Kernan, Doris. *Steps to English.* 6 books. Grades K–6. Webster/McGraw Hill, 1975.
> Lismore, Thomas. *Welcome to English Series.* 5 books. Grades 3–8. Regents Publishing Co., 1973.
> Marquardt, W. F. et al. *English Around the World.* 6 levels. Grades 1–6. Scott, Foresman and Co., 1977.
> Mellgren, Lars, and Walker, Michael. *Yes! English for Children.* 3 levels. Grades K–4. Addison-Wesley Publishing Co., 1977.
> Morton, Lois. *Learning English as a Second Language.* 2 levels. Grades 4–8. Oceana Publications, Inc., 1976.
> Robinett, Ralph et al. *Miami Linguistic Readers.* 2 levels. 15 books. Grades 1–2. D. C. Heath & Co., 1974.
> Slager, W. R. et al. *Core English.* 4 levels. 4 kits. Grades K–3. Ginn and Co., 1972.
> Slager, W. R. et al. *English for Today.* Second Edition. 6 books. Grades 2–8. Webster/McGraw-Hill, 1973.

Extensive Reading

The previous reading stages help the pupils establish the ability to recognize spoken vocabulary in print and to increase the speed and accuracy of word recognition. They further an understanding, from written symbols, of the concepts learned in speech. Finally, they promote the development of desirable habits of oral and silent reading, and an ability to comprehend and interpret what has been read either silently or orally.

Extensive reading should be for pleasure. The school media center and classroom library can contribute to the ESOL program during this stage of reading development, especially if they provide books and stories about the native culture of the young learners. Such books will help reassure the children learning English as a second language that the school respects that culture. Their self-image as responsible members of the class will be strong motivation for undertaking the difficult task of mastering English reading skills. Stories that depict the life of ethnic groups in urban areas are stories with which ESOL children can identify and through which they can be encouraged to learn about many other cultures and life-styles. It is hoped that the children will thus acquire the habit of turning to books for pleasurable experiences.

Forms of Writing

Writing activities reinforce other habits and skills of language learning, and therefore efforts should be exerted to make the activities purposeful. The children may practice on the chalkboard or write the exercises immediately in their loose-leaf binders or workbooks.

All four forms of elementary school ESOL writing should be corrected promptly (either by the teacher or by the boys and girls working under the teacher's supervision). Sample papers can be placed in folders for use during evaluative sessions with parents and pupils. Some children may also wish to keep special notebooks of written work, arranged in a day-by-day progression, to help them evaluate their growth in writing.

Copying

Imitative writing lays the groundwork for correct writing habits. Pupils copy familiar material that they can already understand and read. This visual and manual memorizing of a dialog, story line, or content of an experience chart is always restricted to material over which the boys and girls have thorough aural-oral control.

When the children have had practice in copying single words, they are ready to copy a small number of sentences (one, two, or three each week) that they had mastered aurally weeks earlier. Under their teacher's guidance, the pupils copy the sentence or sentences to be learned, imitating the models carefully and writing each for several lines. They are cautioned to pronounce each sentence naturally but silently before copying it and to make every effort not to allow pronunciation to be affected by spelling. They should insert all punctuation marks correctly. They should write repeatedly until they have mastered the models. Finally the class can write accurately the assigned material without having access to models.

While the first writing activity is simple copying, a more advanced form involves some check on comprehension. Pupils may be instructed to copy certain sentences, as in the following examples, and then react accordingly:

1. Drawing objects
   (Copy the sentences and then draw each object.)
   This is a man
   This is a pan.
   This is a fan.

2. Matching questions and answers
   (Copy the questions and then match each with its correct answer.)
   What is your teacher's name?
   To which school do you go?
   I live in Oregon.
   I go to Miles School.
   In which city do you live?
   My teacher is Mr. Merritt.

Dictation

The initial form of writing demands visual stimulus; the second form, an oral stimulus. Dictation combines pronunciation and knowledge of structural forms with punctuation and capitalization. It offers pupils another opportunity to make sentence patterns a part of their language habits. It allows encoding of phonemes into graphemes. It serves as a testing device to check on individual progress. It gives pupils practice in retaining a phrase in their consciousness long enough to write it down. It teaches them to decide quickly which words to use among those that have similar pronunciations but different spellings and/or meanings. Finally, it helps them realize that the omission or misuse of small function words may be a serious error.

Selections for dictation may be chosen from dialogs, songs, poems, and narratives which have been read and discussed earlier by the pupils. At least one familiar sentence from the selection should be dictated each time during the writing lesson because short, frequent dictations are best.

An acceptable technique for elementary ESOL/FLES dictation involves three readings by the teacher. The first is done at normal speed and without pauses *while the pupils listen.* The second is also at normal tempo, except for pauses after each phrase, *while the pupils write;* the marks of punctuation are preferably not stated and there is no repetition of the text. The third reading by the teacher occurs at normal speed and without pauses, *while the pupils listen and check their writing;* they may fill in omissions and correct the word order on their own papers at this time.

After the dictation the pupils immediately exchange their dictations and check each other's work against the model copy on the chalkboard, overhead transparency, or chart (which was kept out of sight during the dictation). Sometimes a pupil may volunteer to copy his or her version on the board for the class to correct and later use as a model.

A tape-recorded dictation exercise is a useful alternative to the procedure just described.

Prepared Exercises

The third area of writing includes various exercises chosen or adapted by the teacher to meet the needs of his or her group. Prepared exercises may originate in teachers' manuals or in school district curriculum guides, or may be custom-made for one self-contained classroom.

They represent a written response to a visual stimulus. They are based on material that has already been either heard or read (and preferably both) so that the children have an additional opportunity to use familiar structure and vocabulary.

Pupils need to be given drill-type practice exercises only until they can write without making the kinds of errors that native speakers-writers of standard English seldom make.

Only ten types of prepared exercises are listed here, though several more can be developed readily. Each belongs in either one of two categories: (1) those whose answers appear on the same sheet as the questions or statements, and (2) those which are more advanced and therefore do not include the answers on the same sheet.

1. Simple exercises (with accompanying answers)

   a. Multiple-Choice
      (1) Single words

      Example: (They, We, I, He) speaks English.

      (2) Sentences

      Example: What does Raymond eat for lunch?

      He eats meat.
      He eats grass.
      He eats wood.

   b. True or false

      Example: Tom's father works in the city.

      _____True   _____False

   c. Matching of questions and answers

      Example: Where is your mother?   He is in the garden.
      Where is your father?   She is in church.

   d. Core paragraph: Answering various types of questions based on one paragraph, which is written above or below the questions.

      Example: In our classroom, there is a big clock on the wall. School begins at nine o'clock, lunch is at noon, and we all go home at three o'clock. Our class reads at ten o'clock, and I like reading best.

      (1) Where is the clock in our classroom? _____
      (2) Does school begin at eight o'clock? _____ _____
      Yes   No
      (3) Lunch is at _____.
      (4) When do we read?   We go home at three o'clock.
          When do we go home?   We read at ten o'clock.

2. Advanced exercises (without nearby answers)

   a. Completion
     (1) Single words

       Example: Mary has one book but John has two _____.

     (2) Phrases

       Example: "How are you?" asked Mr. Brown.
             "_____" answered his friend.

   b. Simple response

     Example: Where is your book? _____
             What color is her dress? _____

   c. Interrogation: Statements are changed to questions.

     Example: Henry plays football.   (Does Henry play football?)
             Jim doesn't have a dog.   (Doesn't Jim have a dog?)

   d. Negation: Positive statements or questions are changed to negative ones.

     Example: Are you going to the movies?
             (Aren't you going to the movies?)
             She is nine years old.
             (She is not nine years old.)

   e. Replacement: The underlined word or words are replaced by a substitute.

     Example: My <u>father</u> is a doctor.   (My brother is a doctor)
             <u>Jack</u> is buying an <u>apple</u>.   (Bill is buying an orange)

   f. Controlled sentence construction: Out of a given group of words, a sentence is to be constructed which uses the items in the order presented and adds others when necessary.

     Example: go, school, with, brother
             I can go to school with your brother.

Independent Composition

The previous writing activities all involve procedures in which certain controls are imposed by the teacher as a means to an end—the ability to write independent or free compositions. The controlled compositions offer writers some practice in correct forms in order to help pupils eventually develop the ability to express their own ideas exactly, albeit briefly, in free compositions.

Compositions are "free" when they are written under the guidance, not control, of the teacher. The teacher can, however, encourage the students to express their own ideas and feelings in writing by using pictures, newspaper articles, films, walking trips, telecasts, and even personal experiences that will promote discussion and reflection. Since the goal of this form of ESOL writing is the expression of children's ideas, creativity, and emotional reactions, the teacher accepts whatever forms or structures the writers use. Then at a later date, the teacher will sit down with each child in an individual conference to guide him or her into proofreading skills for improved punctuation, capitalization, and spelling.

Learning Games for ESOL

The games described in this section can help reinforce structural patterns and vocabulary. They do not entail excessive preparation. The pictures, realia, or sentence cards which some of the games require are the sorts of materials routinely found in ESOL/FLES classrooms.

Auction

1. Realia is placed on the "auction" table in front of the room, with one item secretly tagged by the teacher, who is the first "auctioneer." All the players come to the auction.
2. The auctioneer describes each item on the table as it comes up for auction, and each interested player is allowed to shout a bid only when he or she has been recognized by the auctioneer.
3. A fixed number of bids should be agreed upon in advance, and the player winning the bid then walks up to the auctioneer to collect his or her purchase.
4. The player purchasing the secret item becomes the next auctioneer.
5. Suggestions: (a) The auctioneer should be garrulous. (b) Objects for sale may be brought from home or constructed in the classroom. (c) The player with the most purchases may be designated as the "big spender."

Baseball

1. The teacher selects one umpire, one scorekeeper, and two teams; and provides large picture cards or sentence cards.
2. After each team has chosen its own catcher and pitcher, the pitcher of Team A flashes a card to the catcher of Team A and to the first batter of Team B, both of whom are standing at home plate.
3. If the catcher answers first and correctly by identifying the picture or reading the card, there is a strike against the batter. If the catcher and batter answer simultaneously, the umpire calls it a foul ball. If the batter answers first and correctly, he or she advances to first base and the next player on Team B comes to bat. When the batter has three strikes, he or she is out and the next player on Team B is up.
4. Players advance one base at a time, runs are scored, three outs constitute a change of teams' position, and the team with the greater number of runs in the designated time wins Baseball.
5. Suggestion: For simpler scoring among younger children, one strike constitutes an out.

Book Bag Relay	1. Each row receives an empty book bag, school bag or bike bag that is placed on the desk or table of the first player.
	2. Each player in turn takes the bag and puts into it one school article which he or she can identify properly (e.g., "This is my spelling book.").
	3. Though each player in one row must insert a different item from his or her table or desk and must identify it properly (for duplication of items within one row is not permitted) a player may insert more than one specified item (e.g., three pencils, two pens) into the book bag.
	4. The first row to have the greatest number of items correctly identified within a specified time wins Book Bag Relay.

Buried Treasure	1. "Buried treasure" (realia or pictures) is placed into a large box in front of the room, and teams are chosen.
	2. One player at a time from each team walks to the box and draws out a buried treasure. If the player can identify or describe the treasure correctly, his or her team retains it. If the player fails, he or she must return the treasure to the box.
	3. Each team continues to choose and identify items until one of its players misses, and the team with the most treasures when time is called wins Buried Treasure.

Eraser Relay	1. Each row, consisting of the same number of players, receives an eraser that is placed on the desk or table of the first player.
	2. The teacher asks the first player of the first row a question (e.g., "What day is this?"), and if the player can answer it successfully, he or she passes the eraser down the row to the next player. If any player in the row fails to answer, he or she retains the eraser; the teacher then proceeds with the second row of players, questioning each briefly until one player is unable to respond or responds incorrectly.
	3. The row that first passes its eraser down to its last player wins Eraser Relay.
	4. Variation: For less advanced classes, the teacher reads some questions aloud and each player in turn responds "Yes" or "No" followed by a short sentence to indicate reasonable comprehension.

Hot Potato	1. The teacher is "It" first. While the teacher turns his or her back to the class, the players pass a small rubber ball quickly around the circle or up and down the rows as if it were a "hot potato."
	2. As each player receives the ball, he or she must say, "I have the ball" before passing it on.
	3. Each time "It" turns around and calls, "Stop," the player holding the hot potato must come up and stand in front of the room. Then the game continues until each player has passed the ball at least once.
	4. "It" must then issue simple penalties (e.g., "Count from 20 to 30," "Draw a cat on the board," or "Give the names of three vegetables") to all players who are standing in front of the room.

5. Suggestion: A baseball, tennis ball, or football may be used to stimulate interest during different seasons of the year.

1. The teacher must provide an assortment of paper masks or a collection of paper hats.   **Knock, Knock**
2. All the players close their eyes, and the teacher quietly taps one player to be "It." "It" dons one of the masks or hats to assume a different identity.
3. "It" now hides under the teacher's desk or behind a screen. When "It" begins to "knock, knock," the other players open their eyes and demand, "Who is there?"
4. "It" answers, "Guess if you can," and begins to describe his or her new identity (e.g., fire fighter, cowboy).
5. The first player to identify "It" correctly becomes "It" for the next round.
6. Suggestions: (a) Players may construct simple masks or hats during an art period. (b) Whenever possible, with older children, masks of famous national heroes of the United States or the native lands of the ESOL players may be used.

1. The teacher selects a timekeeper, and space is cleared for "It" to perform.   **Look at Me**
2. The player chosen as "It" mimes an action, and the other players, either individually or chorally, offer guesses as to what "It" is doing (e.g., "You are drinking water" or "You are washing your hands").
3. The first player to identify the action correctly becomes "It" for the next round. When there has been a choral response, "It" selects his or her successor.
4. The player chosen as "It" who can puzzle the class the longest with a pantomime wins Look at Me.
5. Suggestions: This game is especially appropriate when the children have been overactive.

1. The teacher chooses a player to be "It" and allows "It" to hide the "red ball" somewhere in the room while the other players close their eyes.   **Red Ball**
2. Once the red ball has been hidden, all eyes are opened and each player is allowed one guess as to the location of the ball; for example, "The ball is on the window sill."
3. If a player's identifying statement is correct, he or she is permitted to look for the red ball in that place.
4. The first player to find the ball is "It" during the next round.
5. Suggestion: Instead of using the relatively large red playground ball, the teacher may prefer to paint a golf ball red or substitute a red tennis ball since a small ball is easier to hide.

1. The teacher places large pictures on the chalk tray, and chooses one player to be "It."   **Robber, Robber**

2. While the other players close their eyes, "It" removes one of the pictures and places it facedown on the teacher's desk.
3. All eyes are opened, and the class shouts, "Robber, Robber, what do you have?"
4. Then, each player is allowed one chance to identify correctly the missing picture, and the first player to do so successfully becomes "It" for the next round.
5. Variations: (a) "It" is permitted to rearrange the pictures each time; (b) Instead of using pictures, the teacher places objects on a table where everyone can see them, and "It" must remove one of the objects.

Show Me

1. Large pictures are placed on the chalk tray in front of the room or on the bulletin board, two teams are chosen, and a scorekeeper is selected.
2. The first player on Team A asks the first player on Team B, "Show me a duck," and the first player on Team B must walk up and point to the correct picture and identify it (e.g., "This is a duck"). Then the second player on Team B asks the second player on Team A, "Show me. . . ."
3. The scorekeeper allows one point for each command that is properly issued, and one point for each correct identification. The team with the greater number of points wins the Show Me game.
4. Variation: The game may be called Draw Me if sufficient chalkboard space is available and the students are talented.

Super Chair

1. The players sit in a semicircle, with the teacher seated at one end on a "super chair" (high stool). A timekeeper stands nearby.
2. While holding up picture or sentence cards, one at a time, the teacher calls on a player in the semicircle to identify the item(s) shown or read the card. If the player succeeds, all the players remain in their own seats. If the player fails, he or she moves to the end of the line and the other players move up clockwise.
3. The teacher is soon replaced by the player who formerly sat at his or her right but who now has succeeded to the super chair and must continue the game.
4. The player who remains longest in the super chair is declared the winner.

Three Chances

1. After one player leaves the room, the teacher selects another player to be "It" and describes "It" softly to the class (e.g., "He has brown hair, blue eyes, and wears a red shirt").
2. The outsider now returns to the room and must guess which player is "It" by asking three questions (e.g., "Is it a boy?"; "Is he tall?"; "Is he wearing a sweater?"); the class answers chorally "Yes" or "No."
3. Then, the outsider has three chances to identify "It." If the outsider is successful, he or she may select the next player to leave the room. Should the outsider fail, the player who has been "It" becomes the next outsider.

4. Suggestion: In the primary grades, the outsider is told, before beginning his or her questioning, the row or part of the room in which "It" is seated.

Triple Play

1. Three teams are chosen, a scorekeeper is selected, and everyone stands.
2. The teacher holds a stack of large pictures or large sentence cards which can be readily seen about halfway across the room. The first players on all three teams try simultaneously to identify the picture or read the card which the teacher flashes to them.
3. The first player to succeed scores one point for his or her team and the game continues with the next trio of players. In case of a tie identification or reading during the "triple play," the teacher puts the cards back into the pile, and the next trio steps up.
4. The team with the most points after a specified period of time wins Triple Play.
5. Suggestion: If the class is small or if the game is played for a long time, a Most Valuable Player can be chosen.

Evaluation of Pupils' and Teachers' Progress

Elementary teachers who are responsible for classroom ESOL programs, and the paraprofessionals who in some districts assist them, may use self-evaluation sheets. They may also periodically employ individual checklists to rate children's aural-oral progress. Typical checklists are found in Figures 14.3, 14.4, 14.5, and 14.6.

To help teachers and their aides evaluate literacy skills of the pupils, individual files may be kept of reading work papers, dictation or written exercises, independent compositions, or informal written group tests.

Informal tests are also administered individually in some districts in an attempt to assess children's oral competency in English structure and vocabulary. These tests generally employ many visuals and some realia, require less than thirty minutes for tape-recording each administration, and have been used either as a pretest diagnostic/placement tool or as a posttest achievement instrument. Sample items from the teacher's manual of one such test are shown in Figure 14.7.

There are presently eight standardized tests available to assess the English language skills of foreign students applying for admission to American universities or colleges.[7] None is appropriate for use with children. This circumstance makes it difficult to place or advance non-English-speaking children in the elementary school on a definitive basis.

There are also two unpublished tests in the form of research instruments which are not available commercially but may be ordered on microfilm (for a fee) from ERIC Document Reproduction Service.[8] The first is for the primary age range (grades one to three) only and the second is for either the primary or intermediate age range (grades four to six); each is listed by title, author, date of construction, purpose, and ordering information:

Figure 14.3.	Self-Evaluation of Teacher	Frequency		
Teacher's Self-Evaluation Checklist in the ESOL Program —FORM A.	Item	Occasionally	Often	Always

Do I:

1. Use a tape recorder for language models or for student performance? _____ _____ _____

2. Involve all of the students in classroom activities? _____ _____ _____

3. Have beginning students spend most of their time listening and speaking? _____ _____ _____

4. Vary materials to maintain the interest of my students? _____ _____ _____

5. Introduce materials at a controlled rate and review frequently? _____ _____ _____

6. Use a normal rate of speech and normal pronunciation in class? _____ _____ _____

7. Use choral responses? _____ _____ _____

8. Arrange lessons so that English model is followed by choral response, individual response, and communication among students? _____ _____ _____

9. Teach vocabulary in a meaningful context? _____ _____ _____

10. Use visual aids? _____ _____ _____

11. Use games as supporting activities to provide additional practice? _____ _____ _____

12. Incorporate culture of the United States into my classroom? _____ _____ _____

13. Know community agencies and facilities that are beneficial to my students? _____ _____ _____

14. Evaluate students according to what has been presented in class? _____ _____ _____

Source: Abridged from *Handbook for Teachers of English as a Second Language.* (Sacramento, California: State Department of Education, 1969), pp. 69–71.

Figure 14.4. Teacher's Self-Evaluation Checklist in the ESOL Program—FORM B.

Self-Evaluation of Teacher	Yes	No
1. Do I demonstrate adequate planning and sequencing?	___	___
2. Do I use material that is relevant to the students' world and at an appropriate level for the students?	___	___
3. Is the aim of my lesson clear to the students, i.e., is the target structure or activity clearly delineated and reflected in my preparation?	___	___
4. Do I have a clear understanding of the structure so that I will not be "surprised" by irregular items?	___	___
5. Are my directions clear and to the point?	___	___
6. Do I keep rules, diagrams and explanations to a minimum?	___	___
7. Are my handouts well prepared and legible and NOT poor duplications characterized by light print or minute type which students, already struggling in a second language, must struggle to read?	___	___
8. Do I speak naturally, at normal speed?	___	___
9. Do I maintain an appropriate pace to keep the class alert and interested?	___	___
10. Do I have good rapport with my class, respecting the students' time as well as exhibiting sensitivity to the students as children and offering positive reinforcement?	___	___
11. Do I listen to my students and am I aware of student errors, limiting correction to what is necessary and relevant?	___	___
12. Do I promote student self-editing?	___	___
13. Do I utilize peer correction?	___	___
14. Do I respect students' abilities to use their own grey matter to come up with new items, and do I invite them to use their own powers of analogy or analysis to make "educated guesses"?	___	___
15. Do I promote student participation and activity?	___	___
16. Am I aware of the ratio of student and teacher talk, keeping teacher talk to a minimum rather than dominating the class?	___	___
17. Do my students have an opportunity to communicate with each other in real language activities so that the emphasis is not on pattern practice?	___	___
18. Is my class arranged for successful communication between students and easy accessibility to the teacher?	___	___
19. Can my students do something new linguistically after the class?	___	___
20. Would I, as a student, enjoy my own class?	___	___

Source: Abridged from the New York State Teachers of English to Speakers of Other Languages and Bilingual Education Association guidelines.

Figure 14.5.	Self-Evaluation of Paraprofessional Aide		Frequency	
Paraprofessional's Self-Evaluation Checklist in the ESOL Program.	Item	Occasionally	Often	Always
	Do I:			
	Prepare carefully?	———	———	———
	Demonstrate enthusiasm?	———	———	———
	Provide for individual differences?	———	———	———
	Use a variety of materials?	———	———	———
	Invent new activities?	———	———	———
	Read professional literature?	———	———	———
	Do boys and girls with whom I work:			
	Attend class regularly?	———	———	———
	Show enthusiasm?	———	———	———
	Participate willingly?	———	———	———
	Continue to understand more English?	———	———	———
	Continue to use more English?	———	———	———

Source: *Guidelines for the Tutor in Teaching English as a Second Language.* (Los Angeles: Los Angeles City Schools, 1970), p. 126.

Figure 14.6.
Teacher's Evaluation of Pupil Growth in the ESOL Program.

Pupil's Name _____ Age _____ Grade _____

Progress in ESOL

Item	Little Improvement	Fair Improvement	Good Improvement	Excellent Improvement
Listens with interest	———	———	———	———
Listens with accuracy	———	———	———	———
Understands directions	———	———	———	———
Understands concepts	———	———	———	———
Repeats sentence structures accurately	———	———	———	———
Recalls sentence structures accurately	———	———	———	———
Repeats vocabulary words accurately	———	———	———	———
Uses language spontaneously	———	———	———	———

Source: *Guidelines for the Tutor in Teaching English as a Second Language.* (Los Angeles: Los Angeles City Schools, 1970), p. 125.

What the Examiner Should Do	What the Examiner Should Say	What the Student Should Say
Give the student a pencil.	*Do you have a book?* **What do you have?* **Tell me that you have a pencil.*	
		(No), I have a pencil.
Take the pencil.		
Give the student an eraser.	*Do you have an eraser?* **Do you?* **Tell me that you do.*	
		(Yes), I do.
Take the eraser.		
Show picture #28 and point to the boy with the brush.	*Ask me who he is.*	
		Who's ⎫ *he?* *Who is* ⎭
	He's Joe.	
Continue with picture #29. Point to José again.	*Does José have a box?* **Does he?* **Tell me that he does.*	
		(Yes), he does.

Figure 14.7. Sample Items from Individually Administered ESOL Informal Test.

* These are additional test stimuli for use with students giving incomplete responses. Students giving no response do not receive a so-called branch test item.
Source: *Examiner's Manual for Test of Oral English Production, Level IA,* rev. (Santa Ana, California: Santa Ana Unified School District, 1972).

1. *Linguistic Capacity Index,* Frederick Brengelman and John C. Manning, 1964, to assess pupil achievement in learning English as a foreign language and to assist the classroom teacher in grouping native Spanish-speaking pupils for English language instruction. (ED 091 753).
2. *Categories for Tallying Problems in Oral Language,* Walter Loban, 1966, to identify the most crucial and frequent oral language deviations from standard English in order to assist teachers in deciding where to place instructional emphasis. (ED 023 653).

Discussion Questions

1. Why has the FLES method succeeded?
2. How can the teacher determine when ESOL pupils are ready to read?
3. Which writing activities would you choose to use with young ESOL learners?

4. How should the teacher evaluate the progress of ESOL students? How can the teacher adequately inform their parents about the program and his or her concern for the students?

Suggested Projects

1. Develop an ESOL dialog which could be taught to five- or six-year-old children.
2. Choose one traditional folktale to tell to a group of primary ESOL boys and girls.
3. Present a learning game to a group of ESOL pupils in an elementary school where you are observing or assisting.
4. Examine one of the readers suitable for ESOL classes.
5. Prepare a unit about the culture of the nearby country or territory—such as Mexico or Puerto Rico—from which some of the community's ESOL students have emigrated.
6. Set up the learning center on ESOL shown in Figure 14.8.

Figure 14.8. Language Arts Learning Center: English as a Second Language.

TYPE OF CENTER: Oral Language   TIME: 15 minutes

GRADE LEVEL: 1–3   NUMBER OF STUDENTS: 1

INSTRUCTIONAL OBJECTIVE: Given stimuli the child should be able to carry on a conversation on the telephone.

MATERIALS: Display board, toy telephone, tape recorder, people pictures, "Talk About" cards, a make-believe switchboard with plugs, directions.

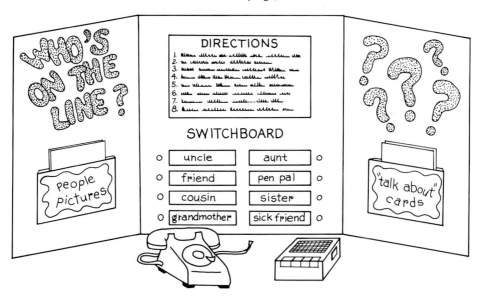

Andersson, T., and Boyer, M. 1978. *Bilingual Schooling in the United States.* 2nd Edition. Austin, Texas: National Educational Laboratory Publishers, Inc.

Donoghue, M. R. 1973. "FLES and International Understanding." *Hispania* 56: 1059–65.

Donoghue, M. R., and Kunkle, J. F. 1979. *Second Languages in Primary Education.* Rowley, Massachusetts: Newbury House Publishers, Incorporated.

Hakuta, K. 1976. "A Case Study of a Japanese Child Learning English As a Second Language." *Language Learning* 26: 321–52.

McLaughlin, B. 1978. *Second-Language Acquisition in Childhood.* Somerset, New Jersey: Halsted Press.

Marks, M., and Heffernan-Cabrera, P. 1977. "Teachers' Attitudes Towards Minority Group Students—Is Pygmalion Turning the Tables?" *TESOL Quarterly* 11: 401–6.

Met, M. 1978. "Bilingual Education for Speakers of English." *Foreign Language Annals* 11: 35–40.

Richards, R. G. 1975. "Singing: A Fun Route to a Second Language." *Reading Teacher* 29: 283–85.

Related Readings

DIRECTIONS TO STUDENTS:

1. Take a picture from the pocket on the left.
2. Pick something you would like to talk about from the pocket on the right.
3. Put the plug in the hole next to the person on the switchboard to whom you are going to talk.
4. Push the two flowered buttons on the recorder at the same time.
5. Pick up the phone receiver, say "Hello!," and begin talking.
6. When you are through, push the "Stop" button on the recorder.
7. Pull the plug out carefully.
8. Hang up the phone and put your "Talk About" card and people picture back in their pockets.

EVALUATION:

The teacher will listen to the tape, noting the vocabulary used and the sequence of events as related by the child, and later confer with the child, offering constructive ideas.

SUGGESTIONS:

People pictures could include:

aunt	uncle
grandparents	sick friend
pen pal	cousin
friend	sister

"Talk About" cards could say:

1. What happened one time on your birthday.
2. Some new place you would like to visit.
3. A vacation you took with your family.
4. What you would do with a million dollars.
5. What you would like to be when you grow up.
6. Your favorite story.
7. A trick you played on someone.
8. A pet you have or would like to have.
9. Your favorite television show.
10. A story you made up.

Source: From *Language Arts Learning Centers and Activities* by Angela Reeke and James Laffey. Copyright 1979 by Goodyear Publishing Company. Reprinted by permission.

Sampson, G. P. 1977. "A Real Challenge to ESOL Methodology." *TESOL Quarterly* 11: 241–55.

Zirkel, P. A. 1976. "The Whys and Ways and Testing Bilinguality Before Teaching Bilingually." *Elementary School Journal* 76: 323–30.

Chapter Notes

1. Bryant Fillion, Frank Smith, and Merrill Swain, "Language 'Basics' for Language Teachers: Towards a Set of Universal Considerations," *Language Arts* 53 (1976): 740–45.
2. Walter T. Petty, Dorothy C. Petty, Anabel P. Newman, and Eloise M. Skeen, "Language Competencies Essential for Coping in Our Society," in *The Teaching of English,* James R. Squire, ed. (Chicago: National Society for the Study of Education, 1977), pp. 88–91. Reprinted with permission of Kenneth J. Rehage, editor for the society.
3. This section abridged from Bloomington Public Schools, *Language Arts Curriculum Guide: K–6* (Bloomington, Minnesota: Bloomington Public Schools, 1971), pp. 1–21.
4. Lillian Weber, "The Classroom Community and the Need to Communicate" in *The Open Classroom Reader,* Charles E. Silberman, ed. (New York: Vintage Books, 1973), pp. 541–50.
5. Joan Ganz Cooney, *Children's Television Workshop: Progress Report* (New York: Children's Television Workshop, 1974). Available also from ERIC Document Reproduction Service as ED 095 892.

Chapter 2

1. Frederic L. Darley and Harris Winitz, "Age of First Word: Review of Research," *Journal of Speech and Hearing Disorders* 26 (1961): 288–89.
2. J. Zonshin, "One-Word Utterances of Hebrew-Speaking Children" (Master's thesis, University of Tel Aviv, 1974).
3. Roger Brown, "Development of the First Language in the Human Species," *American Psychologist* 20 (1973): 97–106.
4. David McNeill, *The Acquisition of Language* (New York: Harper & Row, 1970), p. 2.
5. Walter Loban, *Language Development: Kindergarten Through Grade Twelve,* Research Report No. 18 (Urbana, Illinois: National Council of Teachers of English, 1976), pp. 81–84.
6. Kellogg W. Hunt, *Grammatical Structures Written at Three Grade Levels,* Research Report No. 3 (Urbana, Illinois: National Council of Teachers of English, 1965); A. F. Watts, *The Language and Mental Development of Children* (Boston: D. C. Heath & Company, 1948); Roy C. O'Donnell, William J. Griffin, and Raymond C. Norris, *Syntax of Kindergarten and Elementary School Children: A Transformational Analysis,* Research Report No. 8 (Urbana, Illinois: National Council of Teachers of English, 1967).
7. In this section the author has drawn upon Department of Education, *Elementary Language Arts Handbook* (Edmonton, Alberta: The Department, 1973), pp. 15–17.
8. Ann M. Bingham-Newman and Ruth A. Saunders, "Take a New Look at Your Classroom with Piaget as a Guide," *Young Children* 32 (1977): 62–72.
9. Oscar K. Buros, ed., *Seventh Mental Measurements Yearbook* (Highland Park, New Jersey: Gryphon Press, 1972), Vol. II.

10. William T. Fagan, Charles R. Cooper, and Julie M. Jensen, *Measures for Research and Evaluation in the English Language Arts* (Urbana, Illinois: ERIC Clearinghouse on Reading and Communication Skills and the National Council of Teachers of English, 1975), pp. 3–51.

Chapter 3

1. Catheryn Eisenhardt, *Applying Linguistics in the Teaching of Reading and the Language Arts* (Columbus, Ohio: Charles E. Merrill, 1972), pp. 96–98; and R. C. O'Donnell, W. J. Griffin, and R. C. Norris, *Syntax of Kindergarten and Elementary School Children: A Transformational Analysis*. Research Report No. 8 (Urbana, Illinois: National Council of Teachers of English, 1967).
2. California State Department of Education, *English Language Framework for California Public Schools* (Sacramento: The Department, 1976), p. 48.
3. Jean Malmstrom, *Understanding Language* (New York: St. Martin's Press, 1977), p. 65.
4. Ibid., p. 66.
5. Paraphrased from Dell Hymes, "Models of the Interaction of Language and Social Life," in *Directions in Sociolinguistics: The Ethnography of Communication*, J. J. Gumperz and D. Hymes, eds. (New York: Holt, Rinehart & Winston, 1972), pp. 35–71.
6. Marilyn Rosenthal, *The Magic Boxes: Children and Black English* (Arlington, Va.: ERIC Clearinghouse on Language and Linguistics/Center for Applied Linguistics, 1977).
7. William H. Rupley and Carol Robeck, "Black Dialect and Reading Achievement," *Reading Teacher* 31 (1978): 598–601.
8. Beatrice L. Kachuck, "Dialect in the Language of Inner-City Children," *Elementary School Journal* 76 (1975): 105–12.
9. Frederick Williams, Robert Hopper, and Diana S. Natalicio, *The Sounds of English* (Englewood Cliffs, New Jersey: Prentice-Hall, 1977), pp. 73–74.
10. Paraphrased from Susan Shafer, "Messin' wif Language," *Elementary School Journal* 76 (1976): 500–506.

Chapter 4

1. Adapted from *English Language Framework for California Public Schools* (Sacramento: The Department, 1976), p. 45.
2. Marv Klein, *Teaching Sentence Structure and Sentence-Combining in the Middle Grades* (Madison: Wisconsin Department of Public Instruction, 1976), pp. 4–5. Reference is made to J. Mellon, *Transformational Sentence Combining: A Method for Enhancing the Development of Syntactic Fluency in English Composition* (Urbana, Illinois: National Council of Teachers of English, 1969) and to F. O'Hare, *Sentence Combining: Improving Student Writing Without Formal Grammar Instruction* (Urbana, Illinois: National Council of Teachers of English, 1973).
3. Carl Lefevre, "A Concise Structural Grammar," *Education* 86 (1965): 131–37.
4. Klein, *Teaching Sentence Structure,* pp. 32–33, 36–37, 40–41, 50–51.
5. Bloomington Public Schools, *Language Arts Curriculum Guides K–6* (Bloomington, Minnesota: Bloomington Public Schools, 1971). This two-volume guide is one of the few English language arts curriculum guides recommended by the National Council of Teachers of English.

6. Oscar K. Buros, ed., *Seventh Mental Measurements Yearbook* (Highland Park, New Jersey: Gryphon Press, 1972), Vol. 1.

Chapter 5

1. Gertrude A. Boyd and E. Gene Talbert, *Spelling in the Elementary School* (Columbus, Ohio: Charles E. Merrill Publishing Co., 1971), p. 17.
2. Ronald L. Cramer, "An Investigation of First-Grade Spelling Achievement," *Elementary English* 47 (1970): 230–37.
3. Wendy M. Golladay, "The Teaching of Spelling to Low Ability Students," *Elementary English* 48 (1971): 366–70.
4. J. Richard Gentry and Edmund H. Henderson, "Three Steps to Teaching Beginning Readers to Spell," *Reading Teacher* 32 (1978): 632–37; James Beers, Carol Beers, and Karen Grant, "The Logic Behind Children's Spelling," *Elementary School Journal* 77 (1977): 238–42; James Beers and Edmund H. Henderson, "A Study of Developing Orthographic Concepts Among First Graders," *Research in the Teaching of English* 11 (1977): 133–48; Rhea Paul, "Invented Spelling in Kindergarten," *Young Children* 31 (1976): 195–200; Ronald L. Cramer, "The Write Way to Teach Spelling," *Elementary School Journal* 76 (1976): 464–67; Charles Read, *Children's Categorization of Speech Sounds in English*, Research Report No. 17 (Urbana, Illinois: National Council of Teachers of English, 1975); James Beers, "First- and Second-Grade Children's Developing Orthographic Concepts of Short and Long Vowels" (Paper presented at the Southeast Regional International Reading Association Conference, 1974); Charles Read, "Children's Judgments of Phonetic Similarities in Relation to English Spelling," *Language Learning* 23 (1973): 17–38; Carol Chomsky, "Beginning Reading Through Invented Spelling" in *Selected Papers from the New England Kindergarten Conference* (Cambridge, Massachusetts: Lesley College, 1973); Carol Chomsky, "Write First, Read Later" in C. Cazden (ed.) *Language in Early Childhood* (Washington, D.C.: National Association for the Education of Young Children, 1972); Dorsey Hammond, "Language Experience in Word and Deed" (Paper presented at the Fifteenth Annual Reading Conference, University of Virginia, 1971); and Charles Read, "Preschool Children's Knowledge of English Phonology," *Harvard Educational Review* 41 (1971): 1–34.
5. Cramer, "Write Way," pp. 465–66.
6. Read, "Preschool Children's Knowledge," p. 33.
7. Paul, "Invented Spelling," p. 199.
8. Read, *Children's Categorization*, p. 30.
9. Hammond, "Language Experience."
10. Noam Chomsky and Morris Halle, *The Sound Pattern of English* (New York: Harper & Row, 1968).
11. Paula Russell, *An Outline of English Spelling* (Los Alamitos, California: SWRL Educational Research and Development, 1975), pp. 1–2.
12. Frederick H. Brengelman, "Dialect and the Teaching of Spelling," *Research in the Teaching of English* 4 (1970): 129–38.
13. Carol Chomsky, "Reading, Writing, and Phonology," *Harvard Educational Review* 40 (1970): 287–309.
14. Ibid.

15. George Manolakes, "The Teaching of Spelling: A Pilot Study," *Elementary English* 52 (1975): 243–47.
16. California State Department of Education, *English Language Framework for California Public Schools* (Sacramento: The Department, 1976), p. 43.
17. Beers, Beers, and Grant, "The Logic," p. 239.
18. Ibid., p. 242.
19. Carl Personke and Albert H. Yee, *Comprehensive Spelling Instruction* (Scranton, Pennsylvania: Intext Educational Publishers, 1971), pp. 35–51.
20. Lillie S. Davis, "The Applicability of Phonic Generalizations to Selected Spelling Programs," *Elementary English* 49 (1972): 706–13.
21. Russell, *An Outline,* pp. 37–41.
22. Hazel Smith, "Teaching Spelling," *British Journal of Educational Psychology* 45 (1975): 68–72.
23. Herbert Rieth et al., "Influence of Distributed Practice and Daily Testing on Weekly Spelling Tests," *Journal of Educational Research* 68 (1974): 73–77.
24. Donald D. Hammill, Stephen Larsen, and Gaye McNutt, "The Effects of Spelling Instruction: A Preliminary Study," *Elementary School Journal* 78 (1977): 67–72.
25. Manolakes, "The Teaching," p. 246.
26. Beers, Beers, and Grant, "The Logic," p. 242.
27. Manolakes, "The Teaching," p. 244.
28. Personke and Yee, *Spelling Instruction,* p. 67.
29. Mae L. Jackson, "Individualized Spelling Lists," *Teacher* 91 (1974): 86–88.
30. Adapted from Theodore E. Glim and Frank S. Manchester, *Basic Spelling,* rev. ed. C (Philadelphia: J. B. Lippincott, 1977).
31. Adapted from Theodore E. Glim and Frank S. Manchester, *Basic Spelling,* rev. ed. E (Philadelphia: J. B. Lippincott, 1977); and from William Kottmeyer and Audrey Claus, *Basic Goals in Spelling,* Level 5, 5th ed. (New York: Webster Division, McGraw-Hill Book Company, 1976).
32. Perry R. Childers, "Snow White and the Seven Dwarfs," *Journal of Experimental Education* 40 (1971): 5–8.
33. Shirley Partoll, "Spelling Demonology Revisited," *Academic Therapy* 11 (1976): 339–47.
34. Sister J. Kowalski, "A Spelling Method That Works," *Academic Therapy* 12 (1977): 365–67.
35. Jerry N. Kuhn and Howard H. Schroeder, "A Multi-Sensory Approach for Teaching Spelling," *Elementary English* 48 (1971): 865–69.

Chapter 6

1. Noam Chomsky, "Phonology and Reading" in *Basic Studies on Reading,* ed. H. Levin and J. Williams (New York: Basic Books, 1970), pp. 3–18.
2. Dale D. Johnson and Thomas C. Barrett, "Johnson's Basic Vocabulary for Beginning Reading and Current Basal Readers: Are They Compatible?" *Journal of Reading Behavior* 4 (1972): 1–11.
3. Ibid.; and Dale Johnson and Emily Majer, "Johnson's Basic Vocabulary: Words for Grades 1 and 2," *Elementary School Journal* 77 (1976): 74–82.
4. Edgar Dale and Joseph O'Rourke, *Techniques of Teaching Vocabulary* (Addison, Illinois: Field Educational Enterprises, Inc., 1971), p. 8.
5. Frank Smith, *Comprehension and Learning* (New York: Holt, Rinehart and Winston, 1975), p. 10.

6. Joseph O'Rourke, *Toward a Science of Vocabulary Development* (The Hague: Mouton, 1974), pp. 83–86.

7. James E. Turnure, "Types of Verbal Elaboration in the Paired-Associate Performance of Educable Mentally Retarded Children," *American Journal of Mental Deficiency* 76 (1971): 306–12.

8. Arthur M. Taylor, Martha L. Thurlow, and James E. Turnure, "Vocabulary Development of Educable Retarded Children," *Exceptional Children* 43 (1977): 444–50.

9. Paraphrased from Dale and O'Rourke, *Techniques*, pp. 28–34.

10. Quality children's magazines as well as selected adult periodicals of interest to children are indexed in Peter Madden et al., "Magazines and Newspapers for Children," *Childhood Education* 53 (1977): 328–36.

11. Dale and O'Rourke, *Techniques*, pp. 20–26.

Chapter 7

1. Sara W. Lundsteen, *Listening: Its Impact on Reading and the Other Language Arts* (Urbana, Illinois: National Council of Teachers of English, 1971), p. 9.

2. Ibid., pp. 58–60.

3. S. W. Weaver and W. L. Rutherford, "A Hierarchy of Listening Skills," *Elementary English* 51 (1974): 1146–50.

4. H. S. Wetstone and B. Z. Friedlander, "The Effect of Live, TV, and Audio Story Narration on Primary Grade Children's Listening Comprehension," *Journal of Educational Research* 68 (1974): 32–35.

5. R. W. Woodcock and C. R. Clark, "Comprehension of a Narrative Passage by Elementary School Children as a Function of Listening Rate, Retention Period, and IQ," *Journal of Communication* 18 (1968): 259–71.

6. Imogene Ramsey, "A Comparison of First Grade Negro Dialect Speaker's Comprehension of Standard English and Negro Dialect," *Elementary English* 49 (1972): 688–96; and Thomas Frentz, "Children's Comprehension of Standard and Negro Nonstandard English Sentences," *Speech Monographs* 38 (1971): 489–96.

7. Jimmie Ellis Cook, "A Study in Critical Listening Using Eight to Ten Year Olds in An Analysis of Commercial Propaganda Emanating from Television," *Dissertation Abstracts International* 33 (1973): 3146A–3147A.

8. Roger A. Richards in *Seventh Mental Measurements Yearbook,* ed. Oscar K. Buros (Highland Park, New Jersey: Gryphon Press, 1972), p. 905.

Chapter 8

1. Frederick Williams, Jack Whitehead, and Jane Traupmann, "Teachers' Evaluations of Children's Speech," *Speech Teacher* 20 (1971): 247–54; and Frederick Williams, "The Psychological Correlates of Speech Characteristics: On Sounding Disadvantaged," *Journal of Speech and Hearing Research* 13 (1970): 472–79.

2. California State Department of Education, *English Language Framework for California Public Schools* (Sacramento: The Department, 1976), pp. 23–24.

3. Ann Seidler, *Experimental Speech Improvement Program* (Glassboro, New Jersey: Glassboro Public School System, 1970), pp. 13–14.

4. Oscar K. Buros, ed., *Seventh Mental Measurements Yearbook* (Highland Park, New Jersey: Gryphon Press, 1972), Vol. 2.

5. Marvin L. Klein, *Talk in the Language Arts Classroom* (Urbana, Illinois: ERIC

Clearinghouse on Reading and Communication Skills and National Council of Teachers of English, 1977), pp. 34–37.

6. Dorothy Nelson, "D. and E.: Show and Tell, Grown Up," *Language Arts* 53 (1976): 203–5.

7. Klein, *Talk,* pp. 41–44.

8. Mary A. Wilcox, "When Children Discuss: A Study of Learning in Small Groups," *Elementary School Journal* 76 (1976): 302–9.

9. Sheila Fitzgerald, "Teaching Discussion Skills and Attitudes," *Language Arts* 52 (1975): 1094–96.

10. James N. Blake, *Speech Education Activities for Children* (Springfield, Illinois: Charles C Thomas, Publisher, 1970), p. 87.

11. Alan W. Huckleberry and Edward S. Strother, *Speech Education for the Elementary Teacher* (Boston: Allyn and Bacon, Inc., 1973), pp. 228–29.

12. Answers to these questions are: (a) They come from the rules and customs of the British Parliament; (b) A motion is made, seconded, and then stated in full by the president; (c) "Is there any discussion?"; (d) A member does not need to be recognized to second a motion; (e) It is not necessary to rise to second a motion; (f) "Here is another suggestion" or "We might try another way"; and (g) No one should speak until he or she has the chairperson's permission.

13. E. Cowe, "Interviewing by Young Children," *Language Arts* 53 (1976): 32–33.

14. Nancy Renfro, *Puppets for Play Production* (New York: Funk and Wagnalls, Inc., 1969).

15. Margaret C. Bryne and Chris C. Shervanian, *Introduction to Communicative Disorders* (New York: Harper & Row, 1977), p. 4.

16. Charles Van Riper, *Speech Correction: Principles and Methods,* 6th ed. (Englewood Cliffs, New Jersey: Prentice-Hall, 1978), p. 29.

17. Bryne and Shervanian, *Communicative Disorders,* p. 5.

18. Stanley Dickson and Gladys R. Jann, "Diagnostic Principles and Procedures" in Stanley Dickson (ed.), *Communication Disorders: Remedial Principles and Practices* (Glenview, Illinois: Scott, Foresman & Company, 1974), p. 25.

19. Anne S. Morency, Joseph W. Wepman, and Sarah K. Hass, "Developmental Speech Inaccuracy and Speech Therapy in the Early School Years," *Elementary School Journal* 70 (1970): 219–24.

20. C. L. Woods, "Social Position and Speaking Competence of Stuttering and Normally Fluent Boys," *Journal of Speech and Hearing Research* 17 (1974): 740–47.

21. Freeman McConnell, Russell Love, and Bertha Smith Clark, "Language Remediation in Children" in Dickson, *Communication Disorders,* pp. 57–58.

Chapter 9

1. Patrick Groff, "Can Pupils Read What Teachers Write?" *Elementary School Journal* 76 (1975): 33–37.

2. Dan W. Andersen, "Correlates of Handwriting Legibility: What Makes Writing Readable?" in *Forum For Focus,* eds. Martha L. King, Robert Emans, and Patricia J. Cianciolo (Urbana, Illinois: National Council of Teachers of English, 1973), pp. 137–43.

3. Sir A. Bullock, *A Language for Life* (London: Her Majesty's Stationery Office, 1975).

4. Eunice N. Askov and Kasper N. Greff, "Handwriting: Copying Versus Tracing as the Most Effective Type of Practice," *Journal of Educational Research* 69

(1975): 96–98; and Edward Hirsch, "The Effects of Letter Formation Practice and Letter Discrimination Training on Kindergarten Handwriting Performance," *Dissertation Abstracts International* 33 (1973): 6648A–49A.

5. Robert M. Forster, "An Experiment in Teaching Transitional, Cursive Handwriting by Educational Television with Teacher Attitude Toward the Teaching of Handwriting as a Factor," *Dissertation Abstracts International* 32 (1971): 1184A.

6. Jone P. Wright and Elizabeth G. Allen, "Ready to Write!" *Elementary School Journal* 75 (1975): 430–35.

7. Bert C. L. Touwen, "Laterality and Dominance," *Developmental Medicine and Child Neurology* 14 (1972): 747–55.

8. C. Sinclair, "Dominance Patterns of Young Children: A Follow-Up Study," *Perceptual and Motor Skills* 32 (1971): 142.

9. Walter Pryzwansky, "Effects of Perceptual-Motor Training and Manuscript Writing on Reading Readiness Skills in Kindergarten," *Journal of Educational Psychology* 63 (1972): 110–15; and Beatrice Furner, "An Analysis of the Effectiveness of a Program of Instruction Emphasizing the Perceptual-Motor Nature of Learning in Handwriting," *Elementary English* 47 (1970): 61–69.

10. Groff, "Can Pupils Read," p. 38.

11. Gertrude Halpin and Gerald Halpin, "Special Paper for Beginning Handwriting: An Unjustified Practice?," *Journal of Educational Research* 69 (1976): 267–69.

12. Dolores Durkin, *Teaching Young Children to Read* (Boston: Allyn & Bacon, 1976), p. 143.

13. Lowell W. Horton, "Illegibilities in the Cursive Handwriting of Sixth-Graders," *Elementary School Journal* 70 (1970): 446–50.

14. Grace Petitclerc, *Young Fingers on a Typewriter* (San Rafael, California: Academic Therapy Publications, 1975), p. 9.

15. Mary Lou Ray, "Type and Learn," *Teacher* 94 (1977): 45–47.

16. Thomas A. Sinks and Jay F. Thurston, "Effect of Typing on School Achievement in Elementary Grades," *Educational Leadership Research Supplement,* January 1972, pp. 344–48.

17. Lowell Horton, "Nurturing Individual Growth in Handwriting," in *Forum for Focus,* pp. 144–47; and Glenn E. Tagatz et al., "Effect of Three Methods of Instruction upon the Handwriting Performance of Third and Fourth Graders," *American Educational Research Journal* 5 (1968): 81–90.

18. John L. Carter and Donald Synolds, "Effects of Relaxation Training upon Handwriting Quality," *Journal of Learning Disabilities* 7 (1974): 53–55.

19. In this section the author has drawn heavily upon *Correcting Handwriting Problems: Integration of Children with Special Needs in a Regular Classroom* (Lexington, Massachusetts: Public Schools, 1974), pp. 6–17.

20. Curtis Hardyck and Lewis F. Petrinovich, "Left-Handedness," *Psychological Bulletin* 84 (1977): 385–404.

21. Curtis Hardyck, Lewis F. Petrinovich, and Roy D. Goldman, "Left-Handedness and Cognitive Deficit," *Cortex* 12 (1976): 266–79.

22. Teachers with several left-handed children may be interested in securing a catalog from the Aristera Organization which sells only products designed for "leftys." The company is located in Westport, Connecticut 06880.

23. Polly Addy and Richard E. Wylie, "The 'Right' Way to Write," *Childhood Education* 49 (1973): 253–55.

Chapter 10

1. E. Paul Torrance and J. Pansy Torrance, *Is Creativity Teachable?* (Blooming-ton, Indiana: Phi Delta Kappa Educational Foundation, 1973), p. 46.

2. E. Paul Torrance, "Give the Devil His Due" in *Creativity: Its Educational Implications,* comp. J. C. Gowan, G. D. Demos, and E. P. Torrance (New York: John Wiley, 1967).

3. The teacher may wish to examine a specimen set of the *Torrance Tests of Creative Thinking* (Lexington, Massachusetts 02173: Personnel Press) designed to measure fluency, flexibility, originality, and elaboration. It can be used with children grades K–6 and consists of a word test (Verbal Test, forty-five to sixty minutes) and a picture test (Figural Test, thirty to forty-five minutes). It has not been well received critically, but appears to be useful as a basis for further study into the nature and nurture of creativity.

4. National Assessment of Educational Progress, *Expressive Writing* (Denver, Colorado: NAEP, 1976); Richard Smith and Lee Hansen, "Integrating Reading and Writing: Effects on Children's Attitudes," *Elementary School Journal* 76 (1976): 238–45; William Harpin, *The Second 'R'* (London: George Allen & Unwin Ltd., 1976); E. Jane Porter, "Research Report," *Language Arts* 52 (1975): 1019–26; Donald H. Graves, "An Examination of the Writing Process of Seven-Year-Old Children," *Research in the Teaching of English* 9 (1975): 227–41; Patrick Groff, "Does Negative Criticism Discourage Children's Compositions?" *Language Arts* 52 (1975): 1032–34; Nancy Roser and James Britt, "Writing with Flair," *Elementary English* 52 (1975): 180–82; Margaret W. Sawkins, "An Analysis of the Oral Responses of Selected Fifth-Grade Children to Questions Concerning Their Written Expression," *Elementary English* 57 (1974): 145–47; Barbara W. Graves, "A Kinesthetic Approach to Building Language Power," *Elementary English* 49 (1972): 818–22; Tillie Hilfman, "Can Second-Grade Children Write More Complex Sentences?" *Elementary English* 47 (1970): 209–14; Joseph S. Krzeski, "Effect of Different Writing Tools and Paper on Performance of the Third Grader," *Elementary English* 48 (1971): 821–24; Robert L. Hillerich, "Evaluation of Written Language," *Elementary English* 48 (1971): 839–42; Ernest McDaniel and Thomas Pietras, "Conventional Test Scores and Creative Writing Among Disadvantaged Pupils," *Research in the Teaching of English* 6 (1972): 181–86; Lester S. Golub and Wayne C. Frederick, "An Analysis of Children's Writing Under Different Stimulus Conditions," *Research in the Teaching of English* 4 (1970): 168–80; Kellogg W. Hunt, "Syntax, Science, and Style" in *A Forum for Focus,* eds. Martha L. King, Robert Emans, and Patricia J. Cianciolo (Urbana, Illinois: National Council of Teachers of English, 1973), pp. 111–25; Samuel S. Zeman, "Reading Comprehension and Writing of Second and Third Graders," *Reading Teacher* 23 (1969): 144–50; June Brooks Ewing, "A Study of the Influence of Various Stimuli on the Written Composition of Selected Third Grade Children," *Dissertation Abstracts* 28 (1968): 4525A; Roy C. O'Donnell et al., *Syntax of Kindergarten and Elementary School Children: A Transformational Analysis,* Research Report No. 8 (Urbana, Illinois: National Council of Teachers of English, 1967); Barbara D. Miller and James W. Ney, "The Effect of Systematic Oral Exercises on the Writing of Fourth-Grade Students," *Research in the Teaching of English* 2 (1968): 44–61; Howard E. Blake and Donald D. Hammill, "Structural Linguistics and Children's Writing," *Elementary English* 44 (1967): 275–78; Syra Elizabeth Benson Nikoloff, "The Rela-

tionship of Teacher Standards to the Written Expression of Fifth and Sixth Grade Children," *Dissertation Abstracts* 26 (1966): 6560; Winifred F. Taylor and Kenneth C. Hoedt, "The Effect of Praise upon the Quality and Quantity of Creative Writing," *Journal of Educational Research* 40 (1966): 80–83; Mary Jo Woodfin, "The Quality of Written Expression of Third Grade Children under Differing Time Limits," *Journal of Experimental Education* 37 (1969): 89–91; and Phyllis and Bernard Shapiro, "Two Methods of Teaching Poetry Writing in the Fourth Grade," *Elementary English* 48 (1971): 225–28.

5. Harpin, *Second 'R'*, pp. 83–84.

6. Wisconsin Department of Public Instruction, *Composition in the Language Arts, Grades 1–8: An Instructional Framework* (Madison: The Department, 1976), p. 4.

7. Carol Gay, "Reading Aloud and Learning to Write," *Elementary School Journal* 77 (1976): 87–93.

8. Richard Gebhardt, "The Timely Teetertotter: Balancing Discipline and Creativity in Writing Classes," *Language Arts* 54 (1977): 673–78.

9. This section has been adapted from Dorothy Grant Hennings and Barbara M. Grant, *Content and Craft* (Englewood Cliffs, New Jersey: Prentice-Hall, Inc., 1973), pp. 9–11.

10. Lester S. Golub, "Syntactic and Lexical Deviations in Children's Written Sentences," *Elementary English* 51 (1974): 144–45.

11. Margaret L. Peters, "Spelling: Caught or Taught?" in *Spelling: Task and Learner,* eds. B. Wade and K. Wedell (Birmingham, England: Educational Review/Occasional Publications 5, 1974).

12. Robert L. Fichtenau, "Teaching Rhetorical Concepts," *Elementary English* 49 (1972): 376–81.

13. Smith and Hansen, "Integrating Reading and Writing," pp. 243–44.

14. Examples are taken from *Impressions,* Vol. 26, 27, and 28 (San Diego, California: San Diego City Schools, 1970, 1971, 1972) and from Nancy Welbourn et al. (eds.), *Let the Children Speak* (Washington, D.C.: Teacher Corps, U.S. Office of Education, 1976).

15. Groff, "Criticism," p. 1034.

16. Hugh Lytton, *Creativity and Education* (New York: Schocken Books, 1972), pp. 100–101; and E. Paul Torrance and R. E. Myers, *Creative Learning and Teaching* (New York: Dodd, Mead, and Co., 1970), pp. 105–6.

17. Donald H. Graves, "Let's Get Rid of the Welfare Mess in the Teaching of Writing," *Language Arts* 53 (1976): 645–51.

18. Laura E. Williams, "Methods of Teaching Composition in Open Classes—England, Canada, and the United States," *Innovator* 9 (1978): 1–3.

19. P. A. Alpren, "The Grading of Original Stories—A Survey," *Elementary English* 51 (1973): 1237–38.

20. W. Don Martin, "Sex, Semantics, and Children's Writing," *Elementary English* 51 (1973): 1238–40.

21. Lydia R. Markham, "Influences of Handwriting Quality on Teacher Evaluation of Written Work," *American Educational Research Journal* 13 (1976): 277–83.

22. Oscar K. Buros, ed., *Seventh Mental Measurements Yearbook* (Highland Park, New Jersey: Gryphon Press, 1972), Vol. 1.

23. Ibid.

24. William T. Fagan, Charles R. Cooper, and Julie M. Jensen, *Measures for Research and Evaluation in the English Language Arts* (Urbana, Illinois: ERIC Clearinghouse on Reading and Communication Skills and the National Council of Teachers of English, 1975), pp. 183–206.

Chapter 11

1. Hampton City Schools, *English Language Arts: A Curriculum Guide K–6* (Hampton, Virginia: City Schools, 1976), p. 73.
2. Helen Huus, "Teaching Literature at the Elementary School Level," *Reading Teacher* 26 (1973): 797–98.
3. Gordon Peterson, "Behavioral Objectives for Teaching Literature," *Language Arts* 52 (1975): 969–71; and with Patrick Groff, "Behavioral Objectives for Children's Literature?" *Reading Teacher* 30 (1977): 652–63. In the second article, Groff offers substantial opposition to Peterson's position.
4. Rebecca J. Lukens, *A Critical Handbook of Children's Literature* (Glenview, Illinois: Scott, Foresman, and Company, 1976), pp. 1–6.
5. Roy E. Toothaker, "Curiosities of Children That Literature Can Satisfy," *Childhood Education* 52 (1976): 262–67.
6. Patricia J. Cianciolo, "Children's Literature in the Seventies," in *Adventuring with Books* (Urbana, Illinois: National Council of Teachers of English, 1977), pp. 1–10.
7. Lin Oliver, "Reading Interests of Children in the Primary Grades," *Elementary School Journal* 77 (1977): 401–6; E. J. Porter, "Research Report: Children's Reading Interests," *Elementary English* 51 (1974): 1003–13; Helen M. Robinson and Samuel Weintraub, "Research Related to Children's Interests and to Developmental Values of Reading," *Library Trends* 22 (1973): 81–108; Cynthia Rose, S. G. Zimet, and G. Blom, "Content Counts: Children Have Preferences in Reading Textbook Stories," *Elementary English* 49 (1972): 14–19; Lian-Hwang Chiu, "Reading Preferences of Fourth Grade Children Related to Sex and Reading Ability," *Journal of Educational Research* 66 (1973): 269–73; L. F. Ashley, "Children's Reading Interests and Individualized Reading," *Elementary English* 47 (1970): 1088–96; Sue Ann Peterson, "Attitudes of Children toward Literary Characters Who Speak Regional Dialects of American English," unpublished doctoral dissertation, University of Minnesota, 1970; Joan T. Feeley, "Interest Patterns and Media Preferences of Boys and Girls in Grades Four and Five," unpublished doctoral dissertation, New York University, 1972; and G. Charles Peterson, "A Study of Library Books Selected by Second Grade Boys and Girls in the Iowa City, Iowa Schools," *Dissertation Abstracts International* 32 (1972): 4847A.
8. F. André Favat, *Child and Tale: The Origins of Interest.* Research Report No. 19 (Urbana, Illinois: National Council of Teachers of English, 1977).
9. *The Bowker Annual of Library and Book Trade Information* (New York: R. R. Bowker, 1977).
10. Ursula Nordstrom, "Stuart, Wilbur, Charlotte: A Tale of Tales," *New York Times Book Review* (May 12, 1974), p. 8.
11. Zena Sutherland and May Hill Arbuthnot, *Children and Books* (Glenview, Illinois: Scott, Foresman, 1977), pp. 444–48.
12. Nancy Larrick, "Wordless Picture Books and the Teaching of Reading," *Reading Teacher* 30 (1976): 743–46.

13. Ann Terry, *Children's Poetry Preferences: A National Survey of Upper Elementary Grades*. Research Report No. 13 (Urbana, Illinois: National Council of Teachers of English, 1974).

14. Mary Lou Roush, "Is the Role of Literature Different in Urban, Suburban, and Rural Classrooms Throughout the Nation?" Research Report, *Elementary English* 50 (1973): 745–47.

15. "Classroom Choices for 1977: Books Chosen by Children," *Reading Teacher* 31 (1977): 6–23.

16. Henry Olsen, "Bibliotherapy to Help Children Solve Problems," *Elementary School Journal* 75 (1975): 423–29.

17. All titles listed were in print in hardbound form during 1974 and were chosen from more than 3000 children's books field-tested in 1976 in six states and one Canadian province. The final selection of 1031 titles appears in Sharon S. Dreyer's *The Bookfinder: A Guide to Children's Literature about the Needs and Problems of Youth Aged 2–15* (Circle Pines, Minn.: American Guidance Service, Inc., 1977).

18. Esther Jenkins, "Multi-Ethnic Literature: Promise and Problems," *Elementary English* 50 (1973): 695.

19. Patrick Groff, "Let's Update Storytelling," *Language Arts:* 54 (1977): 274.

20. Elsie M. Ziegler, "A Study of the Effects of Creative Dramatics on the Progress in the Use of the Library, Reading Interests, Reading Achievement, Self-Concept, Creativity, and Empathy of Fourth and Fifth Grade Children," *Dissertation Abstracts International* 31 (1971): 6482A.

21. Chow Loy Tom, "A National Survey of What Teachers Read to Children in the Middle Grades," unpublished doctoral dissertation, The Ohio State University, 1969.

22. Bernard J. Lonsdale and Helen K. Mackintosh, *Children Experience Literature* (New York: Random House, 1973), pp. 493–94.

23. California State Department of Education, *English Language Framework for California Public Schools* (Sacramento: The Department, 1976), p. 57.

24. Oscar K. Buros, ed. *Seventh Mental Measurements Yearbook* (Highland Park, New Jersey: Gryphon Press, 1972), Vol. 1.

1. California State Department of Education, *Drama/Theatre Framework for California Public Schools* (Sacramento: State Department of Education, 1974), pp. 6–7.

2. Elaine C. Smith, "Drama and the Schools: A Symposium," *Elementary English* 49 (1972): 300.

3. Moses Goldberg, *Children's Theatre: A Philosophy and a Method* (Englewood Cliffs, New Jersey: Prentice-Hall, Inc., 1974), pp. 127–35.

4. Martha L. Larson, "Reader's Theatre: New Vitality for Oral Reading," *Reading Teacher* (1976): 359–60.

5. Edwina Hartshorn and John C. Brantley, "Effects of Dramatic Play on Classroom Problem-Solving Ability," *Journal of Educational Research* 66 (1973): 243–46; Eleanor C. Irwin, "The Effect of a Program of Creative Dramatics Upon Personality as Measured by the California Test of Personality, Sociograms, Teacher Ratings, and Grades," *Dissertation Abstracts* 24 (1963): 2188; "Creative Dramatics Spurs Verbal Development," *Nation's Schools* 90 (1972):

Chapter 12

51–52; and Lessie Carlton and Robert H. Moore, *Reading, Self-Directive Dramatization and Self-Concept* (Columbus, Ohio: Charles E. Merrill Publishing Co., 1968).

6. Emily Gillies, *Creative Dramatics for All Children* (Washington, D.C.: Association for Childhood Education International, 1973), p. 48.

7. John W. Stewig, *Spontaneous Drama: A Language Art* (Columbus, Ohio: Charles E. Merrill Publishing Co., 1973), pp. 92–93.

8. Fannie R. Shaftel and George Shaftel, *Role-Playing for Social Values* (Englewood Cliffs, New Jersey: Prentice-Hall, Inc., 1967), pp. 134–35.

9. Ibid., pp. 203–425.

10. Abridged from Jack Strauss and Richard DuFour, "Discovering Who I Am: A Humanities Course for Sixth Grade Students," *Elementary English* 47 (1970): 100–103.

11. Donald J. Bissett, "From Literature to Drama to Life," in *Reading Ladders for Human Relations,* ed. Virginia M. Reid (Washington, D.C.: American Council on Education, 1972), p. 38.

12. Gillies, *Creative Dramatics,* p. 19.

13. Adapted from Stewig, *Spontaneous Drama,* pp. 9–10.

Chapter 13

1. American Association of School Librarians, ALA, and Association for Educational Communications and Technology, *Media Programs: District and School* (Chicago: ALA; and Washington, D.C.: AECT, 1975), p. 4.

2. Board of Education of the City of New York, *The School Library Media Center: A Force for Learning* (New York: The Board, 1975), p. 101.

3. Eugene P. Sheehy, comp., *Guide to Reference Books,* 9th ed. (Chicago: American Library Association, 1976), pp. 101–2.

4. Kenneth Kister, *Encyclopedia Buying Guide, 1975–76* (New York: R. R. Bowker Company, 1976).

5. Morris L. Mower and LeRoy Barney, "Which Are the Most Important Dictionary Skills?" *Elementary English* 45 (1968): 468–71.

6. J. Harlan Shores and James E. Snoddy, "Organizing and Teaching the Research Study Skills in the Elementary School," *Elementary English* 48 (1971): 648–51.

7. Ruth Ann Davies, *The School Library Media Center: A Force for Educational Excellence* (New York: R. R. Bowker Co., 1974).

8. H. Thomas Walker and Paula K. Montgomery, *Teaching Media Skills* (Littleton, Colorado: Libraries Unlimited, 1977), pp. 34–36.

9. In this section the author has drawn upon Board of Education of the City of New York, *The School Library Media Center,* pp. 145–58.

Chapter 14

1. There are also 350,000 French-speaking children; 180,000 American Indian (including Eskimo) children; 60,000 Portuguese children; 40,000 Chinese children; and 45,000 other non-English-speaking children. Maria M. Swanson, "Bilingual Education: The National Perspective" in *Responding to New Realities* (Skokie, Illinois: National Textbook Co., 1974) ed. Gilbert A. Jarvis, p. 82.

2. Muriel Saville-Troike, *Foundations for Teaching English as a Second Language* (Englewood Cliffs, New Jersey: Prentice-Hall, Inc., 1976), p. 134.

3. Ventura County (California) Superintendent of Schools Office, *Handbook for*

Goals and Objective for Learning English as a Second Language (Ventura, California: County Schools Office, 1972), p. 3.

4. Morris L. Krear and Charles R. Boucher, "A Comparison of Special Programs of Classes in English for Elementary School Pupils," *Modern Language Journal* 51 (1967): 335–37.

5. Clare Burstall et al., *Primary French in the Balance* (Atlantic Highlands, New Jersey: Humanities Press, Inc., 1974).

6. The ACTFL, located at 2 Park Avenue, New York 10016, is one of the two groups especially interested in helping ESOL teachers. The other is TESOL (Teachers of English to Speakers of Other Languages) located at 455 Nevils Building, Georgetown University, Washington, D.C. 20057. Both organizations publish excellent journals which are distributed at no charge to the members.

7. Oscar K. Buros, ed. *Seventh Mental Measurements Yearbook* (Highland Park, New Jersey: Gryphon Press, 1972), Vol. 1.

8. William T. Fagan, Charles R. Cooper, and Julie M. Jensen, *Measures for Research and Evaluation in the English Language Arts* (Urbana, Illinois: ERIC Clearinghouse on Reading and Communication Skills and the National Council of Teachers of English, 1975), pp. 150–56.

Appendix 1

Language Arts Textbook Evaluation*

Directions for use:

1. In each section indicated by a roman numeral, place a 3 before each item on which you think the text is outstandingly satisfactory.
2. Place a 2 before each item on which you think the text is more satisfactory than unsatisfactory.
3. Place a 1 before each item on which you think the text is more unsatisfactory than satisfactory.
4. Place a 0 before each item on which you think the text is completely unsatisfactory.
5. Total your points within each section. Record these totals on the Summary Sheet and compare them with those from other textbooks being evaluated. The book having the highest total is the most effective for your purposes.

I. Attitudes toward Language

_____ A. How effectively does the text capitalize on students' native understanding of language?

_____ B. How effectively does the text recognize that students may speak various dialects of English?

_____ C. How effectively does the text emphasize that several styles of speech and writing are appropriate to various situations?

_____ D. How effectively does the text emphasize that language changes constantly?

_____ E. How much attention does the text give to teaching reading, writing, listening, and speaking as skills of communication?

_____ F. How much attention does the text give to language as used outside the classroom in television, newspapers, magazines, and advertising?

_____ G. How much attention does the text give to the regional and social dialects of the United States?

_____ H. How much attention does the text give to the history of the English language?

_____ I. How much attention does the text give to the making and using of dictionaries?

_____ J. How clearly does the text explain that dictionaries describe usage and do *not* prescribe it?

Explanatory Notes and Comments: _____

_____

_____

* Reprinted with permission from Jean Malmstrom's *Understanding Language,* St. Martin's Press, Inc., 1977.

II. Motivation of Students

_____ A. How effectively will the text motivate the better students?
_____ B. How effectively will the text motivate the slower students?
_____ C. How effectively will the text encourage inductive thinking?
_____ D. How effectively will the text encourage deductive thinking?
_____ E. How successfully does the text describe options rather than present rules?
_____ F. How well does the text interrelate language study, composition, and literature?
_____ G. How originally does the text present material?
_____ H. How effectively does the text emphasize ideas and minimize linguistic terminology?

Explanatory Notes and Comments: _____

_____

_____

III. Adaptability

_____ A. How adaptable is the text for slow students?
_____ B. How adaptable is the text for average students?
_____ C. How adaptable is the text for superior students?
_____ D. How adaptable is the text for speakers of nonstandard dialects?
_____ E. How useful is the text as a reference tool?
_____ F. How useful is the text as a supplement to the curriculum?
_____ G. How useful is the text as a curriculum guide?

Explanatory Notes and Comments: _____

_____

_____

IV. Diction and Style

_____ A. How well will students like the writing style of the text?
_____ B. How accurately is word choice adjusted to the students for whom the text is intended? (Consider using a cloze test in reaching your conclusions.)
_____ C. How effectively does sentence variety increase the text's appeal?
_____ D. How much will the style of the text enhance your own effectiveness in the classroom?

Explanatory Notes and Comments: _____

_____

_____

_____ A. How clearly are the instructional goals of the text presented?

_____ B. How effectively do these goals mesh with your own instructional goals?

_____ C. How consistently is the viewpoint of the introductory comments and/or the teacher's manual maintained throughout the text?

Explanatory Notes and Comments: _____

_____

_____

Rate the text on the quality of each of the following.

_____ A. Reference features
(table of contents, index, illustrations)

_____ B. Physical features
(size, binding, printing, margins, paper)

Explanatory Notes and Comments: _____

_____

_____

_____ I. Attitudes toward language

_____ II. Motivation of students

_____ III. Adaptability

_____ IV. Diction and style

_____ V. Authority and reliability

_____ VI. Miscellaneous features

Overall Explanatory Notes and Comments: _____

_____

_____

Appendix 2

Guidelines for Equal Treatment of the Sexes*

The word *sexism* was coined, by analogy to *racism,* to denote discrimination based on gender. In its original sense, *sexism* referred to prejudice against the female sex. In a broader sense, the term now indicates any arbitrary stereotyping of males and females on the basis of their gender. . . . Women as well as men have been leaders and heroes, explorers and pioneers, and have made notable contributions to science, medicine, law, business, politics, civics, economics, literature, the arts, sports, and other areas of endeavor. Books dealing with subjects like these, as well as general histories, should acknowledge the achievements of women. The fact that women's rights, opportunities, and accomplishments have been limited by the social customs and conditions of their time should be openly discussed whenever relevant to the topic at hand.

We realize that the language of literature cannot be prescribed. The recommmendations in these guidelines, thus, are intended primarily for use in teaching materials, reference works, and nonfiction works in general.

Nonsexist Treatment of Women and Men

Men and women should be treated primarily as people, and not primarily as members of opposite sexes. Their shared humanity and common attributes should be stressed—not their gender difference. Neither sex should be stereotyped or arbitrarily assigned to a leading or secondary role.

1. a. Though many women will continue to choose traditional occupations such as homemaker or secretary, women should not be typecast in these roles but shown in a wide variety of professions and trades: as doctors and dentists, not always as nurses; as principals and professors, not always as teachers; as lawyers and judges, not always as social workers; as bank presidents, not always as tellers; as members of Congress, not always as members of the League of Women Voters.

   b. Similarly, men should not be shown as constantly subject to the "masculine mystique" in their interests, attitudes, or careers. They should not be made to feel that their self-worth depends entirely upon their income level or the status level of their jobs. They should not be conditioned to believe that a man ought to earn more than a woman or that he ought to be the sole support of a family.

   c. An attempt should be made to break job stereotypes for both women and men. No job should be considered sex-typed, and it should never be implied that certain jobs are incompatible with a woman's "femininity" or a man's "masculinity." Thus, women as well as men should be shown

* McGraw-Hill Book Company, New York, 1975.

as accountants, engineers, pilots, plumbers, bridge-builders, computer operators, TV repairers, and astronauts, while men as well as women should be shown as nurses, grade-school teachers, secretaries, typists, librarians, file clerks, switchboard operators, and baby-sitters.

Women within a profession should be shown at all professional levels, including the top levels. Women should be portrayed in positions of authority over men and over other women, and there should be no implication that a man loses face or that a woman faces difficulty if the employer or supervisor is a woman. All work should be treated as honorable and worthy of respect; no job or job choices should be downgraded. Instead, women and men should be offered more options than were available to them when work was stereotyped by sex.

d. Books designed for children at the preschool, elementary, and secondary levels should show married women who work outside the home and should treat them favorably. Teaching materials should not assume or imply that most women are wives who are also full-time mothers, but should instead emphasize the fact that women have choices about their marital status, just as men do: that some women choose to stay permanently single and some are in no hurry to marry; that some women marry but do not have children, while others marry, have children, and continue to work outside the home. Thus, a text might say that some married people have children and some do not, and that sometimes *one or both parents* work outside the home. Instructional materials should never imply that all women have a "mother instinct" or that the emotional life of a family suffers because a woman works. Instead they might state that when both parents work outside the home there is usually either greater sharing of the child-rearing activities or reliance on day-care centers, nursery schools, or other help.

According to Labor Department statistics for 1972, over 42 percent of all mothers with children under eighteen worked outside the home, and about a third of these working mothers had children under six. Publications ought to reflect this reality.

Both men and women should be shown engaged in home maintenance activities, ranging from cooking and housecleaning to washing the car and making household repairs. Sometimes the man should be shown preparing the meals, doing the laundry, or diapering the baby, while the woman builds bookcases or takes out the trash.

e. Girls should be shown as having, and exercising, the same options as boys in their play and career choices. In school materials, girls should be encouraged to show an interest in mathematics, mechanical skills, and active sports, for example, while boys should never be made to feel ashamed of an interest in poetry, art, or music, or an aptitude for cooking, sewing, or child care. Course materials should be addressed to students of both sexes. For example, home economics courses should apply to boys as well as girls, and shop to girls as well as boys. Both males and females should be shown in textbook illustrations depicting career choices.

When as a practical matter it is known that a book will be used primarily by women for the life of the edition (say, the next five years), it is pointless to pretend that the readership is divided equally between males and females. In such cases it may be more beneficial to address the book fully to women and exploit every opportunity (1) to point out to them a broader set of options than they might otherwise have considered, and (2) to encourage them to aspire to a more active, assertive, and policymaking role than they might otherwise have thought of.

f. Women and girls should be portrayed as active participants in the same proportion as men and boys in stories, examples, problems, illustrations, discussion questions, test items, and exercises, regardless of subject matter. Women should not be stereotyped in examples by being spoken of only in connection with cooking, sewing, shopping, and similar activities.

2. a. Members of both sexes should be represented as whole human beings with *human* strengths and weaknesses, not masculine or feminine ones. Women and girls should be shown as having the same abilities, interests, and ambitions as men and boys. Characteristics that have been traditionally praised in males—such as boldness, initiative, and assertiveness —should also be praised in females. Characteristics that have been praised in females—such as gentleness, compassion, and sensitivity— should also be praised in males.

b. Like men and boys, women and girls should be portrayed as independent, active, strong, courageous, competent, decisive, persistent, serious-minded, and successful. They should appear as logical thinkers, problem-solvers, and decision makers. They should be shown as interested in their work, pursuing a variety of career goals, and both deserving of and receiving public recognition for their accomplishments.

c. Sometimes men should be shown as quiet and passive, or fearful and indecisive, or illogical and immature. Similarly, women should sometimes be shown as tough, aggressive, and insensitive. Stereotypes of the logical, objective male and the emotional, subjective female are to be avoided. In descriptions, the smarter, braver, or more successful person should be a woman or girl as often as a man or boy. In illustrations, the taller, heavier, stronger, or more active person should not always be male, especially when children are portrayed.

3. Women and men should be treated with the same respect, dignity, and seriousness. Neither should be trivialized or stereotyped, either in text or in illustrations. Women should not be described by physical attributes when men are being described by mental attributes or professional position. Instead, both sexes should be dealt with in the same terms. References to a man's or a woman's appearance, charm, or intuition should be avoided when irrelevant.

No

Henry Harris is a shrewd lawyer and his wife Ann is a striking brunette.

Yes

The Harrises are an attractive couple. Henry is a handsome blond and Ann is a striking brunette.

Or

The Harrises are highly respected in their fields. Ann is an accomplished musician and Henry is a shrewd lawyer.

The Harrises are an interesting couple. Henry is a shrewd lawyer and Ann is very active in community (*or* church *or* civic) affairs.

a. In descriptions of women, a patronizing or girl-watching tone should be avoided, as should sexual innuendoes, jokes, and puns. Examples of practices to be avoided: focusing on physical appearance (a buxom blonde); using special female-gender word forms (poetess, aviatrix, usherette); treating women as sex objects or portraying the typical woman as weak, helpless, or hysterical; making women figures of fun or objects of scorn and treating their issues as humorous or unimportant.

   Examples of stereotypes to be avoided: scatterbrained female, fragile flower, goddess on a pedestal, catty gossip, henpecking shrew, apron-wearing mother, frustrated spinster, ladylike little girl. Jokes at women's expense—such as the woman driver or nagging mother-in-law cliches—are to be avoided.

No
the fair sex; the weaker sex

Yes
women

No
the distaff side

Yes
the female side or line

No
the girls or the ladies (when adult females are meant)

Yes
the women

No
girl, as in: I'll have my *girl* check that.

Yes
I'll have my *secretary* (or my *assistant*) check that. (Or use the person's name.)

No

lady used as a modifier, as in *lady* lawyer

Yes

lawyer (A woman may be identified simply through the choice of pronouns, as in: *The lawyer made her summation to the jury.* Try to avoid gender modifiers altogether. When you *must* modify, use *woman* or *female,* as in: *a course on women writers,* or *the airline's first female pilot.*)

No

the little woman; the better half; the ball and chain

Yes

wife

No

female-gender word forms, such as *authoress, poetess, Jewess*

Yes

author, poet, Jew

No

female-gender or diminutive word forms, such as *suffragette, usherette, aviatrix*

Yes

suffragist, usher, aviator (or pilot)

No

libber (a put-down)

Yes

feminist; liberationist

No

sweet young thing

Yes

young woman; girl

No

coed (as a noun)

Yes

student

> (*Note:* Logically, *coed* should refer to any student at a coeducational college or university. Since it does not, it is a sexist term.)

No

housewife

Yes

homemaker for a person who works at home, or rephrase with a more precise or more inclusive term

No

career girl or career woman

Yes

name the woman's profession: *attorney Ellen Smith; Marie Sanchez, a journalist* or editor or business executive or doctor or lawyer or agent

No

cleaning woman, cleaning lady, or *maid*

Yes

housekeeper; house or *office cleaner*

No

The sound of the drilling disturbed the housewives in the neighborhood.

Yes

The sound of the drilling disturbed everyone within earshot (or everyone in the neighborhood).

No

Housewives are feeling the pinch of higher prices.

Yes

Consumers (customers or shoppers) are feeling the pinch of higher prices.

b. In descriptions of men, especially men in the home, references to general ineptness should be avoided. Men should not be characterized as dependent on women for meals, or as clumsy in household maintenance, or as foolish in self-care.

To be avoided: characterizations that stress men's dependence on women for advice on what to wear and what to eat, inability of men to care for themselves in times of illness, and men as objects of fun (the henpecked husband).

c. Women should be treated as part of the rule, not as the exception.

Generic terms, such as doctor and nurse, should be assumed to include both men and women, and modified titles such as "woman doctor" or "male nurse," should be avoided. Work should never be stereotyped as "woman's work" or as "a man-sized job." Writers should avoid showing a "gee-whiz" attitude toward women who perform competently; ("Though a woman, she ran the business as well as any man" or "Though a woman, she ran the business efficiently.")

d. Women should be spoken of as participants in the action, not as possessions of the men. Terms such as *pioneer, farmer,* and *settler* should not be used as though they applied only to adult males.

No
Pioneers moved West, taking their wives and children with them.

Yes
Pioneer families moved West.

Pioneer men and women (or pioneer couples) moved West, taking their children with them.

e. Women should not be portrayed as needing male permission in order to act or to exercise rights (except, of course, for historical or factual accuracy).

No
Jim Weiss allows his wife to work part-time.

Yes
Judy Weiss works part-time.

4. Women should be recognized for their own achievements. Intelligent, daring, and innovative women, both in history and in fiction, should be provided as role-models for girls, and leaders in the fight for women's rights should be honored and respected, not mocked or ignored.

5. In references to humanity at large, language should operate to include women and girls. Terms that tend to exclude females should be avoided whenever possible.

a. The word *man* has long been used not only to denote a person of male gender, but also generically to denote humanity at large. To many people today, however, the word *man* has become so closely associated with the first meaning (a male human being) that they consider it no longer broad enough to be applied to any person or to human beings as a whole. In deference to this position, alternative expressions should be used in place of *man* (or derivative constructions used generically to signify humanity at large) whenever such substitutions can be made without producing an awkward or artificial construction. In cases where *man*-words must be used, special efforts should be made to ensure that pictures and other devices make explicit that such references include women.

Here are some possible substitutions for *man*-words:

No
mankind

Yes
humanity, human beings, human race, people

No

primitive man

Yes

primitive people or peoples; primitive human beings; primitive men and women

No

man's achievements

Yes

human achievements

No

If a man drove 50 miles at 60 mph . . .

Yes

If a person (or driver) drove 50 miles at 60 mph . . .

No

the best man for the job

Yes

the best person (or candidate) for the job

No

manmade

Yes

artificial; synthetic, manufactured; constructed; of human origin

No

manpower

Yes

human power; human energy; workers; workforce

No

grow to manhood

Yes

grow to adulthood; grow to manhood or womanhood

b. The English language lacks a generic singular pronoun signifying *he* or *she,* and therefore it has been customary and grammatically sanctioned to use masculine pronouns in expressions such as "one . . . *he,*" "anyone . . . *he,*" and "each child opens *his* book." Nevertheless, avoid when possible the pronouns *he, him,* and *his* in reference to the hypothetical person or humanity in general.

Various alternatives may be considered:

(1) Reword to eliminate unnecessary gender pronouns.

No

The average American drinks his coffee black.

Yes

The average American drinks black coffee.

(2) Recast into the plural.

Yes

Most Americans drink their coffee black.

(3) Replace the masculine pronoun with *one, you, he* or *she, her* or *his,* as appropriate. (Use *he* or *she* and its variations sparingly to avoid clumsy prose.)

(4) Alternate male and female expressions and examples.

No

I've often heard supervisors say, "He's not the right man for the job," or "He lacks the qualifications for success."

Yes

I've often heard supervisors say, "She's not the right person for the job," or "He lacks the qualifications for success."

(5) To avoid severe problems of repetition or inept wording, it may sometimes be best to use the generic *he* freely, but to add, in the preface and as often as necessary in the text, emphatic statements to the effect that the masculine pronouns are being used for succinctness and are intended to refer to both females and males.

These guidelines can only suggest a few solutions to difficult problems of rewording. The proper solution in any given passage must depend on the context and on the author's intention. For example, it would be wrong to pluralize in contexts stressing a one-to-one relationship, as between teacher and child. In such cases, the expression *he or she* or either *he* or *she* as appropriate will be acceptable.

c. Occupational terms ending in *man* should be replaced whenever possible by terms that can include members of either sex unless they refer to a particular person.

No

congressman

Yes

member of Congress; representative (but Congress*man* Koch and Congress*woman* Holzman)

No
businessman

Yes
business executive; business manager

No
fireman

Yes
fire fighter

No
mailman

Yes
mail carrier; letter carrier

No
salesman

Yes
sales representative; salesperson; salesclerk

No
insurance man

Yes
insurance agent

No
statesman

Yes
leader; public servant

No
chairman

Yes
the person presiding at (or chairing) a meeting; the presiding officer; the chair; head; leader; coordinator; moderator

No
cameraman

Yes
camera operator

No
foreman

Yes
supervisor

d. Language that assumes all readers are male should be avoided.

No
you and your wife
when you shave in the morning

Yes
you and your spouse
when you brush your teeth (or wash up) in the morning

6. The language used to designate and describe females and males should treat the sexes equally.
   a. Parallel language should be used for women and men.

   No
   the men and the ladies

   Yes
   the men and the women
   the ladies and the gentlemen
   the girls and the boys

   No
   man and wife

   Yes
   husband and wife

   Note that *lady* and *gentleman, wife* and *husband,* and *mother* and *father* are role words. *Ladies* should be used for women only when men are being referred to as *gentlemen.* Similarly, women should be called *wives* and *mothers* only when men are referred to as *husbands* and *fathers.* Like a male shopper, a woman in a grocery store should be called a *customer,* not a *housewife.*
   b. Women should be identified by their own names (e.g., Indira Gandhi). They should not be referred to in terms of their roles as wife, mother, sister, or daughter unless it is in these roles that they are significant in context. Nor should they be identified in terms of their marital relationships (Mrs. Gandhi) unless this brief form is stylistically more convenient (than, say Prime Minister Gandhi) or is paired up with similar references to men.

(1) A woman should be referred to by name in the same way that a man is. Both should be called by their full names, by first or last name only, or by title.

No
Bobby Riggs and Billie Jean

Yes
Bobby Riggs and Billie Jean King

No
Billie Jean and Riggs

Yes
Billie Jean and Bobby

No
Mrs. King and Riggs

Yes
King and Riggs
Ms. King (because she prefers Ms.) and Mr. Riggs

No
Mrs. Meir and Moshe Dayan

Yes
Golda Meir and Moshe Dayan or Mrs. Meir and Dr. Dayan

(2) Unnecessary reference to or emphasis on a woman's marital status should be avoided. Whether married or not, a woman may be referred to by the name by which she chooses to be known, whether her name is her original name or her married name.

c. Whenever possible, a term should be used that includes both sexes. Unnecessary references to gender should be avoided.

No
college boys and coeds

Yes
students

d. Insofar as possible, job titles should be nonsexist. Different nomenclature should not be used for the same job depending on whether it is held by a male or by a female. (See also paragraph 5c for additional examples of words ending in *man*.)

No
steward or purser or stewardess

Yes

flight attendant

No

policeman and policewoman

Yes

police officer

No

maid and houseboy

Yes

house or office cleaner; servant

e. Different pronouns should not be linked with certain work or occupations on the assumption that the worker is always (or usually) female or male. Instead either pluralize or use *he or she* and *she or he*.

No

the consumer or shopper . . . she

Yes

consumers or shoppers . . . they

No

the secretary . . . she

Yes

secretaries . . . they

No

the breadwinner . . . his earnings

Yes

the breadwinner . . . his or her earnings *or* breadwinners . . . their earnings.

f. Males should not always be first in order of mention. Instead, alternate the order, sometimes using: *women and men, gentlemen and ladies, she or he, her or his.*

The Caldecott Medal is named in honor of Randolph Caldecott (1846–1886), an English illustrator of children's books. The Medal is presented annually by a committee of the Children's Service Division of the American Library Association to "the artist of the most distinguished American picture book for children." The book must be an original work by a citizen or resident of the United States.

Caldecott Medal Books

1978 Award: *Noah's Ark: Story of the Flood.* Written and illustrated by Peter Spier. Doubleday.

Honor books: *It Could Always Be Worse.* Illustrated and retold by Margot Zemach. Farrar.
Castle. Written and illustrated by David Macaulay. Houghton Mifflin.

1977 Award: *Ashanti to Zulu: African Traditions.* Illustrated by Leo and Diane Dillon. Written by Margaret Musgrove. Dial.

Honor books: *The Golem: A Jewish Legend.* Illustrated and retold by Beverly McDermott. Lippincott.
The Contest: An Armenian Folktale. Adapted and illustrated by Nonny Hogrogian. Greenwillow.
Hawk, I'm Your Brother. Illustrated by Peter Parnall. Written by Byrd Baylor. Scribner.
The Amazing Bone. Written and illustrated by William Steig. Farrar.
Fish for Supper. Written and illustrated by M. B. Goffstein. Dial.

1976 Award: *Why Mosquitos Buzz in People's Ears.* Illustrated by Leo and Diane Dillon. Retold by Verna Aardema. Dial.

Honor books: *The Desert Is Theirs.* Illustrated by Peter Parnall. Written by Byrd Baylor. Scribner.
Strega Nona. Illustrated and retold by Tomie de Paola. Prentice.

1975 Award: *Arrow to the Sun.* Adapted and illustrated by Gerald McDermott. Viking.

Honor books: *Jambo Means Hello—Swahili Alphabet Book.* Illustrated by Tom Feelings. Written by Muriel Feelings. Dial.

1974 Award: *Duffy and the Devil*. Illustrated by Margot Zemach. Retold by Havre Zemach. Farrar.
Honor books: *Cathedral: The Story of Its Construction*. Written and illustrated by David Macaulay. Houghton Mifflin.
               Three Jovial Huntsmen. Adapted and illustrated by Susan Jeffers. Bradbury.

1973 Award: *The Funny Little Woman*. Illustrated by Blair Lent. Written by Arlene Mosel. Dutton.
Honor books: *Anansi the Spider*. Adapted and illustrated by Gerald McDermott. Holt.
               Hosie's Alphabet. Illustrated by Leonard Baskin. Written by Hosea, Tobias, and Lisa Baskin. Viking.
               Snow-White and the Seven Dwarfs. Illustrated by Nancy Ekholm Burkert. Translated from the Brothers Grimm by Randall Jarrell. Farrar.
               When Clay Sings. Illustrated by Tom Bahti. Written by Byrd Baylor.

1972 Award: *One Fine Day*. Illustrated and retold by Nonny Hogrogian. Macmillan.
Honor books: *If All the Seas Were One Sea*. Written and illustrated by Janina Domanska. Macmillan.
               Moja Means One: Swahili Counting Book. Illustrated by Tom Feelings. Written by Muriel Feelings. Dial.
               Hildilid's Night. Illustrated by Arnold Lobel. Written by Cheli Duran Ryan. Macmillan.

1971 Award: *A Story, a Story: An African Tale*. Retold and illustrated by Gail E. Haley. Atheneum.
Honor books: *The Angry Moon*. Illustrated by Blair Lent. Retold by William Sleator. Little, Brown.
               Frog and Toad Are Friends. Written and illustrated by Arnold Lobel. Harper.
               In the Night Kitchen. Written and illustrated by Maurice Sendak. Harper.

1970 Award: *Sylvester and the Magic Pebble*. Written and illustrated by William Steig. Windmill/Simon.
Honor books: *Goggles!* Written and illustrated by Ezra Jack Keats. Macmillan.
               Alexander and the Wind-up Mouse. Written and illustrated by Leo Lionni. Pantheon.
               Pop Corn and Ma Goodness. Illustrated by Robert Andrew Parker. Written by Edna Mitchell Preston. Viking.
               Thy Friend Obadiah. Written and illustrated by Brinton Burkle. Viking.

The Judge: An Untrue Tale. Illustrated by Margot Zemach. Written by Harve Zemach. Farrar.

1969 Award: *The Fool of the World and the Flying Ship: A Russian Tale.* Illustrated by Uri Shulevitz. Retold by Arthur Ransome. Farrar.

Honor books: *Why the Sun and the Moon Live in the Sky: An African Folk Tale.* Illustrated by Blair Lent. Retold by Elphinstone Dayrell. Houghton Mifflin.

1968 Award: *Drummer Hoff.* Illustrated by Ed Emberley. Adapted by Barbara Emberley. Prentice.

Honor books: *Frederick.* Written and illustrated by Leo Lionni. Pantheon.
Seashore Story. Written and illustrated by Taro Yashima. Viking.
The Emperor and the Kite. Illustrated by Ed Young. Written by Jane Yolen. World.

1967 Award: *Sam, Bangs and Moonshine.* Written and illustrated by Evaline Ness. Holt.

Honor books: *One Wide River to Cross.* Illustrated by Ed Emberley. Adapted by Barbara Emberley. Prentice.

1966 Award: *Always Room for One More.* Illustrated by Nonny Hogrogian. Written by Sorche Nic Leodhas, *pseud.* (Leclaire Alger). Holt.

Honor books: *Hide and Seek Fog.* Illustrated by Roger Duvoisin. Written by Alvin Tresselt. Lothrup.
Just Me. Written and illustrated by Marie Hall Ets. Viking.
Tom Tit Tot. Illustrated by Evaline Ness. Edited by Joseph Jacobs. Scribner.

1965 Award: *May I Bring a Friend?* Illustrated by Beni Montresor. Written by Beatrice Schenk de Regniers. Atheneum.

Honor books: *Rain Makes Applesauce.* Illustrated by Marvin Bileck. Written by Julian Scheer. Holiday House.
The Wave. Illustrated by Blair Lent. Written by Margaret Hodges. Houghton Mifflin.
A Pocketful of Cricket. Illustrated by Evaline Ness. Text by Rebecca Caudill. Holt.

1964 Award: *Where the Wild Things Are.* Written and illustrated by Maurice Sendak. Harper.

Honor books: *Swimmy.* Story and pictures by Leo Lionni. Pantheon.
All in the Morning Early. Illustrated by Evaline Ness. Text by Sorche Nic Leodhas, *pseud.* (Leclaire Alger). Holt.
Mother Goose and Nursery Rhymes. Illustrated by Philip Reed. Atheneum.

1963 Award:	*The Snowy Day*. Story and pictures by Ezra Jack Keats. Viking.
Honor books:	*The Sun is a Golden Earring*. Illustrated by Bernarda Bryson. Text by Natalia M. Belting. Holt.
	Mr. Rabbit and the Lovely Present. Illustrated by Maurice Sendak. Written by Charlotte Zolotow. Harper.
1962 Award:	*Once a Mouse*. Retold and illustrated by Marcia Brown. Scribner.
Honor books:	*The Fox Went Out on a Chilly Night*. Illustrated by Peter Spier. Doubleday.
	Little Bear's Visit. Illustrated by Maurice Sendak. Written by Else H. Minarik. Harper.
	The Day We Saw the Sun Come Up. Illustrated by Adrienne Adams. Written by Alice E. Goudey. Scribner.
1961 Award:	*Baboushka and the Three Kings*. Illustrated by Nicolas Sidjakov. Written by Ruth Robbins. Parnassus Press.
Honor books:	*Inch by Inch*. Written and illustrated by Leo Lionni. Ivan Obolensky, Inc.
1960 Award:	*Nine Days to Christmas*. Illustrated by Marie Hall Ets. Written by Marie Hall Ets and Aurora Labastida. Viking.
Honor books:	*Houses from the Sea*. Illustrated by Adrienne Adams. Written by Alice E. Goudey. Scribner.
	The Moon Jumpers. Illustrated by Maurice Sendak. Written by Janice May Udry. Harper.
1959 Award:	*Chanticleer and the Fox*. Adapted from Chaucer's *The Canterbury Tales* and illustrated by Barbara Cooney. Crowell.
Honor books:	*The House that Jack Built: La Maison Que Jacques A Batie*. Text and illustrations by Antonio Frasconi. Harcourt.
	What Do You Say, Dear? Illustrated by Maurice Sendak. Written by Sesyle Joslin. W. R. Scott.
	Umbrella. Story and pictures by Taro Yashima. Viking.
1958 Award:	*Time of Wonder*. Written and illustrated by Robert McCloskey. Viking.
Honor books:	*Fly High, Fly Low*. Story and pictures by Don Freeman. Viking.
	Anatole and the Cat. Illustrated by Paul Galdone. Written by Eve Titus. McGraw-Hill.
1957 Award:	*A Tree Is Nice*. Illustrated by Marc Simont. Written by Janice May Udry. Harper.
Honor books:	*Mr. Penny's Race Horse*. Written and illustrated by Marie Hall Ets. Viking.
	1 Is One. Story and pictures by Tasha Tudor. Walck.

Anatole. Illustrated by Paul Galdone. Written by Eve Titus. McGraw-Hill.

Gillespie and the Guards. Illustrated by James Daugherty. Written by Benjamin Elkin. Viking.

Lion. Written and illustrated by William Pène du Bois. Viking.

1956 Award: *Frog Went A-Courtin'*. Illustrated by Feodor Rojankovsky. Text retold by John Langstaff. Harcourt.

Honor books: *Play With Me*. Story and pictures by Marie Hall Ets. Viking.

Crow Boy. Written and illustrated by Taro Yashima. Viking.

1955 Award: *Cinderella, or the Little Glass Slipper*. Illustrated and translated from Charles Perrault by Marcia Brown. Scribner.

Honor books: *Book of Nursery and Mother Goose Rhymes*. Illustrated by Marguerite de Angeli. Doubleday.

Wheel on the Chimney. Illustrated by Tibor Gergely. Written by Margaret Wise Brown. Lippincott.

The Thanksgiving Story. Illustrated by Helen Sewell. Text by Alice Dalgliesh. Scribner.

1954 Award: *Madeline's Rescue*. Written and illustrated by Ludwig Bemelmans. Viking.

Honor books: *Journey Cake, Ho!* Illustrated by Robert McCloskey. Text by Ruth Sawyer. Viking.

When Will the World Be Mine? Illustrated by Jean Charlot. Written by Miriam Schlein. W. R. Scott.

The Steadfast Tin Soldier. Illustrated by Marcia Brown. Story by Hans Christian Andersen, trans. by M. R. James. Scribner.

A Very Special House. Illustrated by Maurice Sendak. Written by Ruth Krauss. Harper.

Green Eyes. Story and pictures by A. Birnbaum. Capitol Pub.

1953 Award: *The Biggest Bear*. Written and illustrated by Lynd Ward. Houghton Mifflin.

Honor books: *Puss in Boots*. Illustrated and translated from Charles Perrault by Marcia Brown. Scribner.

One Morning in Maine. Written and illustrated by Robert McCloskey. Viking.

Ape in a Cape: An Alphabet of Odd Animals. Text and pictures by Fritz Eichenberg. Harcourt.

The Storm Book. Illustrated by Margaret Bloy Graham. Written by Charlotte Zolotow. Harper.

Five Little Monkeys. Story and illustrations by Juliet Kepes. Houghton Mifflin.

1952 Award: *Finders Keepers*. Illustrated by Nicolas, *pseud*. (Nicolas Mordvinoff). Written by Will, *pseud*. (William Lipkind). Harcourt.

Honor books:	*Mr. T. W. Anthony Woo*. Story and pictures by Marie Hall Ets. Viking.

Honor books: *Mr. T. W. Anthony Woo*. Story and pictures by Marie Hall Ets. Viking.

Skipper John's Cook. Written and illustrated by Marcia Brown. Scribner.

All Falling Down. Illustrated by Margaret Bloy Graham. Written by Gene Zion. Harper.

Bear Party. Written and illustrated by William Pène du Bois. Viking.

Feather Mountain. Written and illustrated by Elizabeth Olds. Houghton Mifflin.

1951 Award: *The Egg Tree*. Written and illustrated by Katherine Milhous. Scribner.

Honor books: *Dick Whittington and His Cat*. Told and illustrated by Marcia Brown. Scribner.

The Two Reds. Illustrated by Nicolas, *pseud.* (Nicolas Mordvinoff). Written by Will, *pseud.* (William Lipkind). Harcourt.

If I Ran the Zoo. Written and illustrated by Dr. Seuss, *pseud.* (Theodor Seuss Geisel). Random House.

The Most Wonderful Doll in the World. Illustrated by Helen Stone. Written by Phyllis McGinley. Lippincott.

T-Bone, the Baby Sitter. Story and pictures by Claire Turlay Newberry. Harper.

1950 Award: *Song of the Swallows*. Written and illustrated by Leo Politi. Scribner.

Honor books: *America's Ethan Allen*. Pictures by Lynd Ward. Story by Stewart Holbrook. Houghton Mifflin.

The Wild Birthday Cake. Illustrated by Hildegard Woodward. Written by Lavinia R. Davis. Doubleday.

The Happy Day. Pictures by Marc Simont. Story by Ruth Krauss. Harper.

Bartholomew and the Oobleck. Written and illustrated by Dr. Seuss, *pseud.* (Theodor Seuss Geisel). Random House.

Henry—Fisherman. Written and illustrated by Marcia Brown, Scribner.

1949 Award: *The Big Snow*. Written and illustrated by Berta and Elmer Hader. Macmillan.

Honor books: *Blueberries for Sal*. Written and illustrated by Robert McCloskey. Viking.

All Around the Town. Illustrated by Helen Stone. Text by Phyllis McGinley. Lippincott.

Juanita. Written and illustrated by Leo Politi. Scribner.

Fish in the Air. Story and pictures by Kurt Wiese. Viking.

1948 Award: *White Snow, Bright Snow.* Illustrated by Roger Duvoisin. Written by Alvin Tresselt. Lothrop.

Honor books: *Stone Soup.* Told and illustrated by Marcia Brown. Scribner.
McElligot's Pool. Written and illustrated by Dr. Seuss, *pseud.* (Theodor Seuss Geisel). Random House.
Bambino the Clown. Text and pictures by George Schreiber. Viking.
Roger and the Fox. Pictures by Hildegard Woodward. Text by Lavinia Davis. Doubleday.
Song of Robin Hood. Designed and illustrated by Virginia Lee Burton. Selected and edited by Anne Malcolmson. Houghton Mifflin.

1947 Award: *The Little Island.* Illustrated by Leonard Weisgard. Written by Golden MacDonald, *pseud.* (Margaret Wise Brown). Doubleday.

Honor books: *Rain Drop Splash.* Illustrated by Leonard Weisgard. Story by Alvin Tresselt. Lothrop.
Boats on the River. Illustrated by Jay Hyde Barnum. Text by Marjorie Flack. Viking.
Timothy Turtle. Illustrated by Tony Palazzo. Written by Al Graham. Robert Welch Pub. Co.
Pedro, the Angel of Olvera Street. Text and illustrations by Leo Politi. Scribner.
Sing in Praise: a Collection of the Best Loved Hymns. Illustrated by Marjorie Torrey. Stories of hymns and musical arrangements by Opal Wheeler. Dutton.

1946 Award: *The Rooster Crows . . .* Illustrated by Maud and Miska Petersham. Macmillan.

Honor books: *Little Lost Lamb.* Illustrated by Leonard Weisgard. Text by Golden MacDonald, *pseud.* (Margaret Wise Brown). Doubleday.
Sing Mother Goose. Illustrated by Marjorie Torrey. Music by Opal Wheeler. Dutton.
My Mother Is the Most Beautiful Woman in the World. Illustrated by Ruth Gannett. Retold by Becky Reyher. Lothrop.
You Can Write Chinese. Text and illustrations by Kurt Wiese. Viking.

1945 Award: *Prayer for a Child.* Illustrated by Elizabeth Orton Jones. Written by Rachel Field. Macmillan.

Honor books: *Mother Goose.* Illustrated by Tasha Tudor. Walck.
In the Forest. Story and pictures by Marie Hall Ets. Viking.
Yonie Wondernose. Written and illustrated by Marguerite de Angeli. Doubleday.

The Christmas Anna Angel. Illustrated by Kate Seredy. Written by Ruth Sawyer. Viking.

1944 Award: *Many Moons.* Illustrated by Louis Slobodkin. Written by James Thurber. Harcourt.

Honor books: *Small Rain: Verses from the Bible.* Illustrated by Elizabeth Orton Jones. Verses selected by Jessie Orton Jones. Viking.

Pierre Pidgeon. Illustrated by Arnold E. Bare. Text by Lee Kingman. Houghton Mifflin.

The Mighty Hunter. Story and pictures by Berta and Elmer Hader. Macmillan.

A Child's Good Night Book. Illustrated by Jean Charlot. Text by Margaret Wise Brown. W. R. Scott.

Good-Luck Horse. Illustrated by Plato Chan. Text by Chih-Yi Chan. Whittlesey.

1943 Award: *The Little House.* Written and illustrated by Virginia Lee Burton. Houghton Mifflin.

Honor books: *Dash and Dart.* Story and pictures by Mary and Conrad Buff. Viking.

Marshmallow. Story and pictures by Clare Turlay Newberry. Harper.

1942 Award: *Make Way for Ducklings.* Written and illustrated by Robert McCloskey. Viking.

Honor books: *An American ABC.* Text and pictures by Maud and Miska Petersham. Macmillan.

In My Mother's House. Illustrated by Velino Herrera. Text by Ann Nolan Clark. Viking.

Paddle-to-the-Sea. Written and illustrated by Holling C. Holling. Houghton Mifflin.

Nothing At All. Story and pictures by Wanda Gag. Coward-McCann.

1941 Award: *They Were Strong and Good.* Written and illustrated by Robert Lawson. Viking.

Honor books: *April's Kittens.* Story and pictures by Clare Turlay Newberry. Harper.

1940 Award: *Abraham Lincoln.* Written and illustrated by Ingri and Edgar d'Aulaire. Doubleday.

Honor books: *Cock-a-Doodle Doo . . .* Story and pictures by Berta and Elmer Hader. Macmillan.

Madeline. Story and pictures by Ludwig Bemelmans. Viking.

The Ageless Story. Illustrated by Lauren Ford. Dodd Mead.

1939 Award: *Mei Li.* Illustrated and written by Thomas Handforth. Doubleday.

Honor books: *The Forest Pool.* Story and pictures by Laura Adams Armer. Longmans.

Wee Gillis. Illustrated by Robert Lawson. Text by Munroe Leaf. Viking.

Snow White and the Seven Dwarfs. Freely translated and illustrated by Wanda Gag. Coward-McCann.

Barkis. Story and pictures by Clare Newberry. Harper.

Andy and the Lion. Written and illustrated by James Daugherty. Viking.

1938 Award: *Animals of the Bible, A Picture Book.* Illustrated by Dorothy P. Lathrop. Text selected by Helen Dean Fish. Lippincott.

Honor books: *Seven Simeons: a Russian Tale.* Retold and illustrated by Boris Artzybasheff. Viking.

Four and Twenty Blackbirds . . . Illustrated by Robert Lawson. Compiled by Helen Dean Fish. Stokes.

Newbery Medal Books

The Newbery Medal is named in honor of John Newbery (1713–1767), an English bookseller and publisher. The Medal is presented annually by a committee of the Children's Service Division of the American Library Association to "the author of the most distinguished contribution to American literature for children." The book must be an original work by a citizen or resident of the United States.

1978 Award: *Bridge to Terabithia.* Katherine Paterson. Crowell.

Honor books: *Anpao: An American Indian Odyssey.* Jamake Highwater. Lippincott.

Ramona and Her Father. Beverly Cleary. Morrow.

1977 Award: *Roll of Thunder, Hear My Cry.* Mildred Taylor. Dial.

Honor books: *A String in the Harp.* Nancy Bond. Atheneum.

Abel's Island. William Steig. Farrar.

1976 Award: *The Grey King.* Susan Cooper. Atheneum/McElderry.

Honor books: *The Hundred Penny Box.* Sharon Bell Mathis. Viking.

Dragonwings. Lawrence Yep. Harper.

1975 Award: *M. C. Higgins, the Great.* Virginia Hamilton. Macmillan.

Honor books: *My Brother Sam Is Dead.* James Lincoln Collier and Christopher Collier. Four Winds.

Philip Hall Likes Me, I Reckon Maybe. Bette Greene. Dial.

Figgs & Phantoms. Ellen Raskin. Dutton.

The Perilous Gard. Elizabeth Marie Pope. Houghton.

1974 Award:	*The Slave Dancer*. Paula Fox. Bradbury.
Honor book:	*The Dark Is Rising*. Susan Cooper. Atheneum.
1973 Award:	*Julie of the Wolves*. Jean Craighead George. Harper.
Honor books:	*Frog and Toad Together*. Arnold Lobel. Harper.
	The Upstairs Room. Johanna Reiss. Crowell.
	The Witches of Worm. Zilpha Keatley Snyder. Atheneum.
1972 Award:	*Mrs. Frisby and the Rats of NIMH*. Robert C. O'Brien. Atheneum.
Honor books:	*Incident at Hawk's Hill*. Allan W. Eckert. Little, Brown.
	The Planet of Junior Brown. Virginia Hamilton. Macmillan.
	The Tombs of Atuan. Ursula K. Le Guin. Atheneum.
	Annie and the Old One. Miska Miles. Little, Brown.
	The Headless Cupid. Zilpha Keatley Snyder. Atheneum.
1971 Award:	*The Summer of the Swans*. Betsy Byars. Viking.
Honor books:	*Kneeknock Rise*. Natalie Babbitt. Farrar.
	Enchantress from the Stars. Sylvia Louis Engdahl. Atheneum.
	Sing Down the Moon. Scott O'Dell. Houghton.
1970 Award:	*Sounder*. William Armstrong. Harper.
Honor books:	*Our Eddie*. Sulamith Ish-Kishor. Pantheon.
	The Many Ways of Seeing: An Introduction to the Pleasures of Art. Janet Gaylord Moore. World.
	Journey Outside. Mary Q. Steele. Viking.
1969 Award:	*The High King*. Lloyd Alexander. Holt.
Honor books:	*To Be a Slave*. Julius Lester. Dial.
	When Schlemiel Went to Warsaw and Other Stories. Isaac Bashevis Singer. Farrar.
1968 Award:	*From the Mixed-Up Files of Mrs. Basil E. Frankweiler*. E. L. Konigsburg. Atheneum.
Honor books:	*Jennifer, Hecate, Macbeth, William McKinley, and Me, Elizabeth*. E. L. Konigsburg. Atheneum.
	The Black Pearl. Scott O'Dell. Houghton.
	The Fearsome Inn. Isaac Bashevis Singer. Scribner.
	The Egypt Game. Zilpha Keatley Snyder. Atheneum.
1967 Award:	*Up A Road Slowly*. Irene Hunt. Follett.
Honor books:	*The King's Fifth*. Scott O'Dell. Houghton Mifflin.
	Zlateh the Goat and Other Stories. Isaac Bashevis Singer. Harper.
	The Jazz Man. Mary Hays Weik. Atheneum.
1966 Award:	*I, Juan de Pareja*. Elizabeth Borton de Trevino. Farrar.
Honor books:	*The Black Cauldron*. Lloyd Alexander. Holt.

The Animal Family. Randall Jarrell. Pantheon.
The Noonday Friends. Mary Stolz. Harper.

1965 Award: *Shadow of a Bull*. Maia Wojciechowska. Atheneum.
Honor books: *Across Five Aprils*. Irene Hunt. Follett.

1964 Award: *It's Like This, Cat*. Emily Neville. Harper.
Honor books: *Rascal*. Sterling North. Dutton.
The Loner. Ester Wier. McKay.

1963 Award: *A Wrinkle in Time*. Madeleine L'Engle. Farrar, Straus.
Honor books: *Thistle and Thyme: Tales and Legends from Scotland*. Sorche Nic Leodhas, *pseud*. (Leclaire Alger). Holt.
Men of Athens. Olivia Coolidge. Houghton Mifflin.

1962 Award: *The Bronze Bow*. Elizabeth George Speare. Houghton Mifflin.
Honor books: *Frontier Living*. Edwin Tunis. World.
The Golden Goblet. Eloise Jarvis McGraw. Coward-McCann.
Belling the Tiger. Mary Stolz. Harper.

1961 Award: *Island of the Blue Dolphins*. Scott O'Dell. Houghton Mifflin.
Honor books: *America Moves Forward*. Gerald W. Johnson. Morrow.
Old Ramon, Jack Schaeffer. Houghton Mifflin.
The Cricket in Times Square. George Seldon, *pseud*. (George Thompson). Farrar, Straus.

1960 Award: *Onion John*. Joseph Krumgold. Crowell.
Honor books: *My Side of the Mountain*. Jean George. Dutton.
America Is Born. Gerald W. Johnson. Morrow.
The Gammage Cup. Carol Kendall. Harcourt.

1959 Award: *The Witch of Blackbird Pond*. Elizabeth George Speare. Houghton Mifflin.
Honor books: *The Family Under the Bridge*. Natalie S. Carlson. Harper.
Along Came a Dog. Meindert DeJong. Harper.
Chicaro: Wild Pony of the Pampa. Francis Kalnay. Harcourt.
The Perilous Road. William O. Steele. Harcourt.

1958 Award: *Rifles for Watie*. Harold Keith. Crowell.
Honor books: *The Horsecatcher*. Mari Sandoz. Westminster.
Gone-Away Lake. Elizabeth Enright. Harcourt.
The Great Wheel. Robert Lawson. Viking.
Tom Paine, Freedom's Apostle. Leo Gurko. Crowell.

1957 Award: *Miracles on Maple Hill*. Virginia Sorensen. Harcourt.
Honor books: *Old Yeller*. Fred Gipson. Harper.
The House of Sixty Fathers. Meindert DeJong. Harper.
Mr. Justice Holmes. Clara Ingram Judson. Follett.
The Corn Grows Ripe. Dorothy Rhoads. Viking.
The Black Fox of Lorne. Marguerite de Angeli. Doubleday.

1956 Award: *Carry On, Mr. Bowditch.* Jean Lee Latham. Houghton Mifflin.
Honor books: *The Secret River.* Marjorie Kinnan Rawlings. Scribner.
The Golden Name Day. Jennie Lindquist. Harper.
Men, Microscopes, and Living Things. Katherine Shippen. Viking.

1955 Award: *The Wheel on the School.* Meindert DeJong. Harper.
Honor books: *The Courage of Sarah Noble.* Alice Dalgliesh. Scribner.
Banner in the Sky. James Ullman. Lippincott.

1954 Award: *. . . and now Miguel.* Joseph Krumgold. Crowell.
Honor books: *All Alone.* Claire Huchet Bishop. Viking.
Shadrach. Meindert DeJong. Harper.
Hurry Home, Candy. Meindert DeJong. Harper.
Theodore Roosevelt, Fighting Patriot. Clara Ingram Judson. Follett.
Magic Maize. Mary and Conrad Buff. Houghton Mifflin.

1953 Award: *Secret of the Andes.* Ann Nolan Clark. Viking.
Honor books: *Charlotte's Web.* E. B. White. Harper.
Moccasin Trail. Eloise McGraw. Coward-McCann.
Red Sails to Capri. Ann Weil. Viking.
The Bears on Hemlock Mountain. Alice Dalgliesh. Scribner.
Birthdays of Freedom. Genevieve Foster. Scribner.

1952 Award: *Ginger Pye.* Eleanor Estes. Harcourt.
Honor books: *Americans Before Columbus.* Elizabeth Baity. Viking.
Minn of the Mississippi. Holling C. Holling. Houghton Mifflin.
The Defender. Nicholas Kalashnikoff. Scribner.
The Light at Tern Rock. Julia Sauer. Viking.
The Apple and the Arrow. Mary and Conrad Buff. Houghton Mifflin.

1951 Award: *Amos Fortune, Free Man.* Elizabeth Yates. Aladdin.
Honor books: *Better Known as Johnny Appleseed.* Mabel Leigh Hunt. Lippincott.
Gandhi, Fighter Without a Sword. Jeanette Eaton. Morrow.
Abraham Lincoln, Friend of the People. Clara Ingram Judson. Wilcox and Follett.
The Story of Appleby Capple. Anne Parrish. Harper.

1950 Award: *The Door in the Wall.* Marguerite de Angeli. Doubleday.
Honor books: *Tree of Freedom.* Rebecca Caudill. Viking.
The Blue Cat of Castle Town. Catherine Coblentz. Longmans.
Kildee House. Rutherford Montgomery. Doubleday.
George Washington. Genevieve Foster. Scribner.
Song of the Pines. Walter and Marion Havighurst. Winston.

1949 Award: *King of the Wind*. Marguerite Henry. Rand McNally.
Honor books: *Seabird*. Holling C. Holling. Houghton Mifflin.
Daughter of the Mountain. Louis Rankin. Viking.
My Father's Dragon. Ruth Gannett. Random House.
Story of the Negro. Arna Bontemps. Knopf.

1948 Award: *The Twenty-One Balloons*. William Pène du Bois. Viking.
Honor books: *Pancakes—Paris*. Claire Huchet Bishop. Viking.
Li Lun, Lad of Courage. Carolyn Treffinger. Abingdon.
The Quaint and Curious Quest of Johnny Longfoot. Catherine Besterman. Bobbs-Merrill.
The Cow-tail Switch, and Other West African Stories. Harold Courlander. Holt.
Misty of Chincoteague. Marguerite Henry. Rand McNally.

1947 Award: *Miss Hickory*. Carolyn Sherwin Bailey. Viking.
Honor books: *The Wonderful Year*. Nancy Barnes. Messner.
Big Tree. Mary and Conrad Buff. Viking.
The Heavenly Tenants. William Maxwell. Harper.
The Avion My Uncle Flew. Cyrus Fisher, *pseud.* (Darwin L. Teilhet). Appleton.
The Hidden Treasure of Glaston. Eleanore Jewett. Viking.

1946 Award: *Strawberry Girl*. Lois Lenski. Lippincott.
Honor books: *Justin Morgan Had a Horse*. Marguerite Henry. Rand McNally.
The Moved-Outers. Florence Crannell Means. Houghton Mifflin.
Bhimsa, the Dancing Bear. Christine Weston. Scribner.
New Found World. Katherine Shippen. Viking.

1945 Award: *Rabbit Hill*. Robert Lawson. Viking.
Honor books: *The Hundred Dresses*. Eleanor Estes. Harcourt.
The Silver Pencil. Alice Dalgliesh. Scribner.
Abraham Lincoln's World. Genevieve Foster. Scribner.
Lone Journey: The Life of Roger Williams. Jeanette Eaton. Harcourt.

1944 Award: *Johnny Tremain*. Esther Forbes. Houghton Mifflin.
Honor books: *These Happy Golden Years*. Laura Ingalls Wilder. Harper.
Fog Magic. Julia Sauer. Viking.
Mountain Born. Elizabeth Yates. Coward-McCann.
Rufus M. Eleanor Estes. Harcourt.

1943 Award: *Adam of the Road*. Elizabeth Jane Gray. Viking.
Honor books: *The Middle Moffat*. Eleanor Estes. Harcourt.
"Have You Seen Tom Thumb?" Mabel Leigh Hunt. Lippincott.

1942 Award: *The Matchlock Gun.* Walter D. Edmonds. Dodd, Mead.
Honor books: *Little Town on the Prairie.* Laura Ingalls Wilder. Harper.
George Washington's World. Genevieve Foster. Scribner.
Indian Captive: the Story of Mary Jemison. Lois Lenski. Lippincott.
Down Ryton Water. Eva Roe Gaggin. Viking.

1941 Award: *Call It Courage.* Armstrong Sperry. Macmillan.
Honor books: *Blue Willow.* Doris Gates. Viking.
Young Mac of Fort Vancouver. Mary Jane Carr. Crowell.
The Long Winter. Laura Ingalls Wilder. Harper.
Nansen. Anna Gertrude Hall. Viking.

1940 Award: *Daniel Boone.* James Daugherty. Viking.
Honor books: *The Singing Tree.* Kate Seredy. Viking.
Runner of the Mountain Tops. Mabel Robinson. Random House.
By the Shores of Silver Lake. Laura Ingalls Wilder. Harper.
Boy with a Pack. Stephen W. Meader. Harcourt.

1939 Award: *Thimble Summer.* Elizabeth Enright. Rinehart.
Honor books: *Nino.* Valenti Angelo. Viking.
Mr. Popper's Penguins. Richard and Florence Atwater. Little, Brown.
"Hello, the Boat!" Phyllis Crawford. Holt.
Leader by Destiny: George Washington, Man and Patriot. Jeanette Eaton. Harcourt.
Penn. Elizabeth Janet Gray. Viking.

1938 Award: *The White Stag.* Kate Seredy. Viking.
Honor books: *Pecos Bill.* James Cloyd Bowman. Little, Brown.
Bright Island. Mabel Robinson. Random House.
On the Banks of Plum Creek. Laura Ingalls Wilder. Harper.

1937 Award: *Roller Skates.* Ruth Sawyer. Viking.
Honor books: *Phebe Fairchild: Her Book.* Lois Lenski. Stokes.
Whistlers' Van. Idwal Jones. Viking.
The Golden Basket. Ludwig Bemelmans. Viking.
Winterbound. Margery Bianco. Viking.
Audubon. Constance Rourke. Harcourt.
The Codfish Musket. Agnes Hewes. Doubleday.

1936 Award: *Caddie Woodlawn.* Carol Brink. Macmillan.
Honor books: *Honk, the Moose.* Phil Stong. Dodd, Mead.
The Good Master. Kate Seredy. Viking.
Young Walter Scott. Elizabeth Janet Gray. Viking.
All Sail Set. Armstrong Sperry. Winston.

1935 Award:	*Dobry*. Monica Shannon. Viking.
Honor books:	*The Pageant of Chinese History*. Elizabeth Seeger. Longmans.
	Davy Crockett. Constance Rourke. Harcourt.
	A Day on Skates. Hilda Van Stockum. Harper.

1934 Award: *Invincible Louisa*. Cornelia Meigs. Little, Brown.
Honor books: *The Forgotten Daughter*. Caroline Snedeker. Doubleday.
Swords of Steel. Elsie Singmaster. Houghton Mifflin.
ABC Bunny. Wanda Gag. Coward-McCann.
Winged Girl of Knossos. Erik Berry, *pseud.* (Allena Best). Appleton-Century.
New Land. Sarah Schmidt. McBride.
Big Tree of Bunlahy. Padraic Colum. Macmillan.
Glory of the Seas. Agnes Hewes. Knopf.
Apprentice of Florence. Anne Kyle. Houghton Mifflin.

1933 Award: *Young Fu of the Upper Yangtze*. Elizabeth Lewis. Winston.
Honor books: *Swift Rivers*. Cornelia Meigs. Little, Brown.
The Railroad to Freedom. Hildegarde Swift. Harcourt.
Children of the Soil. Nora Burglon. Doubleday.

1932 Award: *Waterless Mountain*. Laura Adams Armer. Longmans.
Honor books: *The Fairy Circus*. Dorothy Lathrop. Macmillan.
Calico Bush. Rachel Field. Macmillan.
Boy of the South Seas. Eunice Tietjens. Coward-McCann.
Out of the Flame. Eloise Lownsbery. Longmans.
Jane's Island. Marjorie Allee. Houghton Mifflin.
Truce of the Wolf and Other Tales of Old Italy. Mary Gould Davis. Harcourt.

1931 Award: *The Cat Who Went to Heaven*. Elizabeth Coatsworth. Macmillan.
Honor books: *Floating Island*. Anne Parrish. Harper.
The Dark Star of Itza. Alida Malkus. Harcourt.
Queer Person. Ralph Hubbard. Doubleday.
Mountains Are Free. Julia Davis Adams. Dutton.
Spice and the Devil's Cave. Agnes Hewes. Knopf.
Meggy MacIntosh. Elizabeth Janet Gray. Doubleday.
Garram the Hunter. Herbert Best. Doubleday.
Ood-le-uk the Wanderer. Alice Lide and Margaret Johansen. Little, Brown.

1930 Award: *Hitty, Her First Hundred Years*. Rachel Field. Macmillan.
Honor books: *Daughter of the Seine*. Jeanette Eaton. Harper.
Pran of Albania. Elizabeth Miller. Doubleday.
The Jumping-Off Place. Marian Hurd McNeely. Longmans.
Tangle-Coated Horse and Other Tales. Ella Young. Longmans.

Vaino. Julia Davis Adams. Dutton.
Little Blacknose. Hildegarde Swift. Harcourt.

1929 Award:	*The Trumpeter of Krakow*. Eric P. Kelly. Macmillan.
Honor books:	*Pigtail of Ah Lee Ben Loo*. John Bennett. Longmans.
	Millions of Cats. Wanda Gag. Coward-McCann.
	The Boy Who Was. Grace Hallock. Dutton.
	Clearing Weather. Cornelia Meigs. Little, Brown.
	Runaway Papoose. Grace Moon. Doubleday.
	Tod of the Fens. Elinor Whitney. Macmillan.

1928 Award: *Gay-Neck, the Story of a Pigeon*. Dhan Gopal Mukerji. Dutton.

Honor books: *The Wonder Smith and His Son*. Ella Young. Longmans.
Downright Dencey. Caroline Snedeker. Doubleday.

1927 Award: *Smoky, the Cowhorse*. Will James. Scribner.
Honor books: No record.

1926 Award: *Shen of the Sea*. Arthur Bowie Chrisman. Dutton.
Honor books: *The Voyagers*. Padraic Colum. Macmillan.

1925 Award: *Tales from Silver Lands*. Charles Finger. Doubleday.
Honor books: *Nicholas*. Anne Carroll Moore. Putnam.
Dream Coach. Anne Parrish. Macmillan.

1924 Award: *The Dark Frigate*. Charles Hawes. Little, Brown.
Honor books: No record.

1923 Award: *The Voyages of Doctor Dolittle*. Hugh Lofting. Lippincott.
Honor books: No record.

1922 Award: *The Story of Mankind*. Hendrik Willem van Loon. Liveright.
Honor books: *The Great Quest*. Charles Hawes. Little, Brown.
Cedric the Forester. Bernard Marshall. Appleton-Century.
The Old Tobacco Shop. William Bowen. Macmillan.
The Golden Fleece and the Heroes Who Lived Before Achilles. Padraic Colum. Macmillan.
Windy Hill. Cornelia Meigs. Macmillan.

1979 Award-Winning Children's Books

Caldecott Medal Books

1979 Award: *The Girl Who Loved Wild Horses*. Written and illustrated by Paul Goble. Bradbury.

Honor books: *Freight Train*. Written and illustrated by Donald Crews. Greenwillow.
The Way to Start a Day. Illustrated by Paul Parnall. Written by Byrd Baylor. Scribner.

Newbery Medal Books

1979 Award: *The Westing Game*. Ellen Raskin. Dutton.
Honor books: *The Great Gilly Hopkins*. Katherine Paterson. Crowell.

Grade	Producer	Medium	Title	Other Information
I	Miller	. . . .	*Across Five Aprils (I. Hunt)	record, cassette, or filmstrips w/records or cassettes
P	Coronet	filmstrips	Aesop's Fables	set of 4 w/records or cassettes
I	Coronet	filmstrips	African Folktales	set of 6 w/records or cassettes
I	Barr	film	*All About Bobby	15 min.
P	Miller	. . . .	*All Upon a Stone (J. C. George)	cassette, or filmstrips w/records or cassettes
PI	BFA	film	All In the Morning Early (N. Leodhas)	10 min.
P	Coronet	filmstrips	*Alphabet Fun	set of 4 w/records or cassettes
P	Spoken	filmstrips	*Amelia Bedelia (P. Parish)	set of 4 w/records or cassettes
PI	Coronet	filmstrips	American Folklore	set of 6 w/records or cassettes
I	Coronet	filmstrips	American Indian Legends	set of 6 w/records or cassettes
P	Ency Brit	filmstrips	American Indian Legends	set of 6 w/records or cassettes
I	Miller	filmstrips	*American Revolution: History Through Art	set of 2 w/records or cassettes
PI	Coronet	film	American Tall Tale Heroes	15 min.
I	Miller	. . . .	*Amos Fortune, Free Man (E. Yates)	record, cassette, or filmstrips w/records or cassettes
PI	Texture	film	*Anansi the Spider (G. McDermott)	10 min., animation
I	Miller	. . . .	*And Now, Miguel (J. Krumgold)	records, cassettes, or filmstrips w/records or cassettes
P	Prentice	filmstrips	And Then What Happens?	set of 5 w/records or cassettes
PI	Coronet	filmstrips	Andersen's Fairy Tales	set of 8 w/records or cassettes
P	Weston	. . . .	Andy and the Lion (J. Daugherty)	film, filmstrip w/cassette, or cassette
P	Weston	. . . .	Angus and the Cat (M. Flack)	filmstrip w/cassette, or cassette
P	BFA	film	*Animal Friends	10 min.
P	Coronet	film	Animals of Africa	13 min.
I	Scholastic	record	Anthology of Negro Poetry for Young People	one 10-inch LP
P	Weston	. . . .	Apt. 3 (E. J. Keats)	film, filmstrip w/cassette, or cassette

NOTE: In this list, the proper names which appear in parentheses after the titles are those of narrators (complete names) or authors (shortened names). All films and filmstrips are in color unless otherwise noted. Under the *Title* category, an asterisk (*) indicates an award-winning production. Under the *Medium* category, dots (. . . .) indicate that the title is available in several media from the same producer as exemplified under *Other Information*. A complete list of producers follows the list.

Grade	Producer	Medium	Title	Other Information
PI	Texture	film	*Arrow to the Sun (G. McDermott)	12 min., animation
I	Scholastic	record	Ashanti Folk Tales from Ghana	one 12-inch LP
PI	Sterling	film	Autumn Impressions	11 min., no narration
PI	McGraw	filmstrips	Basic Goals in Spelling: Fourth Edition (W. Kottmeyer and A. Claus)	set of 6 per grade, grades 1 to 8
P	Viking	filmstrip	Bear Party (W. P. du Bois)	w/record or cassette
P	Coronet	filmstrips	Being You	set of 6 w/records or cassettes
P	Troll	tapes	Best in Children's Literature	set of 20 cassettes
P	Sterling	film	*Big People—Little People	9 min.
P	Weston	....	Big Snow, The (B. & E. Hader)	filmstrip w/cassette or cassette
P	Weston	....	Biggest Bear, The (L. Ward)	filmstrip w/cassette or cassette
PI	Barr	film	Birds in Your Backyard (Rev. Ed.)	11 min.
I	Caedmon	....	Black Fairy Tales (Claudia McNeil)	one 12-inch LP or one cassette
PI	Ency Brit	film	*Blue Dashiki, The	14 min., no narration
I	Viking	....	Blue Willow (D. Gates)	record or cassette w/book
P	Weston	....	Blueberries for Sal (R. McCloskey)	film, filmstrip w/cassette, or cassette
P	Library	filmstrip	*Books Talk Back	w/record or cassette
I	Library	filmstrip	Books Tell Their Story	w/record or cassette
PI	Barr	film	Box, The	10 min.
P	Films	film	Bremen Town Musicians	15 min., puppetry
P	Weston	....	Brian Wildsmith's Fishes	filmstrip w/cassette or cassette
P	Weston	....	Brian Wildsmith's Wild Animals	filmstrip w/cassette or cassette
I	Learning	film	*Brown Wolf (J. London)	26 min.
I	Coronet	film	Building Better Paragraphs: Second Edition	12 min.
PI	Churchill	film	*Buttercup	11 min.
I	Barr	film	*By The Sea	14 min.
I	Miller	....	Caddie Woodlawn (C. R. Brink)	record, cassette, or filmstrips w/records or cassettes
P	Weston	filmstrips	Caldecott Honor Titles	20 w/cassettes
P	Weston	filmstrips	Caldecott Medal Titles	23 w/cassettes
P	Weston	....	Camel Who Took a Walk, The (J. Tworkov)	film, filmstrip w/cassette, or cassette
P	Weston	....	Caps for Sale (E. Slobodkina)	film, filmstrip w/cassette, or cassette
I	Library	filmstrip	Card Catalog: Dewey Decimal Classification	w/record or cassette
I	Caedmon	....	Carroll, Lewis and Edward Lear: Nonsense Verse (Beatrice Lillie, Cyril Ritchard, Stanley Holloway)	one 12-inch LP or one cassette

Grade	Producer	Medium	Title	Other Information
I	Miller	. . . .	*Carry On, Mr. Bowditch (J. L. Latham)	record, cassette, or filmstrips w/ records or cassettes
I	Sterling	film	Casey at the Bat (E. Thayer)	6 min.
P	Weston	. . . .	Cat and the Collector, The (L. Glovach)	film, filmstrip w/ cassette, or cassette
P	BFA	film	Cat in the Hat, The (Dr. Seuss)	24 min.
P	Weston	. . . .	Charlie Needs a Cloak (T. dePaola)	film, filmstrip w/ cassette, or cassette
PI	Pathways	records	Charlotte's Web (E. B. White)	four 12-inch LPs
P	Churchill	film	*Chick, Chick, Chick	12 min.
P	Spoken	records	Child's Garden of Verses, A (R. Stevenson)	two 12-inch LPs
PI	Sterling	film	Child's Garden of Verses, A (R. Stevenson)	10 min.
I	Prentice	filmstrips	*Chinese Tales	set of 4 w/ records or cassettes
P	Viking	filmstrips	*Christmas in Noisy Village (A. Lindgren)	w/ cassette
PI	Coronet	filmstrips	Christmas Tales from Many Lands	set of 6 w/ records or cassettes
PI	Spoken	records	Ciardi (John) Poetry	three 12-inch LPs
PI	Spoken	tapes	Ciardi Collection, John	set of 6 cassettes
P	Caedmon	. . . .	Cinderella and Other Fairy Tales (Claire Bloom)	one 12-inch LP or one cassette
P	Coronet	filmstrips	Circus!	set of 4 w/ records or cassettes
P	Weston	. . . .	Circus Baby, The (M. & M. Petersham)	film, filmstrip w/ cassette, or cassette
PI	Barr	film	Circus Day (Revised Edition)	18 min.
PI	Churchill	film	*City Awakens, A	14 min., no narration
I	Barr	film	*City I See, The	14 min.
P	Ency Brit	kit	Classic Fairy Tales	set of 10, w/ records or cassettes, book, etc.
I	Caedmon	. . . .	Classics of American Poetry for the Elementary Curriculum	two 12-inch LPs or two cassettes
I	Caedmon	. . . .	Classics of English Poetry for the Elementary Curriculum	one 12-inch LP or one cassette
PI	Learning	film	*Clown	15 min., no narration
I	Churchill	film	Clubhouse Boat, The (F & G Shaftel)	19 min., open-ended
I	Ency Brit	transparencies	Composition Skills	set of 262 in 7 cases, w/ reprod. masters
I	Pyramid	film	Concert, The	12 min., no narration
PI	BFA	film	*Conch Shell, The	5 min.
P	Viking	filmstrip	Corduroy (D. Freeman)	w/ record or cassette
P	Barr	film	Courtesy: A Good Eggsample	10 min.
PI	Learning	film	Cow-Tail Switch, The	8 min.
PI	Churchill	films	Creative Writing (A Series)	set of 4, 16 min. each
P	Churchill	film	*Creeps Machine, The	9 min.

Grade	Producer	Medium	Title	Other Information
P	Weston	. . . .	*Crow Boy* (T. Yashima)	film, filmstrip w/cassette, or cassette
P	Spoken	filmstrips	*Curious George* (A Series) (H. A. Rey)	set of 6 w/records or cassettes
P	Weston	. . . .	*Curious George Rides a Bike* (H. A. Rey)	film, filmstrip w/cassette, or cassette
P	Weston	. . . .	*Custard the Dragon* (O. Nash)	filmstrip w/cassette or cassette
P	Viking	filmstrip	*Dandelion* (D. Freeman)	w/record or cassette
I	BFA	film	*Day Grandpa Died, The*	11 min.
I	Coronet	filmstrips	*Developing Study Skills*	set of 8 w/records or cassettes
P	Sterling	film	*Dick Whittington and His Cat*	16 min.
I	Prentice	transparencies	*Dictionary Skills*	set of 51, w/28 overlays
PI	Miller	records	*Discover the Sounds of Poetry*	set of two 12-inch LPs
I	Coronet	films	*Discovering Language: A Series*	6 titles, 9–13 min. each
PI	Caedmon	. . . .	*Discovering Rhythm and Rhyme in Poetry* (Julie Harris, David Wayne)	one 12-inch LP or one cassette
PI	Coronet	film	*Discovering the Library* (Second Edition)	11 min.
P	Coronet	filmstrips	*Discovering Your Senses*	set of 6 w/records or cassettes
I	Coronet	film	*Do Words Ever Fool You?*	11 min.
PI	Churchill	film	*Dogs*	15 min.
I	Weston	film	*Doughnuts, The* (from *Homer Price* by R. McCloskey)	26 min., color or b/w
P	Miller	tapes	*Dr. Seuss Presents*	set of 3 cassettes
I	Barr	film	*Drop of Water, A*	14 min.
P	Weston	. . . .	*Drummer Hoff* (B & E Emberley)	film, filmstrip w/cassette, or cassette
PI	Barr	film	*Education—Why Language Arts?*	11 min.
PI	Barr	film	*Education—Why Science?*	11 min.
PI	Barr	film	*Education—Why Social Science?*	11 min.
I	Barr	film	*Education—Why Tests?*	10 min.
PI	Sterling	film	*Electric Imagination, The*	10 min.
I	Library	filmstrip	*Encyclopedias: Basic Knowledge* (Part I)	w/record or cassette
P	BFA	film	*Evan's Corner* (E. Hill)	24 min.
I	Sterling	film	*Eyes Are for Seeing*	9 min.
P	Prentice	filmstrips	*Fables of Aesop*	set of 6 w/records or cassettes
PI	Sterling	film	*Fair Play*	8 min., open-ended
P	Ency Brit	filmstrips	*Fairy Tale Magic*	set of 10 w/records or cassettes
PI	BFA	film	*Fast Is Not a Ladybug* (M. Schlein)	11 min.
P	Churchill	films	*Feelings* (A Series)	set of 6, 8–10 min. each
I	Learning	film	*Felipa—North of the Border*	17 min.

Grade	Producer	Medium	Title	Other Information
P	Harcourt	kit	*Find Your Own Way*	6 filmstrips w/records or cassettes, activity cards, books, etc.
PI	Sterling	film	*Finders Keepers*	8 min., open-ended
P	Ency Brit	film	*Fir Tree, The* (H. G. Andersen)	27 min.
P	Ency Brit	film	*Fire to the Sea	10 min., no narration
I	Sterling	film	*First Step Typing*	13 min.
P	Weston	....	*Five Chinese Brothers, The* (C. Bishop)	film, filmstrip w/cassette, or cassette
P	Sterling	film	*Flash-O Capital Letters*	11 min.
P	Sterling	film	*Flash-O Small Letters*	10 min.
P	Sterling	film	*Flebus	7 min.
I	Barr	film	*Flight—A New Awareness	13 min.
PI	Ency Brit	film	*Fog	9 min., no narration
PI	Guidance	kit	*Folktales Around The World*	set of 10 filmstrips w/records or cassettes, activity cards, map, etc.
P	Caedmon	....	*Frances* (Four stories by R. Hoban)	one 12-inch LP or one cassette
PI	Churchill	film	*Friends	18 min.
P	Weston	....	*Frog Went-A-Courtin'* (J. Langstaff)	film, filmstrip w/cassette, or cassette
P	Ency Brit	....	*Fun with Speech*	set of 3 records or 3 cassettes
P	Coronet	film	*Fun with Speech Sounds* (Second Edition)	14 min.
P	Coronet	films	*Fun with Words* (A Series)	set of 8, 11 min. each, color or b/w
P	Weston	....	*Funny Little Woman, The* (A. Mosel)	filmstrip w/cassette or cassette
PI	Caedmon	....	*Gathering of Great Poetry for Children* (Julie Harris, David Wayne, Cyril Ritchard)	four cassettes or four 12-inch LPs
P	Weston	....	*Georgie* (R. Bright)	film, filmstrip w/cassette, or cassette
P	Sterling	film	*Georgie to the Rescue* (R. Bright)	10 min.
I	Learning	film	*Geronimo Jones*	21 min.
I	Troll	filmstrips	*Getting Ready to Write Creatively*	set of 6 w/cassettes
PI	Barr	film	*Gift, The	11 min.
PI	Learning	film	*Glob Family, The*	8 min., no narration
P	Weston	....	*Goggles!* (E. J. Keats)	film, filmstrip w/cassette, or cassette
P	Coronet	film	*Goldilocks and the Three Bears	11 min.
P	Caedmon	....	*Goldilocks and the Three Bears and Other Stories* (Claire Bloom)	one 12-inch LP or one cassette

Grade	Producer	Medium	Title	Other Information
P	Ency Brit	filmstrips	*Good Manners Are Me*	set of 3 w/records or cassettes
I	Caedmon	. . . .	*Great Quillow, The* (J. Thurber, Peter Ustinov)	one 12-inch LP or one cassette
P	Spoken	records	*Grimm's Fairy Tales*	three 12-inch LPs
PI	Barr	film	**Greenhouse*	11 min.
I	Coronet	film	*Haiku: An Introduction to Poetry*	11 min.
PI	Sterling	film	**Hailstones and Halibut Bones*	
			Part I	6 min.
			Part II	7 min.
P	Coronet	film	*Handwriting for Beginners: Manuscript*	13 min.
I	Learning	film	*Handy-Dandy-Do-It-Yourself Filmmaking Film*	8 min.
I	Prentice	filmstrips	*Hans Christian Andersen (A Series)*	set of 5, w/records or cassettes
I	Spoken	records	*Hans Christian Andersen Tales*	seven 12-inch LPs
P	BFA	film	**Hansel and Gretel*	11 min.
P	Weston	. . . .	*Happy Owls, The* (C. Piatti)	film, filmstrip w/cassette, or cassette
P	Ency Brit	film	*Hare and the Tortoise* (Aesop)	11 min., b/w
P	Weston	. . . .	*Harold and the Purple Crayon* (C. Johnson)	film, filmstrip w/cassette, or cassette
PI	Learning	film	**Hello, Up There*	8 min.
P	Weston	. . . .	*Hercules* (H. Gramatky)	film, filmstrip w/cassette, or cassette
PI	Sterling	film	*Here Comes the Circus*	11 min.
I	Spoken	. . . .	*Heroes, Gods, and Monsters of the Greek Myths* (Julie Harris and Richard Kiley)	six 12-inch LPs or six cassettes
I	Miller	filmstrip	**High King, The* (L. Alexander)	w/records or cassettes
	Ency Brit	filmstrip	*Higher Roads to Meaning*	set of 6 w/records or cassettes
P	Weston	tapes	*Homer Price* (Stories by R. McCloskey)	set of 3 cassettes
P	Churchill	film	*Hopscotch*	12 min., animation
PI	Texture	film	*Horse Flickers*	10 min.
I	Miller	. . . .	**House of Sixty Fathers, The* (M. DeJong)	record, cassette, or filmstrip w/record or cassette
P	Sterling	film	**House That Jack Built, The*	6 min.
P	Learning	film	*How the Elephant Got His Trunk* (Kipling)	8 min.
P	Learning	film	*How the First Letter Was Written*	8 min.
P	Learning	film	*How the Whale Got His Throat*	8 min.
I	Ency Brit	film	*Hunter and the Forest, The*	8 min., b/w, no narration
I	Miller	. . . .	**I, Juan de Pareja* (E. B. de Treviño)	record, cassette, or filmstrip w/record or cassette

Grade	Producer	Medium	Title	Other Information
P	Pathways	record	*I Met A Man* (J. Ciardi)	one 12-inch LP
P	Barr	film	*I Want. . . . You Want*	7 min.
I	Sterling	film	*Icarus and Daedalus*	6 min.
I	Coronet	film	*Improving Your Vocabulary*	11 min.
P	Weston	. . . .	*In the Forest* (M. H. Ets)	film, filmstrip w/cassette, or cassette
I	Miller	. . . .	**Invincible Louisa* (C. Meigs)	record or cassette
PI	Spoken	records	*Irish Fairy Tales* (Siobhan McKenna)	two 12-inch LPs
I	Caedmon	. . . .	*James and the Giant Peach* (R. Dahl)	one 12-inch LP or one cassette
PI	Coronet	filmstrips	*Japanese Stories of Magic*	set of 6 w/records or cassettes
P	Weston	. . . .	*Jenny's Birthday Book* (E. Averill)	filmstrip w/cassette or cassette
P	Viking	filmstrip	*Joey's Cat* (R. Burch)	w/record or cassette
I	Miller	. . . .	**Johnny Tremain* (E. Forbes)	record or cassette
P	Miller	film	**Judge, The* (H. and M. Zemach)	9 min.
I	Caedmon	. . . .	*Julie of the Wolves* (J. C. George)	one 12-inch LP or one cassette
P	Spoken	filmstrips	*Jungle Books* (R. Kipling)	2 sets of 4 w/records or cassettes
PI	BFA	film	**Junkyard*	10 min., no narration
PI	Coronet	filmstrips	*Just So Stories* (R. Kipling)	set of 4 w/records or cassettes
PI	Churchill	film	**Kite Story*	25 min., no narration
I	Guidance	filmstrips	**Language Skills: Speaking of Spelling*	set of 2 w/records or cassettes
P	Ency Brit	film	*Late for Dinner: Was Dawn Right?*	8 min., open-ended
I	Coronet	filmstrips	**Latin American Folktales*	set of 6 w/records or cassettes
I	Guidance	filmstrips	*Learn to Be a Wise Consumer*	set of 4 w/records or cassettes
P	McGraw	filmstrips	*Learning About Our Language* (A Series)	4 sets of 6 each
I	Barr	filmstrips	*Learning Language Through Songs and Symbols*	3 sets of 4 each w/cassettes
PI	Spoken	filmstrips	*Legends from the Lands of Sun and Snow*	set of 4 w/records or cassettes
I	Pyramid	film	*Legend of John Henry*	11 min., animation
P	Ency Brit	kits	*LEIR*	three levels, each with 2 kits: filmstrips w/cassettes, resource cards, reprod. masters, etc.
P	Ency Brit	film	*Lemonade Stand: What's Fair?*	14 min.
P	Weston	. . . .	*Lentil* (R. McCloskey)	film, filmstrip w/cassette, or cassette
I	Guidance	filmstrips	**Let's Learn to Study*	set of 2 w/records or cassettes
P	Coronet	filmstrips	**Let's Listen*	set of 2 w/records or cassettes
P	Coronet	filmstrips	*Let's Tell Picture Stories*	set of 4 w/records or cassettes

Grade	Producer	Medium	Title	Other Information
I	Guidance	filmstrips	*Let's Write a Poem*	set of 2 w/records or cassettes
PI	Churchill	film	*Let's Write a Story*	11 min.
P	Weston	. . . .	*Letter to Amy, A* (E. Keats)	film, filmstrip w/cassette, or cassette
PI	Coronet	film	*Letter Writing for Beginners*	11 min., color or b/w
I	Prentice	filmstrips	*Library, The*	set of 2 w/cassettes
I	Ency Brit	film	*Library—A Place for Discovery*	16 min.
I	BFA	filmstrips	*Library Skills* (A Series)	set of 6 w/records or cassettes
I	Troll	tapes	*Library Skills Box*	set of 10 cassettes w/reprod. masters
I	Barr	film	*Library World*	16 min.
P	Sterling	film	*Lickety-Split Licorice*	8 min., no narration
P	Houghton	kit	*Listen and Do: Consonants*	16 cassettes or records, reprod. masters, etc.
P	Houghton	kit	*Listen and Do: Vowels*	11 cassettes or records, reprod. masters, etc.
I	Troll	tapes	*Listen and Think*	set of 12 cassettes w/reprod. masters
PI	Coronet	film	*Listen Well, Learn Well* (Second Edition)	11 min.
P	Churchill	film	*Listening*	14 min.
P	Houghton	kit	*Listening and Learning*	20 lessons on 10 cassettes or 5 records, reprod. masters, etc.
P	Scholastic	kit	*Listening Skills Program* Unit I: Easy Ears Unit II: Earpower	40 lessons on 10 cassettes, reprod. masters, guide, etc.
PI	Learning	film	**Little Airplane That Grew, The*	9 min., no narration
PI	Pathways	records	*Little House in the Big Woods, The* (L. Wilder, Julie Harris)	four 12-inch LPs
P	Coronet	film	**Little Red Hen, The*	11 min.
P	Weston	. . . .	*Little Red Lighthouse, The* (H. Swift)	film, filmstrip w/cassette, or cassette
P	Caedmon		*Little Red Riding Hood and The Dancing Princesses* (Claire Bloom)	one 12-inch LP or one cassette
P	Weston	. . . .	*Little Tim and the Brave Sea Captain* (E. Ardizzone)	film, filmstrip w/cassette, or cassette
P	Weston	. . . .	*Little Toot* (H. Gramatky)	filmstrip w/cassette, or cassette
P	Caedmon	. . . .	*Little Toot: Five Stories* (H. Gramatky)	one 12-inch LP or one cassette
PI	Coronet	filmstrips	**Living on a Farm*	set of 6 w/records or cassettes
I	Troll	filmstrips	*Look It Up*	set of 4 w/cassettes
I	Ency Brit	film	*Loon's Necklace, The*	11 min.
PI	BFA	film	**Lorax, The* (Dr. Seuss)	24 min.
I	Barr	film	**Lost Pigeon*	15 min.
P	Churchill	film	*Lost Puppy*	14 min., open-ended
P	Learning	film	**Madeline* (L. Bemelmans)	7 min.

Grade	Producer	Medium	Title	Other Information
PI	Learning	film	*Magic Balloons, The	18 min., no narration
P	Ency Brit	films	Magic Moments (A Series)	5 sets of 4 each, 3 to 8 min. each
PI	Texture	film	Magic Tree, The (G. McDermott)	10 min., animation
P	Weston	....	Make Way for the Ducklings (R. McCloskey)	film, filmstrip w/cassette, or cassette
I	Coronet	film	Making Sense with Outlines (Second Edition)	11 min.
I	Coronet	film	Making Sense with Sentences (Second Edition)	15 min.
I	Caedmon	....	Many Moons (J. Thurber, Peter Ustinov)	one 12-inch LP or one cassette
P	Weston	....	May I Bring a Friend? (B. Schenk de Regniers)	filmstrip w/cassette or cassette
I	Learning	film	*Me and You Kangaroo	19 min., no narration
I	Ency Brit	filmstrips	Media Resources for Discovery	set of 8 w/records or cassettes
I	Library	filmstrip	Meet the Card Catalog	w/record or cassette
I	Miller	filmstrips	*Meet the Newbery Author Alexander, Lloyd Estes, Eleanor George, Jean Craighead Hamilton, Virginia Singer, Isaac Bashevis	each w/record or cassette
PI	Coronet	film	Mermaid Princess, The (H. C. Andersen)	13 min.
P	Learning	film	*Merry-Go-Round Horse, The	17 min., no narration
I	Learning	film	*Miguel—Up from Puerto Rico	15 min.
P	Weston	....	Mike Mulligan and His Steam Shovel (V. L. Burton)	film, filmstrip w/cassette, or cassette
P	Weston	....	Millions of Cats (W. Gag)	film, filmstrip w/cassette, or cassette
PI	Films	film	Milo's Journey (N. Juster)	15 min., animation
I	Viking	....	Miss Hickory (C. S. Bailey)	record or cassette
P	Weston	....	Mr. Gumpy's Outing (J. Burningham)	filmstrip w/cassette or cassette
P	Miller	....	*Mr. Popper's Penguins (R. and F. Atwater)	record or cassette
I	Miller	....	*Mrs. Frisby and the Rats of NIMH (R. C. O'Brien)	record, cassette, or filmstrip w/record or cassette
PI	BFA	film	*Movement Explanation: What Am I?	11 min.
I	Library	filmstrip	Multimedia Center	w/record or cassette
PI	Barr	film	*My Grandson Lew (C. Zolotow)	13 min.
PI	BFA	film	My Mother is the Most Beautiful Woman in the World (B. Reyher)	9 min.

Grade	Producer	Medium	Title	Other Information
I	BFA	film	*Mythology of Greece and Rome	16 min.
I	Troll	filmstrips	New Adventures in Language	set of 15 w/cassettes
I	Miller	kits	Newbery Literature Activities Packs	12 titles, each w/records or cassettes, reprod. masters, poster, guide, etc.
I	BFA	film	*Newspaper Serves Its Community, A	14 min.
P	Sterling	film	Night's Nice	10 min.
P	Weston	. . . .	Norman the Doorman (D. Freeman)	film, filmstrip w/cassette, or cassette
I	BFA	film	North American Indian Legends	21 min.
P	Barr	film	Now I Am Bigger	10 min.
P	Viking	filmstrip	Obadiah the Bold (B. Turkle)	w/record or cassette
P	Weston	. . . .	One Monday Morning (U. Shulevitz)	film, filmstrip w/cassette, or cassette
I	Ency Brit	kit	Open Box	set of 10 short strips, picture cards, 3 cassettes, guide, etc.
I	Coronet	filmstrips	Our Language	set of 6 w/records or cassettes
P	Guidance	filmstrips	Outset: Places to Go	set of 2 w/records or cassettes
P	Weston	. . . .	Over in the Meadow (J. Langstaff)	film, filmstrip w/cassette, or cassette
P	Weston	. . . .	Owl and the Pussy-Cat, The (E. Lear)	film, filmstrip w/cassette, or cassette
P	Weston	. . . .	Pancho (B. & E. Hader)	film, filmstrip w/cassette or cassette
I	Barr	film	Park Community, A	10 min.
I	Coronet	film	Parliamentary Procedure in Action (Second Edition)	16 min.
PI	Reader's	kits	Pathways of Sound: A Children's Literature Program	5 units: each w/cassettes, reprod. masters, etc.
P	Weston	. . . .	Patrick (Q. Blake)	film, filmstrip w/cassette, or cassette
PI	BFA	film	*Paul Bunyan	11 min.
PI	Churchill	film	*Perils of Priscilla	16 min., no narration
PI	Caedmon	. . . .	Peter Pan, Story of (Glynis Johns)	one 12-inch LP or one cassette
P	Weston	. . . .	Peter's Chair (E. Keats)	film, filmstrip w/cassette, or cassette
P	Weston	. . . .	Petunia (R. Duvoisin)	film, filmstrip w/cassette, or cassette
P	Spoken	filmstrips	Pick a Peck o' Poems	set of 6 w/records or cassettes
PI	Pathways	record	Pickety Fence and Other Poems by David McCord	one 12-inch LP
I	BFA	film	Pied Piper of Hamelin, The (R. Browning)	11 min.

Grade	Producer	Medium	Title	Other Information
I	McGraw	kits	*Plus 10 Vocabulary Booster* (W. Kottmeyer)	five levels: cassettes, mastery tests, notebooks, etc.
I	Guidance	filmstrips	*Pocketful of Poetry	set of 2 w/records or cassettes
P	Guidance	filmstrips	*Poems for Glad, Poems for Sad*	set of 2 w/records or cassettes
P	Weston	filmstrips	*Poetry*	set of 15 w/cassettes
I	Ency Brit	filmstrips	*Poetry Alive*	set of 6 w/records or cassettes
P	Coronet	filmstrips	*Poetry and Me*	set of 4 w/records or cassettes
P	Coronet	film	*Poetry for Beginners*	11 min.
I	Spoken	filmstrips	*Project Independence*	set of 4 w/cassettes
P	Sterling	film	*Puffed-Up Dragon, The*	11 min.
PI	Barr	film	*Pulling Together*	10 min.
I	Coronet	film	*Punctuation-Mark Your Meaning* (Second Edition)	12 min.
P	Spoken	filmstrips	*Puppet Theater Filmstrips*	set of 6 w/cassettes
I	Troll	filmstrips	*Putting Words in Order*	set of 6 w/cassettes
I	Viking	. . . .	*Queenie Peavy* (R. Burch)	record or cassette
P	Spoken	kit	*Quickwick, Your Library Guide*	5 filmstrips w/records or cassettes, reprod. masters, game, etc.
I	Viking	. . . .	*Rabbit Hill* (R. Lawson)	record or cassette
I	Caedmon	. . . .	*Rain God's Daughter and Other African Folktales* (Ruby Dee)	one cassette or one 12-inch LP
PI	Churchill	film	*Rainshower	14 min., no narration
P	Sterling	film	*Red and Black*	7 min.
P	Weston	. . . .	*Red Carpet, The* (R. Parkin)	film, filmstrip w/cassette, or cassette
P	Caedmon	. . . .	*Reluctant Dragon, The* (K. Grahame)	one 12-inch LP or one cassette
P	Coronet	film	*Rhythm, Rhythm Everywhere*	10 min.
I	Barr	film	*Rodeo Cowboy	22 min.
PI	Learning	film	*Rug Maker, The*	9 min.
PI	Sterling	film	*Rumpelstiltskin*	11 min.
PI	Films	film	*Runt of the Litter* (E. B. White)	12 min.
PI	Churchill	film	*Safe Play: Danger Places*	14 min.
PI	Pyramid	film	*Seashore	8 min.
PI	Harcourt	filmstrips	*Self Expression and Conduct: The Humanities*	
			Beginning Level	set of 6 w/records or cassettes
			Level One	set of 8 w/records or cassettes
			Level Two	set of 6 w/records or cassettes
P	Weston	. . . .	*Selfish Giant, The* (O. Wilde)	film, filmstrip w/cassette, or cassette
P	Learning	film	*Seven Ravens, The* (Grimm)	21 min.
I	Sterling	film	*Shakespeare: Selection for Children* (Maurice Evans)	6 min.
P	Coronet	film	*Sharing Time in Our Class*	11 min.

Grade	Producer	Medium	Title	Other Information
P	Films	film	*Shoemaker and the Elves, The	15 min., puppetry
PI	Barr	film	*Show Biz—A Job Well Done	12 min.
PI	Ency Brit	filmstrips	*Show Me a Poem	set of 6 w/records or cassettes
P	Coronet	film	Signals for Sense: Punctuation Marks	10 min.
PI	Ency Brit	films	Silent Safari (A Series)	set of 5, 11 min. each, no narration
I	Prentice	filmstrips	Simply Shakespeare	set of 5 w/records or cassettes
I	Miller	. . . .	*Sing Down the Moon (S. O'Dell)	record, cassette, filmstrip w/record or cassette
P	Films	film	Singing Bone, The (Grimm Brothers)	13 min.
P	Sterling	film	*Smallest Elephant in the World, The	6 min.
P	Weston	. . . .	Snowy Day, The (E. Keats)	film, filmstrip w/cassette, or cassette
I	Pyramid	film	*Solo	15 min.
I	Miller	. . . .	*Sounder (W. H. Armstrong)	record or cassette
P	Ency Brit	. . . .	Speech Improvement	set of 5 records or 5 cassettes
P	Coronet	film	Spelling for Beginners	11 min.
I	Coronet	film	Spelling Is Easy (Second Edition)	11 min.
PI	Scholastic	kits	Spelling Monsters	4 units (A–D): each with 5 filmstrips w/records or cassettes, reprod. masters, etc.
I	Prentice	kits	Spelling Spree	set of 3 with filmstrips w/cassettes, word cards, reprod. masters, etc.
I	Barr	film	*Spring—Six Interpretations	13 min.
PI	Sterling	film	Spring Impressions	10 min., no narration
P	Viking	filmstrip	Squawk to the Moon, Little Goose (E. M. Preston)	w/cassette
PI	Churchill	film	Squeak the Squirrel	11 min.
PI	McGraw	kits	Steps to English	four levels, each w/cassettes, cue cards, books, etc.
P	Weston	. . . .	Stone Soup (M. Brown)	film, filmstrip w/cassette, or cassette
P	Weston	. . . .	Stonecutter, The (G. McDermott)	film, filmstrip w/cassette, or cassette
P	Churchill	film	Stories!	14 min.
P	Coronet	filmstrips	Stories to Think About	set of 6 w/records or cassettes
P	Weston	. . . .	Story About Ping, The (M. Flack)	film, filmstrip w/cassette, or cassette
PI	Prentice	kit	Story Starters	set of 12 filmstrips w/records or cassettes and w/prints
PI	Churchill	film	Storymaker	14 min.
PI	Pathways	records	Stuart Little (Julie Harris)	two 12-inch LPs

Grade	Producer	Medium	Title	Other Information
I	Viking	. . . .	*Summer of the Swans, The* (B. Byars)	record or cassette
P	Caedmon	. . . .	*Tale of Flopsy Bunnies and Other Beatrix Potter Stories* (Claire Bloom)	one 12-inch LP or one cassette
P	Weston	. . . .	*Tale of Peter Rabbit, The* (B. Potter)	filmstrip w/cassette, or cassette
P	Caedmon	. . . .	*Tale of Peter Rabbit and Other Stories* (Claire Bloom)	one 12-inch LP or one cassette
P	Ency Brit	film	*Tale of Rumpelstiltskin*	21 min.
PI	Barr	film	*Taleb and His Lamb	16 min.
PI	Coronet	filmstrips	*Tales from Japan*	set of 8 w/records or cassettes
I	Sterling	film	*Tales of Hiawatha*	19 min., animation
P	Troll	kit	*Talking Picture Dictionary*	set of 16 cassettes w/books, guide, etc.
P	Spoken	tapes	*Talking with Mike*	cassettes or open-reel tapes, w/37 lessons
P	Viking	filmstrip	*Talking Without Words* (M. H. Ets)	w/record or cassette
PI	Coronet	filmstrips	*Tall Tales in American Folklore*	set of 6 w/records or cassettes
PI	Ency Brit	film	*Tchou, Tchou	15 min., no narration
I	Sterling	film	*Terminus	26 min., b/w, no narration
I	Miller	. . . .	*Thimble Summer (E. Enright)	record, cassette, or filmstrip w/record or cassette
I	Weston	film	*This Is New York* (M. Sasek)	12 min., iconographic
I	Pyramid	film	*Thoroughbred*	22 min., no narration
P	Weston	. . . .	*Three Billy Goats Gruff, The*	filmstrip w/cassette or cassette
PI	Ency Brit	film	*Three Fox Fables* (Aesop)	11 min., b/w
P	Weston	. . . .	*Three Robbers, The* (T. Ungerer)	film, filmstrip w/cassette, or cassette
PI	Learning	film	*Thunderstorm	9 min., no narration
P	Viking	filmstrip	*Thy Friend, Obadiah* (B. Turkle)	w/record or cassette
P	Weston	. . . .	*Tikki, Tikki, Tembo* (A. Mosel)	film, filmstrip w/cassette, or cassette
P	Weston	. . . .	*Time of Wonder* (R. McCloskey)	film, filmstrip w/cassette, or cassette
PI	Viking	filmstrip	*Tower of Babel, The* (W. Wiesner)	w/cassette
P	Spoken	kits	*Treasury of Animal Stories* (B. Potter)	2 sets of 4 filmstrips each w/records or cassettes, guide, reprod. masters, etc.
P	Spoken	filmstrips	*Treasury of Grimm's Fairy Tales*	set of 6 w/records or cassettes
P	Spoken	kit	*Treasury of Nursery Rhymes*	set of 4 filmstrips w/records or cassettes, reprod. masters, guides, etc.

Grade	Producer	Medium	Title	Other Information
PI	Viking	filmstrip	*Two Hundred Rabbits* (L. Andersen and A. Adams)	w/cassette
I	Viking	....	*Twenty-One Balloons, The* (W. P. Du Bois)	record or cassette
PI	Coronet	film	*Ugly Duckling, The* (H. C. Andersen)	11 min.
I	Learning	film	*Unicorn in the Garden, A* (J. Thurber)	7 min.
PI	Barr	film	*Use Your Ears*	9 min.
P	Miller	....	*Velveteen Rabbit, The* (M. Williams)	record, cassette, or filmstrip w/record or cassette
P	Spoken	filmstrips	*Velveteen Rabbit, The* (M. Williams)	set of 2 w/records or cassettes
I	Troll	filmstrips	*Vocabulary Development: Words, Words, Words*	set of 6 w/cassettes
I	Barr	film	*Watch Out for My Plant*	13 min.
PI	BFA	film	*Wave, The: Japanese Folktale*	9 min.
I	Coronet	film	*We Discover the Dictionary* (Second Edition)	11 min.
I	Coronet	film	*We Discover the Encyclopedia*	11 min.
I	Coronet	filmstrips	*Weather is Poetry*	set of 4 w/records or cassettes
P	Coronet	film	*What Are Animal Tails For?*	11 min.
P	Ency Brit	films	*What Happens Next? (A Series)*	set of 5, 14–16 min. each
PI	Guidance	kit	*What Is a Folktale?*	set of 3 filmstrips w/records or cassettes, activity cards, map, etc.
PI	Barr	film	*What Is Nothing?*	9 min.
I	Coronet	filmstrips	*What Is Poetry?* Part I: *Sound and Image* Part II: *Sense and Nonsense*	 set of 5 w/cassettes set of 5 w/cassettes
I	BFA	film	*What's in a Story*	14 min.
I	Houghton	filmstrips	*What's the Word?*	set of 12, captioned
P	Ency Brit	film	*Whazzat?*	10 min., animation
P	Weston	....	*Wheel on the Chimney* (M. W. Brown)	film, filmstrip w/cassette, or cassette
PI	Barr	film	*Where Should a Squirrel Live?*	11 min., no narration
P	Weston	....	*Where the Wild Things Are* (M. Sendak)	film, filmstrip w/cassette, or cassette
P	Weston	....	*Whistle for Willie* (E. J. Keats)	film, filmstrip w/cassette, or cassette
I	Barr	filmstrips	*Why Don't People Say What They Mean?*	set of 4 w/cassettes
P	Miller	....	*Why Noah Chose the Dove* (I. B. Singer)	filmstrip w/record or cassette, or cassette
PI	Learning	film	*Why People Have Special Jobs: The Man Who Made Spinning Tops*	7 min., animation

Grade	Producer	Medium	Title	Other Information
PI	Learning	film	*Why We Have Elections: The Kings of Snark*	9 min., animation
PI	Learning	film	*Why We Have Laws: Shiver, Gobble, and Snore*	7 min., animation
PI	Learning	film	*Why We Have Taxes: The Town That Had No Policemen*	7 min., animation
PI	Learning	film	*Why We Need Each Other: The Animals' Picnic Day*	10 min., animation
PI	Learning	film	*Why We Use Money: The Fisherman Needed a Knife*	8 min., animation
PI	Films	film	*Wilbur's Story* (E. B. White)	15 min., animation
I	Learning	film	*William—from Georgia to Harlem*	17 min.
I	Pathways	records	*Wind in the Willows, The* (Robert Brooks, Jessica Tandy, Hume Cronyn)	four 12-inch LPs
P	Caedmon	....	*Winnie-the-Pooh* (Carol Channing)	one 12-inch LP or one cassette
P	Pathways	records	*Winnie-the-Pooh* (Maurice Evans)	two 12-inch LPs
PI	Sterling	film	*Winter Impressions*	12 min., no narration
PI	Learning	film	**Winter of the Witch* (Burgess Meredith)	25 min.
I	Miller	....	**Witch of Blackbird Pond, The* (E. G. Speare)	record or cassette
P	Sterling	film	*Wonderful Lollypop Rooster, The*	8 min., no narration
P	Prentice	kits	*Wonderworm: Values in Story and Song*	3 kits of filmstrips w/records or cassettes, reprod. masters, posters, etc.
PI	Churchill	film	*Words!*	14 min.
I	Coronet	filmstrips	*World Myths and Folktales*	set of 8 w/records or cassettes
I	Reader's	kits	*Write to Communicate: The Language Arts in Process*	four levels, each w/record, cards, portfolio books, posters, guides, etc.
I	Guidance	filmstrips	*Write Now: Workshop*	5 sets of 2 each w/records or cassettes
I	Coronet	film	*Writing a Report*	11 min.
I	Coronet	film	*Writing Different Kinds of Letters*	11 min.
I	Guidance	filmstrips	**Writing: From Assignment to Composition*	set of 2 w/records or cassettes
P	Weston	....	*Wynken, Blynken and Nod* (E. Field)	film, filmstrip w/cassette, or cassette
PI	Troll	filmstrips	*You Decide/Open-Ended Tales*	set of 6 w/cassettes
I	McGraw	records	*You Learn to Type*	twenty 12-inch LPs

Grade	Producer	Medium	Title	Other Information
I	Coronet	film	*You'll Find It in the Library*	12 min.
PI	Library	filmstrip	*Your Library—Place of Living Learning*	w/record or cassette
I	Coronet	filmstrips	**Your Newspaper*	set of 6 w/records or cassettes
I	Coronet	films	*Your Study Skills* (A Series)	set of 6, 10–13 min. each
PI	Texture	film	*Zebras*	10 min., animation
P	Ency Brit	film	**Zoo's Eye View*	11 min., no narration

Producers

BFA Educational Media, Santa Monica, California   90406

Barr Films, Pasadena, California   91107

Caedmon Records, New York   10018

Churchill Films, Los Angeles   90069

Coronet Instructional Media, Chicago   60601

Encyclopaedia Britannica Educational Corporation, Chicago   60611

Films Incorporated, Wilmette, Illinois   60091

Guidance Associates, New York   10017

Harcourt Brace Jovanovich, Inc., New York   10017

Houghton Mifflin Company, Boston   02107

Learning Corporation of America, New York   10019

Library Filmstrip Center, Wichita, Kansas   67211

McGraw-Hill Book Company, Webster Division, New York   10020

Miller-Brody Productions, Inc., New York   10017

Pathways of Sound, Inc., Cambridge, Massachusetts   02138

Prentice-Hall Media, Tarrytown, New York   10591

Pyramid Films, Santa Monica, California   90406

Reader's Digest Services, Inc., Education Division, Pleasantville, New York   10570

Scholastic Book Services, Englewood Cliffs, New Jersey   07632

Spoken Arts, New Rochelle, New York   10801

Sterling Educational Films, New York   10016

Texture Films, Inc., New York   10019

Troll Associates, Mahwah, New Jersey   07430

Viking Press, New York   10022

Weston Woods, Weston, Connecticut   06883

Author Index

l

Lahey, M., 202
Laird, C., 57
Laird, H., 57
Lampman, E., 323
Landau, E., 323
Landes, J., 82
Langstaff, C., 317
Langstaff, J., 317
Larrick, N., 312, 317, 318, 319, 455
Larsen, S., 448
Larson, G., 163
Larson, M., 352, 455
Larson, R., 294
Lasker, J., 321
Lawson, R., 312, 328
Leach, M., 326
Lear, E., 315, 316, 340
Lebrun, Y., 243
Lecron, H., 317
Lee, M., 321
Lee, R., 322
Leeming, J., 304
Lefevre, C., 446
Leitch, S., 41
L'Engle, M., 321
Lenski, L., 319, 321, 326, 337
Le Shan, E., 301
Lessenberry, D., 227
Lester, J., 332
Levin, H., 448
Levine, E., 321
Lewis, C., 327
Lewis, G., 369
Lewis, R., 315, 317
Lewis, S., 193
Lindgren, A., 311
Lindsay, V., 173, 317, 339, 340
Lionni, L., 193, 311
Lisker, S., 313
Lismore, T., 428
Little, J., 321, 322
Livingston, M., 319
Lloyd, A., 227
Loban, W., 25, 441, 445
Lobel, A., 307
Longfellow, H., 314
Lonsdale, B., 455
Lorge, I., 128
Loss, J., 131
Love, R., 450
Lovelace, T., 347
Ludovici, L., 57

Lukens, R., 454
Lundsteen, S., 141, 294, 449
Lytton, H., 453

m

McCaslin, N., 369
McClanahan, T., 202
McCloskey, R., 150, 311, 332, 343
McClung, R., 312
McConnell, F., 450
McCord, D., 313, 319
McDaniel, E., 452
MacKintosh, H., 455
McKown, R., 312
McKuen, R., 314
McLaughlin, B., 443
MacManus, S., 326
McNamara, T., 40
McNaught, H., 308
McNeer, M., 312
McNeill, D., 445
McNutt, G., 448
Madden, P., 449
Mahmoud, C., 138
Majer, E., 448
Malmstrom, J., 47, 446, 459
Manchester, F., 448
Mann, P., 307
Manning, J., 441
Manolakes, G., 448
Marcus, A., 40
Marcus, M., 138
Mari, E., 313
Mari, I., 313
Markham, L., 453
Marks, M., 443
Marquardt, W., 428
Martin, B., 358
Martin, W., 453
Mason, G., 243
Matsuno, M., 322
Mattleman, M., 410
Mavrogenes, N., 138
Maxim, G., 112
Mayer, M., 313, 358
Mazor, R., 369
Meade, R., 82
Means, F., 324
Meeks, E., 304
Mehdevi, A., 326
Meigs, C., 312, 313, 316
Meisterheim, M., 294
Mellgren, L., 428

Mellon, J., 62, 293, 446
Meltzer, M., 324
Mendelson, A., 163
Mendoza, M., 243
Merriam, E., 131, 314, 317, 319
Met, M., 443
Miller, B., 452
Mills, M., 324
Milne, A., 266, 308
Moe, J., 358
Molarsky, O., 323
Molnar, J., 324
Momaday, N., 324
Monjo, F., 310, 332
Montessori, M., 210
Montgomery, P., 456
Moore, C., 314, 332, 367
Morey, W., 307
Morton, L., 428
Mountain, L., 138
Mower, M., 456
Musgrove, M., 307
Myers, R., 453

n

Nash, O., 317
Natalicio, D., 53, 446
Nathan, D., 323
Nelson, D., 449
Ness, E., 335
Neville, E., 324
Newbery, J., 299
Newman, A., 445
Ney, J., 452
Nic Leodhas, S., 326
Niemeyer, M., 324
Nikoloff, S., 452
Nilsen, A., 59
Nilsen, D., 59
Nordstrom, U., 321, 455
Norris, G., 321
Norris, R., 25, 445, 446
Noyce, R., 59
Noyes, A., 314

o

O'Dell, S., 343
O'Donnell, H., 163
O'Donnell, R., 25, 293, 445, 446, 452
Ogg, O., 57
O'Hare, F., 62, 446
Oliver, L., 454

Subject Index

Bilingual education, 413–14
Biography for children, 303, 306, 307, 312
Biological theory of language acquisition, 20
Black Americans in children's literature, 323–24
Black English dialect (SEE Dialect, Black English)
Book clubs, juvenile, 330–31
Book fairs, 328
Book reports/reviews, 268, 330, 337–38
    picture, 336, 337
    written, 337–38
Box stage for puppets, 195
Buzz groups (SEE Discussion, buzz groups)
BVD strategy for vocabulary, 125

C

Caldecott Medal Books, 477–85
Calendar, The, 329
Capitalization, 257, 259
Card catalog, using, 378–85
Cassette tapes, 327–28, 493–508
Catalog cards, sample, 380, 381–84
Categories for Tallying Problems in Oral Language (Test), 441
Chair stage for puppets, 195
Chalkboard writing, 216, 237
Checklist, pupils; in area of
    ESOL, 440–41
    handwriting difficulties, 233
    language behavior (preschool), 22–23
    nonstandard English dialect, 51
    speech, 175–76
Checklist, pupils' self-evaluation (SEE Evaluation, pupil's self)
Checklist, teacher's, for guiding role-playing, 362–63
Checklist, teacher's self-evaluation, in area of
    ESOL, 438–39
    listening, 161
    literature, 346
    speech, 174
Children's Book Council, 329
Children's drama (SEE Children's theater AND Drama, creative)
Children's literature (SEE Literature, children's)
Children's theater, 328, 350–52
    agencies producing, 351
    defined, 349
    objectives of, 351
Children's Theater Association, 351, 354

Chinese-Americans in children's literature, 324
Choral reading, 338–45
    arrangements for, 339–42
    evaluation of, 344–45
    pitfalls of, 344
Choral speaking (SEE Choral reading)
Chronological age (SEE Age, chronological)
Classroom environment, 145, 166
    open, 12
    traditional, 12
Cognitive domain (SEE Domains, educational, cognitive)
Collages, 270, 332
Competencies, English language, 5–7
Composition, written,
    content of, 254–57
    dictation and, 252–53
    evaluation of pupils' progress in, 289–93
    factors affecting performance in, 247–49
    guidelines for teaching, 249–52
    in ESOL, 429–33
    samples of children's, 275–88
    skill of, 257–59
    stages of, 252–54
    stimuli for, 263–75
Comprehension skills in listening, 142–43
Comprehensive Tests of Basic Skills (CTBS), 135, 292, 409
Concept development and
    spelling ability, 85–86
    vocabulary, 122
Concrete operations period (Piaget), 29–30
Conferences, teacher–pupil, in
    handwriting, 238
    written composition, 251, 289–91
Consonant sounds, symbols for, 90
Constituents, 66–67
Construction, English, 46, 66–67
Context clue methods of word attack,
    external, 126–27
    internal, 126, 127–28
Controlled test reading (ESOL) (SEE Reading, ESOL)
Conversation and dialogue, 16, 180–82
Cooperative Primary Tests, 158
Copying,
    in ESOL, 429–30
    in handwriting, 205, 208
    in written composition, 253
Creative drama (SEE Drama, creative)
Creativity, 244–47, 251, 289
Cumulative arrangement in choral reading, 340–42
Cursive writing (SEE Handwriting, cursive)

d

Debating, 184–85, 268
Decoding, 5, 84
Deductive method, 85
Derivational affixes (SEE Affixes, derivational)
Determiners, noun, 68, 79
Development, child,
  growth patterns, 26
  Piagetian principles, 30–31
Dewey Decimal Classification System, 376–78
Dialect, 47–53
  Black English, 50–53
  nonstandard, 50–53
  regional, 49
  regions of United States, 49
  social, 50
  standard, 50
Dialog arrangement in choral reading, 339
Dialog in FLES, 418, 420–21
Dialogue and conversation (SEE Conversation and dialogue)
Diamante, 275, 287
Dictation in written composition,
  group, 252, 253
  individual, 253
  in ESOL, 430
Dictionaries, 124, 129, 258, 388–93
  activities for using, 391–93
  elementary, 390–91
  picture, 388–89
  skills for, 390
Diphthongs, 21
Discrimination drill (SESD) (SEE Drills (SESD), discrimination)
Discrimination skills (SEE Auditory discrimination)
Discussion, 182–84
  buzz group, 183
  panel, 183, 335
  round table, 183
Disorders, speech (SEE Speech disorders)
Divergent thinking, 246
Domains, educational,
  affective, 9, 301
  cognitive, 8–9, 301
  evaluation of, 9–10
  psychomotor, 9
Dominance, lateral, 214
Doorway stage for puppets, 195
Double-base transformation (SEE Transformation, double-base)
Drama, children's, 349–71

Drama, creative (SEE ALSO Children's theater; Dramatic play; Pantomime; Sociodrama; AND Story dramatization)
  definition of, 349, 352
  evaluation of pupils' progress in, 368–69
  teacher's role in, 354
  values and objectives of, 350, 352–53
Dramatic play, 15, 358–60
  developmental steps in, 360
  sequence of growth in, 359
Dramatization, story (SEE Story dramatization)
Drills (SESD),
  discrimination, 53
  response, 53
  translation, 53
Durrell Listening-Reading Series, 158

e

Editing (SEE Proofreading)
Educational domains (SEE Domains, educational)
Elaborations, 125–26
"Electric Company, The", 16, 271
Elementary and Secondary Education Act, 351, 413
Elicited Imitation (test), 40
Empiricist theory of language acquisition, 19
Encoding, 84
Encyclopedias, using, 387–88
English for Speakers of Other Languages (ESOL), 413–43
  evaluation of, 437–41
  handwriting and, 234
  learning games in, 433–37
  literacy skills in, 423–33
  method of instruction in, 415–18
  oral skills in, 418–23
  program goals of, 415
English language (SEE ALSO Grammar, English)
  as a second dialect (SESD), 53
  as a second language (ESOL), 413–43
  history of, 54–57
English programs,
  competencies for, 4–7
  goals of, 7–8
  structures in, 11
Environment,
  classroom and/or school, 10–14, 145, 166, 181, 248, 250, 359
  processing of, 27
Environmental skills in listening, 143

Graphemes, 84, 86, 89
Growth and development, child (SEE Development, child)
Growth patterns of children K-6, 26

h

Haiku poetry, 271, 275, 282, 315, 316
Hand dominance (SEE Dominance, lateral)
Handedness,
   tests for, 235–36
   written composition and, 248
Handicapped children (SEE Exceptional children)
Hand puppets (SEE Puppets)
Handwriting, 205–44
   alphabets, 218–19, 222–23
   cursive, 220–26
   evaluation of pupils' progress in, 238–42
   individualized instruction in, 230–31
   left-handed children and, 235–38
   legibility in, 207, 239–40, 241, 258
   manuscript, 215–20
   materials and tools for, 216, 237
   readiness for, 209–215, 221
   scales, 242
   slant print, 220
   speed and, 207, 238–39
   typewriting, 226–40
   written composition and, 258, 292
Haptics, 85, 106
Hardback books for children, 307
Hard-of-hearing children (SEE Exceptional children)
Historical fiction for children, 302, 307
History, language (SEE Language, English)
Holophrases, 21
Homophones, 91, 129
"House that Jack Built, The", 340–42

i

Ideolect, 49
Illinois Test of Psycholinguistic Abilities, 157
Imitation-Comprehension-Production Test, 40
Improvisation (SEE Story dramatization, improvisation)
Indexes of Syntactic Maturity (test), 293
Indexes, skills in using, 386–87
Indians, American, in children's literature, 324
Individual differences, providing for, 31–35

Individualized instruction in
   handwriting, 230–31
   spelling, 97–100
Indo-European language family, 55
Inductive method, 86
Inflectional affixes (SEE Affixes, inflectional)
Informational books for children, 303, 306, 312
Instructional activities (SEE Activities, instructional)
Intelligence and
   creativity, 246
   handwriting, 206
   listening ability, 143
   typewriting ability, 230
   vocabulary growth, 121
   written composition, 247
Interpretation (SEE Story dramatization, interpretation)
Interviewing, 187–88
Intonation, 44, 65, 167
Introductions, making, 189–90
Invented spelling (SEE Spelling, invented)
Invention in written composition, 261–62
Iowa Tests of Basic Skills, 111

j

Japanese-Americans in children's literature, 324
Jews, American, in children's literature, 324
Juncture phonemes (SEE Phonemes, juncture)
Juvenile best sellers, 307–8

k

Kansas Elementary Spelling Test, 110–11
Kansas Intermediate Spelling Test, 110–11
Kernel (SEE Kernel sentence)
Kernel sentence, 67–68
Kindergarten, 86, 88, 148, 187, 203, 211, 235, 314, 358, 398–99
Kinesics, 354
Kits, multimedia, 443–508
K-Ratio Index, 40

l

Language arts program, English, 1–18
Language arts textbooks, evaluation of, 459–61

r

Rationalist theory of language acquisition, 20
Reader's theater, 352
Readiness,
  for cursive writing, 221
  for ESOL reading, 424
  for handwriting, 209–15
  for language, 14–17
Reading (SEE ALSO Bibliotherapy; Choral reading; Readers' theater; AND Reading, ESOL)
  and listening, 141
  and spelling, 84
  and vocabulary, 115
  and written composition, 247
Reading, ESOL
  charts, 425
  controlled text, 427–28
  extensive, 428–29
  readiness for, 424
  recognition, 424–26
  recombination, 426–27
  series for use in, 428
  stages of, 423–29
Recognition reading (ESOL) (SEE Reading, ESOL)
Recombination reading (ESOL) (SEE Reading, ESOL)
Records, 16, 327–28, 493–508
Reference books, using, 393–94
Refrain arrangement in choral reading, 339
Regional dialect (SEE Dialect, regional)
Reporting, 177, 178–79
Response drill (SESD) (SEE Drills, (SESD), response)
Revising written composition, 289, 290
Robert's Rules of Order Newly Revised, 185
Role-playing (SEE Sociodrama)
Root words, 95, 128
Round table discussion (SEE Discussion, round table)

s

Sager Writing Scale, 293
Scales, handwriting (SEE Handwriting Scales)
Schema for Testing Language Arts Concept Attainment, 40
School, elementary,
  organizational models, 12–13
Schroeder Composition Scale, 293

Semantic Differential Scales for Use with Inner-City Pupils, 40
Semantics, 47
Senryu poetry, 275, 315
Sensorimotor period (Piaget), 28
Sentence patterns, 46–47, 61, 63, 65
"Sesame Street", 16
Sesquipedalian words, 132
Setting in children's fiction, 310–11
Sex differences in
  handwriting, 207
  literary interests, 305
  speech, 165
  stuttering, 200
  vocabulary development, 122
  written composition, 247
Sexes, equal treatment of, publication guidelines, 463–76
Sexism, definition, 463
Shadow puppets (SEE Puppets, shadow)
Show-and-Tell, 178–79
Single-base transformation (SEE Transformation, single-base)
Skills of written composition (SEE Composition, written, skills of)
Skimming, 394–95
Slant print (SEE Handwriting, slant print)
Social courtesies, participating in, 188–91
Social dialect (SEE Dialect, social)
Sociodrama, 360–63
Socioeconomic status,
  and vocabulary performance, 121
  and writing composition, 248
Sociolect (SEE Social dialect)
Southern (Dialect) Region, 49
Spacing in handwriting, 218, 225
Speaking (SEE Speech arts; Speech correction; AND Speech improvement)
SPEAKING (acronym), 48
Special education pupils (SEE Exceptional children)
Speech arts, 173, 176–96
  choral reading, 338–45
  conversation and dialogue, 177
  drama, creative, 352–67
  debating, 177
  discussion, 177
  following parliamentary procedure, 177
  giving talks, 177, 178–80
  interviewing, 177
  participating in social courtesies, 177, 188–91
  puppetry, 177
  storytelling, 325–26
Speech community, 49, 65